W9-CII-793

ACCOUNTING

VOLUME TWO

NINTH CANADIAN EDITION

CHARLES T. HORNGREN
Stanford University

WALTER T. HARRISON, JR.
Baylor University

JO-ANN L. JOHNSTON
British Columbia Institute of Technology

CAROL A. MEISSNER
Georgian College

PETER R. NORWOOD
Langara College

PEARSON

Toronto

Library and Archives Canada Cataloguing in Publication

Accounting / Charles T. Horngren ... [et al.]. — 9th Canadian ed.

Includes bibliographical references and indexes.

ISBN 978-0-13-269009-6 (v. 1)–ISBN 978-0-13-269008-9 (v. 2)

1. Accounting—Textbooks. I. Horngren, Charles T., 1926–2011

HF5635.H8125 2013   657'.044   C2012-904344-3

Copyright © 2014, 2011, 2007, 2005, 2002, 1999, 1996, 1993, 1991 Pearson Canada Inc. All rights reserved.

Manufactured in Canada.   This publication is protected by copyright and permission should be obtained from the publisher prior to any prohibited reproduction, storage in a retrieval system, or transmission in any form or by any means, electronic, mechanical, photocopying, recording, or likewise. To obtain permission(s) to use material from this work, please submit a written request to Pearson Canada Inc., Permissions Department, 26 Prince Andrew Place, Don Mills, Ontario, M3C 2T8, or fax your request to 416-447-3126, or submit a request to Permissions Requests at **www.pearsoncanada.ca.**

Original edition published by Pearson Education, Inc., Upper Saddle River, New Jersey, USA. Copyright © 2012 Pearson Education, Inc. This edition is authorized for sale only in Canada.

Credits and acknowledgments of material borrowed from other sources and reproduced, with permission, in this textbook appear on the appropriate page within the text below.

If you purchased this book outside the United States or Canada, you should be aware that it has been imported without the approval of the publisher or author.

10 9 8 7 6 5 4 3 2

Vice-President, Editorial Director: Gary Bennett
Editor-in-Chief: Nicole Lukach
Acquisitions Editor: Megan Farrell
Marketing Manager: Claire Varley
Developmental Editor: Anita Smale
Project Manager: Deborah Starks
Manufacturing Manager: Jane Schell
Production Editor: GEX Publishing Services
Copy Editor: Anita Smale
Proofreader: GEX Publishing Services
Compositor: GEX Publishing Services
Photo Researcher: Rachel Irwin
Permissions Researcher: Rachel Irwin
Art Director: Julia Hall
Cover and Interior Designer: Miriam Blier
Cover Image: Getty Images/Romeo Banias

Photo Credits

753 with permission of Osler, Hoskin & Harcourt LLP; **809** Frances Roberts / Alamy; **861** AlamyBR2C5R; **917** PhotoEdit / Alamy; **989** Courtesy Kinross Corporation; **1051** Aaron Vincent Elkaim / CP; **1127** Courtesy Winpak Ltd.

PEARSON

BRIEF
Contents

Contents

*In each chapter, Assignment Material includes Questions, Starters, Exercises (including Serial and Challenge Exercises),
   Beyond the Numbers, and Ethical Issue, and Problems (Group A and B, and Challenge Problems).
**Extending Your Knowledge includes Decision Problems, Financial Statement Cases, and, in select chapters, IFRS Mini-Cases.

18 Financial Statement Analysis 1126

About the Authors

CHARLES T. HORNGREN was the Edmund W. Littlefield Professor of Accounting, Emeritus, at Stanford University. A graduate of Marquette University, the late Professor Horngren received his MBA from Harvard University and his PhD from the University of Chicago. He is also the recipient of honorary doctorates from Marquette University and DePaul University.

A Certified Public Accountant, Horngren served on the Accounting Principles Board for six years, the Financial Accounting Standards Board Advisory Council for five years, and the Council of the American Institute of Certified Public Accountants for three years. For six years, he served as a trustee of the Financial Accounting Foundation, which oversees the Financial Accounting Standards Board and the Government Accounting Standards Board. Horngren is a member of the Accounting Hall of Fame.

A member of the American Accounting Association, Horngren has been its President and its Director of Research. He received its first annual Outstanding Accounting Educator Award. The California Certified Public Accountants Foundation gave Horngren its Faculty Excellence Award and its Distinguished Professor Award. He is the first person to have received both awards. The American Institute of Certified Public Accountants presented its first Outstanding Educator Award to Horngren. Horngren was named Accountant of the Year, Education, by the national professional accounting fraternity, Beta Alpha Psi.

Professor Horngren was also a member of the Institute of Management Accountants, from whom he received its Distinguished Service Award. He was also a member of the Institute's Board of Regents, which administers the Certified Management Accountant examinations.

Horngren is the author of other accounting books published by Pearson Prentice Hall: *Cost Accounting: A Managerial Emphasis*, Thirteenth Edition, 2008 (with Srikant Datar and George Foster); *Introduction to Financial Accounting*, Ninth Edition, 2006 (with Gary L. Sundem and John A. Elliott); *Introduction to Management Accounting*, Fourteenth Edition, 2008 (with Gary L. Sundem and William Stratton); *Financial & Managerial Accounting*, Second Edition, 2009 and *Financial Accounting*, Eighth Edition, 2009 (with Walter T. Harrison, Jr. and M. Suzanne Oliver).

Horngren was the Consulting Editor for the Charles T. Horngren Series in Accounting.

WALTER T. HARRISON, JR. is Professor Emeritus of Accounting at the Hankamer School of Business, Baylor University. He received his BBA from Baylor University, his MS from Oklahoma State University, and his PhD from Michigan State University.

Professor Harrison, recipient of numerous teaching awards from student groups as well as from university administrators, has also taught at Cleveland State Community College, Michigan State University, the University of Texas, and Stanford University.

A member of the American Accounting Association and the American Institute of Certified Public Accountants, Professor Harrison has served as Chairman of the Financial Accounting Standards Committee of the American Accounting Association, on the Teaching/Curriculum Development Award Committee, on the Program Advisory Committee for Accounting Education and Teaching, and on the Notable Contributions to Accounting Literature Committee.

Professor Harrison has lectured in several foreign countries and published articles in numerous journals, including *Journal of Accounting Research*, *Journal of Accountancy*, *Journal of Accounting and Public Policy*, *Economic Consequences of Financial Accounting Standards*, *Accounting Horizons*, *Issues in Accounting Education*, and *Journal of Law and Commerce*.

He is co-author of *Financial & Managerial Accounting*, Second Edition, 2009 and *Accounting*, Eighth Edition, 2009 (with Charles T. Horngren and M. Suzanne Oliver), published by Pearson Prentice Hall. Professor Harrison has received scholarships, fellowships, and research grants or awards from PriceWaterhouseCoopers, Deloitte & Touche, the Ernst & Young Foundation, and the KPMG Foundation.

JO-ANN L. JOHNSTON is a program head and instructor in the Accounting, Finance and Insurance Department at the British Columbia Institute of Technology (BCIT). She obtained her Diploma of Technology in Financial Management from BCIT, her Bachelor in Administrative Studies from British Columbia Open University, and her MBA from Simon Fraser University. She is also a Certified General Accountant and completed the Canadian Securities Course.

Prior to entering the field of education, Mrs. Johnston worked in public practice and industry for over ten years. She is a past member of the Board of Governors of the Certified General Accountants Association of British Columbia and has served on various committees for the Association. She was also a member of the Board of Directors for the BCIT Faculty and Staff Association, and served as Treasurer during that tenure. She currently serves as chair of the CGA Student Advisory Group and is a member of CGA-BC Education Foundation and the Strategic Planning Committee for the Certified General Accountants Association of British Columbia.

In addition to teaching duties and committee work for the British Columbia Institute of Technology, Mrs. Johnston is the financial officer for a family-owned business.

CAROL A. MEISSNER is a professor in the School of Business at Georgian College in Barrie, Ontario, where she is a member of several curriculum committees. She is also a professor and program coordinator for the Bachelor of Business (Automotive Management) degree at the Automotive Business School of Canada, which is part of Georgian's School of Business. She teaches in both degree and diploma programs, primarily in the areas of introductory financial accounting for non-majors and dealership financial analysis, both in class and online.

A self-professed "learning junkie," Professor Meissner holds a Bachelor of Commerce degree, a Master of Business Administration degree, a Master of Arts degree in Education (Community College concentration), and is a Certified General Accountant. She has also earned Georgian College's Professional Development Teaching Practice Credential and is a graduate of Georgian's Aspiring Leaders program in addition to attending numerous conferences related to teaching, accounting, and the automotive industry. She is currently a member of the National Association of Fleet Administrators Student Advisory Task Force.

Professor Meissner has always been a teacher. She started as a part-time College instructor when she completed her first degree and moved to full-time teaching in 2005. Her "real world" experience includes car dealership controllership, and self-employment as a part-time controller and consultant for a wide variety of businesses. Professor Meissner has recently worked on several online projects for publishers as a subject-matter expert.

PETER R. NORWOOD is an instructor in accounting and coordinator of the Accounting program at Langara College in Vancouver. A graduate of the University of Alberta, he received his MBA from the University of Western Ontario. He is a Certified Public Accountant, Chartered Accountant, a Fellow of the Institute of Chartered Accountants of British Columbia, a Certified Management Accountant, and a Fellow of the Society of Management Accountants of Canada.

Before entering the academic community, Mr. Norwood worked in public practice and industry for over fifteen years. He is a Past President of the Institute of Chartered Accountants of British Columbia and Chair of the Chartered Accountants School of Business (CASB). He is also the Chair of the Chartered Accountants Education Foundation for the British Columbia Institute of Chartered Accountants, and has been active on many provincial and national committees, including the Board of Evaluators of the Canadian Institute of Chartered Accountants. Mr. Norwood is also a sessional lecturer in the Sauder School of Business, University of British Columbia.

Making Connections in *Accounting*

NEW

Key Questions are the important concepts in the chapter expressed in everyday language.

Learning Objectives are the important concepts in each chapter.

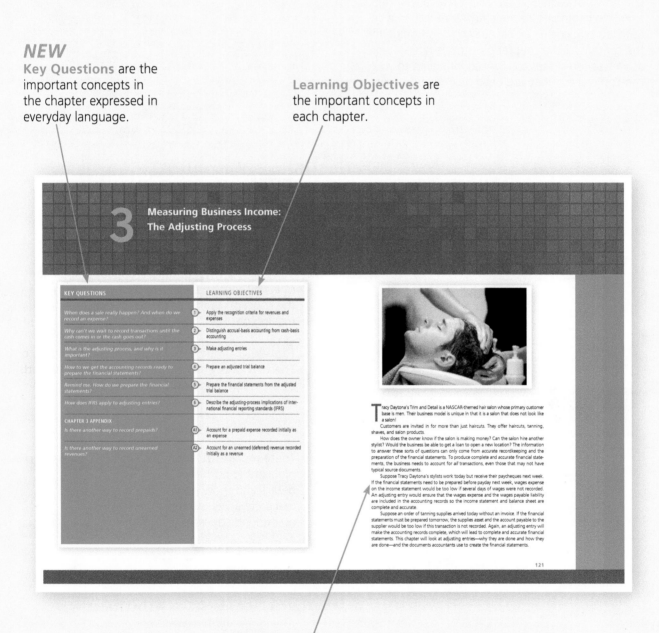

A **chapter-opening story** shows why the topics in the chapter are important to real companies and business people. We refer to this story throughout the chapter.

NEW

Connecting Chapter "X" appears at the beginning of each chapter. Don't read a chapter from the beginning to the end? Need to find a topic quickly when you're studying? This guide to the content of the chapter gives page references, as well as references to MyAccountingLab so you can connect to what you need quickly and easily.

CONNECTING CHAPTER 1

①	②	③	④	⑤	⑥
Define accounting, and describe the users of accounting information	Explain why ethics and rules of conduct are crucial in accounting and business	Describe and discuss the forms of business organizations	Explain the development of accounting standards, and describe the concepts and principles	Describe and use the accounting equation to analyze business transactions	Prepare and evaluate the financial statements
Why is accounting important, and who uses the information? page 5	*Why is it important for accountants to be ethical? page 7*	*In what form can we set up a company? page 9*	*What are the rules of accounting, and why do we need them? page 11*	*How do business transactions affect the accounting records of a company? page 16*	*What financial statements are prepared by a company, and how do we create them? page 23*
Accounting: The Language of Business, page 5	Ethical Considerations in Accounting and Business, page 7	Forms of Business Organizations, page 9	Accounting Concepts, page 11	The Accounting Equation, page 16	The Financial Statements, page 23
Decision Makers: The Users of Accounting Information, page 5				Accounting for Business Transactions, page 17	Relationships among the Financial Statements, page 24
The History and Development of Accounting, page 7				Evaluating Business Transactions, page 22	
			MyAccountingLab **Video:** Accounting Concepts and Principles	MyAccountingLab **Videos:** The Accounting Equation – Accounting Equation: Impact on Owner's Equity – Operating Activities and Their Impact on the Accounting Equation – Financing and Investing Activities and Their Impact on the Accounting Equation	MyAccountingLab **Animation:** Relationships among the Financial Statements **Video:** Introduction to Financial Statements

MyAccountingLab
- Chapter 1: Accounting Cycle Tutorial
- Chapter 1: DemoDoc covering Basic Transactions
- Chapter 1: Student PowerPoint Slides
- Chapter 1: Audio Chapter Summary

All MyAccountingLab resources can be found in the Chapter Resources section and in the Multimedia Library.

The **Summary** for Chapter 1 appears on page 30.
Accounting Vocabulary with definitions appears on page 33.

Connecting Chapter "X" appears at the beginning of each chapter and gives a guide to the content of the chapter with page references, as well as references to MyAccountingLab so you can connect to what you need quickly and easily.

What role does accounting play in Lisa Hunter's situation? Lisa had to decide how to organize her company. She set up her business as a proprietorship—a single-owner company—with herself as the owner. As her business grows, she may decide to expand it by taking on a partner. She might also choose to incorporate—that is, to form a corporation. In this chapter, we discuss all three forms of business organization: proprietorships, partnerships, and corporations.

You may already know various accounting terms and relationships, because accounting affects people's behaviour in many ways. This first accounting course will sharpen your focus by explaining how accounting works. As you progress

4   Part 1 The Basic Structure of Accounting

✓ JUST CHECKING

13. a. If the assets of a business are $75,000 and the liabilities total $65,000, how much is the owner's equity?
    b. If the owner's equity in a business is $50,000 and the liabilities are $20,000, how much are the assets?

14. Indicate whether each account listed below is a(n) asset (A), liability (L), owner's equity (OE), revenue (R), or expense (E) account.

Accounts Receivable	_____	Salaries Expense	_____
Computer Equipment	_____	Consulting Service Revenue	_____
S. Scott, Capital	_____	Cash	_____
Rent Expense	_____	Notes Payable	_____
Supplies	_____	Supplies Expense	_____
S. Scott, Withdrawals	_____	Accounts Payable	_____

15. A customer pays a deposit of $20,000 to your company for a service that you will begin to provide six months from now. How do you account for this transaction?

Just Checking Solutions appear at the end of this chapter and on MyAccountingLab.

MyAccountingLab

Videos: The Accounting Equation
• Accounting Equation: Impact on Owner's Equity
• Operating Activities and Their Impact on the Accounting Equation
• Financing and Investing Activities and Their Impact on the Accounting Equation

Just Checking questions appear at the end of each Learning Objective. Test your mastery of the concepts in this Learning Objective before moving on.

NEW

The **Just Checking Solutions** appear at the end of the chapter and on MyAccountingLab.

JUST CHECKING Solutions for Chapter 1

1. Accounting is the information system that measures business financial activities, processes that information into reports, and communicates the results to decision makers.
2. Individuals use accounting in day-to-day affairs. Businesses use accounting information to set goals for their organization. Investors need accounting information to evaluate their investments or potential investments. Creditors could use financial information to evaluate their ongoing relationship with a company.
3. Financial accounting communicates financial information about a company to interested users who are external to the company (investors, creditors, and regulators, for example). Management accounting is a branch of accounting that is used within a company to help make better future-oriented decisions.

13. To answer both questions, use the accounting equation:
    a. **Assets − Liabilities = Owner's Equity**
    $75,000 − $65,000 = $10,000
    b. **Assets = Liabilities + Owner's Equity**
    $70,000 = $20,000 + $50,000

14. Indicate whether each account listed below is a(n) asset (A), liability (L), owner's equity (OE), revenue (R), or expense (E) account.

Accounts Receivable	A
Computer Equipment	A
S. Scott, Capital	OE
Rent Expense	E

These **margin items** highlight important details and show how real companies use the accounting concepts.

WHY IT'S DONE THIS WAY

A primary focus in this chapter has been on various types of adjustments. You now know that these adjustments are all "non-cash" and they are recorded to provide more relevant financial statements to users. In terms of the accounting framework in Exhibit 1–6 in Chapter 1 (and on the back inside cover of this book), let's take a closer look at the role of adjustments.

A good example of this role can be found by examining prepaid accounts. Assume that a company has purchased its business insurance for the next year. If we look at *Level 4* of the accounting framework, we quickly realize that this transaction should be recognized as a financial transaction and we should measure the transaction at its cost. *Level 3* of the accounting framework tells us that the company would categorize this transaction as an asset, since there is future economic benefit to the company—the company has insurance coverage for the next year. Thus, we have now recognized an asset, which is prepaid

insurance. By recording and measuring the transaction in this manner, we have provided information that is relevant and reliable at the time the insurance is purchased.

As the year goes along, however, we use up the prepaid asset. The insurance coverage will expire a year from the date it was purchased, so the value of the prepaid asset declines with the passage of time. If we were to prepare the financial statements five months after the insurance was purchased, would the balance sheet be relevant if it still showed the prepaid insurance at its original cost? The answer is no. Since the insurance policy only has seven months of coverage remaining, we need to adjust the value of the prepaid insurance by expensing the used-up portion. By completing the adjustment, our financial statements remain both reliable and relevant to users (*Level 2* of the accounting framework) and the balance sheet and income statement will communicate useful information to users (*Level 1*).

NEW

Why It's Done This Way links "how" the accounting is done to "why it's done the way it's done" by connecting the chapter topic back to the basic principles of financial reporting described in Chapter 1.

Adjusting-Process Implications of International Financial Reporting Standards (IFRS)

The concept of accrual accounting is accepted around the world. The accounting guidelines for all countries recommend the use of accrual accounting. Consequently, the adjustment process that has been described in this chapter is applicable in all developed countries that provide standards for the preparation of financial statements.

The use of IFRS for publicly accountable enterprises has no direct impact on the adjusting process for these companies. Companies reporting under IFRS and ASPE go through the same adjusting process. In terms of the accrual journal entries we have seen in this chapter, the most significant difference between IFRS and ASPE is in the terms used in the amortization journal entries. IFRS specify that *depreciation* is the term to be used, whereas ASPE allow both *amortization* and *depreciation* to be used. Thus, you will see the terms *Accumulated Depreciation* and *Depreciation Expense* on IFRS financial statements for PPE. ASPE companies might choose to use the IFRS terms to be consistent with companies reporting under IFRS.

As we will see in future chapters, there is an impact on the way the financial statements are presented for companies reporting under IFRS versus ASPE. This topic will be discussed in Chapter 4.

LO ⑥
How does IFRS apply to adjusting entries?

International financial reporting standards (IFRS) is covered in the final Learning Objective in each chapter (except Chapter 1). How is IFRS different from accounting standards for private enterprises (ASPE)? Here is where we highlight the similarities and differences.

✓ JUST CHECKING

13. Do international financial reporting standards (IFRS) for publicly accountable enterprises in Canada have an impact on the adjusting process for these companies?

Just Checking Solutions appear at the end of this chapter and on MyAccountingLab.

Summary Problem for Your Review

Summary Problem for Your Review pulls together the chapter concepts. It comes with hints and reminders for solving the problem, and full solutions.

The unadjusted trial balance of Retail Employment Specialists pertains to November 30, 2014, which is the end of its year-long (fiscal) accounting period.

RETAIL EMPLOYMENT SPECIALISTS Unadjusted Trial Balance November 30, 2014		
Cash	$ 13,800	
Accounts receivable	10,000	
Supplies	2,000	
Furniture	20,000	
Accumulated amortization—furniture		$ 8,000
Building	100,000	
Accumulated amortization—building		60,000
Land	44,000	
Accounts payable		4,000
Salaries payable		0
Unearned service revenue		16,000
Gerry Barg, capital		64,000
Gerry Barg, withdrawals	50,000	

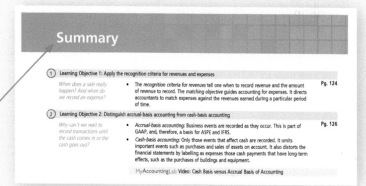

Summary appears at the end of each chapter, organized by Learning Objective. The point-form format with key diagrams and formulas keeps it concise. Page references help you find the topics you want to review.

SELF-STUDY QUESTIONS

Test your understanding of the chapter by marking the correct answer for each of the following questions:

1. The organization that formulates generally accepted accounting principles is the (p. 12)
   a. Ontario Securities Commission (OSC)
   b. Public Accountants Council of Canada
   c. Accounting Standards Board
   d. Canada Revenue Agency (CRA)

2. Which of the following forms of business organization is an "artificial person" and must obtain legal approval from the federal government or a province to conduct business? (p. 10)
   a. Law firm
   b. Proprietorship
   c. Partnership
   d. Corporation

3. You have purchased some T-shirts for $6,000 and can sell them immediately for $8,000. What accounting consideration, assumption, or characteristic governs the amount at which to record the goods you purchased? (p. 15)
   a. Economic-entity assumption
   b. Reliability characteristic
   c. Cost principle
   d. Going-concern assumption

4. The economic resources of a business are called (p. 16)
   a. Assets
   b. Liabilities
   c. Owner's equity
   d. Accounts payable

5. If the assets of a business are $200,000 and the liabilities are $90,000, how much is the owner's equity? (p. 16)
   a. $290,000
   b. $110,000
   c. $200,000
   d. $90,000

6. A business has assets of $160,000 and liabilities of $180,000. How much is its owner's equity? (p. 16)
   a. $0
   b. ($20,000)
   c. $160,000
   d. $340,000

7. If the owner's equity in a business is $70,000 and the liabilities are $35,000, how much are the assets? (p. 16)
   a. $35,000
   b. $70,000
   c. $105,000
   d. $45,000

8. Purchasing office supplies on account will (p. 18)
   a. Increase an asset and increase a liability
   b. Increase an asset and increase owner's equity
   c. Increase one asset and decrease another asset
   d. Increase an asset and decrease a liability

9. Performing a service for a customer or client and receiving the cash immediately will (p. 19)
   a. Increase one asset and decrease another asset
   b. Increase an asset and increase owner's equity
   c. Decrease an asset and decrease a liability
   d. Increase an asset and increase a liability

10. Paying an account payable will (p. 20)
    a. Increase one asset and decrease another asset
    b. Decrease an asset and decrease owner's equity
    c. Decrease an asset and decrease a liability
    d. Increase an asset and increase a liability

11. The financial statement that summarizes assets, liabilities, and owner's equity is called the (p. 24)
    a. Cash flow statement
    b. Balance sheet
    c. Income statement
    d. Statement of owner's equity

12. The financial statements that are dated for a time period (rather than for a specific point in time) are the (pp. 24–25)
    a. Balance sheet and income statement
    b. Balance sheet and statement of owner's equity
    c. Income statement, statement of owner's equity, and cash flow statement
    d. All financial statements are dated for a time period.

Answers to Self-Study Questions

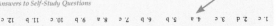

1. c 2. d 3. c 4. a 5. b 6. b 7. c 8. a 9. b 10. c 11. b 12. c

---

ACCOUNTING VOCABULARY

Accounting period Time frame, or period of time, covered by financial statements and other reports (p. 123).

Accrual-basis accounting Accounting that recognizes (records) the impact of a business event as it occurs, regardless of whether the transaction affected cash (p. 126).

Accrued expense An expense that has been incurred but not yet paid in cash (p. 135).

Accrued revenue A revenue that has been earned but not yet received in cash (p. 136).

Accumulated amortization The cumulative sum of all amortization expense from the date of acquiring a capital asset (p. 133).

Adjusted trial balance A list of all the ledger accounts with their adjusted balances (p. 141).

Adjusting entry Entry made at the end of the period to assign revenues to the period in which they are earned and expenses to the period in which they are incurred. Adjusting entries help measure the period's income and bring the related asset and liability accounts to correct balances for the financial statements (p. 129).

Amortization The term the *CICA Handbook* uses to describe the writing off to expense of the cost of capital assets; also called *depreciation* (p. 132).

Carrying value (of property, plant, and equipment) The asset's cost less accumulated amortization (p. 134).

Cash-basis accounting Accounting that records only transactions in which cash is received or paid (p. 126).

Contra account An account that always has a companion account and whose normal balance is opposite that of the companion account (p. 133).

Deferred revenue Another name for unearned revenue (p. 137).

Intangible asset An asset with no physical form giving a special right to current and expected future benefits (p. 132).

Matching objective The basis for recording expenses. Directs accountants to identify all expenses incurred during the period, measure the expenses, and match them against the revenues earned during that same span of time (p. 125).

Prepaid expense A category of miscellaneous assets that is an advance payment of an expense that typically expires or gets used up in the near future. Examples include prepaid rent, prepaid insurance, and supplies (p. 130).

Property, plant, and equipment (PPE) Long-lived tangible capital assets, such as land, buildings, and equipment, used to operate a business (p. 132).

SIMILAR ACCOUNTING TERMS

Accounting period	Reporting period
Accrual-basis accounting	Accrual accounting
Adjusting the accounts	Making the adjusting entries; adjusting the books
Amortization	Depreciation; depletion
Carrying value	Book value
Deferred	Unearned
Property, plant, and equipment (PPE)	Capital asset; plant asset; fixed asset; tangible capital asset

All question numbers in red appear on **MyAccountingLab**.

Excel Spreadsheet Template appears in the margin when a spreadsheet is available to complete the question.

All questions come with a brief description and the Learning Objective(s) covered.

Check figures are given in the margin when appropriate so you can be sure you're "on track."

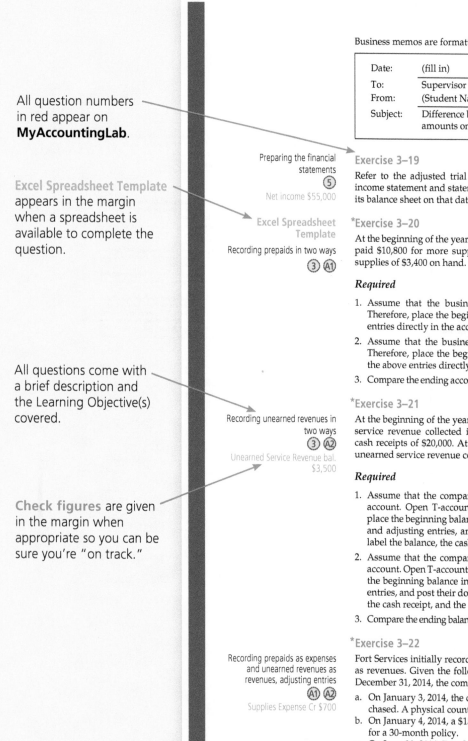

Business memos are formatted as follows:

Date:	(fill in)
To:	Supervisor
From:	(Student Name)
Subject:	Difference between the *unadjusted* and the *adjusted* amounts on an adjusted trial balance

Preparing the financial statements
⑤
Net income $55,000

Excel Spreadsheet Template
Recording prepaids in two ways
③ Ⓐ1

Recording unearned revenues in two ways
③ Ⓐ2
Unearned Service Revenue bal. $3,500

Recording prepaids as expenses and unearned revenues as revenues, adjusting entries
Ⓐ1 Ⓐ2
Supplies Expense Cr $700

Exercise 3–19

Refer to the adjusted trial balance in Exercise 3–16. Prepare Smith / income statement and statement of owner's equity for the month ended its balance sheet on that date. Draw the arrows linking the three stateme

*Exercise 3–20

At the beginning of the year, supplies of $4,800 were on hand. During the paid $10,800 for more supplies. At the end of the year, the count of supplies of $3,400 on hand.

Required

1. Assume that the business records supplies by initially debiting Therefore, place the beginning balance in the Supplies T-account, and entries directly in the accounts without using a journal.

2. Assume that the business records supplies by initially debiting ar Therefore, place the beginning balance in the Supplies Expense T-ac the above entries directly in the accounts without using a journal.

3. Compare the ending account balances under both approaches. Are they

*Exercise 3–21

At the beginning of the year, a business had a liability to customers of $. service revenue collected in advance. During the year, the business cash receipts of $20,000. At year end, the company's liability to custom unearned service revenue collected in advance.

Required

1. Assume that the company records unearned revenues by initially (account. Open T-accounts for Unearned Service Revenue and Ser place the beginning balance in Unearned Service Revenue. Journalize and adjusting entries, and post their dollar amounts. As references label the balance, the cash receipt, and the adjustment.

2. Assume that the company records unearned revenues by initially (account. Open T-accounts for Unearned Service Revenue and Service F the beginning balance in Service Revenue. Journalize the cash collec entries, and post their dollar amounts. As references in the T-accounts the cash receipt, and the adjustment.

3. Compare the ending balances in the two accounts. Explain why they are th

*Exercise 3–22

Fort Services initially records all prepaid expenses as expenses and all u as revenues. Given the following information, prepare the necessary a December 31, 2014, the company's year-end.

a. On January 3, 2014, the company's first day of operations, $2,500 of s chased. A physical count revealed $700 of supplies still on hand at Do

b. On January 4, 2014, a $15,000 payment for insurance was made to ar for a 30-month policy.

c. On June 30, 2014, Fort Services received nine months' rent totalling $ from a tenant.

---

* These Exercises cover Chapter 3 Appendix topics.

Working Papers are available for purchase. They are a set of tear-out forms to use to solve all the Exercises and Problems in Volume 2. Avoid time-consuming set-up and focus on the accounting right away.

The **Group A Problems** have check figures in the margin, but the **Group B Problems** do not.

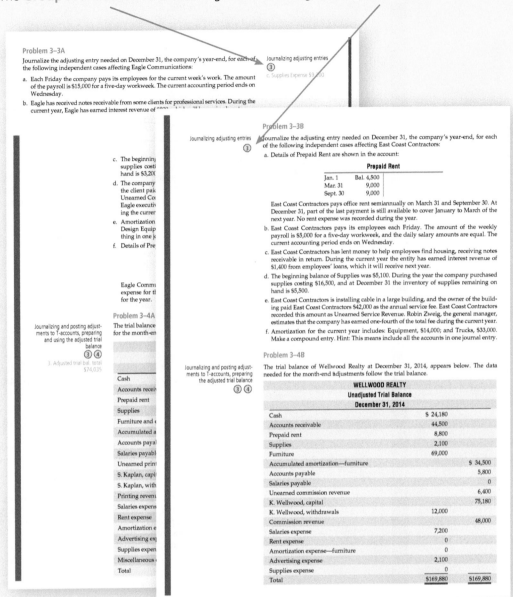

Problem 3–3A

Journalize the adjusting entry needed on December 31, the company's year-end, for each of the following independent cases affecting Eagle Communications:

a. Each Friday the company pays its employees for the current week's work. The amount of the payroll is $15,000 for a five-day workweek. The current accounting period ends on Wednesday.

b. Eagle has received notes receivable from some clients for professional services. During the current year, Eagle has earned interest revenue of $...

Journalizing adjusting entries
③
c. Supplies Expense $9,...

c. The beginning ...
supplies costi...
hand is $3,200...

d. The company...
the client paid...
Unearned Co...
Eagle executiv...
ing the curren...

e. Amortization...
Design Equip...
thing in one j...

f. Details of Pre...

Eagle Commu...
expense for th...
for the year.

Problem 3–4A

Journalizing and posting adjustments to T-accounts, preparing and using the adjusted trial balance
③ ④
3. Adjusted trial bal. total
$74,035

The trial balance...
for the month-en...

Cash
Accounts receiv...
Prepaid rent
Supplies
Furniture and e...
Accumulated a...
Accounts payabl...
Salaries payabl...
Unearned print...
S. Kaplan, capi...
S. Kaplan, with...
Printing revenu...
Salaries expens...
Rent expense
Amortization e...
Advertising exp...
Supplies expen...
Miscellaneous...
Total

Journalizing adjusting entries
③

Problem 3–3B

Journalize the adjusting entry needed on December 31, the company's year-end, for each of the following independent cases affecting East Coast Contractors:

a. Details of Prepaid Rent are shown in the account:

Prepaid Rent	
Jan. 1 Bal. 4,500	
Mar. 31 9,000	
Sept. 30 9,000	

East Coast Contractors pays office rent semiannually on March 31 and September 30. At December 31, part of the last payment is still available to cover January to March of the next year. No rent expense was recorded during the year.

b. East Coast Contractors pays its employees each Friday. The amount of the weekly payroll is $5,000 for a five-day workweek, and the daily salary amounts are equal. The current accounting period ends on Wednesday.

c. East Coast Contractors has lent money to help employees find housing, receiving notes receivable in return. During the current year the entity has earned interest revenue of $1,400 from employees' loans, which it will receive next year.

d. The beginning balance of Supplies was $5,100. During the year the company purchased supplies costing $16,500, and at December 31 the inventory of supplies remaining on hand is $5,500.

e. East Coast Contractors is installing cable in a large building, and the owner of the building paid East Coast Contractors $42,000 as the annual service fee. East Coast Contractors recorded this amount as Unearned Service Revenue. Robin Zweig, the general manager, estimates that the company has earned one-fourth of the total fee during the current year.

f. Amortization for the current year includes: Equipment, $14,000; and Trucks, $33,000. Make a compound entry. Hint: This means include all the accounts in one journal entry.

Problem 3–4B

Journalizing and posting adjustments to T-accounts, preparing the adjusted trial balance
③ ④

The trial balance of Wellwood Realty at December 31, 2014, appears below. The data needed for the month-end adjustments follow the trial balance.

WELLWOOD REALTY Unadjusted Trial Balance December 31, 2014		
Cash	$ 24,180	
Accounts receivable	44,500	
Prepaid rent	8,800	
Supplies	2,100	
Furniture	69,000	
Accumulated amortization—furniture		$ 34,500
Accounts payable		5,800
Salaries payable		0
Unearned commission revenue		6,400
K. Wellwood, capital		75,180
K. Wellwood, withdrawals	12,000	
Commission revenue		48,000
Salaries expense	7,200	
Rent expense	0	
Amortization expense—furniture	0	
Advertising expense	2,100	
Supplies expense	0	
Total	$169,880	$169,880

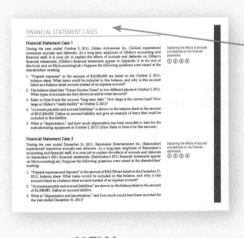

FINANCIAL STATEMENT CASES

Financial Statement Case 1

During the year ended October 2, 2011, Gildan Activewear Inc. (Gildan) experienced numerous accruals and deferrals. As a long-term employee of Gildan's accounting and financial staff, it is your job to explain the effects of accruals and deferrals on Gildan's financial statements. (Gildan's financial statements appear in Appendix A at the end of this book and on MyAccountingLab.) Suppose the following questions were raised at the shareholders' meeting:

1. "Prepaid expenses" in the amount of $10,966,000 are listed on the October 2, 2011, balance sheet. What items would be included in this balance, and why is this account listed as a balance sheet account instead of an expense account?
2. The balance sheet lists "Future Income Taxes" in two different places at October 2, 2011. What types of accounts are they shown as and at what amounts?
3. Refer to Note 8 and the account "long-term debt." How large is the current loan? How large is Gildan's "credit facility" at October 2, 2011?
4. "Accounts payable and accrued liabilities" is shown on the balance sheet in the amount of $315,269,000. Define an accrued liability and give an example of items that could be included in this liability.
5. What is "depreciation," and how much depreciation has been recorded to date for the manufacturing equipment at October 2, 2011? (Hint: Refer to Note 4 for this amount.)

Financial Statement Case 2

During the year ended December 31, 2011, Rainmaker Entertainment Inc. (Rainmaker) experienced numerous accruals and deferrals. As a long-term employee of Rainmaker's accounting and financial staff, it is your job to explain the effects of accruals and deferrals on Rainmaker's 2011 financial statements. (Rainmaker's 2011 financial statements appear on MyAccountingLab.) Suppose the following questions were raised at the shareholders' meeting:

1. "Prepaid expenses and deposits" in the amount of $923,760 are listed on the December 31, 2011, balance sheet. What items would be included in this balance, and why is this account listed as a balance sheet account instead of an expense account?
2. "Accounts payable and accrued liabilities" are shown on the balance sheet in the amount of $1,308,881. Define an accrued liability.
3. What is "depreciation and amortization," and how much would have been recorded for the year ended December 31, 2011?

Explaining the effects of accruals and deferrals on the financial statements
① ② ③ ④

Explaining the effects of accruals and deferrals on the financial statements
① ② ③ ④

Financial Statement Cases appear in almost every chapter, giving practice using real-company financial information.

IFRS MINI-CASE

Lisa Hunter has been in business for two years and her company, Hunter Environmental Consulting (HEC), has been very successful. Lisa would like to expand the business by opening offices in central and eastern Canada, and eventually in the United States. However, Lisa realizes these plans require more money than she can borrow from a bank. One option she is considering is to make Hunter Environmental Consulting a corporation so she can list the company on a stock exchange and sell shares in the company to the general public. Lisa knows you are studying accounting and asks you whether HEC has to change the way it is reporting—HEC reports under ASPE currently—if HEC becomes a publicly traded company. Answer Lisa's question and explain why there are two sets of reporting standards in Canada.

NEW

IFRS Mini-Cases appear in selected chapters and highlight the similarities and differences between ASPE and IFRS.

Supplements for Students and Instructors

The primary goal of the supplements that accompany *Accounting* is to help instructors deliver their course with ease, using any delivery method—traditional, self-paced, or online—and for students to learn and practise accounting in a variety of ways that meet their learning needs and study preferences.

MyAccountingLab

The moment you know.

Educators know it. Students know it. It's that inspired moment when something that was difficult to understand suddenly makes perfect sense. MyAccountingLab has been designed and refined with a single purpose in mind—to help educators create that moment of understanding with their students.

MyAccountingLab delivers **proven results** in helping individual students succeed. It provides **engaging experiences** that personalize, stimulate, and measure learning for each student. And, it comes from a **trusted partner** with educational expertise and an eye on the future. MyAccountingLab is the portal to an array of learning tools for all learning styles—practice questions with guided solutions are only the beginning. MyAccountingLab now includes Knewton, the latest technology in Adaptive Assessment for individualized learning and mastery. Students can access MyAccountingLab at www.myaccountinglab.com.

MyAccountingLab can be used by itself or linked to any learning management system. To learn more about how MyAccountingLab combines proven learning applications with powerful assessment, instructors can visit www.myaccountinglab.com.

Study on the Go

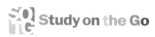

Featured at the end of each chapter, you will find a unique barcode providing access to Study on the Go. Study on the Go brings material from your textbook to you and your smartphone. Now wherever you are—whatever you are doing—you can study by listening to the Audio Summaries, quizzing yourself, or using the awesome Glossary Flashcards. Go to one of the sites below to see how you can download an app to your smartphone for free. Once the app is installed, your phone will scan the code and link to a website containing Pearson's Study on the Go content that you can access anytime.

ScanLife
http://get.scanlife.com/

NeoReader
http://get.neoreader.com/

QuickMark
http://www.quickmark.com.tw/

MyAccountingCourse Premium Online Courseware

Pearson's MyAccountingCourse™ is a premium online course solution that combines fully customizable course lessons and tutorials and the personalized homework and assessment features of MyAccountingLab™. Designed to be used in fully online or blended learning environments, MyAccountingCourse can accommodate various term lengths and includes an integrated eBook and comprehensive Instructor Resource Guide.

Features of MyAccountingCourse include:

- A flexible, customizable solution where an instructor may add to, delete, and reorganize content. Each topic-based MyAccountingCourse module is built to specific learning outcomes, and MyAccountingCourse includes a comprehensive Instructor Resource Guide complete with course outcomes, lesson objectives, and teaching tips.
- Interactive lesson presentations with a proven learning model, robust content, and relevant video, audio, eBook, downloadable MP3 lectures, and other rich media assets.
- Rich MyAccountingLab-based assessment, pre-tests, quizzes, homework, and tests.

CourseSmart for Students

CourseSmart goes beyond traditional expectations, providing instant, online access to the textbooks and course materials you need at an average savings of 60%. With instant access from any computer and the ability to search your text, you'll find the content you need quickly, no matter where you are. And with online tools like highlighting and note-taking, you can save time and study efficiently. See all the benefits at www.coursesmart.com/students.

Pearson eText

Pearson eText gives you access to the text whenever and wherever you have access to the Internet. eText pages look exactly like the printed text, offering powerful new functionality for students and instructors. Users can create notes, highlight text in different colours, create bookmarks, zoom, click hyperlinked words and phrases to view definitions, and view in single-page or two-page view. Pearson eText allows for quick navigation to key parts of the eText using a table of contents and provides full-text search.

Technology Specialists

Pearson's Technology Specialists work with faculty and campus course designers to ensure that Pearson technology products, assessment tools, and online course materials are tailored to meet your specific needs. This highly qualified team is dedicated to helping schools take full advantage of a wide range of educational resources, by assisting in the integration of a variety of instructional materials and media formats. Your local Pearson Education sales representative can provide you with more details on this service program.

Instructor's Resources on the Online Catalogue at http://catalogue.pearsoned.ca

This password-protected site provides a collection of resources to help faculty with lecture preparation, presentation, and assessment. It contains the following supplements:

- **Instructor's Solutions Manual** Now provided in both Adobe PDF and MS Word format for ease of use.

- **Instructor's Resource Manual** Also provided in both Adobe PDF and MS Word format, the Instructor's Resource Manual includes Chapter Overviews and Outlines, Assignment Grids, Ten-Minute Quizzes, and other valuable teaching resources including how to integrate MyAccountingLab and MyAccountingCourse in your course. In addition, there is a new section describing all the supplements that come with *Accounting*, along with suggestions for how and when they can be used, written by an instructor who has used them all!

- **TestGen** This powerful and user-friendly computerized test bank includes well over 100 questions per chapter, ranging from True False, Multiple-Choice, and Matching to Problems and Critical Thinking Exercises.

- **PowerPoint Teaching Transparencies** For instructors and students, we provide a comprehensive set of PowerPoint files with 40 to 60 slides per chapter.

- **Exhibits** We are pleased to provide the exhibits from the text in GIF format for use in the classroom and easy conversion to acetate format.

- **Adapting Your Lecture Notes** These detailed transition notes, including comparison of tables of content, chapter objectives, and chapter content, will facilitate your course preparation if you make the switch to *Accounting* from another introductory accounting text.

Other items include:

- **Group Projects**
- **Solutions to Group Projects**
- **Check Figures**
- **Excel Spreadsheet Templates**
- **Gildan Activewear Inc. 2011 Annual Report**
- **Rainmaker Entertainment Inc. 2011 Annual Report**

Pearson Custom Publishing

We know that not every instructor follows the exact order of a course text. Some may not even cover all the material in a given volume. Pearson Custom Publishing provides the flexibility to select the chapters you need, presented in the order you want, to tailor fit your text to your course and your students' needs. Contact your Pearson Education Canada Sales and Editorial Representative to learn more.

We hope you enjoy *Accounting*!

Acknowledgements for the Ninth Canadian Edition of *Accounting*

We would like to thank the late Charles Horngren, and Tom Harrison for their encouragement and support.

Thanks are due to the following instructors for reviewing the previous edition of this text during the planning and development of this new edition, and for their excellent suggestions and ideas:

Dr. Andrea Chance, George Brown College
Robin Day, British Columbia Institute of Technology
Andrew Dykstra, Georgian College
Carol Fearon, Seneca College
Dave Flemming, George Brown College
Paul Griffin, Humber Institute of Technology and Advanced Learning
Gerry La Rocca, Vanier College
Jeff Oestreicher, Humber Institute of Technology and Advanced Learning
Doug Ringrose, Grant MacEwan University
Don Smith, Georgian College
Glen Stanger, Douglas College
Selina Tang, Douglas College

Thanks are due to the instructors who reviewed some or all of the chapters in Volumes 1 and 2 of this new edition of *Accounting*:

Bharat Aggarwal, Seneca College
Mina Ally, Seneca College
Alym Amlani, Kwantlen Polytechnic University
Joanne Belliveau, Northern Alberta Institute of Technology
Robin Day, British Columbia Institute of Technology
Denise Dodson, Nova Scotia Community College
Cynthia Duncan, Seneca College
Burchell Hanson, Humber Institute of Technology and Advanced Learning
John Harris, Centennial College
Gerry La Rocca, Vanier College
Doug Ringrose, Grant MacEwan University
Jeff Oestreicher, Humber Institute of Technology and Advanced Learning
Ann Overton, Centennial College
Angelo Papadatos, Dawson College
Paul Pickett, Conestoga College
Don Smith, Georgian College
Glen Stanger, Douglas College
Brad Witt, Humber Institute of Technology and Advanced Learning
John Tataryn, Assiniboine Community College
Jeanine Wall, Red River College

Special thanks to Doug Ringrose, Grant MacEwan University, for being a "super reviewer" of Volume 1—his comments helped us to improve the chapters even further.

Thanks to the 2012/2013 Pearson Editorial Advisory Board in Accounting. This group of subject-matter experts helped us develop improved content for our print-based products and online resources:

Susan Fisher, Algonquin College
Deirdre Fitzpatrick, George Brown College
Ho Yee Low, Kwantlen University
Doug Ringrose, Grant McEwan University
Don Smith, Georgian College
Glen Stanger, Douglas College
Brad Witt, Humber College

Thanks to the 2012 Pearson Student Editorial Advisory Board in Accounting. This group of students helped us develop improved content for MyAccountingLab by providing feedback on its content, platform structure, and functionality:

Patrick Belliveau, Sheridan College
Connor Bildfell, University of Victoria
Jennifer McAllister, Algonquin College
Carla Winter, Grant MacEwan University
Andrea Yeung, University of British Columbia

Thanks to the many student focus groups from a variety of schools, in particular British Columbia Institute of Technology and Algonquin College, whose comments helped us to develop new features to increase student accessibility and student engagement in both the textbook and MyAccountingLab. Special thanks to student Stefan Muntean from Northern Alberta Institute of Technology who provided detailed feedback that helped us improve this new edition of *Accounting*.

Thanks are extended to Gildan Activewear Inc. and Rainmaker Entertainment Inc. for permission to use their annual reports in Volumes 1 and 2 of this text and on MyAccountingLab. We acknowledge the support provided by the websites of various news organizations, and by the annual reports of a large number of public companies.

The Canadian Institute of Chartered Accountants, as the official promulgator of generally accepted accounting principles in Canada, and the *CICA Handbook*, are vital to the conduct of business and accounting in Canada. We have made every effort to incorporate the most current *Handbook* recommendations in this new edition of *Accounting* for both private enterprises (ASPE) and for publicly accountable enterprises subject to international financial reporting standards (IFRS).

We would like to give special thanks to Amy Lam, CA, Senior Director of Member Services, Institute of Chartered Accountants of British Columbia, for her guidance and technical support during this time of great changes in the accounting-standards environment. Her willingness to review and discuss portions of the manuscript was very generous and insightful, and it is gratefully acknowledged.

We would like to acknowledge the people of Pearson Education Canada, in particular V-P Editorial Director Gary Bennett, Editor-in-Chief Nicole Lukach, Acquisitions Editor Megan Farrell, and Marketing Manager Claire Varley. Special thanks to Lead Project Manager Avinash Chandra, Production Managers Sarah Gallagher and Deborah Starks, as well as Project Managers Marisa Taylor and Lynn Brownell and the team at GEX Publishing Services for their superior efforts in guiding this edition through the various phases of preparation and production. We would like to thank Media Content Developers Victoria Naik and Imee Salumbides, and their team for their excellent work on the MyAccountingLab that accompanies this textbook. We would also like to acknowledge the editorial and technical support of Anita Smale, CPA, CA.

I would like to thank my husband Bill and family for their encouragement and support.

Jo-Ann L. Johnston

I would like to thank my students for keeping me on my toes. Hearing their new ideas and ways of thinking about accounting makes teaching such a wonderful job.
Carol A. Meissner

I would like to thank my wife, Helen, and my family very much for their support and encouragement. I would also like to acknowledge the support of my co-authors and the outstanding work of our developmental editor, Anita Smale.
Peter R. Norwood

12 Partnerships

KEY QUESTIONS		LEARNING OBJECTIVES
What are the characteristics of a partnership?	1	Identify the characteristics of a partnership
How do we account for partners' investments in a partnership?	2	Account for partners' initial investments in a partnership
How can we allocate profits and losses to the partners?	3	Allocate profits and losses to the partners by different methods
How do we account for a new partner?	4	Account for the admission of a new partner
How do we account for the withdrawal of a partner?	5	Account for the withdrawal of a partner
How do we account for the ending of a partnership?	6	Account for the liquidation of a partnership
How does IFRS affect partnerships?	7	Identify the impact on partnerships of international financial reporting standards (IFRS)

Osler, Hoskin & Harcourt LLP (limited liability partnership) is one of Canada's largest law firms. In 2012, the firm had over 500 lawyers who provided a variety of legal services to Canadian clients, as well as U.S. and international clients with interests in Canada. The firm has offices in Toronto, Montreal, Ottawa, Calgary, and New York. Osler, Hoskin & Harcourt LLP has a long list of areas of expertise and has been very successful. The firm deals with issues that cross Canada's internal borders as well as issues that cross international borders.

"Increasingly, our clients are looking for seamless legal support across the United States–Canada border and we are uniquely positioned to offer this support in the areas sought most often by our clients.... We understand the importance of being familiar with our clients' business and industry and of aligning our work to support their business objectives. We know that we perform best when we integrate our advice within the context of the business imperatives facing our clients, combining our efforts to assist our clients in overcoming their challenges and achieving their goals. By engaging Osler, our clients gain access to the expertise and experience they need from the best of our firm. Our 'one firm' approach is based on teamwork and collaboration to deliver superior legal advice efficiently and effectively for our clients."[1]

In this chapter, we will explain the partnership form of business organization and examine many of the issues that affect partnerships.

---

[1] From the Osler, Hoskin & Harcourt website www.osler.com/AboutUs/, accessed August 9, 2012.

① Identify the characteristics of a partnership	② Account for partners' initial investments in a partnership	③ Allocate profits and losses to the partners by different methods	④ Account for the admission of a new partner	⑤ Account for the withdrawal of a partner	⑥ Account for the liquidation of a partnership	⑦ Identify the impact on partnerships of international financial reporting standards (IFRS)
What are the characteristics of a partnership? page 756	*How do we account for partners' investments in a partnership? page 761*	*How can we allocate profits and losses to the partners? page 762*	*How do we account for a new partner? page 768*	*How do we account for the withdrawal of a partner? page 772*	*How do we account for the ending of a partnership? page 776*	*How does IFRS affect partnerships? page 780*
Characteristics of a Partnership, page 756	Forming a Partnership, page 761	Sharing Partnership Profits and Losses, page 762	Admission of a Partner, page 768	Withdrawal of a Partner from the Business, page 772	Liquidation of a Partnership, page 776	The Impact on Partnerships of International Financial Reporting Standards (IFRS), page 780
Types of Partnerships, page 759		Partner Withdrawals (Drawings) of Cash and Other Assets, page 766		Death of a Partner, page 775		
Partnership Financial Statements, page 759						

MyAccountingLab
- Chapter 12: DemoDoc covering Partnerships
- Chapter 12: Student PowerPoint Slides
- Chapter 12: Audio Chapter Summary

All MyAccountingLab resources can be found in the Chapter Resources section and the Multimedia Library.

The **Summary** for Chapter 12 appears on page 782.
Accounting Vocabulary with definitions appears on page 784.

The partnership form of business introduces some complexities that a proprietorship avoids:

- How much cash should a new partner contribute to the business?
- How should the partners divide profits and losses?
- How should a partner who leaves the firm be compensated for her or his share of the business?

A **partnership** is an association of two or more persons who co-own a business for profit. This definition is common to the various provincial partnership acts, which tend to prescribe similar rules with respect to the organization and operation of partnerships in their jurisdictions.

Forming a partnership is easy. It requires no permission from government authorities and involves no legal procedures, with the exception that most provinces require most partnerships to register information such as the names of the partners and the name under which the business will be conducted.[2] When two people decide to go into business together, a partnership is automatically formed.

A partnership combines the assets, talents, and experience of the partners. Business opportunities closed to an individual may open up to a partnership. As the chapter-opening story illustrates, this is an important characteristic of a partnership. Osler, Hoskin & Harcourt LLP is successful because it is able to combine the skills of its very specialized lawyers and provide its clients with a complete roster of legal services. It is unlikely a lawyer operating as a proprietorship could offer the same level of expertise.

Partnerships come in all sizes. Many partnerships have fewer than 10 partners. Some medical practices may have 10 or more partners, while some of the largest law firms in Canada have more than 300 partners. The largest accounting firm in Canada has more than 500 partners.[3] Exhibit 12–1 lists the 10 largest public accounting firms in Canada. The majority of them are partnerships.

EXHIBIT **12–1** | The Ten Largest Accounting Firms in Canada

Rank 2011	Firm	Revenue (Millions)	Number of Partners/Principals
1	Deloitte & Touche LLP	$1,505	538
2	PricewaterhouseCoopers LLP	1,180	420
3	KPMG LLP	1,138	429
4	Ernst & Young LLP	870	331
5	Grant Thornton Canada (includes Grant Thornton LLP and Raymond Chabot Grant Thornton (Quebec))	515	416
6	BDO Canada LLP	426	382
7	MNP LLP	374	283
8	Collins Barrow National Co-operative	143	177
9	RSM Richter	84	76
10	Mallette	53	59

Source: "Canada's Accounting Top 30," *The Bottom Line*, April 2012, online at www.thebottomlinenews.ca/documents/Canadas_Accounting_Top_30.pdf, accessed August 15, 2012. Courtesy of *The Bottom Line*.

WHY IT'S DONE THIS WAY

Beginning with this chapter, you will learn more about the different types of organization structures that were first mentioned in Chapter 1. To this point, proprietorships were studied extensively. This chapter covers partnerships and the remaining chapters after this focus on corporations.

The good news is that the principles and concepts in the accounting framework described in Chapter 1 (and repeated on the back inside cover of this book) apply equally to all types of organizations, including partnerships. Accounting differences among types of organizations only relate to the equity section of the balance sheet. Therefore, the **Level 4** recognition and measurement criteria and constraints apply equally to partnerships as well as proprietorships and corporations. The **Level 3** elements of financial statements are the same for the three types of organizations except for an expansion in the partnership's equity section (and further expansion in the corporation's equity section). For partnerships, the **Level 2** qualitative characteristics of accounting information are the same as for proprietorships and corporations, and the **Level 1** objective of financial reporting continues to be to communicate useful information to users of partnership financial information.

---

[2] Smyth, J.E., D.A. Soberman, A.J. Easson, and S.S. McGill, *The Law and Business Administration in Canada,* 13th edition (Toronto: Pearson Canada Inc., 2013), pp. 598–602.

[3] "Canada's Accounting Top 30," *The Bottom Line*, April 2012, online at www.thebottomlinenews.ca/documents/Canadas_Accounting_Top_30.pdf, accessed August 15, 2012.

Characteristics of a Partnership

LO ①
What are the characteristics of a partnership?

Starting a partnership is voluntary. A person cannot be forced to join a partnership, and partners cannot be forced to accept another person as a partner (unless existing partners vote and the majority accept the new partner). The following characteristics distinguish partnerships from proprietorships and from corporations.

The Written Partnership Agreement

KEY POINTS

A partnership is not required to have a formal written agreement. But a written agreement prevents confusion as to the sharing of profits and losses, partners' responsibilities, admission of new partners, how the partnership will be liquidated, and so on. However, there can still be disagreements even when there is a written agreement.

A business partnership is somewhat like a marriage. To be successful, the partners must cooperate. However, business partners do not vow to remain together for life. To make certain that each partner fully understands how the partnership operates, partners should draw up a **partnership agreement**. Although the partnership agreement may be oral, a written agreement between the partners reduces the chance of a misunderstanding. This agreement is a contract between the partners, so transactions under the agreement are governed by contract law. The provincial legislatures in Canada have passed their respective versions of a partnership act, the terms of which apply in the absence of a partnership agreement or in the absence of particular matters in the partnership agreement.[4]

The partnership agreement should specify the following points:

1. Name, location, and nature of the business
2. Name, capital investment, and duties of each partner
3. Procedures for admitting a new partner
4. Method of sharing profits and losses among the partners
5. Withdrawals of assets allowed to the partners
6. Procedures for settling disputes among the partners
7. Procedures for settling with a partner who withdraws from the firm
8. Procedures for removing a partner who will not withdraw or retire from the partnership voluntarily
9. Procedures for liquidating the partnership—selling the assets, paying the liabilities, and giving any remaining cash to the partners

As partners enter and leave the business, the old partnership is dissolved and a new partnership is formed. Drawing up a new agreement for each new partnership may be expensive and time-consuming.

Limited Life

A partnership has a limited life. If one partner withdraws from the business, the partnership dissolves and its books are closed. If the remaining partners want to continue as partners in the same business, they form a new partnership with a new set of books. **Dissolution** is the ending of a partnership and does not require liquidation; that is, the assets need not be sold to outside parties for a new partnership to be created. Often the new partnership continues the former partnership's business, and the new partnership may choose to continue to use the dissolved partnership's name. Large partnerships such as PricewaterhouseCoopers retain the firm name even after partners resign from the firm.

---

[4] Smyth, J.E., D.A. Soberman, A.J. Easson, and S.A. McGill, *The Law and Business Administration in Canada*, 13th edition (Toronto: Pearson Canada Inc., 2013), pp. 598–618.

Mutual Agency

Mutual agency means that every partner is a mutual agent of the firm. Any partner can bind the business to a contract within the scope of the partnership's regular business operations. If a partner enters into a contract with a person or another business to provide a service, then the firm—not just the partner who signed the contract—is bound to provide that service. If the partner signs a contract to buy her own car, however, the partnership is not liable because the car is a personal matter. It is not within the scope of the regular business operations of the partnership.

The following example shows the impact mutual agency can have on a partnership. Richard Harding and Simon Davis formed a partnership to deal in lumber and other building material. The partners agreed that their company should not handle brick or any stone materials and that neither partner had the right to purchase these commodities. While Harding was away during the summer, Davis purchased a quantity of these materials for the company because he could buy them at a cheap price. Two months later, when Harding returned, business was very slow, and brick and stone were selling at a price lower than Davis had paid for them. Harding, therefore, refused to abide by the contract Davis had made with the brick and stone supplier, and refused to accept any more deliveries under the contract. Harding argued that Davis had no authority to buy these goods since the partnership was not organized to deal in brick and stone. The supplier of the brick and stone said that he did not know the partnership was not in the brick and stone business. In fact, he believed that it did handle these goods since all of the other lumber companies in the town bought or sold brick and stone. Because the supplier acted in good faith, he claimed that Harding and Davis should abide by the contract and accept the remaining deliveries of brick and stone. Who was correct? Under normal circumstances, the brick-and-stone supplier is correct because the mutual agency characteristic of a partnership allows partners to bind each other in business contracts. The agreements made within the partnership would not be known by an outside party like the supplier, so the supplier would have a solid case and could sue the partnership to abide by the contract.[5]

Unlimited Liability

Each partner has **unlimited personal liability** for the debts of the business. When a partnership cannot pay its debts with business assets, the partners must pay with their personal assets. (There are exceptions, which are described in the next section, Types of Partnerships.) Proprietors also have unlimited personal liability for the debts of their business.

Suppose the partnership of Willis & Jones cannot pay a $20,000 business debt that Jones created. Willis and Jones each become personally liable (must pay this amount with their personal assets) because each partner has *unlimited liability* for their business debts. If either partner is unable to pay his or her part of the debt, the other partner (or partners) must make payment.

Unlimited liability and mutual agency are closely related. A dishonest partner or a partner with poor judgment may commit the partnership to a contract under which the business loses money. In turn, creditors may force *all* the partners to pay the debt from their personal assets. Hence, a business partner should be chosen with great care. This was shown in the Harding and Davis partnership described above.

---

[5] This case is based on the scenario described on http://chestofbooks.com/business/law/
Case-Method/B-Apparent-Scope-Of-Authority.html#ixzz1qimHxY2o, accessed on August 14, 2012.

KEY POINTS

A personal investment of assets in a partnership becomes the joint property of all the partners.

Co-ownership of Property

Any asset—cash, inventory, machinery, computers, and so on—that a partner invests into the partnership becomes the joint property of all the partners. The partner who invested the asset is no longer its sole owner.

No Partnership Income Tax

A partnership pays no income tax on its business income. Instead, the net income of the partnership is divided and flows through to become the taxable income of the partners. Suppose the Willis & Jones partnership earned net income of $150,000, shared equally by the two partners. The partnership would pay no income tax *as a business entity*. However, each partner would pay income tax *as an individual* on his or her $75,000 share of partnership income.

Partners' Equity Accounts

Recall from Chapter 1, page 16, that owner's equity for a proprietorship has only one account, entitled "Capital." Accounting for a partnership is much like accounting for a proprietorship. We record buying and selling goods and services, collecting and paying cash for a partnership just as we do for a proprietorship. But, because a partnership has more than one owner, the partnership must have a separate owner's equity account for each partner. For example, the equity account for Leslie Willis is "L. Willis, Capital." Just as a proprietor has a drawings or withdrawal account (a temporary account), each partner in a partnership has a withdrawal account, such as "L. Willis, Withdrawals."

Exhibit 12–2 lists the advantages and disadvantages of partnerships (compared with proprietorships and corporations). Most features of a proprietorship also apply to a partnership, most importantly

- Limited life
- Unlimited liability
- No business income tax

EXHIBIT 12–2 | Advantages and Disadvantages of Partnerships

Partnership Advantages	Partnership Disadvantages
Versus Proprietorships:	1. A partnership agreement may be difficult to formulate. Each time a new partner is admitted or a partner leaves the partnership, the business needs a new partnership agreement.
1. A partnership can raise more capital since capital comes from more than one person.	
2. A partnership brings together the abilities of more than one person.	2. Relationships among partners may be fragile.
3. Partners working well together can achieve more than by working alone: $1 + 1 > 2$ in a good partnership.	3. Mutual agency and unlimited liability create personal obligations for each partner.
Versus Corporations:	
4. A partnership is less expensive to organize than a corporation, which requires articles of incorporation from a province or the federal government.	
5. A partnership is subject to fewer governmental regulations and restrictions than is a corporation.	

Types of Partnerships

There are two basic types of partnerships: general and limited.

General Partnerships

A **general partnership** is the basic form of partnership organization. Each partner is a co-owner of the business with all the privileges and risks of ownership. The general partners share the profits, losses, and the risks of the business. The partnership *reports* its income to the government tax authority (Canada Revenue Agency, or CRA), but the partnership pays *no* income tax. The profits and losses of the partnership pass through the business to the partners, who then pay personal income tax on their income. All the other features just covered also apply to a general partnership.

Limited Partnerships

Partners can avoid unlimited personal liability for partnership obligations by forming a *limited partnership*. A **limited partnership** has at least two classes of partners. There must be at least one *general partner*, who takes primary responsibility for the management of the business. The general partner also takes most of the risk of failure if the partnership goes bankrupt (liabilities exceed assets). In some limited partnerships, such as real-estate limited partnerships, the general partner often invests little cash in the business. Instead, the general partner's contribution is her or his skill in managing the organization. Usually, the general partner is the last owner to receive a share of partnership profits and losses. But the general partner may earn all excess profits after the limited partners get their share of the income.

The *limited partners* are so named because their personal obligation for the partnership's liabilities is limited to the amount they have invested in the business. Limited partners have limited liability similar to the limited liability that shareholders in a corporation have. Usually, the limited partners have invested the bulk of the partnership's assets and capital. They, therefore, usually have the first claim to partnership profits and losses, but only up to a specified limit. In exchange for their limited liability, their potential for profits usually has a limit as well.

Most professionals, such as doctors, lawyers, and most public accounting firms in Canada—including almost all of those in Exhibit 12–1—are now organized as **limited liability partnerships (LLPs)**. An LLP can only be used by eligible professions—accounting is an eligible profession—and is designed to protect innocent partners from negligence damages that result from another partner's actions. This means that each partner's personal liability for other partners' negligence is limited to a certain dollar amount, although liability for a partner's own negligence is still unlimited. The LLP must carry an adequate amount of malpractice insurance or liability insurance to protect the public.

KEY POINTS

Since all partners are personally liable for any debt of the business, it is extremely important to choose a partner carefully. This is one reason some investors/partners prefer the *limited partnership* form of business organization.

Partnership Financial Statements

Partnership financial statements are much like those of a proprietorship. However, a partnership income statement includes a section showing the division of net income to the partners. A partnership balance sheet reports a separate Capital account for each partner in the section now called Partners' Equity. Large partnerships may show one balance, the total for all partners. For example, the Willis & Jones partnership of Leslie Willis and Andrew Jones might report its financial statements for the year ended December 31, 2014, as shown in Panel A of Exhibit 12–3 on the next page. A proprietorship's financial statements are presented in Panel B for comparison.

PANEL A—PARTNERSHIP

WILLIS & JONES
Income Statement
For the Year Ended December 31, 2014

Revenues	$460
Expenses	(270)
Net income	$190
Allocation of net income:	
To Leslie Willis	$114
To Andrew Jones	76 $190

WILLIS & JONES
Statement of Owners' Equity*
For the Year Ended December 31, 2014

	Willis	Jones
Capital, January 1, 2014	$ 50	$40
Additional investments	10	—
Net income	114	76
Subtotal	174	116
Withdrawals	(72)	(48)
Capital, December 31, 2014	$102	$68

WILLIS & JONES
Balance Sheet
December 31, 2014

Assets	
Cash and other assets	$170
Partners' Equity	
Leslie Willis, capital	$102
Andrew Jones, capital	68
Total equity	$170

*This statement could also be called a Statement of Partners' Equity.

PANEL B—PROPRIETORSHIP

WILLIS CONSULTING
Income Statement
For the Year Ended December 31, 2014

Revenues	$460
Expenses	(270)
Net income	$190

WILLIS CONSULTING
Statement of Owner's Equity
For the Year Ended December 31, 2014

Capital, January 1, 2014	$ 90
Additional investments	10
Net income	190
Subtotal	290
Withdrawals	(120)
Capital, December 31, 2014	$170

WILLIS CONSULTING
Balance Sheet
December 31, 2014

Assets	
Cash and other assets	$170
Owner's Equity	
Leslie Willis, capital	$170

✓ JUST CHECKING

1. John Richards and Patricia Quinn would like to form a partnership to open up a night club—Endelay's. They each have $100,000 and have decided that since they have been life-long friends, they do not need a written partnership agreement. Detail the contents of a partnership agreement and explain the importance of a written agreement to Richards and Quinn.

2. Suppose you were giving the friends in the previous question advice on their decision to form a partnership. Detail the advantages and disadvantages of their decision.

3. Richards and Quinn may, at some point, want to bring in a partner who does not want any day-to-day responsibility for managing the operations; he or she may simply want to receive a return on his or her investment. Describe the type of partner this person would be.

Just Checking Solutions appear at the end of this chapter and on MyAccountingLab.

Forming a Partnership

Let's examine the start up of a partnership. Partners in a new partnership may invest assets and their related liabilities in the business. These contributions are journalized in the same way as for proprietorships, by debiting the assets and crediting the liabilities at their agreed-upon values. Each person's net contribution—assets minus liabilities—is credited to the equity account for that person. Often the partners hire an independent firm to appraise their assets and liabilities at current market value at the time a partnership is formed. This outside evaluation assures an objective valuation for what each partner brings into the business.

Suppose Katie Zheng and Dan Chao form a partnership on June 1, 2014 to develop and sell computer software. The partners agree on the following values based on an independent appraisal:

LO ②

How do we account for partners' investments in a partnership?

Zheng's contributions

- Cash, $10,000; inventory, $40,000; and accounts payable, $80,000 (The appraiser believes that the current market values for these items equal Zheng's book values.)
- Computer equipment: cost, $800,000; accumulated amortization, $200,000; current market value, $450,000

Chao's contributions

- Cash, $5,000
- Computer software: cost, $50,000; current market value, $100,000

REAL WORLD EXAMPLE

There is a way for a partner to allow the partnership to use a personal asset, such as a car or money, without losing his or her claim to that asset. The partner could lease the car to the partnership. If the partnership were liquidated, the car would have to be returned to its owner. The partner could also lend money to the partnership instead of investing it. Upon liquidation, the partnership would have to repay the loan to the lending partner before any distribution of capital to the partners.

The partnership records receipts of the partners' initial investments at the current market values of the assets and liabilities because, in effect, the partnership is buying the assets and assuming the liabilities at their current market values. The partnership entries are as follows:

Zheng 's investment			
2014			
Jun. 1	Cash	10,000	
	Inventory	40,000*	
	Computer Equipment	450,000*	
	Accounts Payable		80,000*
	Katie Zheng, Capital		420,000
	To record Zheng's investment in the		
	partnership ($500,000 – $80,000).		

Chao's investment			
2014			
Jun. 1	Cash	5,000	
	Computer Software	100,000*	
	Dan Chao, Capital		105,000
	To record Chao's investment in the		
	partnership.		

*The assets were appraised and their current market values were used.

KEY POINTS

The major difference in accounting for a proprietorship versus a partnership is the number of Capital and Withdrawal accounts. The partnership balance sheet shows a separate Capital account for each partner, and there is a separate Withdrawals account for each partner. The asset and liability sections on the balance sheet and the income statement are the same for a proprietorship and a partnership.

The initial partnership balance sheet appears in Exhibit 12–4. Note that the asset and liability sections on the balance sheet are the same for a proprietorship and a partnership.

EXHIBIT **12–4** | Partnership Balance Sheet

ZHENG AND CHAO
Balance Sheet
June 1, 2014

Assets		Liabilities	
Cash	$ 15,000	Accounts payable	$ 80,000
Inventory	40,000	**Partners' Equity**	
Computer equipment	450,000	Katie Zheng, capital	420,000
Computer software	100,000	Dan Chao, capital	105,000
		Total partners' equity	525,000
		Total liabilities	
Total assets	$605,000	and equity	$605,000

✓ JUST CHECKING

4. Marty Kaur invests land in a partnership with Lee Manors. Kaur purchased the land in 2011 for $20,000. Three independent real estate appraisers now value the land at $50,000. Kaur wants $50,000 capital in the new partnership, but Manors objects. Manors believes that Kaur's capital investment should be measured by the book value of his land. Manors and Kaur seek your advice. Which value of the land is appropriate for measuring Kaur's capital—book value or current market value? State the reason for your answer.

5. Refer to the previous question. Give the partnership's journal entry to record Kaur's investment in the business.

Just Checking Solutions appear at the end of this chapter and on MyAccountingLab.

Sharing Partnership Profits and Losses

— LO ③ —
How can we allocate profits and losses to the partners?

Allocating profits and losses among partners can be challenging and can be a major source of disputes. Any division of profits and losses is allowed as long as the partners agree and it is in the partnership agreement. Typical arrangements include the following:

1. Sharing profits and losses based on a stated fraction for each partner, such as 50/50, or 2/3 and 1/3, or 4:3:3 (which means 40 percent to Partner A, 30 percent to Partner B, and 30 percent to Partner C).
2. Sharing based on each partner's capital investment.
3. Sharing based on each partner's service.
4. Sharing based on a combination of stated fractions, investments, service, and other items.

If the partners have not drawn up an agreement, or if the agreement does not state how the partners will divide profits and losses, then, by law, the partners must share profits and losses equally. If the agreement specifies a method for sharing profits but not losses, then losses are shared in the same proportion as profits. For example, a partner receiving 75 percent of the profits would likewise absorb 75 percent of any losses.

In some cases, an equal division is not fair. One partner may perform more work for the business than the other partner, or one partner may make a larger capital contribution. In the preceding example, Dan Chao might agree to work longer hours for the partnership than Katie Zheng in order to earn a greater share of profits. Zheng could argue that she should receive more of the profits because she contributed more net assets ($420,000) than Chao did ($105,000). Chao might contend that his computer software program is the partnership's most important asset, and that his share of the profits should be greater than Zheng's share. Arriving at fair sharing of profits and losses in a partnership may be difficult. We now demonstrate some options available in determining partners' shares of profits and losses.

Sharing Based on a Stated Fraction

The ratio of 2:1 is equal to fractions of 2/3 and 1/3, where the denominator of the fraction is the sum of the numbers in the ratio. The ratio of 2:1 is also a 66.7-percent: 33.3-percent sharing ratio.

The partnership agreement may state each partner's fraction of the total profits and losses. Suppose the partnership agreement of Shannon Kerry and Raoul Calder allocates two-thirds of the business profits and losses to Kerry and one-third to Calder. This sharing rule can also be expressed as 2:1. If net income for the year is $60,000, and all revenue and expense accounts have been closed, the Income Summary account has a credit balance of $60,000 prior to its closing:

Income Summary

Bal.	60,000

The entry to close this account and allocate the net income to the partners' Capital accounts is

Dec. 31	Income Summary	60,000	
	Shannon Kerry, Capital		40,000
	Raoul Calder, Capital		20,000
	To allocate net income to partners.		
	(Kerry: $60,000 × ⅔; Calder: $60,000 × ⅓)		

Suppose Kerry's beginning Capital balance were $50,000 and Calder's were $10,000. After posting, the accounts appear as follows:

Income Summary		Shannon Kerry, Capital		Raoul Calder, Capital	
Clo. 60,000	60,000		Beg. 50,000		Beg. 10,000
			Clo. 40,000		Clo. 20,000
			End. 90,000		End. 30,000

If the partnership had a net loss of $15,000, the Income Summary account would have a debit balance of $15,000. In that case, the closing entry to allocate the loss to the partners' Capital accounts would be

Dec. 31	Shannon Kerry, Capital	10,000	
	Raoul Calder, Capital	5,000	
	Income Summary		15,000
	To allocate net loss to partners.		
	(Kerry: $15,000 × ⅔; Calder: $15,000 × ⅓)		

A profit or loss will increase or decrease each partner's Capital account, but cash will not change hands.

Sharing Based on Capital Investments

Profits and losses are often allocated in proportion to the partners' capital investments in the business. Suppose John Abbot, Erica Baxter, and Tony Craven are partners in ABC Company. Their Capital accounts at the end of the first year of business have the following balances, before closing entries. These amounts are equal to the original capital investments for each of the partners, since no earnings or withdrawals have yet been posted to these accounts.

John Abbot, Capital	$120,000
Erica Baxter, Capital	180,000
Tony Craven, Capital	150,000
Total Capital balances	$450,000

Assume that the partnership earned a profit of $300,000 for the year. To allocate this amount based on capital investments, each partner's percentage share of the partnership's total capital investment amount must be computed. We simply divide each partner's investment by the total capital investment amount. These figures, multiplied by the $300,000 profit amount, yield each partner's share of the year's profits:

Abbot:	($120,000 ÷ $450,000) × $300,000	=	$ 80,000
Baxter:	($180,000 ÷ $450,000) × $300,000	=	120,000
Craven:	($150,000 ÷ $450,000) × $300,000	=	100,000
	Net income allocated to partners	=	$300,000

The closing entry to allocate the profit to the partners' Capital accounts is

Dec. 31	Income Summary	300,000	
	John Abbot, Capital		80,000
	Erica Baxter, Capital		120,000
	Tony Craven, Capital		100,000
	To allocate net income to partners.		

After this closing entry, the partners' Capital balances are

John Abbot, Capital ($120,000 + $80,000)	$200,000
Erica Baxter, Capital ($180,000 + $120,000)	300,000
Tony Craven, Capital ($150,000 + $100,000)	250,000
Total Capital balances after allocation of net income	$750,000

Sharing Based on Capital Investments and on Service

One partner, regardless of his or her capital investment, may put more work into the business than the other partners. Even among partners who log equal service time, one person's superior experience and knowledge may be worth more to the firm. To reward the harder-working or more valuable person, the profit-and-loss-sharing method may be based on a combination of partner capital investments *and* service to the business.

Assume Michelle Wallas and Carolyn Borugian formed a partnership in which Wallas invested $50,000 and Borugian invested $50,000, a total of $100,000. Borugian devotes more time to the partnership and earns the larger payout from the partnership. Accordingly, the two partners have agreed to share profit as follows:

1. The first $50,000 of partnership profit is to be allocated based on partners' capital investments in the business.

2. The next $60,000 of profit is to be allocated based on service (Borugian works 60 percent of the time and Wallas 40 percent of the time), with Wallas receiving $24,000 and Borugian receiving $36,000.

3. Any remaining profit is allocated equally.

LEARNING TIPS

To calculate each partner's share of profit or loss, follow these steps, shown using John Abbot's data:

1. $120,000 ÷ $450,000 = 26.6667%*
2. 26.6667% × $300,000 = $80,000.10, rounded to $80,000

*Do not round the % amount but round the $ amount.

If net income for the first year is $125,000, the partners' shares of this profit are computed as follows:

	Wallas	Borugian	Total
Total net income			$ 125,000
Sharing the first $50,000 of net income,			
based on capital investments:			
Wallas ($50,000 ÷ $100,000 × $50,000)	$25,000		
Borugian ($50,000 ÷ $100,000 × $50,000)		$25,000	
Total			50,000
Net income remaining for allocation			75,000
Sharing of next $60,000, based on service:			
Wallas	24,000		
Borugian		36,000	
Total			60,000
Net income left for allocation			15,000
Remainder shared equally:			
Wallas ($15,000 × $^1/_2$)	7,500		
Borugian ($15,000 × $^1/_2$)		7,500	
Total			15,000
Net income left for allocation			$ 0
Net income allocated to the partners	$56,500	$68,500	$ 125,000

On the basis of this allocation, the closing entry is

Dec. 31	Income Summary	125,000	
	Michelle Wallas, Capital		56,500
	Carolyn Borugian, Capital		68,500
	To allocate net income to partners.		

Sharing Based on "Salaries" and Interest

Partners may be rewarded for their service and their capital investments to the business in other ways. In one sharing plan, the partners are allocated "salaries" (which are predetermined sums to be withdrawn, *not* employee salaries) plus interest on their Capital balances. It is important to remember that the "salaries" and interest amounts discussed above are not the business expenses for salaries and interest in the usual sense. "Salaries" and interest in partnership agreements are ways of expressing the allocation of profits and losses to the partners. The "salary" component rewards service to the partnership. The interest component rewards a partner's investment of cash or other assets in the business. But the partners' "salary" and interest amounts are *not* salary expense and interest expense in the partnership's accounting or tax records.

Assume Edward Meyers and Pierre Zrilladich form an oil-exploration partnership. At the beginning of the year, their Capital balances are $200,000 and $250,000, respectively. The partnership agreement allocates an annual "salary" of $107,000 to Meyers and $88,000 to Zrilladich. After these amounts are allocated, each partner earns 8 percent interest on his beginning Capital balance. Any remaining net income is divided equally. Partnership profit of $240,000 for 2014 will be allocated as follows:

	Meyers	Zrilladich	Total
Total net income			$240,000
First, "salaries":			
Meyers	$107,000		
Zrilladich		$ 88,000	
Total			195,000
Net income remaining for allocation			45,000
Second, interest on beginning capital balances:			
Meyers ($200,000 × 0.08)	16,000		
Zrilladich ($250,000 × 0.08)		20,000	
Total			36,000
Net income remaining for allocation			9,000
Third, remainder shared equally:			
Meyers ($9,000 × 1/2)	4,500		
Zrilladich ($9,000 × 1/2)		4,500	
Total			9,000
Net income remaining for allocation			$ 0
Net income allocated to the partners	$127,500	$112,500	$240,000

In the preceding illustration, net income exceeded the sum of "salary" and interest. If the partnership profit is less than the allocated sum of "salary" and interest, a negative remainder will occur at some stage in the allocation process. Even so, the partners use the same method for allocation purposes. For example, assume that Meyers and Zrilladich Partnership earned only $205,000 in 2014.

REAL WORLD EXAMPLE

In some large partnerships, a "units" system of profit and loss allocation is used. Each partner is awarded a particular number of units, which becomes the numerator in the fraction used for allocation. The total number of units awarded is the denominator in the fraction. The units method can allow a partnership to continue even as partners enter and withdraw from the partnership if unit formulas (rather than partner names) are a part of the partnership agreement.

	Meyers	Zrilladich	Total
Total net income			$205,000
First, "salaries":			
Meyers	$107,000		
Zrilladich		$88,000	
Total			195,000
Net income remaining for allocation			10,000
Second, interest on beginning capital balances:			
Meyers ($200,000 × 0.08)	16,000		
Zrilladich ($250,000 × 0.08)		20,000	
Total			36,000
Net income remaining for allocation			(26,000)
Third, remainder shared equally:			
Meyers ($26,000 × 1/2)	(13,000)		
Zrilladich ($26,000 × 1/2)		(13,000)	
Total			(26,000)
Net income remaining for allocation			$ 0
Net income allocated to the partners	$110,000	$95,000	$205,000

A net loss would be allocated to Meyers and Zrilladich in the same manner outlined for net income. The sharing procedure would begin with the net loss, and then allocate "salary," interest, and any other specified amounts to the partners.

For example, assume that Meyers and Zrilladich Partnership had a loss of $30,000 in 2014.

	Meyers	Zrilladich	Total
Total net income (net loss)			($30,000)
First, "salaries":			
Meyers	$107,000		
Zrilladich		$88,000	
Total			195,000
Net income (loss) remaining for allocation			(225,000)
Second, interest on beginning Capital balances:			
Meyers ($200,000 × 0.08)	16,000		
Zrilladich ($250,000 × 0.08)		20,000	
Total			36,000
Net income (loss) remaining for allocation			(261,000)
Third, remainder shared equally:			
Meyers ($261,000 × ½)	(130,500)		
Zrilladich ($261,000 × ½)		(130,500)	
Total			(261,000)
Net income remaining for allocation			$ 0
Net income (loss) allocated to the partners	($ 7,500)	($22,500)	($30,000)

We see that partners may allocate profits and losses based on a stated fraction, capital investments, service, interest on Capital balances, or any combination of these factors. Each partnership shapes its profit-and-loss-sharing ratio to fit its own needs.

Partner Withdrawals (Drawings) of Cash and Other Assets

Partners need cash for personal living expenses like anyone else. Partnership agreements usually allow partners to withdraw cash or other assets from the business. These withdrawals are sometimes called *drawings*, and are recorded in a separate Withdrawals or Drawings account for each partner. (Drawings from a partnership are recorded exactly as for a proprietorship.) Assume that both Edward Meyers and Pierre Zrilladich are allowed a monthly withdrawal of $12,500. The partnership records the March 2014 withdrawal with this entry:

REAL WORLD EXAMPLE

According to the *Income Tax Act*, partners are taxed on their share of partnership income, not on the amount of their withdrawals.

Mar. 31	Edward Meyers, Withdrawals	12,500	
	Cash		12,500
	Monthly partner withdrawal of cash—cheque #101.		

Mar. 31	Pierre Zrilladich, Withdrawals	12,500	
	Cash		12,500
	Monthly partner withdrawal of cash—cheque #102.		

During the year, each partner's Withdrawal account accumulates 12 such amounts, a total of $150,000 ($12,500 × 12). At the end of the year, the general ledger shows the following account balances immediately after net income has been closed to the partners' Capital accounts. Assume the January 1, 2014, balances for Meyers and Zrilladich are shown below, and that $205,000 of profit has been allocated on the basis of the illustration on page 766.

Edward Meyers, Capital

		Jan. 1, 2014 Bal.	200,000
		Dec. 31, 2014	
		Net income	110,000

Pierre Zrilladich, Capital

		Jan. 1, 2014 Bal.	250,000
		Dec. 31, 2014	
		Net income	95,000

Edward Meyers, Withdrawals

Dec. 31, 2014 Bal. 150,000	

Pierre Zrilladich, Withdrawals

Dec. 31, 2014 Bal. 150,000	

The Withdrawals accounts must be closed at the end of the period (as must be done for a proprietorship).

2014			
Dec. 31	Edward Meyers, Capital	150,000	
	Edward Meyers, Withdrawals		150,000
	To close the Withdrawals account to Capital.		
Dec. 31	Pierre Zrilladich, Capital	150,000	
	Pierre Zrilladich, Withdrawals		150,000
	To close the Withdrawals account to Capital.		

The amount of the withdrawal does not depend on the partnership's income or loss for the year. In fact, it is possible for a partner to withdraw more than the balance in the Capital account if, for example, profits were expected to be higher than they proved to be and withdrawals were made in anticipation of these high profits. This situation can only occur if the partnership has the cash required for the withdrawal and the other partners agree with the withdrawal and the ending Capital balance.

✓ JUST CHECKING

6. List the factors that can influence the way profits and losses are shared.

7. Calculate the net income or net loss to be allocated to each partner under the following partnership agreements:

   a. Burns and White share profits and losses 60/40. Net partnership income was $50,000.

   b. Betty, Luella, and Pius share profits and losses 3:4:3. Net partnership loss was $200,000.

   c. Locke and Barnel share profits 1/3 and 2/3. The partnership agreement does not address the sharing of losses. Net partnership loss was $60,000.

   d. Hampton and Kirk do not have a partnership agreement. Hampton does one-third of the work and Kirk does two-thirds of the work. Partnership net income was $90,000.

8. Harper, Cheves, and Calderon have capital investments of $20,000, $30,000, and $50,000, respectively. The partners share profits and losses as follows:

   a. The first $40,000 is divided based on the partner's capital investments.

   b. The next $40,000 is based on service, shared equally by Harper and Cheves.

   c. The remainder is divided equally.

   Compute each partner's share of the $92,000 net income for the year.

Just Checking Solutions appear at the end of this chapter and on MyAccountingLab.

Admission of a Partner

LO ④

How do we account for a new partner?

A partnership lasts only as long as its current set of partners remain in the business. Admitting a new partner dissolves the old partnership and begins a new one.

Often the new partnership continues the former partnership's business. In fact, the new partnership may choose to retain the dissolved partnership's name, as is the case with accounting firms. PricewaterhouseCoopers LLP, for example, is an accounting firm that retires and admits partners during the year. Thus the former partnership dissolves and a new partnership begins many times. The business, however, retains the name and continues operations. Other partnerships may dissolve and then re-form under a new name. Let's look at the ways that a new owner can be added to a partnership.

Admission by Purchasing a Partner's Interest

A person can become a member of a partnership by purchasing an existing partner's interest in the business. First, however, the new person must gain the approval of the other partners.

Let's assume that Stephanie Spelacy and Carlo Lowes have a partnership that carries these figures:

Cash	$ 40,000	Total liabilities	$120,000
Other assets	360,000	Stephanie Spelacy, capital	170,000
		Carlo Lowes, capital	110,000
		Total liabilities	
Total assets	$400,000	and equity	$400,000

Business is so successful that Spelacy receives an offer from Linda Drake, an outside party, to buy her $170,000 interest in the business for $200,000. Lowes approves Drake as a new partner, and Spelacy agrees to accept $200,000. The firm records the transfer of capital with this entry:

Apr. 16	Stephanie Spelacy, Capital	170,000	
	Linda Drake, Capital		170,000
	To transfer Spelacy's equity to Drake.		

The debit closes Spelacy's Capital account because she is no longer a partner in the firm. The credit opens Drake's Capital account because Spelacy's equity has been transferred to Drake, as shown in the T-accounts. The entry amount is Spelacy's Capital balance ($170,000) and not the $200,000 price that Drake paid Spelacy to buy into the business. The full $200,000 goes to Spelacy, including the $30,000 difference between her Capital balance and the price received from Drake.

In this example, the partnership does not receive cash because the transaction was between Drake and Spelacy, not between Drake and the partnership. Suppose Drake pays Spelacy less than Spelacy's Capital balance. The entry on the partnership books is not affected. Spelacy's equity is transferred to Drake at book value ($170,000).

The old partnership of Spelacy and Lowes has dissolved. Lowes and Drake draw up a new partnership agreement, with a new profit-and-loss-sharing ratio, and continue business operations. If Lowes does not accept Drake as a partner, the Spelacy and Lowes partnership might be dissolved, and Drake would be unable to buy Spelacy's interest.

Stephanie Spelacy, Capital

170,000	170,000

Linda Drake, Capital

	170,000

Carlo Lowes, Capital

	110,000

KEY POINTS

The profit or loss on the sale of a partnership interest belongs personally to the partner selling the interest and will not appear on the partnership's books.

Admission by Investing in the Partnership

A person may be admitted as a partner by investing directly in the partnership rather than by purchasing an existing partner's interest. The new partner invests assets—for example, cash, inventory, or equipment—in the business. Let's consider several possible, independent investment scenarios for a new partner.

Admission by Investing in the Partnership at Book Value—No Bonus Assume that the partnership of Robin Hardy and Michael May has the following assets, liabilities, and capital:

Cash	$ 20,000	Total liabilities	$ 60,000
Other assets	200,000	Robin Hardy, capital	70,000
		Michael May, capital	90,000
		Total liabilities	
Total assets	$220,000	and equity	$220,000

Devan Mann wants to join the Hardy and May partnership. Mann can invest equipment and land (Other assets) with a market value of $80,000. Hardy and May agree to dissolve their partnership and to start up a new one, giving Mann one-third interest in exchange for the contributed assets, as follows:

LEARNING TIPS

Always add the new partner's investment to the existing partners' capital total *first* before calculating the new partner's ownership interest amount in the partnership.

Partnership capital before Mann is admitted ($70,000 + $90,000)	$160,000
Mann's investment in the partnership	80,000
Partnership capital after Mann is admitted	$240,000
Mann's capital in the partnership ($240,000 × 1/3)	$ 80,000

Notice that Mann is buying into the partnership at book value because her one-third investment ($80,000) equals one-third of the new partnership's total capital ($240,000). The partnership's entry to record Mann's investment is

Jul. 18	Other Assets	80,000	
	Devan Mann, Capital		80,000
	To admit D. Mann as a partner with a one-third interest in the business.		

After this entry, the partnership books show:

Cash	$ 20,000	Total liabilities	$ 60,000
Other assets		Robin Hardy, capital	70,000
($200,000 + $80,000)	280,000	Michael May, capital	90,000
		Devan Mann, capital	80,000
		Total liabilities	
Total assets	$300,000	and equity	$300,000

Mann's one-third interest in the partnership does not necessarily entitle her to one-third of the profits. The sharing of profits and losses is a separate element in the partnership agreement.

Admission by Investing in the Partnership—Bonus to the Old Partners   A successful partnership may require a higher payment from a new partner entering the business. The old partners may demand a bonus, which will increase their Capital accounts.

Suppose that Hiro Nagasawa and Lisa Wendt's partnership has earned above-average profits for 10 years. The two partners share profits and losses equally. The balance sheet carries these figures:

Cash	$ 40,000	Total liabilities	$100,000
Other assets	210,000	Hiro Nagasawa, capital	70,000
		Lisa Wendt, capital	80,000
		Total liabilities	
Total assets	$250,000	and equity	$250,000

Nagasawa and Wendt agree to admit Alana Moor to a one-fourth interest in return for Moor's cash investment of $90,000. Moor's Capital balance on the new partnership books is only $60,000, computed as follows:

Partnership capital before Moor is admitted ($70,000 + $80,000)	$150,000
Moor's investment in the partnership	90,000
Partnership capital after Moor is admitted	$240,000
Moor's capital in the partnership ($240,000 × 1/4)	$ 60,000
Bonus to the old partners ($90,000 − $60,000)	$ 30,000

In effect, Moor had to buy into the partnership at a price ($90,000) above the book value of her one-fourth interest ($60,000). Moor's greater-than-book-value investment of $30,000 creates a *bonus* for Nagasawa and Wendt. The entry on the partnership books to record Moor's investment is

Mar. 1	Cash	90,000	
	Alana Moor, Capital		60,000
	Hiro Nagasawa, Capital		15,000
	Lisa Wendt, Capital		15,000
	To admit A. Moor as a partner with a		
	one-fourth interest in the business.		
	Nagasawa and Wendt each receive a		
	bonus of $15,000 ($30,000 × ¹/₂).		

LEARNING TIPS

Notice in the March 1 journal entry that Nagasawa's and Wendt's Capital accounts increased because of Moor's investment, but that Nagasawa and Wendt have not received cash. All the cash went into the partnership. Their increased Capital accounts include the bonus amount contributed by Moor, calculated according to the original partners' profit-and-loss ratio.

Moor's Capital account is credited for her one-fourth interest in the partnership. The bonus is allocated to the original partners (Nagasawa and Wendt) based on their profit-and-loss ratio.

The new partnership's balance sheet reports these amounts:

Cash ($40,000 + $90,000)	$130,000	Total liabilities	$100,000
Other assets	210,000	Hiro Nagasawa, capital	
		($70,000 + $15,000)	85,000
		Lisa Wendt, capital	
		($80,000 + $15,000)	95,000
		Alana Moor, capital	60,000
		Total liabilities	
Total assets	$340,000	and equity	$340,000

Admission by Investing in the Partnership—Bonus to the New Partner A potential new partner may be so important that the old partners offer a partnership share that includes a bonus to the new partner. A law firm may strongly desire a former premier, cabinet minister, or other official as a partner because of the person's reputation. A restaurant owner may want to go into partnership with a famous sports personality like Sidney Crosby or a singer like Shania Twain.

Suppose Jan Page and Miko Goh have a restaurant. Their partnership balance sheet appears as follows:

Cash	$140,000	Total liabilities	$120,000
Other assets	360,000	Jan Page, capital	230,000
		Miko Goh, capital	150,000
		Total liabilities	
Total assets	$500,000	and equity	$500,000

The partners admit Martin Santiago, a famous hockey player, as a partner with a one-third interest in exchange for Santiago's cash investment of $100,000. At the time of Santiago's admission, the firm's capital is $380,000—Page, $230,000 plus Goh, $150,000. Page and Goh share profits and losses in the ratio of two-thirds to Page and one-third to Goh. The computation of Santiago's equity in the new partnership is

Partnership capital before Santiago is admitted ($230,000 + $150,000)	$380,000
Santiago's investment in the partnership	100,000
Partnership capital after Santiago is admitted	$480,000
Santiago's Capital in the partnership ($480,000 × ¹/₃)	$160,000
Bonus to new partner ($160,000 − $100,000)	$ 60,000

In this case, Santiago entered the partnership at a price ($100,000) below the book value of his equity ($160,000). The bonus of $60,000 went to Santiago from the other partners. The Capital accounts of Page and Goh are debited for the $60,000 difference between the new partner's equity ($160,000) and his investment ($100,000). The old partners share this decrease in capital, which is accounted for as though it were a loss, based on their profit-and-loss ratio. The entry to record Santiago's investment is

Aug. 24	Cash	100,000	
	Jan Page, Capital ($60,000 × $^2/_3$)	40,000	
	Miko Goh, Capital ($60,000 × $^1/_3$)	20,000	
	Martin Santiago, Capital		160,000
	To admit M. Santiago as a partner with a		
	one-third interest in the business.		

The new partnership's balance sheet reports these amounts:

Cash		Total liabilities	$120,000
($140,000 + $100,000)	$240,000	Jan Page, capital	
Other assets	360,000	($230,000 − $40,000)	190,000
		Miko Goh, capital	
		($150,000 − $20,000)	130,000
		Martin Santiago, capital	160,000
		Total liabilities	
Total assets	$600,000	and equity	$600,000

In the next section, we will see how to account for the withdrawal of a partner from a business.

✓ JUST CHECKING

9. Tina and Jean are partners with Capital balances of $25,000 and $75,000, respectively. They share profits and losses in a 30:70 ratio. Tina and Jean admit Phyllis to a 10 percent interest in a new partnership when Phyllis invests $20,000 in the business.

   a. Compute the bonus to Tina and Jean.

   b. Journalize the partnership's receipt of Phyllis's investment.

   c. What is each partner's Capital in the new partnership?

10. Refer to the previous question. If Phyllis had invested only $10,000 into the partnership for a 10 percent interest, journalize the partnership's receipt of Phyllis's investment.

Just Checking Solutions appear at the end of this chapter and on MyAccountingLab.

Withdrawal of a Partner from the Business

LO ⑤
How do we account for the withdrawal of a partner?

A partner may leave the business for many reasons, including retirement or a dispute with the other partners. The withdrawal of a partner dissolves the old partnership. The partnership agreement should specify how to settle with a withdrawing partner.

In the simplest case, a partner may withdraw by selling his or her interest to another party in a personal transaction. This is the same as admitting a new person who purchases an old partner's interest, as we saw earlier. The journal entry simply debits the withdrawing partner's Capital account and credits the new partner's Capital account. The dollar amount of the entry is the old partner's Capital balance, regardless of the price paid by the purchaser, as illustrated for Spelacy and Drake on page 769. The accounting when one current partner buys a second partner's interest is the same as when an outside party buys a current partner's interest.

If the partner withdraws in the middle of the accounting period, the partnership books should be updated to determine the withdrawing partner's Capital balance. The business must measure net income or net loss for the fraction of the year up to the withdrawal date, and allocate profit or loss according to the existing ratio. This is the same process as having a year end on the date the partner withdraws from the partnership. An alternative is to set an amount in the partnership agreement to be allocated regardless of the final annual results. This could be appropriate in businesses that have seasonal fluctuations, where the selection of withdrawal date could lead to unfair allocations. After the books have been closed, the business then accounts for the change in partnership capital.

The withdrawing partner may receive his or her share of the business in partnership assets other than cash. The question then arises of what value to assign the partnership assets—book value or current market value? The settlement procedure often specifies an independent appraisal of the assets to determine their current market value because market values may have changed. In that case, the partnership must revalue the partnership assets, known as an **asset revaluation**. Thus the partners share any market-value changes according to their profit-and-loss ratio.

Suppose Ben Wolfe is retiring in midyear from the partnership of Sheldon, Greis, and Wolfe. After the books have been adjusted for partial-period income but before the asset appraisal, revaluation, and closing entries are recorded, the balance sheet reports the following:

LEARNING TIPS

The accounting when one current partner buys a second partner's interest is the same as when an outside party buys a current partner's interest.

REAL WORLD EXAMPLE

When a partner leaves a partnership, she or he ceases to be an agent and no longer has the authority to bind the business to contracts. Third parties with whom the partnership has dealt should be notified that the exiting partner no longer can bind the partnership. All others can be told with a newspaper advertisement.

Cash		$ 70,000	Total liabilities		$ 80,000
Inventory		40,000	Joan Sheldon, capital		50,000
Land		50,000	George Greis, capital		40,000
Building	$90,000		Ben Wolfe, capital		20,000
Less: Accumulated					
amortization	60,000	30,000	Total liabilities		
Total assets		$190,000	and equity		$190,000

An independent appraiser revalues the inventory at $34,000 (down from $40,000), and the land at $100,000 (up from $50,000). The partners share the differences between market value and book value based on their profit-and-loss ratio of 1:2:1.

The entries to record the revaluation of the inventory and land are

LEARNING TIPS

The ratio of 1:2:1 is equal to 1/4, 1/2, 1/4, or a 25-percent, 50-percent, 25-percent sharing ratio.

Jun. 30	Joan Sheldon, Capital ($6,000 × $\frac{1}{4}$)	1,500	
	George Greis, Capital ($6,000 × $\frac{1}{2}$)	3,000	
	Ben Wolfe, Capital ($6,000 × $\frac{1}{4}$)	1,500	
	Inventory ($40,000 − $34,000)		6,000
	To revalue the inventory and allocate the		
	loss in value to the partners.		

Jun. 30	Land ($100,000 − $50,000)	50,000	
	Joan Sheldon, Capital ($50,000 × $\frac{1}{4}$)		12,500
	George Greis, Capital ($50,000 × $\frac{1}{2}$)		25,000
	Ben Wolfe, Capital ($50,000 × $\frac{1}{4}$)		12,500
	To revalue the land and allocate the gain		
	in value to the partners.		

After the revaluations, the partnership balance sheet reports:

Cash		$ 70,000	Total liabilities	$ 80,000
Inventory		34,000	Joan Sheldon, capital ($50,000 −	61,000
Land		100,000	$1,500 + $12,500)	
Building	$90,000		George Greis, capital ($40,000 −	62,000
Less: Accumulated			$3,000 + $25,000)	
amortization	60,000	30,000	Ben Wolfe, capital ($20,000 −	
			$1,500 + $12,500)	31,000
			Total liabilities	
Total assets		$234,000	and equity	$234,000

The books now carry the assets at current market value, which becomes the new book value, and the Capital accounts are up to date. As the balance sheet shows, Wolfe has a claim to $31,000 in partnership assets. Now we can account for Wolfe's withdrawal from the business.

Withdrawal at Book Value

If Ben Wolfe withdraws by taking cash equal to the book value of his owner's equity, the entry would be

Jun. 30	Ben Wolfe, Capital	31,000	
	Cash		31,000
	To record the withdrawal of B. Wolfe		
	from the partnership.		

This entry records the payment of partnership cash to Wolfe and the closing of his Capital account upon his withdrawal from the business.

Withdrawal at Less Than Book Value

KEY POINTS

Whenever a new partnership is formed, a new partnership agreement and a new profit-and-loss ratio are needed and should be created.

The withdrawing partner may be so eager to depart that she or he is willing to take less than her or his equity. Assume Ben Wolfe withdraws from the business and agrees to receive cash of $10,000 and the new partnership's $15,000 note payable. This $25,000 settlement is $6,000 less than Wolfe's $31,000 equity in the business. The remaining partners share this $6,000 difference—which is a bonus to them—according to their profit-and-loss ratio.

Because Wolfe has withdrawn from the partnership, Wolfe's capital account is closed, and Greis and Sheldon may or may not continue the partnership. Assuming they agree to form a new partnership, a new agreement—and a new profit-and-loss ratio—is needed. In forming a new partnership, Greis and Sheldon may decide on any ratio they wish. Assume Greis and Sheldon agree on a profit-and-loss ratio of $2/3$ for Greis and $1/3$ for Sheldon.

The entry to record Wolfe's withdrawal at less than book value is

Jun. 30	Ben Wolfe, Capital	31,000	
	Cash		10,000
	Note Payable to Ben Wolfe		15,000
	Joan Sheldon, Capital		2,000
	George Greis, Capital		4,000
	To record withdrawal of B. Wolfe from		
	the partnership. Sheldon's bonus is		
	$2,000 ($6,000 × $1/3$) and Greis's		
	bonus is $4,000 ($6,000 × $2/3$).		

Withdrawal at More Than Book Value

A withdrawing partner may receive assets worth more than the book value of her or his equity. This situation creates

- A bonus to the withdrawing partner
- A decrease in the remaining partners' Capital accounts, shared in their profit-and-loss ratio

The accounting for this situation follows the pattern illustrated previously for withdrawal at less than book value—with one exception. In this situation, the remaining partners' Capital accounts are debited because they are paying a bonus to the withdrawing partner.

Refer back to our previous example. Suppose Wolfe withdraws from the partnership and agrees to receive $40,000 cash. Greis and Sheldon agree that Greis will get two-thirds of the new partnership's profits and losses, and Sheldon one-third. The entry to record Wolfe's withdrawal at more than book value is

Jun. 30	Ben Wolfe, Capital	31,000	
	Joan Sheldon, Capital	3,000	
	George Greis, Capital	6,000	
	Cash		40,000
	To record withdrawal of B. Wolfe from the partnership. Sheldon's Capital is reduced by $3,000 ($9,000 × $^1/_3$) and Greis's Capital is reduced by $6,000 ($9,000 × $^2/_3$).		

Death of a Partner

As with any other form of partnership withdrawal, the death of a partner dissolves a partnership. The partnership accounts are adjusted to measure net income or loss for the fraction of the year up to the date of death. The accounts are then closed to determine all partners' Capital balances on that date. Settlement with the deceased partner's estate is based on the partnership agreement. There may or may not be an asset revaluation. The estate commonly receives partnership assets equal to the partner's Capital balance. The partnership closes the deceased partner's Capital account with a debit and credits an asset account or a payable to the estate.

Suppose Joan Sheldon (of the partnership on page 773) dies after all accounts have been adjusted to current market value. Sheldon's Capital balance is $61,000 after the revaluation of the inventory and land on page 774. Sheldon's estate may request cash for her final share of the partnership's assets. The partnership's journal entry is

REAL WORLD EXAMPLE

Partners commonly carry life insurance on themselves, with the partners as beneficiaries. In the event of a death, the partners receive the cash flow necessary to settle with the deceased partner's estate, without putting the partnership into financial jeopardy.

Jul. 1	Joan Sheldon, Capital	61,000	
	Cash		61,000
	To record withdrawal of Sheldon from the business.		

Alternatively, a remaining partner may purchase the deceased partner's equity. The deceased partner's Capital account is debited and the purchaser's Capital account is credited. The amount of this entry is the ending Capital balance of the deceased partner.

11. Suppose Ruth is withdrawing from the partnership of Ruth, Nick, and Adriana. The partners share profits and losses in a 1:2:3 ratio for Ruth, Nick, and Adriana, respectively. After the revaluation of assets, Ruth's Capital balance is $40,000, and the other partners agree to pay her $50,000. Nick and Adriana agree to a new profit-and-loss ratio of 2:3 for Nick and Adriana, respectively. Journalize the payment to Ruth for her withdrawal from the partnership.

12. Refer to the previous question. Suppose the situation is the same except that the other partners agree to pay Ruth $30,000. Journalize the payment to Ruth for her withdrawal from the partnership.

13. Refer to Question 11 above. Suppose the situation is the same except that Ruth died the day after revaluation of the assets, and her estate requests cash for her final share of the partnership's assets. Journalize the payment to Ruth's estate for her withdrawal from the partnership.

Just Checking Solutions appear at the end of this chapter and on MyAccountingLab.

Liquidation of a Partnership

LO ⑥

How do we account for the ending of a partnership?

As we have seen, the admission or withdrawal of a partner dissolves the partnership. However, the business may continue operating with no apparent change to outsiders such as customers and creditors. In contrast, business **liquidation** is the process of going out of business by selling the entity's assets and paying its liabilities. The business shuts down. The final step in liquidation of a business is to *distribute any remaining cash to the owners.* Before the business is liquidated, the books should be adjusted and closed. After closing, only asset, liability, and partners' Capital accounts remain open.

Liquidation of a partnership includes three basic steps:

1. Sell the assets. Allocate the gain or loss to the partners' Capital accounts based on the profit-and-loss ratio.

2. Pay all the partnership liabilities.

3. Pay the remaining cash to the partners in proportion to their Capital balances.

The liquidation of a business can stretch over weeks or months, even years for a large company. Selling every asset and paying every liability of the entity takes time. For example, in one case the liquidation of a law firm of over 75 partners took almost a year.

To avoid excessive detail in our illustrations, we include only two asset categories—Cash and Noncash Assets—and a single liability category—Liabilities. Our examples also assume that the business sells the assets in a single transaction and then pays the liabilities at once. (In actual practice, each asset and its related amortization would be accounted for separately when it is sold, and each liability would be accounted for separately when it is paid.)

Assume that Ryan Lauren, Alexis Andrews, and Scott Benroudi have shared profits and losses in the ratio of 3:1:1. (This ratio is equal to 3/5, 1/5, 1/5, or a 60-percent, 20-percent, 20-percent sharing ratio.) The partners decide to liquidate their partnership. After the books are adjusted and closed, these accounts remain:

LEARNING TIPS

The ratio of 3:1:1 is equal to 3/5, 1/5, 1/5, or a 60-percent, 20-percent, 20-percent sharing ratio.

Cash	$ 10,000	Liabilities	$ 30,000
Noncash assets	90,000	Ryan Lauren, capital	40,000
		Alexis Andrews, capital	20,000
		Scott Benroudi, capital	10,000
		Total liabilities	
Total assets	$100,000	and equity	$100,000

Sale of Assets at a Gain

Step 1—Sell the Assets Assume the Lauren, Andrews, and Benroudi partnership sells its noncash assets for $150,000 (book value, $90,000). The partnership realizes a gain of $60,000, which is allocated to the partners based on their profit-and-loss-sharing ratio. The entry to record this sale and allocate the gain is

Oct. 31	Cash	150,000	
	Noncash Assets		90,000
	Ryan Lauren, Capital		36,000
	Alexis Andrews, Capital		12,000
	Scott Benroudi, Capital		12,000
	To sell noncash assets in liquidation and		
	allocate gain to partners. Lauren's share		
	of the gain is $36,000 ($60,000 × 0.60),		
	Andrews' and Benroudi's are $12,000 ($60,000 × 0.20).		

Now the partners' Capital accounts have the following balances:

Ryan Lauren, Capital		Alexis Andrews, Capital		Scott Benroudi, Capital	
	40,000		20,000		10,000
	36,000		12,000		12,000
Bal.	76,000	Bal.	32,000	Bal.	22,000

This journal entry could be broken down into two steps: recording the gain or loss on liquidation, and recording the allocation of the gain or loss to the partners. If this is done, the journal entries would be

Oct. 31	Cash	150,000	
	Noncash Assets		90,000
	Gain on Liquidation		60,000
31	Gain on Liquidation	60,000	
	Ryan Lauren, Capital		36,000
	Alexis Andrews, Capital		12,000
	Scott Benroudi, Capital		12,000

Step 2—Pay all the Partnership Liabilities The partnership then pays off its liabilities:

Oct. 31	Liabilities	30,000	
	Cash		30,000
	To pay liabilities in liquidation.		

Step 3—Pay the Remaining Cash to the Partners in Proportion to Their Capital Balances The final liquidation transaction pays all remaining cash to the partners *according to their Capital balances.* (By contrast, *gains* and *losses* on the sale of assets are shared by the partners based on their profit-and-loss-sharing ratio.) The amount of cash left in the partnership is $130,000, as follows:

Cash			
Beg. bal.	10,000	Payment of liabilities	30,000
Sale of assets	150,000		
End. bal.	130,000		

The partners divide the remaining cash according to their Capital balances:

Oct. 31	Ryan Lauren, Capital	76,000	
	Alexis Andrews, Capital	32,000	
	Scott Benroudi, Capital	22,000	
	Cash		130,000
	To disburse cash to partners in liquidation.		

A convenient way to summarize the transactions in a partnership liquidation is given in Exhibit 12–5. Remember:

- Upon liquidation, gains and losses on the sale of assets are divided according to the *profit-and-loss ratio*.
- The final cash payment to the partners is based on *Capital balances*.

EXHIBIT 12–5 | Partnership Liquidation—Sale of Assets at a Gain

					Capital		
					Lauren	Andrews	Benroudi
	Cash	+ Noncash Assets	= Liabilities	+	(60%) +	(20%) +	(20%)
Balances before sale of assets	$ 10,000	$90,000	$30,000		$ 40,000	$ 20,000	$ 10,000
Step 1, Sale of assets and sharing of gain	150,000	(90,000)	—		36,000	12,000	12,000
Balances	160,000	0	30,000		76,000	32,000	22,000
Step 2, Payment of liabilities	(30,000)		(30,000)				
Balances	130,000	0	0		76,000	32,000	22,000
Step 3, Disbursement of cash to partners	(130,000)				(76,000)	(32,000)	(22,000)
Balances	$ 0	$ 0	$ 0		$ 0	$ 0	$ 0

KEY POINTS

Keep in mind that, upon liquidation, gains and losses on the sale of assets are divided according to the profit-and-loss ratio. The final cash disbursement to the partners is based on Capital balances.

After the disbursement of cash to the partners, the business has no assets, liabilities, or equity. All final balances are zero. By the accounting equation, partnership assets *must* equal partnership liabilities plus partnership capital.

Sale of Assets at a Loss

Liquidation of a business often includes the sale of assets at a loss. When a loss occurs, the partners' Capital accounts are debited based on the profit-and-loss-sharing ratio. Otherwise, the accounting follows the pattern illustrated for the sale of assets at a gain.

Suppose the Lauren, Andrews, and Benroudi partnership sold its noncash assets for $30,000 and all other details in Exhibit 12–5 remained the same. This creates a loss of $60,000 on the sale of the noncash assets. Exhibit 12–6 summarizes the transactions in a partnership liquidation when the assets are sold at a loss.

KEY POINTS

There are a few ways to deal with a capital deficiency upon liquidation. The decision of which method to use must be made *before* the ending cash is distributed.

Capital Deficiencies

Notice that Benroudi's Capital account has a negative balance. This is known as a *capital deficiency*. The capital deficiency must be dealt with *before* the ending cash is distributed. One way of dealing with the $2,000 capital deficiency in Benroudi's Capital

EXHIBIT 12–6 | Partnership Liquidation—Sale of Assets at a Loss

| | | | | | Capital | | |
	Cash +	Noncash Assets =	Liabilities +	Lauren (60%) +	Andrews (20%) +	Benroudi (20%)
Balances before sale of assets	$ 10,000	$ 90,000	$ 30,000	$ 40,000	$ 20,000	$ 10,000
Step 1, Sale of assets and						
sharing of loss	30,000	(90,000)		(36,000)	(12,000)	(12,000)
Balances	40,000	0	30,000	4,000	8,000	(2,000)
Step 2, Payment of liabilities	(30,000)		(30,000)			
Balances	10,000	0	0	4,000	8,000	(2,000)
Step 3, Disbursement of cash						
to partners	(10,000)			(4,000)	(8,000)	2,000
Balances	$ 0	$ 0	$ 0	$ 0	$ 0	$ 0

account is for Benroudi to contribute $2,000 of assets to the partnership to erase his capital deficiency. If Benroudi contributes cash, the journal entry to record this is

Cash	2,000	
Scott Benroudi, Capital		2,000
Contributed cash to erase capital deficiency on liquidation.		

Another option for dealing with Benroudi's $2,000 capital deficiency is for Benroudi's partners, Lauren and Andrews, to agree to absorb Benroudi's capital deficiency by decreasing their own Capital balances in proportion to their remaining profit-sharing percentages: Lauren, 60/80; Andrews, 20/80. The journal entry to record this is

Ryan Lauren, Capital	1,500	
Alexis Andrews, Capital	500	
Scott Benroudi, Capital		2,000
To absorb the Bebroudi capital deficiency by decreasing remaining partners' Capital balances.		

How do partners deal with a situation where two of the three partners have capital deficiencies? Both partners could contribute assets in the amount of their deficiencies to the third partner. However, if the deficient partners cannot contribute personal assets, then the deficits must be absorbed by the remaining partner. If the remaining partner then still has a balance in his or her Capital account, any remaining cash balance would be paid to that partner.

When a business liquidates, there may not be enough cash from the sale of the assets to pay the liabilities. The partners (who are personally liable for the partnership debts) must contribute cash on the basis of their profit-and-loss ratio to cover unpaid debts.

✓JUST CHECKING

14. Refer to the Lauren, Andrews, and Benroudi partnership on page 776. Suppose the partnership sold its noncash assets for $20,000 and all other details in Exhibit 12–5 remained the same.

   a. What is the profit or loss created on the sale of the noncash assets?

   b. Allocate the profit or loss calculated in part (a) to the partners.

   c. How can the partnership deal with any capital deficiencies in this situation?

Just Checking Solutions appear at the end of this chapter and on MyAccountingLab.

The Impact on Partnerships of International Financial Reporting Standards (IFRS)

LO ⑦
How does IFRS affect partnerships?

The principles and requirements used to record transactions and prepare financial statements for partnerships, as shown in this chapter, are set out in the "Unincorporated Businesses" section of the *CICA Handbook*. There is no corresponding accounting standard for partnerships reporting under IFRS. Partnerships can report under IFRS, and may want to, especially if the partnership intends to become a corporation in the future and trade its shares on a stock exchange. However, IFRS do not include specific guidance on how to account for partnerships. IFRS do require that partnerships disclose information equivalent to that provided by limited companies. Accounting for limited companies will be covered in Chapters 13 and 14. The important point is that IFRS do not include specific guidance on how to account for partnerships.

✓ JUST CHECKING

15. Suppose your partnership prepares its financial statements in accordance with IFRS. How does the IFRS approach for partnerships differ from the approach described in this chapter?

Just Checking Solutions appear at the end of this chapter and on MyAccountingLab.

MyAccountingLab

DemoDoc: Partnerships

Summary Problem for Your Review

The partnership of Espranza and Boiko admits Steven Franzen as a partner on January 2, 2014. The partnership has these balances on that date:

Cash	$ 9,000	Total liabilities	$ 50,000
Other assets	110,000	Debby Espranza, capital	45,000
		Thomas Boiko, capital	24,000
Total assets	$119,000	Total liabilities and equity	$119,000

Debby Espranza's share of profits and losses is 60 percent and Thomas Boiko's share is 40 percent.

Required

(Items 1 and 2 are independent.)

1. Suppose Franzen pays Boiko $30,000 to acquire Boiko's interest in the business after Espranza approves Franzen as a partner.

   a. Record the transfer of owner's equity on the partnership books.

   b. Prepare the partnership balance sheet immediately after Franzen is admitted as a partner.

2. Suppose Franzen becomes a partner by investing $31,000 cash to acquire a one-fourth interest in the business.

   a. Compute Franzen's Capital balance and determine whether there is any bonus. If so, who gets the bonus?

   b. Record Franzen's investment in the business.

   c. Prepare the partnership balance sheet immediately after Franzen is admitted as a partner. Include the appropriate heading.

3. Which way of admitting Franzen to the partnership increases its total assets? Give your reason.

Key Fact: Partnership admitting a new partner
Date: January 2, 2014

SOLUTION

Requirement 1

a. 2014

Jan. 2	Thomas Boiko, Capital	24,000	
	Steven Franzen, Capital		24,000
	To transfer Boiko's equity in the partnership to Franzen.		

When a new partner acquires an old partner's interest, the new partner purchases the old partner's equity balance on the books and *replaces* the old partner. Any amount paid in excess goes to the old partner personally.

b. The balance sheet for the partnership of Espranza and Franzen is identical to the balance sheet given for Espranza and Boiko in the problem, except Steven Franzen's name replaces Thomas Boiko's name in the title and in the listing of Capital accounts.

Requirement 2

a. Computation of Franzen's Capital balance:

Partnership capital before Franzen is admitted	
($45,000 + $24,000)	$ 69,000
Franzen's investment in the partnership	31,000
Partnership capital after Franzen is admitted	$100,000
Franzen's capital in the partnership ($100,000 × 1/4)	$ 25,000
Bonus to the old partners ($31,000 − $25,000)	$ 6,000

When a new partner acquires an interest in a partnership, the new partner *joins the existing partners* by adding cash to the pool of capital, then dividing the pool among the old and new partners. Any amount paid in excess increases the old partners' Capital balances.

b. 2014

Jan. 2	Cash	31,000	
	Steven Franzen, Capital		25,000
	Debby Espranza, Capital		3,600
	Thomas Boiko, Capital		2,400
	To admit Franzen as a partner with a one-fourth interest in the business. Espranza's bonus is $3,600 [($31,000 − $25,000) × 0.60] and Boiko's bonus is $2,400 [($31,000 − $25,000) × 0.40].		

Any amount paid in excess increases the old partners' Capital balances by giving each old partner a bonus. The bonus is based on the profit-and-loss percentage in place before the new partner joined.

c.

ESPRANZA, BOIKO, AND FRANZEN
Balance Sheet
January 2, 2014

Cash*	$ 40,000	Total liabilities	$ 50,000
Other assets	110,000	Debby Espranza, capital**	48,600
		Thomas Boiko, capital***	26,400
		Steven Franzen, capital	25,000
Total assets	$150,000	Total liabilities and equity	$150,000

*$9,000 + $31,000 = $40,000

**$45,000 + $3,600 = $48,600

***$24,000 + $2,400 = $26,400

The Cash and Capital accounts will change when a new partner joins existing partners. Add the bonus to each of the old partners' Capital balances and add the new partner's Capital balance, all from the January 2, 2014, journal entry.

A partnership's total assets are increased only when a new partner joins existing partners, not when a new partner "replaces" an old partner by purchasing the old partner's Capital.

Requirement 3

Franzen's investment in the partnership increases its total assets by the amount of his contribution. Total assets of the business are $150,000 after his investment, compared with $119,000 before. By contrast, Franzen's purchase of Boiko's interest in the business is a personal transaction between the two individuals. It does not affect the assets of the partnership, regardless of the amount Franzen pays Boiko.

Summary

① Learning Objective 1: Identify the characteristics of a partnership

What are the characteristics of a partnership?

A *partnership* is a business co-owned by two or more persons for profit.
The characteristics of partnerships are

- Ease of formation
- Limited life
- Mutual agency
- Unlimited liability
- No partnership income taxes

In a *limited partnership*, the limited partners have limited personal liability for the obligations of the business.

- A written *partnership agreement* establishes procedures for admission of a new partner
- Withdrawals of a partner
- The sharing of profits and losses among the partners

When a new partner is admitted to the firm or an existing partner withdraws, the old partnership is *dissolved*, or ceases to exist. A new partnership may or may not emerge to continue the business.

Pg. 756

② Learning Objective 2: Account for partners' initial investment in a partnership

How do we account for partners' investments in a partnership?

Accounting for a partnership is similar to accounting for a proprietorship. However, a partnership has more than one owner.

- Each partner has an individual Capital account and a Withdrawal account; the Capital accounts for each partner are shown on the balance sheet.
- The partnership income statement includes a section showing the division of net income to the partners.

Pg. 761

③ Learning Objective 3: Allocate profits and losses to the partners by different methods

How can we allocate profits and losses to the partners?

Partners share net income or loss in any manner they choose.
Common sharing agreements base the *profit-and-loss ratio* on:

- A stated fraction
- Partners' capital investments
- Partners' service to the partnership
- Other methods, including a combination of "salaries" and "interest" which, despite their name, are not expenses of the business.

Partner withdrawals, also called drawings, reduce the partner capital accounts, but are not a form of net income allocation.

Pg. 762

Learning Objective 4: Account for the admission of a new partner

How do we account for a new partner?

If the old partners agree to admit a new partner to the partnership, the old partnership is dissolved and a new partnership is created.

Pg. 768

An outside person may become a partner by:

- Purchasing a current partner's interest (the transaction is between the partners and does not increase the total partnership equity)
- Investing in the partnership (the transaction increases the total partnership equity by the amount of the investment)

In some cases, the new partner must pay the current partners a bonus to join. In other situations, the new partner may receive a bonus to join.

Learning Objective 5: Account for the withdrawal of a partner

How do we account for the withdrawal of a partner?

The steps for accounting for the withdrawal of a partner are:

Pg. 772

1. Adjust and close the books up to the date of the partner's withdrawal from the business.
2. Appraise the assets and the liabilities to determine their current market value. Allocate the gain or loss in value to the partners' Capital accounts based on their profit-and-loss-sharing ratio.
3. Account for the partner's withdrawal
   a. At book value (no change in remaining partners' Capital balances)
   b. At less than book value (increase the remaining partners' Capital balances)
   c. At greater than book value (decrease the remaining partners' Capital balances).

Learning Objective 6: Account for the liquidation of a partnership

How do we account for the ending of a partnership?

In *liquidation*, a partnership goes out of business by:

Pg. 776

1. Selling the assets
2. Paying the liabilities
3. Paying any remaining cash to the partners.

Learning Objective 7: Identify the impact on partnerships of international financial reporting standards (IFRS)

How does IFRS affect partnerships?

IFRS does not provide specific guidance on how to account for partnerships. The *CICA Handbook* section "Unincorporated Businesses" gives guidance on recording transactions and preparing financial statements for partnerships reporting under ASPE.

Pg. 780

Check Accounting Vocabulary on page 784 for all key terms used in Chapter 12 and the Glossary on page 1246 for all key terms used in the textbook.

CHAPTER REVIEW:

MyAccountingLab   DemoDoc covering Partnerships

MyAccountingLab   Student PowerPoint Slides

MyAccountingLab   Audio Chapter Summary

Note: All MyAccountingLab resources can be found in the Chapter Resources section and the Multimedia Library.

SELF-STUDY QUESTIONS

Test your understanding of the chapter by marking the correct answer for each of the following questions:

1. Which of these characteristics identifies a partnership? (*pp. 754–758*)
   a. Unlimited life
   b. No income tax paid by the business entity
   c. Limited personal liability
   d. All of the above

2. A partnership records a partner's investment of assets in the business at (*p. 761*)
   a. The partner's book value of the assets invested
   b. The market value of the assets invested
   c. A special value set by the partners
   d. Any of the above, depending upon the partnership agreement

3. The partnership of Hungerford, LaPlante, and Egly divides profits in the ratio of 4:5:3. There is no provision for losses. During 2014, the business earned $40,000. Egly's share of this income is (pp. 762–763)

    a. $10,000

    b. $13,333

    c. $16,000

    d. $16,667

4. Suppose the partnership of Hungerford, LaPlante, and Egly in the preceding question lost $40,000 during 2014. LaPlante's share of this loss is (p. 763)

    a. Not determinable because the ratio applies only to profits

    b. $13,333

    c. $10,000

    d. $16,667

5. The partners of Martin, Short, and Chase share profits and losses 1/5, 1/6, and 19/30. During 2014, the first year of their partnership, the business earned $120,000, and each partner withdrew $50,000 for personal use. What is the balance in Chase's Capital account after all closing entries? (p. 763)

    a. Not determinable because Chase's beginning Capital balance is not given

    b. Minus $10,000

    c. Minus $50,000

    d. $70,000

6. Elaine Robinson buys into the partnership of Quantz and Goodwin by purchasing a one-third interest for $55,000. Prior to Robinson's entry, Edward Quantz's Capital balance was $46,000, and Louisa Goodwin's balance was $52,000; profits and losses were shared equally. The entry to record Robinson's buying into the business is (pp. 769–771)

a.	Cash	55,000	
	Elaine Robinson, Capital		55,000

b.	Edward Quantz, Capital	27,500	
	Louisa Goodwin, Capital	27,500	
	Elaine Robinson, Capital		55,000

c.	Cash	55,000	
	Elaine Robinson, Capital		51,000
	Edward Quantz, Capital		2,000
	Louisa Goodwin, Capital		2,000

d.	Cash	51,000	
	Edward Quantz, Capital	2,000	
	Louisa Goodwin, Capital	2,000	
	Elaine Robinson, Capital		55,000

7. The partners of Tsui, Valik, and Wollenberg share profits and losses equally. Their Capital balances are $40,000, $50,000, and $60,000, respectively, when Wollenberg sells her interest in the partnership to Valik for $90,000. Tsui and Valik continue the business. Immediately after Wollenberg's retirement, the total assets of the partnership are (pp. 772–774)

    a. Increased by $30,000

    b. Increased by $90,000

    c. Decreased by $60,000

    d. The same as before Wollenberg sold her interest to Valik

8. Prior to Bill Ching's withdrawal from the partnership of Ching, Han, and Lee, the partners' Capital balances were $140,000, $110,000 and $250,000, respectively. The partners share profits and losses 1/3, 1/4, and 5/12. The appraisal indicates that assets should be written down by $36,000. Arthur Han's share of the write-down is (pp. 772–774)

    a. $7,920   c. $12,000

    b. $9,000   d. $18,000

9. The process of closing the business, selling the assets, paying the liabilities, and disbursing remaining cash to the owners is called (p. 776)

    a. Dissolution   c. Withdrawal

    b. Forming a new partnership   d. Liquidation

10. Mike Marr and Pamela Coombs have shared profits and losses equally. Immediately prior to the final cash disbursement in a liquidation of their partnership, the books show:

    Cash $100,000 = Liabilities $0 + Mike Marr, Capital $60,000 + Pamela Coombs, Capital $40,000

    How much cash should Marr receive? (p. 777)

    a. $40,000   c. $60,0000

    b. $50,000   d. None of the above

Answers to Self-Study Questions

1. b 2. b 3. a ($40,000 × 3/12 = $10,000) 4. d ($40,000 × 5/12 = $16,667) 5. a
6. c [($46,000 + $52,000 + $55,000) × 1/3 = $51,000; $55,000 − $51,000 = $4,000; $4,000 ÷ 2 = $2,000 each to Quantz and Goodwin] 7. d 8. b ($36,000 × 1/4 = $9,000) 9. d 10. c

ACCOUNTING VOCABULARY

Asset revaluation Adjust asset values to reflect current market values usually based on an independent appraisal of the assets (p. 773).

Dissolution Ending of a partnership (p. 756).

General partnership A form of partnership in which each partner is an owner of the business, with all the privileges and risks of ownership (p. 759).

Limited liability partnership (LLP) A partnership in which each partner's personal liability for the business's debts is limited to a certain dollar amount *(p. 759).*

Limited partnership A partnership with at least two classes of partners: a general partner and limited partners *(p. 759).*

Liquidation The process of going out of business by selling the entity's assets and paying its liabilities. The final step in liquidation of a business is the distribution of any remaining cash to the owners *(p. 776).*

Mutual agency Every partner can bind the business to a contract within the scope of the partnership's regular business operations *(p. 757).*

Partnership An unincorporated business with two or more owners *(p. 754).*

Partnership agreement Agreement that is the contract between partners specifying such items as the name, location, and nature of the business; the name, capital investment, and duties of each partner; and the method of sharing profits and losses by the partners *(p. 756).*

Unlimited personal liability When a partnership (or a proprietorship) cannot pay its debts with business assets, the partners (or the proprietor) must use personal assets to meet the debt *(p. 757).*

SIMILAR ACCOUNTING TERMS

Limited Liability Partnership	LLP
Liquidation	Shutting down the business; going out of business
Partners' equity	Partners' Capital; Capital
Withdrawals	Drawings

Assignment Material

QUESTIONS

1. List nine items that the partnership agreement should specify.

2. Ron Montgomery, who is a partner in M&N Associates, commits the firm to a contract for a job within the scope of its regular business operations. What term describes Montgomery's ability to obligate the partnership?

3. If a partnership cannot pay a debt, who must make payment? What term describes this obligation of the partners?

4. How is income of a partnership taxed?

5. Identify the advantages and disadvantages of the partnership form of business organization.

6. Chris Higgins and Taylor Pyett's partnership agreement states that Higgins gets 60 percent of profits and Pyett gets 40 percent. If the agreement does not discuss the treatment of losses, how are losses shared? How do the partners share profits and losses if the agreement specifies no profit-and-loss-sharing ratio?

7. What determines the amount of the credit to a partner's Capital account when the partner contributes assets other than cash to the business?

8. Do partner withdrawals of cash for personal use affect the sharing of profits and losses by the partner? If so, explain how. If not, explain why not.

9. Name two events that can cause the dissolution of a partnership.

10. Briefly describe how to account for the purchase of an existing partner's interest in the business.

11. Jeff Malcolm purchases Sheila Wilson's interest in the Wilson & Conners partnership. What right does Malcolm obtain from the purchase? What is required for Malcolm to become Paula Conners' partner?

12. Sal Assissi and Hamza Zahari each have capital of $150,000 in their business. They share profits in the ratio of 55:45. Sheetal Kaur acquires a one-fifth share in the partnership by investing cash of $100,000. What are the Capital balances of the three partners immediately after Kaur is admitted?

13. When a partner resigns from the partnership and receives assets greater than her or his Capital balance, how is the difference shared by the other partners?

14. Distinguish between dissolution and liquidation of a partnership.

15. Name the three steps in liquidating a partnership.

16. The partnership of Ralls and Sauls is in the process of liquidation. How do the partners share (a) gains and losses on the sale of noncash assets, and (b) the final cash disbursement?

17. Compare and contrast the financial statements of a proprietorship and a partnership.

18. Summarize the situations in which partnership allocations are based on (a) the profit-and-loss ratio, and (b) the partners' Capital balances.

MyAccountingLab   Make the grade with MyAccountingLab: The Starters, Exercises, and Problems marked in red can be found on MyAccountingLab. You can practise them as often as you want, and most feature step-by-step guided instructions to help you find the right answer.

STARTERS

The partnership form of business

①

Starter 12–1 For each of the three independent situations below, indicate if you would recommend the partnership form of business organization. State your reasons for your recommendation.

1. Sarah, Alisha, and Connie just graduated from a two-year college program and would like to start a bookkeeping business called SAC Bookkeeping. They each have equivalent assets to bring to the business.
2. Philip Harcourt just joined the law practice of Osler and Hoskins. He thinks he will be making a huge salary and is worried about the tax effects of this income. He thinks the partners should incorporate the partnership and avoid the tax bill.
3. Fred Klaus and Felix Cadeau would like to form a construction company. Fred has the contacts, cash, and estimating skills, while Felix has equipment and field experience. There will be minimal profits until the business has a few projects.

Statement of owners' equity

①

Asanti, $76,900.

Starter 12–2 Asanti and Quall are partners. Using the following information, prepare a statement of owners' equity on December 31, 2014.

	Capital Jan. 1, 2014	Capital Contributions	Net Income Allocated	Partner Drawings
Asanti	$45,000	$10,000	$33,900	$12,000
Quall	$60,000	$10,000	$22,100	$12,000

Partners' profits, losses, and Capital balances

③

2. Abel, Capital $43,000

Starter 12–3 Abel and Baker decided to form a partnership. Abel contributed equipment (book value $65,000), inventory (paid $20,000), and $10,000 cash. The equipment and inventory have a current market value of $40,000 and $15,000 respectively. Abel also had a debt of $20,000 for the equipment. Baker contributed office equipment (book value $20,000) and cash of $50,000. The current market value of the office equipment is $10,000. The two partners fail to agree on a profit-and-loss-sharing ratio. For the first month (June 2014), the partnership lost $4,000.

1. How much of this loss goes to Abel? How much goes to Baker?
2. The partners withdrew no assets during June. What is each partner's Capital balance at June 30? Prepare a T-account for each partner's Capital.

Starter 12-4 Friesen, Walters, and Onley have Capital balances of $12,000, $6,000, and $6,000, respectively. The partners share profits and losses as follows:

Dividing partnership profits based on capital contributions and service

Friesen $43,000

a. The first $40,000 is divided based on the partners' capital investments.
b. The next $30,000 is based on service, shared equally by Friesen and Onley.
c. The remainder is divided equally.
   Compute each partner's share of the $94,000 net income for the year.

Starter 12-5 The partnership of Bosch and Cutler had these balances at September 30, 2014:

Partnership income statement

Net income for Bosch $36,000

Cash..	$ 20,000	Service Revenue	$145,000
Liabilities	40,000	Bosch, Capital	30,000
Cutler, Capital	10,000	Total expenses.......................	85,000
Other assets............................	120,000		

Bosch gets 60 percent of profits and losses, and Cutler 40 percent. Prepare the partnership's income statement and ending Capital balances for the year ended September 30, 2014.

Starter 12-6 Todd has a Capital balance of $60,000; Carlson's balance is $50,000. Reynaldo pays $200,000 to purchase Carlson's interest in the Todd & Carlson partnership. Carlson gets the full $200,000.

Admitting a partner who purchases an existing partner's interest

Journalize the partnership's transaction to admit Reynaldo to the partnership.

Starter 12-7 The partnership of Evans and Falconi has these Capital balances:

Admitting a partner who invests in the business

1. No bonus

- Judy Evans $60,000
- Julie Falconi $80,000

Joan Gray invests cash of $70,000 to acquire a one-third interest in the partnership.

1. Does Gray's investment in the firm provide a bonus to the partners? Show your work.
2. Journalize the partnership's receipt of the $70,000 from Gray.

Starter 12-8 Bo and Go have partner Capital balances of $115,000 and $75,000, respectively. Bo gets 60 percent of profits and losses, and Go gets 40 percent. Assume Mo invests $70,000 to acquire a 25 percent interest in the new partnership of Bogomo. Is there a bonus? If so, who gets it? Journalize the partnership's receipt of cash from Mo.

Admitting a new partner; bonus to the old partners

Bonus $5,000

Starter 12-9 Adams, Everett, and Chapman each have a $50,000 Capital balance. They share profits and losses as follows: 25 percent to Adams, 50 percent to Everett, and 25 percent to Chapman. Suppose Chapman is withdrawing from the business, and the partners agree that no appraisal of assets is needed. How much in assets can Chapman take from the partnership? Give the reason for your answer. What role does the profit-and-loss ratio play in this situation?

Withdrawal of a partner

Starter 12-10 Simpson, Locke, and Job each have a $25,000 Capital balance. Simpson is very old and is retiring from the business. The partners agree to revalue the assets at current market value. A real-estate appraiser values the land at $70,000 (book value is $50,000). The profit-and-loss ratio is 1:2:1. Journalize (a) the revaluation of the land on July 31, and (b) payment of $30,000 to Simpson upon his retirement the same day.

Withdrawal of a partner; asset revaluation

(a) Debit Land $20,000

Starter 12-11 Use the data in Exhibit 12-5. Suppose the partnership of Lauren, Andrews, and Benroudi liquidates by selling all noncash assets for $80,000. Complete the liquidation schedule as shown in Exhibit 12-5.

Liquidation of a partnership at a loss

Starter 12-12 This Starter builds on the solution to Starter 12-11. After completing the liquidation schedule in Starter 12-11, journalize the partnership's (a) sale of noncash assets for $80,000 (use a single account for Noncash Assets), (b) payment of liabilities, and (c) payment of cash to the partners. Include an explanation with each entry.

Liquidation of a partnership

(c) Lauren, $34,000; Andrews, $18,000; Benroudi, $8,000 payments of cash

Capital deficit upon liquidation
of a partnership
6

Starter 12–13 This Starter builds on the solution to Starter 12–12. After completing the liquidation schedule in Starter 12–12, you notice that Benroudi has a final balance of negative $8,000. What are the options for dealing with this capital deficit?

EXERCISES

Exercise 12–1

Partnership characteristics

Mark Giltrow and Denise Chan are forming a business to imprint T-shirts. Giltrow suggests that they organize as a partnership in order to avoid the unlimited liability of a proprietorship. According to Giltrow, partnerships are not very risky.

Giltrow explains to Chan that if the business does not succeed, each partner can withdraw from the business, taking the same assets that she or he invested at its beginning. Giltrow states that the main disadvantage of the partnership form of organization is double taxation: First, the partnership pays a business income tax; second, each partner also pays personal income tax on her or his share of the business's profits.

Correct the errors in Giltrow's explanation.

Exercise 12–2

Organizing a business as a
partnership

Joanna Volescu, a friend from college, approaches you about forming a partnership to export software. Since graduation, Joanna has worked for the World Bank, developing important contacts among government officials and business leaders in Poland and Hungary. Joanna believes she is in a unique position to capitalize on expanding markets. With your expertise in finance, you would have responsibility for accounting and finance in the partnership.

Required Discuss the advantages and disadvantages of organizing the export business as a partnership rather than a proprietorship. Comment on the way partnership income is taxed.

Exercise 12–3

Investments by partners

2. Total assets $56 mil.

Jackson Cooke and Julia Bamber are forming a partnership to develop an amusement park near Ottawa. Cooke contributes cash of $3 million and land valued at $30 million. When Cooke purchased the land, its cost was $16 million. The partnership will assume Cooke's $6 million note payable on the land. Bamber invests cash of $15 million and construction equipment that she purchased for $14 million (accumulated amortization to date, $6 million). The equipment's market value is equal to its book value.

Required

1. Journalize the partnership's receipt of assets and liabilities from Cooke and from Bamber. Record each asset at its current market value with no entry to accumulated amortization.

2. Compute the partnership's total assets, total liabilities, and total owners' equity immediately after organizing.

Exercise 12–4

Recording a partner's investment

2

Janice Partington, Capital
$376,000

Janice Partington has operated a management consulting business as a proprietorship. She and Alison Morse have decided to reorganize the business as a partnership, effective April 1. Partington's investment in the partnership consists of cash, $88,000; accounts receivable, $50,000 less allowance for uncollectibles, $4,000; office furniture, $14,000 less accumulated amortization, $4,000; a small building, $242,000 less accumulated amortization, $120,000; accounts payable, $18,000; and a note payable to the bank, $44,000.

To determine Partington's equity in the partnership, she and Morse hire an independent appraiser. This outside party provides the following market values of the assets and liabilities that Partington is contributing to the business: cash, accounts receivable, office furniture, accounts payable, and note payable—the same as Partington's book value; allowance for uncollectible accounts, $12,000; building, $310,000; and accrued expenses payable (including interest on the note payable), $8,000.

Required Make the entry on the partnership books to record Partington's investment.

Exercise 12–5

Ken Danolo and Jim Goldman form a partnership, investing $96,000 and $168,000, respectively. Determine their shares of net income or net loss for each of the following situations:

a. Net loss is $124,800, and the partners have no written partnership agreement.

b. Net income is $105,600, and the partnership agreement states that the partners share profits and losses based on their capital investments.

c. Net income is $264,000. The first $132,000 is shared based on the partner capital investments. The next $100,000 is shared based on partner service, with Danolo receiving 40 percent and Goldman receiving 60 percent. The remainder is shared equally.

Excel Spreadsheet Template

Computing partners' shares of net income and net loss

c. Danolo $104,000

Exercise 12–6

Ken Danolo withdrew cash of $148,000 for personal use, and Jim Goldman withdrew cash of $120,000 during the year. Using the data from situation (c) in Exercise 12–5, journalize the entries to close to each Capital account (a) the net income to the partners, and (b) the partners' Withdrawal accounts. Explanations are not required. Indicate the amount of increase or decrease in each partner's Capital balance. What was the overall effect on partnership capital?

Computing partners' Capital balances

Overall effect $4,000 decrease

Exercise 12–7

Goertz Accounting Services has a capital balance of $30,000 after adjusting assets to the fair market value. Leonard Goertz wants to form a partnership with Morley Neilson, who will receive a 30-percent interest in the new partnership. Neilson contributes $17,000 for his 30-percent interest. Determine Neilson's equity after admission and any bonus if applicable.

Admitting a new partner

Neilson's equity $14,100

Exercise 12–8

Joanna Wang is admitted to a partnership. Prior to the admission of Wang, the partnership books show Tanya Wird's Capital balance at $79,000 and Alan Bales' Capital balance at $39,500. Wird and Bales share profits and losses equally.

Admitting a new partner

c. Wang $47,500

Required

1. Compute the amount of each partner's equity on the books of the new partnership under each of the following plans:

   a. Wang purchases Bales's interest in the business, paying $47,250 directly to Bales.

   b. Wang invests $39,250 to acquire a one-fourth interest in the partnership.

   c. Wang invests $71,500 to acquire a one-fourth interest in the partnership.

2. Make the partnership journal entry to record the admission of Wang under plans a, b, and c in Requirement 1. Explanations are not required.

Exercise 12–9

The Simra Brothers Partnership had the following statement of partners' equity for the years ended December 31, 2013 and 2014. (This is similar to the statement of owners' equity shown in Exhibit 12–3 on page 760.)

Using a partnership financial statement, admitting a new partner

a. Harry Simra 40%
   Sunny Simra 60%

Simra Brothers Partnership Statement of Partners' Equity For the Years Ended December 31, 2013 and 2014				
	Harry Simra, Capital	Sunny Simra, Capital	Amin Simra, Capital	Total Partnership Capital
Balance, Jan. 1, 2013	$75,000	$ 50,000		$125,000
Net income for 2013	20,000	30,000		50,000
Balance, Dec. 31, 2013	95,000	80,000		175,000
Amin's contribution	2,000	3,000	$45,000	50,000
Net income for 2014	8,000	56,000	16,000	80,000
Less partner withdrawals	(12,000)	(16,000)	(10,000)	(38,000)
Balance, Dec. 31, 2014	$93,000	$123,000	$51,000	$267,000

Required

1. What was the profit-and-loss-sharing ratio in 2013?
2. Refer to Amin's contribution, which was made in cash. How much cash did Amin contribute to the partnership?
3. What percentage of interest did Amin obtain?
4. Why do Harry and Sunny have additions to their balances as a result of Amin's contribution?
5. What was the profit-and-loss-sharing ratio in 2014?

Exercise 12–10

Withdrawal of a partner from a business

2. $42,000

After closing the books, Stihl & Laksa's partnership balance sheet reports owner's equity of $40,500 for Stihl and $54,000 for Laksa. Stihl is withdrawing from (leaving) the firm. He and Laksa agree to write down partnership assets by $18,000. They have shared profits and losses in the ratio of one-third to Stihl and two-thirds to Laksa. The partnership agreement states that a partner withdrawing from the firm will receive assets equal to the book value of his owner's equity.

1. How much will Stihl receive?
2. Laksa will continue to operate the business as a proprietorship. What is Laksa's beginning Capital on the proprietorship books?

Exercise 12–11

Withdrawal of a partner

b. Debit Bruno, Capital $122,400

Alana Bruno is retiring from the partnership of Bruno, Teale, and White on May 31. The partner Capital balances are Bruno, $108,000; Teale, $153,000; and White, $66,000. The partners agree to have the partnership assets revalued to current market values. The independent appraiser reports that the book value of the inventory should be decreased by $24,000, and the book value of the land should be increased by $96,000. The partners agree to these revaluations. The profit-and-loss ratio has been 2:4:4 for Bruno, Teale, and White, respectively. In retiring from the firm, Bruno received $150,000 cash.

Required Journalize (a) the asset revaluations, and (b) Bruno's withdrawal from the firm.

Exercise 12–12

Liquidation of a partnership

2. Jonas $53,500

Jonas, Teese, and Moyer are liquidating their partnership. Before selling the noncash assets and paying the liabilities, the Capital balances are Jonas, $57,500; Teese, $34,500; and Moyer, $23,000. The partnership agreement divides profits and losses equally.

Required

1. After selling the noncash assets and paying the liabilities, suppose the partnership has cash of $115,000. How much cash will each partner receive in final liquidation?
2. After selling the noncash assets and paying the liabilities, suppose the partnership has cash of $103,000. How much cash will each partner receive in final liquidation?

Exercise 12–13

Liquidation of a partnership

Payment of cash: Garcia $26,400

Prior to liquidation, the accounting records of Garcia, Woods, and Mickelson included the following balances and profit-and-loss-sharing percentages:

				Capital		
		Noncash		Garcia	Woods	Mickelson
	Cash +	Assets =	Liabilities +	(40%) +	(30%) +	(30%)
Balances before						
sale of assets	$10,000	$62,500	$26,500	$20,000	$15,000	$11,000

The partnership sold the noncash assets for $78,500, paid the liabilities, and disbursed the remaining cash to the partners. Complete the summary of transactions in the liquidation of the partnership. Use the format illustrated in Exhibit 12–5.

Exercise 12–14

The partnership of Linus, Lebrun, and Beale is liquidating. Business assets, liabilities, and partners' Capital balances prior to dissolution follow. The partners share profits and losses as follows: Shelly Linus, 20 percent; Peter Lebrun, 30 percent; and Cathy Beale, 50 percent.

Liquidation of a partnership

Shelly Linus, Capital $29,600

Required Create a spreadsheet or solve manually—as directed by your instructor—to show the ending balances in all accounts after the noncash assets are sold for $280,000. Determine the unknown amounts, represented by (?):

	A	B	C	D	E	F
	Cash	**Noncash Assets**	**Liabilities**	**Shelly Linus, Capital**	**Peter Lebrun, Capital**	**Cathy Beale, Capital**
1			LINUS, LEBRUN, AND BEALE			
2			Sale of Noncash Assets			
3			(For $280,000)			
4				Shelly	Peter	Cathy
5		Noncash		Linus,	Lebrun,	Beale,
6	Cash	Assets	Liabilities	Capital	Capital	Capital
7						
8	$ 12,000	$252,000	$154,000	$24,000	$74,000	$12,000
9	280,000	(252,000)	_____	? †	?	?
10						
11	$292,000	$ 0	$154,000	$?	$?	$?
12						
13						†($A9 − $B8)*.2

SERIAL EXERCISE

This exercise continues the Kerr Consulting situation from Chapter 11 and will continue it in Volume 2. If you did not complete any Serial Exercises in earlier chapters, you can still complete Exercise 12–15 as it is presented.

Exercise 12–15

Alex Kerr has been running Kerr Consulting as a proprietorship but is planning to expand operations in the near future. The Kerr Consulting January 31, 2014, balance sheet appears on the next page, with all amounts reflected at current market value. Alex Kerr is considering forming a partnership with Jill Monroe, who provides the market-value financial information shown on the next page. Create the Kerr and Monroe Consulting partnership balance sheet at January 31, 2014.

Preparing a partnership balance sheet

Total assets $219,797

Assets	Kerr Consulting	Monroe's Business
Cash	$32,350	$100,000
Accounts receivable	4,900	50,000
Inventory	2,713	5,000
Supplies	100	1,000
Prepaid rent	2,000	0
Equipment	2,000	10,000
Accumulated amortization—equipment	(66)	0
Furniture	6,000	4,000
Accumulated amortization—furniture	(200)	0
Total assets	$49,797	$170,000
Liabilities and Equity		
Accounts payable	$10,700	$ 20,000
Salary payable	1,400	0
Unearned service revenue	1,333	0
Notes payable	0	50,000
Alex Kerr, capital	36,364	—
Jill Monroe, capital	—	100,000
Total liabilities and capital	$49,797	$170,000

CHALLENGE EXERCISE

Exercise 12–16

Preparing a partnership balance sheet

Total assets $1,425,000

On December 31, 2014, Jim Austin and Mike Mundy agree to combine their proprietorships as a partnership. Their balance sheets on December 31 are as follows:

Assets	Austin's Business		Mundy's Business	
	Book Value	Current Market Value	Book Value	Current Market Value
Cash..	$ 30,000	$ 30,000	$ 25,000	$ 25,000
Accounts receivable (net).............	110,000	100,000	40,000	35,000
Inventory...	255,000	230,000	170,000	180,000
Capital assets (net)........................	610,000	525,000	270,000	300,000
Total assets.....................................	$1,005,000	$885,000	$505,000	$540,000

Liabilities and Capital				
Accounts payable...........................	$ 120,000	$120,000	$ 50,000	$ 50,000
Accrued expenses payable............	10,000	10,000	10,000	10,000
Notes payable	275,000	275,000		
Jim Austin, capital.........................	600,000	480,000		
Mike Mundy, capital			445,000	480,000
Total liabilities and capital...........	$1,005,000	$885,000	$505,000	$540,000

Required

1. Prepare the partnership balance sheet on December 31, 2014.

2. Assume John Allen wants to join the partnership by paying $212,000 for a ¼ interest. The partnership equity before John joins is $960,000, and Jim Austin and Mike Mundy shared profits 60 percent for Austin and 40 percent for Mundy. Prepare the journal entry to record John's admission to the partnership on January 1, 2015.

3. What percent of the profits will John Allen receive after becoming a partner?

BEYOND THE NUMBERS

Beyond the Numbers 12–1

The following questions relate to issues faced by partnerships.

Partnership issues

① ⑤

1. The text suggests that a written partnership agreement should be drawn up between the partners in a partnership. One benefit of an agreement is that it provides a mechanism for resolving disputes between the partners. What are five areas of dispute that might be resolved by a partnership agreement?

2. The statement has been made that "If you must take on a partner, make sure the partner is richer than you are." Why is this statement valid?

3. Frizzell, Clamath & Legree is a partnership of lawyers. Clamath is planning to move to Australia. What are the options open to her to convert her share of the partnership assets to cash?

ETHICAL ISSUE

Feng Li and Tanya Ng operate The Party Centre, a party supply store in Red Deer, Alberta. The partners split profits and losses equally, and each takes an annual withdrawal of $90,000. To even out the workload, Ng does the buying and Li serves as the accountant. From time to time, they use small amounts of store merchandise for personal use. In preparing for a large private party, Li took engraved invitations, napkins, place mats, and other goods that cost $3,000. She recorded the transaction as follows:

Cost of Goods Sold.....................................	3,000	
Inventory...		3,000

Required

1. How should Li have recorded this transaction?

2. Discuss the ethical dimension of Li's action.

PROBLEMS (GROUP A)

MyAccountingLab

Problem 12–1A

Vince Sharma and Klaus Warsteiner formed a partnership on January 1, 2014. The partners agreed to invest equal amounts of capital. Sharma invested his proprietorship's assets and liabilities (all accounts have normal balances):

Investments by partners

②

2. Total assets $252,000

	Sharma's Book Value	Current Market Value
Accounts receivable...	$24,000	$20,000
Inventory..	86,000	62,000
Prepaid expenses..	13,000	12,000
Store equipment..	72,000	52,000
Accounts payable...	40,000	40,000

On January 1, Warsteiner invested cash in an amount equal to the current market value of Sharma's partnership capital. The partners decided that Sharma would earn 70 percent of partnership profits because he would manage the business. Warsteiner agreed to accept 30 percent of profits. During the period ended December 31, 2014, the partnership earned $432,000. Warsteiner's withdrawals were $128,000 and Sharma's withdrawals were $172,800.

Required

1. Journalize the partners' initial investments.
2. Prepare the partnership balance sheet immediately after its formation on January 1, 2014.
3. Calculate the partners' Capital balances on December 31, 2014.

Problem 12–2A

Admitting a new partner
④
3. B. Peller, Capital $20,000

SuddenValley Resort is a partnership, and its owners are considering admitting Ben Peller as a new partner. On July 31, 2014, the Capital accounts of the three existing partners and their shares of profits and losses are as follows:

	Capital	Profit-and-Loss Percent
Eleanor Craven................	$20,000	20%
Amy Osler	30,000	30
Brian Harmon..................	40,000	50

Required Journalize the admission of Peller as a partner on July 31, 2014, for each of the following independent situations:

1. Peller pays Harmon $55,000 cash to purchase Harmon's interest.
2. Peller invests $30,000 in the partnership, acquiring a one-quarter interest in the business.
3. Peller invests $30,000 in the partnership, acquiring a one-sixth interest in the business.

Problem 12–3A

Excel Spreadsheet
Template

Computing partners' shares of
net income and net loss
③
1. b. Net income allocated to:
Sasso$58,000

Sheila Sasso, Karen Schwimmer, and Jim Perry have formed a partnership. Sasso invested $60,000, Schwimmer $120,000, and Perry $180,000. Sasso will manage the store, Schwimmer will work in the store three-quarters of the time, and Perry will not work in the business.

Required

1. Compute the partners' shares of profits and losses under each of the following plans:
   a. Net loss is $70,500, and the partnership agreement allocates 45 percent of profits to Sasso, 35 percent to Schwimmer, and 20 percent to Perry. The agreement does not discuss the sharing of losses.
   b. Net income for the year is $136,500. The first $45,000 is allocated on the basis of partners' Capital investments. The next $75,000 is based on service, with $45,000 going to Sasso and $30,000 going to Schwimmer. Any remainder is shared equally.
   c. Net loss for the year is $136,500. The first $45,000 is allocated on the basis of partners' Capital investments. The next $75,000 is based on service, with $45,000 going to Sasso and $30,000 going to Schwimmer. Any remainder is shared equally.
2. Revenues for the year were $858,000 and expenses were $721,500. Under plan (b), prepare the partnership income statement for the year. Assume a year end of September 30, 2014.
3. How will what you have learned in this problem help you manage a partnership?

Problem 12–4A

Recording changes in
partnership Capital
④ ⑤
3. Debit Karen Tenne, Capital
$248,000

Trail Equipment is a partnership owned by three individuals. The partners share profits and losses in the ratio of 30 percent to Karen Tenne, 40 percent to Frank Durn, and 30 percent to Erin Hana. At December 31, 2014, the firm has the following balance sheet amounts:

Cash		$ 354,000	Total liabilities	$ 520,000
Accounts receivable	$ 88,000			
Less: Allowance				
for uncollectibles	4,000	84,000		
Inventory		432,000	Karen Tenne, capital	248,000
Equipment	460,000		Frank Durn, capital	160,000
Less: Accumulated			Erin Hana, capital	270,000
amortization	132,000	328,000	Total liabilities	
Total assets		$1,198,000	and capital	$1,198,000

Karen Tenne withdraws from the partnership on this date.

Required Record Tenne's withdrawal from the partnership under the following independent plans:

1. In a personal transaction, Tenne sells her equity in the partnership to Michael Adams, who pays Tenne $176,000 for her interest. Durn and Hana agree to accept Adams as a partner.

2. The partnership pays Tenne cash of $72,000, and gives her a note payable for the remainder of her book equity in settlement of her partnership interest.

3. The partnership pays Tenne $260,000 cash for her equity in the partnership.

4. The partners agree that the equipment is worth $548,000 (net). After the revaluation, the partnership settles with Tenne by giving her cash of $44,000 and inventory for the remainder of her book equity.

Problem 12–5A

The partnership of Malkin, Neale, & Staal has experienced operating losses for three consecutive years. The partners, who have shared profits and losses in the ratio of Lisa Malkin, 20 percent, John Neale, 40 percent, and Brian Staal, 40 percent, are considering the liquidation of the business. They ask you to analyze the effects of liquidation under various assumptions about the sale of the noncash assets. They present the following partnership balance sheet amounts at December 31, 2014:

Liquidation of a partnership

1. b. Cash distributed to partners $228,000

Cash	$ 41,000	Liabilities	$151,000
Noncash assets	367,000	Lisa Malkin, capital	57,500
		John Neale, capital	158,500
		Brian Staal, capital	41,000
		Total liabilities	
Total assets	$408,000	and capital	$408,000

Required

1. Prepare a summary of liquidation transactions (as illustrated in the chapter) for each of the following situations:

   a. The noncash assets are sold for $420,000.

   b. The noncash assets are sold for $338,000.

2. Make the journal entries to record the liquidation transactions in requirement 1(b).

Problem 12–6A

The partnership of Telliher, Bachra, and Lang has experienced operating losses for three consecutive years. The partners, who have shared profits and losses in the ratio of Thea Telliher, 60 percent, Denis Bachra, 20 percent, and Alan Lang, 20 percent, are considering the liquidation of the business. They ask you to analyze the effects of liquidation under various possibilities about the sale of the noncash assets. *None of the partners have personal assets if they go into a deficit financial position.* They present the following partnership balance sheet amounts at December 31, 2014:

Liquidation of a partnership (deficits)

1a. Loss allocated to Telliher $49,500

Cash	$ 6,750	Liabilities	$ 28,350
Noncash assets	118,800	Thea Telliher, capital	46,600
		Denis Bachra, capital	30,000
		Alan Lang, capital	20,600
		Total liabilities	
Total assets	$125,550	and capital	$125,550

Required

1. Prepare a summary of liquidation transactions (as illustrated in Exhibits 12–5 or 12–6) for each of the following situations:

   a. The noncash assets are sold for $36,300.

   b. The noncash assets are sold for $27,600.

2. What legal recourse do the remaining partners have to be reimbursed for deficit balances?

3. Suppose, after allocating Telliher's deficit balance, Lang now has a deficit balance. How would the partnership deal with this deficiency?

Problem 12–7A

Capital amounts for the balance sheet of a partnership
② ③

2. K. Santiago, Capital $41,500

SAC & Company is a partnership owned by K. Santiago, R. Astorga, and J. Camino, who share profits and losses in the ratio of 1:3:4. The adjusted trial balance of the partnership (in condensed form) at June 30, 2014, follows.

SAC & COMPANY Adjusted Trial Balance June 30, 2014		
Cash	$ 166,000	
Noncash assets	800,000	
Liabilities		$ 690,000
K. Santiago, capital		152,000
R. Astorga, capital		282,000
J. Camino, capital		428,000
K. Santiago, withdrawals	126,000	
R. Astorga, withdrawals	272,000	
J. Camino, withdrawals	312,000	
Revenues		748,000
Expenses	624,000	
Totals	$2,300,000	$2,300,000

Required

1. Prepare the June 30, 2014, entries to close the Revenue, Expense, Income Summary, and Withdrawals accounts.

2. Using T-accounts, insert the opening balances in the partners' Capital accounts, post the closing entries to the Capital accounts, and determine each partner's ending Capital balance.

Problem 12–8A

Accounting for partners' investments; allocating profits and losses; accounting for the admission of a new partner; accounting for the withdrawal of a partner; preparing a partnership balance sheet
② ③ ④ ⑤

2. A. Buckner, Capital $387,209

2011

Jun. 10   Adam Buckner and Amber Kwan have agreed to pool their assets and form a partnership to be called B&K Consulting. They agree to share all profits equally and make the following initial investments:

	Buckner	Kwan
Cash..	$15,000	$30,000
Accounts receivable (net).................	33,000	27,000
Office furniture.....................................	36,000	24,000

Dec. 31   The partnership's reported net income was $195,000 for the year ended December 31, 2011.

2012

Jan.   1   Buckner and Kwan agree to accept Heidi Nguen into the partnership with a $180,000 investment for 30 percent of the business. The partnership agreement is amended to provide for the following sharing of profits and losses:

	Buckner	Kwan	Nguen
Annual "salary"....................................	$90,000	$120,000	$75,000
Interest on capital balance	5%	5%	5%
Balance in ratio of..............................	3 :	2 :	5

Dec. 31   The partnership's reported net income was $480,000.

2013

Oct. 10   Buckner withdrew $84,000 cash from the partnership and Kwan withdrew $57,000 (Nguen did not make any withdrawals).

Dec. 31   The partnership's reported net income was $255,000.

2014

Jan. 2   After a disagreement as to the direction in which the partnership should be moving, Nguen decided to withdraw from the partnership. The three partners agreed that Nguen could take cash of $300,000 in exchange for her equity in the partnership.

Required

1. Journalize all of the transactions for the partnership.
2. Prepare the partners' equity section of the balance sheet as of January 2, 2014.

Problem 12–9A

Dennis Devlin, Gary Freemont, and Jean London started a partnership to operate a management consulting business. The partnership (DFL Partners) had the following transactions:

Accounting for partners' investments; allocating profits and losses; accounting for the admission of a new partner; accounting for the liquidation of a partnership

②③④⑤⑥

Dec. 31, 2013
Debit Dennis Devlin, Capital
$90,000

2012

Jan. 2   Devlin, Freemont, and London formed the partnership by signing an agreement that stated that all profits would be shared in a 3:2:5 ratio and by making the following investments:

	Devlin	Freemont	London
Cash...	$ 24,000	$ 42,000	$138,000
Accounts receivable (net)..................	84,000	126,000	180,000
Office furniture....................................	0	66,000	0
Computer equipment.........................	156,000	0	54,000

Dec. 31   The partnership reported net income of $252,000 for the year.

2013

Jun. 7   Devlin and London agreed that Freemont could sell his share of the partnership to André Hughes for $390,000. The new partners agreed to keep the same profit-sharing arrangement (3:2:5 for Devlin:Hughes:London).

Dec. 31   The partnership reported a net loss of $300,000 for the year.

2014

Jan. 3   The partners agreed to liquidate the partnership. On this date the balance sheet showed the following items, all at their normal balances:

Cash..	$ 78,000
Accounts receivable...	1,476,000
Allowance for uncollectible accounts......................................	72,000
Office furniture..	360,000
Computer equipment..	600,000
Accumulated amortization (total)	180,000
Accounts payable..	1,440,000

The assets were sold for the following amounts:

Accounts receivable...	$ 720,000
Office furniture..	390,000
Computer equipment..	360,000

Devlin and Hughes both have personal assets, but London does not.

Required

Journalize all the transactions for the partnership.

Problem 12–1B

Investments by partners

②

On January 1, 2014, Svitlana Yaeger and Val Havlac formed a partnership. The partners agreed to invest equal amounts of capital. Havlac invested her proprietorship's assets and liabilities (all accounts have normal balances) as follows:

	Havlac's Book Value	Current Market Value
Accounts receivable	$20,200	$20,000
Inventory	44,000	48,000
Prepaid expenses	4,800	4,000
Office equipment	92,000	56,000
Accounts payable	48,000	48,000

On January 1, 2014, Yaeger invested cash in an amount equal to the current market value of Havlac's partnership capital. The partners decided that Havlac would earn two-thirds of partnership profits because she would manage the business. Yaeger agreed to accept one-third of profits. During the remainder of the year, the partnership earned $276,000. Havlac's withdrawals were $76,000, and Yaeger's withdrawals were $56,000.

Required

1. Journalize the partners' initial investments.
2. Prepare the partnership balance sheet immediately after its formation on January 1, 2014.
3. Calculate the partners' Capital balances at December 31, 2014.

Problem 12–2B

Admitting a new partner

④

Pineridge Consulting Associates is a partnership, and its owners are considering admitting Helen Fluery as a new partner. On March 31, 2014, the Capital accounts of the three existing partners and their shares of profits and losses are as follows:

	Capital	Profit-and-Loss Ratio
Jim Zook	$ 50,000	40%
Richard Land	100,000	20
Jennifer Lowe	150,000	40

Required Journalize the admission of Fluery as a partner on March 31, 2014, for each of the following independent situations:

1. Fluery pays Lowe $200,000 cash to purchase Lowe's interest in the partnership.
2. Fluery invests $100,000 in the partnership, acquiring a one-fourth interest in the business.
3. Fluery invests $80,000 in the partnership, acquiring a one-fourth interest in the business.

Problem 12–3B

Excel Spreadsheet Template

Computing partners' shares of net income and net loss

② ③

Sav Berlo, Silvio Felini, and Louis Valente have formed a partnership. Berlo invested $30,000, Felini $40,000, and Valente $50,000. Berlo will manage the store, Felini will work in the store half time, and Valente will not work in the business.

Required

1. Compute the partners' shares of profits and losses under each of the following plans:
   a. Net loss is $200,000, and the partnership agreement allocates 40 percent of profits to Berlo, 25 percent to Felini, and 35 percent to Valente. The agreement does not discuss the sharing of losses.
   b. Net income for the year is $354,000. The first $150,000 is allocated based on partner capital investments. The next $72,000 is based on service, with Berlo receiving $56,000 and Felini receiving $16,000. Any remainder is shared equally.

2. Revenues for the year were $1,014,000 and expenses were $660,000. Under plan (b), prepare the partnership income statement for the year. Assume a January 31, 2014, year end.

3. How will what you learned in this problem help you manage a partnership?

Problem 12–4B

Vector Financial Planning is a partnership owned by three individuals. The partners share profits and losses in the ratio of 20 percent to Katherine Depatie, 40 percent to Sam Seamus, and 40 percent to Emily Hudson. At December 31, 2014, the firm has the following balance-sheet amounts:

Recording changes in partnership capital

Cash		$ 350,400	Total liabilities		$ 573,000
Accounts receivable	$ 92,400				
Less: Allowance					
for uncollectibles	16,800	75,600			
Building	1,102,000		Katherine Depatie, capital		390,600
Less: Accumulated			Sam Seamus, capital		210,000
amortization	294,000	808,000	Emily Hudson, capital		260,400
Land		200,000	Total liabilities		
Total assets		$1,434,000	and capital		$1,434,000

Seamus withdraws from the partnership on December 31, 2014, to establish his own consulting practice.

Required Record Seamus's withdrawal from the partnership under the following independent plans:

1. In a personal transaction, Seamus sells his equity in the partnership to Rea Pearlman, who pays Seamus $120,000 for one-half of his interest. Depatie and Hudson agree to accept Pearlman as a partner.

2. The partnership pays Seamus cash of $163,000, and gives him a note payable for the remainder of his book equity in settlement of his partnership interest.

3. The partnership pays Seamus cash of $336,000.

4. The partners agree that the building is worth $682,000 (net). After the revaluation, the partnership settles with Seamus by giving him cash of $82,000 and a note payable for the remainder of his book equity.

Problem 12–5B

The partnership of Du, Chong, and Quing has experienced operating losses for three consecutive years. The partners, who have shared profits and losses in the ratio of Jia Du, 10 percent, Denis Chong, 30 percent, and Alan Quing, 60 percent, are considering the liquidation of the business. They ask you to analyze the effects of liquidation under various possibilities about the sale of the noncash assets. They present the following partnership balance-sheet amounts at December 31, 2014:

Liquidation of a partnership
⑥

Cash	$ 70,000	Liabilities	$316,000
Noncash assets	526,000	Jia Du, capital	80,000
		Denis Chong, capital	102,000
		Alan Quing, capital	98,000
Total assets	$596,000	Total liabilities and capital	$596,000

Required

1. Prepare a summary of liquidation transactions (as illustrated in the chapter) for each of the following situations:
   a. The noncash assets are sold for $552,000.
   b. The noncash assets are sold for $448,000.

2. Make the journal entries to record the liquidation transactions in Requirement 1(b).

Problem 12–6B

Liquidation of a partnership
(deficit)
⑥

The partnership of Pavelski, Ovechin, and Oh has experienced operating losses for three consecutive years. The partners, who have shared profits and losses in the ratio of Steven Pavelski, 60 percent, Eddie Ovechin, 20 percent, and Kwan Oh, 20 percent, are considering the liquidation of the business. They ask you to analyze the effects of liquidation under various possibilities about the sale of the noncash assets. None of the partners has personal assets if they go into a deficit financial position. They present the following partnership balance-sheet amounts at December 31, 2014:

Cash	$ 27,000	Liabilities	$113,400
Noncash assets	475,200	Steven Pavelski, capital	186,400
		Eddie Ovechin, capital	120,000
		Kwan Oh, capital	82,400
Total assets	$502,200	Total liabilities and capital	$502,200

Required

1. Prepare a summary of liquidation transactions (as illustrated in Exhibits 12–5 or 12–6) for each of the following situations:

   a. The noncash assets are sold for $145,200.

   b. The noncash assets are sold for $110,400.

2. What legal recourse do the remaining partners have to be reimbursed for deficit balances?

Problem 12–7B

Capital amounts for the balance
sheet of a partnership
② ③

SY&I is a partnership owned by T. Shitang, D. Yamamoto, and J. Ishikawa, who share profits and losses in the ratio of 2:3:5. The adjusted trial balance of the partnership (in condensed form) at September 30, 2014, follows.

SY&I		
Adjusted Trial Balance		
September 30, 2014		
Cash	$ 110,000	
Noncash assets	389,000	
Liabilities		$ 319,000
T. Shitang, capital		125,000
D. Yamamoto, capital		97,000
J. Ishikawa, capital		46,000
T. Shitang, withdrawals	99,000	
D. Yamamoto, withdrawals	81,000	
J. Ishikawa, withdrawals	40,000	
Revenues		928,000
Expenses	796,000	
Totals	$1,515,000	$1,515,000

Required

1. Prepare the September 30, 2014, entries to close the Revenue, Expense, Income Summary, and Withdrawals accounts.

2. Using T-accounts, insert the opening Capital balances in the partner Capital accounts, post the closing entries to the Capital accounts, and determine each partner's ending Capital balance.

Problem 12–8B

Accounting for partners' investments; allocating profits and losses; accounting for the admission of a new partner; accounting for the withdrawal of a partner; preparing a partnership balance sheet ② ③ ④ ⑤

2011

Jun. 10 Steven Hodgson and Sarah Asham have agreed to pool their assets and form a partnership to be called H&A Distributors. They agree to share all profits equally and make the following initial investments:

	Hodgson	Asham
Cash...	$21,000	$36,000
Accounts receivable (net).................	42,000	21,000
Office furniture (net)........................	48,000	27,000

Dec. 31 The partnership's reported net income was $228,000 for the year ended December 31, 2011.

2012

Jan. 1 Hodgson and Asham agree to accept Myra Sirroca into the partnership with a $210,000 investment for 40 percent of the business. The partnership agreement is amended to provide for the following sharing of profits and losses:

	Hodgson	Asham	Sirroca
Annual "salary"..................................	$120,000	$90,000	$80,000
Interest on end-of-period capitial balance	10%	10%	10%
Balance in ratio of.............................	2 :	3 :	5

Dec. 31 The partnership's reported net income is $570,000.

2013

Oct. 10 Hodgson withdrew $90,000 cash from the partnership and Asham withdrew $60,000 (Sirroca did not make any withdrawals).

Dec. 31 The partnership's reported net income is $225,000.

2014

Jan. 2 After a disagreement as to the direction in which the partnership should be moving, Sirroca decided to withdraw from the partnership. The three partners agreed that Sirroca could take cash of $510,000 in exchange for her equity in the partnership.

Required

1. Journalize all of the transactions for the partnership.
2. Prepare the partners' equity section of the balance sheet as of January 2, 2014.

Problem 12–9B

Accounting for partners' investments; allocating profits and losses; accounting for the admission of a new partner; accounting for the liquidation of a partnership ② ③ ④ ⑤ ⑥

William Dione, Julie Porter, and Regina Westlake started a partnership to operate a courier service. The partnership (DP&W Couriers) had the following transactions:

2012

Jan. 2 Dione, Porter, and Westlake formed the partnership by signing an agreement that stated that all profits would be shared in a 2:3:5 ratio and by making the following investments:

	Dione	Porter	Westlake
Cash...	$12,000	$ 8,000	$14,000
Accounts receivable (net).................	20,000	14,500	60,000
Office furniture (net)........................	0	0	15,000
Vehicles (net)	21,000	38,500	0

Dec. 31 The partnership reported net income of $53,500 for the year.

2013

Jun. 7 Dione and Westlake agreed that Porter could sell her share of the partnership to Ray Ewing for $82,500. The new partners agreed to keep the same profit-sharing arrangement (2:3:5 for Dione:Ewing:Westlake).

Dec. 31 The partnership reported a net loss of $67,000 for the year.

2014

Jan. 3   The partners agreed to liquidate the partnership. On this date, the balance sheet showed the following items (all accounts have their normal balances):

Cash	$ 17,500
Accounts receivable	316,000
Allowance for uncollectible accounts	22,500
Office furniture	74,500
Vehicles	240,000
Accumulated amortization (total)	49,500
Accounts payable	386,500

The assets were sold for the following amounts:

Accounts receivable	$190,000
Office furniture	82,500
Vehicles	106,000

Dione and Ewing both have personal assets, but Westlake does not.

Required Journalize all of the transactions for the partnership.

CHALLENGE PROBLEMS

Problem 12–1C

Deciding on a capital structure
① ②

Nancy Wesla and Jordon Dugger have been in a partnership for five years. The principal business of the partnership is systems design for financial institutions. Gross revenues have increased from $330,000 in 2010 to $3,800,000 in 2014, the year just ended. The number of employees has increased from two in the first year to nine in the most recent year. Wesla and Dugger realized that they had to build up the partnership's capital and have withdrawn only part of the annual profits. As a result, their Capital accounts have increased from $200,000 (Wesla, $140,000; Dugger, $60,000) in 2010 to $2,000,000 (Wesla, $1,080,000; Dugger, $920,000) in 2014.

The two partners realize that they must expand their capital base to expand their operations in order to meet the increasing demand for their systems designs. At the same time, they wish to take personal advantage of the partnership's earnings. They have been trying to determine whether they should continue the partnership and borrow the necessary funds, take on one or more partners (several of their employees have expressed interest and have capital to invest), or incorporate and sell a portion of the business to outsiders. With respect to incorporation, Faisal Jamal, a former classmate of Wesla's who works for a stockbroker, has indicated he knows of investors who would be interested in buying a share of the business.

Required Wesla and Dugger have come to you to ask for advice. Provide an analysis of the situation and make a recommendation. In response to your questions, they indicate they will need additional capital of $1,600,000 to $2,000,000.

Problem 12–2C

The effects of accounting decisions on profits
③

Simone Perrier, Mary Salter, and Sean Patten have been partners in a systems design business for the past eight years. Perrier and Patten work full-time in the business; Salter has a public accounting practice and works about five to 10 hours per week on the administrative side of the business. The business has been successful and the partners are considering expansion.

The partnership agreement states that profits will be distributed as follows:

1. Partners will get 6 percent interest on their average Capital balances.
2. Perrier will get a "salary" of $75,000; Salter will get a "salary" of $9,375; Patten will get a "salary" of $75,000.
3. The balance remaining will be distributed on the basis of Perrier, 40 percent; Salter, 20 percent; and Patten, 40 percent.

The agreement also stipulates that the distributions outlined in parts 1 and 2 of the agreement will be made even if there are not sufficient profits and that any deficiency will be shared on the basis of part 3.

The capital structure was as follows at December 31, 2014, and reflects the average Capital balances for 2014:

Perrier	$ 228,750
Salter	1,091,250
Patten	491,250
Total	$1,811,250

There has been some stress in the partnership of late because Perrier believes that she is contributing a major part of the effort but is earning much less than Patten; Salter is upset because she believes that she is earning the least even though her capital is essentially funding the partnership.

Required Perrier, Salter, and Patten have come to you to ask for advice as to how they might amicably settle the present dispute. Analyze the situation and make a recommendation. Assume net income in 2014 was $400,000.

Extending Your Knowledge

DECISION PROBLEM

Lori Barclay invested $30,000 and Vanesa Resultan invested $15,000 in a public relations firm that has operated for 10 years. Neither partner has made an additional investment. They have shared profits and losses in the ratio of 2:1, which is the ratio of their investments in the business. Barclay manages the office, supervises the 16 employees, and does the accounting. Resultan, the moderator of a television talk show, is responsible for marketing. Her high profile generates important revenue for the business. During the year ended December 2014, the partnership earned net income of $75,000, shared in the 2:1 ratio. On December 31, 2014, Barclay's Capital balance was $152,500 and Resultan's Capital balance was $105,000.

Settling disagreements among partners

Required

Respond to each of the following situations:

1. What explains the difference between the ratio of partner Capital balances at December 31, 2014, and the 2:1 ratio of partner investments and profit sharing?
2. Resultan believes the profit-and-loss-sharing ratio is unfair. She proposes a change, but Barclay insists on keeping the 2:1 ratio. What two factors may underlie Resultan's unhappiness?

3. During January 2014, Barclay learned that revenues of $24,000 were omitted from the reported 2013 income. She brings this to Resultan's attention, pointing out that her share of this added income is two-thirds, or $16,000, and Resultan's share is one-third, or $8,000. Resultan believes they should share this added income based on their Capital balances: 60 percent (or $14,400) to Barclay, and 40 percent (or $9,600) to Resultan. Which partner is correct? Why?

4. Assume that an account payable of $18,000 for an operating expense in 2013 was omitted from 2013 reported income. On what basis would the partners share this amount?

FINANCIAL STATEMENT CASE

Lisogar, Philip & Walters (LPW) is a regional accounting firm with four offices. Summary data from the partnership's annual report follow:

	Years Ended June 30				
	(Dollars in thousands, except where indicated)				
	2014	2013	2012	2011	2010
Revenues					
Assurance services	$1,234	$1,122	$1,064	$1,093	$1,070
Consulting services	1,007	775	658	473	349
Tax services	743	628	567	515	557
Total Revenues	$2,984	$2,525	$2,289	$2,081	$1,976
Operating Summary					
Revenues	$2,984	$2,525	$2,289	$2,081	$1,976
Personnel costs	1,215	1,004	887	805	726
Other costs	712	630	517	458	415
Income to Partners	$1,057	$ 891	$ 885	$ 818	$ 835
Statistical Data					
Average number of partners	9	9	9	8	8

Required

1. What percentages of total revenues did LPW earn by performing assurance services (similar to audit), consulting services, and tax services during 2010? What were the percentages in 2014? Which type of service grew the most from 2010 to 2014?

2. Compute the average revenue per partner in 2014. Assume each partner works 1,900 hours per year. On average, how much does each partner charge a client for one hour of time?

3. How much net income did each LPW partner earn, on average, in 2014?

1. The partnership agreement is a contract, so transactions under the agreement are governed by contract law. If or when disputes arise, both partners are legally protected. A partnership agreement should contain the following items:

   - Name, location, and nature of the business
   - Name, capital investment, and duties of each partner
   - Procedures for admitting a new partner
   - Method of sharing profits and losses among the partners
   - Withdrawals of assets allowed to the partners
   - Procedures for settling disputes among the partners
   - Procedures for settling with a partner who withdraws from the firm
   - Procedures for removing a partner who will not withdraw or retire from the partnership voluntarily
   - Procedures for liquidating the partnership

2. Advantages as compared to proprietorships: Partnerships can raise more capital, partnerships bring together the abilities of more than one person, and partners working well together can achieve more than by working alone. Compared to corporations, partnerships are less expensive to organize than a corporation, and are subject to fewer governmental regulations and restrictions than a corporation. The main disadvantage of partnerships is that partnership agreements may be difficult to formulate. Each time a new partner is admitted or a partner leaves the partnership, the business needs a new partnership agreement. Other disadvantages are that relationships among partners may be fragile, and mutual agency and unlimited liability create personal obligations for each partner.

3. This person would be a limited partner, so named because his or her personal obligation for the partnership's liabilities is limited to the amount he or she invested in the business.

4. The appraised value or current market value is the appropriate value to use because that is what the land is worth now, and the current market value was verified by independent professionals.

5.

Land	50,000	
Marty Kaur, Capital		50,000

6. The factors that can influence the way profits and losses are shared are:

   - Each partner's contribution of assets and liabilities
   - The fair market value of the assets contributed
   - The time each partner will devote to the business
   - The skills, abilities, reputation, clients, and other benefits that each partner contributes.

7. a. Burns: $50,000 \times 60\% = \$30,000$ net income
      White: $50,000 \times 40\% = \$20,000$ net income
   b. Betty: $200,000 \times 3/10 = \$60,000$ net loss
      Luella: $200,000 \times 4/10 = \$80,000$ net loss
      Pius: $200,000 \times 3/10 = \$60,000$ net loss
   c. Losses are shared the same way as profits.
      Locke: $60,000 \times 1/3 = \$20,000$ net loss
      Barnel: $60,000 \times 2/3 = \$40,000$ net loss
   d. When there is no agreement, profits and losses are shared equally.
      Hampton: $90,000 \times 1/2 = \$45,000$ net income
      Kirk: $90,000 \times 1/2 = \$45,000$ net income

8. Each partner's share of the $92,000 net income for the year:

	Harper	Cheves	Calderon	Total
Total net income				$92,000
First, interest on capital investments:				
Harper ($20,000 ÷ 100,000 × 40,000)	$ 8,000			
Cheves ($30,000 ÷ 100,000 × 40,000)		$12,000		
Calderon ($50,000 ÷ 100,000 × 40,000)			$20,000	
Total				40,000
Net income remaining for allocation				52,000
Second, based on service:				
Harper	20,000			
Cheves		20,000		
Total				40,000
Net income remaining for allocation				12,000
Third, remainder shared equally:				
Harper ($12,000 × 1/3)	4,000			
Cheves ($12,000 × 1/3)		4,000		
Calderon ($12,000 × 1/3)			4,000	
Total				12,000
Net income remaining for allocation				$ 0
Net income allocated to the partners	$32,000	$36,000	$24,000	$92,000

9.

a.

Partnership capital before Phyllis is admitted ($25,000 + $75,000)		$100,000
Phyllis's investment in the partnership		20,000
Partnership capital after Phyllis is admitted		$120,000
Phyllis's capital in the partnership ($120,000 × 1/10)		$ 12,000
Bonus to the old partners ($20,000 − $12,000)		$ 8,000

b.

Cash	20,000	
Phyllis, Capital		12,000
Tina, Capital ($8,000 × 0.30)		2,400
Jean, Capital ($8,000 × 0.70)		5,600
To admit Phyllis with a 10% interest in the business.		

c. Partners' capital balances:

Tina, capital ($25,000 + $2,400)	$ 27,400
Jean, capital ($75,000 + $5,600)	80,600
Phyllis, capital	12,000
Total partnership capital	$120,000

10.

Partnership capital before Phyllis is admitted ($25,000 + $75,000)	$ 100,000
Phyllis's investment in the partnership	10,000
Partnership capital after Phyllis is admitted	$ 110,000
Phyllis's capital in the partnership ($110,000 × 1/10)	$ 11,000
Bonus to the new partner ($11,000 − $10,000)	$ 1,000

Cash	10,000	
Tina, Capital ($1,000 × 0.30)	300	
Jean, Capital ($1,000 × 0.70)	700	
Phyllis, Capital		11,000
To admit Phyllis with a 10% interest in the business.		

11.

Ruth, Capital	40,000	
Nick, Capital	4,000	
Adriana, Capital	6,000	
Cash		50,000
To record withdrawal of Ruth from the business. Nick's capital is reduced by $4,000 [($50,000 − $40,000) × 2/5] and Adriana's capital is reduced by $6,000 [($50,000 − $40,000) × 3/5].		

12.

Ruth, Capital	40,000	
Nick, Capital		4,000
Adriana, Capital		6,000
Cash		30,000
To record withdrawal of Ruth from the business. Nick's capital is increased by $4,000 [($40,000 − $30,000) × 2/5] and Adriana's capital is increased by $6,000 [($54,000 − $30,000) × 3/5].		

13.

Ruth, Capital	40,000	
Cash		40,000
To record withdrawal of Ruth from the business.		

14. a. The sale of the noncash assets for $20,000 creates a loss of $70,000 on the sale of noncash assets ($90,000 − $20,000 = $70,000).

b.

	Cash +	Noncash Assets =	Liabilities +	Lauren (60%) +	Capital Andrews (20%) +	Benroudi (20%)
Balances before sale of assets	$10,000	$90,000	$30,000	$40,000	$ 20,000	$ 10,000
Sale of assets and sharing of loss	20,000	(90,000)		(42,000)	(14,000)	(14,000)
Balances	30,000	0	30,000	(2,000)	6,000	(4,000)
Payment of liabilities	(30,000)		(30,000)			
Balances	0	0	0	(2,000)	6,000	(4,000)
Disbursement of cash to partners	0			2,000	(6,000)	4,000
Balances	$ 0	$ 0	$ 0	$ 0	$ 0	$ 0

c. Lauren and Benroudi both have capital deficiencies. Both of these partners could contribute assets in the amount of their deficiencies to Andrews. However, if the deficient partners cannot contribute personal assets, then the deficits must be absorbed by Andrews. If Andrews absorbs the deficits, then she has a zero balance in her capital account. Since there is no remaining cash balance to distribute, she would be paid nothing more at liquidation.

15. IFRS does not include any specific guidance on accounting for partnerships. Rather, IFRS requires that partnerships disclose information equivalent to that provided by limited companies.

13 Corporations: Share Capital and the Balance Sheet

KEY QUESTIONS	LEARNING OBJECTIVES
What is a corporation, and why is it an important form of business?	**1** Identify the characteristics of a corporation
How do we record and present share information?	**2** Record the issuance of shares, and prepare the shareholders' equity section of a corporation's balance sheet
What are cash dividends, and how do we account for them?	**3** Account for cash dividends
What is the difference between book value and market value of shares?	**4** Use different share values in decision making
What are ROA and ROE, and how do we calculate them?	**5** Evaluate a company's return on assets (ROA) and return on shareholders' equity (ROE)
How does IFRS apply to share capital?	**6** Identify the impact of international financial reporting standards (IFRS) on share capital

Tim Hortons® restaurants are a Canadian icon. Founded in 1964 in Hamilton, Ontario, Tim Hortons enjoyed steady growth for the next three decades and, in 1995, was acquired by Wendy's International. The Tim Hortons chain was wholly owned by Wendy's until 2006, when part of the ownership was sold to the investing public through a process known as an *initial public offering* (IPO).

Tim Hortons was first incorporated in the United States, but its head office was in Canada. It reorganized itself as a Canadian public company in September 2009. It kept the name Tim Hortons Inc. Canada's falling corporate tax rate was the main lure, although Tim Hortons earns 90 percent of its revenue from its Canadian operations.

Tim Hortons lists its shares of stock on the New York Stock Exchange and the Toronto Stock Exchange with the stock symbol THI. It is the fourth-largest publicly traded quick-service restaurant chain in North America and the largest in Canada.

Tim Hortons' success continues. In 2011, the company declared several dividends of $0.17 per common share so that it could share some of its profit with investors, and it increased the dividend to $0.21 per common share in February 2012. Tim Hortons also repurchased $200 million of its common shares, or about 10 percent of its common shares available to the public, between March 5, 2012, and December 28, 2012.

"Our decision to proceed with our sixth consecutive major share repurchase program reflects our strong financial foundation and confidence in our cash flows, growth strategies and continued performance," said Cynthia Devine, Chief Financial Officer.

Source: Tim Hortons Inc. website, Corporate Profile; and 2011, Q4 2011 Quarterly Report to Shareholders from www.timhortons.com, accessed August 27, 2012, and updated on April 30, 2013.

①	②	③	④	⑤	⑥
Identify the characteristics of a corporation	Record the issuance of shares, and prepare the shareholders' equity section of a corporation's balance sheet	Account for cash dividends	Use different share values in decision making	Evaluate a company's return on assets (ROA) and return on shareholders' equity (ROE)	Identify the impact of international financial reporting standards (IFRS) on share capital
What is a corporation, and why it is an important form of business? page 810	*How do we record and present share information? page 816*	*What are cash dividends, and how do we account for them? page 824*	*What is the difference between book value and market value of shares? page 828*	*What are ROA and ROE, and how do we calculate them? page 831*	*How does IFRS apply to share capital? page 833*
Corporations: An Overview, page 810	Issuing Shares, page 816	Accounting for Cash Dividends, page 824	Different Values of Shares, page 828	Evaluating Operations, page 831	The Impact on Share Capital of International Financial Reporting Standards (IFRS), page 833
Shareholders' Equity Basics, page 814	Ethical Considerations in Accounting for the Issuance of Shares, page 823				
	Organization Costs, page 823				

MyAccountingLab

- Chapter 13: DemoDoc covering Common Shares
- Chapter 13: Student PowerPoint Slides
- Chapter 13: Audio Chapter Summary

All MyAccountingLab resources can be found in the Chapter Resources section and the Multimedia Library.

The **Summary** for Chapter 13 appears on page 836.
Accounting Vocabulary with definitions appears on page 838.

Like Gildan Activewear Inc. and Rainmaker Entertainment Inc., Tim Hortons Inc. is a corporation. From this point forward, we will focus on corporations, so this chapter marks a turning point. We begin with the start-up of a corporation and also cover the corporate balance sheet, which differs from proprietorships and partnerships only in the equity section. Fortunately, most of the accounting you have learned thus far also applies to corporations.

Corporations: An Overview

LO ①
What is a corporation, and why is it an important form of business?

Corporations dominate business activity in Canada. Tim Hortons Inc. and Canadian Tire Corporation, Limited are two familiar examples. Although proprietorships and partnerships are more numerous, corporations transact more business and are larger in terms of total assets, sales revenue, and number of employees. Most well-known businesses, such as grocery store chain Loblaw Companies Limited, oil and gas producer EnCana Corporation, and drugstore chain The Jean Coutu Group (PJC) Inc., are corporations. Their full names include *Limited, Incorporated,* or *Corporation* (abbreviated *Ltd., Inc.,* or *Corp.*) to show they are corporations.

A corporation can be set up as a *public corporation*, such as the businesses just mentioned, or as a *private corporation*. A **public corporation** is a company organized as a corporation that is listed and sells its shares on a stock exchange.

Canadian generally accepted accounting principles (GAAP) require that these publicly accountable enterprises follow international financial reporting standards (IFRS). A **private corporation** is a company organized as a corporation that is not listed and does not sell its shares on a stock exchange. According to GAAP, private enterprises have the choice to follow either IFRS or accounting standards for private enterprises (ASPE). The majority of this chapter will focus on ASPE and what is common between the standards. At the end of the chapter, a few differences between the standards will be highlighted.

Characteristics of a Corporation

What makes the corporate form of organization so attractive? What are some of the reasons other forms of business organization are chosen?

Separate Legal Entity   A corporation is a separate legal entity formed under federal or provincial law. The government issues **articles of incorporation**, which is a document giving the owners permission to form a corporation. Neither a proprietorship nor a partnership requires federal or provincial approval to do business, because in the eyes of the law the business and the owner or owners are not separate entities. From a legal perspective, a corporation is a distinct entity, an artificial person that exists apart from its owners, who are called **shareholders**.

A corporation has many of the rights that a person has. For example, a corporation may buy, own, and sell property. Assets and liabilities in the business belong to the corporation rather than to the corporation's owners. The corporation may enter into contracts, sue, and be sued, just like an individual.

Continuous Life and Transferability of Ownership   The owners' equity of a corporation is divided into **shares** of **stock**. The articles of incorporation specify how many shares the corporation can issue (sell) and lists the other details of its relationships with the federal or provincial government under whose laws it is incorporated. Most corporations have *continuous lives* regardless of changes in the ownership of their shares. In contrast, proprietorships and partnerships end when their ownership changes.

The shareholders of Tim Hortons, Barrick Gold, or any other corporation may sell or trade the shares to another person, give them away, bequeath them in a will, or dispose of them in any other way they desire. The transfer of the shares does not affect the continuity of the corporation.

No Mutual Agency   **Mutual agency** means that all the owners act as agents of the business. A contract signed by one owner is binding for the whole company. Mutual agency operates in partnerships, but *not* in corporations. A shareholder of Imperial Oil Limited cannot commit the corporation to a contract (unless the shareholder is also an officer of the corporation).

Limited Liability of Shareholders   Shareholders have **limited liability** for corporation debts. That means they have no personal obligation for corporation liabilities. The most that a shareholder can lose on an investment in a corporation's shares is the cost of the investment. In contrast, proprietors and partners are personally liable for all the debts of their businesses, unless the partnership is a limited liability partnership (LLP).

The combination of limited liability and no mutual agency means that investors can invest in a corporation without fear of losing all their personal wealth if the business fails. This feature enables a corporation to raise more money than proprietorships and partnerships can.

Separation of Ownership and Management   Shareholders own a corporation, but a *board of directors*—elected by the shareholders—appoints corporate officers to manage the business. Shareholders may invest $100 or $1 million without having to manage the company.

Corporate Taxation   Corporations are separate taxable entities. They pay a variety of taxes not borne by proprietorships or partnerships, such as federal and provincial corporate income taxes. Corporate earnings are subject to some **double taxation**.

- First, corporations pay their own income taxes on corporate income.

REAL WORLD EXAMPLE

Just because a company is a private corporation does not mean it is small. Manufacturer's Life Insurance Canada is the largest private corporation in Canada according to *The Globe and Mail*, with over $37 million in revenues in 2010.

KEY POINTS

Corporations can have one or more shareholders. For simplicity and ease of reading, this text will refer to "shareholders" rather than "shareholder(s)."

REAL WORLD EXAMPLE

Because of limited shareholder liability, many banks will lend money to a small corporation only if a third party (usually a corporate officer) guarantees payment of the loan personally in the event of default by the corporation.

KEY POINTS

Corporations are owned by investors, who usually are not involved in the daily operations. A corporation's financial statements should provide the information for investors to make sound decisions about whether to invest in the business.

- The shareholders then pay personal income tax on the dividends (distributions) that they receive from corporations, although the tax rate is usually lower than for regular income to minimize double taxation.

Proprietorships and partnerships pay no business income tax. Instead, owners are taxed on their share of the proprietorship or partnership income on their personal income tax return.

Government Regulation Because of shareholders' limited liability for corporation debts, outsiders doing business with the corporation can look no further than the corporation for payment of its debts. To protect persons who lend money to a corporation or who invest in its shares, the federal and provincial governments monitor the affairs of corporations. This government regulation consists mainly of ensuring that corporations disclose adequate business information for investors and creditors. This government regulation can be expensive for corporations.

Unique Costs for Corporations In Canada, legally, the directors of a corporation (defined below) have unlimited liability. However, insurance is available to cover any costs incurred by directors who may be sued by outsiders doing business with the corporation. If the corporation did not purchase this insurance for its directors, no one would agree to be a director of a corporation. In many small corporations, there may only be one or a few shareholders, who would also be directors of the corporation. The cost for directors' insurance is unique to corporations—proprietorships or partnerships would not incur this cost.

Exhibit 13–1 summarizes the advantages and disadvantages of corporations.

REAL WORLD EXAMPLE

Public corporations are required to have an audit and file certain reports with the applicable provincial securities commission. These requirements add to a corporation's expenses without increasing its income, but are necessary.

EXHIBIT **13–1** | Advantages and Disadvantages of a Corporation

Corporation Advantages	Corporation Disadvantages
1. Can raise more money than a proprietorship or partnership.	1. Ownership and management are separated.
2. Has a continuous life.	2. Corporate earnings are subject to some double taxation.
3. Transferring ownership is easy.	
4. No mutual agency exists among the shareholders.	3. Government regulation can be expensive.
5. Shareholders have limited liability.	4. Corporations may incur costs unique to corporations.

Organization of a Corporation

The process of creating a corporation begins when its organizers, called the *incorporators,* submit articles of incorporation to the federal or provincial government for approval. The articles of incorporation include the **authorization of shares** for the corporation to issue a certain number of shares of stock, which are shares of ownership in the corporation. The incorporators pay fees and file the required documents with the incorporating jurisdiction. Then the corporation comes into existence and becomes a legal entity. The incorporators agree to a set of **bylaws,** which act as the constitution for governing the corporation.

The ultimate control of the corporation rests with the shareholders, who usually receive one vote for each voting share they own. The shareholders elect the members of the **board of directors**, which:

- Sets policy for the corporation.
- Elects a **chairperson**, who is often the most powerful person in the corporation.
- Appoints the **president**, who is the chief executive officer (CEO) in charge of managing day-to-day operations.

Most corporations have a number of vice-presidents. Exhibit 13–2 shows a typical authority structure in a corporation.

EXHIBIT **13–2** | Typical Authority Structure in a Corporation

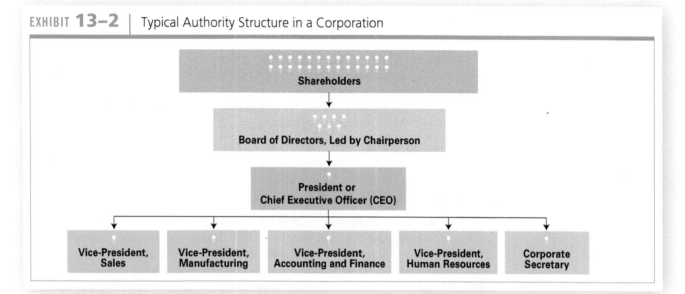

All corporations have an annual meeting at which the shareholders elect directors and make other shareholder decisions such as appointing the external auditors. Shareholders unable to attend this annual meeting may vote on corporation matters by use of a **proxy**, which appoints another person to cast the vote on their behalf.

Share Capital

A corporation issues *share certificates* to its owners when they invest in the business. Shareholders rarely see or receive share certificates. Instead, their share purchase and sale transactions are listed on the monthly summary of activity in their brokerage or trading accounts. Because shares represent the corporation's capital, they are often called *share capital*. The basic unit of share capital is called a *share*. A corporation may issue a share certificate for any number of shares it wishes—one share, 100 shares, or any other number. Exhibit 13–3 depicts an actual share certificate for 200 Intrawest Corporation shares and highlights key information found on a share certificate.

EXHIBIT **13–3** | Share Certificate

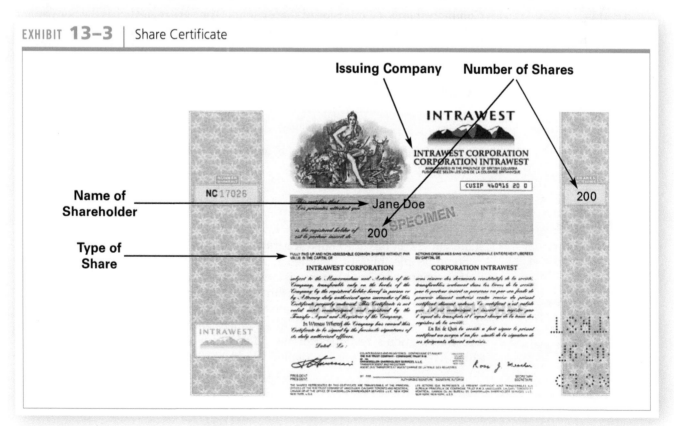

Shareholders' Equity Basics

KEY POINTS

The two main different sources of owners' equity are owner investment and earnings not withdrawn by the owner. In a proprietorship, the owner's investment and earnings are both recorded in the Capital account. In a corporation, the owners' investment is called *contributed capital* and the earnings not paid out to the owners (shareholders) are called *retained earnings*.

A corporation reports assets and liabilities the same way as a proprietorship or a partnership. However, owners' equity of a corporation—called **shareholders' equity**—is reported differently. Business laws require corporations to report their sources of capital because some of the capital must be maintained by the company. The two most basic sources of capital are

- **Contributed capital,** which represents investment amounts received from the shareholders of the corporation. Contributed surplus, which will be discussed later, is also a component of contributed capital; and

- **Retained earnings,** which is capital earned from profitable operations.

While the *Canada Business Corporations Act* and several of the provincial incorporating acts use the term *stated capital* to describe share capital, this text will use the more common term, share capital. Exhibit 13–4 is a summarized version of the shareholders' equity section of the balance sheet of Canadian Tire Corporation, Limited used to show how to report these categories of shareholders' equity.

EXHIBIT **13–4**	Summarized Shareholders' Equity at December 31, 2011, of Canadian Tire Corporation, Limited. (adapted, amounts in millions)

Shareholders' Equity	
Contributed capital	$ 710.5
Retained earnings	3,698.5
Total shareholders' equity	$4,409.0

Contributed Capital Comes from the Shareholders

Common shares are one type of share capital. They are regarded as the permanent capital of the business because the balance in the Common Shares account *cannot* be withdrawn by the shareholders. The entry to record the receipt of $200,000 cash and the issuance of common shares to shareholders is

Oct. 20	Cash	200,000	
	Common Shares		200,000
	Issued common shares.		

Issuing shares increases both the assets and the shareholders' equity of a corporation.

Retained Earnings Comes from Profitable Operations

KEY POINTS

Sometimes students incorrectly view Retained Earnings as an asset, like cash. Remember, Retained Earnings is a part of shareholders' equity and therefore should have a normal *credit* balance. A *debit* balance in Retained Earnings is called a *deficit*.

Profitable operations produce net income for the corporation, which increases shareholders' equity through a separate account called Retained Earnings.

Some people think of Retained Earnings as a fund of cash. It is not, because Retained Earnings is not an asset; it is an element of shareholders' equity. Retained earnings has no particular relationship to cash or any other asset.

Corporations close their revenues and expenses into Income Summary, and then they close net income to Retained Earnings. To illustrate, Canadian Tire Corporation's revenues for the 52 weeks ended December 31, 2011, were $10,387,100,000 and expenses totalled $9,643,400,000.

The closing entries would be

2011			
Dec. 31	Revenues (detailed)	10,387,100,000	
	Income Summary		10,387,100,000
	To close revenue.		

2011			
Dec. 31	Income Summary	9,643,400,000	
	Expenses (detailed)		9,643,400,000
	To close expenses.		

Now, Income Summary holds revenues, expenses, and net income.

Income Summary

Expenses	9,643,400,000	Revenues	10,387,100,000
		Balance	
		(net income)	743,700,000

Finally, the Income Summary's balance is closed to Retained Earnings.

2011			
Dec. 31	Income Summary	743,700,000	
	Retained Earnings		743,700,000
	To close net income to Retained Earnings.		

This closing entry completes the closing process. Income Summary is zeroed out, and Retained Earnings now holds net income.

If Canadian Tire had had a net loss, Income Summary would have had a debit balance. To close an assumed $100,000 loss, the closing entry credits Income Summary and debits Retained Earnings as follows:

2011			
Dec. 31	Retained Earnings	100,000	
	Income Summary		100,000
	To close Income Summary by transferring		
	net loss to Retained Earnings.		

Negative Retained Earnings Is Called a Deficit A loss or an accumulation of several years of losses may cause a debit balance in the Retained Earnings account. This condition—called a Retained Earnings or accumulated **deficit**—is reported as a negative amount in shareholders' equity. B2Gold Corp., which has its head office in Vancouver, reported the following (adapted) in its 2011 annual report:

Shareholders' Equity (in thousands of U.S. dollars)	
Contributed capital (357,570,170 shares issued)	$312,829
Contributed surplus	19,971
Deficit	(42,669)
Total shareholders' equity	$290,131

A Corporation May Pay Dividends to Shareholders

A profitable corporation may distribute cash to its shareholders. Such distributions are called **dividends**. Dividends are similar to the withdrawals of cash made by the owner of a proprietorship or by a partner of a partnership. Dividends decrease both the assets and retained earnings (and therefore, shareholders' equity) of the corporation. Dividends are discussed in detail later in this chapter.

Shareholders' Rights

The owner of a share has certain rights that are set out in the corporation's articles of incorporation; these vary from company to company, and even between classes of shares within a company. In addition, the shareholder may have other rights granted by the legislation under which the corporation wrote its articles. The articles of incorporation, for example, may specify that the shareholder of one class of common shares is entitled to one vote per share at shareholders' meetings, while the shareholder of another class of common shares is not entitled to vote. An example of a shared right is that, under the *Canada Business Corporations Act,* shareholders may require the directors of the company to call a meeting of the shareholders.

Some of the rights generally attached to common shares[1] are

- The right to sell the shares.
- The right to vote at shareholders' meetings.
- The right to receive a **proportionate share** of any dividends declared by the directors for that class of shares.
- The right to receive a proportionate share of any assets on the winding-up of the company, after the creditors and any classes of shares that rank above that class have been paid.
- A **preemptive right**—the right to maintain one's proportionate ownership in the corporation. If a shareholder owns 5 percent of the outstanding common shares and the corporation decides to issue 100,000 new shares, the shareholder would be entitled to purchase 5,000 of the new shares ($0.05 \times 100,000$).

REAL WORLD EXAMPLE

Some corporations issue several classes of common shares—Class A shares and Class B shares. In a case like this, one class may have the rights of common shares and the other may have some restrictions or enhancements. For example, Magna International Inc., a major auto-parts supplier, has Class A shares with one vote each, while their Class B shares have 300 votes each.

✓ JUST CHECKING

1. Compare and contrast the characteristics of proprietorships and corporations.
2. Describe the authority structure of a corporation, starting with the group or position that has the greatest authority.
3. List any three of the five rights typically attached to common shares.

Just Checking Solutions appear at the end of this chapter and on MyAccountingLab.

Issuing Shares

LO ②
How do we record and present share information?

Large corporations such as George Weston Limited, BCE Inc., and Kinross Gold Corp. need huge quantities of money to operate. They cannot expect to finance all their operations through borrowing. They can raise these funds by issuing shares. The articles of incorporation include an *authorization of shares*—that is, a provision for the business to issue (sell) a certain number of shares. Corporations may sell their shares directly to the shareholders; however, they typically use the services of an **underwriter** to sell their shares, such as the brokerage firm RBC Dominion Securities or Scotia Capital Inc. The agreement between a corporation and its underwriter will vary, but typically the underwriter will commit to placing (selling)

---

[1] For a more complete listing, the interested reader is referred to the *Canada Business Corporations Act in The Revised Statutes of Canada.*

all of the share issue it can with its customers, and to buying any unsold shares for its own account. In another form of contract, the underwriter agrees to do its best to sell all of the share issue but makes no guarantees. The underwriter makes its money by selling the shares for a higher price than it pays to the corporation issuing the shares.

The corporation need not issue all the shares that the articles of incorporation allow—the number of **authorized shares** can, and often does, exceed the number of issued shares. Management may hold some shares back and issue them later if the need for additional capital arises. The shares that the corporation does issue to shareholders are called **issued shares**. Only by issuing shares—not by receiving authorization—does the corporation increase the asset and shareholders' equity amounts on its balance sheet. Shares held by shareholders are considered **outstanding shares**. The total number of a corporation's shares outstanding at any time represents 100 percent of its ownership.

Most corporations are authorized to issue many more shares than they intend to issue originally. If the corporation wants to issue more than the authorized shares, the articles of incorporation must be amended. Amendment of the articles of incorporation requires shareholder approval and may require government approval as well.

The price that the shareholder pays to acquire shares from the corporation is called the **issue price**. A combination of market factors—including the company's comparative earnings record, financial position, prospects for success, and general business conditions—determines issue price.

The shares of a corporation may be either common or preferred. We will examine common shares first.

Common Shares

Every corporation issues *common shares*, the most basic form of share capital. Companies may issue different classes of common shares. For example, Rogers Communications Inc. has issued Class A common shares, which carry the right to vote, and Class B common shares, which are nonvoting. (Classes of common shares may also be designated Series A, Series B, and so on, with each series having unique features.) There is a separate general-ledger account for each class of common shares.

Investors who buy common shares take a risk with a corporation. They are the owners of the business, but the corporation makes no promises to pay them. If the corporation succeeds, it may distribute dividends to its shareholders, but if retained earnings and cash are too low, the shareholders may receive no dividends. The market value (selling price) of the shares of successful corporations increase, and investors enjoy the benefit of selling the shares at a gain. Thus, the holder of common shares can earn income both from dividends and from increases in the value of the shares.

But share prices can decrease, possibly leaving the investors with nothing of value. Because common shareholders take a risky investment position, they demand increases in share prices, high dividends, or both. If the corporation does not accomplish these goals and many shareholders sell their shares, the market price will fall. Short of bankruptcy, this is one of the worst things that can happen to a corporation because it means that the corporation cannot easily raise capital as needed. The period from the autumn of 2008 to the first part of 2009 highlighted this as most stock markets around the world saw share prices plummet. Exhibit 13–5 on the next page shows the performance of the Canadian stock market, represented by the performance of a group of corporate shares on the Toronto Stock Exchange. Notice the steep decline in values in 2008 and 2009. Imagine how difficult it must have been for shareholders and managers of corporations during that period.

KEY POINTS

Note the differences between the following terms:

Authorized shares—the maximum number of shares the corporation can issue according to the articles of incorporation. This can be increased (although not easily).

Issued and outstanding shares—shares that have been sold to and are held by shareholders. The total number of a corporation's shares issued and outstanding at any time represents 100 percent of its ownership.

KEY POINTS

The common shareholders are the owners of the business.

REAL WORLD EXAMPLE

The U.S. term for common shares is *common stock*.

EXHIBIT **13-5** | Canadian Stock Market Performance (TSX Composite)

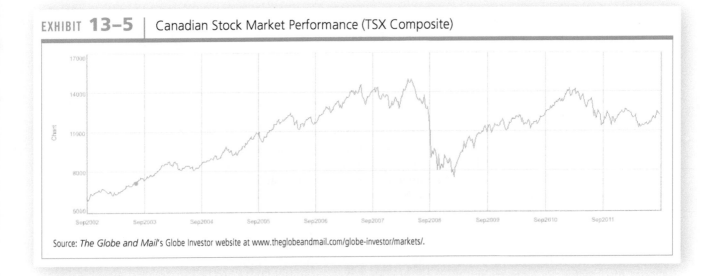

Source: *The Globe and Mail*'s Globe Investor website at www.theglobeandmail.com/globe-investor/markets/.

Issuing Common Shares

Companies often advertise the issuance of their shares to attract investors. A good source of such information is SEDAR (System for Electronic Document Analysis and Retrieval). SEDAR is the website developed under the authority of the Canadian Securities Administrators and administered by each of the provincial securities regulatory authorities. Exhibit 13–6 is a reproduction of a portion of the *prospectus* dated March 24, 2006, of Tim Hortons Inc.'s *initial public offering* of 29,000,000 common shares at $27.00 per share. A **prospectus** is a required legal document that describes the investment offering to potential purchasers. An **initial public offering** is the first time a corporation's shares are sold to investors or members of the public.

No-Par-Value Shares **No-par-value shares** are shares that do not have a value assigned to them by the articles of incorporation. The *Canada Business Corporations Act* (CBCA) requires all newly issued shares in Canada to be no-par-value. **Par value** is an arbitrary value assigned to each share, and might be seen in Canadian corporations that were established before the CBCA came into effect or when certain complex tax-planning arrangements are made.

Stated Value of Shares The board of directors may assign a value to the shares when they are issued; this value is known as the **stated value**. For example, Dajol Inc. has authorization to issue 100,000 common shares, having no par value assigned to them by the articles of incorporation. Dajol Inc. needs $50,000 at incorporation, and might issue 10,000 shares for $5.00 per share, 2,000 shares at $25.00 per share, or 1,000 shares at $50.00 per share, and so on. The point is that Dajol Inc. can assign whatever value to the shares the board of directors wishes; however, the price the shares sell for on the market may be very different from the stated value. To illustrate this, refer to the announcement of the share issue by Tim Hortons Inc. in Exhibit 13–6. The initial price to the public at the bottom of the announcement of $27.00 per share is the stated value. Once the market opened, the price was $37.00 per share, and at the end of the first day of trading, the price was $33.10 per share.

The full amount of the proceeds from the sale of shares by a company must be allocated to the capital account for those shares, as shown in the next section.

REAL WORLD EXAMPLE

If you looked at the balance sheet of a U.S. corporation, you might see that its common shares had been issued at *par value*. This means the board of directors assigned a value to the common shares. If the shares were sold for more than par value, the difference was credited to Paid-in Capital in Excess of Par, or Additional Paid-in Capital. Most Canadian corporations credit the capital account for common shares for the full amount of the net proceeds from the sale of the shares.

EXHIBIT **13–6** | Announcement of Share Issue by Tim Hortons Inc.

Supplemented Prep Prospectus

Initial Public Offering   March 24, 2006

TIM HORTONS INC.

C$783,000,000

29,000,000 Shares of Common Stock

This prospectus qualifies the distribution (the "offering") of 29,000,000 shares of common stock in the capital of Tim Hortons Inc. Unless the context otherwise requires, any reference in this prospectus to "we", "our" and the "Company" refer to Tim Hortons Inc. and its consolidated subsidiaries.

We are offering our common stock for sale concurrently in Canada under the terms of this prospectus and in the United States under the terms of registration statement on Form S-1 filed with the United States Securities and Exchange Commission. Our common stock is being offered in Canada by Goldman Sachs Canada Inc., RBC Dominion Securities Inc., J.P. Morgan Securities Canada Inc., Scotia Capital Inc., BMO Nesbitt Burns Inc., CIBC World Markets Inc., Merrill Lynch Canada Inc. and TD Securities Inc. (the "Canadian Underwriters") and in the United States by Goldman, Sachs & Co., RBC Capital Markets Corporation, J.P. Morgan Securities Inc., Scotia Capital (USA) Inc., Bear, Stearns & Co. Inc., CIBC World Markets Corp., Cowen & Co., LLC, Harris Nesbitt Corp., Lazard Capital Markets LLC, Merrill Lynch, Pierce, Fenner & Smith Incorporated, TD Securities (USA) LLC, Huntington Capital Corp., Loop Capital Markets, LLC, NatCity Investments, Inc. and The Williams Capital Group, L.P. (together with the Canadian Underwriters, the "underwriters"). In connection with this distribution, the underwriters may over-allot or effect transactions which stabilize, maintain or otherwise affect the market price of the common stock at levels other than those which otherwise might prevail on the open market. See "Underwriting". **After the initial offering, the offering price may be changed by the underwriters as described under "Underwriting".**

There is currently no market through which the common stock may be sold and purchasers may not be able to resell shares purchased under this prospectus. The Toronto Stock Exchange has conditionally approved the listing of the common stock under the symbol "THI." Listing is subject to our fulfilling all of the requirements of the Toronto Stock Exchange, including distribution of the common stock to a minimum number of public securityholders. Our common stock has been approved for listing on the New York Stock Exchange under the symbol "THI". An Investment in the common stock is subject to a number of risks that should be considered by a prospective purchaser. Investors should carefully consider the risk factors described under "Risk Factors" before purchasing the common stock.

Price: C$27.00 per Share

	Price to the Public	Underwriters Discounts and Commissions	Net Proceeds to Tim Hortons Inc.
Per Share	C$27.00	C$1.62	C$25.38
Total offering	C$783,000,000	C$46,980,000	C$736,020,000

REAL WORLD EXAMPLE

Take a look at how much the underwriters made on this deal—almost $47 million! Might this be time to consider a career in finance?

KEY POINTS

Issuance of new shares increases the corporation's assets and shareholders' equity. Sales of shares by shareholders after this date are not reflected in the corporation's balance sheet.

Issuing Common Shares at a Stated Value Using the Tim Hortons's information found in Exhibit 13–6 , the share issuance entry (including fees and commissions) is

Jan. 8	Cash	736,020,000	
	Discounts and Commissions Expense	46,980,000	
	Common Shares		783,000,000
	To issue 29,000,000 common shares at		
	$27.00 per share, the stated value,		
	less discounts and commissions expenses.		

REAL WORLD EXAMPLE

Stock exchanges, brokers, and other companies provide the market price of a company's shares and the dividend per share, as well as the dividend yield (which is the dividend per share ÷ market price per share) on the internet.

The amount invested in the corporation, $783,000,000 in this case, is called share capital. The credit to Common Shares records an increase in the share capital of the corporation.

This next example shows the Research in Motion (RIM; now called BlackBerry) shareholders' equity section in its annual report for the year ended February 26, 2011. RIM's annual report in Note 9 (a) "Share Capital" indicates that RIM's articles of incorporation permit it to issue " . . . an unlimited number of voting common shares . . . " At Feb. 26, 2011, RIM had issued 523,868,644 common shares for US$2,359,000,000. The common shares were issued at an average value of $4.50 (calculated as $2,359,000,000 ÷ 523,868,644 common shares). The corporation reported shareholders' equity (adapted) as follows:

Shareholders' Equity (in millions of U.S. dollars)	
Contributed capital	
Common shares, unlimited number of shares	
authorized, 523,868,644 shares issued	$2,359
Retained earnings	6,579
Total shareholders' equity	$8,938

LEARNING TIPS

Whenever a corporation receives assets in exchange for share capital, assets and shareholders' equity will *increase*. Whenever a corporation distributes assets to shareholders (by paying dividends or retiring shares), assets and shareholders' equity will *decrease*.

Issuing Common Shares for Assets Other Than Cash   A corporation may issue shares in exchange for assets other than cash. It debits the assets received for their current market value and credits the common shares or preferred shares accounts accordingly. The assets' prior book value does not matter. Suppose Gillan Corporation issued 25,000 common shares for equipment worth $25,000 plus a building worth $125,000. The entry is

Nov. 12	Equipment	25,000	
	Building	125,000	
	Common Shares		150,000
	To issue 25,000 common shares in		
	exchange for equipment and a building.		

Common Shares increases by the amount of the assets' *current market value,* $150,000 in this case; the stated value or value assigned to the shares would be $6.00 ($150,000 ÷ 25,000) per share.

Preferred Shares

Preferred shares have special rights or preferences that give their owners certain advantages over common shareholders. Investors who buy preferred shares take less risk than do common shareholders. Most notably,

- Preferred shareholders receive dividends before the common shareholders.
- Preferred shareholders receive assets before the common shareholders if the corporation liquidates.
- Corporations often pay a fixed dividend on preferred shares. Investors usually buy preferred shares to earn those fixed dividends.

Often, preferred shares are **cumulative**, which means that if the preferred dividend is not paid in a year, the dividend from that year must be paid to the preferred shareholders before the common shareholders can receive a dividend in a later year. Because of the preferred shareholders' priorities, common shares represent the *residual ownership* in the corporation's assets after the liabilities and the claims of preferred shareholders have been subtracted. Often the right to vote is withheld from preferred shareholders. Companies may issue different classes of preferred shares (Class A and Class B or Series A and Series B, for example). Each class is recorded in a separate account.

The preferred dividend may be a set amount or a fixed percentage of some number, such as the prime interest rate at the date of declaration of the dividend.

For example, Bombardier Inc.'s January 31, 2011, annual report showed the company had the following classes of common and preferred shares:

	Number of Shares Authorized	Number of Shares Issued and Outstanding	Dividends
Class A Shares (Multiple Voting)	1,892,000,000	315,084,537	—
Class B Shares (Subordinate Voting)	1,892,000,000	1,410,626,970	—
Series 2 Cumulative Redeemable Preferred	12,000,000	8,464,920	80% of the Canadian prime rate payable monthly
Series 3 Cumulative Redeemable Preferred	12,000,000	2,535,080	5.267% or $1.31675 per share payable quarterly
Series 4 Cumulative Redeemable Preferred	9,400,000	9,400,000	6.25% or $1.5625 per share payable quarterly

Investors usually buy preferred shares to earn these fixed dividends. Preferred shares' market values do not fluctuate much, so investor income from owning preferred shares is mostly from dividends rather than share-price increases. Individuals might also prefer to hold preferred shares because the income tax rate they pay on dividends they receive is lower than the income tax rate they pay on interest they receive. It's for that reason that the dividend rate on a company's preferred shares is usually lower than the interest rate on bonds the company issues (the bonds pay interest; the preferred shares pay dividends).

Corporations are faced with a number of choices when raising capital. Some of the things a corporation should consider when choosing to sell shares or issue long-term debt are:

	Common Shares	Preferred Shares	Long-term Debt
Annual Cost/Liability	None	Flexible. There may be dividends but only if declared by the board of directors	Required interest payment
Control	Vote	Usually no voting rights, so no change in control	Lenders have no voting rights
Repayment	No	No	Yes, fixed per terms of loan
Tax Implications for the corporation	None	Dividends are not tax deductible because they are a distribution of earnings	Interest is a deductible expense for tax purposes

Not all corporations issue preferred shares. However, all corporations must issue at least one common share.

Issuing Preferred Shares

Accounting for preferred shares follows the pattern illustrated for common shares.

Assume Cendant Corporation's articles of incorporation authorize issuance of 10,000 preferred shares with an annual dividend of $10.00 per share. On July 31, the company issues 1,000 shares at a stated price of $100.00 per share and receives a cash payment of $100,000. The issuance entry is

Jul. 31	Cash	100,000	
	Preferred Shares		100,000
	To issue 1,000 preferred shares for $100.00 per share (1,000 × $100).		

REAL WORLD EXAMPLE

Another investment vehicle available to investors is called an *income trust* or *investment trust*. It is a portfolio of assets that is designed to provide safety of principal and a regular fixed income. An example of an income trust is Big Rock Brewery Income Trust. Unitholders receive monthly cash payments, but at the same time they maintain their equity position in the company. The monthly cash payments are roughly equivalent to dividends paid by corporations, but their tax treatment in the hands of unitholders is different.

Convertible Preferred Shares

Convertible preferred shares are preferred shares that may be exchanged by the preferred shareholders, if they choose, for another specified class of shares in the corporation. For example, the preferred shares of Renewal Resources Inc. are convertible into the company's common shares. A note to Renewal's balance sheet describes the conversion terms as follows:

> **The . . . preferred shares are convertible at the rate of 7.00 common shares for each preferred share outstanding.**

If you owned 100 Renewal convertible preferred shares, you could convert them into 700 (100 × 7.00) common shares. Under what condition would you exercise the conversion privilege? You would do so if the market value of the common shares that you could receive from conversion was greater than the market value of the preferred shares that you presently held. This way, you as an investor could increase your personal wealth.

Renewal Resources Inc.'s convertible preferred shares were issued at $100.00 per share, and the common shares at $1.00. The company would record the conversion at the value of the 100 preferred shares on the Renewal Resources Inc. books, or $10,000 (100 × $100). The conversion of the 100 preferred shares into 700 common shares would be recorded as follows:

KEY POINTS

No gain or loss is reported on a conversion of shares.

Mar. 7	Preferred Shares	10,000	
	Common Shares		10,000
	Conversion of preferred shares into common.		
	(100 preferred shares converted into 700 common shares.)		

At this point, the new common shares cannot be converted back to preferred shares.

The balance sheet would be updated to show the change in the equity section by reflecting the new numbers of each type of share.

The Shareholders' Equity Section of a Balance Sheet

The shareholders' equity section of Chang Corporation's balance sheet at December 31, 2014, appears in Exhibit 13–7. Note the two sections of shareholders' equity: contributed capital and retained earnings. Also observe the order of the contributed capital accounts: preferred shares, then common shares.

KEY POINTS

In the contributed capital section, "Preferred shares, $5.00," means the annual dividend is $5.00 per preferred share. The dividend can also be stated as a percent.

EXHIBIT 13–7 | Part of Chang Corporation's Balance Sheet

CHANG CORPORATION
Partial Balance Sheet
December 31, 2014

Shareholders' Equity

Contributed capital

Preferred shares, $5.00, 10,000 shares authorized,	
1,000 shares issued and outstanding	$ 50,000
Common shares, 10,000 shares authorized,	
4,000 shares issued and outstanding	80,000
Total contributed capital	130,000
Retained earnings	50,000
Total shareholders' equity	$180,000

Ethical Considerations in Accounting for the Issuance of Shares

Issuance of shares for *cash* poses no serious ethical challenge because the value of the asset received (cash) is clearly understood. The company simply receives cash and issues the shares to the shareholders. However, issuing shares for assets other than cash can pose an ethical challenge. The company issuing the shares wants to look successful, so it often wishes to record a large amount for the noncash asset received (such as land or a building) and for the shares being issued. Why? Because large asset and equity amounts make the business look prosperous, and financial ratios can be affected in a positive way. This can motivate a company to record a high amount for the assets.

A company is supposed to record an asset received at its current market value. However, one person may appraise land at a market value of $400,000. Another may honestly believe the land is worth only $300,000. A company receiving land in exchange for its shares must decide whether to record the land at $300,000, at $400,000, or at some amount in between based on external, independent evidence.

The ethical course of action is to record the asset at its current market value, as determined by independent appraisers. Corporations are rarely found guilty of *understating* their assets, but companies have been sued for *overstating* asset values.

REAL WORLD EXAMPLE

Sometimes, with publicly traded corporations, it is most objective to use the market value of the shares given in exchange for an asset as a measure of the asset's value.

Organization Costs

The costs of organizing a corporation include legal fees for preparing documents and advising on procedures and fees paid to the incorporating jurisdiction, and charges by promoters for selling the company's shares. These costs are grouped in an account titled Organization Costs, which is an asset because these costs contribute to a business's start-up. Suppose BBV Holdings Inc. pays legal fees and incorporation fees of $5,000 to organize the corporation under the *Canada Business Corporations Act* in Newfoundland. In addition, an investment dealer charges a fee of $15,000 for selling 30,000 common shares of BBV Holdings Inc. to investors for $225,000. Instead of being paid in cash, the broker receives 2,000 common shares as payment. BBV Holdings Inc.'s journal entries to record these organization costs are

Mar. 31	Organization Costs	5,000	
	Cash		5,000
	Legal fees and incorporation fees to organize the corporation.		
Apr. 3	Cash	225,000	
	Organization Costs	15,000	
	Common Shares		240,000
	To record receipt of funds from sale of 30,000 common shares and issue of 2,000 shares to investment dealer for selling shares in organization.		

Organization costs is an *intangible asset,* reported on the balance sheet along with patents, trademarks, goodwill, and any other intangibles. The *Income Tax Act* allows corporations to expense a portion of organization costs against taxable income. While the *CICA Handbook* does not require them to be amortized, most

REAL WORLD EXAMPLE

Notice there is no rule for how long to amortize the organization costs. As you learn more accounting, you will find there are fewer rules and more room for professional judgment when recording transactions.

companies amortize organization costs over a short time period because of their relatively small size. As is true with other intangibles, amortization expense for the year should be disclosed in the financial statements.

✓ JUST CHECKING

4. Explain why the following comment is false: Preferred shares are a riskier investment than common shares.

5. Assume WCP Corporation's articles of incorporation authorize issuance of 10,000 convertible preferred shares with an annual dividend of $10.00 per share and an unlimited number of common shares. On July 31, the company issued 1,000 preferred shares at a stated price of $100.00 per share and 2,000 common shares at $50.00 per share, and received total cash of $200,000.

   a. Record the issuance of the shares.
   b. Calculate total contributed capital and total shareholders' equity, assuming retained earnings is now $50,000.
   c. Record the conversion of 10 of the $100.00 convertible preferred shares (now having a market value of $90). Each preferred share is convertible into two common shares.

6. Indicate whether each of the following favours the use of long-term debt to raise capital or the issuance of common shares.

   a. Annual payment is optional.
   b. Money must be repaid.
   c. Issuance means dilution of existing control.
   d. Annual cost is tax deductible.

Just Checking Solutions appear at the end of this chapter and on MyAccountingLab.

Accounting for Cash Dividends

LO ③
What are cash dividends, and how do we account for them?

Corporations share their wealth with the shareholders through dividends. Corporations declare dividends from *retained earnings* and usually pay the dividends with *cash*. The corporation must have enough retained earnings to declare the dividend and also have enough cash to pay the dividend. Companies also have the option to issue stock dividends. Stock dividends are discussed in Chapter 14.

Dividend Dates

KEY POINTS

To declare cash dividends, a corporation must have (1) a credit balance in Retained Earnings, (2) adequate cash, and (3) approval from the board of directors.

A corporation must declare a dividend before paying it. The corporation has no obligation to pay a dividend until the board of directors declares one. However, once the dividend is declared, it becomes a legal liability. Three dates for dividends are relevant:

① *Declaration date* On the **declaration date**, the board of directors announces the intention to pay the dividend. The declaration creates a current liability called Dividends Payable for the corporation.

② *Date of record* Those shareholders holding the shares on the **date of record**—a few weeks after declaration—will receive the dividend.

③ *Payment date* Payment of the dividend usually follows the record date by two to four weeks.

KEY POINTS

Dividends are *not* an expense, but a distribution of earnings to owners. Cash dividends, like withdrawals, reduce assets and shareholders' equity.

Dividend announcements are published in the financial press and online to ensure that shareholders or potential shareholders are kept fully aware of the corporation's dividend policy. Notice that the important dates mentioned above are shown in Exhibit 13–8.

EXHIBIT 13-8 | Example of a Dividend Notice for Laurentian Bank of Canada

Laurentian Bank of Canada - Dividend Notice ①**Declaration Date**

MONTREAL, Feb. 22, 2012 /CNW Telbec/ - The Board of Directors of the Laurentian Bank of Canada declared today the following dividends:

- a dividend of $0.375 on the preferred shares Series 9, payable on March 15, 2012 to shareholders of record at the close of business on March 7, 2012; and

- a dividend of $0.328125 on the preferred shares Series 10, payable on March 15, 2012 to shareholders of record at the close of business on March 7, 2012.

②**Date of Record**

③**Payment Date**

For the year 2012, all dividends declared will be eligible dividends, unless otherwise indicated. The dividends declared on February 22, 2012, are eligible dividends for income tax legislation purposes.

For further information:

Gladys Caron

Vice-President,

Public Affairs, Communications and Investor Relations

Office: (514) 284-4500, extension 7511

Cellular: (514) 893-3963

gladys.caron@banquelaurentienne.ca

Source: http://www.newswire.ca/en/story/925541/laurentian-bank-of-canada-dividend-notice

Declaring and Paying Dividends

Declaration of a cash dividend is recorded by debiting Retained Earnings and crediting the current liability, Dividends Payable, as follows (amounts assumed):[2]

Oct. 3	Retained Earnings	20,000	
	Dividends Payable		20,000
	To declare a cash dividend for shareholders		
	on the October 31 date of record. Payment		
	date is November 15.		

There is no journal entry on October 31, the date of record. Shareholders who own shares on this date will receive the dividend on November 15.

To pay the dividend on the payment date, the transaction is recorded as follows:

Nov. 15	Dividends Payable	20,000	
	Cash		20,000
	To pay a cash dividend.		

When a company has issued both preferred and common shares, the preferred shareholders receive their dividends first. The common shareholders receive dividends only if the total declared dividend is large enough to satisfy the preferred requirements. Let's see how dividends are divided between preferred and common shares.

---

[2] Some accountants debit a Dividends account, a temporary account that is later closed to Retained Earnings, but most businesses debit Retained Earnings directly, as shown here.

Guthrie Industries Inc. has 10,000 shares of $1.50 preferred shares outstanding plus common shares. Exhibit 13–9 shows the division of dividends between the preferred shares and common shares for two situations.

EXHIBIT **13–9**	Dividing a Dividend between the Preferred Shares and Common Shares of Guthrie Industries Inc.	
Case A:	**Total dividend of $15,000**	
	Preferred dividend (The full $15,000 goes to the preferred shares because the annual preferred dividend is $15,000 ($1.50 × 10,000).)	$15,000
	Common dividend (None, because the total dividend declared did not exceed the preferred dividend for the year.)	0
		$15,000
Case B:	**Total dividend of $50,000**	
	Preferred dividend ($1.50 × $10,000)	$15,000
	Common dividend ($50,000 – $15,000)	35,000
		$50,000

If the year's dividend is just equal to or less than the preferred dividend (Case A in Exhibit 13–9), the preferred shareholders receive the entire dividend, and the common shareholders receive nothing that year. However, if Guthrie Industries Inc.'s annual dividend is large enough to exceed the preferred dividend for the year (Case B in Exhibit 13–9), the preferred shareholders receive their regular dividend and the common shareholders receive the remainder.

The dividend preference is normally stated as a dollar amount. For example, the preferred shares may be "Preferred shares, $5.00," meaning that the shareholders are entitled to an annual dividend of $5.00 per share (see Exhibit 13–7 on page 822).

When a company has more than one class of preferred shares or common shares, the division of dividends among the various classes of shares depends on the order of priority created when each of the classes was issued.

Dividends on Cumulative and Noncumulative Preferred Shares

The allocation of dividends will involve additional calculations if the preferred shares are *cumulative*. If a corporation fails to pay the preferred dividend, the missed dividends are said to be *in arrears*. The owners of **cumulative preferred shares** must receive all dividends in arrears plus the current year's dividend before the corporation pays dividends to the common shareholders. "Cumulative" means that any dividends in arrears will accumulate, or carry over, to the future. The cumulative feature is not automatic to preferred shares but must be assigned to the preferred shares in the articles of incorporation. Common shares are never cumulative.

Let's assume the preferred shares of Guthrie Industries Inc. are cumulative and the company did not distribute the 2013 preferred dividend of $15,000. Before paying dividends to its common shareholders in 2014, the company must first pay preferred dividends of $15,000 for each of 2013 and 2014, a total of $30,000.

If Guthrie Industries declares a $55,000 dividend in 2014, how much of this dividend goes to the preferred shareholders if the preferred shares are cumulative? How much goes to the common shareholders? The allocation of this $55,000 dividend is shown in Exhibit 13–10.

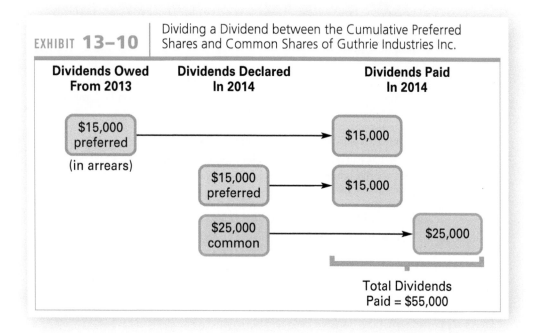

| EXHIBIT **13–10** | Dividing a Dividend between the Cumulative Preferred Shares and Common Shares of Guthrie Industries Inc. |

Dividends Owed From 2013

Dividends Declared In 2014

Dividends Paid In 2014

$15,000 preferred (in arrears) → $15,000

$15,000 preferred → $15,000

$25,000 common → $25,000

Total Dividends Paid = $55,000

The entry to record the declaration of this dividend is

2014			
Sept. 6	Retained Earnings	55,000	
	Dividends Payable, Preferred Shares		30,000
	Dividends Payable, Common Shares		25,000
	To declare a cash dividend. Preferred		
	dividends are $30,000 ($15,000 × 2); common		
	dividends are $25,000 ($55,000 − $30,000).		

If the preferred shares are not designated as cumulative, the corporation is not obligated to pay any dividends in arrears. Suppose that the Guthrie Industries Inc. preferred shares were noncumulative, and the company did not distribute a dividend in 2013. The preferred shareholders would lose the 2013 dividend forever. Of course, the common shareholders would not receive a 2013 dividend either. Before paying any common dividends in 2014, the company would have to pay only the 2014 preferred dividend of $15,000 as shown in Case A in Exhibit 13–9.

Having dividends in arrears on cumulative preferred shares is *not* a liability to the corporation. (A liability for dividends arises only after the board of directors declares the dividend.) Nevertheless, a corporation must report cumulative preferred dividends in arrears in the notes to the financial statements. This information alerts common shareholders to how much in cumulative preferred dividends must be paid before the common shareholders will receive any dividends.

Note disclosure of cumulative preferred dividends might take the following form on the balance sheet. Observe the two references to Note 3. The "$1.50" after "Preferred shares" is the dividend rate.

Preferred shares, $1.50, 50,000 shares authorized, 10,000 shares issued (Note 3)	$ 80,000
Common shares, 100,000 shares authorized, 40,000 shares issued	200,000
Retained earnings (Note 3)	414,000

> **Note 3: Cumulative preferred dividends in arrears.** At December 31, 2014, dividends on the company's $1.50 preferred shares were in arrears for 2013 and 2014, in the amount of $30,000 ($1.50 × 10,000 × 2 years).

7. CRS Robotics Inc. was organized on January 1, 2013, with 500,000 shares authorized; 200,000 shares were issued on January 5, 2013. CRS Robotics Inc. earned $250,000 during 2013 and declared a dividend of $0.25 per share on December 16, 2013, payable to shareholders on January 6, 2014.
   a. Journalize the declaration and payment of the dividend.
   b. Compute the balance of Retained Earnings on December 31, 2013.

8. Trivision Corp. has outstanding 20,000 common shares and 10,000 $2.00 cumulative preferred shares. The company has declared no dividends for the past two years but plans to pay $90,000 this year.
   a. Compute the dividends for the preferred and common shares.
   b. By how much will the dividends reduce Retained Earnings?

9. Preferred shares usually have preference over common shares when dividends are distributed. What other alternative features of preferred shares give them an advantage over common shares?

Just Checking Solutions appear at the end of this chapter and on MyAccountingLab.

Different Values of Shares

—— LO ④ ——
What is the difference between book value and market value of shares?

The business community refers to several different *share values*. Both market value and book value are used for decision making.

Market Value

REAL WORLD EXAMPLE

A change in the market price of a company's shares does not affect the corporation unless the corporation decides to issue additional shares or repurchase its own shares. Most share transactions are between shareholders and are carried out through a stock exchange.

A share's **market value**, or *market price*, is the price for which a person can buy or sell a share. The issuing corporation's net income, financial position, future prospects, and the general economic conditions determine market value. Most companies' websites track their share prices as do many business news sites and brokerage firms. *In almost all cases, shareholders are more concerned about the market value of a share than any other value.* At February 2, 2012, the common shares of Winpak Ltd., the Winnipeg-based manufacturer of packaging, were *listed at* (an alternative term is *quoted at*) $12.85, which meant they sold for, or could be bought for, $12.85 per share. The purchase of 1,000 common shares of Winpak Ltd. would cost $12,850 ($12.85 × 1,000), plus a commission. If you were selling 1,000 common shares, you would receive cash of $12,850 less a commission. The commission is the fee an investor pays to a stockbroker for buying or selling the shares. If you buy shares in Winpak Ltd. from another investor, Winpak Ltd. gets no cash. The transaction is a sale between investors. Winpak Ltd. records only the change in shareholder name.

Book Value

LEARNING TIPS

Book value per share uses the number of shares *outstanding*, not the number of shares authorized.

The **book value** of a share is the amount of shareholders' equity on the company's books for each share. If the company has only common shares outstanding, divide total shareholders' equity by the number of shares *outstanding*. If a company has both common shares and preferred shares, the preferred shareholders have the first claim to shareholders' equity. Therefore, the preferred shareholders' equity must be subtracted from total shareholders' equity to calculate the shareholders' equity available for the common shareholders. This is shown by the formula:

$$\text{Book value per common share} = \frac{\text{Total shareholders' equity} - \text{Preferred equity}}{\text{Number of common shares outstanding}}$$

For example, a company with shareholders' equity of $180,000, no preferred shares, and 5,000 common shares outstanding has a book value of $36.00 per common share, calculated as follows:

$$\text{Book value per common share} = \frac{\text{Total shareholders' equity} - \text{Preferred equity}}{\text{Number of common shares outstanding}}$$

$$= \frac{\$180,000 - \$0}{5,000}$$

$$= \$36.00$$

If the company has both preferred and common shares outstanding, the preferred shareholders' equity must be calculated before the common shareholders' equity can be calculated. Ordinarily, preferred shares have a specified **liquidation value**, or redemption value, or call value. The book value of preferred shares is usually their liquidation value plus any cumulative dividends in arrears on the shares. The book value *per share* equals the sum of the liquidation value and any cumulative dividends in arrears divided by the number of preferred shares outstanding. This is shown by the formula:

$$\text{Book value per preferred share} = \frac{\text{Liquidation value} + \text{Dividends in arrears}}{\text{Number of preferred shares outstanding}}$$

To illustrate, Garner Corp. reports the following amounts:

Shareholders' Equity	
Contributed capital	
Preferred shares, $7.00, $90 liquidation value, 5,000 shares authorized,	
1,000 shares issued and outstanding	$100,000
Common shares, 20,000 shares authorized,	
5,000 shares issued and outstanding	150,000
Total contributed capital	250,000
Retained earnings	90,000
Total shareholders' equity	$340,000

Suppose that three years of cumulative preferred dividends are in arrears. The current year preferred dividend must also be paid.

The book value for the preferred shares must be calculated first:

$$\text{Book value per preferred share} = \frac{\text{Liquidation value} + \text{Dividends in arrears}}{\text{Number of preferred shares outstanding}}$$

$$= \frac{(\$90 \times 1,000) + (\$7.00 \times 1,000 \times 4^*)}{1,000}$$

$$= \frac{\$90,000 + \$28,000}{1,000}$$

$$= \frac{\$118,000}{1,000}$$

$$= \$118.00$$

*4 years of dividends = 3 years in arrears + current year

The book value for the common shares can then be calculated, as follows:

$$\text{Book value per common share} = \frac{\text{Total shareholders' equity} - \text{Preferred equity}}{\text{Number of common shares outstanding}}$$

$$= \frac{\$340,000 - \$118,000}{5,000}$$

$$= \$44.40$$

Using Book Value in Decision Making   How is book value per share used in decision making? Book value may be a factor in determining the price to pay for a *closely held* corporation. A corporation is **closely held** when it is a private corporation that has only a few shareholders Also, a company may buy out a shareholder by agreeing to pay the book value of the shareholder's shares.

Some investors compare the book value of a share with its market value. The idea is that shares selling below book value are underpriced and thus are a good buy. But the relationship between book value and market value is far from clear. Other investors believe that, if shares sell at a price below book value, the company must be experiencing difficulty. Exhibit 13–11 contrasts the book values and market prices for the common shares of three Canadian companies. In all cases, the share price, which is the market value, exceeds book value—a sign of success.

EXHIBIT 13–11 | Book Value and Market Value

	Book Value	Approximate Fourth-Quarter Market-Value Range
Enbridge Inc. (fiscal year end September 30, 2011)	$10.12	$33.46–$36.35
Barrick Gold Corp. (year end December 31, 2011)	$22.38	$44.92–$54.05
Winpak Ltd. (fiscal year end February 7, 2012)	US$6.58	C$10.82–$14.57

✓ JUST CHECKING

10. Castle Corporation's balance sheet at year end shows the following:

Shareholders' Equity	
Contributed capital	
Preferred shares, 7%, $13.00 liquidation value, 5,000 shares authorized, 3,500 shares issued	$ 45,500
Common shares, 140,000 shares authorized and issued	74,500
Total contributed capital	120,000
Retained earnings	260,000
Total shareholders' equity	$380,000

Compute the shareholders' equity allocated to the preferred shareholders. Five years of cumulative preferred dividends are in arrears including the current year.

11. Refer to the Castle Corporation data in the previous question. Compute the shareholders' equity available for the common shareholders and the book value per common share.

Just Checking Solutions appear at the end of this chapter and on MyAccountingLab.

Evaluating Operations

Investors and creditors are constantly comparing companies' profits. The Tim Hortons Inc. net income may not be comparable to that of a company in the oil and gas business, such as EnCana Corporation, or of a brewery, such as Sleeman Breweries Ltd. It is difficult to compare an established company, such as Canadian Tire Corporation, Limited, to a relatively young company, such as Infowave Software Inc. of Burnaby, B.C. To compare companies, investors, creditors, and managers use standard profitability ratios. Two important ratios are the rate of return on total assets and the rate of return on shareholders' equity. We will calculate both ratios using the figures from the Gildan Activewear Inc. annual report found in Appendix A and on MyAccountingLab.

LO ⑤
What are ROA and ROE, and how do we calculate them?

Rate of Return on Total Assets

The **rate of return on total assets**, or simply **return on assets (ROA)**, measures a company's success in using its assets to earn income. Two groups invest money to finance a corporation:

- Shareholders—they invest in shares and expect the company to earn net income.
- Creditors—they lend money to the corporation to earn interest.

The sum of net income and interest expense is the return to the two groups that have financed the corporation's assets, and this is the numerator of the return on assets ratio. The denominator is average total assets ((beginning + ending total assets) ÷ 2). Return on assets is computed as follows (amounts in thousands of U.S. dollars):

$$\frac{\text{Rate of return on total assets}}{} = \frac{\text{Net income} + \text{Interest expense}}{\text{Average total assets}} = \frac{\$239,904 + \$5,485}{(\$1,889,721 + \$1,327,532)/2} = \frac{\$245,389}{\$1,608,627} = 0.1525, \text{ or } 15.3\%$$

Net income and interest expense are taken from the income statement (or in Gildan's case, from the consolidated statements of earnings and comprehensive income). Average total assets are computed from the beginning and ending balance sheets. How is this profitability measure used in decision making? It is used to compare companies. By relating the sum of net income and interest expense to average total assets, we have a standard measure that describes the profitability of all types of companies.

What is a good rate of return on total assets? There is no single answer to this question because rates of return vary widely by industry. For example, consumer products companies earn much higher returns than do utilities or grocery store chains. In most industries, a return on assets of 10 percent is considered very good.

Rate of Return on Common Shareholders' Equity

Rate of return on common shareholders' equity, often called **return on equity (ROE)**, shows the relationship between net income and average common shareholders' equity. The numerator is net income minus preferred dividends. This information is taken from the income statement and statement of retained earnings. Preferred dividends are subtracted because the preferred shareholders have the first claim to dividends from the company's net income. The denominator is average *common shareholders' equity*—total shareholders' equity minus preferred equity. Gildan's rate of return on common shareholders' equity for October 2, 2011, is computed as follows (amounts in thousands of U.S. dollars):

$$\begin{array}{c}\text{Rate of}\\\text{return on}\\\text{common}\\\text{share-}\\\text{holders'}\\\text{equity}\end{array} = \frac{\begin{array}{c}\text{Net income} -\\\text{Preferred}\\\text{dividends}\end{array}}{\begin{array}{c}\text{Average}\\\text{common}\\\text{shareholders'}\\\text{equity}\end{array}} = \frac{\$239{,}904 - \$0}{(\$1{,}327{,}315 + 1{,}114{,}429)/2} = \frac{\$239{,}904}{\$1{,}220{,}872} = 0.197, \text{ or } 19.7\%$$

Observe that the return on equity (19.7 percent) is higher than the return on assets (15.3 percent). This difference results from the interest expense component of return on assets. Companies such as Gildan borrow at one rate, say, 7.5 percent, and invest the funds to earn a higher rate, say, 9.5 percent. Borrowing at a lower rate than the return on investments is called *using leverage*. During good times, leverage produces high returns for shareholders. However, too much borrowing can make it difficult to pay the interest on the debt. The company's creditors are guaranteed a fixed rate of return on their loans. The shareholders, conversely, have no guarantee that the corporation will earn net income, so their investments are riskier. Consequently, shareholders demand a higher rate of return than do creditors, and this explains why return on equity should exceed return on assets.

Investors and creditors use return on common shareholders' equity in much the same way as they use return on total assets—to compare companies. The higher the rate of return, the more successful the company. A 12-percent return on common shareholders' equity is considered quite good in many industries. Investors also compare a company's return on shareholders' equity to interest rates available in the market. If interest rates are almost as high as return on equity, many investors will lend their money to earn interest or deposit it in a bank rather than invest in common shares. They choose to forego the extra risk of investing in shares when the rate of return on equity is too low.

✓ JUST CHECKING

12. The financial statements of Riley Resources Corp. reported the following:

	2014	2013
Net income	$ 80,000	$ 90,000
Interest expense	20,000	24,000
$6.00 Preferred shares (1,000 shares)	100,000	100,000
Common shares	200,000	200,000
Retained earnings	180,000	160,000
Total assets	840,000	760,000

Dividends were paid to preferred shareholders in 2013 and 2014. Dividends of $54,000 were declared and paid to common shareholders in 2014. Compute the return on assets for 2014.

13. Refer to the Riley Resources Corp. financial information in the previous question. Compute the return on common shareholders' equity for 2014.

14. Refer to the previous two questions. Compare the return on assets (ROA) and return on equity (ROE). Is there a favourable or unfavourable relationship between the two ratios?

Just Checking Solutions appear at the end of this chapter and on MyAccountingLab.

The Impact on Share Capital of International Financial Reporting Standards (IFRS)

The principles governing accounting for share capital are essentially the same under accounting standards for private enterprises (ASPE), as described in this chapter, and under IFRS. The primary difference in the two sets of accounting standards has to do with the required disclosure for share capital. Under IFRS, companies must make certain disclosures about *all* classes of shares authorized by the corporation, whether those classes of shares have been issued or not. The requirements under ASPE are less rigorous—they only require that disclosure be made for classes of shares that have actually been issued.

Another difference exists in how organization costs are treated. As shown in this chapter, organization costs are capitalized under ASPE—recorded as an intangible asset—and then amortized. Under IFRS, these costs are expensed. The remaining details of accounting for and reporting share capital under IFRS are highly technical in nature and beyond the scope of this text.

LO ⑥

How does IFRS apply to share capital?

REAL WORLD EXAMPLE

According to the CICA, there are approximately 4,500 publicly accountable enterprises in Canada that *must* follow IFRS. Every other corporation has a choice to follow IFRS or ASPE.

✓ JUST CHECKING

15. How does accounting for share capital under IFRS differ from that required under ASPE as shown in this chapter?

Just Checking Solutions appear at the end of this chapter and on MyAccountingLab.

WHY IT'S DONE THIS WAY

Before this chapter, we studied proprietorships and partnerships. In this chapter and in the remainder of this text (and, in all likelihood, in the more advanced financial accounting courses that you may take), the focus will be on corporations.

As with partnerships, the principles and concepts in the accounting framework described in Chapter 1 (and repeated on the back inside cover of this book) apply equally to corporations. Accounting differences among types of organizations only relate to the equity section of the balance sheet, with corporations having contributed capital and retained earnings. The details about the classes and number of shares in the contributed capital are given on the balance sheet or in the notes that accompany the financial statements. Information is presented this way because corporations can have more "owners" who may not have access to the financial details like a proprietor or a partner would.

For corporations, the disclosure of financial information may change, but the objectives

expressed in the conceptual framework do not. In fact, there is no change in any of the components of the framework. The *Level 4* recognition and measurement criteria are the same, except the role of disclosure is more pronounced. The *Level 3* financial–statement elements are the same except, again, for the more detailed presentation of shareholders' equity. The *Level 2* qualitative characteristics of financial information remain, and the *Level 1* objective of financial reporting continues to be to communicate useful information to users of corporate financial information.

For publicly traded corporations, the financial statements are intended for a larger audience than a private corporation, including a greater number of shareholders who are not involved in operating the business, so many items in the financial statements have to be explained more fully. As a result, publicly traded companies *must* follow International Financial Reporting Standards (IFRS), which, along with some accounting changes, require much more detailed information to be disclosed.

Presented below are the accounts and related balances for ECOM Finance Ltd. at September 30, 2014.

Common Shares,		Inventory	$ 85,000
60,000 shares authorized,		Property, Plant, and	
25,000 shares issued	$95,000	Equipment, net	204,000
Salary Payable	3,000	Accounts Receivable, net	25,000
Cash	15,000	Preferred Shares, $6.00, cumulative,	
Accounts Payable	20,000	20,000 shares authorized,	
Retained Earnings	80,000	3,000 shares issued	50,000
Organization Costs, net	1,000	Income Tax Payable	12,000
Long-term Note Payable	70,000		

Required

1. Prepare the classified balance sheet at September 30, 2014. Use the account format of the balance sheet.

2. Are the preferred shares cumulative or noncumulative? How can you tell?

3. What is the total amount of the annual preferred dividend?

4. Assume the common shares were all issued at the same time. What was the selling price per share?

5. Compute the book value per share of the preferred shares and the common shares. No prior-year preferred dividends are in arrears, and ECOM Finance Ltd. has not declared the current-year dividend.

MyAccountingLab

DemoDoc: Common Shares

SOLUTIONS

1.

1. The classified balance sheet must specify current assets and current liabilities. Make sure that
Total assets = Total liabilities + Shareholders' equity.

ECOM FINANCE LTD.
Balance Sheet
September 30, 2014

Assets		Liabilities	
Current:		Current:	
Cash	$ 15,000	Accounts payable	$ 20,000
Accounts receivable, net	25,000	Salary payable	3,000
Inventory	85,000	Income tax payable	12,000
Total current assets	125,000	Total current liabilities	35,000
Property, plant, and equipment, net	204,000	Long-term note payable	70,000
Intangible assets:		Total liabilities	105,000
Organization costs, net	1,000	**Shareholders' Equity**	
		Contributed capital:	
		Preferred shares, $6.00, cumulative,	
		20,000 shares authorized,	
		3,000 shares issued	$ 50,000
		Common shares,	
		60,000 shares authorized,	
		25,000 shares issued	95,000
		Total contributed capital	145,000
		Retained earnings	80,000
		Total shareholders' equity	225,000
		Total liabilities and	
Total assets	$330,000	shareholders' equity	$330,000

2. The preferred shares are cumulative as is noted in their description.

3. Total annual preferred dividend: $18,000 (3,000 × $6.00)

4. Price per share: $3.80 ($95,000 ÷ 25,000 shares issued)

5. Book values per share of preferred and common shares:

Preferred	
Book value	$ 50,000
Cumulative dividend for current year (3,000 × $6.00)	18,000
Shareholders' equity allocated to preferred	$ 68,000
Book value per share ($68,000 ÷ 3,000 shares)	$ 22.67
Common	
Total shareholders' equity	$225,000
Less: Shareholders' equity allocated to preferred	68,000
Shareholders' equity available	
for common shareholders	$157,000
Book value per share ($157,000 ÷ 25,000 shares)	$ 6.28

2. All features must be specified in the financial statements.

3. Details are given on the balance sheet.

4. Use the number of shares issued, *not* the number of shares authorized.

5. Preferred: Remember to *add* any dividends in arrears, including the current year's dividends if they were not paid.

5. Common: Book value per common share must exclude any amounts pertaining to preferred shares.

Chapter 13 Corporations: Share Capital and the Balance Sheet **835**

Summary

① Learning Objective 1: Identify the characteristics of a corporation

What is a corporation, and why is it an important form of business?

A corporation is a separate legal and business entity. Shareholders are the owners of a corporation.

Advantages of a corporation:

- Continuous life
- Ease of raising large amounts of capital
- Ease of transferring ownership
- Limited liability

Disadvantages:

- A degree of double taxation
- Separation of ownership and management
- Expensive government regulation
- Additional costs

Pg. 810

② Learning Objective 2: Record the issuance of shares, and prepare the shareholders' equity section of a corporation's balance sheet

How do we record and present share information?

- Shares are classified as common or preferred, and there may be several classes or series. Preferred shares are further defined to include: cumulative or noncumulative, redeemable, and convertible.
- The balance sheet carries the capital raised through share issuance under the heading Contributed Capital in the shareholders' equity section. Retained Earnings is listed last.

Pg. 816

③ Learning Objective 3: Account for cash dividends

What are cash dividends, and how do we account for them?

- There is a liability to pay dividends when the board of directors declares a dividend. Dividends are given to shareholders who own shares on the date of record and are paid after the date of record.
- Preferred shares have priority over common shares when dividends are paid. Preferred dividends are usually stated as a dollar amount per share.
- Preferred shares have a claim to dividends in arrears if the preferred shares are cumulative.

Pg. 824

④ Learning Objective 4: Use different share values in decision making.

What is the difference between book value and market value of shares?

- A share's *market value* is the price for which a share may be bought or sold.
- *Book value* is the amount of shareholders' equity per share.

$$\text{Book value per common share} = \frac{\text{Total shareholder's equity} - \text{Preferred equity}}{\text{Number of common shares outstanding}}$$

$$\text{Book value per preferred share} = \frac{\text{Liquidation value} + \text{Dividends in arrears}}{\text{Number of preferred shares outstanding}}$$

Pg. 828

⑤ Learning Objective 5: Evaluate a company's return on assets (ROA) and return on shareholders' equity (ROE)

What are ROA and ROE, and how do we calculate them?

- These are two standard measures of profitability. A healthy company's return on equity will exceed its return on assets.

Rate of return on total assets (ROA):

$$\text{ROA} = \frac{\text{Net income} + \text{Interest expense}}{\text{Average total assets}}$$

Rate of return on common shareholders' equity (ROE):

$$\text{ROE} = \frac{\text{Net income} - \text{Preferred dividends}}{\text{Average common shareholders' equity}}$$

Pg. 831

How does IFRS apply to share capital?

- Accounting for shares under ASPE and IFRS is the same.
- IFRS requires that certain disclosures be made for classes of shares that have been authorized but not issued.
- Organization costs are expensed under IFRS but capitalized as intangible assets and amortized under ASPE.

Pg. 833

Check **Accounting Vocabulary** on page 836 for all key terms used in Chapter 13 and the **Glossary** on page 1246 for all key terms used in the textbook.

CHAPTER REVIEW:

MyAccountingLab   DemoDoc covering Common Shares

MyAccountingLab   Student PowerPoint Slides

MyAccountingLab   Audio Chapter Summary

Note: All MyAccountingLab resources can be found in the Chapter Resources section and the Multimedia Library.

SELF-STUDY QUESTIONS

Test your understanding of the chapter by marking the correct answer to each of the following questions:

1. Which characteristic of a corporation is most attractive to an owner (shareholder)? (*pp. 811–812*)
   a. Limited liability
   b. Double taxation
   c. Mutual agency
   d. All of the above

2. The person with the most power in a corporation often is the (*p. 812*)
   a. Accountant
   b. Chairperson of the board
   c. President
   d. Vice-president

3. The dollar amount of the shareholder investments in a corporation is called (*p. 814*)
   a. Outstanding shares
   b. Total shareholders' equity
   c. Contributed capital
   d. Retained earnings

4. The arbitrary value assigned to a share by the board of directors is called (*p. 818*)
   a. Market value   c. Book value
   b. Liquidation value   d. Stated value

5. Shares issued by a corporation incorporated under the *Canada Business Corporations Act* normally have (*p. 818*)
   a. No par value
   b. A par value set by management

   c. A par value set by the government
   d. A par value of $1.00

6. Magnum Corporation receives a building for 10,000 common shares. The building's book value is $275,000 and its current market value is $640,000. This transaction increases Magnum's share capital by (*p. 820*)
   a. $0 because the corporation received no cash
   b. $365,000
   c. $275,000
   d. $640,000

7. Organization costs is classified as a(n) (*pp. 823–824*)
   a. Operating expense
   b. Current asset
   c. Contra item in shareholders' equity
   d. None of the above

8. Glanville Inc. has 10,000 $3.50 cumulative preferred shares and 100,000 common shares issued and outstanding. Two years' preferred dividends are in arrears.

   Glanville Inc. declares a cash dividend large enough to pay the preferred dividends in arrears, the preferred dividend for the current period, and a $1.50 dividend per common share. What is the total amount of the dividend? (*p. 770*)
   a. $255,000   c. $150,000
   b. $220,000   d. $105,000

9. The preferred shares of Glanville Inc. in the preceding question were issued at $55.00 per share. Each preferred share can be converted into 10 common shares.

The entry to record the conversion of these preferred shares into common is (p. 822)

a. Cash   550,000
      Preferred Shares   500,000
      Common Shares   50,000
b. Preferred Shares   500,000
      Cash   50,000
      Common Shares   550,000

c. Preferred Shares   550,000
      Common Shares   550,000
d. Common Shares   550,000
      Preferred Shares   550,000

10. When an investor is buying shares as an investment, the value of most direct concern is (p. 828)
   a. Par value   c. Liquidation value
   b. Market value   d. Book value

Answers to Self-Study Questions

1. a 2. b 3. c 4. d 5. a 6. d 7. d Intangible asset
8. a [(10,000 × $3.50 × 3 = $105,000) + (100,000 × $1.50 = $150,000) = $255,000] 9. c 10. b

ACCOUNTING VOCABULARY

Articles of incorporation   The document issued by the federal or provincial government giving the incorporators permission to form a corporation   (p. 811).

Arrears   To be behind or overdue in a debt payment   (p. 826).

Authorization of shares   Provision in a corporation's articles of incorporation that permits a corporation to sell a certain number of shares of stock   (p. 812).

Authorized shares   The number of shares a corporation is allowed to sell according to the articles of incorporation   (p. 812).

Board of directors   Group elected by the shareholders to set policy for a corporation and to appoint its officers   (p. 812).

Book value   Amount of shareholders' equity on the company's books for each of its shares   (p. 828).

Bylaws   Constitution for governing a corporation   (p. 812).

Chairperson (of board)   Elected person on a corporation's board of directors; usually the most powerful person in the corporation   (p. 812).

Closely held   Describes a corporation with only a few shareholders   (p. 830).

Common shares   The most basic form of share capital. In describing a corporation, the common shareholders are the owners of the business   (p. 814).

Contributed capital   A corporation's capital from investments by the shareholders. Also called *share capital* or *capital stock*   (p. 814).

Convertible preferred shares   Preferred shares that may be exchanged by the preferred shareholders, if they choose, for another class of shares in the corporation   (p. 822).

Cumulative preferred shares   Preferred shares whose owners must receive all dividends in arrears before the corporation pays dividends to the common shareholders   (p. 826).

Date of record   On this date, which is a few weeks after the declaration of the dividend, the list of shareholders who will receive the dividend is compiled   (p. 824).

Declaration date   The date on which the board of directors announces the dividend. There is a liability created on this date   (p. 824).

Deficit   Debit balance in the retained earnings account   (p. 815).

Dividends   Distributions by a corporation to its shareholders   (p. 815).

Double taxation   Corporations pay their own income taxes on corporate income. Then, the shareholders pay personal income tax on the cash dividends that they receive from corporations   (p. 811).

Initial public offering (IPO)   The first time a particular class of a corporation's shares are sold to investors   (p. 818).

Issue price   The price at which shareholders first purchase shares from the corporation   (p. 817).

Issued shares   Shares that are offered for sale to investors   (p. 817).

Leverage   The use of financial instruments to increase the potential return on investment; in other words, borrowing money at a particular interest rate and using it to make investments that earn a higher rate of return than that interest rate   (p. 832).

Liquidation value   (redemption value or call value) The amount of capital that a preferred shareholder would receive per preferred share upon liquidation of the corporation   (p. 829).

Limited liability   No personal obligation of a shareholder for corporation debts. The most that a shareholder can lose on an investment in a corporation's shares is the cost of the investment   *(p. 811)*.

Market value   Price for which a person could buy or sell a share   *(p. 828)*.

Mutual agency   All owners act as agents of the business and can bind it to contracts. This does not exist in a corporation   *(p. 811)*.

No-par-value shares   Shares that do not have a value assigned to them by the articles of incorporation   *(p. 818)*.

Organization costs   The costs of organizing a corporation, including legal fees and charges by promoters for selling the shares. Organization costs is an intangible asset under ASPE but is written off as an expense under IFRS   *(p. 823)*.

Outstanding shares   Shares in the hands of a shareholder   *(p. 817)*.

Par value   An arbitrary value assigned when certain shares are initially offered to the public; these types of shares are not common in Canada   *(p. 818)*.

Preemptive right   Existing shareholders are given the right to purchase additional shares of the company before the shares are offered to others. This would give existing shareholders the opportunity to maintain the same percentage of ownership as they would have had before the new shares were issued   *(p. 816)*.

Preferred shares   Shares of stock that give their owners certain advantages over common shareholders, such as the priority to receive dividends before the common shareholders and the priority to receive assets before the common shareholders if the corporation liquidates   *(p. 820)*.

President   Chief operating officer in charge of managing the day-to-day operations of a corporation   *(p. 812)*.

Private corporation.   A corporation that does not issue shares that are traded on a stock exchange   *(p. 811)*.

Proportionate share   The same amount of shares in relation to others before and after an event such as a new issue of shares   *(p. 816)*.

Prospectus   A mandatory legal document that describes an investment to potential purchasers   *(p. 818)*.

Proxy   A formal appointment of one person to cast a vote for another person   *(p. 813)*.

Public corporation   A corporation that issues shares that are traded on a stock exchange   *(p. 810)*.

Rate of return on common shareholders' equity   Net income minus preferred dividends, divided by average common shareholders' equity. A measure of profitability. Also called *return on equity (ROE)* or *return on common shareholders' equity*   *(p. 831)*.

Rate of return on total assets   The sum of net income plus interest expense divided by average total assets. This ratio measures the success a company has in using its assets to earn income for the persons who finance the business. Also called *return on assets (ROA)*   *(p. 831)*.

Retained earnings   A corporation's capital that is earned through profitable operation of the business   *(p. 814)*.

Return on assets (ROA)   Another name for *rate of return on total assets*   *(p. 831)*.

Return on equity (ROE)   Net income minus preferred dividends, divided by average common shareholders' equity. A measure of profitability. Also called *return on common shareholders' equity*   *(p. 831)*.

Shareholder   A person or a company that owns shares in a corporation   *(p. 811)*.

Shareholders' equity   Owners' equity of a corporation   *(p. 814)*.

Shares   Units into which the owners' equity of a corporation is divided   *(p. 811)*.

Stated value   An arbitrary amount assigned to a share of stock when it is issued   *(p. 818)*.

Stock   Shares into which the owners' equity of a corporation is divided   *(p. 811)*.

Underwriter   An independent firm that is hired to sell shares on a corporation's behalf   *(p. 816)*.

SIMILAR ACCOUNTING TERMS

Initial public offering	IPO
Liquidation value	Redemption value; Call value; Call price
Market value	Market price
Rate of return on common shareholders' equity	Return on equity; ROE
Rate of return on total assets	Return on assets; ROA
Share capital	Capital stock; Stated capital
Shareholder	Stockholder (US terminology)

Assignment Material

QUESTIONS

1. Identify the characteristics of a corporation.
2. Explain how corporate earnings are subject to a degree of double taxation.
3. Briefly outline the steps in the organization of a corporation.
4. Compare the characteristics of a partnership and a corporation.
5. Name the five rights of a common shareholder. Are preferred shares automatically nonvoting?
6. Which event increases the assets of the corporation: authorization of shares or issuance of shares? Explain.
7. Suppose Bala Ltd. issued 1,400 shares of its $4.50 preferred shares for $110.00 per share. By how much would this transaction increase the company's contributed capital? By how much would it increase retained earnings? By how much would it increase annual cash dividend payments?
8. United Inc. issued 150 common shares for $9.00 per share and 250 shares for $8.50 per share. What would be the journal entry to record the combined issue?
9. How does issuance of 1,500 common shares for land and a building, together worth $200,000, affect contributed capital?
10. List the following accounts in the order in which they would appear on the balance sheet: Common Shares, Organization Costs, Preferred Shares, Retained Earnings, Dividends Payable. Also, give each account's balance-sheet classification.
11. What type of account is Organization Costs? Briefly describe how to account for organization costs.
12. Briefly discuss the three important dates for a dividend.
13. Tapin Inc. has 2,500 shares of its $1.75 preferred shares outstanding. Dividends for 2012 and 2013 are in arrears. Assume that Tapin Inc. declares total dividends of $35,000 at the end of 2014. Show how to allocate the dividends to preferred and common (a) if preferred is cumulative, and (b) if preferred is noncumulative.
14. As a preferred shareholder, would you rather own cumulative or noncumulative preferred? If all other factors are the same, would the corporation rather issue cumulative or noncumulative preferred shares? Give your reasons.
15. How are cumulative preferred dividends in arrears reported in the financial statements? When do dividends become a liability of the corporation?
16. Distinguish between the market value of shares and the book value of shares. Which is more important to investors?
17. How is book value per common share computed when the company has both preferred shares and common shares outstanding?
18. Why should a healthy company's rate of return on shareholders' equity exceed its rate of return on total assets?

MyAccountingLab   Make the grade with MyAccountingLab: The Starters, Exercises, and Problems marked in red can be found on MyAccountingLab. You can practise them as often as you want, and most feature step-by-step guided instructions to help you find the right answer.

STARTERS

Authority structure in a corporation

Starter 13–1 Answer these questions about corporations.

1. Who is the most powerful person in the corporation?
2. What group holds the ultimate power in a corporation?
3. Who is in charge of day-to-day operations?
4. Who is in charge of accounting?

The balance sheets of a corporation and a proprietorship ①

Starter 13–2 How does a proprietorship's balance sheet differ from a corporation's balance sheet? How are the two balance sheets similar?

Issuing shares ②

Starter 13–3 Eagle Looking Incorporated has two classes of shares: common and preferred. Journalize Eagle Looking's issuance of

a. 1,000 common shares for $70.00 per share
b. 1,000 preferred shares for a total of $32,000

Explanations are not required.

Starter 13–4   Munsters Inc. issued all its shares during 2014 and reported the following on its balance sheet at December 31, 2014:

Issuing shares and interpreting shareholders' equity
②

Common shares	
Authorized: 5,000 shares	
Issued and outstanding: 3,000 shares	$ 2,900
Retained earnings	49,000

Journalize the company's issuance of the shares for cash.

Starter 13–5   At December 31, 2014, KD Corporation reported the following on its comparative balance sheet, which included 2013 amounts for comparison:

Issuing shares and analyzing retained earnings
②

1. Increased $6,000

	December 31,	
	2014	**2013**
Common shares		
Authorized: 10,000 shares		
Issued: 3,600 shares in 2014	$85,000	
3,490 shares in 2013		$79,000
Retained earnings	50,800	46,800

1. How much did KD Corporation's total contributed capital increase during 2014? What caused total contributed capital to increase? How can you tell?
2. Assuming no dividends were declared during 2014, did KD Corporation have a profit or a loss for 2014? How can you tell?

Starter 13–6   Hatteras Corporation reported the following accounts (a partial list):

Preparing the shareholders' equity section of a balance sheet
②

Total shareholder's equity
$37,500

Cost of Goods Sold	$29,400	Accounts Payable	$3,000
Common Shares,		Retained Earnings	8,000
40,000 shares issued		Unearned Revenue	2,600
and outstanding	29,500	Cash	12,000
Long-term Note Payable	3,800	Total assets	?

Prepare the shareholders' equity section of the Hatteras balance sheet.

Starter 13–7   Use the Hatteras Corporation data in Starter 13–6 to compute the company's

Using shareholders' equity data
②

b. Total assets $46,900

a. Total liabilities
b. Total assets

Starter 13–8   Solve for the missing amounts in the partial balance sheet using the additional information provided below.

Calculating shareholders' equity data
②

D = $125,000 deficit

Shareholders' Equity	
Contributed Capital	
Preferred shares, $2.50, __(A)__ issued, outstanding	$175,000
Common shares, 150,000 issued and outstanding	(B)
Total contributed capital	(C)
Deficit	(D)
Total Equity	$500,000

All of the shares were issued at one time. Common shares were sold for $3.00 per share and preferred shares were sold for $5.00 each. No dividends were paid for the year.

Starter 13–9 Mboko Corporation earned net income of $85,000 during the year ended December 31, 2013. On December 15, Mboko Corporation declared the annual cash dividend on its 5,000 $5.00 preferred shares and a $0.60 per share cash dividend on its 50,000 common shares. Mboko Corporation then paid the dividends on January 4, 2014.

Journalize for Mboko Corporation:

a. Declaring the cash dividends on December 15, 2013

b. Paying the cash dividends on January 4, 2014

Dividing cash dividends between
preferred and common shares
③
3. Preferred $3,375
Common $11,625

Starter 13–10 Golda Inc. has the following shareholders' equity:

Preferred shares, $0.025, cumulative, liquidation value $0.50, 50,000 shares authorized, 45,000 shares issued and outstanding..................	$ 20,000
Common shares, 1,000,000 shares authorized and issued and outstanding	200,000
Retained earnings...	130,000
Total shareholders' equity	$350,000

Answer these questions about Golda's dividends:

1. Are Golda Inc.'s preferred shares cumulative or noncumulative? How can you tell?

2. Suppose Golda Inc. declares cash dividends of $15,000 for 2014. How much of the dividends goes to preferred shares? How much goes to common shares?

3. Suppose Golda Inc. did not pay the preferred dividend in 2012 and 2013. In 2014, the company declares cash dividends of $15,000. How much of the dividends goes to preferred shares? How much goes to common shares?

Starter 13–11 Refer to the shareholders' equity information of Golda Inc. in Starter 13–10. Golda Inc. has not declared preferred dividends for five years (including the current year). Compute the book value per share of Golda Inc.'s common shares. Round your answer to two decimal places.

Computing return on assets and
return on equity
⑤
ROA 13.9%

Starter 13–12 Township Corp.'s 2014 financial statements reported the following items—with 2013 figures given for comparison.

	2014	2013
Balance sheet		
Total assets	$49,000	$44,800
Total liabilities	$25,400	$22,000
Total shareholders' equity (all common)	23,600	22,800
Total liabilities and equity	$49,000	$44,800
Income statement		
Net sales	$39,130	
Cost of goods sold	14,210	
Gross margin	24,920	
Selling and administrative expenses	14,000	
Interest expense	400	
All other expenses, net	4,420	
Net income	$ 6,100	

Compute Township Corp.'s rate of return on total assets and rate of return on common shareholders' equity for 2014. Do these rates of return look high or low?

EXERCISES

Exercise 13–1

Suppose you are forming a business and you need some outside money from other investors. Assume you have decided to organize the business as a corporation that will issue shares to raise the needed funds. Briefly discuss your most important reason for organizing as a corporation rather than as a partnership. If you had decided to organize as a partnership, what would be your most important reason for not organizing as a corporation?

Characteristics of a corporation

Exercise 13–2

David Johnston and Lisa Jacobs are opening a decorating business to be named Student Decor Ltd. They need outside capital, so they plan to organize the business as a corporation. Because your accounting course is next to their design class, they come to you for advice. Write a memorandum informing them of the steps in forming a corporation. Identify specific documents used in this process, and name the different parties involved in the ownership and management of a corporation.

Organizing a corporation

Exercise 13–3

Is each of the following statements true or false? For each false statement, explain why it is false.

Types of shares

a. A shareholder may bind (obligate) the corporation to a contract.

b. The policy-making body in a corporation is called the board of directors.

c. The owner of 100 preferred shares has greater voting rights than the owner of 100 common shares.

d. A company incorporated under the *Canada Business Corporations Act* must assign the proceeds of a share issue to the capital account for that type of share.

e. All common shares issued and outstanding have equal voting rights.

f. Issuance of 1,000 common shares at $12.00 per share increases shareholders' equity by $12,000.

g. The stated value of a share is the value assigned to the shares by the company issuing them at the date issued.

h. A corporation issues its preferred shares in exchange for land and a building with a combined market value of $200,000. This transaction increases the corporation's shareholders' equity by $200,000 regardless of the assets' prior book value.

Exercise 13–4

East Ltd. made the following share issuance transactions:

Issuing shares

2. Contributed capital $136,500

Jan. 19	Issued 4,500 common shares for cash of $11.00 per share.
Feb. 3	Sold 1,000 $1.50 Class A preferred shares for $14,000 cash.
11	Received inventory valued at $30,000 and equipment with market value of $17,000 for 5,800 common shares.
15	Issued 2,000 $1.00 Class B preferred shares for $13.00 per share.

Required

1. Journalize the transactions. Explanations are not required.
2. How much contributed capital did these transactions generate for East Ltd?

Exercise 13–5

Shapalov Supplies Ltd. imports farm equipment. The corporation issues 10,000 common shares for $15.00 per share. Record issuance of the shares.

Recording issuance of common shares

Chapter 13 Corporations: Share Capital and the Balance Sheet **843**

Exercise 13–6

Issuing shares to finance the purchase of assets
②

Sutherland Equipment Ltd. has a choice about how it records the acquisition of property, plant, and equipment in return for shares. Make the journal entries for each of the following cases:

Case A—Issue shares and buy the assets in separate transactions:
Sutherland Equipment Ltd. issued 7,000 common shares for cash of $1,460,000. In a separate transaction, Sutherland then used the cash to purchase an office building for $900,000 and equipment for $560,000. Journalize the two transactions.

Case B—Issue shares to acquire the assets:
Sutherland Equipment Ltd. issued 7,000 common shares to acquire an office building valued at $900,000 and equipment worth $560,000. Journalize this transaction.

Compare the balances in all accounts in Case A and Case B. Are the account balances similar or different?

Exercise 13–7

Issuing shares and preparing the shareholders' equity section of the balance sheet
②

2. Total shareholders' equity $465,000

The articles of incorporation for Mid-way Consulting Inc. authorize the company to issue 500,000 $5 preferred shares and 1,000,000 common shares. During its first year of operations, Mid-way Consulting Inc. completed the following selected transactions:

2014

Jan.	4	Issued 5,000 common shares to the consultants who formed the corporation, receiving cash of $140,000.
	13	Issued 500 preferred shares for cash of $55,000.
	14	Issued 4,000 common shares in exchange for land valued at $120,000.
Dec.	31	Earned a profit for the fiscal year and closed the $150,000 net income into Retained Earnings.

Required

1. Record the transactions in the general journal.
2. Prepare the shareholders' equity section of the Mid-way Consulting Inc. balance sheet at December 31, 2014.

Exercise 13–8

Contributed capital for a corporation
②

Total contributed capital $545,000

Yippee Corp. has recently organized. The company issued common shares to a lawyer who provided legal services worth $7,500 to help organize the corporation. It issued common shares to another person in exchange for his patent with a market value of $50,000. In addition, Yippee Corp. received cash both for 2,500 of its $1.50 preferred shares at $20.00 per share and for 35,000 of its common shares at $12.50 per share. Without making journal entries, determine the total contributed capital created by these transactions.

Exercise 13–9

Shareholders' equity section of a balance sheet
②

2. Total shareholders' equity $271,500

The articles of incorporation for Novak Technology Inc. authorize the issuance of 100,000 preferred shares and 250,000 common shares. During a two-month period, Novak Technology Inc. completed these share-issuance transactions:

Mar. 23	Issued 12,000 common shares for cash of $10.00 per share.
Apr. 12	Received inventory valued at $60,000 and equipment with a market value of $10,000 for 5,000 common shares.
17	Issued 1,500 $2.25 preferred shares. The issue price was cash of $11.00 per share.

Required

1. Journalize the transactions, with explanations.
2. Prepare the shareholders' equity section of the Novak Technology Inc. balance sheet for the transactions given in this exercise. Retained Earnings has a balance of $65,000.

Exercise 13–10

Skeet Corporation has the following selected account balances at June 30, 2014. Prepare the shareholders' equity section of the company's balance sheet.

Common Shares,		Inventory	$70,000
500,000 shares authorized,		Machinery and Equipment	82,500
100,000 shares issued	$100,000	Preferred Shares, $1.25,	
Accumulated Amortization—		100,000 shares authorized,	
Machinery and Equipment	32,500	10,000 shares issued	87,500
Retained Earnings	97,000	Organization Costs, net	2,500
Cost of Goods Sold	42,500		

Excel Spreadsheet Template

Shareholders' equity section of a balance sheet
②
Total shareholders' equity $284,500

Exercise 13–11

Refer to the shareholders' equity of Chang Corporation in Exhibit 13–7, page 822. Answer these questions about Chang's dividends.

1. How much in dividends must Chang Corporation declare each year before the common shareholders receive cash dividends for the year?

2. Suppose Chang Corporation declares cash dividends of $20,000 for 2014. How much of the dividends go to preferred shareholders? How much goes to common shareholders?

3. Are Chang Corporation's preferred shares cumulative or noncumulative? How can you tell?

4. Suppose Chang Corporation did not pay the preferred dividend in 2012 and 2013. In 2014, Chang declares cash dividends of $40,000. How much of the dividends go to preferred shareholders? How much goes to common shareholders?

Dividing cash dividends between preferred and common shares
③
4. Common $35,000

Exercise 13–12

The following elements of shareholders' equity are adapted from the balance sheet of Brzynski Marketing Ltd:

Computing dividends on preferred and common shares
③
Common gets $29,000

Shareholders' Equity	
Preferred shares, $0.10, cumulative,	
100,000 shares authorized, 60,000 shares issued and outstanding	$ 60,000
Common shares, 2,000,000 shares authorized, 900,000 shares issued	
and outstanding	1,500,000

The company has paid all dividends through 2012.

Required Compute the dividends paid to preferred shareholders and to common shareholders for 2013 and 2014 if total dividends are $0 in 2013, and $41,000 in 2014. Round your answers to the nearest dollar.

Exercise 13–13

The balance sheet of Nature's Design Technology Inc. reported the following:

Book value per share of preferred and common shares
④
Common $12.10 per share

Cumulative preferred shares; 300 shares issued and outstanding,	
liquidation value $15,000	$ 15,000
Common shares; 25,000 shares issued and outstanding	187,500

Assume that Nature's Design had paid preferred dividends for the current year and all prior years (no dividends in arrears). Retained earnings was $115,000.

Required Compute the book value per share of the preferred shares and the common shares.

Exercise 13–14

Refer to Exercise 13–13. Compute the book value per share of the preferred shares and the common shares, assuming that four years of preferred dividends (including dividends for the current year) are in arrears. Assume the preferred shares are cumulative and their dividend rate is $7.00 per share.

Book value per share of preferred and common shares; preferred dividends in arrears
③ ④
Preferred $78.00 per share; common $11.76 per share

Exercise 13–15

Woldenga Equipment Inc. reported the figures shown below for 2014 and 2013.

	2014	2013
Income statement:		
Interest expense	$ 5,200	$ 3,700
Net income	3,250	5,200
Balance sheet:		
Total assets	105,000	95,000
Preferred shares, $1.15,		
200 shares issued and outstanding	1,000	1,000
Common shareholders' equity	46,700	43,000
Total shareholders' equity	47,700	44,000

Compute the rate of return on total assets (ROA) and the rate of return on common share-holders' equity (ROE) for 2014. Do these rates of return suggest strength or weakness? Give your reasons.

SERIAL EXERCISE

This exercise continues the Kerr Consulting situation from Exercise 12–15 of Chapter 12. If you did not complete Exercise 12–15, you can still complete Exercise 13–16 as it is presented.

Exercise 13–16

Alex Kerr has been running Kerr Consulting as a proprietorship but is planning to expand operations in the near future. In Chapter 12, Alex had considered taking on a partner, but decided not to form a partnership after all. To raise cash for future expansion, he has now decided to incorporate and create Kerr Consulting Corporation. He has gone through all the legal steps to incorporate his business; as of February 1, 2014, Kerr Consulting Corporation is authorized to issue an unlimited number of common shares and 50,000 $2.00 preferred shares.

The Kerr Consulting January 31, 2014, balance sheet appears below. All amounts in the accounting records reflect current market value.

Kerr Consulting	
Assets	
Cash	$32,350
Accounts receivable	4,900
Inventory	2,713
Supplies	100
Prepaid rent	2,000
Equipment	2,000
Accumulated amortization—equipment	(66)
Furniture	6,000
Accumulated amortization—furniture	(200)
Total assets	$49,797
Liabilities and Equity	
Accounts payable	$10,700
Salary payable	1,400
Unearned service revenue	1,333
Alex Kerr, capital	36,364
Total liabilities and capital	$49,797

Required

1. Create the journal entry to record the incorporation of the business on February 1, 2014. To do this, you need to record each asset and liability account at its current market value. For equipment and furniture, this would be the net book value of each—there would not be any accumulated amortization accounts at the beginning of the new corporation's life. The Alex Kerr, Capital balance would become the value of the 20,000 common shares Alex issues to himself.

2. To raise $50,000 in additional cash, Kerr Consulting Corporation issued 1,000 of the preferred shares for $50.00 per share on February 1, 2014. Journalize this transaction.

3. Kerr Consulting Corporation incurred $1,500 in legal fees and incorporation fees to organize the corporation under the *Canada Business Corporations Act* in Ontario. Prepare the journal entry for these organization costs.

CHALLENGE EXERCISE

Exercise 13–17

Mussalem Motors Inc. reported these comparative shareholders' equity data:

Accounting for shareholders' equity transactions

	December 31,	
	2014	**2013**
Common shares	$1,530,000	$ 300,000
Retained earnings	2,318,000	1,538,000

During 2014, Mussalem Motors Inc. completed these transactions and events:

a. Net income, $1,430,000.

b. Cash dividends, $650,000.

c. Issuance of common shares for cash, 3,000 shares at $60.00 per share.

d. Issuance of common shares to purchase another company (Mussalem Motors debited the Investments account), 15,000 shares at $70.00 per share.

Required Without making journal entries, show how Mussalem Motors Inc.'s 2014 transactions and events accounted for the changes in the shareholders' equity accounts. For each shareholders' equity account, start with the December 31, 2013, balance and work toward the balance at December 31, 2014.

BEYOND THE NUMBERS

Beyond the Numbers 13–1

Answering the following questions will enhance your understanding of the shareholders' equity of corporations.

Characteristics of corporations' shareholders' equity

1. Why do you think contributed capital and retained earnings are shown separately in the shareholders' equity section?
2. Vivien Chan, major shareholder of Nah Inc., proposes to sell some land she owns to the company for common shares in Nah Inc. What problem does Nah Inc. face in recording the transaction?
3. Preferred shares generally have preference over common shares for dividends and on liquidation. Why would investors buy common shares when preferred shares are available?
4. If you owned 100 shares of Tim Hortons Inc. and someone offered to buy the shares for their book value, would you accept the offer? Why or why not?
5. What is a convertible preferred share? Why would an investor exercise the conversion privilege?

ETHICAL ISSUE

Note: This case is based on a real situation.

Jason Wertz paid $50,000 for a franchise that entitled him to market Success software programs in the countries of the European Union. Wertz intended to sell individual franchises for the major language groups of Western Europe—German, French, English, Spanish, and Italian. Naturally, investors considering buying a franchise from Wertz asked to see the financial statements of his business.

Believing the value of the franchise to be greater than $50,000, Wertz sought to capitalize his own franchise at $375,000. The law firm of St. Charles and LaDue helped Wertz form a corporation authorized to issue 500,000 common shares. Lawyers suggested the following chain of transactions:

1. A third party borrows $375,000 and purchases the franchise from Wertz.

2. Wertz pays the corporation $375,000 to acquire all its shares.

3. The corporation buys the franchise from the third party, who repays the loan.

In the final analysis, the third party is debt-free and out of the picture. Wertz owns all the corporation's shares, and the corporation owns the franchise. The corporation balance sheet lists a franchise acquired at a cost of $375,000. This balance sheet is Wertz's most valuable marketing tool.

Required

1. What is unethical about this situation?

2. Who can be harmed? How can they be harmed? What role does accounting play?

PROBLEMS (GROUP A)

MyAccountingLab

Problem 13–1A

Organizing a corporation

Mark Mathews and Karen Willamas are opening a software company. They have developed a new and effective software to manage small business operations. Their most fundamental decision is how to organize the business. Mathews thinks the partnership form is best. Willamas favours the corporate form of organization. They seek your advice.

Required Write a memo to Mathews and Willamas to make them aware of the advantages and the disadvantages of organizing the business as a corporation. Use the following format for your memo:

Date:	_____
To:	Mark Mathews and Karen Willamas
From:	Student Name
Subject:	Advantages and disadvantages of the corporate form of business organization

Problem 13–2A

Journalizing corporation transactions and preparing the shareholders' equity section of the balance sheet

(2)

2. Total shareholders' equity $667,500

The partnership of Nuan Zhang and Jen Phuah needed additional capital to expand into new markets, so the business incorporated as A-1 Services Inc. The articles of incorporation under the *Canada Business Corporations Act* authorize A-1 Services Inc. to issue 500,000 $2.50 preferred shares and 2,000,000 common shares. In its first year, A-1 Services Inc. completed the following share-related transactions:

2014

Aug. 2   Paid incorporation fees of $6,000 and paid legal fees of $16,000 to organize as a corporation.

2   Issued 20,000 common shares to Zhang and 25,000 common shares to Phuah in return for cash. Zhang paid $150,000 cash, and Phuah paid $187,500 cash.

Dec. 10   Issued 1,000 preferred shares to acquire a computer system with a market value of $80,000.

16   Issued 15,000 common shares for cash of $120,000.

Required

1. Record the transactions in the general journal.
2. Prepare the shareholders' equity section of the A-1 Services Inc. balance sheet at December 31, 2014. The ending balance in Retained Earnings is $130,000.

Problem 13–3A

Riverbend Inc. was organized in 2013. At December 31, 2013, Riverbend Inc.'s balance sheet reported the following shareholders' equity:

Issuing shares and preparing the shareholders' equity section of the balance sheet

5. Total shareholders' equity $613,750

Preferred shares, $4.00, 200,000 shares authorized, none issued	$ 0
Common shares, 1,000,000 shares authorized, 150,000 shares issued and outstanding	225,000
Retained earnings (Deficit)	(50,000)
Total shareholders' equity	$175,000

Required

Answer the following questions, making journal entries as needed.

1. What does the $4.00 mean for the preferred shares? If Riverbend Inc. issues 2,500 preferred shares, how much in cash dividends will it expect to pay?
2. At what average price per share did Riverbend Inc. issue the common shares during 2013?
3. Were first-year operations profitable? Give your reason.
4. During 2014, the company completed the following selected transactions:

   a. Issued for cash 1,500 preferred shares at $20.00 per share.

   b. Issued for cash 5,000 common shares at a price of $1.75 per share.

   c. Issued 100,000 common shares to acquire a building valued at $250,000.

   d. Net income for the year was $150,000, and the company declared no dividends. Make the closing entry for net income.

   Journalize each transaction. Explanations are not required.
5. Prepare the shareholders' equity section of the Riverbend Inc. balance sheet at December 31, 2014.

Problem 13–4A

Excel Spreadsheet Template

Shareholders' equity section of the balance sheet

② ③

Play-time Equipment Ltd. Total shareholders' equity $590,000

The following summaries for Play-time Equipment Ltd. and Lil-tikes Products Inc. provide the information needed to prepare the shareholders' equity section of each company's balance sheet. The two companies are independent.

Play-time Equipment Ltd. This company is authorized to issue 200,000 common shares. All the shares were issued at $3.00 per share. The company incurred a net loss of $75,000 in 2011 (its first year of operations) and a net loss of $30,000 in 2012. It earned net incomes of $35,000 in 2013 and $60,000 in 2014. The company declared no dividends during the four-year period.

Lil-tikes Products Inc. Lil-tikes Products Inc.'s articles of incorporation authorize the company to issue 200,000 cumulative preferred shares and 1,000,000 common shares. Lil-tikes Products Inc. issued 2,000 preferred shares at $12.50 per share. It issued 100,000 common shares for $300,000. The company's Retained Earnings balance at the beginning of 2014 was $75,000. Net income for 2014 was $50,000, and the company declared the specified preferred share dividend for 2014. Preferred share dividends for 2013 were in arrears. The preferred dividend was $1.10 per share per year.

Required For each company, prepare the shareholders' equity section of its balance sheet at December 31, 2014. Show the computation of all amounts. Journal entries are not required.

Problem 13–5A

Analyzing the shareholders' equity of a corporation

4. Dividends Payable— Common $125,000

Redfern Limited reported the following information in its December 31, 2013, annual report:

Shareholders' Equity	
Preferred shares, $2.75, cumulative;	
600,000 shares authorized; 100,000 shares issued and outstanding	$ 400,000
Common shares, unlimited number of shares	
authorized, 1,300,000 shares issued and outstanding	1,850,000
Retained earnings	5,850,000
Total shareholders' equity	$8,100,000

Required

1. Identify the different issues of shares that Redfern Limited has outstanding.

2. What is the average issue price per preferred share?

3. Make two summary journal entries to record issuance of all the Redfern shares for cash. Explanations are not required.

4. Assume no preferred dividends are in arrears. Journalize the declaration of a $400,000 dividend at June 30, 2014. Use separate Dividends Payable accounts for preferred and common shares. An explanation is not required.

Problem 13–6A

Preparing a corporation balance sheet; measuring profitability
②⑤

1. Total assets, Dec. 31, 2014, $759,000

The following accounts and related balances of Etse Manufacturing Inc. are arranged in no particular order.

Accounts Payable	$ 36,000	Accrued Liabilities	$ 23,000
Retained Earnings	?	Long-term Note Payable	100,500
Common Shares,		Accounts Receivable, net	100,000
100,000 shares		Preferred Shares, $0.15	
authorized, 33,000 shares		25,000 shares authorized,	
issued and outstanding	165,000	6,000 shares issued	30,000
Dividends Payable	4,500	Cash	35,000
Total assets, Dec. 31, 2013	567,500	Inventory	190,500
Net income	140,750	Property, Plant, and	
Common Shareholders'		Equipment, net	381,000
Equity, Dec. 31, 2013	520,000	Prepaid Expenses	15,500
Interest Expense	10,850	Patent, net	37,000

Required

1. Prepare the company's classified balance sheet in the report format at December 31, 2014.

2. Compute the rate of return on total assets and the rate of return on common shareholders' equity for the year ended December 31, 2014.

3. Do these rates of return suggest strength or weakness? Give your reason.

Problem 13–7A

Excel Spreadsheet Template

Computing dividends on preferred and common shares

1. b. 2012: Common $74,000

Everest Corporation has 50,000 $0.50 preferred shares and 600,000 common shares issued and outstanding. During a three-year period, Everest Corporation declared and paid cash dividends as follows: 2011, $0; 2012, $124,000; and 2013, $260,000.

Required

1. Compute the total dividends to preferred shares and common shares for each of the three years if
   a. Preferred shares are noncumulative.
   b. Preferred shares are cumulative.
2. For requirement 1b, record the declaration of the 2013 dividends on December 22, 2013, and the payment of the dividends on January 12, 2014.

Problem 13–8A

The balance sheet of Tulameen Systems Inc. reported the following:

Analyzing the shareholders'
equity of a corporation
③ ④
4. Book value per share—
Common $14.36

Shareholders' Equity	
Preferred shares, cumulative convertible; authorized 25,000 shares	$200,000
Common shares, authorized 50,000 shares; issued 44,000 shares	528,000
Retained earnings	168,000
Total shareholders' equity	$896,000

Notes to the financial statements indicate that 10,000 $1.20 preferred shares were issued and outstanding. The preferred shares have a liquidation value of $24.00 per share. Preferred dividends are in arrears for two years, including the current year. On the balance sheet date, the market value of the Tulameen Systems Inc. common shares was $28.00 per share.

Required

1. Are the preferred shares cumulative or noncumulative? How can you tell?
2. What is the total contributed capital of the company?
3. What is the total market value of the common shares?
4. Compute the book value per share of the preferred shares and of the common shares.

Problem 13–9A

At January 1, 2012, Computer Metals Processing Ltd.'s balance sheet reported the following shareholders' equity:

Recording the issuance
of shares; allocating cash
dividends; calculating book
value; preparing the liability and
shareholders' equity sections of
the balance sheet
② ③ ④
2. Total shareholders' equity
$2,430,000

Shareholders' Equity	
Contributed capital:	
Preferred shares, $1.25, cumulative (2 years in arrears),	
liquidation price of $20, 100,000 shares authorized,	
30,000 shares issued and outstanding	$ 200,000
Common shares,	
Class A, 20,000 shares authorized and issued and outstanding	125,000
Class B, unlimited number of shares authorized,	
150,000 shares issued and outstanding	1,500,000
Total contributed capital	1,825,000
Retained earnings	300,000
Total shareholders' equity	$2,125,000

The company had the following transactions on the dates indicated:

2012

Dec. 1   The company declared dividends of $180,000, payable on January 15, 2013, to the shareholders of record on December 31, 2012. Indicate the amount that would be payable to the preferred shareholders and to the common shareholders. The dividend rate for Class A and Class B shares is the same.

31   The company reported net income after taxes of $60,000 for the year and then closed the Income Summary account.

2013

Jan. 7   The company sold 10,000 preferred shares at $23.50 per share.

15   The company paid the dividend declared on December 1, 2012.

Feb. 14   The company sold 15,000 Class B common shares at $11.00 per share.

Dec. 2   The company declared dividends of $120,000, payable on January 15, 2014, to the shareholders of record on December 31, 2013. Indicate the amount that would be payable to the preferred shareholders and to the common shareholders.

31   The company reported net income after taxes of $145,000 and then closed the Income Summary account.

2014

Jan. 15   Paid the dividend declared on December 2, 2013.

Required

1. Record the transactions in the general journal.
2. Prepare the liability and shareholders' equity sections of the balance sheet as of the close of business on December 31, 2013.
3. Calculate the book value per share of the preferred shares and of the common shares (Class A and Class B combined) on December 31, 2013.
4. What was the average price at which the Class A common shares were issued?

PROBLEMS (GROUP B)   MyAccountingLab

Problem 13–1B

Organizing a corporation
①

Jack Rudd and Pam Kines are opening an office supply store. The area where the store is located is growing, and no competitors are located in the immediate vicinity. Their most fundamental decision is how to organize the business. Rudd thinks the partnership form is best. Kines favours the corporate form of organization. They seek your advice.

Required

Write a memo to Rudd and Kines to make them aware of the advantages and disadvantages of organizing the business as a corporation. Use the following format for your memo:

Date:	_____
To:	Jack Rudd and Pam Kines
From:	[Student Name]
Subject:	Advantages and disadvantages of the corporate form of business organization

Problem 13–2B

Journalizing corporation transactions and preparing the shareholders' equity section of the balance sheet
②

The articles of incorporation authorize Gingrich Solutions Ltd. to issue 100,000 $2.00 preferred shares and 250,000 common shares. In its first year, Gingrich Solutions Ltd. completed the following selected transactions:

2014

Jan. 2   Paid incorporation costs of $2,500 and legal fees of $6,000 to organize as a corporation.

6   Issued 20,000 common shares for equipment with a market value of $175,000.

12   Issued 100 preferred shares to acquire software with a market value of $19,500.

22   Issued 5,000 common shares for $7.00 cash per share.

Required

1. Record the transactions in the general journal.
2. Prepare the shareholders' equity section of the Gingrich Solutions Ltd. balance sheet at December 31, 2014. The ending Retained Earnings balance is $60,000.

Problem 13–3B

Sloboda Corporation was organized in 2013. At December 31, 2013, Sloboda Corporation's balance sheet reported the following shareholders' equity:

Issuing shares and preparing the shareholders' equity section of the balance sheet

Preferred shares, $0.20, 50,000 shares authorized, none issued	$ 0
Common shares, 100,000 shares authorized, 10,000 shares issued	
and outstanding	87,500
Retained earnings (Deficit)	(20,000)
Total shareholders' equity	$67,500

Required

1. What does the $0.20 mean for the preferred shares? If Sloboda Corporation issued 4,000 preferred shares, how much in cash dividends will Sloboda Corporation expect to pay per year?

2. At what average price per share did Sloboda Corporation issue the common shares?

3. Were first-year operations profitable? Give your reason.

4. During 2014, the company completed the following selected transactions. Journalize each transaction. Explanations are not required.

   a. Issued for cash 10,000 preferred shares at $2.50 per share.

   b. Issued for cash 1,000 common shares at a price of $9.00 per share.

   c. Issued 25,000 common shares to acquire a building valued at $235,000.

   d. Net income for the year was $62,500, and the company declared no dividends. Make the closing entry for net income.

5. Prepare the shareholders' equity section of the Sloboda Corporation balance sheet at December 31, 2014.

Problem 13–4B

Excel Spreadsheet Template

Shareholders' equity section of the balance sheet

Shareholders' equity information is given for Rexell Inc. and Raonic Corp. The two companies are independent.

Rexell Inc. Rexell Inc. is authorized to issue 100,000 common shares. All the shares were issued at $10.00 per share. The company incurred a net loss of $30,000 in 2012, its first year of business. It earned net income of $45,000 in 2013 and $50,000 in 2014. The company declared no dividends during the three-year period.

Raonic Corp. Raonic Corp.'s articles of incorporation authorize the company to issue 50,000 $1.25 cumulative preferred shares and 500,000 common shares. Raonic Corp. issued 4,000 preferred shares at $10.00 per share. It issued 60,000 common shares for a total of $150,000. The company's retained earnings balance at the beginning of 2014 was $55,000, and net income for the year was $62,500. During 2014, the company declared the specified dividend on preferred and a $0.50 per share dividend on common. Preferred dividends for 2013 were in arrears.

Required For each company, prepare the shareholders' equity section of its balance sheet at December 31, 2014. Show the computation of all amounts. Journal entries are not required.

Problem 13–5B

Analyzing the shareholders' equity of a corporation

Reckless Phones Ltd. included the following shareholders' equity on its year-end balance sheet at December 31, 2014:

Shareholders' Equity	
Preferred shares, $0.25, cumulative, unlimited authorization,	
10,000 shares issued and outstanding	$ 32,500
Common shares, unlimited authorization, 230,000 shares issued	
and outstanding	100,000
Retained earnings	1,000,000
	$1,132,500

Required

1. Identify the different issues of shares that Reckless has outstanding.

2. Are the preferred shares cumulative or noncumalative? How can you tell?

3. Give two summary journal entries to record issuance of all the Reckless shares. All the shares were issued for cash. Explanations are not required.

4. Assume that preferred dividends are in arrears for 2013. Record the declaration of a $15,000 dividend on December 31, 2014. Use separate Dividends Payable accounts for preferred shares and common shares.

Problem 13–6B

Preparing a corporation balance sheet; measuring profitability
② ⑤

The accounts and related balances of Labelle Systems Ltd. are arranged in no particular order.

Trademark, net	$19,000	Common Shareholders'	
Preferred Shares, $0.20,		Equity, June 30, 2013	$200,000
10,000 shares authorized,		Net income	25,000
issued and outstanding	29,500	Total assets,	
Cash	15,000	June 30, 2013	410,000
Accounts Receivable, net	52,500	Interest Expense	7,200
Accrued Liabilities	30,000	Property, Plant, and	
Long-term Note Payable	48,500	Equipment, net	300,000
Inventory	93,500	Common Shares, 500,000	
Dividends Payable	10,500	shares authorized; 272,000	
Retained Earnings	?	shares issued and outstanding	300,000
Accounts Payable	36,000	Prepaid Expenses	12,000

Required

1. Prepare the company's classified balance sheet in report format at June 30, 2014.

2. Compute the rate of return on total assets and the rate of return on common shareholders' equity for the year ended June 30, 2014.

3. Do these rates of return suggest strength or weakness? Give your reason.

Problem 13–7B

Excel Spreadsheet Template

Computing dividends on preferred and common shares
③

Brappit Broadcasting Inc. has 15,000 $2.50 preferred shares and 75,000 common shares outstanding. Brappit Broadcasting Inc. declared and paid the following dividends during a three-year period: 2012, $45,000; 2013, $0; and 2014, $130,000.

Required

1. Compute the total dividends on preferred shares and common shares for each of the three years if

   a. Preferred shares are noncumulative.

   b. Preferred shares are cumulative.

2. For requirement 1b, record the declaration of the 2014 dividends on December 28, 2014, and the payment of the dividends on January 17, 2015. Use separate Dividends Payable accounts for preferred shares and common shares.

Problem 13–8B

Analyzing the shareholders' equity of a corporation
③ ④

The balance sheet of Sonic Sales Limited reported the following at December 31, 2014:

Shareholders' Equity	
Preferred shares, redeemable, nonvoting, cumulative;	
authorized 16,000 shares (liquidation value $350,000)	$350,000
Common shares, authorized 200,000 shares; issued 90,000 shares	340,000
Retained earnings	120,000
Total shareholders' equity	$810,000

Notes to the financial statements indicate that 16,000 of the cumulative preferred shares were issued and outstanding. The shares paid a dividend of $1.40. Preferred dividends have not been paid for three years, including the current year. On the balance sheet date, the market value of Sonic Sales Limited's common shares was $3.00 per share.

Required

1. Are the preferred shares cumulative or noncumulative? How can you tell?
2. Which class of shareholders controls the company? Give your reason.
3. What is the total contributed capital of the company?
4. What was the total market value of the common shares?
5. Compute the book value per share of the preferred shares and the common shares.

Problem 13–9B

At January 1, 2012, Bohemia Nursery Ltd.'s balance sheet reported the following shareholders' equity:

Recording the issuance of shares; allocating cash dividends; calculating book value; preparing the shareholders' equity section of the balance sheet ② ③ ④

Shareholders' Equity	
Contributed capital:	
Preferred shares, $0.75, cumulative (3 years in arrears),	
liquidation price of $25, 100,000 shares authorized,	
40,000 shares issued and outstanding	$ 800,000
Common shares:	
Class A, 15,000 shares authorized, issued, and outstanding	120,000
Class B, unlimited number of shares authorized,	
75,000 shares issued and outstanding	375,000
Total contributed capital	1,295,000
Retained earnings	300,000
Total shareholders' equity	$1,595,000

The company had the following transactions on the dates indicated:

2012

Dec. 1 The company declared dividends of $170,000, payable on January 14, 2013, to the shareholders of record on December 31, 2012. Indicate the amount that would be payable to the preferred shareholders and to the common shareholders. Class A and Class B shares receive the same per-share dividend.

31 The company reported net income after taxes of $80,000 and closed the Income Summary account.

2013

Jan. 7 The company sold 10,000 preferred shares at $22.50 per share.

14 The company paid the dividend declared on December 1, 2012.

Feb. 14 The company sold 15,000 Class B common shares at $5.00 per share.

Dec. 2 The company declared dividends of $75,000, payable on January 13, 2014, to the shareholders of record on December 31, 2013. Indicate the amount that would be payable to the preferred shareholders and to the common shareholders.

31 The company reported net income after taxes of $63,000 and closed the Income Summary account.

2014

Jan. 13 Paid the dividend declared on December 2, 2013.

Required

1. Record the transactions in the general journal.
2. Prepare the shareholders' equity section of the balance sheet as of the close of business on December 31, 2013.

3. Calculate the book value per share of the preferred shares and of the common shares on December 31, 2013.

4. What was the average price at which the Class A common shares were issued?

CHALLENGE PROBLEMS

Problem 13–1C

The pros and cons of incorporation
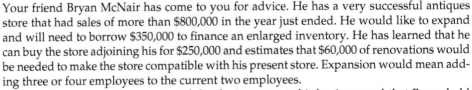
①

Your friend Bryan McNair has come to you for advice. He has a very successful antiques store that had sales of more than $800,000 in the year just ended. He would like to expand and will need to borrow $350,000 to finance an enlarged inventory. He has learned that he can buy the store adjoining his for $250,000 and estimates that $60,000 of renovations would be needed to make the store compatible with his present store. Expansion would mean adding three or four employees to the current two employees.

Bryan's accountant has suggested that he incorporate his business and that Bryan hold all the shares. He has cited several reasons to Bryan, including the benefits of limited liability. Bryan has talked to his banker about the possibility of incorporating; the banker has pointed out that if Bryan does incorporate, the bank will need personal guarantees for any loans Bryan arranges with the bank.

Required Consider Bryan's situation and discuss the pros and cons of incorporation for Bryan. What would you suggest?

Problem 13–2C

Issuing shares; preparing and analyzing the shareholders' equity section
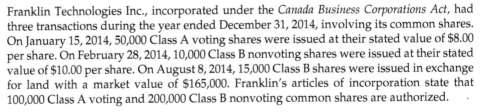
②

Franklin Technologies Inc., incorporated under the *Canada Business Corporations Act*, had three transactions during the year ended December 31, 2014, involving its common shares. On January 15, 2014, 50,000 Class A voting shares were issued at their stated value of $8.00 per share. On February 28, 2014, 10,000 Class B nonvoting shares were issued at their stated value of $10.00 per share. On August 8, 2014, 15,000 Class B shares were issued in exchange for land with a market value of $165,000. Franklin's articles of incorporation state that 100,000 Class A voting and 200,000 Class B nonvoting common shares are authorized.

Required

1. Prepare the journal entry to record the transaction of January 15, 2014.

2. Prepare the journal entry to record the transaction of February 28, 2014.

3. Prepare the journal entry to record the transaction of August 8, 2014.

4. Create the shareholders' equity section for Franklin Technologies Inc. after the three transactions have taken place. Assume retained earnings was $100,000 at this time.

5. What was the average issue price of each Class B common share?

6. How did Franklin Technologies Inc. withhold the voting privilege from its Class B common shareholders?

Problem 13–3C

Deciding on an investment in shares; evaluating different types of shares

④ ⑤

You have just received a bequest of $2,000 from an aunt and you have decided to invest the money in shares of Electronic Recycling Inc., a company that is listed on the Toronto Stock Exchange. Electronic Recycling Inc. (ERI) has common shares; cumulative preferred shares; noncumulative, convertible preferred shares; and noncumulative preferred shares. The common shares are trading at $40.00 and currently have been paying a dividend of $2.40 per share. The cumulative preferred shares are selling at $50.00 and have a stated dividend of $3.50. The convertible preferred shares are selling for $78.50 and are convertible at the rate of 2 common for 1 preferred; the dividend rate is $5.30. The noncumulative preferred shares are trading at $25.00 and have a dividend rate of $1.55.

Required Evaluate each of the four different shares as an investment opportunity. After performing your analysis, select which shares you will buy and explain your choice.

Extending Your Knowledge

DECISION PROBLEM

Kimberly Carlyle and Erron Friesen have written a spreadsheet program (Viacalc) to rival Excel. They need additional capital to market the product, and they plan to incorporate the business. They are considering the capital structure. Their primary goal is to raise as much capital as possible without giving up control of the business. Carlyle and Friesen plan to sell the Viacalc software to the corporation in exchange for 100,000 common shares. The partners have been offered $100,000 for the software.

The corporation's plans for the articles of incorporation include an authorization to issue 10,000 preferred shares and 1,000,000 common shares. Carlyle and Friesen are uncertain about the most desirable features for the preferred shares. Prior to incorporating, the partners have discussed their plans with two investment groups. The corporation can obtain capital from outside investors under either of the following plans:

Plan 1 Group 1 will invest $100,000 to acquire 1,000 shares of $7.50, cumulative preferred shares and $72,000 to acquire 60,000 common shares. Each preferred share will receive 50 votes if preferred dividends are more than two years in arrears.

Plan 2 Group 2 will invest $150,000 to acquire 1,200 shares of $8.50 nonvoting, noncumulative preferred shares.

Required

Assume the corporation receives its articles of incorporation.

1. Journalize the issuance of common shares to Kimberly Carlyle and Erron Friesen.
2. Journalize the issuance of shares to the outsiders under both plans.
3. Assume that net income for the first year is $184,000, and total dividends of $34,800 are properly subtracted from retained earnings. Prepare the shareholders' equity section of the corporation balance sheet under both plans.
4. Recommend one of the plans to Carlyle and Friesen. Give your reasons.

Evaluating alternative ways of raising capital

FINANCIAL STATEMENT CASES

Financial Statement Case 1

The Gildan Activewear Inc. fiscal 2011 financial statements appear in Appendix A at the end of this book and on MyAccountingLab. Answer the following questions about the company's share capital.

Shareholders' equity

1. Where can you find information about Gildan's share capital? What classes of shares does Gildan have issued and outstanding? How many shares are authorized and how many are issued and outstanding?
2. Were any shares issued during the year? How do you know?

Financial Statement Case 2

The Rainmaker Entertainment Inc. 2011 financial statements appear on MyAccountinglab. Answer the following questions about the company's share capital.

Shareholders' equity

2. Book value per share $0.58

1. What classes of shares has Rainmaker Entertainment Inc. issued? How many shares are authorized and how many are issued and outstanding?
2. What is the book value per share at December 31, 2011? The market price of the shares closed at $0.44 on that date. Why is the market price different from the book value per share?
3. What did Rainmaker Entertainment Inc. earn per common share in 2011? Where did you find that information?

Plaid Robots Inc. is a small, privately held corporation that had a great first year of operations. Management is considering taking the company public in the next three to five years. Since this is its first year of operations, its CEO, Pete Seckler, must now ask the accounting department to prepare its year-end financial statements. He still hasn't decided if the company will report using accounting standards for private enterprises (ASPE) or international financial reporting standards (IFRS). Pete has heard that there is "more" disclosure needed if the company follows IFRS but does not know what that means. Since he is not an accountant, he would like to see the shareholders' equity section of the balance sheet for this company prepared under both ASPE and IFRS to see for himself what all the fuss is about.

The following information is available to you to prepare the comparison:

- 250,000 Class A common shares were issued and outstanding at $5 each. There are 1,000,000 authorized Class A shares.
- 400,000 Class B common shares have been authorized but none have been issued.
- 10,000 preferred shares issued and outstanding at $10 each, 50,000 authorized
- Net income for the period May 1, 2013 to April 30, 2014 was $110,000

Required

1. Prepare the shareholders' equity section of the balance sheet as it would be presented under ASPE. Use the minimum acceptable disclosure.

2. Prepared the shareholders' equity section of the balance sheet as it would be presented if Plaid Robots reported under IFRS.

3. Would IFRS allow another presentation than what you have shown in Requirement 2?

JUST CHECKING Solutions for Chapter 13

1. *Proprietorship*
   - Legally, the owner and the business are one entity.
   - Limited to life of proprietor.
   - Unlimited liability of the owner.
   - Management by owner.
   - Business income is included in calculating owner's taxable income.

   Corporation
   - Separate legal entity.
   - Continuous life.
   - Limited liability of shareholders.
   - Often separation of ownership and management.
   - Pays corporate income tax.
   - May incur additional costs compared to proprietorships.

2. The authority structure in a corporation typically begins with the *shareholders*, who have the ultimate control in a corporation. The shareholders elect a *board of directors*, who elect a *chairperson of the board*. The board and its chairperson elect a *president* or *chief executive officer (CEO)*, who manages day-to-day operations; then *vice-presidents* are hired.

3. The five rights typically attached to common shares are:
   - The right to sell the shares.
   - The right to vote at shareholders' meetings.

- The right to receive a proportionate share of any dividends declared on the common shares.
- The right to receive a proportionate share of assets remaining on the winding-up of the company after creditors and more senior classes of shareholders are paid.
- The right to maintain a proportionate ownership in the corporation (the preemptive right).

4. Preferred shares are less risky because they usually have a fixed dividend rate and are repaid before common shares.

5. a. July 31

Cash	200,000	
Preferred Shares		100,000
Common Shares		100,000

   To issue 1,000 preferred shares with stated value of $100 per share, and 2,000 common shares at $50 per share.

   b. Contributed capital:

Preferred Shares	$ 100,000
Common Shares	100,000
Total contributed capital	200,000
Retained earnings	50,000
Total shareholders' equity	$250,000

c. Converting preferred shares into common shares occurs at the original value of the preferred shares, not at their current market value.

Preferred Shares	1,000	
Common Shares		1,000
To record conversion of 10 preferred shares into 20 common shares (10 preferred shares × 2 common shares/preferred share).		

6. a. common shares   c. long-term debt
   b. common shares   d. long-term debt

7. a. December 16, 2013, declaration of the dividend:

Retained Earnings	50,000	
Dividends Payable		50,000
To declared a dividend on common shares to be paid on January 6, 2014 (200,000 shares × $0.25 per share).		

January 6, 2014, payment of the dividend:

Dividends Payable	50,000	
Cash		50,000
To pay the dividend on common shares declared on December 16, 2013.		

b. The balance in retained earnings is $200,000 ($250,000 − $50,000). The declaration on December 16, 2013—not the payment on January 6, 2014—reduces retained earnings.

8. a.

Preferred Shares:	
Dividends in arrears ($2.00 × 10,000 × 2 years)	$40,000
Current dividend	20,000
Total to Preferred Shares	$60,000
Common Shares:	
Remainder of dividend ($90,000 − $60,000)	30,000
Total dividend	$90,000

b. Dividends will reduce retained earnings by $90,000.

9. Preferred shares may be cumulative or not cumulative, and convertible or not convertible. In addition, preferred shares have priority over common shares when the assets are distributed to shareholders upon liquidation of the company.

10. Shareholders' equity allocated to preferred shareholders:

Preferred shares ($13 × 3,500)	$ 45,500
Dividends in arrears ($45,500 × 7% × 5 years)	15,925
Shareholders' equity for preferred shares	$ 61,425

11. Shareholders' equity allocated to common shareholders:

Total shareholders' equity	$380,000
Less: Shareholders' equity allocated to preferred	61,425
Shareholders' equity available for common shareholders	$318,575
Book value per common share = ($318,575 ÷ 140,000 shares)	$ 2.28

12. Return on assets is 12.5%:
(Net income + Interest expense) ÷ Average total assets
= ($80,000 + $20,000) ÷ [($840,000 + $760,000) ÷ 2]
= $100,000 ÷ $800,000
= 0.125, or 12.5%

13. Return on equity is 20%:
(Net income − Preferred dividends) ÷ Average common shareholders' equity
= ($80,000 − $6.00 × 1,000) ÷ [($380,000 + $360,000) ÷ 2]
= $74,000 ÷ $370,000
= 0.20, or 20%

14. The return on equity (ROE) is higher than the return on assets (ROA), which indicates that the company is using leverage favourably.

15. Under IFRS, a company is required to disclose information about all classes of shares authorized by the corporation, whether or not those shares have been issued. IFRS differs from ASPE in that the latter set of standards only requires companies to report this information for the classes of shares that have been issued.

14

Corporations: Retained Earnings and the Income Statement

KEY QUESTIONS		LEARNING OBJECTIVES
How do we account for stock dividends and stock splits?	1	Account for stock dividends and stock splits
Why are shares repurchased, and how do we account for them?	2	Account for repurchased shares
How do we prepare a corporate income statement?	3	Prepare a detailed corporate income statement
How do we prepare a statement of retained earnings and a statement of shareholders' equity?	4	Prepare a statement of retained earnings and a statement of shareholders' equity
What is the impact of IFRS on the income statement and the statement of shareholders' equity?	5	Identify the impact on the income statement and the statement of shareholders' equity of international financial reporting standards (IFRS)

Dollarama is Canada's largest dollar store chain, a Canadian retail success story in an economy dominated by large, American retailers. And this is a store that doesn't advertise! It relies on store locations that have a lot of people passing by. In 2011/2012, the company added new stores at the rate of about one per week. As of June 2012, it had 721 locations across Canada.

Dollarama carries at least 4,000 seasonal and consumable products, and general merchandise in each store. Products are now offered beyond its original $1.00 price point. Since 2009, some merchandise is priced at $1.25, $1.50, or $2.00. This move has been extremely successful as almost half of the company's sales are from products priced over a dollar. The company tries to change a quarter of the products each year to keep the product fresh and relevant for customers, who come from all walks of life. One downtown Toronto store manager said that some local trendy restaurants buy wineglasses at his store!

Dollarama Inc. (listed as DOL on the Toronto Stock Exchange) is a Canadian public corporation. It is unusual because it is still managed by members of the family that started it. The retail enterprise has its roots in a store started in 1910 by Salim Rossy. His chain of stores was expanded by his son George and again by George's son Larry, who founded Dollarama in its present form in 1992. Larry is the current CEO and his son, Neil, is the chief merchandising officer.

Dollarama had a very successful 2011 fiscal year. Annual sales increased to over $1.6 billion. Per-store sales increased as did the average purchase by each customer. Profits have also increased. In the first three months of the 2012 fiscal year, the company earned $63,600,000 or $0.84 per diluted share. One way that companies share these profits with shareholders is by issuing dividends. Dollarama declared a quarterly dividend of $0.11 per share in June 2012.

Dollarama's management wanted to further increase shareholder value, so it also announced that the company was going to buy back its own shares. A *Globe and Mail* reporter commented, "The company's earnings have been so strong, it is throwing off a

①	②	③	④	⑤
Account for stock dividends and stock splits	Account for repurchased shares	Prepare a detailed corporate income statement	Prepare a statement of retained earnings and a statement of shareholders' equity	Identify the impact on the income statement and the statement of shareholders' equity of international financial reporting standards (IFRS)
How do we account for stock dividends and stock splits? page 864	*Why are shares repurchased, and how do we account for them? page 869*	*How do we prepare a corporate income statement? page 873*	*How do we prepare a statement of retained earnings and a statement of shareholders' equity? page 879*	*What is the impact of IFRS on the income statement and the statement of shareholders' equity? page 885*
Retained Earnings, page 863	Repurchase of Its Shares by a Corporation, page 869	The Corporate Income Statement – Analyzing Earnings, page 873	Statement of Retained Earnings, page 879	The Impact of IFRS on the Income Statement and the Statement of Shareholders' Equity, page 885
Stock Dividends, page 864	Ethical and Legal Issues for Share Transactions, page 873		Statement of Shareholders' Equity, page 880	
Stock Splits, page 867			Accounting for Errors and Changes in Accounting Policy, page 883	
Similarities and Differences between Stock Dividends and Stock Splits, page 869			Restrictions on Retained Earnings, page 884	

MyAccountingLab

- Chapter 14: DemoDoc covering Stock Splits and Stock Dividends
- Chapter 14: Student PowerPoint Slides
- Chapter 14: Audio Chapter Summary

All MyAccountingLab resources can be found in the Chapter Resources section and the Multimedia Library.

The **Summary** for Chapter 14 appears on page 889.
Accounting Vocabulary with definitions appears on page 892.

steady stream of cash and the board wanted to add the ability to buy back shares as part of a plan to return capital to shareholders."[1]

Investors seem to be agreeing with the company's choices. Dollarama's share price has increased from $44 per share when it went public in 2009 to $63.75 in June 2012.

Chapter 13 introduced corporations and covered the basics of shareholders' equity. We saw that a corporation's balance sheet is the same as that for a proprietorship or a partnership, except for the owners' equity section, which is called shareholders' equity for a corporation and has some different accounts.

---

[1] Boyd Erman, "Dollarama Would Pay Top Dollar in Buyback," *The Globe and Mail*, June 13, 2012, online at http://www.theglobeandmail.com/globe-investor/investment-ideas/streetwise/dollarama-would-pay-top-dollar-in-buyback/article4256717. Also Ross Marowits, "Dollarama Hikes Dividend as Profit Jumps 51%," The Canadian Press, April 11, 2012, online at http://www.theglobeandmail.com/globe-investor/dollarama-hikes-dividend-as-profit-jumps-51/article4099396/, and John Daly, "How Dollarama Turns Pocket Change Into Billions," *The Globe and Mail's Report on Business Magazine*, March 29, 2012, online at http://www.theglobeandmail.com/report-on-business/rob-magazine/how-dollarama-turns-pocket-change-into-billions/article4097813/, and the Dollarama Inc. website, "Dollarama Announces the Launch of a Normal Course Issuer Bid" at http://www.dollarama.com/wp-content/uploads/2012/06/Dollarama-Announces-the-Launch-of-a-Normal-Course-Issuer-Bid.pdf. All articles and websites accessed September 13, 2012.

Chapter 13 began with the issuance of common shares, and also covered the declaration and payment of cash dividends. The topics covered in Chapter 13 apply to private corporations, whose shares tend to be held by a small number of shareholders and are not traded on a stock exchange, as well as public corporations, whose shares trade on stock exchanges.

All corporations' financial reporting is governed by Canadian generally accepted accounting principles (GAAP). Public corporations are governed by international financial reporting standards (IFRS), which are discussed in Learning Objective 5 in this chapter. Private enterprises have a choice to follow either IFRS or accounting standards for private enterprises (ASPE). While ASPE forms the basis for this textbook, some examples in this chapter use public corporations to illustrate concepts more easily and to acknowledge that the accounting information students will see in the business press and in everyday dealings will be generated mainly by public corporations.

This chapter takes corporate equity a few steps further, as follows:

Chapter 13 covered	Chapter 14 covers
Contributed capital	Retained earnings
Issuing shares	Repurchasing shares
Cash dividends	Stock dividends and stock splits
Corporate balance sheet	Corporate income statement

Retained Earnings

We have seen that the owners' equity section of a corporation's balance sheet is called *shareholders' equity*. The contributed capital accounts and retained earnings make up the shareholders' equity section. We studied contributed capital in Chapter 13. Now let's focus on retained earnings.

Retained Earnings carries the balance of the business's accumulated lifetime net income less all net losses from operations and less all dividends. *Retained* means "held onto" or "kept." Retained earnings is the shareholders' stake in total assets that come from profits. Successful companies grow by reinvesting the assets they generate from profitable operations. The normal balance of Retained Earnings is a credit. A debit balance in Retained Earnings is called a *deficit*. Retained earnings deficits are not common because they often indicate that the corporation may be facing corporate failure and bankruptcy.

When you see a balance sheet, remember these facts about Retained Earnings:

KEY POINTS

Retained Earnings is not a cash account. A $500,000 balance in Retained Earnings means that $500,000 of capital has been created by profits left in or reinvested in the business over its lifetime.

- *Credits to the Retained Earnings account arise only from net income.* Retained Earnings shows how much net income a corporation has earned and retained in the business. Its balance is the cumulative, lifetime earnings of the company less all net losses and all dividends.

- *The Retained Earnings account is not a reservoir of cash.* Instead, Retained Earnings represents no particular asset. In fact, the corporation may have a large balance in Retained Earnings but too little cash to pay a dividend.

  - To *declare* a dividend, the company must have a credit balance in Retained Earnings both before and after the declaration of dividends.

  - To *pay* the dividend, it must have the cash.

Retained Earnings and Cash are two very different accounts, unrelated to each other.

- Recall that, in a proprietorship, investments, net income, and withdrawals are all recorded in the Capital account. In a corporation, *shareholders' equity*

LEARNING TIPS

Remember:

Beginning Retained Earnings
+ Net Income, or
− Net Loss
− Dividends
= Ending Retained Earnings

Retained Earnings	
	Beginning balance
Net loss	Net income
Dividends	
	Ending balance

—— LO ① ——
How do we account for stock
dividends and stock splits?

is split into Contributed Capital and Retained Earnings. The Contributed Capital section holds capital invested, or contributed. Retained Earnings is used to record net income, net loss, and dividends.

- *Retained Earnings' ending balance is computed as follows* (amounts assumed):

Beginning balance	$ 70,000
Add: Net income for the year	80,000
Less: Net loss* (none this year)	
Dividends for the year	(50,000)
Ending balance	$100,000

*In a particular year, a corporation can have a net income or a net loss, but not both.

Stock Dividends

A **stock dividend**, also called a **share dividend**, is a distribution of a corporation's own shares to its shareholders. Stock dividends are fundamentally different from cash dividends because stock dividends do not give any cash to the shareholders. Stock dividends increase Common Shares and decrease Retained Earnings. Both of these accounts are elements of shareholders' equity, so total shareholders' equity is unchanged. There is merely a transfer from Retained Earnings to Common Shares, as shown in the example below and in Exhibit 14–1.

To illustrate the effects of a stock dividend, assume Sugar Bay Parts Inc. offered a 10 percent stock dividend to its shareholders. Since 75,000 shares were issued and outstanding before the stock dividend, then 7,500 new shares would be issued as a result of the stock dividend (75,000 × 10% = 7,500). This gives a total of 82,500 shares issued and outstanding after the stock dividend (75,000 + 7,500 = 82,500). Assume the market price of the shares was $1.50 per share on the date of the stock dividend, so the total value of the new 7,500 shares was $11,250.

The shareholders' equity section of Sugar Bay Parts Inc. before and after the stock dividend appears in Exhibit 14–1. Notice the change in the Retained Earnings and Common Shares balances after the stock dividend—each balance has changed by the $11,250 value of the 7,500 shares from the stock dividend.

EXHIBIT 14–1 | Effects of a Stock Dividend

Before		**After**	
Shareholders' equity:		Shareholders' equity:	
Retained earnings	$150,000	Retained earnings	$138,750 (↓ by $11,250)
Common shares (75,000)	100,000	Common shares (82,500)	111,250 (↑ by $11,250)
Total shareholders'		Total shareholders'	
equity	$250,000	equity	$250,000

Suppose you owned 20 percent of Sugar Bay Parts Inc.'s shares before the stock dividend, which is 15,000 shares (75,000 × 20% = 15,000). A 10 percent stock dividend gives you 1,500 new shares (15,000 × 10% = 1,500), for a total of 16,500 shares (15,000+1,500=16,500). After the stock dividend, you own 20 percent of the total shares (16,500 ÷ 82,500 = 20%). This proves that you are in the same relative ownership position (20 percent ownership) after the stock dividend as you were before the stock dividend. Notice that Total Shareholders' Equity remains the same before and after the stock dividend.

KEY POINTS

When a shareholder receives a stock dividend, the shareholder's percentage ownership in the company does not change.

Amount of Retained Earnings Transferred in a Stock Dividend Stock dividends are said to be *capitalized retained earnings* because they transfer an amount from retained earnings to contributed capital. The contributed capital accounts are more permanent than retained earnings because they cannot be paid out as dividends. Many shareholders view stock dividends as distributions little different from cash dividends.

Stock dividends, like cash dividends, are taxable in the hands of the recipient. The value of the stock dividend is equal to the amount of the increase in the capital of the company paying the dividend. The increase is usually the fair market value of the shares issued.

Reasons for Stock Dividends

Why do companies issue stock dividends? There are several reasons:

- *To continue dividends but conserve cash.* A company may wish to continue dividends in some form but may need to keep its cash in the business.

- *To reduce the market price per share of its shares.* For companies whose shares trade on a stock exchange, a stock dividend may cause the market price of a company's shares to fall because of the increased supply of the shares. Fairfax Financial Holdings Limited's common shares traded at $430.00 in January 2012. If the company doubled the number of its shares outstanding by issuing a stock dividend, it would be likely to drop the market price of the shares by approximately half, or $215.00 per share. The objective of such a large stock dividend would be to make the shares less expensive, and thus more affordable and attractive to investors.

Recording Stock Dividends

As with a cash dividend, there are three key dates for a stock dividend:

- Declaration date
- Date of record
- Distribution date (payment date)

The board of directors announces stock dividends on the declaration date. The date of record and the distribution date follow. (This is the same sequence of dates used for a cash dividend.) The declaration of a stock dividend does *not* create a liability because the corporation is not obligated to pay out assets. (Recall that a liability is a claim on *assets.*) Instead, the corporation has declared its intention to distribute its shares.

One concern about stock dividends is how to determine the amount to transfer from retained earnings to the Common Shares account. The *Canada Business Corporations Act* suggests that the market value of the shares issued is the appropriate amount to transfer, while other incorporating acts allow the directors to set a value on the shares. If market value were to be used, it would be the market value on the date the dividend is declared. This is the valuation used in this text.

KEY POINTS

A cash dividend involves the payment of a current asset (cash). A stock dividend is a distribution of a company's own shares, which are not an asset but rather a component of equity.

Assume General Communications Corporation has the following shareholders' equity prior to a stock dividend:

Shareholders' Equity	
Contributed capital	
Common shares, 100,000 shares authorized, 40,000 shares issued	$400,000
Retained earnings	100,000
Total shareholders' equity	$500,000

KEY POINTS

Never credit a payable account for a stock dividend. No liability is created when a stock dividend is declared, as compared to a cash dividend, which does create a liability.

Assume General Communications Corporation declares a 10 percent common stock dividend on November 17. The company will distribute 4,000 (40,000 × 0.10) shares in the dividend. On November 17, the market value of its common shares is $16.00 per share. Using the market value approach, Retained Earnings is debited for the market value of the 4,000 dividend shares and Common Stock Dividend Distributable is credited. Common Stock Dividend Distributable is a shareholders' equity account and not a liability because it is not a distribution of assets. General Communications Corporation makes the following entry on the declaration date.

Nov. 17	Retained Earnings	64,000	
	Common Stock Dividend Distributable		64,000
	To declare a 10 percent common stock dividend.		
	(40,000 × 0.10 × $16)		

The accounting equation for this transaction shows that a stock dividend does not affect assets, liabilities, or total shareholders' equity. It merely rearranges the information within the shareholders' equity accounts.

Assets	=	Liabilities	+	Shareholders' Equity	
				−64,000	Retained Earnings
0	=	0		+64,000	Common Stock Dividend Distributable

If the company prepares financial statements after the declaration of the stock dividend but before issuing it, Common Stock Dividend Distributable is reported in the shareholders' equity section of the balance sheet immediately after Common Shares. However, this account holds the value of the dividend shares only from the declaration date to the date of distribution.

On the distribution date, the company records issuance of the dividend shares as follows:

Dec. 12	Common Stock Dividend Distributable	64,000	
	Common Shares		64,000
	To issue common shares in a stock dividend.		

The following tabulation shows the changes in shareholders' equity caused by the stock dividend:

Shareholders' Equity	Before the Dividend	After the Dividend	Change
Contributed capital			
Common shares, 100,000 shares authorized 40,000 shares issued	$400,000		
44,000 shares issued		$464,000	Up by $64,000
Total contributed capital	400,000	464,000	Up by $64,000
Retained earnings	100,000	36,000	Down by $64,000
Total shareholders' equity	$500,000	$500,000	Unchanged

Stock Splits

A **stock split** is fundamentally different from a stock dividend. A stock split increases the number of authorized and outstanding shares with a proportionate reduction in the book value per share. For example, if the company splits its stock 2 for 1, the number of outstanding shares is doubled and each share's book value is halved. Many large companies in Canada—Lululemon, Bank of Nova Scotia, Loblaw Companies Limited, and others—have split their stock.

Assume that the market price of one common share of Marcato Corp. is $100 and that the company wishes to decrease the market price to approximately $50. Marcato decides to split the common shares 2 for 1 in the expectation that the share's market price would fall from $100 to $50. A 2-for-1 stock split means that the company would have two times as many shares outstanding after the split as it had before and that each share's book value would be halved. Assume Marcato had 400,000 common shares issued and outstanding before the split. Exhibit 14–2 shows how a 2-for-1 stock split affects Marcato Corp.'s shareholders' equity:

- It doubles the number of shares authorized and issued
- It leaves all account balances and total shareholders' equity unchanged

REAL WORLD EXAMPLE

Stock splits are more common than stock dividends. Bell Canada Enterprises has split its stock 3 times: 4 for 1 in 1948, 3 for 1 in 1979, and 2 for 1 in 1997.

EXHIBIT 14–2 | A 2-for-1 Stock Split

Shareholders' Equity before 2-for-1 Stock Split	
Contributed capital	
Common shares, unlimited number of shares authorized,	
400,000 shares issued and outstanding	$4,000,000
Retained earnings	1,800,000
Total shareholders' equity	$5,800,000

Shareholders' Equity after 2-for-1 Stock Split	
Contributed capital	
Common shares, unlimited number of shares authorized,	
800,000 shares issued and outstanding	$4,000,000
Retained earnings	1,800,000
Total shareholders' equity	$5,800,000

Because the stock split affects no account balances, no formal journal entry is necessary. Instead, the split is often recorded in a **memorandum entry**—a note in the journal without debits or credits—such as the following:

Aug. 19	Distributed one new common share for each old share previously outstanding. This increased the number of common shares issued and outstanding from 400,000 to 800,000.

Consolidation

A company may engage in a **consolidation** (or **reverse split**) to decrease the number of shares outstanding and increase the market price per share. If the number of shares outstanding is decreased, then existing shareholders may have a better chance of maintaining control over a corporation's shares. There are fewer shares available to be traded and purchased by new shareholders. For example, Marcato Corp. could consolidate its stock 1 for 4, which would reduce the number of shares issued from 400,000 to 100,000 and increase the share price from, for example, $25.00 per share

REAL WORLD EXAMPLE

Luna Gold Corporation, a Vancouver gold exploration company working in Brazil, consolidated its shares in early 2012 when it was selling at $0.64 per share. The 5-for-1 consolidation raised the share price to $3.20 on the day it happened.

to $100.00 per share. Consolidations are rare but are sometimes done to allow companies to continue trading their shares on stock exchanges that require a minimum share price if the company's share price falls below the minimum.

Similarities and Differences between Stock Dividends and Stock Splits

A 2-for-1 stock split and a 100 percent stock dividend appear remarkably similar on the surface, but there are a number of differences between the two choices.

Similarities

- Both increase the number of shares owned per shareholder.
- Neither a stock dividend nor a stock split changes the investor's total cost of the shares owned. For example, assume you paid $32,000 to acquire 1,000 common shares of Western AquaCulture Ltd. If Western AquaCulture Ltd. distributes a 100 percent stock dividend, your 1,000 shares increase to 2,000, but your total cost is still $32,000. Likewise, if Western AquaCulture Ltd. performs a 2-for-1 stock split, your shares increase in number to 2,000, but your total cost is unchanged.
- Both a stock dividend and a stock split increase the corporation's number of shares issued and outstanding. For example, a 100 percent stock dividend and a 2-for-1 stock split both double the outstanding shares and are likely to cut the stock's market price per share in half.

Differences

REAL WORLD EXAMPLE

Dividend reinvestment plans (or DRIPs) are a popular investment product. They result in taxable dividends, because a cash dividend is received and is used to buy additional shares immediately.

- Stock splits and stock dividends differ in the way they are treated for tax purposes. A stock *split* does not create taxable income to the investor, but a stock *dividend* does because stock dividends are taxed in the same way as cash dividends. The stock dividend is valued at the market value of the shares on the date the stock dividend is declared, and this amount is included as taxable income. This is one reason why stock dividends are less popular than stock splits; investors must pay income tax on a stock dividend even though no cash is received.
- A stock *dividend* shifts an amount from retained earnings to contributed capital, leaving the total book value unchanged. However, the book value per share will decrease because of the increased number of shares outstanding. A stock *split* affects no account balances whatsoever but instead changes the book value of each share.

Exhibit 14–3 provides a summary of the effects.

MyAccountingLab

DemoDoc: Stock Splits and Stock Dividends

EXHIBIT **14–3** | Effects of Dividends and Stock Splits

Effect on:	Cash Dividend	Stock Dividend	Stock Split
Common Shares account	None	Increase	None
Number of common shares issued and outstanding	None	Increase	Increase
Number of shares authorized	None	None	Increase (except when an unlimited number of shares are authorized)
Retained earnings	Decrease	Decrease	None
Total shareholders' equity	Decrease	None	None
Taxes to be paid by a shareholder	Yes	Yes	No
Book value per share	No	Yes	Yes

✓ JUST CHECKING

1. Answer the following questions to review stock and cash dividends.
   a. How is a stock dividend like a cash dividend?
   b. What happens to total share capital as a result of cash and stock dividends?
   c. What happens to total shareholders' equity as a result of cash and stock dividends?
   d. Which type of dividend gives taxable income to the shareholder?

2. Beachcomber Pool Supply Inc. has 16,000 common shares outstanding for a total contributed capital value of $48,000. Beachcomber declares a 10 percent stock dividend on July 15 when the market value of its shares is $8.00 per share. The date of record is August 15 and the distribution date is August 31.
   a. Journalize the declaration of the stock dividend on July 15 and the distribution on August 31.
   b. What is the overall effect on Beachcomber's total assets?
   c. What is the overall effect on total shareholders' equity?
   d. If Beachcomber declared a 2-for-1 stock split instead of a stock dividend, what would be the journal entry on July 15? On August 31?
   e. What would be the effect of the stock split on shareholders' equity?

3. Stutterstep Corp., an Internet service provider, has prospered during the past seven years, and recently the company's share price has shot up to $61.00. Stutterstep's management wishes to decrease the share price to the range of $29.00 to $31.00, which will be attractive to more investors. Should the company issue a 100 percent stock dividend or split the stock? Why? If you propose a stock split, state the split ratio that will accomplish the company's objective. Show your computations.

Just Checking Solutions appear at the end of this chapter and on MyAccountingLab.

Repurchase of Its Shares by a Corporation

Corporations may **repurchase shares** from their shareholders for several reasons:

— LO ②—
Why are shares repurchased, and how do we account for them?

- The corporation may have issued all its authorized shares and need to recover shares for distributions to officers and employees under bonus plans or share purchase plans.

- The purchase may help support the share's current market price by decreasing the supply of shares available to the public.

- Management may gather in the shares to avoid a takeover by an outside party.

- The corporation may need to meet share-ownership requirements or limits, which may be a percentage of the total for foreign ownership or some other legislated requirement.

REAL WORLD EXAMPLE

It is normal for businesses to repurchase their own shares. There are announcements ahead of time for "normal course issuer bids" that tell the public a repurchase will take place. This is what Dollarama did in 2012.

The *Canada Business Corporations Act* requires a corporation that purchases its own shares to cancel the shares bought. Those shares are then treated as authorized but unissued.

Several of the provincial incorporating acts also require that the shares be cancelled, while other jurisdictions inside and outside of Canada permit the corporation to hold the shares as **treasury shares** (in effect, the corporation holds the shares in its treasury) and resell them. Because of the complex and varied treatment of treasury shares, they are covered more fully in intermediate and advanced accounting courses, so will not be covered further in this text.

Most incorporating acts do not permit a corporation to acquire its own shares if such reacquisition would result in the corporation's putting itself into financial jeopardy and being unable to pay its liabilities as they become due.

The first step in recording a share repurchase is to calculate the average cost per share. How a share repurchase is recorded depends on whether the shares are repurchased at a price equal to or less than or greater than the average cost per share. We will examine each of these situations.

Share Repurchase at Average Issue Price

Assume the articles of incorporation for Dawson Resources Ltd., issued under the *Canada Business Corporations Act*, authorized it to issue 100,000 common shares. By February 28, 2014, Dawson Resources had issued 9,000 shares at an average issue price of $20.00 per share, and its shareholders' equity appeared as follows:

Shareholders' Equity	
Contributed capital	
Common shares, 100,000 shares authorized, 9,000 shares issued	
and outstanding	$180,000
Retained earnings	24,000
Total shareholders' equity	$204,000

On March 20, 2014, Dawson Resources Ltd. repurchases 1,000 shares at $20.00 per share, an amount equal to the average issue price of $20.00 per share. The company records the transaction as follows:

2014			
Mar. 20	Common Shares	20,000	
	Cash		20,000
	Purchased 1,000 shares at $20.00 per share.		

The repurchase of its own shares by a company decreases the company's assets and its shareholders' equity. The Common Shares account is debited and the Cash account is credited to remove the original cost of the shares from the account. The shareholders' equity section of Dawson Resources Ltd.'s balance sheet would appear as follows after the transaction:

Shareholders' Equity	
Contributed capital	
Common shares, 100,000 shares authorized, 8,000 shares issued and	
outstanding (Note 6)	$160,000
Retained earnings	24,000
Total shareholders' equity	$184,000
Note 6: During the year, the company acquired 1,000 common shares at a price of $20.00 per share; the shares had been issued at $20.00 per share.	

Observe that the purchase of the shares decreased the number of shares issued and outstanding. Only *outstanding* shares have a vote, receive cash dividends, and share in assets if the corporation liquidates.

Share Repurchase below Average Issue Price

The *CICA Handbook* requires a company that purchases its own shares at a price less than the *average issue price* to debit Common Shares (or Preferred Shares, as the case may be) for the average issue price. The excess of the average issue price over the purchase price should be credited to a new account: Contributed Surplus—Share Repurchase. (If the company has more than one class or series of shares, the Contributed Surplus—Share Repurchase account name would include the class or series.)

Let's continue the Dawson Resources Ltd. example. On April 30, 2014, Dawson repurchases 1,000 shares at $15.00 per share. The average issue price was $20.00 per share. The company records the transaction as follows:

2014			
Apr. 30	Common Shares	20,000	
	Contributed Surplus—Share Repurchase		5,000
	Cash		15,000
	Purchased 1,000 shares at $15.00 per share.		

Since the common shares repurchased had an issue value of $20,000 (1,000 × $20), and cash was paid in the amount of $15,000, the contributed surplus was $5,000 ($20,000 − $15,000 = $5,000).

The shareholders' equity section of Dawson Resources Ltd.'s balance sheet would appear as follows after the transaction:

Shareholders' Equity	
Contributed capital	
Common shares, 100,000 shares authorized, 7,000 shares issued and outstanding	$140,000
Contributed Surplus—Share Repurchase (Note 6)	5,000
Total contributed capital	145,000
Retained earnings	24,000
Total shareholders' equity	$169,000

Note 6: During the year, the company acquired 1,000 common shares at a price of $20.00 per share and 1,000 common shares at a price of $15.00 per share; the shares had been issued at $20.00 per share.

Dawson Resources Ltd. now has a balance in the Contributed Surplus—Share Repurchase account.

Share Repurchase above Average Issue Price

When a company purchases its own shares at a price greater than the average issue price, the excess should first be debited to Contributed Surplus—Share Repurchase to reduce the balance in this account to $0, and any remaining excess should then be debited to Retained Earnings.

Balance in the Contributed Surplus—Share Repurchase Account Let's continue the Dawson Resources Ltd. example. Suppose Dawson repurchased another 1,000 shares at $30.00 per share on May 10, 2014, and the Contributed Surplus—Share Repurchase account had the balance of $5,000 shown above. The company would reduce the balance in Contributed Surplus—Share Repurchase to nil before reducing the Retained Earnings account, as follows:

2014			
May 10	Common Shares	20,000	
	Contributed Surplus—Share Repurchase	5,000	
	Retained Earnings	5,000	
	Cash		30,000
	Purchased 1,000 shares at $30.00 per share.		

Since the common shares repurchased for $30,000 had an issue value of $20,000 (1,000 × $20), the contributed surplus was reduced to nil by debiting the Contributed Surplus—Share Repurchase account for $5,000. Retained Earnings was debited for the remainder ($30,000 − $20,000 − $5,000 = $5,000).

The shareholders' equity section of Dawson Resources Ltd.'s balance sheet would appear as follows after the transaction:

Shareholders' Equity	
Contributed capital	
Common shares, 100,000 shares authorized, 6,000 shares issued and outstanding (Note 6)	$120,000
Retained earnings	19,000
Total shareholders' equity	$139,000

Note 6: During the year, the company acquired 1,000 common shares at a price of $20.00 per share, 1,000 common shares at a price of $15.00 per share, and 1,000 common shares at a price of $30.00 per share; the shares had been issued at $20.00 per share.

No Balance in the Contributed Surplus—Share Repurchase Account Suppose Dawson Resources Ltd. had repurchased 1,000 of its shares at $30.00 per share on May 10, 2014, and did not have a balance in the Contributed Surplus—Share Repurchase account. Retained Earnings would be debited for the difference between the purchase price and the issue price, which in this case is $10,000 ($30,000 − $20,000). The journal entry would be as follows:

2014			
May 10	Common Shares	20,000	
	Retained Earnings	10,000	
	Cash		30,000
	Purchased 1,000 shares at $30.00 per share.		

Recording the Sale of Repurchased Shares

KEY POINTS

The repurchase and sale of its own shares do not affect a corporation's net income. A share repurchase affects *balance sheet accounts*, not income statement accounts.

A company incorporated under the *Canada Business Corporations Act* may reissue the shares that it previously had repurchased. The sale would be treated like a normal sale of authorized but unissued shares. The Contributed Surplus—Share Repurchase account is *not* affected when a company sells its own repurchased shares.

The repurchase and sale of its own shares do not affect a corporation's net income. A share repurchase affects *balance sheet accounts*, not income statement accounts.

Exhibit 14–4 summarizes the journal entries for share repurchases.

EXHIBIT 14–4 | Summary of Journal Entries for Share Repurchases

Repurchase at average issue price:

Common Shares	Number repurchased × Average cost per share	
Cash		Number repurchased × Price paid per share

Repurchase below average issue price:

Common Shares	Number repurchased × Average cost per share	
Contributed Surplus— Share Repurchase		Difference between Cash and Common Shares amounts
Cash		Number repurchased × Price paid per share

Repurchase above average issue price:

Common Shares	Number repurchased × Average cost per share	
Contributed Surplus— Share Repurchase	Use up the credit balance in this account first	
Retained Earnings	The amount of any remaining difference (the "plug" amount)	
Cash		Number repurchased × Price paid per share

Ethical and Legal Issues for Share Transactions

Share repurchase transactions have a serious ethical and legal dimension. A company buying its own shares must be extremely careful that its disclosures of information are complete and accurate. Otherwise, a shareholder who sold shares back to the company may claim that he or she was deceived into selling the shares at too low a price. For example, what would happen if a company repurchased its own shares at $17.00 per share and one day later announced a technological breakthrough that would generate millions of dollars in new business? The share price would likely increase in response to the new information. If it could be proved that management withheld the information, a shareholder selling shares back to the company might file a lawsuit to gain the difference per share. The shareholder would claim that, with the knowledge of the technological advance, he or she would have held the shares until after the price increase and been able to sell the shares at a higher price.

Insider Trading   To keep the stock markets fair for everyone, people who work for public corporations are not allowed to buy or sell shares of the company when the information they have is not available to the public. They are also not allowed to share this information secretly with their friends. While jail terms for this sort of action are rare, Barry Landen, the former Vice-President of Corporate Affairs at Agnico-Eagle Mines Ltd, was sentenced to 45 days in jail and assessed a $200,000 fine for insider trading under the *Securities Act*. He sold shares to avoid a loss of $115,000 based on "undisclosed material information."[2]

REAL WORLD EXAMPLE

In Canada, the first criminal conviction for insider trading occurred in 2010—it was a 39-month prison sentence. In Canada, the maximum prison term for insider trading under the Criminal Code is 10 years. In the United States, in 2012, a lawyer was sent to federal prison for 12 years—the longest sentence so far.

✓ JUST CHECKING

4. Whippet Industries Corporation has the following partial balance sheet information available at November 30, 2013:

Shareholders' Equity	
Contributed Capital	
Common shares, 400,000 shares authorized,	
150,000 shares issued and outstanding	$ 900,000
Retained earnings	700,000
Total shareholders' equity	$1,600,000

If Whippet Industries repurchased 20,000 common shares on March 1, 2014, at a price of $4.50 per share, prepare the journal entry for the transaction.

5. Refer to the previous question. Suppose Whippet Industries repurchased 20,000 shares on March 1, 2014, at a price of $8.25 per share instead of $4.50. Prepare the journal entry for this transaction.

6. Prepare the shareholders' equity section of the balance sheet after the repurchase in Just Checking question 5.

Just Checking Solutions appear at the end of this chapter and on MyAccountingLab.

The Corporate Income Statement— Analyzing Earnings

As we have seen, the shareholders' equity of a corporation is more complex than the capital of a proprietorship or a partnership. Also, a corporation's income statement includes some features that don't often apply to a proprietorship or a partnership. Most of the income statements you will see belong to corporations, so we turn now to the corporate income statement to explore these new features.

LO ③

How do we prepare a corporate income statement?

---

[2] Megan Harman, "Insider Sentenced to Jail Term," posted February 6, 2009, and retrieved from http://www.investmentexecutive.com/-/news-48051 on November 27, 2012.

Net income is probably the most important piece of information about a company. Net income measures how successfully the company has operated. To shareholders, the larger the corporation's profit, the greater the likelihood of dividends or share-price increases. To creditors, the larger the corporation's profit, the better able it is to pay its debts. Net income builds up a company's assets and shareholders' equity. It also helps to attract capital from new investors who believe the company will be successful in the future.

Suppose you are considering investing in the shares of The Toronto-Dominion Bank, Dollarama Inc., or a private corporation. You would examine these companies' income statements. Of particular interest is the amount of net income they can expect to earn year after year. To understand net income, let's examine Exhibit 14–5, which presents the income statement of Como Technology Inc., a small manufacturer of electronic switching equipment that is owned by a few shareholders who run the company. Its shares do not trade on a stock exchange, so Como Technology Inc. is a private enterprise.

EXHIBIT 14–5 | Corporate Income Statement

COMO TECHNOLOGY INC.
Income Statement
For the Year Ended December 31, 2014

Sales revenue		$1,000,000	
Cost of goods sold		480,000	
Gross margin		520,000	
Operating expenses (listed individually)		362,000	
Operating income		158,000	
Other gains (losses)			Continuing
(a) Loss on restructuring operations	($20,000)		operations
(b) Gain on sale of machinery	42,000	22,000	
Income from continuing operations before income tax		180,000	
(c) Income tax expense		63,000	
Income from continuing operations		117,000	
Discontinued operations			
Operating income, $60,000, less income tax of $21,000	39,000		Discontinued
Gain on disposal, $10,000, less income tax of $3,500	6,500	45,500	operations
Net income		$ 162,500	
Earnings per common share			
(60,000 shares outstanding)			
Income from continuing operations		$ 1.95	Earnings
Income from discontinued operations		0.76	per share
Net income		$ 2.71	

Continuing Operations

Income from a business's continuing operations helps financial statement users make predictions about the business's future earnings. In the income statement of Exhibit 14–5, the topmost section reports income from continuing operations. This part of the business is expected to continue from period to period. In the absence of other information, we may use this information to predict that Como Technology Inc. will earn income of approximately $117,000 next year.

The continuing operations of Como Technology Inc. include three items deserving explanation:

(a) During 2014, the company had a $20,000 loss on restructuring operations. Restructuring costs include severance pay to laid-off workers, moving expenses for employees transferred to other locations, and environmental cleanup expenses. The restructuring loss is part of continuing operations because Como Technology Inc. is remaining in the same line of business. But the restructuring loss is highlighted as an "other" item (unusual item) on the income statement because its cause—restructuring—falls outside Como's main business endeavour, which is selling electronics products.

(b) Como Technology Inc. had a gain on the sale of machinery ($42,000), which is also outside the company's core business activity. This explains why the gain is reported separately from Como's sales revenue, cost of goods sold, and gross margin.

The gains or losses from *any* unusual or infrequent transactions that are outside a company's core business activity would be disclosed separately on the income statement as part of income from continuing operations. Other examples in addition to those shown in Exhibit 14–5 could include:

- Losses due to lawsuits
- Losses due to employee labour strikes
- Losses due to floods, fire, or other forces of nature

These items are *not* shown net of tax effects.

(c) Income tax expense ($63,000) has been deducted in arriving at income before discontinued operations (i.e., income from continuing operations). The tax corporations pay on their income is a significant expense. The combined federal and provincial income tax rates for corporations varies from time to time, for type and size of company, and from province to province; for corporations not eligible for the small business deduction, the current rates range from about 25 percent to a maximum rate of 38 percent. We will use an income tax rate of 35 percent in our illustrations. This is a reasonable estimate of combined federal and provincial income taxes. The $63,000 income tax expense in Exhibit 14–5 equals the pretax income from continuing operations multiplied by the tax rate ($180,000 \times 0.35 = $63,000).

After continuing operations, an income statement may include gains and losses from discontinued operations.

KEY POINTS

Businesses operate to generate profits; without profits a business will not exist for long. The main source of income for an ongoing business must be from regular, continuing operations, not from sources such as selling off a business segment.

Discontinued Operations

Many corporations engage in several lines of business. For example, The Jim Pattison Group of Vancouver is the third-largest private corporation in Canada and includes a diverse group of businesses. They include companies that sell illuminated signs, wholesale food, and retail automobiles, while others are involved in packaging, media, and periodical distribution, to name just a few. We call each significant part of a company a **segment of the business**.

A company may sell a segment of its business. Such a sale is not a regular source of income because a company cannot keep on selling its segments indefinitely. The sale of a business segment is viewed as a one-time transaction. Financial analysts and potential investors typically do not include income or loss on discontinued operations in their predictions about a company's future income. The discontinued segments will generate no income in the future.

The income statement presents information on the segment that has been disposed of under the heading Discontinued Operations. This section of the income statement is divided into two components:

- Operating income (or loss) from the segment that is disposed of.
- Gain (or loss) on the disposal.

Assume income and gains are taxed at the 35-percent rate. They would be reported as follows:

Discontinued operations	
Operating income $60,000, less income tax, $21,000	$39,000
Gain on disposal, $10,000 less income tax, $3,500	6,500
	$45,500

This presentation appears in Exhibit 14–5 on page 874.

It is necessary to separate discontinued operations into these two components because the company may operate the discontinued segment for part of the year. This is the operating income (or loss) component; it should include the results of operations of the segment from the beginning of the period to the disposal date. There is usually also a gain (or loss) on disposal. Both the operating income (or loss) and the gain (or loss) on disposal are shown net of tax. This is because income tax is such a significant component of continuing operations and discontinued operations that investors and analysts need to know the tax effects. Operating losses and losses on disposal generate tax benefits because they reduce net income and thus reduce the amount of tax that needs to be paid.

If the transactions for discontinued operations have not been completed at the company's year end, the gain (or loss) may have to be estimated. To be conservative, the estimated net loss should be recorded in the accounts at year end while an estimated net gain would not be recognized until it was realized.

It is important that the assets, liabilities, and operations of the segment can be clearly identified as separate from those of other operations of the company. The notes to the financial statements should disclose fully the nature of the discontinued operations and other relevant information about the discontinued operations, such as revenue to the date of discontinuance.

Discontinued operations are common in business. General Motors decided to stop producing the Saturn line of vehicles, and Molson Coors Brewing Company sold part of its interest in Cervejarias Kaiser, a Brazilian brewing company.

Earnings Per Share (EPS)

For many corporations, the final segment of a corporation income statement presents the company's earnings per share. **Earnings per share (EPS)** is the amount of a company's net income per outstanding common share. While ASPE does not require that corporations disclose EPS figures on the income statement or in a note to the financial statements, many corporations do provide this information because investors and financial analysts sometimes use it to assess a corporation's profitability. EPS is also widely reported in the financial press, so it is important to know how it is calculated and how it is used. EPS is a key measure of a business's success. Basic EPS is computed as follows:

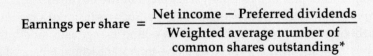

$$\text{Earnings per share} = \frac{\text{Net income} - \text{Preferred dividends}}{\text{Weighted average number of common shares outstanding*}}$$

* How to calculate the *weighted average number of common shares outstanding* is illustrated in the next section. If there is no change in the number of shares outstanding during the period, then use the total number of common shares outstanding.

Just as the corporation lists separately its different sources of income from continuing operations and discontinued operations, it should list separately the EPS figure for income before discontinued operations and net income for the

KEY POINTS

The tax effect of the discontinued segment's operating income (or loss) is not included in income tax expense ($63,000 in Exhibit 14–5 ⓒ); rather, it is added or deducted in the discontinued-operations part of the income statement.

REAL WORLD EXAMPLE

If showing a higher EPS is a good thing, what prevents companies from buying back shares just to make the EPS look better? Nothing really! This is why financial analysis is never done by looking at only one calculation. Prudent investors will look at many different factors when considering where to invest funds.

period to emphasize the significance of discontinued operations to a company's overall results.

Consider the income statement of Como Technology Inc. shown in Exhibit 14–5; in 2014, it had 60,000 common shares outstanding. Income from continuing operations was $117,000 and income from discontinued operations net of tax was $45,500. Como Technology Inc. could present the following EPS information:

Earnings per common share	
Income from continuing operations ($117,000 ÷ 60,000)	$1.95
Income from discontinued operations ($45,500 ÷ 60,000)	0.76
Net income [($117,000 + $45,500) ÷ 60,000]	$2.71

Note that the details of calculations shown above are for illustrative purposes only. They would not appear in formal financial statements.

The income statement user can better understand the sources of the business's EPS amounts when they are presented in this detail.

Weighted Average Number of Common Shares Outstanding Computing EPS is straightforward if the number of common shares outstanding does not change over the entire accounting period. For many corporations, however, this figure varies as the company issues new shares and repurchases its own shares over the course of the year. Consider a corporation that had 100,000 shares outstanding from January through November, then purchased 60,000 of its own shares for cancellation. This company's EPS would be misleadingly high if computed using 40,000 (100,000 − 60,000) shares. To make EPS as meaningful as possible, corporations use the weighted average number of common shares outstanding during the period.

Let's assume the following figures for IMC Communications Corporation. From January through May, 2014, the company had 240,000 common shares outstanding; from June through August, 200,000 shares; and from September through December, 210,000 shares. We compute the weighted average by considering the outstanding shares per month as a fraction of the year:

Number of Common Shares Outstanding		Fraction of Year				Weighted Average Number of Common Shares Outstanding
240,000	×	$5/12$	(January through May)	=		100,000
200,000	×	$3/12$	(June through August)	=		50,000
210,000	×	$4/12$	(September through December)	=		70,000
Weighted average number of common shares outstanding during 2014				=		220,000

LEARNING TIPS

Remember that this is a *weighted* average and not a *simple* average. If you calculated the simple average [(240,000 + 200,000 + 210,000) ÷ 3], you would get an answer of 216,667, which is not weighted. The correct answer is 220,000 as shown at the left because it reflects the fact that there are different amounts of shares held for different lengths of time.

The 220,000 weighted average would be divided into net income to compute the corporation's EPS.

Stock Dividends and Stock Splits The calculation of weighted average number of common shares outstanding becomes complicated when there have been stock dividends or stock splits during the year. For both stock dividends and stock splits, the number of shares outstanding during the year are restated to reflect the stock dividend or stock split *as if it had occurred at the beginning of the year.*

To illustrate, let's extend the IMC Communications Corporation example above by assuming a stock dividend of 10 percent was effective on September 1. The effect of the 10-percent stock dividend is a multiplier of 1.10 for the period January to August to restate the number of outstanding shares as if the stock dividend had occurred at the beginning of the year. The number of outstanding shares for September to December already reflects the 10-percent stock dividend, so the effect is a multiplier of 1.00 for those months. We compute the weighted average by considering the outstanding shares per month as a fraction of the year:

Number of Common Shares Outstanding		Effect of Stock Dividend		Fraction of Year				Weighted Average Number of Common Shares Outstanding
240,000	×	1.10	×	$5/12$	(January through May)		=	110,000
200,000	×	1.10	×	$3/12$	(June through August)		=	55,000
231,000*	×	1.00	×	$4/12$	(September through December)		=	77,000
Weighted average number of common shares outstanding during 2014							=	242,000

* Amount includes the 10-percent stock dividend

The 242,000 weighted average number of common shares outstanding would be divided into net income to compute the corporation's EPS.

To illustrate the results of a stock split, change the IMC Communications Corporation example above by assuming a 2-for-1 stock split on September 1, 2014, instead of the 10-percent stock dividend shown above. The effect of the 2-for-1 stock split is 2.00, to double the number of shares for the period January to August to restate the number of outstanding shares as if the stock split had occurred at the beginning of the year. The number of outstanding shares for September to December already reflects the 2-for-1 stock split, so the effect is 1.00 for those months. Again, we compute the weighted average by considering the outstanding shares per month as a fraction of the year:

Number of Common Shares Outstanding		Effect of Stock Split		Fraction of Year				Weighted Average Number of Common Shares Outstanding
240,000	×	2.00	×	$5/12$	(January through May)		=	200,000
200,000	×	2.00	×	$3/12$	(June through August)		=	100,000
420,000*	×	1.00	×	$4/12$	(September through December)		=	140,000
Weighted average number of common shares outstanding during 2014							=	440,000

* Amount includes the 2-for-1 stock split

The 440,000 weighted average number of common shares outstanding would be divided into net income to compute the corporation's EPS.

Preferred Dividends   Holders of preferred shares have no claim to the business's income beyond the stated preferred dividend. Even though preferred shares have no claims, preferred dividends do affect the EPS figure. Preferred dividends declared in the year are deducted from income to more accurately reflect what is left to be shared by the common shareholders. There is an exception to this rule and that is if there are cumulative preferred shares. For cumulative preferred shares, the annual dividend is deducted in the formula even if it has not been declared.

If Como Technology Ltd. (from Exhibit 14–5) had 10,000 cumulative preferred shares outstanding, each with a $1.50 dividend, the annual preferred dividend would be $15,000 (10,000 × $1.50). The $15,000 would be subtracted from income, resulting in the following EPS computations:

Earnings per common share		
Income from continuing operations	($117,000 − $15,000) ÷ 60,000	$1.70
Income from discontinued operations	$45,500 ÷ 60,000	0.76
Net income	=($162,500 − $15,000) ÷ 60,000	$2.46

KEY POINTS

Dividends in arrears are not used in the EPS calculation. Only current dividends *declared* or the annual amount of cumulative preferred dividends (even if not declared) are deducted from net income.

Dilution   Some corporations make their bonds or preferred shares more attractive to investors by offering conversion privileges, which permit the holder to convert the bond or preferred shares into some specified number of common shares. If in fact the bonds or preferred shares are converted into common shares, then the EPS will be diluted (reduced) because more common shares are divided into net income. Because convertible bonds or convertible preferred shares can be traded for common shares, the common shareholders want to know the amount of the decrease in EPS that would occur if conversion took place. To provide this information, corporations with convertible bonds or preferred shares outstanding present two sets of EPS amounts: EPS based on actual outstanding common shares (basic EPS) and EPS based on outstanding common shares plus the number of additional common shares that would arise from conversion of the convertible bonds and convertible preferred shares into common shares (fully diluted EPS). **Fully diluted EPS** is always lower than basic EPS. The topic of dilution can be very complex and is covered more fully in intermediate accounting texts.

Price-earnings Ratio   EPS is one of the most widely used accounting figures. Many income statement users place top priority on EPS. Also, the market price of a share in a company is related to its EPS. By dividing the market price of a company's share by its EPS, we compute a statistic called the **price-to-earnings ratio** or *price–earnings ratio*. Several websites as well as the business press, such as *The Globe and Mail Report on Business*, report the price–earnings ratios (listed as P/E) daily for hundreds of companies listed on the Toronto Stock Exchange (TSX), the Montréal Exchange, the TSX Venture Exchange, the New York Stock Exchange, and NASDAQ. The price–earnings ratio is explored more fully in Chapter 18.

REAL WORLD EXAMPLE

In the story at the beginning of this chapter, notice that Dollarama quoted two different amounts for earnings per share: basic earnings and diluted earnings. In Note 13 of its January 12, 2012, consolidated financial statements, the company states that the dilution is reported because of "potential common shares that are share options."

✓JUST CHECKING

7. On September 1, 2014, Acme Equipment Corp. sells its division that manufactures mobile homes. The assets are sold at a taxable gain of $1,700,000. The loss from operations for the year up to the date of sale was $960,000. The tax rate is 30 percent. How would you present the loss for the year and the sale of the division on the income statement for the year ended December 31, 2014?

8. The net income of Hart Corp. amounted to $3,750,000 for the year ended December 31, 2014. Hart Corp. had 200,000 $9.00 cumulative preferred shares throughout the year, and 310,000 common shares at the end of the year. At January 1, 2014, Hart Corp. had 270,000 common shares outstanding, and issued 40,000 common shares on April 1. Calculate Hart Corp.'s EPS.

9. Refer to the Hart Corp. data in the previous question. Assume the same details but, in addition, that a 3-for-1 stock split of the common shares occurred on October 1, 2014. Calculate Hart Corp.'s EPS.

Just Checking Solutions appear at the end of this chapter and on MyAccountingLab.

Statement of Retained Earnings

Retained earnings may be a significant portion of a corporation's shareholders' equity. The year's income increases the Retained Earnings balance, and dividends declared decrease it. Retained earnings is so important that some corporations prepare a separate financial statement outlining the major changes in this equity account. The statement of retained earnings for Como Technology Inc. appears in Exhibit 14–6.

> **LO ④**
> How do we prepare a statement of retained earnings and a statement of shareholders' equity?

EXHIBIT **14-6** | Statement of Retained Earnings

COMO TECHNOLOGY INC.	
Statement of Retained Earnings	
For the Year Ended December 31, 2014	
Retained earnings, January 1, 2014	$260,000
Net income for 2014	162,500
	422,500
Dividends for 2014	(42,000)
Retained earnings, December 31, 2014	$380,500

Some companies report income and retained earnings on a single statement. Exhibit 14–7 illustrates how Como Technology Inc. would combine its income statement and its statement of retained earnings.

EXHIBIT **14-7** | Statement of Income and Retained Earnings

COMO TECHNOLOGY INC.		
Statement of Income and Retained Earnings		
For the Year Ended December 31, 2014		
Income statement	Sales revenue	$1,000,000
	Cost of goods sold	480,000
	Gross margin	520,000
	Operating expenses (listed individually)	362,000
Statement of Retained Earnings	Net income for 2014	162,500
	Retained earnings, January 1, 2014	260,000
		422,500
	Dividends for 2014	(42,000)
	Retained earnings, December 31, 2014	$ 380,500
	Earnings per common share (60,000 shares outstanding)	
	Income from continuing operations	$ 1.95
	Income from discontinued operations	0.76
	Net income	$ 2.71

Statement of Shareholders' Equity

REAL WORLD EXAMPLE

Corporations that follow ASPE are not required to prepare the statement of shareholders' equity. Those who follow IFRS must prepare this statement, as discussed further on page 885.

In addition to the balance sheet and income statement, corporations may prepare the **statement of shareholders' equity**, or simply the **statement of equity**, to present changes in all components of equity, much as the statement of owner's equity presents information on changes in the equity of a proprietorship. Sales and repurchases of shares during the year affect contributed capital. The year's income increases the Retained Earnings balance, and dividends decrease it. The statement of shareholders' equity begins with the previous year's shareholders' equity balances and shows the changes that led to the current year's final balances. The statement of shareholders' equity for Como Technology Inc. appears in Exhibit 14–8, with some details added for illustration. Notice that the information from the statement of retained earnings appears in the Retained Earnings column of the statement of shareholders' equity.

EXHIBIT **14–8** | Statement of Shareholders' Equity

COMO TECHNOLOGY INC.
Statement of Shareholders' Equity
For the Year Ended December 31, 2014

	Common Shares	Contributed Surplus— Share Repurchases	Retained Earnings	Total Share- holders' Equity
Balance, December 31, 2013	$360,000	$ 0	$260,000	$620,000
Issuance of shares	100,000			100,000
Net income			162,500	162,500
Cash dividends			(42,000)	(42,000)
Repurchase of common shares	(40,000)	10,000		(30,000)
Balance, December 31, 2014	$420,000	$10,000	$380,500	$810,500

Variations in Reporting Shareholders' Equity

Accountants sometimes report shareholders' equity in ways that differ from our examples. We use a detailed format in this book to help you learn the components of shareholders' equity. Companies assume that investors and creditors understand the details.

An important skill you will learn in this book is how to be comfortable with the information presented in the financial statements of actual companies. In Exhibit 14–9, we present a side-by-side comparison of our teaching format and the format of the Bank of Nova Scotia, taken from its 2011 annual report. Note the following points with respect to the real-world format illustrated in Exhibit 14-9 and also with regard to actual financial statements:

(a) The Bank of Nova Scotia uses the heading Capital Stock. Companies may use Share Capital or other headings instead of Contributed Capital.

(b) Some companies combine all classes of contributed capital into a single line item and provide specifics in the notes to the financial statements. The Bank of Nova Scotia has combined several series of preferred shares in a single line item but does show preferred and common shares separately.

(c) The preferred and common shares are described fully in the notes with respect to shares authorized and issued and outstanding; the information in the balance sheet is limited to a description of the class and total amount for which each of the two classes of shares were issued and outstanding.

(d) Often total shareholders' equity is not specifically labelled.

(e) If this were a statement for a private enterprise following ASPE, the number of *authorized* shares would not need to be disclosed.

EXHIBIT **14–9** | Formats for Reporting Shareholders' Equity***

Textbook Format		Real-World Format	
Shareholders' Equity ($ amounts in millions)		**Shareholders' Equity ($ amounts in millions)**	
Contributed capital		(a) Capital stock	
Preferred shares, unlimited number authorized (e) 175,345,767 issued, outstanding	$ 4,384	Preferred shares (Note 15)*	$ 4,384
Common shares, unlimited number authorized 1,088,972,173 issued, outstanding	8,432	Common shares (Note 16)**	8,432
Retained earnings	24,662	Retained earnings	24,662
Accumulated other comprehensive income (loss) (Note 17)	(4,718)	Accumulated other comprehensive income (loss) (Note 17)	(4,718)
Total shareholders' equity	$32,760	(d)	$32,760

(c) ***Note 15: Preferred Shares (adapted)**
Authorized
An unlimited number of Preferred Shares without nominal or par value.
Issued and fully paid
Preferred shares   175,345,767 shares

**Note 16: Common Shares (adapted)
Authorized
An unlimited number of Common Shares without nominal or par value.
Issued and fully paid
Common shares   1,088,972,173

***ASPE and IFRS suggest the presentation of comparative data; in order to simplify the illustration, data are presented for 2011 only.

WHY IT'S DONE THIS WAY

In this chapter, you were introduced to new features presented on most corporate income statements, specifically the separation of income from continuing and discontinued operations, and earnings-per-share calculations. As we have seen in earlier chapters, the multi-step income statement is designed to communicate useful information to interested users to help them assess the success of the company—this is the *Level 1* objective of the accounting framework described in Chapter 1 (and repeated on the back inside cover of this book). The multi-step income-statement approach is a very useful tool for users for the *Level 2* relevance, and comparability features of the information contained in the statement, as well as the format of the statement.

Users of the financial statements want to assess the future profitability of the company and will use the income statement to achieve that objective. Users are also interested in assessing management's *stewardship* of the company. Stewardship is the concept of how well management uses the company's assets to meet company objectives; company objectives could include earning a profit, serving specific markets, treating employees fairly, minimizing risks that face the company, and providing a good return to shareholders. Conveniently, the corporate multi-step income statement allows both objectives to be achieved. Future profitability can be estimated by studying the income from continuing operations, the ongoing operations that should continue into the future. Reporting unusual or infrequent activities separately on the income statement as part of ongoing operations helps users to adjust their estimates of future profitability even more. Management stewardship may be assessed by examining the composition of the net income or, perhaps, comprehensive income for companies that report under IFRS (see Learning Objective 5). Management is responsible for the "bottom-line" performance of the company, which includes *all* items on the income statement that form the final net income amount, while at the same time meeting the company's other objectives.

The presentation of income from continuing and discontinued operations (and the related earning-per-share amounts) on a multi-step income statement is an example of how the accounting framework influences the type of disclosure typically seen in corporate financial statements.

Accounting for Errors and Changes in Accounting Policy and Circumstances

The consistency principle is an important concept in accounting. But what if situations change and information on financial statements needs to be reported differently? Management might feel a different accounting method would provide better information to investors. Perhaps an error was made. Depending on the reason for the change, there are two ways this should be handled—with either *retrospective* (looking back) or *prospective* (looking forward) treatment.

Errors

What happens when a company makes an error in recording revenues or expenses? Detecting the error in the period in which it occurs allows the company to make a correction before preparing that period's financial statements. But failure to detect the error until a later period means that the business will have reported an incorrect amount of income on its income statement. After the revenue and expense accounts are closed, the Retained Earnings account will absorb the effect of the error, and its balance will be wrong until the error is corrected.

To correct an error, the correcting entry includes a debit or credit to Retained Earnings for the error amount and a debit or credit to the asset or liability account that was misstated.

Assume that Paquette Corporation recorded the closing inventory balance for 2013 as $30,000. When the inventory records were checked, it was discovered that the correct amount was $40,000. This error resulted in overstating 2013 expenses by $10,000 and understating net income by $10,000. The entry to record this error correction in 2014[*] is

Jun. 19	Inventory	10,000	
	Retained Earnings		10,000
	Correction of prior years' error in		
	recording closing inventory in 2013.		

The credit to Retained Earnings adjusts its account balance to reflect the understated income in 2013. If Cost of Goods Sold were credited in 2014 when the correcting entry was recorded, income in 2014 would be overstated. The journal entry properly locates the adjustment in the period prior to 2014 (i.e., to 2013, when the error occurred.) This is an example of **retrospective** treatment because numbers from the prior year are restated to reflect the correction of the error. However, instead of restating prior financial statements, the opening balance of Retained Earnings is adjusted for the error.

The error correction would appear on the statement of retained earnings as shown below, or on the statement of shareholders' equity in the Retained Earnings section (shown in the Summary Problem for Your Review at the end of the chapter):

PAQUETTE CORPORATION Statement of Retained Earnings For the Year Ended December 31, 2014	
Retained earnings, January 1, 2014 as originally reported	$390,000
Adjustment to correct error	
in recording closing inventory in 2013 (see Note XX)	10,000
Retained earnings, January 1, 2014, as adjusted	400,000
Net income for 2014	114,000
	514,000
Dividends for 2014	(41,000)
Retained earnings balance, December 31, 2014	$473,000

---

[*]We disregard the income tax effects to simplify the illustration.

Change in Accounting Policy

A change in accounting policy should be applied *retrospectively*; in other words, prior periods should be restated to reflect the change. This would be done by restating any prior-periods' comparative data provided in the current year's financial statements (not by reprinting the financial statements or annual reports from prior years). In addition, the facts of the restatement should be disclosed in the notes. An example would be a change in amortization method. The effect of the change on prior periods' results would appear as an item on the statement of retained earnings or on the statement of shareholders' equity in the Retained Earnings section, the same way as an error would.

Change in Circumstances

Companies must make estimates about many items on the financial statements, such as the amount of warranties or bad debts, inventory obsolescence, or the useful life of assets for amortization. If these estimates need to change to better reflect a change in circumstances, then the changes are made to the current year and all future financial statements. This **prospective** treatment is in response to new information and is done to make the information more useful. There is no change to past financial statements because the estimates at that time were correct based on what was known at that time.

Restrictions on Retained Earnings

REAL WORLD EXAMPLE

How do restrictions protect creditors? By limiting how much managers can pay as dividends, they guarantee that some equity is left in the company in case it goes out of business. That way, managers who own a company can't sell all the assets and pay themselves a dividend, which leaves the lenders nothing on which to collect the debts.

To ensure that corporations maintain a minimum level of shareholders' equity for the protection of creditors, incorporating acts restrict the amount of its own shares that a corporation may repurchase, and the amount of dividends that can be declared. In addition, companies may voluntarily create reserves, or *appropriations*. Companies report their restrictions in notes to the financial statements.

Appropriations of Retained Earnings

Appropriations are restrictions of retained earnings that are recorded by formal journal entries. A corporation may appropriate—that is, segregate in a separate account—a portion of Retained Earnings for a specific use. For example, the board of directors may appropriate part of Retained Earnings for expanding a manufacturing plant. A debit to Retained Earnings and a credit to a separate account—Retained Earnings Restricted for Plant Expansion—records the appropriation. Appropriated Retained Earnings is normally reported directly above the regular Retained Earnings account, with a footnote where the appropriation is more fully described. *Retained earnings appropriations are rare.* Presentation of this information on the balance sheet may take this form:

Shareholders' Equity		
Total contributed capital		$325,000
Retained earnings:		
Appropriated for plant expansion	$125,000	
Unappropriated	50,000	
Total retained earnings		175,000
Total shareholders' equity		$500,000

Or the retained earnings could be shown with a notation that refers the reader to the notes for more details:

Shareholders' Equity	
Total contributed capital	$325,000
Retained earnings (Note X)	175,000
Total shareholders' equity	$500,000
Note X: The board of directors appropriated part of Retained Earnings to expand a manufacturing plant.	

Limits on Dividends and Share Repurchases   Cash dividends and repurchases of shares require a cash payment. In fact, repurchases of shares are returns of their investment to the shareholders. These outlays decrease assets, so the corporation has fewer resources to pay liabilities. A bank may agree to lend $500,000 only if the borrowing corporation limits dividend payments and repurchases of its shares. A corporation might agree to restrict dividends as a condition for receiving a loan in order to get a lower interest rate.

This type of restriction on the payment of dividends is more often seen, as shown in the following note:

Restriction on Dividends Certain terms of the Company's preferred shares and debt instruments could restrict the Company's ability to declare dividends on preferred and common shares. At year end, such terms did not restrict or alter the company's ability to declare dividends.

✓ JUST CHECKING

10. Complete the following statement of shareholders' equity by calculating the missing amounts a, b, c, and d.

CHECKPOINT INDUSTRIES INC.
Statement of Shareholders' Equity
For the Year Ended April 30, 2014

	Common Shares	Contributed Surplus— Share Repurchases	Retained Earnings	Total Share-holders' Equity
Balance, April 30, 2013	$260,000	$ 0	a.	$360,000
Issuance of shares	100,000			100,000
Net income			62,500	c.
Cash dividends			(22,000)	(22,000)
Repurchase of common shares	(60,000)	b.		(50,000)
Balance, April 30, 2014	$300,000	$10,000	$140,500	d.

11. Identify whether each of the following independent cases is a correction of an error, a change in policy, or a change in estimate:

a. CheckPoint Industries Inc. felt it was better to use the units-of-production method of amortization for its vehicles rather than the straight-line method that had been used so far.

b. CheckPoint Industries Inc. decided that its equipment would last three years longer than it had originally anticipated.

c. During 2014, CheckPoint Industries Inc. discovered that a supplies invoice in the amount of $16,500 had not been recorded in 2013.

12. For each of the situations in the previous question, indicate whether there should be retrospective or prospective changes to the financial statements.

Just Checking Solutions appear at the end of this chapter and on MyAccountingLab.

The Impact of IFRS on the Income Statement and the Statement of Shareholders' Equity

All corporations are governed by Canadian generally accepted accounting principles (GAAP). Private corporations can choose to follow accounting standards for private enterprises (ASPE), which is described in this chapter, or international financial reporting standards (IFRS). Public corporations *must* follow IFRS. ASPE is less complicated and requires fewer disclosures than IFRS because it is assumed that private-corporation shareholders and lenders can get access to the information they need directly from the corporation. Typically, shareholders and lenders cannot get this access to information from large, public corporations. There are a number of differences between the two standards that we will highlight here.

LO ⑤

What is the impact of IFRS on the income statement and the statement of shareholders' equity?

Policy Changes   Companies following IFRS may only change an accounting policy if it meets the criteria of providing more *relevant or reliable* information. This is not explicitly stated this way in ASPE, since ASPE identifies additional possible reasons for management to make an accounting-policy change. When there is a retrospective restatement of information, IFRS requires that a statement of financial position be prepared for the earliest period in which the accounting policy change resulted in a restated balance or a reclassified item. ASPE only requires that the change be reported by restating any prior-periods' comparative data in the current financial statements.

Error Correction   In International Accounting Standard (IAS) 8, IFRS allows a corporation to be exempt from restating financial information retroactively if it is *impractical* to do so. This sort of statement does not appear in Section 1506 of the *CICA Handbook* for ASPE.

Earnings Per Share   One of the main differences in preparing the income statement is that IFRS requires companies to disclose EPS information on the income statement, whereas ASPE does not. However, many private corporations do provide EPS information for current and potential investors. When EPS information is included, it must be shown separately for both basic and diluted amounts, and results from continuing and discontinued operations must be shown separately, even if the results are negative.

No Statement of Retained Earnings   IFRS requires companies to prepare a Statement of Changes in Equity, rather than a Statement of Retained Earnings. The Statement of Changes in Equity is similar to the Statement of Shareholders' Equity described in this chapter.

Statement of Comprehensive Income   Companies have a number of choices for their reporting under IFRS. IFRS requires corporations to report *other comprehensive income*, whereas ASPE does not. IFRS reporters may choose to prepare an income statement and a separate statement of comprehensive income, or combine this information into one statement. Other comprehensive income arises from a number of sources including unrealized gains and losses on certain classes of investment securities due in part to the use of fair value measurement. Exhibit 14–10 shows how the same information can be presented two different ways for the same company. Notice that the amount of income tax is shown separately for each component.

Another difference in an IFRS income statement is that the expenses may be organized by *function*. This alternative presentation is recommended if it more fairly presents the information or if that is how the industry presents the information. Most income statements we have seen in this text are presented by *nature* of the expense.

REAL WORLD EXAMPLE

Expense presentation by *nature* would include depreciation, transportation costs, and advertising whereas by *function* these would be shown on the income statement as administrative costs, distribution costs, and selling costs.

EXHIBIT **14–10**	Examples of a Consolidated Statement of Earnings and Comprehensive Income, and a Statement of Comprehensive Income

Weekee Industries Limited
Statement of Comprehensive Income
For the Years Ended March 31, 2014 and 2013

	2014	2013
Profit before income tax	$799,500	$705,600
Income tax expense	239,850	211,680
Profit from continuing operations	559,650	493,920
Discontinued operations		
Profit (loss) from discontinued operation net of income tax	38,000	
Profit	597,650	493,920
Other comprehensive income		
Foreign currency translation differences		
for foreign operations, net of income tax	8,000	2,000
Net change in fair value of available-for-sale		
financial assets, net of income tax	9,250	7,500
Other comprehensive income for the period, net of income tax	17,250	9,500
Comprehensive income	$614,900	$503,420
		(*Continued*)

Weekee Industries Limited
Consolidated Statement of Earnings and Comprehensive Income
For the Years Ended March 31, 2014 and 2013

	2014	2013
Continuing operations		
Revenue	$1,650,000	$1,400,000
Cost of sales	750,000	600,000
Gross profit	900,000	800,000
Administrative expenses	50,000	45,000
Distribution expenses	30,000	27,000
Research and development expenses	15,000	13,000
Other expenses	5,000	9,000
Results from operating activities	800,000	706,000
Finance income	1,000	800
Finance costs	(1,500)	(1,200)
Net finance costs	(500)	(400)
Profit before income tax	799,500	705,600
Income tax expense	239,850	211,680
Profit from continuing operations	559,650	493,920
Discontinued operation		
Profit (loss) from discontinued operation, net of income tax	38,000	
Profit for the period	597,650	493,920
Other comprehensive income		
Foreign currency translation differences for foreign operations, net of income tax	8,000	2,000
Net change in fair value of available-for-sale financial assets, net of income tax	9,250	7,500
Other comprehensive income for the period, net of income tax	17,250	9,500
Total comprehensive income for the period	$ 614,900	$ 503,420
Earnings per share		
Basic earnings per share	$3.15	$2.58
Earnings per share from continuing operations	$2.87	$2.53

Note: *Earnings per share is presented as part of the income statement if the income statement is separate from the statement of comprehensive income*

✓ JUST CHECKING

13. Companies reporting under IFRS are required to provide two types of information in their financial statements that are not required for companies reporting under ASPE. Describe each type of information and the financial statement on which it is reported.

14. Companies reporting under ASPE, as described in this chapter, sometimes create a Statement of Shareholders' Equity. What is the name of the same statement for companies reporting under IFRS?

15. Prepare a simple statement of comprehensive income for Yoshi Corporation using the following information:

    • For the year ended June 30, 2014
    • Loss for the year is $25,000
    • Gain on equity investments is $60,000
    • Tax rate is 25 percent

Just Checking Solutions appear at the end of this chapter and on MyAccountingLab.

Summary Problem for Your Review

The following information was taken from the ledger of Innisdale Inc. at December 31, 2014:

Loss on sale of discontinued operations	$ 20,000	Selling expenses	$ 78,000
Prior-year error—credit to Retained Earnings	5,000	Common shares, 40,000 shares issued and outstanding	125,000
		Sales revenue	620,000
Gain on sale of property	61,000	Interest expense	30,000
Income tax expense (saving)		Cost of goods sold	380,000
Continuing operations	42,000	Operating income, discontinued operations	30,000
Discontinued operations			
Operating income	10,500	Loss due to lawsuit	11,000
Loss on sale	(7,000)	General expenses	62,000
Total dividends	19,000	Preferred shares, $4.00, cumulative, 1,000 shares issued and outstanding	50,000
Retained earnings, January 1, 2014, as originally reported	108,000		

Required

Sort the ledger items into those that appear on the various statements.

Prepare a single-step income statement first, then a statement of retained earnings, then a statement of shareholders' equity for Innisdale Inc. for the year ended December 31, 2014. Include the EPS presentation and show computations. Assume no changes in the share accounts during the year, and assume a 35-percent tax rate.

SOLUTION

Recall that a single-step income statement shows cost of goods sold as an expense and does not show the calculation for gross profit. In addition, gains and losses are shown as part of income from continuing operations and not as a separate section.

Expenses include all normal operating costs related to the revenue reported. Income tax expense is included here.

Discontinued operations are reported net of income tax of 35 percent.

INNISDALE INC.			
Income Statement			
For the Year Ended December 31, 2014			
Revenue and gains			
Sales revenue			$620,000
Gain on sale of property			61,000
Total revenues and gains			681,000
Expenses and losses			
Cost of goods sold		$380,000	
Selling expenses		78,000	
General expenses		62,000	
Interest expense		30,000	
Loss due to lawsuit		11,000	
Income tax expense		42,000	
Total expenses and losses			603,000
Income from continuing operations			78,000
Discontinued operations (Note A)			
Operating income	$30,000		
Less income tax	(10,500)	19,500	
Loss on sale of discontinued operations	(20,000)		
Less income tax saving	7,000	(13,000)	6,500
Net income			$ 84,500

(Continued)

INNISDALE INC.		*(Continued)*
Earnings per share		
Income from continuing operations		
[($78,000 − $4,000) ÷ 40,000 shares]		$1.85
Income from discontinued operations ($6,500 ÷ 40,000 shares)		0.16
Net income [($84,500 − $4,000) ÷ 40,000 shares]		$2.01

Computations:

$$\text{Earnings per share} = \frac{\text{Net income} - \text{Preferred dividends}}{\text{Weighted average number of common shares outstanding}}$$

Preferred dividends: 1,000 × $4.00 = $4,000

The EPS are calculated by using net income from various parts of the income statement less preferred dividends. Use the common shares and preferred shares information from the data given to calculate preferred dividends and the number of common shares outstanding.

INNISDALE INC.
Statement of Retained Earnings
For the Year Ended December 31, 2014

Retained earnings, January 1, 2014, as originally reported	$108,000
Correction of prior-year error—credit (Note X)	5,000
Retained earnings, January 1, 2014, as adjusted	113,000
Net income for current year	84,500
	197,500
Dividends for 2014	(19,000)
Retained earnings, December 31, 2014	$178,500

Prior-period adjustments must be disclosed in a separate line in the statement of retained earnings.

Given in the list of data.

INNISDALE INC.
Statement of Shareholders' Equity
For the Year Ended December 31, 2014

	Common Shares	Preferred Shares	Retained Earnings	Total Share-holders' Equity
Balance, December 31, 2013	$125,000	$50,000	$108,000	$283,000
Adjustment to correct error			5,000	5,000
Net income			84,500	84,500
Cash dividends			(19,000)	(19,000)
Balance, December 31, 2014	$125,000	$50,000	$178,500	$353,500

The Retained Earnings column of the statement of shareholders' equity contains the same information as the statement of retained earnings created earlier.

Summary

① Learning Objective 1: Account for stock dividends and stock splits

How do we account for stock dividends and stock splits?

- *Stock dividends*, or *share dividends*, are distributions of the corporation's own shares to its shareholders. At the date of declaration, the following journal entry would be made: **Pg. 864**

Retained Earnings	Market value	
Common Stock Dividend Distributable		Market value

- *Stock dividends:*

Retained Earnings ↓	Common Shares ↑	Total Shareholders' Equity is unchanged by a stock dividend.

- *Stock splits* do not change any account balances.
- Stock splits and stock dividends increase the number of shares outstanding and, thus, lower the market price per share.

2 Learning Objective 2: Account for repurchased shares

Why are shares repurchased, and how do we account for them?

- *Repurchased shares* are the corporation's own shares that have been issued and reacquired by the corporation.

Pg. 869

Repurchase at average issue price:		
Common Shares	Number repurchased × Average cost per share	
Cash		Number repurchased × Price paid per share
Repurchase below average issue price:		
Common Shares	Number repurchased × Average cost per share	
Contributed Surplus— Share Repurchase		Difference between Cash and Common Shares amounts
Cash		Number repurchased × Price paid per share
Repurchase above average issue price:		
Common Shares	Number repurchased × Average cost per share	
Contributed Surplus— Share Repurchase	Use up the credit balance in this account first	
Retained Earnings	The amount of any remaining difference (the "plug" amount)	
Cash		Number repurchased × Price paid per share

3 Learning Objective 3: Prepare a detailed corporate income statement

How do we prepare a corporate income statement?

- The corporate *income statement* lists separately the various sources of income— *income from continuing operations* (which includes unusual gains and losses), and *discontinued operations*—as well as related *income tax expense*. The bottom line of the income statement reports *net income* or *net loss* for the period. *Earnings-per-share* figures may also appear on the income statement, or may be calculated by investors.

Pg. 873

- $\text{Earnings per share} = \dfrac{\text{Net income} - \text{Preferred dividends}}{\text{Weighted average number of common shares outstanding}}$

4 Learning Objective 4: Prepare a statement of retained earnings and a statement of shareholders' equity

How do we prepare a statement of retained earnings and a statement of shareholders' equity?

- A corporation must prepare a statement of retained earnings, which reports the changes in the Retained Earnings account, including prior-period adjustments, net income or net loss, and dividends paid. This statement may be combined with the income statement.
- Corporations may prepare a statement of shareholders' equity, which reports the changes in all the shareholders' equity accounts, including sales and repurchases of a corporation's own shares, cash and stock dividends paid, and net income or loss.

Pg. 879

5 Learning Objective 5: Identify the impact on the income statement and statement of shareholders' equity of international financial reporting standards (IFRS)

What is the impact of IFRS on the income statement and statement of shareholders' equity?

- Companies that report under IFRS must present EPS information on their income statement and must report comprehensive income in a statement of comprehensive income.
- Under IFRS, the statement of shareholders' equity is called the statement of changes in equity. No statement of retained earnings is prepared.

Pg. 885

Check Accounting Vocabulary on page 892 for all key terms used in Chapter 14 and the Glossary on page 1246 for all key terms used in the textbook.

MyAccountingLab   DemoDoc covering Stock Splits and Stock Dividends

MyAccountingLab   Student PowerPoint Slides

MyAccountingLab   Audio Chapter Summary

Note: All MyAccountingLab resources can be found in the Chapter Resources section and the Multimedia Library.

SELF-STUDY QUESTIONS

Test your understanding of the chapter by marking the best answer for each of the following questions:

1. A corporation has total shareholders' equity of $100,000, including Retained Earnings of $38,000. The Cash balance is $40,000. The maximum cash dividend the company can declare and pay is (pp. 863–864)
   a. $38,000   c. $30,000
   b. $40,000   d. $100,000

2. A stock dividend, or share dividend, (p. 846)
   a. Decreases shareholders' equity
   b. Decreases assets
   c. Leaves total shareholders' equity unchanged
   d. Does none of the above

3. Acres Ltd. has 10,000 common shares outstanding. The shares were issued at $20.00 per share, and now their market value is $40.00 per share. Acres' board of directors declares and distributes a common stock dividend of one share for every 10 held. Which of the following entries shows the full effect of declaring and distributing the dividend? (pp. 865–866)

   a. Retained Earnings........................ 40,000
         Common Stock Dividend
            Distributable.........................   40,000

   b. Retained Earnings........................ 20,000
         Common Shares.......................   20,000

   c. Retained Earnings........................ 20,000
         Cash...   20,000

   d. Retained Earnings........................ 40,000
         Common Shares.......................   40,000

4. Lang Real Estate Investment Corporation declared and distributed a 50 percent stock dividend. Which of the following stock splits would have the same effect on the number of Lang shares outstanding? (p. 867)
   a. 2 for 1   c. 4 for 3
   b. 3 for 2   d. 5 for 4

5. Deer Lake Outfitters Ltd. purchased 10,000 of its common shares that had been issued at $1.50 per share, paying $7.00 per share. This transaction (p. 869)
   a. Has no effect on company assets
   b. Has no effect on shareholders' equity
   c. Decreases shareholders' equity by $15,000
   d. Decreases shareholders' equity by $70,000

6. A restriction of retained earnings (p. 846)
   a. Has no effect on total retained earnings
   b. Reduces retained earnings available for the declaration of dividends
   c. Is usually reported by a note
   d. Does all of the above

7. Which of the following items is not reported on the income statement? (p. 873)
   a. Issue price of shares
   b. Unusual gains and losses
   c. Income tax expense
   d. Earnings per share

8. The income statement item that is likely to be most useful for predicting income from year to year is (pp. 874–875)
   a. Unusual items
   b. Discontinued operations
   c. Income from continuing operations
   d. Net income

9. In computing earnings per share (EPS), dividends on cumulative preferred shares are (p. 876)
   a. Added because they represent earnings to the preferred shareholders
   b. Subtracted because they represent earnings to the preferred shareholders
   c. Ignored because they do not pertain to the common shares
   d. Reported separately on the income statement

10. A corporation accidentally overlooked an accrual of property tax expense at December 31, 2013. Accountants for the company detect the error early in 2014 before the expense is paid. The entry to record this correction in 2014 for a prior year's error is *(pp. 883–884)*

   a. Retained Earnings XXX
         Property Tax Expense   XXX

   b. Property Tax Expense XXX
         Property Tax Payable   XXX

   c. Retained Earnings XXX
         Property Tax Payable   XXX

   d. Property Tax Payable XXX
         Property Tax Expense   XXX

Answers to Self-Study Questions

1.a 2.c 3.d 4.b 5.d 6.d 7.a 8.c 9.b 10.c

ACCOUNTING VOCABULARY

Appropriations Restriction of retained earnings that is recorded by a formal journal entry *(p. 884)*.

Consolidation A decrease in the number of shares outstanding by a fixed ratio. Also called a *reverse split* *(p. 867)*.

Earnings per share (EPS) The amount of a company's net income per outstanding common share *(p. 876)*.

Fully diluted EPS Earnings per share calculated using the number of outstanding common shares plus the number of additional common shares that would arise from conversion of convertible bonds and convertible preferred shares into common shares *(p. 879)*.

Memorandum entry A journal entry without debits and credits *(p. 867)*.

Price-to-earnings ratio (or price-earnings ratio, or P/E) The market price of a share divided by its earnings per share (EPS) *(p. 879)*.

Prospective In the future. For example, changes in accounting estimates are reflected in future financial statements, *not* in past financial statements *(p. 884)*.

Repurchase of own shares A corporation purchases its own shares that it issued previously *(p. 869)*.

Retrospective In the past. For example, changes in accounting policies are reflected in past financial-statement figures as if those policies had always been in place *(p. 883)*.

Reverse split Another name for a consolidation *(p. 867)*.

Segment of the business A significant part of a company *(p. 875)*.

Share dividend Another name for a stock dividend *(p. 864)*.

Stock dividend A proportional distribution by a corporation of its own shares to its shareholders. Also called a *share dividend* *(p. 864)*.

Stock split An increase in the number of authorized and outstanding shares coupled with a proportionate reduction in the book value of each share *(p. 867)*.

Statement of equity Another name for statement of shareholders' equity *(p. 880)*.

Statement of shareholders' equity Presents changes in all components of equity. Also called *statement of equity* *(p. 880)*.

Treasury shares When a corporation repurchases its own shares and holds the shares in its treasury for resale *(p. 869)*.

SIMILAR ACCOUNTING TERMS

Consolidation	Reverse split
Contributed capital	Share capital; Capital stock
Income Statement	Statement of Earnings
Price-to-earnings ratio	Price-earnings ratio; P/E ratio
Shareholders' equity	Stockholders' equity (U.S. term)
Statement of shareholders' equity	Statement of equity; Statement of changes in equity
Stock dividend	Share dividend

Assignment Material

QUESTIONS

1. Identify the two main parts of shareholders' equity and explain how they differ.

2. Identify the account debited and the account credited from the last closing entry a corporation makes each year. What is the purpose of this entry?

3. Hoc Automotive Ltd. reported a Cash balance of $2 million and a Retained Earnings balance of $12 million. Explain how Hoc Automotive Ltd. can have so much more retained earnings than cash. In your answer, identify the nature of retained earnings and state how it ties to cash.

4. Give two reasons for a corporation to distribute a stock dividend.

5. A friend of yours receives a stock dividend on an investment. She believes stock dividends are the same as cash dividends. Explain why the two are not the same.

6. Grek Rentals Inc. declares a stock dividend on June 21 and reports Stock Dividend Payable as a liability on the June 30 balance sheet. Is this correct? Give your reason.

7. What value is normally assigned to shares issued as a stock dividend?

8. Explain the similarity and difference between a 100-percent stock dividend and a 2-for-1 stock split to the corporation issuing the stock dividend and the stock split.

9. Give three reasons why a corporation may repurchase its own shares.

10. What effect does the repurchase and cancellation of common shares have on the (a) assets, (b) authorized shares, and (c) issued and outstanding shares of the corporation?

11. Are there any cases when a company does not cancel its repurchased shares? If so, what are they?

12. Incorporating legislation frequently has a prohibition on a corporation's purchasing its own shares in certain circumstances. What are those circumstances? Why does the prohibition exist?

13. Why do creditors wish to restrict a corporation's payment of cash dividends and repurchases of the corporation's shares?

14. Why is it necessary to use the *weighted* average number of common shares in the earnings per share calculation rather than the average number of common shares?

15. What is the most widely used of all accounting statistics? What is the price–earnings ratio? Compute the price–earnings ratio for a company with earnings per common share of $3.00 and a market price of $21.00 per common share.

16. What is the earnings per share of Phukett Realty Ltd., which had net income of $48,750 and a weighted average number of common shares of 15,000?

17. What are two ways to report a retained earnings restriction? Which way is more common?

18. Identify two items on the income statement that generate income tax expense. What is an income tax saving, and how does it arise?

19. Why is it important for a corporation to report income from continuing operations separately from discontinued operations?

20. Give four examples of gains and losses that are unusual and reported separately in the continuing operations section of the income statement.

21. For errors made in prior periods, what account do all corrections affect? On what financial statement are these corrections reported?

MyAccountingLab

Make the grade with MyAccountingLab: The Starters, Exercises, and Problems marked in red can be found on MyAccountingLab. You can practise them as often as you want, and most feature step-by-step guided instructions to help you find the right answer.

STARTERS

Interpreting retained earnings
①

Starter 14–1 The retained earnings account has the following transactions in 2014 shown in a T-account format.

Retained Earnings

	180,000
20,000	X
	220,000

1. What does X represent?
2. How much is X?
3. What does the amount of $20,000 represent?

Recording a stock dividend
①

1. Dr Retained Earnings $36,000

Starter 14–2 Rad Roadsters Ltd. has 10,000 common shares outstanding. Rad distributes a 20 percent stock dividend when the market value of its shares is $18.00 per share.

1. Journalize Rad's declaration of the stock dividend on September 30, 2014, and the distribution of the stock dividend on October 30, 2014. Explanations are not required.
2. What is the overall effect of the stock dividend on Rad's total assets? On total shareholders' equity?

Comparing and contrasting cash dividends and stock dividends
①

Starter 14–3 Compare and contrast the accounting for cash dividends and stock dividends. In the space provided, insert either "Cash dividends," "Stock dividends," or "Both cash dividends and stock dividends" to complete each of the following statements:

1. _____ decrease Retained Earnings.
2. _____ have no effect on a liability.
3. _____ increase contributed capital by the same amount that they decrease Retained Earnings.
4. _____ decrease both total assets and total shareholders' equity, resulting in a decrease in the size of the company.

Accounting for a stock split
①

1. Total shareholders' equity $332,000

Starter 14–4 Jurgen's Farms Inc. recently reported the following shareholders' equity:

Common shares,	
250,000 shares authorized, 55,000 shares issued and outstanding	$121,500
Retained earnings	210,500
Total shareholders' equity	$332,000

Suppose Jurgen's Farms split its common shares 2 for 1 in order to decrease the market price of its shares. The company's shares were trading at $83.00 immediately before the split.

1. Prepare the shareholders' equity section of Jurgen's Farms Inc.'s balance sheet after the stock split.
2. Which account balances changed after the stock split? Which account balances were unchanged?

Stock dividend and repurchase
① ②

Starter 14–5 Anderson Products Inc. issued 100,000 common shares at $10.00 per share. Later, when the market price was $15.00 per share, the company distributed a 10 percent stock dividend. Then Anderson Products Inc. repurchased 500 shares at $20.00 per share. What is the final balance in the Common Shares account?

Starter 14–6 Boris' Dollar Store Inc. repurchased 1,000 common shares paying cash of $12.00 per share on April 16, 2014. The shares were originally issued for $5.00 per share.

Journalize the transaction. An explanation is not required.

Accounting for the repurchase of common shares
②

Starter 14–7 BLT Corporation's agreement with its bank lender restricts BLT's dividend payments. Why would a bank lender restrict a corporation's dividend payments and share repurchases?

Interpreting a restriction of retained earnings
③

Starter 14–8 List the major parts of a multi-step corporate income statement for Star Soccer Trainers Inc. for the year ended December 31, 2014. Include all the major parts of the income statement, starting with net sales revenue and ending with net income (net loss). Remember to separate continuing operations from discontinued operations. You may ignore dollar amounts and earnings per share.

Preparing a corporate income statement
③

Starter 14–9 Answer these questions about a corporate income statement:

1. How do you measure gross margin?
2. What is the title of those items that are unusual, infrequent, and over which management has no influence or control?
3. Which income number is the best predictor of future net income?
4. What is the "bottom line"?
5. What does *EPS* abbreviate?

Explaining the items on a complex corporate income statement
③

Starter 14–10 Gala Fruit Corp's accounting records include the following items, listed in no particular order, at December 31, 2014.

Preparing a corporate income statement
③

Net income $18,000

Other gains (losses)	$(12,500)	Net sales revenue	$100,000
Cost of goods sold	35,000	Operating expenses	30,000
Gain on discontinued		Accounts receivable	9,500
operations	7,500		

Income tax of 40 percent applies to all items.

Prepare Gala Fruit Corp.'s multi-step income statement for the year ended December 31, 2014. Omit earnings per share.

Starter 14–11 Return to the Gala Fruit Corp. data in Starter 14–10. Gala Fruit had 10,000 common shares outstanding on January 1, 2014. Gala Fruit declared and paid preferred dividends of $1,500 during 2014. In addition, Gala Fruit paid a 20 percent common stock dividend on June 30.

Show how Gala Fruit Corp. reported EPS data on its 2014 income statement.

Reporting earnings per share
③

EPS for net income $1.38

Starter 14–12 Figero Inc. has $350,000 of income in 2014. During that same time, it declared preferred dividends in the amount of $13,000. The following activities affecting common shares occurred during the year:

Calculating earnings-per-share
③

Jan.	1	120,000 common shares were outstanding
Aug.	1	Sold 35,000 common shares
Sept.	1	Issued a 10 percent common stock dividend

1. Calculate the weighted-average number of common shares outstanding during the year.
2. Calculate earnings per share. Round to the nearest cent.

Starter 14–13 Oak Research Inc. (ORI) ended 2013 with Retained Earnings of $37,500. During 2014, ORI earned net income of $40,000 and declared dividends of $15,000. Also during 2014, ORI got a $12,000 tax refund from Canada Revenue Agency. A tax audit revealed that ORI in error paid too much income tax in 2012.

Reporting the correction of a prior-period error
④

Retained Earnings, Dec. 31, 2014, $74,500

Prepare ORI's statement of retained earnings for the year ended December 31, 2014, to report the correction of the prior-period error.

Starter 14–14 Return to the Oak Research Inc. (ORI) data in Starter 14–13. ORI ended 2013 with $20,000 in common shares and $15,000 in $0.50 preferred shares. No shares were sold or repurchased during 2014. Create ORI's statement of shareholders' equity for the year ended December 31, 2014.

Starter 14–15 For each of the following situations, indicate whether there is a change in estimate, or a change of policy, or an error. Then indicate if the correction needs to be applied retroactively (change past statement information) or prospectively (only future statements will be affected).

	Change in estimate	Change in policy	Error	Retroactive statements	Prospective statements
A switch from the weighted-average method of inventory to the FIFO method.					
Management decided the welding equipment will last twelve years and not the original estimate of ten years.					
Missing expense invoices were found after the financial statements were finalized.					

EXERCISES

Exercise 14–1

Journalizing a stock dividend
and reporting shareholders'
equity
①

2. Total shareholders' equity
$680,000

The shareholders' equity for King Paving Inc. on June 30, 2014 (end of the company's fiscal year), follows:

Common shares, 800,000 shares authorized, 80,000 shares issued and outstanding	$300,000
Retained earnings	380,000
Total shareholders' equity	$680,000

On August 8, 2014, the market price of King Paving Inc.'s common shares was $12.00 per share and the company declared a 20 percent stock dividend. King Paving Inc. issued the dividend shares on August 31, 2014.

Required

1. Journalize the declaration and distribution of the stock dividend.
2. Prepare the shareholders' equity section of the balance sheet after the stock dividend distribution.

Exercise 14–2

Poco Travel Ltd. is authorized to issue 500,000 common shares. The company issued 70,000 shares at $7.50 per share. On June 10, 2014, when the Retained Earnings balance was $360,000, Poco Travel Ltd. declared a 10 percent stock dividend, using the market value of $4.00 per share. It distributed the stock dividend on July 20, 2014. On August 5, 2014, Poco Travel Ltd. declared a $0.45 per share cash dividend, which it paid on September 15, 2014.

Required

1. Journalize the declaration and distribution of the stock dividend.
2. Journalize the declaration and payment of the cash dividend.
3. Prepare the shareholders' equity section of the balance sheet after both dividends.

Exercise 14–3

Halifax Metal Products Ltd. had the following shareholders' equity at October 31, 2014:

Reporting shareholders' equity after a stock split

Total shareholders' equity
$600,000

Common shares, unlimited shares authorized, 60,000 shares issued and outstanding	$150,000
Retained earnings	450,000
Total shareholders' equity	$600,000

On November 14, 2014, Halifax Metal Products Ltd. split its common shares 2 for 1. Make the memorandum entry to record the stock split, and prepare the shareholders' equity section of the balance sheet immediately after the split.

Exercise 14–4

Examine Halifax Metal Products Ltd.'s shareholders' equity section for October 31, 2014, in Exercise 14–3. Suppose Halifax Metal Products Ltd. consolidated its common shares 1 for 2 (a reverse stock split) in order to increase the market price of its shares. The company's shares were trading at $6.00 immediately before the reverse split. Make the memorandum entry to record the share consolidation, and prepare the shareholders' equity section of Halifax Metal Products Ltd.'s balance sheet after the share consolidation. What would you expect the market price to be, approximately, after the reverse split?

Accounting for a reverse stock split (consolidation)

Total shareholders' equity
$600,000

Exercise 14–5

Usurp Corp., an Internet service provider, has prospered during the past seven years, and recently the company's share price has shot up to $244.00. Usurp's management wishes to decrease the share price to the range of $116.00 to $124.00, which will be attractive to more investors. Should the company issue a 100-percent stock dividend or split the stock? Why? If you propose a stock split, state the split ratio that will accomplish the company's objective. Show your computations.

Using a stock split or a stock dividend to decrease the market price of a share

Exercise 14–6

Identify the effects of these transactions on shareholders' equity. Has shareholders' equity increased, decreased, or remained the same? Each transaction is independent.

a. A 10-percent stock dividend. Before the dividend, 400,000 common shares were outstanding; market value was $7.50 at the time of the dividend.

b. A 2-for-1 stock split. Prior to the split, 50,000 common shares were outstanding.

c. Repurchase of 5,000 common shares at $7.00 per share. The average issue price of these shares was $5.00.

d. Sale of 2,000 repurchased common shares for $6.50 per share.

Effects of share issuance, dividends, and share repurchase transactions

Exercise 14–7

Journalize the following transactions that Apex Technologies Ltd. conducted during 2014:

Feb. 19	Issued 10,000 common shares at $15.00 per share.
Apr. 24	Repurchased 2,000 common shares at $13.00 per share. The average issue price of the shares was $14.00.
Jun. 30	Repurchased 2,000 common shares at $19.00 per share. The average issue price of the shares was $14.00.

Journalizing share repurchase transactions

Exercise 14–8

Debon Ltd. had the following shareholders' equity on March 26, 2014:

Common shares, unlimited shares authorized, 140,000 shares issued and outstanding	$420,000
Retained earnings	475,000
Total shareholders' equity	$895,000

On May 3, 2014, the company repurchased and cancelled 5,000 common shares at $3.50 per share.

1. Journalize this transaction and prepare the shareholders' equity section of the balance sheet at June 30, 2014.

2. How many common shares are outstanding after the share repurchase?

Journalizing repurchase of company shares and reporting shareholders' equity

1. Total shareholders' equity
$877,500

Exercise 14–9

Accounting for the repurchase of preferred shares

(b) Reduced by $4,384 million

Study Exhibit 14–9 on page 882. Suppose the Bank of Nova Scotia repurchased its preferred shares. What would be the amount of the reduction of the company's total shareholders' equity if the cost to repurchase the preferred shares was (a) $5,000 million? (b) $4,384 million? (c) $4,000 million?

Exercise 14–10

Reporting a retained earnings restriction

②

a. Total shareholders' equity $587,500

The agreement under which Karset Transport Ltd. issued its long-term debt requires the restriction of $150,000 of the company's Retained Earnings balance. Total Retained Earnings is $337,500, and total contributed capital is $250,000.

Required Show how to report shareholders' equity (including retained earnings) on Karset Transport Ltd.'s balance sheet at December 31, 2014, assuming:

a. Karset Transport Ltd. discloses the restriction in a note. Write the note.

b. Karset Transport Ltd. appropriates retained earnings in the amount of the restriction and includes no note in its statements.

Exercise 14–11

Excel Spreadsheet Template

Preparing a multiple-step income statement

③

Net income $24,500

The ledger of Doe Plastics Inc. contains the following information for operations for the year ended September 30, 2014.

Sales revenue	$350,000	Income tax expense—gain on	
Operating expenses		discontinued operations......	$ 8,000
(excluding income tax)	67,500	Other loss..................................	22,500
Cost of goods sold	230,000	Income tax expense—	
Gain on discontinued		operating income..................	10,000
operations	12,500		

Required Prepare a multiple-step income statement for the year ended September 30, 2014. Omit earnings per share. Was 2014 a good year or a bad year for Doe Plastics Inc.? Explain your answer in terms of the outlook for 2015.

Exercise 14–12

Computing earnings per share

③

EPS = $0.78

BMO Solutions Inc. earned net income of $84,000 in 2014. The ledger reveals the following figures:

Preferred shares, $1.50, 4,000 shares issued and outstanding	$ 50,000
Common shares, unlimited shares authorized, 100,000 shares issued	300,000

Required Compute BMO Solutions Inc.'s EPS for 2014, assuming no changes in the share accounts during the year.

Exercise 14–13

Computing earnings per share

③

EPS for net income $0.40

LeDuc Construction Ltd. had 60,000 common shares and 20,000 $0.75 preferred shares outstanding on December 31, 2013. On April 30, 2014, the company issued 6,000 additional common shares and split the common shares 2 for 1 on December 1, 2014. There were no other share issuances and no share repurchases during the year ended December 31, 2014. Income for the year from continuing operations was $70,000, and loss on discontinued operations (net of income tax) was $4,000.

Required Compute LeDuc Construction Ltd.'s EPS amounts for the year ended December 31, 2014.

Exercise 14–14

Pacific Hotels Inc., a large hotel chain, had Retained Earnings of $250.0 million at the beginning of 2014. The company showed these figures at December 31, 2014:

	($ millions)
Net income	$75.0
Cash dividends—preferred	1.5
common	44.5
Debit to retained earnings due to repurchase of preferred shares	4.0

Required Prepare the statement of retained earnings for Pacific Hotels Inc. for the year ended December 31, 2014.

Excel Spreadsheet Template

Preparing a statement of retained earnings

Retained earnings, Dec. 31, 2014, $275.0 million

Exercise 14–15

Lankin Concrete Products Ltd. reported the correction of an error made in the year ended December 31, 2014. An inventory error caused net income of the prior year to be overstated by $50,000. Retained Earnings at January 1, 2014, as previously reported, stood at $2,408,000. Net income for the year ended December 31, 2014, was $448,000, and dividends were $61,000.

Required Prepare the company's statement of retained earnings for the year ended December 31, 2014.

Excel Spreadsheet Template

Preparing a statement of retained earnings with a correction of a prior-period error

Retained earnings, Dec. 31, 2014, $2,745,000

Exercise 14–16

For the year ended December 31, 2013, Evans Inc. reported the following shareholders' equity:

Common shares, 400,000 shares authorized, 140,000 shares issued and outstanding	$1,400,000
Retained earnings	672,000
	$2,072,000

During 2014, Evans Inc. completed these transactions and events (listed in chronological order):

a. Declared and issued a 10-percent stock dividend. At the time, Evans Inc.'s common shares were quoted at a market price of $11.50 per share.

b. Sold 1,000 common shares for $12.50 per share.

c. Sold 1,000 common shares to employees at $10.00 per share.

d. Net income for the year was $397,500.

e. Declared and paid cash dividends of $140,000.

Required Prepare Evans Inc.'s statement of shareholders' equity for 2014.

Preparing a statement of shareholders' equity

Total shareholders' equity, Dec. 31, 2014, $2,352,000

SERIAL EXERCISE

This exercise continues the Kerr Consulting Corporation situation from Exercise 13–16 of Chapter 13. If you did not complete Exercise 13–16, you can still complete Exercise 14–17 as it is presented.

Exercise 14–17

To raise cash for future expansion, Alex Kerr incorporated his proprietorship and created Kerr Consulting Corporation. Kerr Consulting Corporation is authorized to issue an unlimited number of common shares and 50,000 $2.00 preferred shares. On February 1, 2014, Alex Kerr purchased 20,000 common shares for his proprietorship equity of $36,364 to maintain control of the company and issued 1,000 of the preferred shares for $50.00 per share.

Journalizing share sale and repurchase transactions

2. Common Shares ending balance, $47,643

In March 2014, Kerr Consulting Corporation has the following transactions related to its common shares:

Mar. 3   The company sold 1,000 of its common shares for $10.00 per share to a small number of people who believed in the company's potential for profit.

20   The company repurchased 100 of its common shares for $12.00 per share from a shareholder who was having financial difficulties.

30   The company sold 100 shares for $15.00 per share.

Required

1. Journalize the entries related to the transactions.
2. Calculate the ending balance in the Common Shares account.

CHALLENGE EXERCISE

Exercise 14–18

Recording a stock dividend and preparing a statement of retained earnings
① ④

2. Retained Earnings, Dec. 31, 2014, $4,200,000

Tillay Environmental Products Inc. (TEPI) began 2014 with 1.6 million common shares issued and outstanding for $4.0 million. Beginning Retained Earnings was $4.5 million. On February 26, 2014, TEPI issued 100,000 common shares at $3.50 per share. On November 16, 2014, when the market price was $5.00 per share, the board of directors declared a 10 percent stock dividend, which was paid on December 20, 2014. Net income for the year was $550,000.

Required

1. Make the journal entries for the issuance of shares for cash and for the 10 percent stock dividend.
2. Prepare the company's statement of retained earnings for the year ended December 31, 2014.

Exercise 14–19

Analyzing stock split and share repurchase transactions
②

6. b. Common Shares outstanding, 13,000

Scopis Ltd. reported its shareholders' equity as shown below.

Shareholders' Equity	
Preferred shares, $1.00	
Authorized: 10,000 shares	
Issued and outstanding: None	$ 0
Common shares	
Authorized: 100,000 shares	
Issued and outstanding: 14,000 shares	70,000
Retained earnings	84,000
	$154,000

1. What was the average issue price per common share?
2. Journalize the issuance of 1,200 common shares at $8.00 per share. Use Scopis Ltd.'s account titles.
3. After question 2, how many Scopis Ltd. common shares are now outstanding?
4. How many common shares would be outstanding after Scopis Ltd. splits its common shares (computed in question 3) 3 for 1?
5. Using Scopis Ltd. account titles, journalize the declaration of a 10 percent stock dividend when the market price of Scopis Ltd.'s common shares is $6.00 per share. Use the shares outstanding in question 3.

6. Ignore the prior transactions and return to the Scopis Ltd. shareholders' equity information in question 1, which shows 14,000 common shares issued.

   a. Journalize the following share repurchase transactions by Scopis Ltd., assuming they occur in the order given.
      i. Scopis Ltd. repurchases 500 of its own shares at $16.00 per share.
      ii. Scopis Ltd. repurchases 500 of its own shares at $4.00 per share.
   b. How many Scopis Ltd. common shares would be outstanding after the transactions in part a take place?

BEYOND THE NUMBERS

Beyond the Numbers 14–1

The following accounting issues have arisen at Tri-City Computers Corp.:

Reporting special items
②③

1. An investor noted that the market price of shares seemed to decline after the date of record for a cash dividend. Why do you think that would be the case?

2. Corporations sometimes repurchase their own shares. When asked why, Tri-City Computers Corp.'s management responded that the shares were undervalued. What advantage would Tri-City Computers Corp. gain by repurchasing its own shares under these circumstances?

3. Tri-City Computers Corp. earned a significant profit in the year ended June 30, 2014, because land that it held was expropriated for a low-rental housing project. The company proposes to treat the sale of land to the government as operating revenue. Why do you think Tri-City Computers Corp. is proposing such treatment? Is this treatment appropriate?

ETHICAL ISSUE

Gregor Gold Mine Ltd. is a gold mine in Ontario. In February 2014, company geologists discovered a new vein of gold-bearing ore that tripled the company's reserves. Prior to disclosing the new vein to the public, top managers of the company quietly bought most of the outstanding Gregor Gold Mine Ltd. shares for themselves personally. After the discovery announcement, Gregor Gold Mine Ltd.'s share price increased from $4.00 to $30.00.

Required

1. Did Gregor Gold Mine Ltd. managers behave ethically? Explain your answer.
2. Who was helped and who was harmed by management's action?

PROBLEMS (GROUP A)

MyAccountingLab

Problem 14–1A

Assume Frelix Construction Ltd. completed the following selected transactions during the year 2014:

Journalizing shareholders' equity transactions
①②

Apr.	19	Declared a cash dividend on the $8.50 preferred shares (3,000 shares outstanding). Declared a $2.00 per share dividend on the 100,000 common shares outstanding. The date of record was May 2, and the payment date was May 25.
May	25	Paid the cash dividends.
Jun.	7	Split the company's 100,000 common shares 2 for 1; one new common share was issued for each old share held.
Jul.	29	Declared a 5-percent stock dividend on the common shares to holders of record on August 22, with distribution set for September 9. The market value was $36.00 per common share.
Sept.	9	Issued the stock dividend shares.
Nov.	26	Repurchased 5,000 of the company's own common shares at $40.00 per share. They had an average issue price of $28.00 per share.

Required Record the transactions in the general journal.

Excel Spreadsheet
Template

Journalizing dividend and
share-repurchase transactions,
reporting shareholders' equity,
and calculating earnings
per share
① ② ③

2. Total shareholders' equity
$435,000

Problem 14–2A

The balance sheet of Gaitree Ltd. at December 31, 2013, reported 250,000 common shares authorized, with 75,000 shares issued and a Common Shares balance of $187,500. Retained Earnings had a credit balance of $150,000. During 2014, the company completed the following selected transactions:

Mar. 15   Repurchased 10,000 of the company's own common shares at $2.75 per share.

Apr. 29   Declared a 5-percent stock dividend on the 65,000 outstanding common shares to holders of record on May 2, with distribution set for May 16. The market value of Gaitree Ltd. common shares was $6.00 per share.

May 16   Issued the stock dividend shares.

Dec. 19   Split the common shares 2 for 1 by issuing one new share for each old share held on December 30, 2014.

    31   Earned net income of $125,000 during the year.

Required

1. Record the transactions in the general journal. Explanations are not required.
2. Prepare the shareholders' equity section of the balance sheet at December 31, 2014.
3. Calculate the average issue price per share on December 31, 2014. Assume no shares were issued or repurchased after December 19, 2014.

Problem 14–3A

Skiptrace Software Inc. is positioned ideally in the manufacturing and distribution sectors. It is the only company providing highly developed inventory tracking software. The company does a brisk business with companies such as Home Hardware and Roots. Skiptrace Software Inc.'s success has made the company a prime target for a takeover. Against the wishes of Skiptrace Software Inc.'s board of directors, an investment group is attempting to buy 55 percent of Skiptrace Software Inc.'s outstanding shares. Board members are convinced that the investment group would sell off the most desirable pieces of the business and leave little of value.

At the most recent board meeting, several suggestions were advanced to fight off the hostile takeover bid. One suggestion was to increase the shares outstanding by splitting the company's shares two for one.

Required As a significant shareholder of Skiptrace Software Inc., write a short memo to the board advising how a stock split would affect the investor group's attempt to take over Skiptrace Software Inc. Include in your memo a discussion of the effect that the stock split would have on assets, liabilities, and total shareholders' equity; that is, the split's effect on the size of the corporation.

Problem 14–4A

Journalizing dividend and
stock-repurchase transactions;
reporting shareholders' equity;
calculating earnings per share
① ② ③ ④

2. Total shareholders' equity
$1,041,250

The balance sheet of Augen Vision Ltd. at December 31, 2013, reported the following shareholders' equity:

Common shares, 200,000 shares authorized, 50,000 shares issued and outstanding	$ 750,000
Retained earnings	250,000
Total shareholders' equity	$1,000,000

During 2014, Augen Vision Ltd. completed the following selected transactions:

Apr. 29   Declared a 10-percent stock dividend on the common shares. The market value of Augen Vision Ltd.'s common shares was $15.00 per share. The record date was May 20, with distribution set for June 3.

Jun. 3   Issued the stock dividend shares.

Jul.	29	Repurchased 5,000 of the company's own common shares at $13.50 per share; average issue price was $14.91.
Nov.	1	Sold 1,000 common shares for $16.50 per share.
	25	Declared a $0.25 per share dividend on the common shares outstanding. The date of record was December 16, and the payment date was January 6, 2015.
Dec.	31	Closed the $105,000 credit balance of Income Summary to Retained Earnings.

Required

1. Record the transactions in the general journal.
2. Prepare a statement of shareholders' equity at December 31, 2014.
3. Calculate earnings per share at December 31, 2014. (Hint: Use issue dates in your calculations.)

Problem 14–5A

The information below was taken from the ledger and other records of Stahl Metalworks Corp. at September 30, 2014.

Preparing a single-step income statement
① ② ④
Net income $21,450

Cost of goods sold	$157,500	Preferred shares, $1.00,	
Loss on sale of property	17,500	15,000 shares authorized,	
Sales returns	3,500	7,500 shares issued	
Income tax expense (saving)		and outstanding	$ 93,750
Continuing operations	13,500	Retained earnings,	
Discontinued segment:		October 1, 2013	30,500
Operating loss	(1,800)	Selling expenses	50,750
Gain on sale	600	Common shares, 50,000 shares	
Gain on sale of discontinued		authorized, issued	
segment	1,750	and outstanding	165,000
Interest expense	4,250	Sales revenue	315,000
General expenses	42,000	Dividends	11,000
Interest revenue	1,750	Operating loss,	
		discontinued segment	5,250
		Loss on insurance settlement	4,000

Required Prepare a single-step income statement, including earnings per share, for Stahl Metalworks Corp. for the fiscal year ended September 30, 2014. Evaluate income for the year ended September 30, 2014, in terms of the outlook for 2015. Assume 2014 was a typical year and that Stahl Metalworks Corp.'s managers hoped to earn income from continuing operations equal to 10 percent of net sales.

Problem 14–6A

Muriel Thomas, accountant for Duchlorol Ltd., was injured in a hiking accident. Another employee prepared the income statement shown on the next page for the fiscal year ended December 31, 2014.

Preparing a corrected combined statement of income and retained earnings
③ ④
Net income $44,100

The individual amounts listed on the income statement are correct. However, some accounts are reported incorrectly, and others do not belong on the income statement at all. Also, income tax (30 percent) has not been applied to all appropriate figures. Duchlorol Ltd. issued 64,000 common shares in 2009 and has not issued or repurchased common shares since that time. The Retained Earnings balance, as originally reported at December 31, 2013, was $242,500. There were no preferred shares outstanding at December 31, 2014.

DUCHLOROL LTD.
Income Statement
2014

Revenue and gains		
Sales		$295,000
Proceeds from sale of preferred shares		66,000
Gain on repurchase of preferred shares		
(issued for $76,000; repurchased for $66,500)		9,500
Total revenues and gains		370,500
Expenses and losses		
Cost of goods sold	$83,000	
Selling expenses	54,000	
General expenses	58,500	
Sales returns	7,500	
Dividends	5,500	
Sales discounts	4,500	
Income tax expense	29,200	
Total expenses and losses		242,200
Income from operations		128,300
Other gains and losses		
Loss on sale of discontinued operations	$ (2,500)	
Flood loss	(15,000)	
Operating loss on discontinued segment	(7,000)	
Correction for 2013 due to an inventory error	(2,000)	
Total other losses		(26,500)
Net income		$101,800
Earnings per share		$ 1.59

Required Prepare a corrected combined statement of income and retained earnings for the year ended December 31, 2014; include earnings per share. Prepare the income statement portion in single-step format.

Problem 14–7A

Computing earnings per
share and reporting
a retained
earnings restriction

1. EPS for net income $1.14

The capital structure of Renault Marketing Inc. at December 31, 2013, included 50,000 $0.50 preferred shares and 74,000 common shares. The 50,000 preferred shares were issued in 2006. Common shares outstanding during 2014 were 74,000 January through April and 80,000 May through September. A 20-percent stock dividend was paid on October 1. Income from continuing operations during 2014 was $122,000. The company discontinued a segment of the business at a gain (net of tax) of $9,250. The Renault Marketing Inc. board of directors restricts $125,000 of retained earnings for contingencies.

Required

1. Compute Renault Marketing Inc.'s earnings per share. Start with income from continuing operations. Income of $122,000 is net of income tax.

2. Show two ways of reporting Renault Marketing Inc.'s retained earnings restriction. Retained Earnings at December 31, 2013, was $145,500, and total contributed capital at December 31, 2014, is $375,000. The company declared dividends of $49,500 in 2014.

Problem 14–8A

Timpano Communication Inc. had the following shareholders' equity on January 1, 2014:

Accounting for stock dividends, stock splits, share transactions, and the statement of shareholders' equity
① ② ④
2. Total shareholders' equity $1,169,750

Preferred shares, $2.00, cumulative (1 year in arrears),	
liquidation price of $20, 100,000 shares authorized,	
15,000 shares issued and outstanding	$240,000
Common shares, unlimited number of shares	
authorized, 25,000 shares issued and outstanding	200,000
Total contributed capital	440,000
Retained earnings	512,000
Total shareholders' equity	$952,000

The following transactions took place during 2014:

Jan.	14	Declared a $90,000 cash dividend, payable on March 1 to the shareholders of record on February 1. Indicate the amount payable to each class of shareholder.
Feb.	28	Issued 10,000 common shares for $6.00 per share.
Mar.	1	Paid the cash dividend declared on January 14.
Apr.	1	Declared a 10 percent stock dividend on the common shares, distributable on May 2 to the shareholders of record on April 15. The market value of the shares was $6.40 per share.
May	2	Distributed the stock dividend declared on April 1.
Jul.	4	Repurchased 3,000 of the company's own common shares at $7.00 per share.
Sept.	2	Issued 2,500 common shares for $7.50 per share.
Nov.	2	Split the common shares 2 for 1.
Dec.	31	Reported net income of $250,000. Closed the Income Summary account.

Required

1. Record the transactions in the general journal. Explanations are not required.
2. Prepare the statement of shareholders' equity for the year ended December 31, 2014.

Problem 14–9A

ArtnMotion Inc. specializes in truck tires and had the following shareholders' equity on January 1, 2014:

Accounting for stock dividends, stock splits, and errors from a prior period; preparing a combined statement of income and retained earnings; calculating earnings per share
① ③ ④
2. Net income $730,600

Preferred shares, $2.50, convertible to common on	
a 2-for-1 basis, 100,000 shares authorized,	
50,000 shares issued and outstanding	$1,500,000
Common shares, unlimited number of shares	
authorized, 150,000 shares issued and outstanding	1,500,000
Total contributed capital	3,000,000
Retained earnings	1,200,000
Total shareholders' equity	$4,200,000

The following information is available for the year ending December 31, 2014:

Feb.	1	Declared a cash dividend of $275,000, payable on March 1 to the shareholders of record on February 15. Indicate the amount payable to each class of shareholder.
Mar.	1	Paid the cash dividend declared on February 1.
May	2	Declared a 20-percent stock dividend on the common shares, distributable on July 4 to the shareholders of record on June 15. The market value of the shares was $11.00 per share.

Jul.	4	Distributed the common shares dividend declared on May 2.

Aug. 8   The company discovered that amortization expense recorded in 2012 was understated in error by $30,000. (Ignore any tax consequences.)

Dec. 31   ArtnMotion Inc.'s records show the following:

Sales for the year	$3,150,000
Cost of goods sold	1,290,000
Operating expenses	792,000
Income from discontinued operations	132,000
Loss on sale of discontinued operations	76,000

Close the Income Summary account, assuming the company pays taxes at the rate of 35 percent.

Required

1. Record the transactions in the general journal. Explanations are not required.
2. Prepare a combined statement of income and retained earnings for the year ended December 31, 2014. Include earnings-per-share information. For purposes of the earnings-per-share calculation, the weighted average number of common shares is 180,000.

PROBLEMS (GROUP B)   MyAccountingLab

Problem 14–1B

Journalizing shareholders' equity transactions

CNZ Corporation Inc. completed the following selected transactions during 2014:

Feb. 4   Declared a cash dividend on the 30,000 $1.40 preferred shares. Declared a $0.20 per share cash dividend on the 40,000 common shares outstanding.

   The date of record was February 15, and the payment date was February 18.

   18   Paid the cash dividends.

Apr. 18   Declared a 15 percent stock dividend on the common shares to holders of record on April 29, with distribution set for May 31. The market value of the common shares was $14.00 per share.

May 31   Issued the stock dividend shares.

Jun. 17   Repurchased 3,000 shares of the company's own common shares at $11.00 per share; average issue price was $8.00 per share.

Nov. 14   Issued 1,000 common shares for $9.00 per share.

Required Record the transactions in the general journal.

Excel Spreadsheet Template

Journalizing dividend and share-repurchase transactions, reporting shareholders' equity, and calculating earnings per share

Problem 14–2B

The balance sheet of Investtech Inc. at December 31, 2013, reported 2,000,000 common shares authorized with 250,000 shares issued at an average price of $4.00 each. Retained Earnings had a balance of $700,000. During 2014, the company completed the following selected transactions:

Feb. 15   Repurchased 20,000 of the company's own common shares at $4.00 per share.

Mar. 8   Sold 8,000 common shares for $4.25 per share.

Sept. 28   Declared a 5-percent stock dividend on the 238,000 outstanding common shares to holders of record on October 15, with distribution set for October 31. The market value of Investtech Inc. common shares was $4.50 per share.

Oct. 31   Issued the stock dividend shares.

Nov. 5   Consolidated the common shares 1 for 2 (reverse split); one new common share was issued for every two existing shares held. Prior to the split, the corporation had 249,900 shares issued and outstanding.

Dec. 31   Earned net income of $230,000 during the year.

Required

1. Record the transactions in the general journal. Explanations are not required.
2. Prepare the shareholders' equity section of the balance sheet at December 31, 2014.
3. Calculate the average issue price per common share on December 31, 2014.

Problem 14–3B

Fundybay Corporation is positioned ideally in its industry. Located in Nova Scotia, Fundybay Corporation is the only company with a reliable record for its locally managed transport company. The company does a brisk business with local major corporations. Fundybay Corporation's recent success has made the company a prime target for a take-over. An investment group from Halifax is attempting to buy 51 percent of the company's outstanding shares against the wishes of Fundybay Corporation's board of directors. Board members are convinced that the Halifax investors would sell off the most desirable pieces of the business and leave little of value.

Repurchasing shares to fight off a takeover of the corporation

At the most recent board meeting, several suggestions were advanced to fight off the hostile takeover bid. The suggestion with the most promise is to repurchase and cancel a huge quantity of shares. Fundybay Corporation has the cash to carry out this plan.

Required

1. As a significant shareholder of Fundybay Corporation, write a memorandum to explain to the board how the repurchase and cancellation of shares might make it more difficult for the Halifax group to take over Fundybay Corporation. Include in your memo a discussion of the effect that repurchasing shares would have on shares outstanding and on the size of the corporation.
2. Suppose Fundybay Corporation management is successful in fighting off the takeover bid and later issues shares at prices greater than the purchase price. Explain what effect the sale of these shares will have on assets, shareholders' equity, and net income.

Problem 14–4B

The balance sheet of Collingwood International Inc. at December 31, 2013, presented the following shareholders' equity:

Journalizing dividends and stock-repurchase transactions; reporting shareholders' equity ①②③④

Contributed capital	
Common shares, 2,000,000 shares authorized, 500,000 shares issued and outstanding	$3,000,000
Retained earnings	820,000
Total shareholders' equity	$3,820,000

During 2014, Collingwood International Inc. completed the following selected transactions:

Mar. 29	Declared a 10 percent stock dividend on the common shares. The market value of Collingwood International Inc. common shares was $5.00 per share. The record date was April 29, with distribution set for May 29.
May 29	Issued the stock dividend shares.
Jul. 30	Repurchased 30,000 of the company's own common shares at $5.00 per share; average issue price was $5.91.
Oct. 4	Sold 20,000 common shares for $7.50 per share.
Dec. 27	Declared a $0.20 per share dividend on the common shares outstanding. The date of record was January 17, 2015, and the payment date was January 31, 2015.
31	Closed the $650,000 net income to Retained Earnings.

Required

1. Record the transactions in the general journal.
2. Prepare the statement of shareholders' equity for the year ended December 31, 2014.
3. Calculate earnings per share at December 31, 2014. (Hint: Use issue dates in your calculations.)

Problem 14–5B

Preparing a single-step income statement ④

The information below was taken from the ledger and other records of Make a Statement Inc. at September 30, 2014.

General expenses.....................	$220,000	Sales revenue	$1,000,000
Loss on sale of		Operating income, discontinued	
discontinued segment	18,000	segment......................................	8,000
Cost of goods sold.................	570,000	Loss on sale of property,	
Income tax expense (saving)		plant, and equipment	5,000
Continuing operations......	44,000	Dividends on preferred	
Discontinued segment:		shares	12,500
Operating income..........	2,000	Preferred shares, $0.50, cumulative,	
Loss on sale	(6,000)	50,000 shares authorized,	
Interest expense.....................	27,000	25,000 shares issued	
Gain on settlement of		and outstanding	350,000
lawsuit	27,000	Dividends on common	
Sales returns............................	23,000	shares	25,000
Contributed surplus from		Retained earnings,	
repurchase of preferred		October 1, 2013	197,000
shares	18,000	Selling expenses...............................	33,000
Sales discounts........................	7,000	Common shares,	
		unlimited shares authorized,	
		40,000 shares issued	
		and outstanding	433,000

Required Prepare a single-step income statement, including earnings per share, for Make a Statement Inc. for the fiscal year ended September 30, 2014. Evaluate income for the year ended September 30, 2014, in terms of the outlook for 2015. Assume 2014 was a typical year and that Make a Statement's managers hoped to earn income from continuing operations equal to 12 percent of net sales.

Problem 14–6B

Preparing a corrected combined statement of income and retained earnings ③④

Thomas Wong, accountant for APB Bikes Ltd., was injured in a biking accident. Another employee prepared the income statement shown on the next page for the fiscal year ended September 30, 2014.

The individual amounts listed on the income statement are correct. However, some accounts are reported incorrectly, and others do not belong on the income statement at all. Also, income tax (25 percent) has not been applied to all appropriate figures. APB Bikes Ltd. issued 30,000 common shares in 2009 and has not issued or repurchased common shares since that date. The Retained Earnings balance, as originally reported at September 30, 2013, was $660,000. There were no preferred shares outstanding at September 30, 2014.

APB BIKES LTD.

Income Statement

September 30, 2014

Revenues and gains		
Sales		$1,000,000
Gain on repurchase of preferred shares		
(issued for $60,000; repurchased for $48,000)		12,000
Total revenues and gains		1,012,000
Expenses and losses		
Cost of goods sold	$478,000	
Selling expenses	133,000	
General expenses	60,000	
Sales returns	13,000	
Correction of an error from a prior period—		
understated income tax for 2013 due to error	10,000	
Dividends	14,000	
Sales discounts	18,000	
Income tax expense	98,700	
Total expenses and losses		824,700
Income from operations		187,300
Other gains and losses		
Operating income on discontinued segment	16,000	
Loss on sale of discontinued operations	(32,000)	
Total other gains		(16,000)
Net income		$ 171,300
Earnings per share		$ 5.71

Required Prepare a corrected combined statement of income and retained earnings for fiscal year 2014; include earnings per share. Prepare the income statement portion in single-step format.

Problem 14–7B

The capital structure of Redding Design Ltd. at December 31, 2013, included 15,000 $1 preferred shares and 420,000 common shares. Common shares outstanding during 2014 were 330,000 in January through March; 348,000 during April; 385,000 May through September; and 420,000 during October through December. Income from continuing operations during 2014 was $446,000. The company discontinued a segment of the business at a gain of $61,500. The board of directors of Redding Design Ltd. has restricted $82,500 of retained earnings for expansion of the company's office facilities.

Computing earnings per share and reporting a retained earnings restriction
③

Required

1. Compute Redding Design Ltd.'s earnings per share. Start with income from continuing operations. Income and loss amounts are net of income tax.

2. Show two ways of reporting Redding Design Ltd.'s retained earnings restriction. Retained Earnings at December 31, 2013, was $172,000, and total contributed capital at December 31, 2014, is $575,000. Redding Design Ltd. declared cash dividends of $250,000 during 2014.

Orillia Outfitters Ltd. had the following shareholders' equity on January 1, 2014:

Preferred shares, $0.75, cumulative (1 year in arrears), liquidation price of $5.00, 50,000 shares authorized, 15,000 shares issued and outstanding	$150,000
Common shares, unlimited number of shares authorized, 25,000 shares issued and outstanding	125,000
Total contributed capital	275,000
Retained earnings	220,000
Total shareholders' equity	$495,000

The following transactions took place during 2014:

Jan. 28 Declared a $25,000 cash dividend, payable on March 1 to the shareholders of record on February 15. Indicate the amount payable to each class of shareholder.

Feb. 25 Issued 10,000 common shares for $7.00 per share.

Mar. 1 Paid the cash dividend declared on January 28.

Apr. 4 Declared a 10-percent stock dividend on the common shares, distributable on May 15 to the shareholders of record on April 15. The market value of the shares was $8.00 per share.

May 15 Distributed the stock dividend declared on April 4.

Jul. 6 Repurchased 10,000 of the company's own common shares at $8.50 per share.

Sept. 3 Issued 5,000 common shares for $8.50 per share.

Nov. 2 Split the common shares 2 for 1.

Dec. 31 Reported net income of $100,000. Closed the Income Summary account.

Required

1. Record the transactions in the general journal. Explanations are not required.
2. Prepare the statement of shareholders' equity for the year ended December 31, 2014.

Red Deer Hardware Ltd. had the following shareholders' equity on January 1, 2014:

Preferred shares, $0.50 cumulative, convertible to common on a 2-for-1 basis, 50,000 shares authorized, 20,000 shares issued and outstanding	$ 55,000
Common shares, unlimited number of shares authorized, 50,000 shares issued and outstanding	62,500
Total contributed capital	117,500
Retained earnings	110,000
Total shareholders' equity	$227,500

The following information is available for the year ending December 31, 2014:

Mar. 7 Declared a cash dividend of $12,500, payable on April 1 to the shareholders of record on March 15. Indicate the amount payable to each class of shareholder.

Apr. 1 Paid the cash dividend declared on March 7.

Jun. 6 Declared a 5-percent stock dividend on the common shares, distributable on August 5 to the shareholders of record on July 4. The market value of the shares was $1.50 per share.

Aug. 5 Distributed the common shares dividend declared on June 6.

Sept. 15   Received notification from Canada Revenue Agency that Red Deer Hardware Ltd. had made an error in filing 2011 taxes. The reassessment showed that the company had reported and overpaid $4,000 in taxes.

Dec. 31   Red Deer Hardware Ltd.'s records show the following:

Sales for the year	$212,500
Cost of goods sold	95,000
Operating expenses	65,000
Income from discontinued operations	4,000
Loss on sale of discontinued operations	(2,500)

Close the Income Summary account, assuming the income tax on all types of income is 40 percent.

Required

1. Record the transactions in the general journal. Explanations are not required.
2. Prepare a combined multi-step statement of income and retained earnings for the year ended December 31, 2014. Include earnings-per-share information.

CHALLENGE PROBLEM

Problem 14–1C

Assume Watawa Inc., a private corporation with a small number of shareholders, had issued 20,000 common shares at incorporation at a price of $22.00. The book value per share was $34.00 at the most recent year end. The company has been paying an annual dividend of $1.56 per share.

Recently, the company had offered to repurchase 3,000 shares at $28.00 per share.

You and a friend bought 100 shares each when the shares were issued. Your friend wonders whether she should sell her shares back to Watawa Inc. since the company was offering 27 percent more than she had paid.

Required   Analyze the information provided to help your friend decide whether or not she should sell her shares back to the company.

Explaining the effects of a share repurchase

Extending Your Knowledge

DECISION PROBLEM

Fraser Valley Technologies Inc. had the following shareholders' equity on December 31, 2014:

Common shares, 200,000 shares issued and outstanding	$2,000,000
Retained earnings	1,200,000
Total shareholders' equity	$3,200,000

Analyzing cash dividends and stock dividends

2. 2012 dividends $20,000; 2014 dividends $16,500

In the past, Fraser Valley Technologies Inc. has paid an annual cash dividend of $2.00 per share. In 2013, despite a large Retained Earnings balance, the board of directors wished to conserve cash for expansion and did not pay a cash dividend but distributed a 10 percent stock dividend. During 2014, the company's cash position improved, so the board declared and paid a cash dividend of $1.50 per share.

Suppose you own 10,000 Fraser Valley Technologies Inc. common shares, acquired January 2, 2012. The market price was $25.00 per share before any of the above dividends.

Required

1. How did the stock dividend affect your proportionate ownership in the company? Explain.

2. What amount of cash dividends did you receive in 2012? What amount of cash dividends did you receive in 2014? Would you expect the dividend per share to remain unchanged?

3. Immediately after the stock dividend was distributed, the market value of Fraser Valley Technologies Inc. shares decreased from $25.00 per share to $22.72 per share. Does this represent a loss to you? Explain.

4. Suppose Fraser Valley Technologies Inc. announces at the time of the stock dividend that the company will continue to pay the annual $2.00 cash dividend per share, even after the stock dividend. Would you expect the market price of the shares to decrease to $22.72 per share as in Requirement 3 above? Explain.

FINANCIAL STATEMENT CASES

Financial Statement Case 1

Corporate income statement and earnings per share
③ ④ ⑤

Use the Gildan Activewear Inc. financial statements in that appear in Appendix A at the end of this book and on MyAccountingLab to answer the following questions.

1. Which income statement format—single-step or multi-step—does Gildan's consolidated statement of income more closely resemble?

2. Does Gildan present a statement of comprehensive income that is separate from the income statement or combined with it?

3. Gildan's basic earnings per share at October 2, 2011, was $1.97 per share. For purposes of this calculation, what was the weighted average number of shares outstanding?

Financial Statement Case 2

Understanding the financial statements, and the effects of reporting under IFRS
② ③ ④ ⑤

Use the Rainmaker Entertainment Inc. 2011 financial statements that appear on MyAccountingLab to answer the following questions.

1. Rainmaker's 2011 financial statements reveal that the company had some adjustments to the share-capital balance as a result of the change to reporting under IFRS. How much was this change? How do you know?

2. Earnings had a restatement in 2010 because of the change to reporting under IFRS. Briefly explain the reconciliation.

3. Did the company pay dividends in 2011? If so, how much were they?

IFRS MINI-CASE

Preparing financial statements under IFRS
③ ④ ⑤

Golden Goods Ltd is a Canadian importer that does business around the word. To obtain credit to do business in other countries, it has to present its financial statements to suppliers who assess the statements and decide whether to extend credit to Golden. Because of this, Golden prepares its financial statements using IFRS.

Your task as an employee of Golden Goods Ltd. is to complete two key financial statements.

Required

1. Calculate the missing amounts to complete the Golden Goods Ltd. income statement. Show your calculations.

10.

CHECKPOINT INDUSTRIES INC.

Statement of Shareholders' Equity

For the Year Ended April 30, 2014

	Common Shares	Contributed Surplus— Share Repurchases	Retained Earnings	Total Share-holders' Equity
Balance, April 30, 2013	$260,000	$ 0	$100,000 (a)	$360,000
Issuance of shares	100,000			100,000
Net income			62,500	62,500 (b)
Cash dividends			(22,000)	(22,000)
Repurchase of common shares	(60,000)	10,000 (c)		(50,000)
Balance, April 30, 2014	$300,000	$10,000	$140,500	$450,500 (d)

11. a. Policy
   b. Estimate
   c. Error

12. a. Retrospective
   b. Prospective
   c. Retrospective

13. Companies reporting under IFRS must present earnings per share (EPS) information on the income statement. They must also report other comprehensive income on the Statement of Comprehensive Income.

14. Companies reporting under IFRS must prepare a Statement of Changes in Equity.

15.

Yoshi Corporation

Statement of Comprehensive Income

For the Year Ended June 30, 2014

Loss	$(25,000)
Gain on equity investment, net of $15,000 income tax	45,000
Comprehensive income	$ 20,000

15 Long-Term Liabilities

KEY QUESTIONS		LEARNING OBJECTIVES
What are bonds?	1	Define bonds payable and the types of bonds
How do we account for the sale of a bond?	2	Determine the price of a bond, and account for basic bond transactions
How do we allocate a bond discount or premium over the life of a bond?	3	Amortize a bond discount and premium by the straight-line amortization method and the effective-interest amortization method
How do we account for changes in a bond issue?	4	Account for retirement and conversion of bonds
How do we decide whether to issue debt versus equity?	5	Show the advantages and disadvantages of borrowing
How do we account for long-term notes?	6	Account for long-term notes payable
How do we account for leases?	7	Account for operating leases and for assets acquired through a capital lease
How does IFRS affect long-term liabilities?	8	Identify the effects on long-term liabilities of international financial reporting standards (IFRS)

CHAPTER 15 APPENDIX

How do we find the future value of an investment?	A1	Compute the future value of an investment
How do we find the present value of an investment?	A2	Compute the present value of a single future amount and the present value of an annuity

McDonald's Corporation, with its headquarters in Oak Brook, Illinois, is the world's largest restaurant chain with total revenues of over $27 billion in 2011. In 2012, McDonald's intends to spend about $1.45 billion to remodel about 2,400 stores while opening 1,300 restaurants to give it about 35,000 locations worldwide.

How do companies like McDonald's finance the remodelling of their restaurants and the opening of new locations? McDonald's could issue more shares and use the proceeds to remodel and expand. It might also borrow from financial institutions and other investors by issuing bonds. Many companies prefer to issue bonds because it doesn't dilute the voting shares of the company, and it locks in principal and interest payments, which allows a company like McDonald's to manage its cash flow. Using debt to fund company growth is a double-edged sword, however. When the economy is buoyant and things are going well, it is a good strategy because your payments are set and once they are covered, profits earned stay with the company and its shareholders. However, when the economy is performing poorly, interest payments must still be paid, even if earnings decline, which could cause financial distress and even lead to bankruptcy.

In May 2012, McDonald's issued $400 million of 1.875 percent, seven-year bonds and $500 million of 0.75 percent, three-year notes to finance the remodeling and expansion described above. Even with the uncertainty in the world economy, investors regard McDonald's as a sound, steady investment and are willing to receive a lower interest rate on the bonds in exchange for this security. While this bond issue gives the company its highest level of debt in the past five years, the interest rates it must pay to these new bondholders are much lower than the rates on bonds maturing during 2012 (6.25 percent notes

①	②	③	④	⑤
Define bonds payable and the types of bonds	Determine the price of a bond, and account for basic bond transactions	Amortize a bond discount and premium by the straight-line amortization method and the effective-interest amortization method	Account for retirement and conversion of bonds	Show the advantages and disadvantages of borrowing
What are bonds? page 919	*How do we account for the sale of a bond? page 921*	*How do we allocate a bond discount or premium over the life of a bond? page 928*	*How do we account for changes in a bond issue? page 938*	*How do we decide whether to issue debt versus equity? page 940*
Bonds: An Introduction, page 919	Issuing Bonds to Borrow Money, page 924	Amortization of a Bond Discount and a Bond Premium, page 928	Retirement of Bonds, page 938	Advantages and Disadvantages of Issuing Bonds versus Shares, page 940
		Reporting Liabilities and Bonds Payable, page 932	Convertible Bonds and Notes, page 939	
		Adjusting Entries for Interest Expense, page 935		

⑥	⑦	⑧	A1	A2
Account for long-term notes payable	Account for operating leases and for assets acquired through a capital lease	Identify the effects on long-term liabilities of international financial reporting standards (IFRS)	Compute the future value of an investment	Compute the present value of a single future amount and the present value of an annuity
How do we account for long-term notes? page 942	*How do we account for leases? page 943*	*How does IFRS affect long-term liabilities? page 947*	*How do we find the future value of an investment? page 976*	*How do we find the present value of an investment? page 980*
Mortgages and Other Long-Term Liabilities, page 942	Lease Liabilities, page 943	The Effects on Long-Term Liabilities of International Financial Reporting Standards (IFRS), page 947	Future Value, page 976	Present Value, page 980

MyAccountingLab
- Chapter 15: DemoDoc covering Bond Transactions
- Chapter 15: Student PowerPoint Slides
- Chapter 15: Audio Chapter Summary

All MyAccountingLab resources can be found in the Chapter Resources section and the Multimedia Library.

The **Summary** for Chapter 15 appears on page 950.
Accounting Vocabulary with definitions appears on page 953.

in July and 3.25 percent bonds in December). Analysts considered this replacement of higher-interest-rate bonds with lower-interest-rate bonds a wise decision by McDonald's.

This chapter discusses long-term liabilities in general and bonds in great detail. Corporate bonds are a very common form of financing, and it is important to understand not only how to account for them but also how they can be beneficial to companies.

Sources: Charles Mead, McDonald's Bonds Tie Higher-Rate IBM Record: Corporate Finance," May 24, 2012, as cited at http://www.bloomberg.com/news/2012-05-24/mcdonald-s-bonds-tie-higher-rated-ibm-record-corporate-finance.html. Also McDonald's Corporation Annual Report 2011, page 25.

This chapter

discusses the third way to finance a company—borrowing money on long-term liabilities. Recall from Chapter 4 that **long-term liabilities** are debts due to be paid in more than a year or more than one of the entity's operating cycles if an operating cycle is greater than one year. Examples include bonds and debentures payable, long-term notes payable, and lease liabilities. The chapter appendix provides background on the valuation of long-term liabilities.

Before launching into bonds payable, let's compare bonds with shares, which were covered in Chapters 13 and 14.

KEY POINTS

The three ways to finance a company are through contributed capital (selling shares), profitable operations (retained earnings), and borrowing money (long-term liabilities).

Shares	Bonds
1. Shares represent *ownership* (equity) of the corporation. Each shareholder is an *owner*.	1. Bonds represent a *debt* (liability) of the corporation. Each bondholder is a *creditor*.
2. The corporation is *not* obligated to repay the amount invested by the shareholders.	2. The corporation *must* repay the bonds at maturity.
3. The corporation may or may not pay dividends on the shares.	3. The corporation *must* pay interest on the bonds.
4. Dividends are *not* an expense and are not tax deductible by the corporation.	4. Interest is a tax-deductible expense of the corporation.

Bonds: An Introduction

Large companies, such as McDonald's, Canadian National Railway Company (CN), and WestJet, cannot borrow billions from a single lender because no lender will risk lending that much money to a single company. Even for smaller companies, it may be impossible to borrow all they need from a bank.

How, then, do large corporations borrow a huge amount? They may issue bonds to the public. A **bond** is a formal arrangement between the issuer of the bond and the holder of the bond. The bondholder (the person or company that buys the bond) lends a fixed amount of money to the issuer. The issuer promises to pay the fixed amount at some future time and to pay regular payments of interest to the bondholder over the life of the bond. The details of the formal arrangement are contained in the **bond indenture**. A bond is a debt of the company that issued the bond. **Bonds payable** are groups of notes payable issued to multiple lenders, called bondholders. TELUS Corporation, the parent company of TELUS Communications Inc., can borrow large amounts from thousands of individual investors, each investor buying a modest amount of TELUS Corporation bonds.

Purchasers of bonds may receive a bond certificate, which shows the name of the company that borrowed the money, exactly like a note payable. Today, transactions are electronic, thereby reducing the need for paper shares or certificates. The certificate also states the **principal value**, which is the amount that the company has borrowed from the bondholder. The bond's principal amount is also called the bond's **maturity value, par value**, or **face value**. The issuing company must pay each bondholder the principal amount at a specific future date, called the **maturity date**, which also appears on the certificate. In Chapter 11, we saw how to account for short-term notes payable. There is a lot of similarity between accounting for short-term notes payable and long-term notes payable.

— LO ① —
What are bonds?

REAL WORLD EXAMPLE

Banks and other lenders diversify their risk by lending relatively small amounts to numerous customers. That way, if a borrower cannot repay, the lender is not devastated.

Bondholders lend their money to earn interest. The bond certificate states the **coupon rate**, which is the interest rate that the issuer will pay the bondholder and the dates that the interest payments are due (generally twice a year). Some bond certificates name the bondholder (the investor). Exhibit 15–1 shows a bond certificate issued by XYZ Corporation (with legal details in the middle omitted).

Review these bond fundamentals in Exhibit 15–1.

- Principal value (also called maturity value, face, or par value)—the amount the borrower must pay back to the bondholders at maturity.
- Maturity date—the date on which the borrower must pay the principal amount to the lender.
- Stated interest rate—the annual rate of interest that the borrower pays the lender.

EXHIBIT 15–1 | Bond Certificate

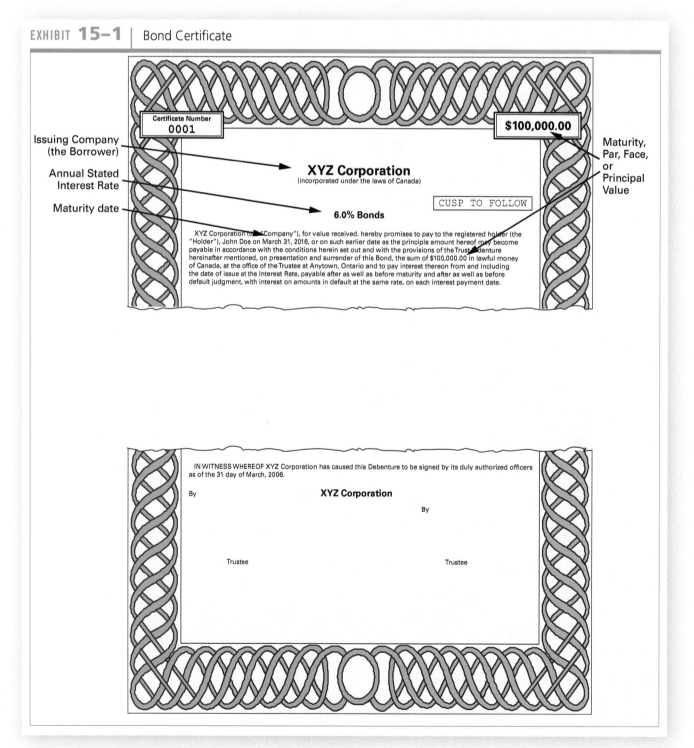

Types of Bonds

There are various types of bonds, including the following:

- **Term bonds** all mature at the same time.
- **Serial bonds** mature in installments at regular intervals. For example, a $500,000, five-year serial bond may mature in $100,000 annual installments over a five-year period.
- **Secured bonds** give the bondholder the right to take specified assets of the issuer (called collateral) if the issuer *defaults*, that is, fails to pay principal or interest. A **mortgage** is an example of a secured bond. Details of the collateral must be provided in the notes to the financial statements.
- **Debentures** are unsecured bonds backed only by the good faith of the issuer. The bond shown in Exhibit 15–1 is a debenture because there are no rights to specific assets given in the first paragraph on the bond.
- **Bearer bonds** are bonds payable to the person that has possession of them. They are also called **unregistered bonds**.

The discussion in this chapter will generally refer to bonds, since secured bonds and debentures (unsecured bonds) are treated essentially the same way for accounting purposes.

REAL WORLD EXAMPLE

A home mortgage is a special type of mortgage bond.

KEY POINTS

A debenture is unsecured and, therefore, is riskier than a bond, which is secured.

✓ JUST CHECKING

1. Refer to the bond certificate illustrated in Exhibit 15–1 and answer the following questions:
   a. What is the name of the corporation issuing the bond?
   b. What is the face value of the bond?
   c. What is the maturity date of the bond?
   d. What is the name of the bondholder?
   e. What is the stated interest rate the issuer will pay the bondholder?

Just Checking Solutions appear at the end of this chapter and on MyAccountingLab.

Bond Prices

A bond can be issued at any price agreed upon by the issuer and the bondholders. There are three basic categories of bond prices. A bond can be issued at

- **Maturity (par, face, or principal) value.** Example: A $1,000 bond issued for $1,000. A bond issued at par has no discount or premium.
- **Discount**, a price below maturity (par) value. Example: A $1,000 bond issued for $980. The discount is $20 ($1,000 − $980).
- **Premium**, a price above maturity (par) value. Example: A $1,000 bond issued for $1,015. The premium is $15 ($1,015 − $1,000).

The issue price of a bond does not affect the required payment at maturity. In all cases, the issuer must pay the maturity value of the bonds when they mature.

Bonds sell at a premium or a discount when the interest rate that will be paid on the bond is different from the interest rate available to investors elsewhere in the market at the time of the bond issuance. This will soon be explained more fully. As a bond nears maturity, its market price moves toward its maturity value. On the maturity date, the market value of a bond equals exactly its maturity value because the company that issued the bond pays that amount to retire the bond.

After a bond is issued, investors may buy and sell it through bond markets. The bond market in Canada is called the over-the-counter (OTC) market. It is a network of investment dealers who trade bonds issued by the Government of Canada and Crown corporations, the provinces, municipalities, regions, and corporations.

LO ②
How do we account for the sale of a bond?

Bond prices are quoted at a percentage of their maturity value, using $100 as a base. For example,

- A $1,000 bond quoted at 100 is bought or sold for 100 percent of maturity value ($1,000).
- A $1,000 bond quoted at 101.5 has a price of $1,015 ($1,000 × 1.015).
- A $1,000 bond quoted at 98.5 has a price of $985 ($1,000 × 0.985).

Exhibit 15–2 contains actual price information for a TELUS Corporation bond, as quoted on the website http://www.pfin.ca/canadianfixedincome/Default.aspx on September 28, 2012. On that date, TELUS Corporation's 5.05-percent par-value bond maturing December 4, 2019, was quoted at 114.87, which was a bid price of $1,148.70 for a $1,000.00 bond. This bid price provided a yield of 2.75 percent (the yield rate of a bond is influenced by the market interest rate and time to maturity).

EXHIBIT **15–2** | Bond Price Information

Bonds	Coupon	Eff. Maturity	Price	Yield
TELUS Corporation	5.05	Dec. 4/19	114.87	2.75

In Exhibit 15–2, "Price" is the **bid price**, the highest price that a buyer is willing to pay for the bond. "Coupon" is the contractual rate of interest that TELUS must pay the bondholders, The "Eff. Maturity" is the date that the bond term ends, and "**Yield**" is the interest rate that an investor will receive, based on a compounding period of one year.

Present Value[1]

🔑 **KEY POINTS**

Present value is always less than future value. You should be able to invest today's money (present value) so that its value will increase (future value). The difference between present value and future value is interest earned.

$$\frac{Present}{Value} + \frac{Interest}{Earned} = \frac{Future}{Value}$$

A dollar received today is worth more than a dollar received in the future. Why? Because you can invest today's dollar and earn income from it. Likewise, deferring any payment until later gives your money a period of time to grow. Money earns income over time, a concept called the *time value of money*. Let's examine how the time value of money affects the pricing of bonds.

Assume a $1,000 bond reaches maturity three years from today and carries no interest. Would you pay $1,000 to purchase this bond? No, because paying $1,000 today to receive the same amount in the future provides you with no income on the investment. You would not be taking advantage of the time value of money. Just how much would you pay today in order to receive $1,000 at the end of three years? The answer is some amount less than $1,000. Suppose $850 is a fair price. By investing $850 now to receive $1,000 later, you earn $150 interest revenue over the three years. The diagram below shows the relationship between a bond's price (present value) and its maturity amount (future value).

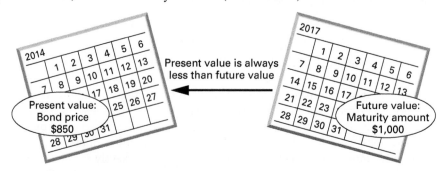

The amount that a person would invest *at the present time* to receive a greater amount at a future date is called the **present value** of the investment or payment.

---

[1] The Chapter 15 Appendix covers present value in more detail.

The present value is the bond's market price. In our example, $850 is the present value (bond price), and the $1,000 maturity value to be received in three years is the future value.

The exact present value of any future amount depends on (1) the amount of the future payment (or receipt), (2) the length of time from the date of the investment to the date when the future amount is to be received (or paid), and (3) the interest rate during the period. We show how to compute present value in this chapter's appendix. We need to be aware of the present-value concept, however, in the discussion of bond prices that follows. If your instructor so directs you, please study the appendix now.

Bond Interest Rates

Bonds are sold at their market price, which is the amount that investors are willing to pay at any given time. Market price is the bond's present value, which equals the present value of the principal payment plus the present value of the cash interest payments. The cash interest payments can be made once every three months (quarterly), once every six months (semiannually), or once per year (annually) over the term of the bond.

Two interest rates work to set the price of a bond:

KEY POINTS

When you buy a bond, you are really "buying" two future cash flows: principal and interest payments. The principal is a single sum received at maturity, and the interest payments are a series of receipts received each period until maturity.

- The **stated interest rate**, or **contract interest rate**, determines the amount of cash interest the borrower pays—and the investor receives—each year. The stated interest rate is printed on the bond and is set by the bond contract. It may be fixed or adjustable. If the rate is fixed, it *does not change* during the life of the bond. For example, XYZ Corporation's 6-percent bonds have a stated interest rate of 6 percent (Exhibit 15–1). Thus, XYZ Corporation pays $6,000 of interest annually on each $100,000 bond. Each semiannual interest payment is $3,000 ($100,000 × 0.06 × 1/2).

- The **market interest rate**, or **effective interest rate**, is the rate that investors demand for lending their money. The market interest rate changes constantly. A company may issue bonds with a stated interest rate that differs from the prevailing market interest rate. XYZ Corporation may issue its 6-percent bonds when the market rate for bonds issued by companies with a similar level of risk has risen to 7 percent. Will the XYZ Corporation bonds attract investors in this market? No, because investors can earn 7 percent on other bonds with a similar level of risk. In order to receive a 7-percent return on their investment, investors will purchase XYZ Corporation bonds only at a price less than the maturity value. The difference between the lower price and the bonds' maturity value is a *discount*. Conversely, if the market interest rate is 5 percent, XYZ Corporation's 6-percent bonds will be so attractive that investors will pay more than the maturity value for them. The difference between the higher price and the maturity value is a *premium*.

KEY POINTS

Because market interest rates fluctuate daily, the stated interest rate will seldom equal the market interest rate on the date the bonds are sold.

Exhibit 15–3 shows how the stated (contract) interest rate and the market interest rate interact to determine the issue price, or selling price, of a bond.

EXHIBIT **15–3**	How the Stated Interest Rate and the Market Interest Rate Interact to Determine the Issue Price of a Bond

Example: Bond with a Stated (Contract) Interest Rate of 5%			
Bond's Stated Interest Rate		Market Interest Rate	Issue Price of the Bond
5%	=	5%	⇒ Maturity value of the bond (face or par value)
5%	<	6%	⇒ Discount (price below maturity value)
5%	>	4%	⇒ Premium (price above maturity value)

KEY POINTS

Bonds sell at a *premium* if the market rate drops below the stated (contract) rate. Bonds sell at a *discount* if the market rate rises above the stated (contract) rate.

Issuing Bonds to Borrow Money

The basic journal entry to record the issuance of bonds debits Cash and credits Bonds Payable. The company may issue bonds for three different bond prices:

- At *maturity* (*par*) value
- At a *discount*
- At a *premium*

Issuing Bonds at Maturity (Par) Value

We begin with the simplest case: issuing bonds at maturity (par) value.

Suppose that UVW Corporation has $100 million in 6 percent bonds that mature in 10 years. Assume that UVW Corporation issued these bonds at par on January 2, 2014. The issuance entry is

2014			
Jan. 2	Cash	100,000,000	
	Bonds Payable		100,000,000
	To issue 6%, 10-year bonds at par.		

UVW Corporation, the borrower, makes this one-time entry to record the receipt of cash and issuance of bonds. Afterward, investors buy and sell the bonds through the bond markets, in a similar way to buying and selling shares through the stock market. Many of these transactions can be completed online. The buy-and-sell transactions between investors do not involve the company that issued the bonds. The company does not keep records of these transactions, except for the names and addresses of the bondholders. (This information is needed for mailing the interest and principal payments. The company may also have bondholder account information so that interest and principal payments can be directly deposited into bondholders' bank or investment accounts.)

Interest payments for these bonds occur each January 2 and July 2. UVW Corporation's entry to record the first semiannual interest payment is

KEY POINTS

Recall that the formula for computing interest is
Amount of interest = Principal × Rate × Time

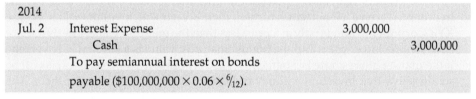

2014			
Jul. 2	Interest Expense	3,000,000	
	Cash		3,000,000
	To pay semiannual interest on bonds		
	payable ($100,000,000 × 0.06 × $\frac{6}{12}$).		

Each semiannual interest payment follows this same pattern.

At maturity, UVW Corporation will record payment of the bonds as follows:

2024			
Jan. 2	Bonds Payable	100,000,000	
	Cash		100,000,000
	To pay bonds payable at maturity.		

Issuing Bonds and Notes Between Interest Dates

The foregoing entries to record UVW Corporation's bond transactions are straightforward because the company issued the bonds on an interest payment date (January 2). However, corporations often issue bonds between interest dates because they may not need the funds in one lump sum or the bonds may take longer to sell than originally planned.

Suppose Manitoba Hydro issues $200 million of 5 percent bonds due June 15, 2020. These bonds are dated June 15, 2014, and carry the price "100 plus accrued interest." An investor purchasing the bonds after the bond date must pay market value *plus accrued interest*. The issuing company will pay the full semiannual interest amount to the bondholder at the next interest payment date. Companies do not split semiannual interest payments among two or more investors who happen to hold the bonds during a six-month interest period since the recordkeeping for this would be difficult.

Assume that Manitoba Hydro sells $100,000 of its bonds on July 15, 2014, one month after the bond date of June 15. Also assume that the market price of the bonds on July 15 is the face value when issuing these bonds. Manitoba Hydro receives one month's accrued interest in addition to the bond's face value, as shown on the following timeline:

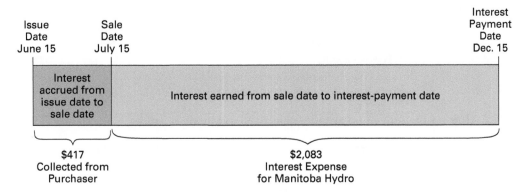

Manitoba Hydro's entry to record issuance of the bonds payable is

2014			
Jul. 15	Cash	100,417	
	Bonds Payable		100,000
	Interest Payable		417
	To issue 5%, 10-year bonds at par, one		
	month after the original issue date. Interest		
	payable is $417 ($100,000 × 0.05 × $\frac{1}{12}$).		

Manitoba Hydro has collected one month's interest in advance. On December 15, 2014, Manitoba Hydro's entry to record the first semiannual interest payment on this $100,000 is

2014			
Dec. 15	Interest Expense	2,083	
	Interest Payable	417	
	Cash		2,500
	To pay semiannual interest on bonds payable.		
	Interest expense is $2,083 ($100,000 × 0.05 × $\frac{5}{12}$);		
	cash paid is $2,500 ($100,000 × 0.05 × $\frac{6}{12}$).		

The debit to Interest Payable eliminates the credit balance in that account from July 15. Manitoba Hydro has now paid that liability.

Note that Manitoba Hydro pays a full six months' interest on December 15. After subtracting the one month's accrued interest received at the time of issuing the bond, Manitoba Hydro has recorded interest expense for five months ($2,083). This interest expense is the correct amount for the five months that the bonds have been outstanding.

When an investor sells bonds or debentures to another investor between interest dates, the price is always "plus accrued interest." Suppose you hold a bond for two months of a semiannual interest period and sell the bonds to another investor before you receive your interest. The person who buys the bonds will receive your two months of interest on the next specified interest date. Thus, you must collect your share of the interest from the buyer when you sell your investment, which happens when the price is "plus accrued interest."

If Manitoba Hydro prepared financial statements immediately after December 15, 2014, it would report nothing on the balance sheet because Interest Payable is $0 and would report Interest Expense of $2,083 on the income statement.

Issuing Bonds at a Discount

Using a financial calculator, the price would be $980,163.82 based on

FV of 1,000,000

N of 20

I of 3.135

PMT of 30,000

Unlike shares, bonds are often issued at a discount. We know that market conditions may force a company like UVW Corporation to accept a discount price for its bonds. Suppose UVW Corporation issues $1,000,000 of its 6-percent, 10-year bonds when the market interest rate is 6.27 percent. As a result, the market price of the bonds drops to a rounded factor of 98.00, which means 98 percent of face or par value. UVW Corporation receives $980,000 ($1,000,000 × 0.98) at issuance and makes the following journal entry:

2014			
Jan. 2	Cash	980,000	
	Discount on Bonds Payable	20,000	
	Bonds Payable		1,000,000
	To issue 6%, 10-year bonds at a discount.		
	Cash received was $980,000 ($1,000,000 × 0.98).		

After posting, the bond accounts have the following balances:

Main Account:	Contra Account:
Bonds Payable	**Discount on Bonds Payable**
1,000,000	20,000

Bond carrying value = $980,000

Discount on Bonds Payable is a contra account to Bonds Payable. Bonds Payable *minus* the discount gives the book value, or carrying value, of the bonds. The relationship between Bonds Payable and the Discount account is similar to the relationships between Equipment and Accumulated Amortization, and between Accounts Receivable and Allowance for Doubtful Accounts. Thus, UVW Corporation's liability is $980,000, which is the amount the company borrowed. UVW Corporation's balance sheet immediately after issuance of the bonds reports:

Long-term liabilities		
Bonds payable, 6%, due 2024	$1,000,000	
Less: Discount on bonds payable	20,000	$980,000

If UVW Corporation were to pay off the bonds immediately (an unlikely occurrence), the company's required outlay would be $980,000 because the market price of the bonds is $980,000.

Interest Expense on Bonds Issued at a Discount We saw earlier that a bond's stated interest rate may differ from the market interest rate. Suppose the market rate is 6.27 percent when UVW Corporation issues its 6-percent bonds. The 0.27 percent interest rate difference creates the $20,000 discount on the bonds. UVW Corporation borrows $980,000 cash but must pay $1,000,000 cash when the bonds mature 10 years later. What happens to the $20,000 balance of the discount account over the life of the bond issue?

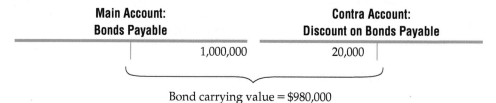

Borrows in 2014	Pays backs in 2024	Discount	
			How do we account for this?
$980,000	$1,000,000	$20,000	

The $20,000 is in reality an additional interest expense to the issuing company. That amount is a cost—beyond the stated interest rate—that the business pays for borrowing the investors' money. The discount has the effect of raising the interest expense on the bonds to the market interest rate of 6.27 percent.

The discount amount is an interest expense not paid until the bond matures. However, the borrower—the bond issuer—benefits from the use of the investors' money each accounting period over the full term of the bond issue. The matching objective directs the business to match an expense against its revenues on a period-by-period basis, so the discount is allocated to interest expense through amortization for each accounting period over the life of the bonds. We will examine this in more detail shortly.

Issuing Bonds at a Premium

To illustrate issuing bonds at a premium, let's change the UVW Corporation example. Assume that the market interest rate is 5.5 percent when the company issues its 6-percent, 10-year bonds. These 6-percent bonds are attractive in a 5.5-percent market, so investors will pay a premium price to acquire them. If the bonds are priced at 103.77 (103.77 percent of par value), UVW Corporation receives $1,037,700 cash upon issuance. The entry is

REAL WORLD EXAMPLE

Why are bonds issued at a premium less common than bonds issued at a discount? Because companies prefer to issue bonds that pay a lower stated interest rate than the market interest rate, so they price the bonds to sell at a discount.

2014			
Jan. 2	Cash	1,037,700	
	Bonds Payable		1,000,000
	Premium on Bonds Payable		37,700
	To issue 6%, 10-year bonds at a premium.		
	Cash received is $1,037,700 ($1,000,000 × 1.0377).		

After posting, the bond accounts have the following balances:

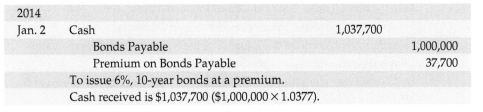

Main Account: Bonds Payable	Companion Account: Premium on Bonds Payable
1,000,000	37,700

Bond carrying value = $1,037,700

UVW Corporation's balance sheet immediately after issuance of the bonds reports:

LEARNING TIPS

Using a financial calculator, the price would be $1,038,068.13, based on

FV of 1,000,000

N of 20

I of 2.75

PMT of 30,000

The difference between $1,038,068.13 and $1,037,700 (which is $368.13) is due to rounding.

Long-term liabilities		
Bonds payable, 6%, due 2024	$1,000,000	
Premium on bonds payable	37,700	$1,037,700

Premium on Bonds Payable is added to Bonds Payable to show the book value, or carrying value, of the bonds. UVW Corporation's liability is $1,037,700, which is the amount that the company borrowed. Immediate payment of the bonds would require an outlay of $1,037,700 because the market price of the bonds at issuance is $1,037,700. The investors would be unwilling to give up bonds for less than their market value.

KEY POINTS

In addition to including the premium or discount in the selling price, all transactions also include accrued interest.

Interest Expense on Bonds Issued at a Premium The 0.5-percent difference between the 6-percent contract rate on the bonds and the 5.5-percent market interest rate creates the $37,700 premium. UVW Corporation borrows $1,037,700 cash but must pay only $1,000,000 cash at maturity.

Borrows in 2014	Pays back in 2024	Premium	
			How do we account for this?
$1,037,700	$1,000,000	$37,700	

We treat the premium as a reduction of interest expense to UVW Corporation. The premium reduces UVW Corporation's cost of borrowing the money and reduces the company's interest expense to an effective interest rate of 5.5 percent, the market rate. We account for the premium much as we handled the discount. We amortize the bond premium as a *decrease* in interest expense over the life of the bonds.

✓ JUST CHECKING

2. In each of the following situations, will the bonds sell at par, at a premium, or at a discount?
   a. 4-percent bonds sold when the market rate is 4.5 percent
   b. 4-percent bonds sold when the market rate is 3.8 percent
   c. 3.5-percent bonds sold when the market rate is 3.5 percent
   d. 3.25-percent bonds sold when the market rate is 3.15 percent
   e. 3.15-percent bonds sold when the market rate is 3.2 percent

3. Sunwood Insurance Corp. issued $1,000,000 of 3.75-percent, 10-year bonds at the market price of 99.00.
   a. Were the bonds issued at par, at a discount, or at a premium?
   b. How much did Sunwood receive on issuance of the bonds?
   c. Make the journal entry for the issuance of the bonds. Include an explanation.
   d. What is the carrying value of the bonds?

4. Parksville Insurance Corp. issued $1,000,000 of 3.75-percent, 10-year bonds at the market price of 101.50.
   a. Were the bonds issued at par, at a discount, or at a premium?
   b. How much did Parksville receive on issuance of the bonds?
   c. Make the journal entry for the issuance of the bonds. Include an explanation.
   d. What is the carrying value of the bonds?

Just Checking Solutions appear at the end of this chapter and on MyAccountingLab.

Amortization of a Bond Discount and a Bond Premium

── LO ③ ──
How do we allocate a bond discount or premium over the life of a bond?

There are two methods for amortizing a bond discount and a bond premium: the straight-line method and the effective-interest method. Each of these will be discussed in turn.

Straight-Line Method of Amortization of a Bond Discount and a Bond Premium·

We can amortize a bond discount or a bond premium by dividing the discount or premium into equal amounts for each interest period. This method is called **straight-line amortization**. (This is very similar to the straight-line method of amortizing assets that we studied in Chapter 10.)

Straight-Line Amortization of a Bond Discount   In our UVW Corporation example on page 926, the beginning discount is $20,000, and there are 20 semiannual interest periods during the bonds' 10-year life. Therefore, 1/20 of the $20,000 bond discount ($20,000 ÷ 20 = $1,000) is amortized each interest period. UVW Corporation's semiannual interest entry on July 2, 2014, is

2014			
Jul. 2	Interest Expense	31,000	
	Cash		30,000
	Discount on Bonds Payable		1,000
	To pay semiannual interest of $30,000 ($1,000,000		
	$\times 0.06 \times {}^{6}\!/_{12}$) and amortize discount on bonds		
	payable, $1,000 ($20,000 ÷ 20).[2]		

Interest expense of $31,000 for each six-month period is the sum of

- The stated interest ($30,000, which is paid in cash)
- *Plus* the amortization of the discount ($1,000)

Discount on Bonds Payable has a debit balance. Therefore, we credit the Discount account to amortize (reduce) its balance. Since Discount on Bonds Payable is a contra account, each reduction in its balance increases the book value or carrying value of Bonds Payable. Twenty amortization entries (semiannual journal entries for 10 years) will decrease the discount balance to zero, which means that the Bonds Payable book value will have increased by $20,000 up to its face value of $1,000,000 by the maturity date. The entry to pay the bonds at maturity is

2024			
Jan. 2	Bonds Payable	1,000,000	
	Cash		1,000,000
	To pay the bonds payable at maturity.		

Straight-Line Amortization of a Bond Premium In our example on page 927, the beginning premium is $37,700, and there are 20 semiannual interest periods during the bonds' 10-year life. Therefore, 1/20 of the $37,700 ($1,885) of bond premium is amortized each interest period. UVW Corporation's semiannual interest entry on July 2, 2014, is

KEY POINTS

When bonds sell at a premium we collect additional revenue. However, to amortize this amount we reduce interest expense rather than set up a separate revenue account.

2014			
Jul. 2	Interest Expense	28,115	
	Premium on Bonds Payable	1,885	
	Cash		30,000
	To pay semiannual interest ($1,000,000 $\times$ 0.06 $\times {}^{6}\!/_{12}$) and		
	amortize premium on bonds payable ($37,700 ÷ 20).[3]		

---

[2] Some accountants record the payment of interest and the amortization of the discount in two separate entries, as follows (both approaches are equally correct):

2014			
Jul. 2	Interest Expense	30,000	
	Cash		30,000
	Paid semiannual interest ($1,000,000 $\times$ 0.06 $\times {}^{6}\!/_{12}$).		
2	Interest Expense	1,000	
	Discount on Bonds Payable		1,000
	Amortized discount on bonds payable ($20,000 ÷ 20).		

[3] The payment of interest and the amortization of the bond premium can be recorded in two separate entries as follows:

2014			
Jul. 2	Interest Expense	30,000	
	Cash		30,000
	Paid semiannual interest ($1,000,000 $\times$ 0.06 $\times {}^{6}\!/_{12}$).		
2	Premium on Bonds Payable	1,885	
	Interest Expense		1,885
	Amortized premium on bonds payable ($37,700 ÷ 20).		

Interest expense of $28,115 is

- The stated interest ($30,000)
- *Minus* the amortization of the premium ($1,885)

The debit to Premium on Bonds Payable reduces its normal balance, which is a credit.

At July 2, 2014, immediately after amortizing the bond premium, the bonds have a carrying amount of

$1,035,815 [calculated as $1,000,000 + ($37,700 − $1,885)]

Long-term liabilities		
Bonds payable, 6%, due 2024	$1,000,000	
Premium on bonds payable	35,815	$1,035,815

At January 2, 2015, the bonds' carrying amount will be

$1,033,930 [calculated as $1,000,000 + ($37,700 − $1,885 − $1,885)]

Long-term liabilities		
Bonds payable, 6%, due 2024	$1,000,000	
Premium on bonds payable	33,930	$1,033,930

At maturity on January 2, 2024, the bond premium will have been fully amortized, and the bonds' carrying amount will be $1,000,000.

Effective-Interest Method of Amortization of a Bond Discount and a Bond Premium

KEY POINTS

The amount of *cash* paid each semiannual interest period is calculated with the formula Interest paid = Par value × (Stated rate ÷ 2). This amount does not change over the term of the bond.

The straight-line amortization method has a theoretical weakness. Each period's amortization amount for a premium or discount is the same dollar amount over the life of the bonds. However, over that time, the bonds' carrying value continues to increase (with a discount) or decrease (with a premium). Thus the fixed dollar amount of amortization changes as a percentage of the bonds' carrying value, making it appear that the bond issuer's interest rate changes over time. This appearance is misleading because in fact the issuer locked in a fixed interest rate when the bonds were issued. The stated (contract) interest *rate* on the bonds does not change.

The **effective-interest amortization** method keeps each interest expense amount at the same percentage of the bonds' carrying value or book value for every interest payment over the bonds' life. The total amount of bond discount or bond premium amortized over the life of the bonds is the same under both methods. Accounting standards for private enterprises (ASPE) specify that the effective-interest method should be used because it does a better job of matching. However, the straight-line method is popular because of its simplicity, and, in practice, if there is no material difference, then the cost/benefit constraint results in companies using straight-line amortization.

Effective-Interest Method of Amortizing a Bond Discount Assume that on January 2, 2014, UVW Corporation issues $1,000,000 of 5-percent bonds at a time when the market rate of interest is 6 percent. Also assume that these bonds mature in five years and pay interest semiannually, so there are 10 semiannual interest payments. The issue price of the bonds is $957,349.[4] The discount on these bonds is $42,651 ($1,000,000 − $957,349). Exhibit 15–4 illustrates amortization of the discount by the effective-interest method.

Recall that we want to present interest expense amounts over the full life of the bonds at a fixed percentage of the bonds' carrying value. The 3-percent rate—the

---

[4] We show how to compute this amount in the Chapter 15 Appendix. The calculation shown here was made with a calculator. In the Chapter 15 Appendix, the amount is computed using the present-value tables that appear in the Appendix.

EXHIBIT **15–4** | Effective-Interest Method of Amortizing a Bond Discount

Panel A: Bond Data

Maturity value—$1,000,000
Stated (contract) interest rate—5%
Interest paid—2.5% semiannually—$25,000 ($1,000,000 × 0.025)
Market interest rate at time of issue—6% annually, 3% semiannually
Issue price—$957,349

Panel B: Amortization Table

	A	B	C	D	E
	Interest	Interest		Unamortized Discount	
	Payment	Expense		Account	Bond
Semiannual	(2.5% of	(3% of	Discount	Balance	Carrying
Interest	Maturity	Preceding Bond	Amortization	(Preceding	Amount
Period	Value)	Carrying Amount)	(B − A)	D − Current C)	($1,000,000 − D)
Issue Date				$42,651	$ 957,349*
1	$25,000	$28,720	$3,720	38,931	961,069
2	25,000	28,832	3,832	35,099	964,901
3	25,000	28,947	3,947	31,152	968,848
4	25,000	29,065	4,065	27,087	972,913
5	25,000	29,187	4,187	22,900	977,100
6	25,000	29,313	4,313	18,587	981,413
7	25,000	29,442	4,442	14,145	985,855
8	25,000	29,576	4,576	9,569	990,431
9	25,000	29,713	4,713	4,856	995,144
10	25,000	29,856	4,856	0	1,000,000

*Minor differences because of the effect of rounding.

Notes

Column A	The semiannual interest payments are constant because they are fixed by the stated interest rate and the bonds' maturity value. (Dark red line in Exhibit 15–5, Panel A, on page 933)
Column B	The interest expense each period is computed by multiplying the preceding bond carrying amount by the market interest rate. The effect of this *effective-interest rate* determines the interest expense each period. The amount of interest each period increases as the effective-interest rate, a constant, is applied to the increasing bond carrying amount (E). (Blue line in Exhibit 15–5, Panel A)
Column C	The excess of each interest expense amount (B) over each interest payment amount (A) is the discount amortization for the period. (Shaded amount in Exhibit 15–5, Panel A)
Column D	The unamortized discount balance decreases by the amount of amortization for the period (C) from $42,651 at the bonds' issue date to zero at their maturity. (Shaded amount in Exhibit 15–5, Panel B) The balance of the discount plus the bonds' carrying amount equals the bonds' maturity value at all times.
Column E	The bonds' carrying amount increases from $957,349 at issuance to $1,000,000 at maturity. (Dark blue line in Exhibit 15–5, Panel B)

effective-interest rate (6 ÷ 2)—*is* that percentage. We have calculated the cost of the money borrowed by the bond issuer—the interest expense—as a constant percentage of the carrying value of the bonds. The *dollar amount* of interest expense varies from period to period but the interest percentage applied to the carrying value remains the same.

KEY POINTS

The amount of semiannual interest expense is calculated with the formula

Interest expense = Bond carrying value × (Market interest rate ÷ 2)

This amount will change each period as the carrying value changes over the term of the bond.

The *accounts* debited and credited under the effective-interest amortization method and the straight-line method are the same. Only the *amounts* differ. We may take the amortization *amounts* directly from the table in Exhibit 15–4. We assume that the first interest payment occurs on July 2 and use the appropriate amounts from Exhibit 15–4, reading across the line for the first interest payment date:

Jul. 2	Interest Expense	28,720	
	Discount on Bonds Payable		3,720
	Cash		25,000
	To pay semiannual interest (Column A) and		
	amortize discount (Column C) on bonds payable.		
	Interest expense is calculated as the cash paid plus		
	the discount amortization (Column B).		

On page 933, Exhibit 15–5, Panel A diagrams the interest expense over the life of bonds issued at a discount. Panel B shows how the carrying amount of the bonds rises to the maturity date. All amounts are taken from Exhibit 15–4. Focus on the highlighted items in Exhibit 15–5 and the references in Exhibit 15–4 to understand the main points of Exhibit 15–5.

Effective-Interest Method of Amortizing a Bond Premium Let's modify the UVW Corporation example to illustrate the effective-interest method of amortizing a bond premium. Assume that, on April 30, UVW Corporation issues $1,000,000 of five-year, 5-percent bonds that pay interest semiannually. If the bonds are issued when the market interest rate is 4 percent, their issue price is $1,044,913.[5] The premium on these bonds is $44,913, and Exhibit 15–6 (on page 934) illustrates amortization of the premium by the effective-interest method.

Assuming that the first interest payment occurs on October 31, we read across the line in Exhibit 15–6 for the first interest payment date and pick up the appropriate amounts.

Oct. 31	Interest Expense	20,898	
	Premium on Bonds Payable	4,102	
	Cash		25,000
	To pay semiannual interest (column A) and		
	amortize premium (column C) on bonds payable.		

On page 935, Exhibit 15–7, Panel A diagrams the interest expense over the life of the bonds issued at a premium. Panel B shows how the carrying amount of the bonds decreases to maturity. All amounts are taken from Exhibit 15–6. Focus on the highlighted items in Exhibit 15–7 and the references in Exhibit 15–6.

Does the method of amortizing a bond premium or discount affect the amount of cash interest paid on a bond? No. The amortization method for a bond premium or discount has *no effect* on the amount of cash interest paid on a bond. The amount of cash interest paid depends on the contract interest rate stated on the bond. That interest rate, and the amount of cash interest paid, are fixed and therefore remain constant over the life of the bond. To see this, examine Column A of Exhibits 15–4 and 15–6.

LEARNING TIPS

The interest and principal portion of the long-term debt should be separated and listed in the current liabilities section of the balance sheet. This was discussed in Chapter 11.

Reporting Liabilities and Bonds Payable

The long-term liabilities are divided into their current and long-term portions for reporting on the balance sheet. For each long-term liability, the portion that is due to be paid within the next year is classified as a current liability and is

---

[5] Again, we compute the present value of the bonds using a calculator. In the Chapter 15 Appendix, the amount is computed using present-value tables.

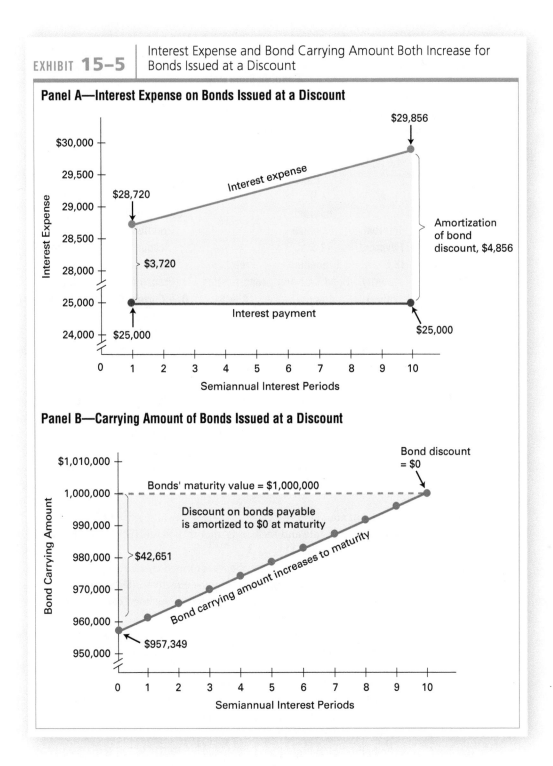

EXHIBIT 15–5 | Interest Expense and Bond Carrying Amount Both Increase for Bonds Issued at a Discount

Panel A—Interest Expense on Bonds Issued at a Discount

Panel B—Carrying Amount of Bonds Issued at a Discount

shown on the balance sheet as the liability "Current portion of long-term debt." The long-term debt is reduced by the same amount so that only the portion of the debt due to be paid in more than a year is listed as a long-term liability on the balance sheet.

Bonds payable are reported on the balance sheet at their maturity amount plus any unamortized premium or minus any unamortized discount. For example, consider the UVW Corporation example on page 929. At December 31, 2015, UVW Corporation would have amortized the Premium on Bonds Payable for three semiannual periods ($1,885 × 3 = $5,655). The issue date is January 2, 2014, first payment is July 2, 2014, second payment is January 2, 2015, and third payment

EXHIBIT 15–6 | Effective-Interest Method of Amortizing a Bond Premium

Panel A: Bond Data

Maturity value—$1,000,000
Stated (contract) interest rate—5%
Interest paid—2.5% semiannually, $25,000 ($1,000,000 × 0.025)
Market interest rate at time of issue—4% annually, 2% semiannually
Issue price—$1,044,913

Panel B: Amortization Table

	A	B	C	D	E
		Interest		Unamortized	
		Expense		Premium	
	Interest	(2% of		Account	Bond
	Payment	Preceding	Premium	Balance	Carrying
Semiannual	(2.5% of	Bond Carrying	Amortization	(Preceding	Amount
Interest	Maturity	Amount)	(A − B)	D − Current C)	(1,000,000 + D)
Period	Value)				
Issue Date				$44,913	$1,044,913
1	$25,000	$20,898	$4,102	40,811	1,040,811
2	25,000	20,816	4,184	36,627	1,036,627
3	25,000	20,733	4,267	32,360	1,032,360
4	25,000	20,647	4,353	28,007	1,028,007
5	25,000	20,560	4,440	23,567	1,023,567
6	25,000	20,471	4,529	19,038	1,019,038
7	25,000	20,381	4,619	14,419	1,014,419
8	25,000	20,288	4,712	9,707	1,009,707
9	25,000	20,194	4,806	4,901	1,004,901
10	25,000	20,099	4,901	0	1,000,000

Notes:

Column A	The semiannual interest payments are a constant amount fixed by the stated interest rate and the bonds' maturity value. (Dark red line in Exhibit 15–7, Panel A)
Column B	The interest expense each period is computed by multiplying the preceding bond carrying amount by the effective-interest rate. The amount of interest decreases each period as the bond carrying amount decreases. (Blue line in Exhibit 15–7, Panel A)
Column C	The excess of each interest payment (A) over the period's interest expense (B) is the premium amortization for the period. (Shaded area in Exhibit 15–7, Panel A)
Column D	The premium balance decreases by the amount of amortization for the period (C) from $44,913 at issuance to zero at maturity. (Shaded area in Exhibit 15–7, Panel B) The bonds' carrying amount minus the premium balance equals the bonds' maturity value.
Column E	The bonds' carrying value decreases from $1,044,913 at issuance to $1,000,000 at maturity. (Dark blue line in Exhibit 15–7, Panel B)

is July 2, 2015. The UVW Corporation balance sheet at December 31, 2015, would show the bonds payable as follows:

Long-term liabilities		
Bonds Payable, 6% due 2024	$1,000,000	
Premium on bonds payable [$37,700 − (3 × $1,885)]	32,045	$1,032,045

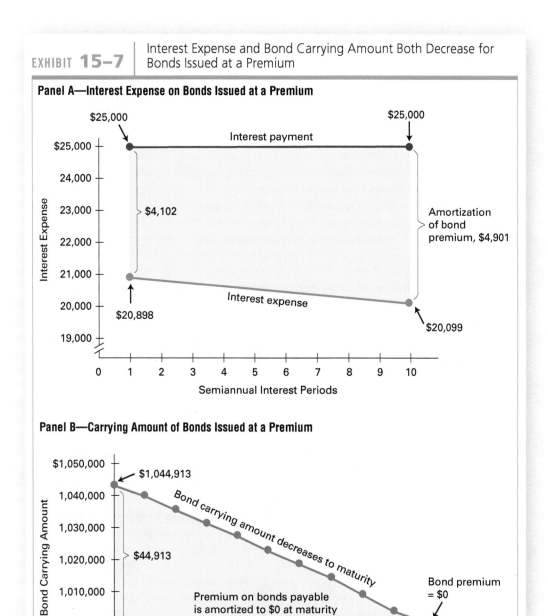

Panel A—Interest Expense on Bonds Issued at a Premium

Panel B—Carrying Amount of Bonds Issued at a Premium

Over the life of the bonds, 20 amortization entries will decrease the premium balance to zero. The payment at maturity will debit Bonds Payable and credit Cash for $1,000,000.

Adjusting Entries for Interest Expense

LEARNING TIPS

Companies issue bonds when they need cash. The interest payments seldom occur on the end of the company's fiscal year. Nevertheless, interest expense must be accrued at the end of the period to measure net income accurately. The accrual entry may often be complicated by the need to amortize a discount or a premium for only a partial interest period.

You may recall that Chapter 3 introduced adjusting entries to accrue expenses. We are now adding a bond discount or premium amortization entry to the interest-accrual entry.

Adjusting Entries Using the Straight-line Method

Suppose B.C. Hydro issues $50,000,000 of 8 percent, 10-year bonds at a $200,000 discount on October 1, 2014. Assume that interest payments occur on March 31 and September 30 each year. If December 31 is its year end, B.C. Hydro records interest for the three-month period (October, November, and December) as follows:

2014			
Dec. 31	Interest Expense	1,005,000	
	Interest Payable		1,000,000
	Discount on Bonds Payable		5,000
	To accrue three months' interest expense		
	($50,000,000 $\times$ 0.08 $\times$ $^3\!/_{12}$) and amortize the		
	discount on bonds payable for three months		
	($200,000 $\div$ 10 $\times$ $^3\!/_{12}$).		

Interest Payable is credited for the three months of cash interest that have accrued since September 30. Discount on Bonds Payable is credited for three months of amortization.

The B.C. Hydro balance sheet at December 31, 2014, reports Interest Payable of $1,000,000 as a current liability. Bonds Payable appears as a long-term liability, presented as follows:

Long-term liabilities		
Bonds payable, 8%, due 2024	$50,000,000	
Less: Discount on bonds payable	195,000	$49,805,000

Observe that the balance of Discount on Bonds Payable decreases by $5,000. The bonds' carrying value increases by the same amount. The bonds' carrying value continues to increase over their 10-year life, reaching $50,000,000 at maturity when the discount will be fully amortized.

The next semiannual interest payment occurs on March 31, 2015, as follows:

2015			
Mar. 31	Interest Expense	1,005,000	
	Interest Payable	1,000,000	
	Cash		2,000,000
	Discount on Bonds Payable		5,000
	To pay semiannual interest ($50,000,000 $\times$ 0.08		
	$\times$ $^6\!/_{12}$), of which $1,000,000 was accrued, and		
	amortize three months' discount on bonds		
	payable ($200,000 $\div$ 10 $\times$ $^6\!/_{12}$).		

Amortization of a premium over a partial interest period is similar except that the account Premium on Bonds Payable is debited.

Adjusting Entries Using the Effective-Interest Method

At year end, it is necessary to make an adjusting entry for accrued interest and amortization of the bond premium for a partial period. In our example on page 932, the last interest payment occurred on October 31. The adjustment for November and December must cover two months, or one-third of a semiannual period.

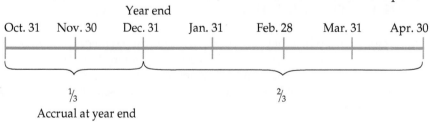

The entry, with amounts drawn from line 2 in Exhibit 15–6 on page 934, is

Dec. 31	Interest Expense	6,939	
	Premium on Bonds Payable	1,395	
	Interest Payable		8,334
	To accrue two months' interest expense ($20,816 × $\frac{2}{6}$), amortize the premium on bonds payable for two months ($4,184 × $\frac{2}{6}$), and record interest payable ($25,000 × $\frac{2}{6}$).		

The second interest payment occurs on April 30 of the following year. The payment of $25,000 includes interest expense for four months (January through April), the reversal of the interest payable liability created at December 31, and premium amortization for four months. The payment entry is the following:

Apr. 30	Interest Expense	13,877	
	Interest Payable	8,334	
	Premium on Bonds Payable	2,789	
	Cash		25,000
	To record semiannual interest for four months ($13,877 = $20,816 × $\frac{4}{6}$), reverse interest payable accrual ($8,334), amortize the premium on bonds payable for four months ($4,184 × $\frac{4}{6}$), and make the cash interest payment of $25,000.		

This timeline shows the total effects of the December 31 accrual and the April 30 semiannual interest payment:

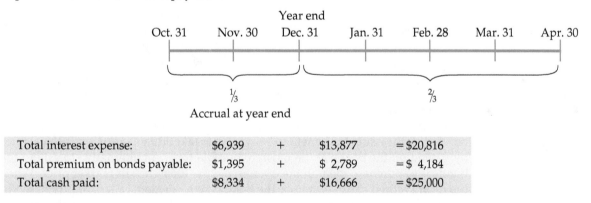

Total interest expense:	$6,939	+	$13,877	= $20,816
Total premium on bonds payable:	$1,395	+	$ 2,789	= $ 4,184
Total cash paid:	$8,334	+	$16,666	= $25,000

If these bonds had been issued at a discount, procedures for these interest entries would be the same, except that Discount on Bonds Payable would be credited.

✓ JUST CHECKING

5. Assume that Ontario Hydro has 6-percent, 10-year bonds that mature on May 1, 2024. Further, assume that $10,000,000 of the bonds are issued at 94.00 on May 1, 2014, and that Ontario Hydro pays interest each April 30 and October 31.

   a. Record issuance of the bonds on May 1, 2014.

   b. Record the interest payment and straight-line amortization of the premium or discount on October 31, 2014.

   c. Accrue interest and amortize the premium or discount on December 31, 2014.

   d. Show how the company would report the bonds on the balance sheet at December 31, 2014.

   e. Record the interest payment on April 30, 2015.

6. Refer to the example of the bonds issued at a premium illustrated in Exhibit 15–6. Use the data in Exhibit 15–6 to accrue interest and amortize the bond premium at the end of the second year, December 31, 2015 (line 4). Then record the April 30, 2016, payment of interest.

7. Refer to Exhibits 15–4 and 15–6 to answer the following questions.

    a. Will the periodic amount of interest expense increase or decrease over the life of a bond issued at a *discount*, under the effective-interest amortization method?

    b. Will the periodic amount of interest expense increase or decrease for a bond issued at a *premium*? Assume the effective-interest method of amortizing the premium.

    c. Consider bonds issued at a discount. Which will be greater, the cash interest paid per period or the amount of interest expense? Answer the same question for bonds issued at a premium.

Just Checking Solutions appear at the end of this chapter and on MyAccountingLab.

Retirement of Bonds

LO ④

How do we account for changes in a bond issue?

KEY POINTS

Callable bonds may be paid off at the corporation's option. The bondholder does not have the choice of refusing but must surrender the bond for retirement.

Normally, companies wait until maturity to pay off, or retire, their bonds payable. All the bond discount or premium has been amortized, and the retirement entry debits Bonds Payable and credits Cash for the bonds' maturity value, as we saw earlier. But companies sometimes retire their bonds prior to maturity. The main reason for retiring bonds early is to relieve the pressure of making interest payments. Interest rates fluctuate. The company may be able to borrow at a lower interest rate and use the proceeds from new bonds to pay off the old bonds, which bear a higher rate. McDonald's did this in the chapter-opening story.

Redeemable bonds are bonds that give the purchaser the option of retiring them at a stated dollar amount prior to maturity. Other bonds are **callable**, which means that the company may *call* or pay off those bonds at a specified price whenever it so chooses. The call price is usually a few percentage points above the face value or par, perhaps 104.00 or 105.00, to make the bonds attractive to lenders. Callable bonds give the issuer the benefit of being able to take advantage of low interest rates by paying off the bonds at the most favourable time. An alternative to calling the bonds is to purchase them in the open market at their current market price. When bonds are retired early—whether the bonds are redeemed, called, or purchased in the open market—the same steps are followed and the journal entry is the same.

When bonds are retired before maturity, follow these steps:

Step 1. Record a partial-period amortization of the premium or discount, if the date is other than an interest payment date.

Step 2. Write off the portion of the premium or discount that relates to the portion of bonds being retired.

Step 3. Calculate any gain or loss on retirement, and record this amount in the retirement journal entry.

Suppose XYZ Corporation has $10,000,000 of bonds outstanding with an unamortized discount of $40,000. Lower interest rates in the market may convince management to retire these bonds on June 30, immediately after an interest date.

Assume that the bonds are callable at 103.00. If the market price of the bonds is 99.50, will XYZ Corporation call the bonds or purchase them in the open market? The market price is lower than the call price, so market price is the better choice. Retiring the bonds at 99.50 results in a gain of $10,000, computed as follows:

MyAccountingLab

DemoDoc: Bond Transactions

Face value of bonds being retired	$10,000,000
Unamortized discount	40,000
[Step 1 (no partial-period amortization in this case) and Step 2]	
Book value, or carrying value	9,960,000
Market price ($10,000,000 × 0.9950) paid to retire the bonds	9,950,000
Gain on retirement of bonds. [Step 3]	$ 10,000

The following entry records retirement of these bonds, which happens to be immediately after an interest date:

Jun. 30	Bonds Payable	10,000,000	
	Discount on Bonds Payable		40,000
	Cash		9,950,000
	Gain on Retirement of Bonds Payable		10,000
	To retire bonds payable before maturity.		

After posting, the bond accounts have zero balances.

Bonds Payable		Discount on Bonds Payable	
Retirement 10,000,000	Prior balance 10,000,000	Prior balance 40,000	Retirement 40,000

The entry removes the bonds payable and the related discount from the accounts and records a gain on retirement. Of course, any existing premium would be removed with a debit to the Premium on Bonds Payable account.

If XYZ Corporation had retired only half of these bonds, the accountant would remove half of the discount or premium. Likewise, if the price paid to retire the bonds exceeded their carrying value, the retirement entry would record a loss with a debit to the account Loss on Retirement of Bonds. ASPE requires that gains and losses on early retirement of debt that are both abnormal in size and unusual be reported separately as a line item on the income statement before the line items for income tax and discontinued operations.

Convertible Bonds and Notes

Corporations often add *sweeteners* to their bonds—features to make the bonds more attractive to potential investors. Many corporate bonds, debentures, and notes payable have the feature of being convertible into the common shares of the issuing company at the option of the investor. These bonds and notes, called **convertible bonds** (or **convertible notes**), combine the safety of assured receipts of principal and interest on the bonds with the opportunity for large gains on the shares. The conversion feature is so attractive that investors usually accept a lower stated, or contract, interest rate than they would on nonconvertible bonds. The lower interest rate benefits the issuer. Convertible bonds are recorded like any other debt at issuance.

If the market price of the issuing company's shares gets high enough, the bondholders will convert the bonds into shares. The corporation records conversion by debiting the bond accounts and crediting the shareholders' equity accounts. Normally, the carrying value of the bonds becomes the book value of the newly issued shares, and no gain or loss is recorded.

REAL WORLD EXAMPLE

Canada Savings Bonds are different from the bonds described in this chapter. Canada Savings Bonds are debentures issued by the Canadian government. They are available in regular and compounding interest, have a guaranteed minimum interest rate, are cashable at any time, and come in denominations of $100, $300, $500, $1000, $5000, and $10,000. The interest rate is guaranteed for one year and fluctuates with market conditions for the remaining nine years until the bonds mature.

Assume that XYZ Corporation bondholders converted $100,000 of XYZ Corporation bonds into 20,000 common shares on May 1, 2014. The bonds were issued at par. XYZ Corporation's entry to record the conversion would be

2014			
May 1	Bonds Payable	100,000	
	Common Shares		100,000
	To record conversion of $100,000 bonds		
	outstanding into 20,000 common shares.		

The entry brings the Bonds Payable account to zero, exactly the same as for a bond retirement. The carrying value of the bonds ($100,000) becomes the amount of increase in shareholders' equity.

✓JUST CHECKING

8. Suppose Shaolin Corporation has $5,000,000 of bonds outstanding with an unamortized premium of $30,000. The call price is 105.00. To reduce interest payments, the company retires half of the bonds at the 100.50 market price. Calculate the gain or loss on retirement, and record the retirement immediately after an interest date.

9. Suppose Shaolin Corporation has $5,000,000 of bonds outstanding with an unamortized premium of $30,000. The bonds are convertible. Assume bondholders converted half of the bonds into 1,000,000 common shares on September 1, 2014. Record the conversion of these bonds into common shares.

10. Suppose Shaolin Corporation has $5,000,000 of bonds outstanding that were issued on different dates, with a total unamortized premium of $30,000. Of these amounts, $1,500,000 of the bonds and $5,000 of the unamortized premium are due in one year. How would Shaolin Corporation report the debt on its year-end balance sheet?

Just Checking Solutions appear at the end of this chapter and on MyAccountingLab.

Advantages and Disadvantages of Issuing Bonds versus Shares

LO ⑤
How do we decide whether to issue debt versus equity?

Businesses acquire assets in different ways. Management may decide to purchase or to lease equipment. If management decides to purchase, the money to pay for the asset may be financed by the business's retained earnings, a note payable, a share issue, or a bond issue. Each financing strategy has its advantages and disadvantages, as follows:

Advantages of Financing Operations by	
Issuing Shares	**Issuing Notes or Bonds**
• Creates no liabilities or interest expense, which must be paid even during bad years; is less risky to the issuing corporation.	• Does not dilute share ownership or control of the corporation.
	• May result in higher earnings per share because interest expense is tax-deductible and ownership is not diluted.
• Raises capital without increasing debt and adversely affecting some key ratios.	
• Carries no obligation to pay dividends.	• Can create greater returns for the shareholders if leveraged profitably.

Exhibit 15–8 illustrates the earnings-per-share (EPS) advantage of borrowing. Recall that earnings per share (EPS) is a company's net income per common share outstanding. Suppose XYZ Corporation has net income of $600,000 and 200,000

common shares outstanding before a new project. The company needs $1,000,000 for expansion, and management is considering two financing plans:

- Plan 1 is to issue $1,000,000 of 10-percent bonds.
- Plan 2 is to issue 100,000 common shares for $1,000,000.

XYZ Corporation management believes the new cash can be invested in operations to earn income of $300,000 before interest and taxes.

EXHIBIT 15–8 | Earnings-per-Share Advantage of Borrowing versus Issuing Shares

	Plan 1: Borrow $1,000,000 at 10%	Plan 2: Issue $1,000,000 of Common Shares
Net income after interest and income tax, before expansion	$600,000	$600,000
Project income before interest and income tax	300,000	300,000
Less: Interest expense ($1,000,000 × 0.10)	100,000	0
Project income before income tax	200,000	300,000
Less: Income tax expense (40%)	80,000	120,000
Project net income	120,000	180,000
Total company net income	$720,000	$780,000
Earnings per share including expansion:		
Plan 1 ($720,000 ÷ 200,000 shares)	$ 3.60	
Plan 2 ($780,000 ÷ 300,000 shares)		$ 2.60

The EPS amount is higher if the company borrows (Plan 1). The business earns more on the investment ($120,000) than the interest it pays on the bonds ($100,000). Earning more income than the cost of borrowing increases the earnings for common shareholders, and is called **trading on the equity**. It is widely used in business to increase earnings per common share.

Borrowing has its disadvantages. Debts must be paid during bad years as well as during good years. Interest expense may be high enough to eliminate net income and lead to a cash crisis and even bankruptcy. This has happened to many internet startups. In contrast, a company that issues shares can omit paying dividends during a bad year.

Computer spreadsheets are useful in evaluating financing alternatives such as issuing common shares, preferred shares, or bonds. This assessment is often called "what if" analysis—for instance, "what if we finance with common shares?" The answers to "what if" questions can be modelled on a spreadsheet to project the company's financial statements over the next few years.

✓ JUST CHECKING

11. If trading on the equity can improve EPS, how might it be to the corporation's *disadvantage* to finance with debt?

12. Suppose Zen Corporation has net income of $600,000 and 200,000 common shares outstanding before a new project. The company needs $1,000,000 for expansion, and management is considering two financing plans:
    - Plan 1 is to issue $1,000,000 of 12 percent bonds.
    - Plan 2 is to issue 50,000 common shares for $1,000,000.

    Zen Corporation management believes the new cash can be invested in operations to earn income of $300,000 before interest and taxes. Which plan seems more favourable given the corporation's tax rate of 40 percent? Why?

Just Checking Solutions appear at the end of this chapter and on MyAccountingLab.

Mortgages and Other Long-Term Liabilities

Mortgages: An Introduction

— LO ⑥ —

How do we account for long-term notes?

REAL WORLD EXAMPLE

The total interest paid on a mortgage can be shocking; paying off a mortgage early can reduce the total interest substantially.

REAL WORLD EXAMPLE

Some mortgages do not require blended mortgage payments of a fixed amount every month. Rather, some mortgages specify that a fixed amount of principal is repaid every month with interest paid on the mortgage balance. Fixed principal payments would ensure that the principal reduction is the constant while the interest and payment amount would change based on a reduced principal base.

A **mortgage** is a *loan secured* by *real property* using a *mortgage note*. The mortgage is repaid in equal monthly installments. A portion of each payment represents interest on the unpaid balance of the loan and the remainder reduces the principal, or the outstanding balance of the loan. Such payments are known as **blended payments**. Mortgage payments can be made at any point in the month, and to pay off a mortgage early, mortgage payments can also be made weekly or biweekly. The principal and interest portions of each mortgage payment can be calculated and presented in a *mortgage installment payment schedule*, also called a *mortgage amortization schedule*. The following is a partial mortgage installment payment schedule for a 10-year, 5 percent, $200,000 mortgage obtained on October 1, 2014, with monthly blended payments of $2,121. All amounts are rounded to the nearest dollar.

	A	B	C	D
	Blended Monthly Mortgage Payment	5% Interest for the Month (Preceding D × 0.05 ÷ 12)	Reduction in Principal (A − B)	Mortgage Balance (Preceding D − Current C)
Period				
Oct. 1, 2014				$200,000
Nov. 1, 2014	$2,121	$833	$1,288	198,712
Dec. 1, 2014	2,121	828	1,293	197,419
Jan. 1, 2015	2,121	823	1,298	196,121

Partial Mortgage Installment Payment Schedule
Blended Mortgage Payments

The blended mortgage payment ($2,121 in Column A) is a blend of both interest and principal. Notice how the reduction in principal (Column C) increases each month so that more of the principal is paid off as the mortgage note matures.

Journal Entry for Mortgage Payments

On November 1, 2014, the journal entry to record the first monthly payment on this $200,000 mortgage is

2014			
Nov. 1	Interest Expense	833	
	Mortgage Payable	1,288	
	Cash		2,121
	To pay monthly mortgage loan and record interest portion of the blended payment.		

Balance Sheet Presentation

The current and long-term portions of mortgage loans are reported on the balance sheet. In the mortgage installment payment schedule above, the mortgage balance in column D represents the total mortgage debt, and this amount is divided into the current portion of the debt due in one year and the long-term portion due after one year. On December 31, 2014, the current portion of the mortgage is classified as a current liability, as well as the interest on the mortgage that has accrued since the December 1, 2014, payment. Using the amounts for the blended mortgage payments shown, the liabilities section of the balance sheet would appear as follows:

December 31, 2014	
Current liabilities	
Interest payable*	$ 823
Current portion of mortgage**	$ 25,452
Long-term debt	
Mortgage***	$171,967

* This is the January 1, 2015, interest from column C of the mortgage installment payment schedule above.

** Calculated as 12 × $2,121, which should normally be split to show the interest and principal portions separately but is not done here for simplicity. If the mortgage installment payment schedule were extended to show all the payments in 2015, you would add the 12 principal payments for the year from the schedule to calculate the current portion of the mortgage.

*** Calculated as $197,419 − $25,452, which is the mortgage balance at December 31, 2014, (from column D) less the current portion of the mortgage shown as a current liability on the balance sheet.

✓ JUST CHECKING

13. Suppose Austin Metal purchases land and a building for $200,000 on October 1, 2014. Austin obtains a mortgage at an annual rate of 5 percent and will make monthly payments for 10 years. Using the installment payment schedule in this section on page 942, journalize the entries for the receipt of the mortgage and for the purchase of the land and building, assuming the land is assessed at $40,000 and the building is assessed at $160,000.

14. Refer to the previous question. Journalize the entry for the second mortgage payment, which was made on December 1, 2014.

Just Checking Solutions appear at the end of this chapter and on MyAccountingLab.

Lease Liabilities

LO ⑦
How do we account for leases?

A **lease** is an agreement in which the asset user (**lessee**) agrees to make regular, periodic payments to the property owner (**lessor**) in exchange for the exclusive use of the asset. Leasing is the way the lessee avoids having to make the large initial cash down payment that purchase agreements require. Accountants divide leases into two types when considering the lease from the lessee's perspective: operating and capital. From the lessor's perspective, there are again two categories of leases, operating and capital, with capital leases further divided into two kinds: *sales-type leases*, in which the lessor is usually a manufacturer or dealer, and *direct financing leases*, in which the lessor is usually not a manufacturer or dealer but provides financing. This text will consider the broader term, *capital lease*, and not the kinds of capital leases.

Operating Leases

Operating leases are usually short-term or cancellable. Many apartment leases and most short-term car-rental agreements extend a year or less. These operating leases give the lessee the right to use the asset, but provide the lessee with no continuing rights to the asset. The lessor retains the usual risks and rewards of owning the leased asset. To account for an operating lease, the lessee makes the following journal entry for a $2,000 lease payment:

Rent Expense (or Lease Expense)	2,000	
Cash		2,000
To record operating lease payment.		

The lessee's books report neither the leased asset nor any lease liability (except perhaps a prepaid rent amount or a rent accrual at the end of the period). However, the future lease payments for each of the next five years should be given in the notes to the financial statements. The nature of the lease commitments should also be stated in the notes.

Capital Leases

REAL WORLD EXAMPLE

Apartments and cars are two examples of items you might lease. With apartments, the lease period is typically one year, so you likely do not consume the apartment's usefulness by the end of the lease and you likely will not obtain ownership of the building at the end of the lease. Therefore, an apartment lease is an operating lease. Since most car leases have lease terms that encourage you to purchase the car at the end of the lease, a car lease like this is probably a capital lease. Businesses typically lease items, including cars and trucks, photocopiers, and expensive equipment, and often these are accounted for as capital leases.

Many businesses use capital leasing to finance the acquisition of some assets. A capital lease is long-term, noncancellable financing that is a form of debt.

How do you distinguish a capital lease from an operating lease? Section 3065 of the *CICA Handbook*, Part II, Accounting Standards for Private Enterprises, defines a **capital lease** as one that substantially transfers all the benefits and risks incident to ownership of property to the lessee. The section goes on to suggest that a lease is a capital lease from the perspective of the lessee if one or more of the following conditions are present at the beginning of the lease:

1. There is reasonable assurance that the lessee will obtain ownership of the leased asset at the end of the lease term.
2. The lease term is of such a length that the lessee will obtain almost all (usually 75 percent or more) of the benefits from the use of the leased asset over its life.
3. The lessor will both recover the original investment and earn a return on that investment from the lease.

A lease that does not meet any of the above conditions is probably an operating lease and should be accounted for as such.

A lease is a capital lease from the perspective of the lessor if any one of the three conditions outlined above is present and *both* of the following are present:

1. The credit risk associated with the lease is normal.
2. The amounts of any unreimbursable costs to the lessor are estimable.

Accounting for a Capital Lease   Accounting for a capital lease is much like accounting for a purchase. The lessor removes the asset on its books by recording a sale of the asset and creating a lease receivable at the beginning of the lease term. The lessee enters the asset into its accounts and records a lease liability at the beginning of the lease term. Thus, the lessee capitalizes the asset on its own financial statements even though the lessee may never take legal title to the property.

How does a lessee compute the cost of an asset acquired through a capital lease? Consider that the lessee gets the use of the asset but does *not* pay for the leased asset in full at the beginning of the lease. A capital lease is, therefore, similar to borrowing money to purchase the leased asset. The lessee must record the leased asset at the present value of the lease liability. The time value of money must be taken into account.

The cost of the asset to the lessee is the sum of any payment made at the beginning of the lease period plus the present value of the future lease payments. The lease payments are equal amounts occurring at regular intervals—that is, they are annuity payments.

Consider a 20-year building lease signed by Sierra Wireless, Inc. The lease starts on January 2, 2014, and requires 20 annual payments of $20,000 each, with the first payment due immediately. If the interest rate in the lease is 10 percent, then the present value of the 19 future payments is $167,298. Sierra's cost of the building is $187,298 (the sum of the initial payment, $20,000, plus the present value of the future payments, $167,298).

This lease meets the second condition for a capital lease given above; this arrangement is similar to purchasing the building on an installment plan. In an installment purchase, Sierra would debit Building and credit Cash and Installment Note Payable. The company would then pay interest and principal on the note payable and record amortization on the building. Accounting for a capital lease

LEARNING TIPS

To compute the present value of the lease asset using a financial calculator, ensure that the BGN key is on, then enter

PMT: $20,000

I: 10%

N: 20

FV: 0

This gives PV of $187,298.

If using the tables, use ($20,000 × PV of annuity at 10 percent for 19 periods, or 8.365 from Exhibit 15A–7 = $187,300). The $2 difference is due to rounding in the tables.

follows this same pattern—debit an asset, credit Cash, and credit a payable for the future lease payments—as shown next.

Sierra records the building at cost, which is the sum of the $20,000 initial payment plus the present value of the 19 future lease payments of $20,000 each, or $187,298 as shown.[6] The company credits Cash for the initial payment and credits Lease Liability for the present value of the future lease payments. At the beginning of the lease term, Sierra Wireless, Inc. makes the following entry:

2014			
Jan. 2	Building under Capital Lease	187,298	
	Cash		20,000
	Capital Lease Liability		167,298
	To lease a building ($20,000 + $167,298) and		
	make the first annual lease payment on the		
	capital lease ($20,000).		

Sierra's lease liability at January 2, 2014, is for 19 payments of $20,000 each on January 2, 2015, to January 2, 2033. However, included in those payments is interest calculated at 10 percent. The lease liability is

Cash payments January 2, 2015, to January 2, 2033 (19 × $20,000)	$380,000
Interest embedded in the lease payments	212,702
Present value of future lease payments	$167,298

If Sierra Wireless, Inc. were to record the liability at $380,000, it would also have to record the interest included in that amount as a contra amount. Most companies net the interest against the cash payments and show the liability as the net amount (principal).

Because Sierra has capitalized the building, the company records amortization (straight-line). Assume the building has an expected life of 25 years. It is amortized over the lease term of 20 years because the lessee has the use of the building only for that period. No residual value enters into the amortization computation because the lessee will have no residual asset when the building is returned to the lessor at the expiration of the lease. Therefore, the annual amortization entry is

2014			
Dec. 31	Amortization Expense	9,365	
	Accumulated Amortization—		
	Building under Capital Lease		9,365
	To record amortization on leased building		
	of $9,365 ($187,298 ÷ 20).		

KEY POINTS

For an operating lease, the lessor, not the lessee, records the amortization expense on the leased asset. For a capital lease, the lessee records the amortization expense.

Note that a lessee, such as Sierra, might obtain ownership of the leased asset at the end of the lease term. In such a situation, the lessee would amortize the leased asset over its useful life instead of over the term of the lease. At year end, Sierra must also accrue interest on the lease liability. Interest expense is computed by multiplying the lease liability by the interest rate on the lease. The following entry credits Capital Lease Liability (not Interest Payable) for this interest accrual:

2014			
Dec. 31	Interest Expense	16,730	
	Capital Lease Liability		16,730
	To accrue interest on the lease liability ($167,298 × 0.10, rounded).		

---

[6]The Chapter 15 Appendix explains present value.

To distinguish between assets that an entity owns and assets it only has a right to use, information about assets acquired through capital leases must be disclosed separately from all other long-term assets. This information includes leased assets' costs, amortization, and interest expense. For the previous example, the balance sheet at December 31, 2014, reports:

Assets		
Capital assets:		
Building under capital lease	$187,298	
Less: Accumulated amortization	9,365	$177,933
Liabilities		
Current liabilities:		
Lease liability (next payment due on Jan. 2, 2015)*		$ 20,000
Long-term liabilities:		
Lease liability		164,028**

* The information in brackets is for student reference only. It would not appear on the balance sheet.
** $164,028 = [Beginning balance ($167,298) + Interest accrual ($16,730) − Current portion ($20,000)]

In addition, the lessee must report the minimum capital lease payments for the next five years in the notes to the financial statements.

The lease liability is split into current and long-term portions because the next payment ($20,000) is a current liability and the remainder is long-term. The January 2, 2015, lease payment is recorded as follows:

2015			
Jan. 2	Lease Liability	20,000	
	Cash		20,000
	To make second annual lease payment on building.		

Other long-term liabilities shown on published balance sheets would include pension obligations, deferred compensation plans, and future income taxes, topics that will be left for more advanced accounting courses.

Off-Balance-Sheet Financing

An important part of business is obtaining the funds needed to acquire assets. To finance operations, a company may issue shares, borrow money, or retain earnings in the business. All three of these financing plans affect the right-hand side of the balance sheet. Issuing shares affects preferred or common shares. Borrowing creates notes or bonds payable. Internal funds come from retained earnings.

Off-balance-sheet financing is the acquisition of assets or services whose resulting debt is not reported on the balance sheet. A prime example is an operating lease. The lessee has the use of the leased asset, but neither the asset nor any lease liability is reported on the balance sheet. In the past, most leases were accounted for by the operating method. More recently, however, Section 3065 in Part II of the *CICA Handbook* has required businesses to account for an increasing number of leases by the capital lease method. Also, Section 3065 has brought about detailed reporting of operating lease payments in the notes to the financial statements; minimum operating lease payments for the next five years must be reported. The inclusion of more lease information, whether for capital or operating leases, makes the accounting information for decision making more complete. Much useful information is reported only in the notes. Experienced investors study the notes as well as the numbers in the financial statements when analyzing a company and deciding whether to invest in it.

✓ JUST CHECKING

15. Bedrock Construction Inc. acquired equipment under a capital lease that requires six annual lease payments of $30,000. The first payment is due when the lease begins on January 2, 2014. Future payments are due on January 2 of each year of the lease term. The interest rate in the lease is 12 percent and the present value of the five future lease payments is $108,143. Journalize (a) the acquisition of the equipment, (b) the amortization for 2014, (c) the accrued interest at December 31, 2014, and (d) the second lease payment on January 2, 2015.

Just Checking Solutions appear at the end of this chapter and on MyAccountingLab.

The Effects on Long-Term Liabilities of International Financial Reporting Standards (IFRS)

We will discuss bonds payable and leases in turn as the accounting treatment for each type of indebtedness does differ.

The two sets of standards governing accounting for bond indebtedness—ASPE and IFRS—are comparable in many key areas. Under ASPE, the liability for bonds is measured at amortized cost. Under IFRS, the liability for bonds is measured at amortized cost as well, but companies are also allowed the option of recording the liability for bonds at fair value. While the fair value option is the primary difference between IFRS and ASPE, there are a number of other differences as well. Variations such as the IFRS requirement to report separately the components of compound financial instruments on the balance sheet are beyond the scope of this text and are covered in more advanced accounting courses.

The principles governing accounting for leases are basically the same under ASPE and IFRS. The only material difference is that companies reporting under IFRS are required to disclose more supplementary information than those reporting under ASPE.

LO ⑧

How does IFRS affect long-term liabilities?

✓ JUST CHECKING

16. When accounting for bonds, what is the primary difference between ASPE and IFRS?

17. When accounting for leases, what is the primary difference between ASPE and IFRS?

Just Checking Solutions appear at the end of this chapter and on MyAccountingLab.

WHY IT'S DONE THIS WAY

Issuing bonds is one common way of raising capital to fund existing or new operations and projects. Corporations may prefer to raise capital with debt—by issuing bonds—because interest payments are tax deductible and the rate of interest paid is, in most cases, fixed. The market, in this case defined as the creditors who purchase the bonds, assess the risk of the company issuing the bonds and compare the bond interest rate with other investments available in the market to determine the interest rate they must earn when they purchase the bonds. This is the market rate of interest we discussed in this chapter.

The action of the market in determining the market rate of interest for bonds leads to either the creation of a discount or a premium, the accounting for which you have studied in this chapter. Since bondholders are always reassessing the risk of their investments, the market rate of interest can change daily. How is this constantly changing market rate of interest reflected in a company's financial statements? Under IFRS, companies can fairly value their bonds at the end of each fiscal period, which means they recalculate the present value of the bonds each year. This annual update to fair value is consistent with the **Level 2** characteristics of relevance and reliability in the accounting framework described in Chapter 1 (and repeated on the back inside cover of this book). Using the current rate of interest to calculate the fair value of bond debt is very relevant information to the users of the financial statements. Since the rate of interest is determined by market forces, it is also very reliable. Under ASPE, companies are not required to recalculate the fair value of their bond debt every year. This is because, typically, there are not as many bondholders in a private corporation and those bondholders have access to information directly from the owners and managers of the company.

Under both ASPE and IFRS, details of the corporation's various bond issues must be disclosed in the notes to the financial statements, as described by the **Level 4** recognition and measurement criteria in the framework. Thus, the valuation of bonds and disclosure of bond information in the financial statements communicate useful information to interested users to help them assess the success of the company—this is the **Level 1** objective of the accounting framework.

Summary Problem for Your Review

Name: Astoria Inc.
Accounting Period:
The years 2014, 2015, 2016

Astoria Inc. has outstanding an issue of 8-percent convertible bonds that mature in 2024. Suppose the bonds were issued October 1, 2014, and pay interest each April 1 and October 1.

Required

1. Complete the following effective-interest amortization table through October 1, 2016.

> Bond data: Maturity value—$2,000,000
> Contract interest rate—8%
> Interest paid—4% semiannually, $80,000 ($2,000,000 × 0.04)
> Market interest rate at time of issue—9% annually, 4.5% semiannually
> Issue proceeds—$1,869,921

Amortization table:

Semiannual Interest Period	A Interest Payment (4% of Maturity Value)	B Interest Expense (4.5% of Preceding Bond Carrying Amount)	C Discount Amortization (B − A)	D Unamortized Discount Account Balance (Preceding D − Current C)	E Bond Carrying Amount ($2,000,000 − D)
Oct. 1, 2014					
Apr. 1, 2015					
Oct. 1, 2015					
Apr. 1, 2016					
Oct. 1, 2016					

2. Using the amortization table, record the following transactions:
   a. Issuance of the bonds on October 1, 2014.
   b. Accrual of interest and amortization of discount on December 31, 2014.
   c. Payment of interest and amortization of discount on April 1, 2015.
   d. Conversion of one-third of the bonds payable into common shares on October 2, 2016.
   e. Retirement of two-thirds of the bonds payable on October 2, 2016. Purchase price of the bonds was 102.00.

SOLUTION

Requirement 1

Amortization table:

Semiannual Interest Period	A Interest Payment (4% of Maturity Value)	B Interest Expense (4.5% of Preceding Bond Carrying Amount)	C Discount Amortization (B − A)	D Unamortized Discount Account Balance (Preceding D − Current C)	E Bond Carrying Amount ($2,000,000 − D)
Oct. 1, 2014				$130,079	$1,869,921
Apr. 1, 2015	$80,000	$84,146	$4,146	125,933	1,874,067
Oct. 1, 2015	80,000	84,333	4,333	121,600	1,878,400
Apr. 1, 2016	80,000	84,528	4,528	117,072	1,882,928
Oct. 1, 2016	80,000	84,732	4,732	112,340	1,887,660

The semiannual interest payment is constant ($80,000). The interest expense is calculated as 4.5 percent of the previous period's carrying value. The unamortized discount account balance reflects that the money received when the bonds were issued ($1,869,921) is less than the maturity value of the bonds ($2,000,000).

Requirement 2

	2014				
a.	Oct. 1	Cash		1,869,921	
		Discount on Bonds Payable		130,079	
		Bonds Payable			2,000,000
		To issue 8%, 10-year bonds at a discount.			

a. The bonds were issued for less than $2,000,000, reflecting a discount. Use the amounts from columns D and E for Oct. 1, 2014 from the amortization table.

<table>
<tr><td>b. The accrued interest is calculated, and the bond discount is amortized. Use 3/6 of the amounts from columns A, B, and C for Apr. 1, 2015.</td><td>b.</td><td colspan="2">Dec. 31</td><td>Interest Expense</td><td>42,073</td><td></td></tr>
</table>

b. The accrued interest is calculated, and the bond discount is amortized. Use 3/6 of the amounts from columns A, B, and C for Apr. 1, 2015.	**b.**	**Dec. 31**	Interest Expense	42,073	
			Discount on Bonds Payable		2,073
			Interest Payable		40,000
			To accrue interest expense for three months ($84,146 × ³⁄₆) and amortize bond discount for three months ($4,146 × ³⁄₆), and record payable for three months ($80,000 × ³⁄₆).		

$$(\$84,146 \times \tfrac{3}{6})$$ and amortize bond discount for three months $(\$4,146 \times \tfrac{3}{6})$, and record payable for three months $(\$80,000 \times \tfrac{3}{6})$.

c. The semiannual interest payment is made ($80,000 from Column A). Only the January–March 2015 interest expense is recorded, since the October–December interest expense was already recorded in Requirement 2b. The same is true for the discount on bonds payable. Reverse Interest Payable from Requirement 2b, since cash is paid now.	**c.**	**2015** **Apr. 1**	Interest Expense	42,073	
			Interest Payable	40,000	
			Discount on Bonds Payable		2,073
			Cash		80,000
			To pay semiannual interest, part of which was accrued on December 31, 2014, and amortize three months' discount on bonds payable ($4,146 × ³⁄₆).		

To pay semiannual interest, part of which was accrued on December 31, 2014, and amortize three months' discount on bonds payable $(\$4,146 \times \tfrac{3}{6})$.

d. When converting bonds to common shares, retire the full amount of the bonds (¹⁄₃ × $2,000,000) and the discount account balance (¹⁄₃ × $112,240 from column D for Oct. 1, 2016).	**d.**	**2016** **Oct. 2**	Bonds Payable	666,667	
			Discount on Bonds Payable		37,447
			Common Shares		629,220
			To record conversion of ¹⁄₃ of the bonds payable ($2,000,000 × ¹⁄₃). Remove ¹⁄₃ of the discount ($112,340 × ¹⁄₃).		

To record conversion of $\tfrac{1}{3}$ of the bonds payable $(\$2,000,000 \times \tfrac{1}{3})$. Remove $\tfrac{1}{3}$ of the discount $(\$112,340 \times \tfrac{1}{3})$.

e. The cash paid on retirement was $102 for every $100 of bonds. Use ²⁄₃ of the amount from column D for Oct. 1, 2016 to calculate Discount on Bonds Payable. The loss on retirement reflects the excess of the book value over the cash received and is the "plug" figure in the journal entry calculated as $1,333,333 − $74,893 − $1,360,000 = $101,560 debit.	**e.**	**Oct. 2**	Bonds Payable	1,333,333	
			Loss on Retirement of Bonds	101,560	
			Discount on Bonds Payable		74,893
			Cash		1,360,000
			To retire remaining bonds payable ($2,000,000 × ²⁄₃) and discount ($112,340 × ²⁄₃) before maturity. Cash paid ($2,000,000 × ²⁄₃ × 1.02).		

To retire remaining bonds payable $(\$2,000,000 \times \tfrac{2}{3})$ and discount $(\$112,340 \times \tfrac{2}{3})$ before maturity.

Cash paid $(\$2,000,000 \times \tfrac{2}{3} \times 1.02)$.

Summary

① **Learning Objective 1: Define bonds payable and the types of bonds**

What are bonds?

- A corporation may borrow money by issuing long-term notes and bonds. **Pg. 919**
- Bondholders are the people or companies that lend the money to the bond or note issuer.
- A bond indenture or contract specifies the maturity value of the bonds, the stated (contract) interest rate, and the dates for paying interest and principal.
- Bonds may be secured (for example, a mortgage) or unsecured (for example, a debenture). Bonds and debentures are accounted for similarly. Mortgages are explored further later in the chapter.

(2) Learning Objective 2: Determine the price of a bond, and account for basic bond transactions

How do we account for the sale of a bond?

- Bonds are traded through organized markets, such as the over-the-counter market.
- Bonds are typically divided into $1,000 units. Their prices are quoted at the price per $100.00 bond.
- Market interest rates fluctuate and may differ from the stated rate on a bond.
- If a bond's stated rate exceeds the market rate, the bond sells at a premium.
- A bond with a stated rate below the market rate sells at a discount.
- Money earns income over time, a fact that gives rise to the present-value concept.
- An investor will pay a price for a bond equal to the present value of the bond principal plus the present value of the stream of bond interest receipts.
- Accrued interest may be factored into the purchase if the bond is sold between interest dates.

Pg. 921

(3) Learning Objective 3: Amortize a bond discount and premium by the straight-line amortization method and the effective-interest amortization method

How do we allocate a bond discount or premium over the life of a bond?

- Straight-line amortization allocates an *equal dollar amount* of premium or discount to each interest period.
- The effective-interest method of amortization allocates a different dollar amount of premium or discount to each interst period because it allocates a *constant percentage* of premium or discount to each interest period. The market rate at the time of issuance is multiplied by the bonds' carrying amount to determine the interest expense for each period and to compute the amount of discount or premium amortization.

Pg. 928

(4) Learning Objective 4: Account for retirement and conversion of bonds

How do we account for changes in a bond issue?

- Companies may retire their bonds payable before maturity.
- Redeemable bonds are bonds that give the purchaser the option of retiring the bonds at a stated dollar amount prior to maturity.
- Callable bonds give the borrower the right to pay off the bonds at a specified call price; otherwise, the company may purchase the bonds in the open market.
- Convertible bonds and notes give the investor the privilege of trading the bonds in for shares of the issuing corporation. The carrying amount of the bonds becomes the book value of the newly issued shares.

Pg. 938

(5) Learning Objective 5: Show the advantages and disadvantages of borrowing

How do we decide whether to issue debt versus equity?

A key advantage of raising money by borrowing versus issuing shares is that interest expense on debt is tax-deductible. Thus, borrowing is less costly than issuing shares.

- If the company can earn more income than the cost of borrowing, EPS will increase.
- Borrowing's disadvantages result from the fact that the company must repay the loan and its interest, unlike issuing shares, where dividends do not have to be declared and paid.

Pg. 940

(6) Learning Objective 6: Account for long-term notes payable

How do we account for long-term notes?

- A mortgage is a loan secured by real property using a mortgage note. The mortgage is repaid in equal monthly installments.
- A portion of each payment represents interest on the unpaid balance of the loan and the remainder reduces the principal, or the outstanding balance of the loan.

Pg. 942

(7) Learning Objective 7: Account for operating leases and for assets acquired through a capital lease

How do we account for leases?

- A lease is an agreement between the lessor who owns an item and rents it to the lessee who has the use of the item.
- In an operating lease, the lessor retains the usual risks and rights of owning the asset. The lessee debits Rent Expense and credits Cash when making lease payments.
- A capital lease is long-term, noncancellable, and similar to an installment purchase of the leased asset. In a capital lease, the lessee capitalizes and amortizes the leased asset, and reports a lease liability on its balance sheet.

Pg. 943

(8) Learning Objective 8: Identify the effects on long-term liabilities of international financial reporting standards (IFRS)

How does IFRS affect long-term liabilities?

- Under ASPE, liabilities for bond indebtedness are reported at amortized cost. Under IFRS, the liability may be reported at amortized cost or fair value.
- Under IFRS, companies are required to disclose more lease information than under ASPE.

Pg. 947

Check Accounting Vocabulary on page 953 for all key terms used in Chapter 15 and the Glossary on page 1246 for all key terms used in the textbook.

CHAPTER REVIEW:

MyAccountingLab   DemoDoc covering Bond Transactions

MyAccountingLab   Student PowerPoint Slides

MyAccountingLab   Audio Chapter Summary

Note: All MyAccountingLab resources can be found in the Chapter Resources section and the Multimedia Library.

SELF-STUDY QUESTIONS

Test your understanding of the chapter by marking the best answer for each of the following questions:

1. Which type of bond is unsecured? (p. 921)
   a. Serial bond
   b. Common bond
   c. Debenture bond
   d. Mortgage bond

2. How much will an investor pay for a $200,000 bond priced at 102.5? (p. 921)
   a. $200,000
   b. $204,000
   c. $205,000
   d. $202,500

3. A bond with a stated interest rate of 6.5 percent is issued when the market interest rate is 6.75 percent. This bond will sell at (p. 923)
   a. Par value
   b. A discount
   c. A premium
   d. A price minus accrued interest

4. Imported Cars Inc. has $1,000,000 of 10-year bonds payable outstanding. These bonds had a discount of $80,000 at issuance, which was five years ago. The company uses the straight-line amortization method. The carrying amount or balance of the Imported Cars Inc. bonds payable is (pp. 926–927)
   a. $920,000
   b. $960,000
   c. $1,000,000
   d. $1,040,000

5. Imported Cars issued its 8-percent bonds payable at a price of $880,000 (maturity value is $1,000,000). The market interest rate was 10 percent when Imported Cars issued its bonds. The company uses the effective-interest method for the bonds. Interest expense for the first year is (pp. 930–931)
   a. $70,400
   b. $80,000
   c. $88,000
   d. $100,000

6. Bonds payable with face value of $1,800,000 and a balance or carrying value of $1,728,000 are retired before their scheduled maturity with a cash outlay of $1,752,000. Which of the following entries correctly records this bond retirement? (pp. 938–939)

a.		
Bonds Payable	1,800,000	
Discount on Bonds Payable	72,000	
Cash		1,752,000
Gain on Retirement of Bonds Payable		120,000

b.		
Bonds Payable	1,800,000	
Loss on Retirement of Bonds Payable	24,000	
Discount on Bonds Payable		72,000
Cash		1,752,000

c.		
Bonds Payable	1,800,000	
Discount on Bonds Payable		36,000
Cash		1,752,000
Gain on Retirement of Bonds Payable		12,000

d.		
Bonds Payable	1,728,000	
Discount on Bonds Payable	72,000	
Gain on Retirement of Bonds Payable		48,000
Cash		1,752,000

7. YYZ Corporation has $3,450,000 of debt outstanding at year end, of which $990,000 is due in one year. What will this company report on its year-end balance sheet? (p. 942)
   a. Long-term debt of $3,450,000
   b. Current liability of $990,000 and long-term debt of $3,450,000
   c. Current liability of $990,000 and long-term debt of $2,460,000
   d. None of the above

8. An advantage of financing operations with debt versus shares is (pp. 946–947)
   a. The tax deductibility of interest expense on debt
   b. The legal requirement to pay interest and principal
   c. Lower interest payments compared to dividend payments
   d. All of the above
9. Which of the following statements is true for mortgage notes payable requiring blended payments? (p. 942)
   a. Payments include an increasing amount of interest and a decreasing amount of principal over the life of the mortgage.
   b. Payments include an increasing amount of principal and a decreasing amount of interest over the life of the mortgage.

   c. Payments include an equal amount of principal and interest for every period over the life of the mortgage.
   d. The total cost of the asset secured by a mortgage is equal to the present value of the mortgage.
10. In a capital lease, the lessee records (pp. 944–945)
   a. A leased asset and a lease liability
   b. Amortization on the leased asset
   c. Interest on the lease liability
   d. All of the above

Answers to Self-Study Questions

1. c   2. c   [$200,000 × 1.025 = $205,000]   3. b   4. b   5. c   6. b   7. c   8. a   9. b   10. d

ACCOUNTING VOCABULARY

Bearer bonds Bonds payable to the person that has possession of them. Also called *unregistered bonds* (p. 921).

Bid price The highest price that a buyer is willing to pay for a bond (p. 922).

Blended payments Payments are a constant amount, and the amount of interest and principal that are applied to the loan change with each payment (p. 943).

Bond A formal agreement in which a lender loans money to a borrower who agrees to repay the money loaned at a future date and agrees to pay interest regularly over the life of the bond (p. 919).

Bond indenture The contract that specifies the maturity value of the bonds, the stated (contract) interest rate, and the dates for paying interest and principal (p. 919).

Bonds payable Groups of notes payable (bonds) issued to multiple lenders called bondholders (p. 919).

Callable bond Bonds that the issuer may call or pay off at a specified price whenever the issuer wants (p. 938).

Capital lease Lease agreement that substantially transfers all the benefits and risks of ownership from the lessor to the lessee (p. 945).

Contract interest rate Interest rate that determines the amount of cash interest the borrower pays and the investor receives each year. Also called the *stated interest rate* (p. 923).

Convertible bond Bonds that may be converted into the common shares of the issuing company at the option of the investor (p. 939).

Coupon rate Represents the contractual rate of interest that the issuer must pay the bondholders (p. 922).

Convertible note Notes that may be converted into the common shares of the issuing company at the option of the investor (p. 939).

Debenture Unsecured bond, backed only by the good faith of the issuer (p. 921).

Discount Amount of bond's issue price under its maturity (par) value (p. 921).

Effective-interest amortization Amortization method in which a different amount of amortization expense is assigned to each year (or period) of the bond's life. The amount of amortization expense is the same percentage of a bond's carrying value for every period over a bond's life (p. 930).

Effective interest rate Interest rate that investors demand in order to loan their money. Also called the *market interest rate* (p. 923).

Face value Another name for the principal or maturity value of a bond (p. 919, 921).

Lease Agreement in which the tenant (lessee) agrees to make rent payments to the property owner (lessor) in exchange for the exclusive use of the asset (p. 944).

Lessee Tenant, or user of the asset, in a lease agreement *(p. 943)*.

Lessor Property owner in a lease agreement *(p. 943)*.

Long-term liabilities Debts due to be paid in more than a year or more than one of the entity's operating cycles if an operating cycle is greater than one year *(p. 919)*.

Market interest rate Interest rate that investors demand in order to loan their money. Also called the *effective interest rate* *(p. 923)*.

Maturity date The date on which the borrower must pay the principal amount to the lender *(p. 919)*.

Maturity value A bond issued at par that has no discount or premium. Also another name for a bond's principal value *(p. 919, 921)*.

Mortgage Borrower's promise to transfer the legal title to certain assets to the lender if the debt is not paid on schedule. A mortgage is a special type of *secured bond* *(p. 921)*.

Off-balance-sheet financing Acquisition of assets or services whose resulting debt is not reported on the balance sheet *(p. 946)*.

Operating lease Usually a short-term or cancellable rental agreement *(p. 943)*.

Par value Another name for the principal or maturity value of a bond *(p. 919, 921)*.

Premium Excess of bond's issue price over its maturity (par) value *(p. 921)*.

Present value Amount a person would invest now to receive a greater amount at a future date *(p. 922)*.

Principal value The amount a company borrows from a bondholder. Also called the bond's *maturity value, par value,* or *face value* *(p. 919, 921)*.

Secured bond A bond that gives the bondholder the right to take specified assets of the issuer if the issuer fails to pay principal or interest *(p. 921)*.

Redeemable bonds Bonds that give the purchaser the option of retiring them at a stated dollar amount prior to maturity *(p. 938)*.

Secured bonds Assets of the issuer are provided as collateral. A mortgage is a special type of secured bond *(p. 921)*.

Serial bond Bond that matures in installments over a period of time *(p. 921)*.

Stated interest rate Interest rate that determines the amount of cash interest the borrower pays and the investor receives each year. Also called the contract interest rate *(p. 923)*.

Straight-line amortization Allocate a bond discount or a bond premium to expense by dividing the discount or premium into equal amounts for each interest period *(p. 928)*.

Term bond Bonds that all mature at the same time for a particular issue *(p. 921)*.

Trading on the equity Earning more income on borrowed money than the related expense, thereby increasing the earnings for the owners of the business *(p. 941)*.

Unregistered bonds Another name for *bearer bonds* *(p. 921)*.

Yield The interest rate that an investor will receive based on a compounding period of one year *(p. 922)*.

SIMILAR ACCOUNTING TERMS

Bond	Secured bond; Mortgage bond
Bond principal	Maturity value; Face value; Par value; Principal value
Stated interest rate	Contract interest rate; Indenture rate
Debenture	Unsecured bond
Market interest rate	Effective interest rate
Capital lease liability	Obligation under capital lease
Operating lease	Short-term lease; Short-term rental
Mortgage installment payment schedule	Mortgage amortization schedule

Assignment Material

QUESTIONS

1. How do bonds payable differ from a note payable?

2. How does an underwriter assist with the issuance of bonds?

3. Compute the price to the nearest dollar for the following bonds with a face value of $10,000:

   a. 93.00   c. 101.375   e. 100.00
   b. 88.75   d. 122.50

4. In which of the following situations will bonds sell at par? At a premium? At a discount?

   a. 9-percent bonds sold when the market rate is 9 percent

   b. 9-percent bonds sold when the market rate is 10 percent

   c. 9-percent bonds sold when the market rate is 8 percent

5. Identify the accounts to debit and credit for transactions (a) to issue bonds at *par*, (b) to pay interest, (c) to accrue interest at year end, and (d) to pay off bonds at maturity.

6. Identify the accounts to debit and credit for transactions (a) to issue bonds at a *discount*, (b) to pay interest, (c) to accrue interest at year end, and (d) to pay off bonds at maturity.

7. Identify the accounts to debit and credit for transactions (a) to issue bonds at a *premium*, (b) to pay interest, (c) to accrue interest at year end, and (d) to pay off bonds at maturity.

8. Why are bonds sold for a price "plus accrued interest"? What happens to accrued interest when bonds are sold by an individual?

9. How does the straight-line method of amortizing a bond discount (or premium) differ from the effective-interest method?

10. A company retires 10-year bonds payable of $100,000 after five years. The business issued the bonds at 104.00 and called them at 103.00. Compute the amount of gain or loss on retirement. How is this gain or loss reported on the income statement? The straight-line method of amortization is used.

11. Bonds payable with a maturity value of $200,000 are callable at 102.50. Their market price is 101.25. If you are the issuer of these bonds, how much will you pay to retire them before maturity?

12. Why are convertible bonds attractive to investors? Why are they popular with borrowers?

13. Ingoldby Corp. has $156 million of bonds outstanding at December 31, 2014. Of the total, $26 million are due in 2015, and the balance in 2016 and beyond. How would Ingoldby Corp. report its bonds payable on the 2014 balance sheet?

14. Contrast the effects on a company of issuing bonds versus issuing shares.

15. Identify the accounts a lessee debits and credits when making operating lease payments.

16. What characteristics distinguish a capital lease from an operating lease?

17. A business signs a capital lease for the use of a building. What accounts are debited and credited (a) to begin the lease term and make the first lease payment, (b) to record amortization, (c) to accrue interest on the lease liability, and (d) to make the second lease payment? The lease payments are made on the first day of the fiscal year.

18. What are blended mortgage payments?

19. Describe how each portion of a blended mortgage payment changes over the life of the mortgage.

20. Show how a lessee reports on the balance sheet any leased equipment and the related lease liability under a capital lease.

21. What is off-balance-sheet financing? Give an example.

MyAccountingLab   Make the grade with MyAccountingLab: The Starters, Exercises, and Problems marked in red can be found on MyAccountingLab. You can practise them as often as you want, and most feature step-by-step guided instructions to help you find the right answer.

STARTERS

Bond terms and definitions
①

Starter 15–1 Match the following terms by entering in the blank space the letter of the phrase that best describes each term.

_____Bond indenture   _____Unregistered bonds

_____Secured bonds   _____Bearer bonds

_____Debentures   _____Serial bonds

_____Convertible bonds   _____Redeemable bonds

a. May be converted into the company's common shares.
b. Matures in installments over a period of time.
c. Unsecured bond, backed only by the good faith of the issuer.
d. Contract agreed to between the issuer of the bonds and the purchaser.
e. Assets of the issuer are provided as collateral.
f. Another name for bearer bonds.
g. Principal is payable to the person that has possession of the bonds.
h. Bonds that give the buyer an option of retiring the bonds before maturity.

Determining if bond price is at par, at a discount, or at a premium
②

Starter 15–2 Determine whether the following bonds payable will be issued at maturity value, at a premium, or at a discount:

a. The market interest rate is 7 percent. Jersey Corp. issues bonds payable with a stated rate of 6.5 percent.
b. Frobisher Bay Inc. issued 7-percent bonds payable when the market rate was 6.75 percent.
c. Carola Corporation issued 8 percent bonds when the market interest rate was 8 percent.
d. Black Hawk Corp. issued bonds payable that pay stated interest of 7 percent. At issuance, the market interest rate was 8.25 percent.

Pricing bonds
②
b. 104,500
d. $102,500

Starter 15–3 Compute the price of the following 4-percent bonds of Lisbon Telecom:

a. $100,000 issued at 98.5   c. $100,000 issued at 92.6
b. $100,000 issued at 104.5   d. $100,000 issued at 102.5

Maturity value of a bond
②

Starter 15–4 For which bond in Starter 15–3 will Lisbon Telecom have to pay the most at maturity? Explain your answer.

Journalizing basic bond payable transactions
②
b. Interest Expense $16,250

Starter 15–5 Hunter Corp. issued a $500,000, 6.5-percent, 10-year bond payable on January 1, 2014. Journalize the following transactions for Hunter Corp. Include an explanation for each entry.

a. Issuance of the bond payable at par on January 1, 2014.
b. Payment of semiannual cash interest on July 1, 2014. (Round to the nearest dollar.)
c. Payment of the bonds payable at maturity. (Give the date.)

Determining bonds payable amounts
②
3. Interest $30,000

Starter 15–6 C&W Drive-Ins Ltd. borrowed money by issuing $1,000,000 of 6-percent bonds payable at 96.5.

1. How much cash did C&W receive when it issued the bonds payable?
2. How much must C&W pay back at maturity?
3. How much cash interest will C&W pay every six months?

Bond interest rates
②

Starter 15–7 A 7-percent, 10-year bond was issued at a price of 93. Was the market interest rate per annum at the date of issuance closer to 6 percent, 7 percent, or 8 percent? Explain.

Issuing bonds payable at a discount, paying interest, and amortizing discount by the straight-line method
② ③
b. Interest Expense $12,500

Starter 15–8 Jobs Inc. issued a $500,000, 4-percent, 10-year bond payable at a price of 90 on January 1, 2014. Journalize the following transactions for Jobs Inc. Include an explanation for each entry.

a. Issuance of the bond payable on January 1, 2014.
b. Payment of semiannual interest and amortization of bond discount on July 1, 2014. Jobs uses the straight-line method to amortize the bond discount.

Starter 15–9 Waves Corp. issued a $400,000, 7-percent, 10-year bond payable at a price of 105 on January 1, 2014. Journalize the following transactions for Waves Corp. Include an explanation for each entry.

a. Issuance of the bond payable on January 1, 2014.
b. Payment of semiannual interest and amortization of bond premium on July 1, 2014. Waves uses the straight-line method to amortize the premium.

Issuing bonds payable at a premium, paying interest, and amortizing premium by the straight-line method
② ③
b. Interest Expense $13,000

Starter 15–10 Reliable Limited issued $800,000 of 3-percent, 10-year bonds payable on October 1, 2014, at par value. Reliable's accounting year ends on December 31. Journalize the following transactions. Include an explanation for each entry.

a. Issuance of the bonds on October 1, 2014.
b. Accrual of interest expense on December 31, 2014.
c. Payment of the first semiannual interest amount on April 1, 2015.

Issuing bonds payable and accruing interest
②
b. Interest Expense $6,000

Starter 15–11 Netwerk Inc. issued $1,500,000 of 5-percent, 10-year bonds payable and received cash proceeds of $1,388,419 on March 31, 2014. The market interest rate at the date of issuance was 6 percent, and the bonds pay interest semiannually.

1. Did the bonds sell at a premium or a discount?
2. Prepare an effective-interest amortization table for the bond discount, through the first two interest payments. Use Exhibit 15–4 as a guide, and round amounts to the nearest dollar. Students can use a financial calculator if so instructed.
3. Record Netwerk Inc.'s issuance of the bonds on March 31, 2014, and on September 30, 2014, payment of the first semiannual interest amount and amortization of the bond discount. Explanations are not required.

Issuing bonds payable and amortizing discount by the effective-interest method
③
3. Interest Expense $41,653

Starter 15–12 Jones Inc. issued $400,000 of 8-percent, 10-year bonds payable at a price of 114.88 on May 31, 2014. The market interest rate at the date of issuance was 6 percent, and the Jones Inc. bonds pay interest semiannually.

The effective-interest amortization table for the bond premium is presented here for the first two interest periods.

Issuing bonds payable and amortizing premium by the effective-interest method
③
3. Interest Expense $13,651

Amortization Table

	A	B	C	D	E
				Unamortized	
End of Semiannual Interest Period	**Interest Payment (4% of Maturity Value)**	**Interest Expense (3% of Preceding Bond Carrying Amount)**	**Premium Amortization (A − B)**	**Premium Account Balance (Previous D − Current C)**	**Bond Carrying Amount ($400,000 + D)**
May 31, 2014				$59,520	$459,520
Nov. 30, 2014	$16,000	$13,786	$2,214	57,306	457,306
May 31, 2015	16,000	13,719	2,281	55,025	455,025

1. How much cash did Jones Inc. receive upon issuance of the bonds payable?
2. Continue the effective-interest amortization table for the bond premium for the next two interest payments. Round amounts to the nearest dollar.
3. Record issuance of the bonds on May 31, 2014, and on November 30, 2015, payment of the third semiannual interest amount and amortization of the bond premium. Explanations are not required.

Starter 15–13 Veltman Corp. issued $750,000 of 4-percent, 10-year bonds at par value on May 1, 2014, four months after the bond's original issue date of January 1, 2014. Journalize the following transactions. Include an explanation for each entry.

a. Issuance of the bonds payable on May 1, 2014.
b. Payment of the first semiannual interest amount on July 1, 2014.

Issuing bonds payable between interest dates and then paying the interest
②
b. Interest Expense $5,000

Accounting for the retirement of bonds payable

④

3. Gain $26,000

Starter 15–14 On January 1, 2014, Ishikawa Inc. issued $500,000 of 9-percent, five-year bonds payable at 104. Ishikawa has extra cash and wishes to retire all the bonds payable on January 1, 2015, immediately after making the second semiannual interest payment. Ishikawa uses the straight-line method of amortization. To retire the bonds, Ishikawa pays the market price of 98.

1. What is Ishikawa's carrying amount of the bonds payable on the retirement date?
2. How much cash must Ishikawa pay to retire the bonds payable?
3. Compute Ishikawa's gain or loss on the retirement of the bonds payable.

Accounting for the conversion of bonds payable

④

1. Carrying amount, $3,030,000

Starter 15–15 Partialfood Corp. has $3,000,000 of convertible bonds payable outstanding, with a bond premium of $30,000 also on the books. The bondholders have notified Partialfood that they wish to convert the bonds into shares. Specifically, the bonds may be converted into 400,000 of Partialfood's common shares.

1. What is Partialfood's carrying amount of its convertible bonds payable prior to the conversion?
2. Journalize Partialfood's conversion of the bonds payable into common shares. No explanation is required.

Reporting liabilities

③ ⑥

Total current liabilities, $28,500

Starter 15–16 Talon Inc. includes the following selected accounts in its general ledger at December 31, 2014:

Notes Payable, Long-term	$50,000	Accounts Payable.....................	$16,000
Bonds Payable..........................	100,000	Discount on Bonds Payable....	3,000
Interest Payable (due next year)	500	Mortgage Payable (payments are $1,000 per month)..............	100,000

Prepare the liabilities section of Talon Inc.'s balance sheet at December 31, 2014, to show how the company would report these items. Report a total for current liabilities.

Applying mortgage concepts to a loan

⑥

Starter 15–17 You qualified for a student loan in the amount of $10,000. Once you graduate, you are required to repay this loan over 10 years at a rate of interest of 4 percent. The monthly interest and principal repayments are calculated like a mortgage. The following table illustrates the first four payments beginning November 1, 2014.

Student Loan Payments				
			Reduction in	
Period	Loan Payment	Interest	Loan	Loan Balance
Nov. 1, 2014				$10,000.00
Dec. 1, 2014	$101.25	$33.33	$67.92	9,932.08
Jan. 1, 2015	101.25	33.11	68.14	9,863.94
Feb. 1, 2015	101.25	32.88	68.37	9,795.57
Mar. 1, 2015	101.25	32.65	68.60	9,726.97

Using the information from the table, record the journal entry for the December 1, 2014, loan payment.

Earnings-per-share effects of financing with bonds versus shares

⑤

EPS: Plan A $3.26

Starter 15–18 T&T Marina needs to raise $2 million to expand. T&T's president is considering two plans:

- Plan A: Issue $2,000,000 of 16 percent bonds payable to borrow the money
- Plan B: Issue 100,000 common shares at $20.00 per share

Before any new financing, T&T expects to earn net income of $600,000, and the company already has 200,000 common shares outstanding. T&T believes the expansion will increase income before interest and income tax by $400,000. The income tax rate is 35 percent.

Prepare an analysis similar to Exhibit 15–8 to determine which plan is likely to result in higher earnings per share. Which financing plan would you recommend?

Starter 15–19 Best Corp. agrees to lease a store in a mall and open a coffee shop. On January 2, 2014, the company pays a non-refundable $20,000 deposit to secure the store and agrees to a lease amount of $10,000 per month for two years. Journalize the initial lease deposit, the first monthly lease payment, and the December 31 year-end adjustment of the $20,000 deposit. Explanations are not required. Would Best Corp. report the lease information in the notes to the financial statements? Why or why not?

Reporting lease liabilities

EXERCISES

MyAccountingLab

Exercise 15–1

Tyler Corp. is planning to issue long-term bonds payable to borrow for a major expansion. The chief executive, Robert Tyler, asks your advice on some related matters, as follows:

a. At what type of bond price will Tyler have total interest expense equal to the cash interest payments?

b. Under which type of price will Tyler's total interest expense be greater than the cash interest payments?

c. The stated interest rate on the bonds is 3 percent, and the market interest rate is 4 percent. What type of price can Tyler expect for the bonds?

d. Tyler could raise the stated interest rate on the bonds to 5 percent (market rate is 4 percent). In that case, what type of price can Tyler expect for the bonds?

Determining whether the bond price will be at par, at a discount, or at a premium

Exercise 15–2

Sea-Link Distributors Inc. issues $2,000,000 of 4-percent, semiannual, 20-year bonds dated on April 30. Record (a) the issuance of bonds at par on April 30 and (b) the next semiannual interest payment on October 31.

Issuing bonds and paying interest

b. Interest Expense $40,000

Exercise 15–3

On February 1, Lasquiti Logistics Inc. issues 20-year, 3-percent bonds payable with a maturity value of $20,000,000. The bonds sell at par and pay interest on January 31 and July 31. Record (a) the issuance of the bonds on February 1, (b) the semiannual interest payment on July 31, and (c) the interest accrual on December 31.

Issuing bonds; paying and accruing interest

b. Interest Expense $300,000

Exercise 15–4

Saturna Corp. issues 20-year, 8-percent bonds with a maturity value of $5,000,000 on April 30. The bonds sell at par and pay interest on March 31 and September 30. Record (a) issuance of the bonds on April 30, (b) payment of interest on September 30, and (c) accrual of interest on December 31.

Issuing bonds; paying and accruing interest

b. Interest Expense $166,667

Exercise 15–5

Refer to the data for Saturna Corp. in Exercise 15–4. If Saturna Corp. issued the bonds on June 30, how much cash would Saturna Corp. receive upon issuance of the bonds?

Issuing bonds between interest dates

Exercise 15–6

On February 1, Harvard Logistics Inc. issued 20-year, 3.5-percent bonds with a maturity value of $5,000,000. The bonds sell at 98.00 and pay interest on January 31 and July 31. Harvard Logistics Inc. amortizes bond discounts by the straight-line method. Record (a) issuance of the bonds on February 1, (b) the semiannual interest payment on July 31, and (c) the interest accrual on December 31.

Issuing bonds, paying and earning interest, and amortizing discount by the straight-line method

b. Interest Expense $90,000

Exercise 15–7

Lafayette Corp. issues $1,500,000 of 20-year, 8-percent bonds on March 31, 2014. The bonds sell at 102.00 and pay interest on March 31 and September 30. Assume Lafayette Corp.

Issuing bonds, paying and accruing interest, and amortizing premium by the straight-line method
b. Interest Expense $59,250

amortizes the premium by the straight-line method. Record (a) the issuance of the bonds on March 31, 2014, (b) payment of interest on September 30, 2014, (c) accrual of interest on December 31, 2014, and (d) payment of interest on March 31, 2015.

Excel Spreadsheet
Template

Preparing an effective-interest
amortization table; recording
interest payments, and the
related discount amortization

③

2. Interest Expense on June 30,
$133,288

Exercise 15–8

Playfair Sports Ltd. is authorized to issue $6,000,000 of 5-percent, 10-year bonds. On January 2, 2014, the contract date, when the market interest rate is 6 percent, the company issues $4,800,000 of the bonds and receives cash of $4,442,941. Interest is paid on June 30 and December 31 each year. Playfair Sports Ltd. amortizes bond discounts by the effective-interest method.

Required

1. Prepare an amortization table for the first four semiannual interest periods. Follow the format of Panel B in Exhibit 15–4 on page 931.

2. Record the issue of bond on January 2, the first semiannual interest payment on June 30, and the second payment on December 31.

3. Show the balance sheet presentation of the bond on the date of issue.

Excel Spreadsheet
Template

Preparing an effective-interest
amortization table; recording
interest accrual and payment,
and the related premium
amortization

③

2. Interest Expense on Dec. 31,
$147,738

Exercise 15–9

On September 30, 2014, when the market interest rate is 6 percent, Yale Ltd. issues $8,000,000 of 8-percent, 20-year bonds for $9,849,182. The bonds pay interest on March 31 and September 30. Yale Ltd. amortizes bond premium by the effective-interest method.

Required

1. Prepare an amortization table for the first four semiannual interest periods. Follow the format of Panel B in Exhibit 15–6 on page 934.

2. Record the issuance of the bonds on September 30, 2014, the accrual of interest at December 31, 2014, and the semiannual interest payment on March 31, 2015.

Excel Spreadsheet
Template

Debt payment and discount
amortization schedule using a
spreadsheet

③

Interest payment $340,000

Exercise 15–10

On January 2, 2014, Omni Industries Inc. issued $4,000,000 of 8.5-percent, 5-year bonds when the market interest rate was 10 percent. Omni Industries pays interest annually on December 31. The issue price of the bonds was $3,772,553.

Required   Create a spreadsheet model to prepare a schedule to amortize the discount on these bonds. Use the effective-interest method of amortization. Round to the nearest dollar, and format your answer as follows:

	A	B	C	D	E	F
1			10%		Unamortized	Bond
2		Interest	Interest	Discount	Discount	Carrying
3	Date	Payment	Expense	Amortization	Balance	Amount
4						
5	Jan. 2, 2014				$227,447	$3,772,553
6	Dec. 31, 2014	$	$	$		
7	Dec. 31, 2015					
8	Dec. 31, 2016					
9	Dec. 31, 2017					
10	Dec. 31, 2018					
		=4,000,000*.085	=F5*.010	=C6–B6	=E5–D6	=F5+D6

Recording retirement of bonds
payable

④

Interest Expense Oct. 1, 2015,
$255,502

Exercise 15–11

Tide Management Inc. issued 8-percent bonds with a maturity value of $6,000,000 for $5,662,980 on October 1, 2014, when the market rate of interest was 9 percent. These bonds mature on October 1, 2022, and are callable at 101.00. Tide Management Inc. pays interest each April 1 and October 1. On October 1, 2015, when the bonds' market price is 104.00, Tide Management Inc. retires the bonds in the most economical way available.

Required Record the payment of interest and the amortization of the bond discount at October 1, 2015; also record the retirement of the bonds on that date. Tide Management Inc. uses the effective-interest method to amortize the bond discount.

Exercise 15–12

Kellogg Imaging Ltd. issued $7,500,000 of 8.5-percent, 15-year convertible bonds payable on July 1, 2014 at a price of 97.0. Each $1,000 face amount of bonds is convertible into 50 common shares. On December 31, 2015, bondholders exercised their right to convert the bonds into common shares.

Recording conversion of bonds payable
(4)
2. Carrying amount at Dec. 31, 2015, $7,252,500

Required

1. What would cause the bondholders to convert their bonds into common shares?
2. Without making journal entries, compute the carrying amount of the bonds payable at December 31, 2015. Kellogg Imaging Ltd. uses the straight-line method to amortize bond premium or discount on an annual basis.
3. All amortization has been recorded properly. Journalize the conversion transaction at December 31, 2015.

Exercise 15–13

Seville Products Ltd. reported the following at September 30, 2014:

Recording early retirement and conversion of bonds payable
(4)
1. Cr Cash $816,000

Long-term liabilities		
Convertible bonds payable, 9%,		
due September 30, 2020	$1,600,000	
Discount on bonds payable	60,000	$1,540,000

Required

1. Record the retirement of one-half of the bonds on October 1, 2014, at the call price of 102.00.
2. Record the conversion of one-fourth (of the original $1,600,000) of the bonds into 10,000 common shares of Seville Products Ltd. on October 1, 2014.

Exercise 15–14

Meadow Transport Ltd. is considering two plans for raising $4,000,000 to expand operations. Plan A is to borrow at 9 percent, and Plan B is to issue 400,000 common shares. Before any new financing, Meadow Transport Ltd. has net income after interest and income tax of $2,000,000 and 400,000 common shares outstanding. Management believes the company can use the new funds to earn income of $840,000 per year before interest and taxes. The income tax rate is 40 percent.

Analyzing alternative plans for raising money
(5)
EPS: Plan A $5.72

Required Analyze Meadow Transport Ltd.'s situation to determine which plan will result in higher earnings per share. Use Exhibit 15–8 on page 941 as a guide.

Exercise 15–15

Aztec Financial Services Ltd. needs to raise $3,000,000 to expand company operations. Aztec's president is considering the issuance of either

Earnings-per-share effects of financing with bonds versus shares
(5)
EPS: Plan A $3.96

• Plan A: $3,000,000 of 4 percent bonds payable to borrow the money
• Plan B: 300,000 common shares at $10.00 per share

Before any new financing, Aztec Financial Services Ltd. expects to earn net income of $900,000, and the company already has 300,000 common shares outstanding. The president believes the expansion will increase income before interest and income tax by $600,000. The company's income tax rate is 40 percent.

Required Prepare an analysis similar to Exhibit 15–8, page 941, to determine which plan is likely to result in the higher earnings per share. Which financing plan would you recommend for Aztec Financial Services Ltd.? Give your reasons.

Exercise 15–16

Reporting long-term debt on the balance sheet
③ ⑥

The chief accounting officer of Platt Productions Ltd. is considering how to report long-term notes. The company's financial accountant has assembled the following for long-term notes payable:

Note 5: Long-Term Debt

Total	$2,400,000
Less: Current portion..	300,000
Less: Unamortized discount...	12,000
Long-term debt...	$2,088,000

None of the unamortized discount relates to the current portion of long-term debt. Show how Platt Productions Ltd.'s balance sheet would report these liabilities.

Exercise 15–17

Recording and reporting mortgage liabilities
⑥

Pacific Spirit Corp. borrowed $500,000 in the form of a mortgage on January 1, 2014, to finance the purchase of a small warehouse. The mortgage rate is 5 percent and the term 20 years, and semiannual payments of $19,918 are made on January 1 and July 1. The following chart shows the first five mortgage payments:

Semiannual Interest Period	A Cash Payment	B Interest Expense 2.5%	C Reduction of Principal	D Principal Balance
Jan. 1, 2014				$500,000
July 1, 2014	$19,918	$12,500	$7,418	492,582
Jan. 1, 2015	19,918	12,315	7,603	484,979
July 1, 2015	19,918	12,124	7,794	477,185
Jan. 1, 2016	19,918	11,930	7,988	469,197
July 1, 2016	19,918	11,730	8,188	461,009

Required

1. Journalize the establishment of the mortgage and the first mortgage payment made on July 1, 2014.

2. Show the balance-sheet presentation of this mortgage on December 31, 2015, separating the current and long-term portions.

Exercise 15–18

Reporting liabilities, including capital lease obligations
⑦
Total liabilities $1,590,000

HMR Associates Inc. includes the following selected accounts in its general ledger at December 31, 2014:

Bonds Payable	$1,040,000	Current Obligation under Capital Lease	$ 12,000
Equipment under Capital Lease	350,000	Accounts Payable	57,000
Interest Payable (due March 1, 2015)	21,000	Long-term Capital Lease Liability	136,000
Current Portion of Bonds Payable	162,000	Discount on Bonds Payable (all long-term)	18,000
Notes Payable, Long-term	180,000		

Required Prepare the liabilities section of HMR Associates Inc.'s balance sheet at December 31, 2014, to show how the company would report these items. Report a total for both current and long-term liabilities.

Exercise 15–19

A capital lease agreement for equipment requires Granger Transport Ltd. to make 10 annual payments of $40,000, with the first payment due on January 2, 2014, the date of the inception of the lease. The present value of the nine future lease payments at 10 percent is $230,360.

Journalizing capital lease and operating lease transactions

2. Dec. 31, 2014, Amortization Expense $27,036

Required

1. Calculate the present value of the lease at 10 percent if your instructor has taught present value.
2. Journalize the following lessee transactions:

   2014

   Jan. 2 Beginning of lease term and first annual payment.

   Dec. 31 Amortization of equipment (10 percent).

      31 Interest expense on lease liability.

   2015

   Jan. 2 Second annual lease payment.

3. Assume now that this is an operating lease. Journalize the January 2, 2014, lease payment.

SERIAL EXERCISE

This exercise continues the Kerr Consulting Corporation situation from Exercise 14–17 of Chapter 14. If you did not complete Exercise 14–17, you can still complete Exercise 15–20 as it is presented.

Exercise 15–20

Kerr Consulting Corporation is considering raising capital for a planned business expansion to a new market. Alex Kerr believes the company will need $500,000 and plans to raise the capital by issuing 6-percent, 10-year bonds on April 1, 2014. The bonds pay interest semiannually on April 1 and October 1. On April 1, 2014, the market rate of interest required by similar bonds by investors is 8 percent, causing the bonds to sell for $431,850.

Bonds transactions

3. Oct. 1, 2014, Interest Expense $17,274

Required

1. Were the Kerr Consulting Corporation's bonds issued at par, a premium, or a discount?
2. Record the cash received on the bond issue date.
3. Journalize the first interest payment on October 1, 2014, and amortize the premium or discount using the effective-interest method.
4. Journalize the entry required, if any, on December 31, 2014, related to the bonds.

CHALLENGE EXERCISE

Exercise 15–21

Analyzing bond transactions
(2) (3)

2. Interest payment $9,000,000

The (partial) advertisement below appeared in the *Financial Post*.

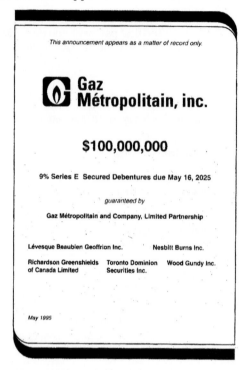

This announcement appears as a matter of record only.

Gaz
Métropolitain, inc.

$100,000,000

9% Series E Secured Debentures due May 16, 2025

guaranteed by

Gaz Métropolitain and Company, Limited Partnership

Lévesque Beaubien Geoffrion Inc.   Nesbitt Burns Inc.

Richardson Greenshields   Toronto Dominion   Wood Gundy Inc.
of Canada Limited   Securities Inc.

May 1995

Interest is payable on November 16 and May 16.

Required Answer these questions about Gaz Métropolitain, Inc.'s secured debentures (bonds):

1. Suppose investors purchased these securities at 98.50 on May 16, 2014. Describe the transaction in detail, indicating who received cash, who paid cash, and how much.
2. Compute the annual cash interest payment on the Gaz Métropolitain, Inc. bonds.
3. Prepare an effective-interest amortization table for Gaz Métropolitain, Inc.'s first two payments, on November 16, 2014, and May 16, 2015. Assume the market rate at the date of issuance was 9.2 percent.
4. Compute Gaz Métropolitain, Inc.'s interest expense for the first full year ended May 16, 2015, under the effective-interest amortization method.
5. Another company's issue of unsecured bonds for $20,000,000 was issued the same day; it bore an interest rate of 12 percent. Why was the rate so much higher for this issue than for the Gaz Métropolitain, Inc. issue?

Exercise 15–22

Analyzing bond transactions
(2) (3)

2. c. $98,563,426

Refer to the bond situation of Gaz Métropolitain, Inc. in Exercise 15–21. Assume Gaz Métropolitain, Inc. issued the bonds at a price of 98.50 and that the company uses the effective-interest amortization method. The company's year end is December 31.

Required

1. Journalize the following bond transactions of Gaz Métropolitain, Inc.:

2014

May 16	Issuance of the bonds.
Nov. 16	Payment of interest expense and amortization of discount on bonds payable. The market rate on the date of issuance was 9.2 percent.
Dec. 31	Accrual of interest expense and amortization of discount on bonds payable.

2. What is Gaz Métropolitain, Inc.'s carrying amount of the bonds payable at
   a. November 16, 2014?
   b. December 31, 2014?
   c. May 16, 2015?

BEYOND THE NUMBERS

Beyond the Numbers 15–1

The following questions are not related.

Questions about long-term debt
②⑥

1. IMAX Corporation obtains the use of most of its theatre properties through leases. IMAX Corporation prefers operating leases over capital leases. Why is this a good idea? Consider IMAX Corporation's debt ratio.

2. IMAX Corporation likes to borrow for longer periods when interest rates are low and for shorter periods when interest rates are high. Why is this a good business strategy?

3. Suppose IMAX Corporation needs to borrow $2,000,000 to open new theatres. The company can borrow $2,000,000 by issuing 8 percent, 20-year bonds at a price of 96. How much will IMAX Corporation actually be borrowing under this arrangement? How much must the company repay at maturity?

ETHICAL ISSUE

Cavell Products Inc., a manufacturer of electronic devices, borrowed heavily during the early 2000s to exploit the advantage of financing operations with debt. At first, Cavell Products Inc. was able to earn operating income much higher than its interest expense and was therefore quite profitable. However, when the business cycle turned down, Cavell Products Inc.'s debt burden pushed the company to the brink of bankruptcy. Operating income was less than interest expense.

Required Is it unethical for managers to commit a company to a high level of debt? Or is it just risky? Who could be hurt by a company's taking on too much debt? Discuss.

PROBLEMS (GROUP A)   MyAccountingLab

Problem 15–1A

The board of directors of Zumbalta Production Co. Ltd. authorizes the issuance of 8-percent, 10-year bonds with a maturity value of $12,000,000. The semiannual interest dates are May 31 and November 30. The bonds are issued through an underwriter on June 30, 2014, at par plus accrued interest from June 1, 2014. Zumbalta's year end is December 31.

Journalizing bond transactions (at par) and reporting bonds payable on the balance sheet
②
1. b. Interest Expense $400,000

Required

1. Journalize the following transactions:
   a. Issuance of the bonds on June 30, 2014.
   b. Payment of interest on November 30, 2014.
   c. Accrual of interest on December 31, 2014.
   d. Payment of interest on May 31, 2015.

2. Report interest payable and bonds payable as they would appear on the Zumbalta Production Co. Ltd. balance sheet at December 31, 2014.

3. Why do we need to accrue interest on June 30 and again on December 31 twice in 2014?

Problem 15–2A

On March 1, 2014, Shaw Systems Ltd. issues 8.5-percent, 20-year bonds payable with a maturity value of $5,000,000. The bonds pay interest on February 28 and August 31. Shaw Systems Ltd. amortizes premium and discount by the straight-line method.

Issuing bonds at a discount, amortizing by the straight-line method, and reporting bonds payable on the balance sheet
②③
3. b. Interest Expense $216,250

Required

1. If the market interest rate is 8 percent when Shaw Systems Ltd. issues its bonds, will the bonds be priced at par, at a premium, or at a discount? Explain.

2. If the market interest rate is 8.875 percent when Shaw Systems Ltd. issues its bonds, will the bonds be priced at par, at a premium, or at a discount? Explain.

3. Assume the issue price of the bonds is 97.00. Journalize the following bond transactions:

   a. Issuance of the bonds on March 1, 2014.
   b. Payment of interest and amortization of discount on August 31, 2014.
   c. Accrual of interest and amortization of discount on November 30, 2014, Shaw Systems Ltd.'s year end.
   d. Payment of interest and amortization of discount on February 28, 2015.

4. Report interest payable and bonds payable as they would appear on the Shaw Systems Ltd. balance sheet at November 30, 2014.

Excel Spreadsheet Template

Analyzing a company's long-term debt, journalizing its transactions, and reporting the long-term debt on the balance sheet

4. Interest Expense $40,000

Problem 15–3A

The notes to Capshaw Biotech Inc.'s financial statements recently reported the following data on September 30, 2014, the company's year end:

NOTE 4: INDEBTEDNESS	
Long-term debt at September 30, 2014, included the following:	
6.00-percent debentures due September 30, 2033, with an effective interest rate of 7.00 percent, net of unamortized discount of $206,712	$1,793,288
Other indebtedness with an interest rate of 5.00 percent, due $408,000 in 2018 and $392,000 in 2019	800,000

Assume Capshaw Biotech Inc. amortizes discount by the effective-interest method.

Required

1. Answer the following questions about Capshaw Biotech Inc.'s long-term liabilities:

   a. What is the maturity value of the 6-percent debentures?
   b. What are Capshaw Biotech Inc.'s annual cash interest payments on the 6-percent debentures?
   c. What is the carrying amount of the 6-percent debentures at September 30, 2014?
   d. How many years remain in the life of the 6-percent debentures?

2. Prepare an amortization table through September 30, 2017, for the 6-percent debentures. Round all amounts to the nearest dollar, and assume Capshaw Biotech Inc. pays interest annually on September 30.

3. Record the September 30, 2016 and 2017, interest payments on the 6-percent debentures.

4. There is no premium or discount on the other indebtedness. Assuming annual interest is paid on September 30 each year, record Capshaw Biotech Inc.'s September 30, 2015, interest payment on the other indebtedness.

Excel Spreadsheet Template

Issuing convertible bonds at a premium, amortizing by the effective-interest method, retiring bonds early, converting bonds, and reporting the bonds payable on the balance sheet

2. b. Interest Expense $161,692

Problem 15–4A

On December 31, 2014, Wynn Holdings Ltd. issues 6-percent, 10-year convertible bonds with a maturity value of $6,000,000. The semiannual interest dates are June 30 and December 31. The market interest rate is 5 percent and the issue price of the bonds is 107.79458. Wynn Holdings Ltd. amortizes any bond premium and discount by the effective-interest method.

Required

1. Prepare an effective-interest-method amortization table for the first four semiannual interest periods.

2. Journalize the following transactions:

   a. Issuance of the bonds on December 31, 2014. Credit Convertible Bonds Payable.
   b. Payment of interest on June 30, 2015.

c. Payment of interest on December 31, 2015.

d. Retirement of bonds with maturity value of $2,000,000 on July 2, 2016. Wynn Holdings Ltd. pays the call price of 104.00.

e. Conversion by the bondholders on July 2, 2016, of bonds with maturity value of $3,000,000 into 40,000 of Wynn Holdings Ltd. common shares.

3. Prepare the balance sheet presentation of the bonds payable that are outstanding at December 31, 2016.

Problem 15–5A

Journalize the following transactions of Mecina Technologies Inc.:

Journalizing bonds payable and capital lease transactions
② ⑦
July 2, 2014, Interest Expense $182,500

2014

Jan.	2	Issued 7-percent, 10-year bonds with a maturity value of $5,000,000 at 97.00.
Jan.	2	Signed a five-year capital lease on equipment. The agreement requires annual lease payments of $400,000, with the first payment due immediately. The present value of the five lease payments is $1,724,851.
Jul.	2	Paid semiannual interest and amortized the discount by the straight-line method on the 7-percent bonds.
Dec. 31		Accrued semiannual interest expense, and amortized the discount by the straight-line method on the 7-percent bonds.
	31	Recorded amortization on the leased equipment, using the straight-line method.
	31	Accrued interest expense at 8 percent on the lease liability.

2024

Jan.	2	Paid the 7-percent bonds at maturity. (Ignore the final interest payment.)

Problem 15–6A

Shield Transport Ltd. is authorized to issue 10-year, 6 percent convertible bonds with a maturity value of $16,000,000. Interest is payable on June 30 and December 31. The bonds are convertible on the basis of 50 common shares for each $1,000 bond. The following bond transactions took place:

Amortizing bond discount and premium by the effective-interest method; retirement of bonds; conversion of bonds
② ③ ④
1. June 30, 2014, Interest Expense $221,209

2014

Jan.	2	Issued bonds with $6,400,000 maturity value. Since the market rate of interest on this date was 8 percent, the bonds sold for $5,530,219.
Jun. 30		Paid semiannual interest and amortized the discount using the effective-interest amortization method.
Dec. 31		Paid semiannual interest and amortized the discount using the effective-interest amortization method.

2015

Jun. 30		Paid semiannual interest and amortized the discount using the effective-interest amortization method.
Jul.	2	Retired bonds with a $3,200,000 maturity value at a rate of 96.00.
	2	Bondholders converted bonds with a $1,600,000 maturity value into common shares.

Required

1. Create an amortization schedule for the first three interest periods for the bonds sold on January 2, 2014. Round all amounts to the nearest whole dollar. Use the values from the schedule and any other information to journalize all the transactions above.

2. Show the balance sheet presentation of the bonds payable on July 2, 2015.

Problem 15–7A

Castlegar Systems Inc. had the following information available on bonds payable outstanding at December 31, 2014, its year end:

Amortizing bond premium by the effective-interest method; accounting for lease transactions
③ ⑦
1. Apr. 2, 2015, Interest Expense $204,452

• $5,000,000—Bonds Payable, 9-percent, interest paid on April 2 and October 2. The bonds had been issued on April 2, 2014, for $5,131,053 when the market rate of interest was 8 percent, and were due April 2, 2017.

The following transactions took place after December 31, 2014:

2015

Jan. 2   Castelgar Systems Inc. signed a lease to rent a warehouse for expansion of its operations. The lease is five years, with an option to renew, and calls for annual payments of $50,000 per year payable on January 2. Castelgar Systems Inc. gave a cheque for the first year upon signing the contract.

2   Castelgar Systems Inc. signed a lease for equipment. The lease is for 10 years with payments of $40,000 per year payable on January 2 (first year's payment was made at the signing). At the end of the lease the equipment will become the property of Castelgar Systems Inc. The future payments on the lease have a present value (at 10 percent) of $270,361. The equipment has a 10-year useful life and zero residual value.

Apr. 2   Paid the interest on the bonds payable and amortized the premium using the effective-interest method. Assume half of the interest expense, amortization of bond premium, and interest payable had been accrued properly on December 31, 2014.

Oct. 2   Paid the interest on the bonds payable and amortized the premium using the effective-interest method.

Dec. 31   Recorded any adjustments required at the end of the year for the bonds payable and the lease(s).

2016

Jan. 2   Made the annual payments on the leases.

Apr. 2   Paid the interest on the bonds payable and amortized the premium using the effective-interest method.

Required

1. For the bonds issued on April 2, 2014, prepare an amortization schedule for the three-year life of the bonds. Round all amounts to the nearest whole dollar.

2. Record the general journal entries for the 2015 and 2016 transactions.

3. Show the liabilities section of the balance sheet on December 31, 2016.

Problem 15–8A

Accounting for a mortgage
⑥

1. Dec. 31, 2016, Principal balance $508,049

Andreas Wines Ltd. issued an $800,000, 5-year, 6 percent mortgage note payable on December 31, 2014, to help finance a new warehouse. The terms of the mortgage provide for semiannual blended payments of $93,784 on June 30 and December 31 of each year.

1. Prepare a mortgage installment payment schedule for the first two years of this mortgage. Round all amounts to the nearest whole dollar.

2. Record the issuance of the mortgage note payable on December 31, 2014.

3. Report interest payable and the mortgage note payable on the December 31, 2014, balance sheet.

4. Journalize the first two installment payments on June 30, 2015, and December 31, 2015.

Problem 15–9A

Financing operations with debt or with shares
⑤

Two businesses must consider how to raise $10,000,000.

Blackburn Inc. is in the midst of its most successful period since it began operations 48 years ago. For each of the past 10 years, net income and earnings per share have increased by 15 percent. The outlook for the future is equally bright, with new markets opening up and competitors unable to manufacture products of Blackburn Inc.'s quality. Blackburn Inc. is planning a large-scale expansion.

Sage Consulting Limited has fallen on hard times. Net income has remained flat for five of the last six years, even falling by 10 percent from last year's level of profits. Top management has experienced unusual turnover, and the company lacks strong leadership. To become competitive again, Sage Consulting Limited desperately needs $10,000,000 for expansion.

Required

1. Propose a plan for each company to raise the needed cash. Which company should borrow? Which company should issue shares? Consider the advantages and disadvantages of raising money by borrowing and by issuing shares, and discuss them in your answer.

2. How will what you have learned in this chapter help you manage a business?

Problem 15–10A

The accounting records of Babine Resources Inc. include the following items:

Reporting liabilities on the balance sheet

Bond payable current portion $103,091

Capital Lease Liability,			Mortgage Note Payable,	
Long-term..............................	$538,000		Long-term...........................	$ 501,000
Bonds Payable, Long-term......	960,000		Building Acquired under	
Premium on Bonds Payable ...	78,000		Capital Lease......................	800,000
Interest Expense	300,000		Bonds Payable, Current	
Interest Payable	98,820		Portion	96,000
Interest Revenue.......................	61,800		Accumulated Amortization,	
Capital Lease Liability,			Building	448,000
Current..................................	74,000		Mortgage Note Payable,	
			short-term...........................	201,000

Required Show how these items would be reported on the Babine Resources Inc. balance sheet, including headings for property, plant, and equipment, current liabilities, long-term liabilities, and so on. Note disclosures are not required. Remember that the premium on bonds payable must be split between the current and long-term portions of the bonds payable.

PROBLEMS (GROUP B)   MyAccountingLab

Problem 15–1B

The board of directors of Farrell Communications Ltd. authorizes the issuance of 6-percent, 20-year bonds with a maturity value of $10,000,000. The semiannual interest dates are March 31 and September 30. The bonds are issued through an underwriter on April 30, 2014, at par plus accrued interest. Farrell's year end is December 31.

Journalizing bond transactions (at par) and reporting bonds payable on the balance sheet
②

Required

1. Journalize the following transactions:
   a. Issuance of the bonds on April 30, 2014.
   b. Payment of interest on September 30, 2014.
   c. Accrual of interest on December 31, 2014.
   d. Payment of interest on March 31, 2015.

2. Report interest payable and bonds payable as they would appear on the Farrell Communications Ltd. balance sheet at December 31, 2014.

3. Why do we need to accrue interest on April 30 and again on December 31, twice in 2014?

Problem 15–2B

On April 1, 2014, Pettington Corp. issues 7-percent, 10-year bonds payable with a maturity value of $3,000,000. The bonds pay interest on March 31 and September 30, and Pettington Corp. amortizes premium and discount by the straight-line method.

Issuing bonds at a premium, amortizing by the straight-line method, and reporting bonds payable on the balance sheet
② ③

Required

1. If the market interest rate is 6 percent when Pettington Corp. issues its bonds, will the bonds be priced at par, at a premium, or at a discount? Explain.

2. If the market interest rate is 8 percent when Pettington Corp. issues its bonds, will the bonds be priced at par, at a premium, or at a discount? Explain.

3. Assume the issue price of the bonds is 103.00. Journalize the following bonds payable transactions:

   a. Issuance of the bonds on April 1, 2014.
   b. Payment of interest and amortization of premium on September 30, 2014.
   c. Accrual of interest and amortization of premium on December 31, 2014, the year end.
   d. Payment of interest and amortization of premium on March 31, 2015.

4. Report interest payable and bonds payable as they would appear on the Pettington Corp. balance sheet at December 31, 2014.

Excel Spreadsheet
Template

Analyzing a company's
long-term debt, journalizing its
transactions, and reporting the
long-term debt on the balance
sheet

Problem 15–3B

Assume that the notes to Pemberton Ltd.'s financial statements reported the following data on September 30, 2014:

NOTE E: LONG-TERM DEBT	
5-percent debentures due 2033, net of unamortized	
discount of $223,162 (effective interest rate of 6.0 percent)	$1,776,838
Pemberton Ltd. amortizes the discount by the effective-interest method.	

Required

1. Answer the following questions about Pemberton Ltd.'s long-term liabilities:

   a. What is the maturity value of the 5-percent debentures?
   b. What is the carrying amount of the 5-percent debentures at September 30, 2014?
   c. What are Pemberton Ltd.'s annual cash interest payments on these debentures?

2. Prepare an amortization table through September 30, 2016, for the 5-percent debentures. Pemberton Ltd. pays interest annually on September 30.

3. Record the September 30, 2016, interest payments on the 5-percent debentures.

4. What is Pemberton Ltd.'s carrying amount of the 5-percent debentures at September 30, 2016, immediately after the interest payment?

Excel Spreadsheet
Template

Issuing convertible bonds at
a discount, amortizing by the
effective-interest method,
retiring bonds early, converting
bonds, and reporting the bonds
payable on the balance sheet
②③④

Problem 15–4B

On December 31, 2014, Monashee Corp. issues 4-percent, 10-year convertible bonds with a maturity value of $4,500,000. The semiannual interest dates are June 30 and December 31. The market interest rate is 5 percent, and the issue price of the bonds is 92.2054. Monashee Corp. amortizes bond premium and discount by the effective-interest method.

Required

1. Prepare an effective-interest method amortization table for the first four semiannual interest periods.

2. Journalize the following transactions:

   a. Issuance of the bonds on December 31, 2014. Credit Convertible Bonds Payable.
   b. Payment of interest on June 30, 2015.
   c. Payment of interest on December 31, 2015.
   d. Retirement of bonds with maturity value of $200,000 on July 2, 2016. Monashee Corp. purchases the bonds at 96.00 in the open market.
   e. Conversion by the bondholders on July 2, 2016, of bonds with maturity value of $400,000 into 5,000 Monashee Corp. common shares.

3. Prepare the balance sheet presentation of the bonds payable that are outstanding at December 31, 2016.

Journalizing bonds payable and
capital lease transactions
②⑦

Problem 15–5B

Journalize the following transactions of Fayuz Communications Inc.:

2014

Jan. 2   Issued $8,000,000 of 7-percent, 10-year bonds payable at 97.00.

      2   Signed a five-year capital lease on machinery. The agreement requires annual lease payments of $80,000, with the first payment due immediately. The present value of the five lease payments is $333,589 using a market rate of 10 percent.

Jul.	2	Paid semiannual interest and amortized the discount by the straight-line method on the 7-percent bonds payable.
Dec.	31	Accrued semiannual interest expense and amortized the discount by the straight-line method on the 7-percent bonds.
	31	Recorded amortization on the leased machinery, using the straight-line method.
	31	Accrued interest expense at 10 percent on the lease liability.

2024

| Jan. | 2 | Paid the 7-percent bonds at maturity. (Ignore the final interest payment.) |

Problem 15–6B

Tasis Ventures Inc. is authorized to issue 10-year, 5-percent convertible bonds with a maturity value of $9,000,000. Interest is payable on June 30 and December 31. The bonds are convertible on the basis of 40 common shares for each $1,000 bond. The following bond transactions took place:

Amortizing bond discount and premium by the effective-interest method; retirement of bonds; conversion of bonds

② ③ ④

2014

Jan.	2	Issued bonds with $5,400,000 maturity value. Since the market rate of interest on this date was 4 percent, the bonds sold for $5,841,488.
Jun.	30	Paid semiannual interest and amortized the premium using the effective-interest method.
Dec.	31	Paid semiannual interest and amortized the premium using the effective-interest method.

2015

Jun.	30	Paid semiannual interest and amortized the premium using the effective-interest method.
Jul.	2	Retired bonds with a $600,000 maturity value at a rate of 101.
	2	Bondholders converted bonds with a $600,000 maturity value into common shares.

Required

1. Create an amortization schedule for the first three interest periods for the bonds sold on January 2, 2014. Round all amounts to the nearest whole dollar. Use the values from the schedule and any other information to journalize all the transactions above.
2. Show the balance sheet presentation of the bonds payable on July 2, 2015.

Problem 15–7B

Moncton Manufacturing Ltd. had the following information available on bonds payable outstanding at December 31, 2013, its year end:

Amortizing bond discount by the effective-interest method; accounting for lease transactions
③ ⑦

- $7,500,000—Bonds Payable, 6 percent, interest paid on April 2 and October 2. The bonds had been sold on October 2, 2013, for $7,330,686 when the market rate of interest was 7 percent. The bonds mature on April 2, 2016.

The following transactions took place after December 31, 2013:

2014

| Jan. | 2 | Moncton Manufacturing Ltd. signed a lease to rent a building for expansion of its operations. The lease is for six years, with an option to renew, and calls for annual payments of $37,500 per year payable on January 2. Moncton Manufacturing Ltd. gave a cheque for the first year upon signing the lease. |
| | 2 | Moncton Manufacturing Ltd. signed a lease for equipment. The lease is for 10 years with payments of $22,500 per year payable on January 2 (first year's payment was made at the signing). At the end of the lease, the equipment will become the property of Moncton Manufacturing Ltd. The future payments on the lease have a present value (at 10 percent) of $129,578. The equipment has a 10-year useful life and zero residual value. |

Apr. 2	Paid the interest on the bonds payable and amortized the discount using the effective-interest method. Assume interest payable of $112,500 had been accrued on December 31, 2013.
Oct. 2	Paid the interest on the bonds payable and amortized the discount using the effective-interest method.
Dec. 31	Recorded any adjustments required at the end of the year for the bonds payable and the lease(s).

2015

Jan. 2	Made the annual payments on the leases.
Apr. 2	Paid the interest on the bonds payable and amortized the discount using the effective-interest method.
Oct. 2	Paid the interest on the bonds payable and amortized the discount using the effective-interest method.
Dec. 31	Recorded any adjustments required at the end of the year for the bonds payable and the lease(s).

Required

1. For the bonds issued on October 2, 2013, prepare an amortization schedule for the life of the bonds. Round all amounts to the nearest whole dollar.

2. Record the general journal entries for the 2014 and 2015 transactions.

3. Show the liabilities section of the balance sheet on December 31, 2015.

Problem 15–8B

Accounting for a mortgage ⑥

Werstirener Brewing Ltd. issued a $600,000, 5-year, 6 percent mortgage note payable on December 31, 2014, to help finance a new distribution centre. The terms of the mortgage provide for semiannual blended payments of $70,338 due June 30 and December 31 of each year.

1. Prepare a mortgage installment payment schedule for the first two years of this mortgage. Round all amounts to the nearest whole dollar.

2. Record the issuance of the mortgage note payable on December 31, 2014.

3. Report interest payable and the mortgage note payable on the December 31, 2014, balance sheet.

4. Journalize the first two installment payments on June 30, 2015, and December 31, 2015.

Problem 15–9B

Financing operations with debt or with shares ⑤

Marketing studies have shown that consumers prefer upscale restaurants, and recent trends in industry sales have supported the research. To capitalize on this trend, Orca Ltd. is embarking on a massive expansion. Plans call for opening five new restaurants within the next 18 months. Each restaurant is scheduled to be 30 percent larger than the company's existing restaurants, furnished more elaborately, with more extensive menus. Management estimates that company operations will provide $15 million of the cash needed for expansion. Orca Ltd. must raise the remaining $15 million from outsiders. The board of directors is considering obtaining the $15 million either through borrowing or by issuing common shares.

Required Write a memo to company management. Discuss the advantages and disadvantages of borrowing and of issuing common shares to raise the needed cash. Use the following format for your memo:

Date:	
To:	Management of Orca Ltd.
From:	Student Name
Subject:	Advantages and disadvantages of borrowing and issuing shares to raise $15 million for expansion

Advantages and disadvantages of borrowing:
Advantages and disadvantages of issuing shares:

Problem 15–10B

The accounting records of Carter Technologies Inc. include the following items:

Reporting liabilities on the balance sheet

Equipment Acquired under		Interest Expense	$171,000
Capital Lease	$591,000	Mortgage Note Payable—	
Bonds Payable—Current		Long-term	238,000
Portion	225,000	Accumulated Amortization—	
Capital Lease Liability—		Equipment	123,000
Long-term	162,000	Capital Lease Liability—	
Discount on Bonds Payable—		Current	64,000
Long-term	21,000	Mortgage Note Payable—	
Interest Revenue	15,000	Current	69,000
Interest Payable	84,000	Bonds Payable—Long-term	900,000

Required Show how these items would be reported on the Carter Technologies Inc. balance sheet, including headings for property, plant, and equipment, current liabilities, long-term liabilities, and so on. Note disclosures are not required. Remember that the premium on bonds payable must be split between the current and long-term portions of the bonds payable.

CHALLENGE PROBLEMS

Problem 15–1C

A friend tells you that she always buys bonds that are at a discount because "You always get more than you paid when the bond matures."

Understanding present value

Required Discuss your friend's understanding of present value.

Problem 15–2C

You have just inherited $50,000 and have decided to buy shares. You have narrowed your choice down to QT Logistics Inc. and Next Systems Ltd. You carefully read each company's annual report to determine which company's shares you should buy. Your research indicates that the two companies are very similar. QT Logistics Inc.'s annual report states "The Company has financed its growth through long- and short-term borrowing," while the Next report contains the statement "The Company has financed its growth out of earnings retained in the business."

Evaluating alternative methods of financing growth

QT's shares are trading at $25.00 while Next's shares are trading at $13.00. You wonder if that is because QT has been paying an annual dividend of $2.00 per share while Next has been paying a dividend of $1.10.

You recall that the morning newspaper had an article about the economy that predicted that interest rates were expected to rise and stay at a much higher rate than at present for the next two to three years.

Required Explain which shares you would buy and indicate why you have selected them.

Extending Your Knowledge

DECISION PROBLEMS

Decision Problem 1

Analyzing alternative ways of raising $10,000,000

1. EPS: Plan A $10.66

Business is going well for Valley Forest Products Inc. The board of directors of this family-owned company believes that the company could earn an additional $9,000,000 in income after interest and taxes by expanding into new markets. However, the $30,000,000 that the business needs for growth cannot be raised within the family. The directors, who strongly wish to retain family control of Valley Forest Products Inc., must consider issuing securities to outsiders. They are considering three financing plans.

Plan A is to borrow at 8 percent. Plan B is to issue 300,000 common shares. Plan C is to issue 300,000 nonvoting, $7.50 cumulative preferred shares. The company presently has net income before tax of $18,000,000 and has 1,500,000 common shares outstanding. The income tax rate is 35 percent.

Required

1. Prepare an analysis similar to Exhibit 15–8 to determine which plan will result in the highest earnings per common share.
2. Recommend one plan to the board of directors. Give your reasons.

Decision Problem 2

Questions about long-term debt

The following questions are not related.

a. Why do you think corporations prefer operating leases over capital leases? How do you think a shareholder would view an operating lease?
b. If you were to win $3,000,000 from Lotto 649, you would receive the $3,000,000 today, whereas if you were to win $3,000,000 in one of the U.S. lotteries, you would receive 20 annual payments of $150,000. Are the prizes equivalent? If not, why not?

FINANCIAL STATEMENT CASES

Financial Statement Case 1

Long-term debt

The Gildan Activewear Inc. financial statements that appear in Appendix A at the end of this book and on MyAccountingLab provide details about the company's long-term debt. Use the data to answer the following questions:

1. How much did Gildan Activewear Inc. borrow on bank and long-term debt during the fiscal year ended October 2, 2011? How much long-term debt did Gildan Activewear Inc. repay during fiscal 2011? During fiscal 2010?
2. What type of long-term debt is listed on the balance sheet at October 2, 2011? See Note 8, and be specific.
3. What is the interest rate charged on the long-term line of credit?
4. What types of shares are outstanding? If dividends were paid during fiscal 2011, what was the amount of the dividends paid?
5. Does Gildan Activewear Inc. have any operating or capital/finance leases outstanding during fiscal 2011?

Financial Statement Case 2

Long-term debt

The Rainmaker Entertainment Inc. income statement and balance sheet on MyAccountingLab provide details about the company's long-term debt and equity. Use the data to answer the following questions:

1. What did Rainmaker have listed as long term debt obligations?
2. List the long-term liability amounts at December 31, 2011 and 2010.

3. What lease payments are due in the year ended December 31, 2012? How much is due in the years beyond 2012?

4. How much interest expense did Rainmaker record on the income statement for 2011 and 2010? How much interest was accrued at December 31, 2010?

5. What types of shares is Rainmaker authorized to issue? Which types of shares were outstanding at December 31, 2011? Were dividends paid during the year ended December 31, 2011? If so, how much were they?

IFRS MINI-CASE

Sun-Rype Products Limited is a manufacturer and marketer of juice-based beverages and fruit-based snacks based in the fruit-growing district of British Columbia but with sales across Canada. Appearing below is an excerpt from the Sun-Rype notes to the consolidated financial statements for the years ended December 31, 2011 and 2010. Sun-Rype reports under IFRS. This chapter discussed disclosure requirements under ASPE. Compare Sun-Rype's reporting below with a company reporting similar information under ASPE.

Note 11 (c) Bank term loans (all amounts in thousands of Canadian dollars)

	Currency	Annual principal payments required	Interest rate	Dec. 31, 2011	Dec. 31, 2010	January 1, 2010
Term loan	U.S. dollar	US$1,480	Bank prime lending rate plus 0.5% (3.75% at December 31, 2011)	$14,035 $ —	$5,470	$ —
Term loan	Canadian dollar	$ 486	Bank prime lending rate plus 0.5% (3.5% at December 31, 2011)	2,308 —	—	—
Term loan	Canadian dollar	$1,500	Bank prime lending rate plus 0.5%	—	—	4,750
Balance outstanding				16,343	5,470	4,750
Current portion				1,961	547	1,500
Non-current portion				$14,382	$4,923	$3,250

During 2011, the Company received secured bank loan advances of US$9.0 million to fund business acquisition payments and $2.4 million to fund capital expenditures.

CHAPTER 15 APPENDIX

Time Value of Money: Future Value and Present Value

The following discussion of future value lays the foundation for present value but is not essential. For the valuation of long-term liabilities, some instructors may wish to begin on page 980.

The phrase *time value of money* refers to the fact that money earns interest over time. Interest is the cost of using money. To borrowers, interest is the expense of renting money. To lenders, interest is the revenue earned from lending. When funds are used for a period of time, we must recognize the interest. Otherwise we overlook an important part of the transaction. Suppose you invest $4,545 in corporate bonds that pay interest of 10 percent each year. After one year, the value of your investment has grown to $5,000. The difference between your original investment ($4,545) and the future value of the investment ($5,000) is the amount of interest revenue you will earn during the year ($455). If you ignored the interest, you would fail to account for the interest revenue you have earned. Interest becomes more important as the time period lengthens because the amount of interest depends on the span of time the money is invested.

Let's consider a second example, but from the borrower's perspective. Suppose you purchase a machine for your business. The cash price of the machine is $8,000, but you cannot pay cash now. To finance the purchase, you sign an $8,000 note payable. The note requires you to pay the $8,000 plus 10-percent interest one year from date of purchase. Is your cost of the machine $8,000, or is it $8,800 [$8,000 plus interest of $800 ($8,000 × 0.10)]? The cost is $8,000. The additional $800 is interest expense and not part of the cost of the machine, although interest expense is certainly a part of the decision of whether or not to purchase the machine.

Future Value

LO **A1**

How do we find the future value of an investment?

The main application of future value *in this book* is to calculate the accumulated balance of an investment at a future date. In our first example, the investment earned 10 percent per year. After one year, $4,545 grew to $5,000, as shown in the timeline in Exhibit 15A–1.

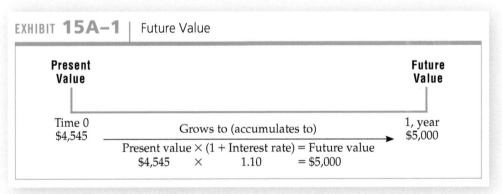

EXHIBIT **15A–1** | Future Value

If the money were invested for five years, you would have to perform five such calculations. You would also have to consider the compound interest that your investment is earning. Compound interest is the interest you earn not only on your principal amount but also the interest you receive on the interest you have already earned. Most business applications include compound interest. The table below shows the interest revenue earned each year at 10 percent:

End of Year	Interest	Future Value
0	—	$4,545
1	$4,545 × 0.10 = $455	5,000
2	5,000 × 0.10 = 500	5,500
3	5,500 × 0.10 = 550	6,050
4	6,050 × 0.10 = 605	6,655
5	6,655 × 0.10 = 666	7,321

Earning 10 percent, a $4,545 investment grows to $5,000 at the end of one year, to $5,500 at the end of two years, and so on. Throughout this discussion we round off to the nearest dollar to keep the numbers simple, although calculations like these are usually rounded to the nearest cent.

Future Value Tables

The process of computing a future value is called *accumulating* or *compounding* because the future value is *more* than the present value. Mathematical tables ease the computational burden. You can also use financial calculators and functions in spreadsheet programs to calculate future value. (In the real world, calculators are used rather than tables—we use tables here to demonstrate the concepts.) Exhibit 15A–2, Future Value of $1, gives the future value for a single sum (a present value), $1, invested to earn a particular interest rate for a specific number of periods. Future value depends on three factors: (1) the amount of the investment, (2) the length of time between investment and future accumulation, and (3) the interest rate.

KEY POINTS

The formula for future value is
$FV = PV(1 + i)^n$
where

FV = future value
PV = present value
 i = interest rate per period
 n = number of compounding periods

EXHIBIT 15A–2 | Future Value of $1 *(An expanded version of this table appears in Appendix B at the end of this text)*

				Future Value of $1						
Periods	2%	3%	4%	5%	6%	7%	8%	9%	10%	12%
1	1.020	1.030	1.040	1.050	1.060	1.070	1.080	1.090	1.100	1.120
2	1.040	1.061	1.082	1.103	1.124	1.145	1.166	1.188	1.210	1.254
3	1.061	1.093	1.125	1.158	1.191	1.225	1.260	1.295	1.331	1.405
4	1.082	1.126	1.170	1.216	1.262	1.311	1.360	1.412	1.464	1.574
5	1.104	1.159	1.217	1.276	1.338	1.403	1.469	1.539	1.611	1.762
6	1.126	1.194	1.265	1.340	1.419	1.501	1.587	1.677	1.772	1.974
7	1.149	1.230	1.316	1.407	1.504	1.606	1.714	1.828	1.949	2.211
8	1.172	1.267	1.369	1.477	1.594	1.718	1.851	1.993	2.144	2.476
9	1.195	1.305	1.423	1.551	1.689	1.838	1.999	2.172	2.358	2.773
10	1.219	1.344	1.480	1.629	1.791	1.967	2.159	2.367	2.594	3.106
11	1.243	1.384	1.539	1.710	1.898	2.105	2.332	2.580	2.853	3.479
12	1.268	1.426	1.601	1.796	2.012	2.252	2.518	2.813	3.138	3.896
13	1.294	1.469	1.665	1.886	2.133	2.410	2.720	3.066	3.452	4.363
14	1.319	1.513	1.732	1.980	2.261	2.579	2.937	3.342	3.797	4.887
15	1.346	1.558	1.801	2.079	2.397	2.759	3.172	3.642	4.177	5.474
16	1.373	1.605	1.873	2.183	2.540	2.952	3.426	3.970	4.595	6.130
17	1.400	1.653	1.948	2.292	2.693	3.159	3.700	4.328	5.054	6.866
18	1.428	1.702	2.026	2.407	2.854	3.380	3.996	4.717	5.560	7.690
19	1.457	1.754	2.107	2.527	3.026	3.617	4.316	5.142	6.116	8.613
20	1.486	1.806	2.191	2.653	3.207	3.870	4.661	5.604	6.727	9.646

LEARNING TIPS

Remember that the number of periods is the number of *compounding periods*. It is *not* the number of years, unless the compounding period happens to be an annual period.

The heading in Exhibit 15A–2 states $1. Future value tables and present value tables are based on $1 because unity (the value 1) is so easy to work with. Observe the Periods column and the Interest Rate columns 2% through 12%. In business applications, interest rates are usually assumed to be for the annual period of one year unless specified otherwise. In fact, an interest rate can be stated for any period, such as 3 percent per quarter or 5 percent for a six-month period. The length of the period is arbitrary. For example, an investment may promise a return (income) of 3 percent per quarter for two quarters (six months). In that case you would be working with 3 percent interest for two periods. It would be incorrect to use 6 percent for one period because the interest is 3 percent compounded quarterly, and that amount differs somewhat from 6 percent compounded semiannually. Take care in studying future value and present value problems to align the interest rate with the appropriate number of periods.

Let's use Exhibit 15A–2. The future value of $1.00 invested at 4 percent for one year is $1.04 ($1.00 × 1.040, which appears at the junction under the 4% column and across from 1 in the Periods column). The figure 1.040 includes both the principal (1.000) and the compound interest for one period (0.040).

Suppose you deposit $5,000 in a savings account that pays annual interest of 4 percent. The account balance at the end of the year will be $5,200. To compute the future value of $5,000 at 4 percent for one year, multiply $5,000 by 1.040 to get $5,200. Now suppose you invest in a 10-year, 6-percent certificate of deposit (CD). What will be the future value of the CD at maturity? To compute the future value of $5,000 at 6 percent for 10 periods, multiply $5,000 by 1.791 (from Exhibit 15A–2) to get $8,955. This future value of $8,955 indicates that $5,000 earning 6 percent interest compounded annually grows to $8,955 at the end of 10 years. In this way, you can find any present amount's future value at a particular future date. Future value is especially helpful for computing the amount of cash you will have on hand for some purpose in the future.

Future Value of an Annuity

In the preceding example, we made an investment of a single amount. Other investments, called annuities, include multiple payments of an equal periodic amount at fixed intervals over the duration of the investment. Consider a family investing for a child's education. The Dietrichs can invest $4,000 annually to accumulate a college fund for 15-year-old Helen. The investment can earn 7 percent annually until Helen turns 18—a three-year investment. How much will be available for Helen on the date of the last investment? Exhibit 15A–3 shows the accumulation—a total future value of $12,860.

The first $4,000 invested by the Dietrichs grows to $4,580 over the investment period. The second $4,000 invested grows to $4,280, and the third $4,000 invested stays at $4,000 because it has no time to earn interest. The sum of the three future

EXHIBIT 15A–3 | Future Value of an Annuity

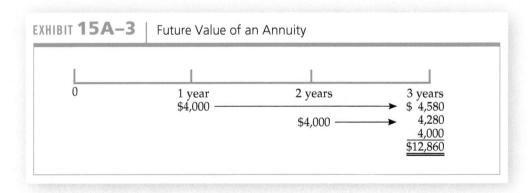

values ($4,580 + $4,280 + $4,000) is the future value of the annuity ($12,860), which can be computed as follows:

End of Year	Annual Investment	Interest	Increase for the Year	Future Value of Annuity
0	—	—	—	0
1	$4,000	—	$4,000	$ 4,000
2	4,000 + ($4,000 × 0.07 = $280) =		4,280	8,280
3	4,000 + ($8,280 × 0.07 = $580) =		4,580	12,860

These computations are laborious. As with the Future Value of $1 (a lump sum), mathematical tables ease the strain of calculating annuities. Exhibit 15A-4, Future Value of Annuity of $1, gives the future value of a series of investments, each of equal amount, at regular intervals.

What is the future value of an annuity of three investments of $1 each that earn 7 percent? The answer 3.215 can be found in the 7% column and across from 3 in the Periods column of Exhibit 15A-4. This amount can be used to compute the future value of the investment for Helen's education, as follows:

KEY POINTS

The formula for the future value of an annuity is

$$S_n = R[(1 + i)^{(n-1)}/i]$$

where

S_n = future value of a simple annuity
R = the periodic payment (rent)
i = interest rate per period
n = number of periodic payments

Amount of each periodic investment	×	Future value of annuity of $1 (Exhibit 15A–4)	=	Future value of investment
$4,000	×	3.215	=	$12,860

EXHIBIT 15A–4	Future Value of Annuity of $1 *(An expanded version of this table appears in Appendix B at the end of this text)*

Future Value of Annuity of $1

Periods	2%	3%	4%	5%	6%	7%	8%	9%	10%	12%
1	1.000	1.000	1.000	1.000	1.000	1.000	1.000	1.000	1.000	1.000
2	2.020	2.030	2.040	2.050	2.060	2.070	2.080	2.090	2.100	2.120
3	3.060	3.091	3.122	3.153	3.184	3.215	3.246	3.278	3.310	3.374
4	4.122	4.184	4.246	4.310	4.375	4.440	4.506	4.573	4.641	4.779
5	5.204	5.309	5.416	5.526	5.637	5.751	5.867	5.985	6.105	6.353
6	6.308	6.468	6.633	6.802	6.975	7.153	7.336	7.523	7.716	8.115
7	7.434	7.663	7.898	8.142	8.394	8.654	8.923	9.200	9.487	10.089
8	8.583	8.892	9.214	9.549	9.897	10.260	10.637	11.028	11.436	12.300
9	9.755	10.159	10.583	11.027	11.491	11.978	12.488	13.021	13.579	14.776
10	10.950	11.464	12.006	12.578	13.181	13.816	14.487	15.193	15.937	17.549
11	12.169	12.808	13.486	14.207	14.972	15.784	16.645	17.560	18.531	20.655
12	13.412	14.192	15.026	15.917	16.870	17.888	18.977	20.141	21.384	24.133
13	14.680	15.618	16.627	17.713	18.882	20.141	21.495	22.953	24.523	28.029
14	15.974	17.086	18.292	19.599	21.015	22.550	24.215	26.019	27.975	32.393
15	17.293	18.599	20.024	21.579	23.276	25.129	27.152	29.361	31.772	37.280
16	18.639	20.157	21.825	23.657	25.673	27.888	30.324	33.003	35.950	42.753
17	20.012	21.762	23.698	25.840	28.213	30.840	33.750	36.974	40.545	48.884
18	21.412	23.414	25.645	28.132	30.906	33.999	37.450	41.301	45.599	55.750
19	22.841	25.117	27.671	30.539	33.760	37.379	41.446	46.018	51.159	63.440
20	24.297	26.870	29.778	33.066	36.786	40.995	45.762	51.160	57.275	72.053

This one-step calculation is much easier than computing the future value of each annual investment and then summing the individual future values. In this way, you can compute the future value of any investment consisting of equal periodic amounts at regular intervals. Businesses make periodic investments to accumulate funds for equipment replacement and other uses—an application of the future value of an annuity.

Present Value

LO **A2**

How do we find the present value of an investment?

Often a person knows a future amount and needs to know the related present value. Recall Exhibit 15A–1, in which present value and future value are on opposite ends of the same time line. Suppose an investment promises to pay you $5,000 at the *end* of one year. How much would you pay *now* to acquire this investment? You would be willing to pay the present value of the $5,000, which is a future amount.

Present value also depends on three factors: (1) the amount of payment (or receipt), (2) the length of time between investment and future receipt (or payment), and (3) the interest rate. The process of computing a present value is called *discounting* because the present value is *less* than the future value.

KEY POINTS

The formula for present value is
$PV = FV \times (1 + i)^n$

where

PV = present value
FV = future value
i = interest rate per period
n = number of compounding periods

In our investment example, the future receipt is $5,000. The investment period is one year. Assume that you demand an annual interest rate of 10 percent on your investment. With all three factors specified, you can compute the present value of $5,000 at 10 percent for one year. The computation is

$$\text{Present value of } \$5,000 \text{ at 10 percent for one year} =$$

$$\frac{\text{Future value}}{1 + \text{Interest rate}} = \frac{\$5,000}{1.10} = \$4,545$$

By turning the problem around, we verify the present value computation:

Amount invested (present value)	$4,545
Expected earnings ($4,545 × 0.10)	455
Amount to be received one year from now (future value)	$5,000

This example illustrates that present value and future value are based on the same equation:

$$\text{Present value} \times (1 + \text{Interest rate}) = \text{Future value}$$

$$\text{Present value} = \frac{\text{Future value}}{1 + \text{Interest rate}}$$

If the $5,000 is to be received two years from now, you will pay only $4,132 for the investment, as shown in Exhibit 15A–5.

EXHIBIT 15A–5 | Two-Year Investment

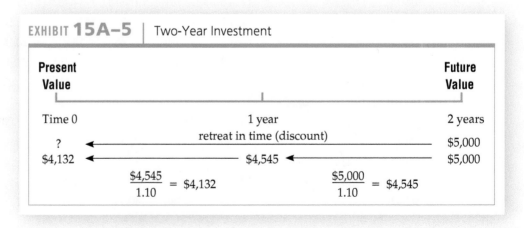

By turning the data around, we verify that $4,132 accumulates to $5,000 at 10 percent for two years.

Amount invested (present value)	$4,132
Expected earnings for first year ($4,132 × 0.10)	413
Amount invested after one year	4,545
Expected earnings for second year ($4,545 × 0.10)	455
Amount to be received two years from now (future value)	$5,000

REAL WORLD EXAMPLE

Notice that earnings for the first year are $413 but the earnings for the second year are $455—this demonstrates the power of compounding. The $42 increase from $413 to $455 comes from earning interest on the interest as well as on the principal.

You would pay $4,132—the present value of $5,000—to receive the $5,000 future amount at the end of two years at 10 percent per year. The $868 difference between the amount invested ($4,132) and the amount to be received ($5,000) is the return on the investment, the sum of the two interest receipts: $413 + $455 = $868.

Present-Value Tables

We have shown the simple formula for computing present value. However, calculating present value "by hand" for investments spanning many years presents too many opportunities for arithmetical errors and it is too much work. Present-value tables ease our work and allow us to see at a glance the relationship between time (in the Periods column) and each interest rate. (In the real world, calculators and computers are used rather than tables—we use tables here to demonstrate the concepts.) Let's re-examine our examples of present value by using Exhibit 15A–6: Present Value of $1.

For the 10 percent investment for one year, we find the junction under 10% and across from 1 in the Period column. The table figure of 0.909 is computed as follows: 1 ÷ 1.10 = 0.909. This work has been done for us, and only the present values are given in the table. The heading in Exhibit 15A–6 states present value for $1. To calculate present value for $5,000, we multiply 0.909 by $5,000. The result is $4,545, which matches the result we obtained by hand.

EXHIBIT 15A–6 | Present Value of $1 *(An expanded version of this table appears in Appendix B at the end of the text)*

Present Value of $1

Periods	2%	3%	4%	5%	6%	7%	8%	10%	12%
1	0.980	0.971	0.962	0.952	0.943	0.935	0.926	0.909	0.893
2	0.961	0.943	0.925	0.907	0.890	0.873	0.857	0.826	0.797
3	0.942	0.915	0.889	0.864	0.840	0.816	0.794	0.751	0.712
4	0.924	0.889	0.855	0.823	0.792	0.763	0.735	0.683	0.636
5	0.906	0.863	0.822	0.784	0.747	0.713	0.681	0.621	0.567
6	0.888	0.838	0.790	0.746	0.705	0.666	0.630	0.564	0.507
7	0.871	0.813	0.760	0.711	0.665	0.623	0.583	0.513	0.452
8	0.854	0.789	0.731	0.677	0.627	0.582	0.540	0.467	0.404
9	0.837	0.766	0.703	0.645	0.592	0.544	0.500	0.424	0.361
10	0.820	0.744	0.676	0.614	0.558	0.508	0.463	0.386	0.322
11	0.804	0.722	0.650	0.585	0.527	0.475	0.429	0.350	0.287
12	0.789	0.701	0.625	0.557	0.497	0.444	0.397	0.319	0.257
13	0.773	0.681	0.601	0.530	0.469	0.415	0.368	0.290	0.229
14	0.758	0.661	0.577	0.505	0.442	0.388	0.340	0.263	0.205
15	0.743	0.642	0.555	0.481	0.417	0.362	0.315	0.239	0.183
16	0.728	0.623	0.534	0.458	0.394	0.339	0.292	0.218	0.163
17	0.714	0.605	0.513	0.436	0.371	0.317	0.270	0.198	0.146
18	0.700	0.587	0.494	0.416	0.350	0.296	0.250	0.180	0.130
19	0.686	0.570	0.475	0.396	0.331	0.277	0.232	0.164	0.116
20	0.673	0.554	0.456	0.377	0.312	0.258	0.215	0.149	0.104

KEY POINTS

Present value payments are assumed to be at the beginning of the year and future value receipts are assumed to be at the end of the year.

REAL WORLD EXAMPLE

Lotteries that pay the winner $1,000 a week for life are an example of an annuity, an equal periodic amount ($1,000) received at a fixed interval (each year for life).

KEY POINTS

The formula for the present value of an annuity is
$A_n = R[(1 - (1+i)^{-n})/i]$

where

A_n = present value of a simple annuity
R = the periodic payment (rent)
i = interest rate per period
n = number of periodic payments

For the two-year investment, we read down the 10% column and across the Period 2 row. We multiply 0.826 (computed as 0.909 ÷ 1.10 = 0.826) by $5,000 and get $4,130, which confirms our earlier computation of $4,132 (the difference is due to rounding in the present-value table). Using the table we can compute the present value of any single future amount.

While we focus on tables in this text, you can also use financial calculators and functions in spreadsheet programs to calculate present value.

Present Value of an Annuity

Return to the investment example beginning on the previous page. That investment provided the investor with only a single future receipt ($5,000 at the end of two years). Annuity investments provide multiple receipts of an equal amount at fixed intervals over the investment's duration.

Consider an investment that promises *annual* cash receipts of $10,000 to be received at the end of each of three years. Assume that you demand a 12-percent return on your investment. What is the investment's present value? What would you pay today to acquire the investment? The investment spans three periods, and you would pay the sum of three present values. The computation is as follows:

Year	Annual Cash Receipt		Present Value of $1 at 12% (Exhibit 15A–6)	Present Value of Annual Cash Receipt
1	$10,000	×	0.893	$ 8,930
2	10,000	×	0.797	7,970
3	10,000	×	0.712	7,120
Total present value of investment				$24,020

The present value of this annuity is $24,020. By paying this amount today, you will receive $10,000 at the end of each of three years while earning 12 percent on your investment.

EXHIBIT 15A–7 | Present Value of Annuity of $1 *(An expanded version of this table appears in Appendix B at the end of the text)*

Present Value of Annuity of $1

Periods	2%	3%	4%	5%	6%	7%	8%	10%	12%
1	0.980	0.971	0.962	0.952	0.943	0.935	0.926	0.909	0.893
2	1.942	1.914	1.886	1.859	1.833	1.808	1.783	1.736	1.690
3	2.884	2.829	2.775	2.723	2.673	2.624	2.577	2.487	2.402
4	3.808	3.717	3.630	3.546	3.465	3.387	3.312	3.170	3.037
5	4.714	4.580	4.452	4.329	4.212	4.100	3.993	3.791	3.605
6	5.601	5.417	5.242	5.076	4.917	4.767	4.623	4.355	4.111
7	6.472	6.230	6.002	5.786	5.582	5.389	5.206	4.868	4.564
8	7.326	7.020	6.733	6.463	6.210	5.971	5.747	5.335	4.968
9	8.162	7.786	7.435	7.108	6.802	6.515	6.247	5.759	5.328
10	8.983	8.530	8.111	7.722	7.360	7.024	6.710	6.145	5.650
11	9.787	9.253	8.760	8.306	7.887	7.499	7.139	6.495	5.938
12	10.575	9.954	9.385	8.863	8.384	7.943	7.536	6.814	6.194
13	11.348	10.635	9.986	9.394	8.853	8.358	7.904	7.103	6.424
14	12.106	11.296	10.563	9.899	9.295	8.745	8.244	7.367	6.628
15	12.849	11.938	11.118	10.380	9.712	9.108	8.559	7.606	6.811
16	13.578	12.561	11.652	10.838	10.106	9.447	8.851	7.824	6.974
17	14.292	13.166	12.166	11.274	10.477	9.763	9.122	8.022	7.120
18	14.992	13.754	12.659	11.690	10.828	10.059	9.372	8.201	7.250
19	15.679	14.324	13.134	12.085	11.158	10.336	9.604	8.365	7.366
20	16.351	14.878	13.590	12.462	11.470	10.594	9.818	8.514	7.469

The example illustrates repetitive computations of the three future amounts, a time-consuming process. One way to ease the computational burden is to add the three present values of $1 (0.893 + 0.797 + 0.712) and multiply their sum (2.402) by the annual cash receipt ($10,000) to obtain the present value of the annuity ($10,000 × 2.402 = $24,020).

An easier approach is to use a present value of an annuity table. Exhibit 15A–7 shows the present value of $1 to be received periodically for a given number of periods. The present value of a three-period annuity at 12 percent is 2.402 (the junction of the Period 3 row and the 12% column). Thus, $10,000 received annually at the end of each of three years, discounted at 12 percent, is $24,020 ($10,000 × 2.402), which is the present value.

Present Value of Bonds Payable

The present value of a bond—its market price—is the present value of the future principal amount at maturity plus the present value of the future contract interest payments. The principal is a single amount to be paid at maturity. The interest is an annuity because it occurs periodically.

Let's compute the present value of 5-percent, five-year bonds of UVW Corporation. The face value of the bonds is $1,000,000, and they pay 2.5 percent contract (cash) interest semiannually. At issuance the market interest rate is 6 percent, but it is computed at 3 percent semiannually. Therefore, the effective-interest rate for each of the 10 semiannual periods is 3 percent. We use 3 percent in computing the present value of the maturity and of the interest. The market price of these bonds is $957,250, as follows:

REAL WORLD EXAMPLE

Using a financial calculator:*

Key	Amount to enter
FV	1,000,000
PMT	25,000
I	3
n	10
COMP	
PV	957,348.99

*Financial calculator keys and results may differ from those shown. Financial calculator results will also differ from those obtained with tables because of the rounding in present-value and future-value tables.

	Effective annual interest rate ÷ 2	Number of semiannual interest payments	
PV of principal:			
$1,000,000 × **PV of single amount** at	3%	for 10 periods	
($1,000,000 × 0.744—Exhibit 15A–6)			$744,000
PV of interest:			
($1,000,000 × 0.025) × **PV of annuity** at	3%	for 10 periods	
($25,000 × 8.530—Exhibit 15A–7)			213,250
PV (market price) of bonds			$957,250

The market price of the UVW Corporation bonds shows a discount because the contract interest rate on the bonds (5 percent) is less than the market interest rate (6 percent). We discuss these bonds in more detail on page 926.

Let's consider a premium price for the UVW Corporation bonds. Assume that UVW Corporation issues $1,000,000 of 5 percent bonds when the market interest rate is 4 percent at issuance. The effective-interest rate is 2 percent for each of the 10 semiannual periods.

	Effective annual interest rate ÷ 2	Number of semiannual interest payments	
PV of principal:			
$1,000,000 × **PV of single amount** at	2%	for 10 periods	
($1,000,000 × 0.820—Exhibit 15A–6)			$ 820,000
PV of interest:			
($1,000,000 × 0.025) × **PV of annuity** at	2%	for 10 periods	
($25,000 × 8.983—Exhibit 15A–7)			224,575
PV (market price) of bonds			$1,044,575

We discuss accounting for these bonds on page 927.

Many calculators and spreadsheet software packages can quickly and accurately perform present value calculations for bonds and leases.

APPENDIX PROBLEMS

Problem 15A–1

Computing the future value of an investment

b. At 6%, $56,370

For each situation, compute the required amount using the tables in this Appendix.

a. Summit Enterprises Ltd. is budgeting for the acquisition of land over the next several years. The company can invest $800,000 at 9 percent. How much cash will Summit Enterprises Ltd. have for land acquisitions at the end of five years? At the end of six years?

b. Alton Associates Inc. is planning to invest $10,000 each year for five years. The company's investment adviser believes that Alton Associates Inc. can earn 6 percent interest without taking on too much risk. What will be the value of Alton's investment on the date of the last deposit if Alton can earn 6 percent? If Alton can earn 8 percent?

Problem 15A–2

Relating the future and present values of an investment

a. $16,080,000

For each situation, compute the required amount using the tables in this Appendix.

a. XS Technologies Inc.'s operations are generating excess cash that will be invested in a special fund. During 2014, XS Technologies Inc. invests $12,000,000 in the fund for a planned advertising campaign for a new product to be released six years later, in 2020. If XS Technologies Inc.'s investments can earn 5 percent each year, how much cash will the company have for the advertising campaign in 2020?

b. XS Technologies Inc. will need $20 million to advertise a new product in 2020. How much must XS Technologies Inc. invest in 2014 to have the cash available for the advertising campaign? XS Technologies Inc. investments can earn 5 percent annually.

c. Explain the relationship between your answers to (a) and (b).

Problem 15A–3

Computing the present values of various notes and bonds

3. $254,280
4. $200,040

Determine the present value of the following notes and bonds using the tables in this Appendix (notes are accounted for in the same way as bonds):

1. $100,000, five-year note payable with contract interest rate of 9 percent, paid annually. The market interest rate at issuance is 10 percent.

2. Ten-year bonds payable with maturity value of $200,000 and contract interest rate of 12 percent, paid semiannually. The market rate of interest is 10 percent at issuance.

3. Same bonds payable as in number 2, but the market interest rate is 8 percent.

4. Same bonds payable as in number 2, but the market interest rate is 12 percent.

Problem 15A–4

Computing a bond's present value; recording its issuance at a discount and interest payments

1. $569,183

On December 31, 2014, when the market interest rate is 8 percent, Churchill Land Corporation issues $600,000 of 10-year, 7.25-percent bonds payable. The bonds pay interest semiannually.

Required

1. Determine the present value of the bonds at issuance using the tables in this Appendix.

2. Assume that the bonds are issued at the price computed in Requirement 1. Prepare an effective-interest method amortization table for the first two semiannual interest periods.

3. Using the amortization table prepared in Requirement 2, journalize issuance of the bonds and the first two interest payments.

Problem 15A–5

Deciding between two payment plans

Ontario Children's Choir needs a fleet of vans to transport the children to singing engagements throughout Ontario. Ford offers the vehicles for a single payment of $120,000 due at the end of four years. Toyota prices a similar fleet of vans for four annual payments of $28,000 each. The children's choir could borrow the funds at 6 percent, so this is the appropriate interest rate. Which company should get the business, Ford or Toyota? Base your decision on present value, and give your reason.

1. a. XYZ Corporation
   b. $100,000.00
   c. March 31, 2016
   d. John Doe
   e. 6% per year; the frequency of interest payments is not shown in Exhibit 15–1, but interest is typically paid twice a year.

2. a. At a discount
   b. At a premium
   c. At par
   d. At a premium
   e. At a discount

3. a. The bonds were issued at a discount.
   b. Sunwood received $990,000 on issuance of the bonds.

   c.
Cash	990,000	
Discount on Bonds Payable	10,000	
Bonds Payable		1,000,000

   To issue 3.75%, 10-year bonds at a discount. Cash received was $990,000 ($1,000,000 × 0.99).

   d. The carrying value of these bonds is $990,000 ($1,000,000 – $10,000 discount).

4. a. The bonds were issued at a premium.
   b. Parksville received $1,015,000 on issuance of the bonds.

   c.
Cash	1,015,000	
Bonds Payable		1,000,000
Premium on Bonds Payable		15,000

   To issue 3.75%, 10-year bonds at a premium. Cash received was $1,015,000 ($1,000,000 × 101.50).

   d. The carrying value of these bonds is $1,015,000 ($1,000,000 + $15,000 premium).

5. a. Compare the bond issue date (May 1, 2014) to the bonds' interest payment dates (April 30 and Oct. 31). If time has passed between the interest payment date and the issue date, then include interest for this time in the amount paid for the bonds. In this case, no time has passed from April 30 to May 1, so no interest needs to be calculated. Also, determine whether there is a premium or a discount. Since bonds were issued at 94.00, which is less than 100.00, there is a discount.

2014			
May 1	Cash	9,400,000	
	Discount on Bonds Payable	600,000	
	Bonds Payable		10,000,000

   Issued 6 percent, 10-year bonds at a discount ($10,000,000 × 0.94).

   b. Check for any interest accruals or partial amortization of a bond premium or discount. Since the six-month period of May 1 to Oct. 31, 2014, occurs before year end, no accruals or partial amortization are necessary on Oct. 31.

Oct. 31	Interest Expense	330,000	
	Cash		300,000
	Discount on Bonds Payable		30,000

   Paid semi-annual interest ($10,000,000 × 0.06 × $\frac{6}{12}$) and amortized discount ($600,000 ÷ 20).

   c. Calculate the time period from the last interest payment (Oct. 31, 2014) to the year end (Dec. 31, 2014). Accrue interest and amortize premium or discount for this time period (2 months).

Dec. 31	Interest Expense	110,000	
	Discount on Bonds Payable		10,000
	Interest Payable		100,000

   Accrued interest ($10,000,000 × 0.06 × $\frac{2}{12}$) and amortized bond discount for two months ($600,000 ÷ 20 × $\frac{2}{6}$).

   d. Make sure all amortization of the bond discount is reflected in Discount on Bonds Payable, including the accrual calculated in part c. Then subtract the discount from Bonds Payable to show the net liability for bonds payable.

Long-term liabilities		
Bonds payable, 6%, due 2024	$10,000,000	
Discount on bonds payable		
($600,000 – $30,000 – $10,000)*	560,000	$9,440,000

   *The calculation is for your reference only. It would not appear on the balance sheet.

   e. The cash payment of interest is always the same: Bonds payable × Stated rate × Time. Reverse the year-end accrual (Interest Payable amount), then calculate interest and amortization of discount or premium for the period Jan. 1 to April 30, 2015.

2015			
Apr. 30	Interest Expense	220,000	
	Interest Payable	100,000	
	Cash		300,000
	Discount on Bonds Payable		20,000

   Paid semi-annual interest ($10,000,000 × 0.06 × $\frac{6}{12}$), part of which was accrued ($100,000), and amortized four months' discount on bonds payable ($600,000 ÷ 20 × $\frac{4}{6}$).

Here are some suggestions for checking your solutions. While you don't have to follow these procedures for every problem, you can use them to check your solutions for reasonableness as well as accuracy.

On April 30, 2015, the bonds have been outstanding for one year. After the entries have been recorded, the account balances should show the results of one year's cash interest payments and one year's bond premium amortization.

Fact 1	Cash interest payments should be $600,000 ($10,000,000 × 0.06).
Accuracy check	Two credits to Cash of $300,000 each = $600,000. Cash payments are correct.
Fact 2	Discount amortization should be $60,000 ($600,000 ÷ 20 semi-annual periods × 2 semi-annual periods in 1 year).
Accuracy check	Three debits to Discount on Bonds Payable ($30,000 + $10,000 + $20,000 = $60,000). Discount amortization is correct.
Fact 3	Also, we can check the accuracy of interest expense recorded during the year ended December 31, 2014.
	The bonds in this problem will be outstanding for a total of 10 years, or 120

(Continued)

(Continued)

(that is, 10×12) months. During 2014, the bonds are outstanding for 8 months (May through December).

Interest expense for 8 months *equals* payment of cash interest for 8 months plus discount amortization for 8 months. Interest expense should therefore be ($10,000,000 \times 0.06 \times 8/12 = \$400,000$) plus [($600,000/120) \times 8 = \$40,000$] or ($400,000 + \$40,000 = \$440,000$).

Accuracy check: Two debits to Interest Expense ($330,000 + \$110,000) = \$440,000$. Interest expense for 2014 is correct.

6.

2015

Dec. 31	Interest Expense	6,882	
	Premium on Bonds Payable	1,451	
	Interest Payable		8,333

To accrue two months' interest expense ($20,647 \times \frac{2}{6}$), amortize premium on bonds payable for two months ($4,353 \times \frac{2}{6}$), and record interest payable ($25,000 \times \frac{2}{6}$).

2016

Apr. 30	Interest Expense	13,765	
	Interest Payable	8,333	
	Premium on Bonds Payable	2,902	
	Cash		25,000

To pay semi-annual interest ($20,647 \times \frac{4}{6}$), some of which was accrued, and amortize premium on bonds payable for four months ($4,353 \times \frac{4}{6}$).

7. a. The periodic amount of interest expense *increases* because the carrying amount of the bond *increases* toward maturity value. To see this, refer to columns B and E of Exhibit 15–4. The upward-sloping line in Exhibit 15–5, Panel A, illustrates the increasing amount of interest expense.

b. The periodic amount of interest expense *decreases* because the carrying amount of the bond *decreases* toward maturity value. To see this, study columns B and E of Exhibit 15–6. The downward-sloping line in Exhibit 15–7, Panel A, illustrates the decreasing amount of interest expense.

c. For bonds issued at a discount, interest expense will be greater than cash interest paid, by the amount of the discount amortized for the period. Remember that the company received less than face value when it issued the bonds. But, at maturity, the company must pay the full value back to the bondholders. Thus, a discount increases the company's interest expense above the amount of cash interest paid each period.

For bonds issued at a *premium*, cash interest paid will be greater than interest expense, by the amount of the premium amortized for the period. This is because the premium amount received at issuance decreases the interest expense below the amount of cash interest paid each period.

8. Calculation of the gain or loss on retirement:

Face value of bonds being retired ($5,000,000 \times \frac{1}{2}$)	$2,500,000
Unamortized premium ($30,000 \times \frac{1}{2}$)	15,000
Book value, or carrying value	2,515,000
Market price paid to retire the bonds ($2,500,000 \times 100.50$)	2,512,500
Gain on retirement of bonds	$ 2,500

The journal entry to record the retirement:

Bonds Payable	2,500,000	
Premium on Bonds Payable	15,000	
Cash		2,512,500
Gain on retirement of bonds		2,500

To retire bonds payable before maturity.

9.

2014

Sept. 1	Bonds Payable	2,500,000	
	Premium on Bonds Payable	15,000	
	Common Shares		2,515,000

To record conversion of $2,515,000 of bonds outstanding into 1,000,000 common shares.

10.

Current liabilities		
Current portion of long-term debt	$1,500,000	
Premium on bonds payable	5,000	$1,505,000
Long-term debt, excluding current portion	3,500,000	
Premium on bonds payable	25,000	3,525,000

11. While trading on the equity can improve EPS, it might be to the corporation's *disadvantage* to finance with debt. This is because the corporation would suffer (1) if the interest rate on its debt is greater than the rate of earnings from that money, and (2) if the company borrows so much that it cannot meet interest and principal payments.

12.

Shares	Plan 1 Borrow $1,000,000 at 10%	Plan 2 Issue $1,000,000 of Common Shares
Net income after interest and income tax, before expansion	$600,000	$600,000
Project income before interest and income tax	$300,000	$300,000
Less: interest expense ($1,000,000 \times 0.12$)	120,000	0
Project income before income tax	180,000	300,000
Less: income tax expense (40%)	72,000	120,000
Project net income	$108,000	$180,000
Total company net income	$708,000	$780,000
Earnings per share including expansion:		
Plan 1 ($708,000 ÷ 200,000 shares)	$ 3.54	
Plan 2 ($780,000 ÷ 250,000 shares)		$ 3.12

Plan 1 seems more favourable because the EPS is higher. However, the EPS is only 13% higher than Plan 2. The company's ability to pay the interest on the bonds must also be considered—at 12 percent, the interest payments may limit the company from making other future expenditures as they are needed, so both plans should be considered carefully.

13.

2014			
Oct. 1	Cash	200,000	
	Mortgage Payable		200,000
	To record the receipt of proceeds from a 10-year, 5 percent mortgage loan.		
Oct. 1	Building	140,000	
	Land	60,000	
	Cash		200,000
	To record the purchase of land and a building for $200,000.		

14.

2014			
Dec. 1	Interest Expense	827	
	Mortgage Payable	1,293	
	Cash		2,121
	To pay monthly mortgage loan and record interest portion.		

15. a.

2014			
Jan. 2	Equipment	138,143	
	Cash		30,000
	Capital Lease Liability		108,143
	To lease equipment and make the first annual lease payment on a capital lease. (Equipment = $30,000 + $108,143 = $138,143). (If using a financial calculator: Pmt – $30,000, N – 6, I – 12% FV – 0, Comp PV – $138,143.29)		

b.

Dec. 31	Amortization Expense	23,024	
	Accumulated Amortization— Leased Equipment		23,024
	To record amortization on leased equipment ($138,143 ÷ 6).		

c.

Dec. 31	Interest Expense	12,977	
	Capital Lease Liability		12,977
	To accrue interest expense on the capital lease liability ($108,143 × 0.12).		

d.

2015			
Jan. 2	Capital Lease Liability	30,000	
	Cash		30,000
	To make second annual lease payment on equipment.		

16. Under ASPE, the liability for bonds is reported at amortized cost. Under IFRS, bond indebtedness can be reported at either amortized cost or fair value.

17. When accounting for leases, IFRS requires companies to disclose more supplementary information than does ASPE.

16 Investments and International Operations

KEY QUESTIONS		LEARNING OBJECTIVES
How do we account for short-term investments?	(1)	Account for short-term investments
How do we account for long-term share investments?	(2)	Account for long-term share investments
What is the equity method, and how do we use it?	(3)	Use the equity method to account for investments
What is consolidation, and how do we perform a simple consolidation?	(4)	Describe and create consolidated financial statements
How do we record investments in bonds?	(5)	Account for investments in bonds
How do we record transactions with foreign currencies?	(6)	Account for foreign-currency transactions
How does IFRS apply to investments and international transactions?	(7)	Identify the impact on accounting for investments of international financial reporting standards (IFRS)

Kinross Gold Corporation is a Canadian-based gold mining company with both Canadian and international operations. The company employs approximately 8,000 people worldwide, and had more than $16 billion in assets and almost $4 billion of metal sales during 2011. Kinross states that its core purpose is to "lead the world in generating value through responsible mining." In 2011, for the third year in a row, it was named as one of Canada's Top 50 Socially Responsible Corporations.[1]

Kinross has more than a dozen subsidiary companies whose results are combined into the corporation's *consolidated* financial statements. In addition, it has a number of companies in which it has a small ownership interest whose results are also reported within the Kinross annual report. The accounting treatment for investments in other companies varies depending on the percentage of ownership acquired (based on the number of shares purchased) and management's intention for the acquired company. The first part of this chapter will explore investments in other companies.

Kinross's investments are mostly in companies located outside of Canada, in places including Russia, Brazil, Chile, Mauritania, Ecuador, and the United States. This is a growing part of Kinross's business. For example, in 2011, Kinross increased its ownership in the Kupol mine in Russia from 75 percent to 100 percent. Interestingly, Kinross is ahead of many companies in investing in businesses in countries with developing economies. It is the largest Canadian investor in Russia. It has spent over $2 billion there from 2007 to 2012. It is also the largest foreign mining investor in that country.[2] Working in different countries means transacting in different currencies. This chapter will also address how foreign-currency transactions are recorded.

---

[1] Kinross Gold Corporation website www.kinross.com, accessed October 16, 2012.

[2] Barrie McKenna and Nicolas Johnson, "In Russia, the Opportunity Still Beckons, and So Do the Pitfalls," *The Globe and Mail*, posted at http://www.theglobeandmail.com/report-on-business/international-business/in-russia-opportunity-still-beckons---and-so-do-the-pitfalls/article552975/published on March 8, 2012, and accessed October 16, 2012.

CONNECTING CHAPTER 16

①	②	③	④	⑤	⑥	⑦
Account for short-term investments	Account for long-term share investments	Use the equity method to account for investments	Describe and create consolidated financial statements	Account for investments in bonds	Account for foreign-currency transactions	Identify the impact on accounting for investments of international financial reporting standards (IFRS)
How do we account for short-term investments? page 993	*How do we account for long-term share investments? page 996*	*What is the equity method, and how do we use it? page 999*	*What is consolidation, and how do we perform a simple consolidation? page 1004*	*How do we record investments in bonds? page 1010*	*How do we record transactions with foreign currencies? page 1014*	*How does IFRS apply to investments and international transactions? page 1019*
Share Investments: An Overview, page 991	Accounting for Long-Term Share Investments, page 996	Long-Term Share Investments Accounted for by the Equity Method, page 999	Consolidated Financial Statements, page 1004	Investments in Bonds and Notes, page 1010	Foreign-Currency Transactions, page 1014	The Impact on Accounting for Investments of International Financial Reporting Standards (IFRS), page 1019
Accounting for Short-Term Investments, page 993						

MyAccountingLab
- Chapter 16: Student PowerPoint Slides
- Chapter 16: Audio Chapter Summary

The **Summary** for Chapter 16 appears on page 1021.
Accounting Vocabulary with definitions appears on page 1024.

Throughout this course, you have become increasingly familiar with the financial statements of companies such as Tim Hortons Inc., Dollarama Inc., Gildan Activewear Inc., and Rainmaker Entertainment Inc.. This chapter continues to examine the real world of accounting by discussing investments and international operations.

Investments range from owning a few shares in another company to the acquisition of an entire company. In earlier chapters we discussed how companies issue shares and bonds. Here we examine shares and bonds from the perspective of a corporate investor who would buy them. Recall that when companies purchase shares, they are considered equity investments because there is a share of ownership that is transferred. Bonds are debt investments.

Why do individuals and corporations invest in shares and bonds? You would probably make an investment in order to earn dividend revenue and to sell the shares at a higher price than you paid for them. Investment companies such as pension funds, mutual funds, insurance companies, bank trust departments, and other corporations buy shares and bonds for this same reason.

Many companies invest in shares and bonds for a second reason: to influence or to control the other company. Kinross Gold Corporation holds 100 percent of the shares of a Canadian company called Underworld Resources Inc. and can exert complete control over the affairs of that company. It owns 25 percent of Compania

Minera Casale (Chile). While Kinross doesn't own all the shares of the Chilean company, it owns "enough" to influence the decisions of its management and, therefore, it reports in the notes to the financial statements that it has influence over the affairs of that company. Different accounting methods apply to different types of investments. We begin with investments in the shares of other companies and then move to investments in bonds and notes before ending the chapter with foreign-exchange transactions.

Share Investments: An Overview

Share Prices

Investors can purchase shares directly from the issuing company or from other investors who wish to sell their shares. Investors buy more shares in transactions with other investors than in purchases directly from the issuing company. Each share is issued only once, but it may be traded among investors multiple times thereafter. People and businesses buy shares from and sell shares to each other in markets, such as the Toronto Stock Exchange (TSX) and the TSX Venture Exchange. Recall that share ownership is transferable. Investors trade millions of shares each day. Brokers like RBC Dominion Securities and Raymond James handle share transactions for a commission. Individuals may also choose to do the trading themselves using discount trading/brokerage accounts to reduce transaction costs. Exhibit 16–1 presents information for the common shares of several Canadian companies listed on Toronto Stock Exchange (TSX).[3]

EXHIBIT 16–1 | Share Price Information for Three Canadian Companies

52 Weeks		Stock	Daily High	Daily Low	Cls or Latest	% Chge	Volume	P/E Ratio
High	Low							
36.47	16.54	Gildan Activewear Inc.	25.69	24.61	25.46	3.12	281,529	18.50
70.56	35.65	Lululemon Athletica Inc.	70.12	69.57	69.50	−0.26	13,623	61.80
15.74	10.30	WestJet Airlines Ltd.	14.10	13.95	14.10	0.05	211,165	13.30

A broker (or website) may "quote a share price," which means the current market price per share. The financial community quotes share prices in dollars and cents. For example, Exhibit 16–1 shows WestJet Airlines Ltd. common shares trading at $14.10 at the close of trading. This information is available instantaneously during the trading day from a variety of websites (such as the website for the Toronto Stock Exchange—tmx.com).

At some point during the previous 52 weeks, WestJet common shares reached a high of $15.74 and, at some other point, a low of $10.30. The TSX website continually updates this information while the stock market is open and then provides a summary at the end of each trading day. The closing price was 0.05 percent higher than the closing price one trading day earlier. From this information, we also learn that 211,165 shares of WestJet stock were traded. The P/E ratio (ratio of the share price to earnings per share) is 13.30 for WestJet shares on this day.

REAL WORLD EXAMPLE

Companies listed on stock exchanges have their name and type of shares shown in short form on many reports. WestJet shares are shown under WJA or WJA.A depending on the class of shares.

Investors and Investees

A person or a company that owns shares in a corporation is an *investor*. The corporation that issued the shares is the *investee*. If you own common shares of WestJet, you are an investor and WestJet is the investee.

---

[3] *Source:* Toronto Stock Exchange website tmx.com for closing information on March 3, 2012. The website was accessed March 5, 2012.

A business may purchase another corporation's shares in the hope of earning dividend revenue and making gains on the sale of the shares. Such investments are rare, however. Most entities prefer to invest in inventory, employees, and capital assets in their own line of business. However, entities do buy the shares of other corporations to gain a degree of control over the investee's operation. An investor holding 25 percent of the outstanding common shares of the investee owns one-fourth of the business. This one-quarter voice in electing the directors of the corporation is likely to give the investor influence over the conduct of the investee's business. The term **significant influence** is used when a company participates in the decision making of another company without having full control over it. Somewhere in the range of 20% to 50% of the ownership of the company is sufficient for this to be the case. This is a decision that requires the use of professional judgment. An investor holding more than 50 percent of the outstanding common shares controls the investee.

Classifying Investments

Short-term investments include **treasury bills, certificates of deposit, money market funds,** and shares and bonds of other companies.

Investments are assets to the investor. The investments may be held for a short term or a long term. **Short-term investments** may also be described as marketable securities or temporary investments, and are current assets. Short-term investments typically are **actively traded**, with the primary objective being to make a profit from changes in short-term market values. To be listed on the balance sheet as current assets, investments must be liquid (readily convertible to cash). Generally, the investor intends to convert the investments to cash within one year but may continue to hold the investments for a longer period.

Management *intent* is the key determinant about whether an investment is categorized as long-term or short-term.

Investments are categorized as current or long-term based on the length of time management intends to hold them. According to accounting standards for private enterprises (ASPE), an investment in the equity of a company that is *not* a short-term investment is categorized as a *long-term investment*. The different types of long-term equity investments are discussed on pages 996 to 997. **Long-term investments** are those investments the investor intends to convert to cash in more than one year. Investments in debt instruments of other companies, such as bonds, can be either short-term or long-term investments. These will also be discussed in this chapter.

Exhibit 16–2 provides an example of the presentation of the investment accounts on the balance sheet. We report assets in order of their liquidity, starting with cash. Short-term investments are shown as current assets, while long-term investments and investments subject to significant influence are reported as long-term assets. Notice that these long-tem investments are reported before property, plant, and equipment, and that there is no subtitle for long-term assets like there is for current assets.

EXHIBIT 16–2 | Reporting Investments on the Balance Sheet

Current assets		
Cash	$x	
Short-term investments	x	
Accounts receivable	x	
Inventories	x	
Prepaid expenses	x	
Total current assets		$x
Long-term investments (or simply **Investments**)—Note X		x
Property, plant, and equipment		x

Note X—Long-Term Investments
Details of the long-term investments in shares where there is no significant influence, long-term investments in shares where there is significant influence, and long-term investments in bonds would be given in this note.

Accounting for Short-Term Investments

The **fair-value method**, or **market-value method**, is used to account for short-term investments in shares. If there is an available market price for the investment, the historic cost is used only as the initial amount for recording investments and as the basis for measuring gains and losses on their sale. These investments are reported on the balance sheet at their fair values. (If there is not an available market price for the investment, it is recorded and reported on the balance sheet at historic cost. Unless otherwise stated, we assume all short-term investments in this chapter have an available market price.)

── LO ① ──
How do we account for short-term investments?

Share Transactions

Let's work through an example to show how share transactions are recorded and the share information is reported on the financial statements.

Investment   All investments are recorded initially at cost. Cost is the price paid for the shares. Section 3856 of Part II of the *CICA Handbook* states that brokerage commission and other transaction costs are expensed. Suppose that Elk Valley Ltd. purchases 1,000 common shares of the 687,000 outstanding shares from Finning International Inc. at the market price of $16.00 per share and pays a $500 commission. Elk Valley Ltd. intends to sell this investment within one year or less and, therefore, classifies it as a short-term investment. Elk Valley Ltd.'s entry to record the investment is

Aug. 22	Short-Term Investments	16,000	
	Brokerage Commissions Expense	500	
	Cash		16,500
	Purchased 1,000 common shares of Finning		
	International Inc. at $16.00 per share		
	(1,000 × $16.00 = $16,000) plus commission of $500.		

Cash Dividend   Assume Elk Valley Ltd. receives a $0.25 per share cash dividend on the Finning shares. Elk Valley Ltd.'s entry to record receipt of the dividends is

Oct. 14	Cash	250	
	Dividend Revenue		250
	Received $0.25 per share cash dividend (1,000 × $0.25) on		
	Finning International Inc. common shares.		

Dividends do not accrue with the passage of time (as interest does). The investee has no liability for dividends until the dividends are declared. An investor makes no accrual entry for dividend revenue at year end in anticipation of a dividend declaration.

However, if a dividend declaration does occur before year end, say, on December 28, the investor *may* debit Dividend Receivable and credit Dividend Revenue on that date. The investor would then report this receivable and the revenue in the December 31 financial statements. Receipt of the cash dividend in January would be recorded by a debit to Cash and a credit to Dividend Receivable. The more common practice, however, is to record the dividend as income when it is received.

Stock Dividend   Receipt of a stock dividend is not income to the investor, and no formal journal entry is needed. As we have seen, a stock dividend increases the number of shares held by the investor but does not affect the total cost of the investment. The *cost per share* of the share investment therefore decreases. The investor usually makes a memorandum entry of the number of stock dividend shares received and the new cost per share. Assume that Elk Valley Ltd. receives

KEY POINTS

Receipts of stock dividends and stock splits are recorded in a memorandum entry. However, for income tax purposes a stock dividend is deemed to be income received by the investor, and tax must be paid on this deemed income.

a 10-percent stock dividend on its 1,000-share investment in Finning International Inc. that cost $16,000. Elk Valley Ltd. would make a memorandum entry like this:

Nov. 22	Received 100 Finning International Inc. common shares in a 10-percent stock dividend. New cost per share is $14.55 ($16,000 ÷ 1,100 shares).

Gain or Loss on Sale Prior to Adjustments to Fair Value   Any gain or loss on the sale of the investment is the difference between the sale proceeds and the carrying value of the investment. Assume that Elk Valley Ltd. sells 400 shares of Finning International Inc. for $20.00 per share, less a $300 commission. The entry to record the sale is

Dec. 18	Cash	7,700	
	Brokerage Commissions Expense	300	
	Short-Term Investments		5,820
	Gain on Sale of Investment		2,180
	Sold 400 common shares of Finning International Inc		
	Cash received was $7,700 [(400 × $20) − $300].		
	Carrying value of common shares sold was $5,820 (400 × $14.55).		

Observe that the carrying value per share of the investment ($14.55) is based on the total number of shares held, including those received as a stock dividend.

Reporting Short-Term Investments at Fair Value   ASPE require that equity investments where there is no significant influence be reported at their fair value, or current market value, at year end. There is no significant influence in this case because Elk Valley owns only a small percentage of the total outstanding shares of Finning International Inc. (Elk Valley owns only 700 of Finning's total of 755,700 common shares after the stock dividend, which is less than one-tenth of 1 percent of Finning's shares.) Any gain or loss resulting from the change in fair value is recognized in net income for the period in which it arises. The gain or loss is recorded as an unrealized gain or loss in the non-operating section of the company's income statement, under "Other gains and losses."

In our previous example, Elk Valley Ltd. had purchased 1,000 shares of Finning International Inc. for $16.00 per share. Ignoring the stock dividend and the December 18 sale, assume that the fair value of the shares at the December 31 year end had increased to $18.00 per share. Elk Valley Ltd. must adjust the value of the short-term investment to $18,000 (1,000 shares × $18.00) from its carrying value of $16,000, which is an increase of $2,000.

To record this adjustment, a Fair-Value Valuation Allowance account is created, which is a **companion account** to the Short-Term Investments or Long-Term Investments account. The following journal entry is recorded to increase the short-term investments value by $2,000:

LEARNING TIPS

Fair-Value Valuation Allowance is a companion account to the main Investments account. We have seen companion accounts before. The Allowance for Doubtful Accounts is a companion account to Accounts Receivable. The companion account may or not be a contra account.

Dec. 31	Fair-Value Valuation Allowance	2,000	
	Unrealized Gain on Fair-Value Adjustment		2,000
	Adjusted Finning International Inc. investment to fair value.		

Elk Valley Ltd.'s balance sheet would report short-term investments and its income statement would report the increase in the short-term investment as follows:

Balance Sheet (partial)			Income Statement (partial)	
Current Assets			Other gains and losses:	
Cash	$ xxx		Unrealized gain on short-term investments	$2,000
Short-term investments, at fair value	18,000		Income before income taxes	xxx
Accounts receivable,			Income tax expense	xxx
net of allowance of $xxx	xxx		Net income (or net loss)	$ xxx

Now assume instead that the Finning International Inc. shares decreased in value, and at the December 31 year end, Elk Valley Ltd.'s investment in the Finning shares is worth $13,000 ($3,000 less than the carrying value of $16,000). The following journal entry is recorded to decrease the short-term investment's value by $3,000:

Dec. 31	Unrealized Loss on Fair-Value Adjustment	3,000	
	Fair-Value Valuation Allowance		3,000
	Adjusted Finning International Inc. investment to fair value.		

Elk Valley Ltd.'s balance sheet would report short-term investments and its income statement would report the decrease in the short-term investments as follows:

Balance Sheet (partial)	
Current Assets	
Cash	$ xxx
Short-term investments, at fair value	13,000
Accounts receivable,	
net of allowance of $xxx	xxx

Income Statement (partial)	
Other gains and losses:	
Unrealized loss on short-term investments	$3,000
Income before income taxes	xxx
Income tax expense	xxx
Net income (or net loss)	$ xxx

Selling a Short-Term Equity Investment When a company sells an equity investment, the gain or loss on the sale is the difference between the sale proceeds and the last carrying amount. If Elk Valley Ltd. sells the Finning International Inc. shares after year end for $12,000, Elk Valley Ltd. would record the sale and the $1,000 loss ($12,000 selling price − $13,000 carrying value) as follows:

Jan. 19	Cash	12,000	
	Loss on Sale of Short-Term Investments	1,000	
	Fair-Value Valuation Allowance	3,000	
	Short-Term Investments		16,000
	Sold Finning International Inc. shares at a loss.		

Notice that:

- Short-Term Investments is credited for the original cost of the investment, adjusted for any stock dividends or stock splits.
- Fair-Value Valuation Allowance is debited, in this case, for the change in fair value since the investment was purchased.
- These entries remove the fair value of the investment from the books.

Companies would normally account for each investment separately, which can be done quite easily with computerized record keeping. Elk Valley Ltd.'s income statement would report the loss on the sale of the short-term investment in the "Other gains and losses" section.

Reporting Short-Term Bond Investments

The fair-value method is used to account for short-term investments in bonds. Like shares, short-term bond investments are valued at fair value, or market value. Premiums or discounts are not amortized as the intent is to hold the bonds for only a short period.

✓ JUST CHECKING

1. Calculate the price per share immediately after each of the following actions. This is a short-term investment and the investor does not have a significant influence on the investee.

   a. 1,000 shares were purchased for $18,700 plus commission of $300.

   b. The shares were split 2 for 1 one month later.

   c. The shares' total market value at year end was $16,000.

   d. All the shares were sold after year end for $20,000 plus commission of $250.

2. Levon Ltd. completed the following investment transactions during 2013 and 2014. Journalize the transactions, providing explanations.

   2013

   Sept. 30   Purchased 1,200 of the 50,000 outstanding common shares of Betam Ltd. at a price of $36.00 per share, intending to sell the investment within the next year. Commissions were $125.

   Dec. 21   Received a cash dividend of $0.09 per share on the Betam Ltd. shares.

   31   At Levon Ltd.'s year end, adjusted the investment to its fair value of $33.50 per share.

   2014

   Apr. 13   Sold the Betam Ltd. shares for $31.00 per share. Commissions were $120.

3. At what amount should the following investment portfolio be reported on the December 31 year-end balance sheet? All the investments are less than 5 percent of the investee's shares. Journalize any adjusting entry required by these data.

Shares	Carrying Value	Current Fair Value
All Seasons Hotels	$ 88,000	$ 97,000
Tangerine Manufacturing Corp.	140,000	124,000
Prairie Grocers Inc.	74,000	76,000

Just Checking Solutions appear at the end of this chapter and on MyAccountingLab.

Accounting for Long-Term Share Investments

LO ②

How do we account for long-term share investments?

LEARNING TIPS

Investments are always long-term unless specifically stated otherwise so the term "long term" does not need to be in the account title. It is shown here just for clarity.

An investor may own numerous investments, some to be held for a short term and others for a long term. For accounting purposes, the two investment portfolios are not mixed. They are reported separately on the balance sheet, as shown in Exhibit 16–2 on page 992. "Long-term" is not often used in the account title for these types of investments. An investment is understood to be long-term unless specifically labelled as short-term and included with current assets.

Long-term investments may be of several different types, depending on the purpose of the investment and thus the percentage of voting interest acquired. Each of the types is introduced in the following paragraphs and summarized in Exhibit 16–3.

EXHIBIT **16–3** | Types of Investments and Accounting Methods under ASPE

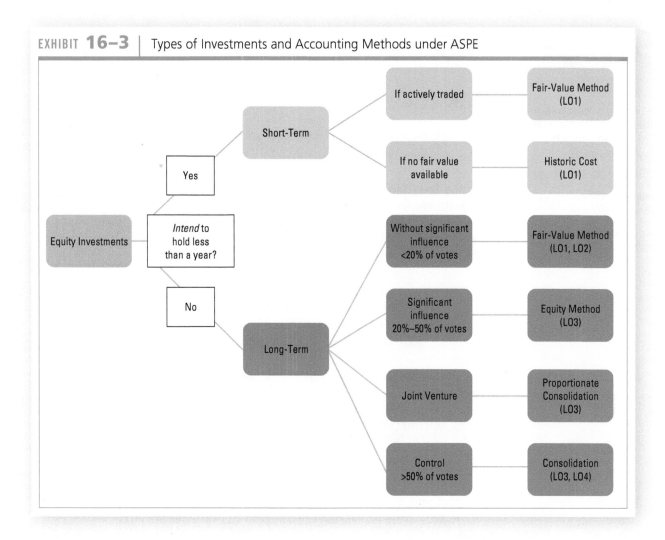

Long-Term Equity Investments Without Significant Influence

An investor may make a long-term investment in the shares of another corporation where the purpose is similar to that of short-term investing—the investor will hold the investment to earn dividend revenue or make profits for selling the investment at a higher price than its purchase price. In such a situation, the investor will generally hold less than 20 percent of the voting interest of the investee and would normally play no important role in the investee's operations. Such an investor would normally account for the investment using the *fair-value method* (*market-value method*), if the market value for the shares of the investee is readily available. ***This is the same treatment as for short-term equity investments.***

Investment   Suppose Elm Corporation purchases 1,000 common shares of Molson Coors Brewing Company at the market price of $48.00 per share, plus a brokerage commission of $1,000. Elm plans to hold these shares for longer than a year and classifies them as a long-term investment. Elm's entry to record the investment is

Feb. 23	Long-Term Investments	48,000	
	Brokerage Commission Expense	1,000	
	Cash		49,000
	Purchased investment (1,000 × $48).		
	Paid brokerage commission fee $1,000.		

Long-Term Investments with No Significant Influence:

The beginning accounting value is shown at cost, which is debited to the Long-Term Investments account at the date of purchase.

Dividends are treated as income.

Brokerage commission fees are expensed.

Gains and losses are recorded on sales.

Cash Dividend   Assume that Elm receives a $1.00 per share cash dividend on the Molson Coors Brewing Company shares. Elm's entry for receipt of the dividend is

Jul. 14	Cash	1,000	
	Dividend Revenue		1,000
	Received dividend on the Molson Coors		
	Brewing Company shares (1,000 × $1.00).		

Reporting Long-Term Investments at Fair Value   Reporting at fair value requires an adjustment to current market value on the balance sheet date. Assume that the fair value of Elm's investment in Molson Coors Brewing Company shares has increased to $50,000 on December 31, its year end. In this case, Elm makes the following adjustment:

Dec. 31	Fair-Value Valuation Allowance	2,000	
	Unrealized Gain on Fair-Value Adjustment		2,000
	Adjusted long-term investment to fair value		
	($50,000 − $48,000).		

Fair-Value Valuation Allowance is a companion account to the Long-Term Investments account. The Allowance account brings the investment to current fair (market) value. Cost ($48,000) plus the Allowance ($2,000) equals the investment carrying amount ($50,000).

Long-Term Investments	Fair-Value Valuation Allowance
48,000	2,000

Investment carrying amount = Market value of $50,000

LEARNING TIPS

Recording and reporting short-term equity investments and long-term equity investments without significant influence is the SAME except for the account name for short-term or long-term. Both use the fair value method.

Here the Fair-Value Valuation Allowance account has a debit balance because the investment has increased in value. If the investment's value declines, the allowance is credited. In that case, the investment carrying amount is cost *minus* the allowance. Fair-Value Valuation Allowance with a credit balance becomes a contra account.

The other side of the December 31 adjustment credits Unrealized Gain on Fair-Value Adjustment. If the investment declines, the company debits Unrealized Loss on Fair-Value Adjustment. *Unrealized* means that the gain or loss resulted from a change in fair value, not from a sale of the investment. A gain or loss on the sale of an investment is said to be *realized* when the company receives cash. For long-term investments where there is no significant influence, the Unrealized Gain (or Loss) is reported in the same manner as the short-term investment gain (or loss): in the non-operating section of the company's income statement, under "other gains and losses."

If there is not an available market price for the long-term investment, it is recorded and reported on the balance sheet at cost, just as short-term investments are. There is no market price when the shares are not traded on a stock exchange. Unless otherwise stated, in this chapter we assume all long-term investments where there is no significant influence have an available market price.

Selling a Long-Term Investment Where There Is No Significant Influence   The sale of a long-term investment where there is no significant influence usually results in a *realized* gain or loss. Suppose Elm Corporation sells its investment in the Molson

Coors Brewing Company shares for $52,000 during the next year, with brokerage commissions of $1,050. Elm would record the sale as follows:

Apr. 16	Cash	50,950	
	Brokerage Commissions Expense	1,050	
	Gain on Sale of Long-Term Investment		2,000
	Long-Term Investments		48,000
	Fair-Value Valuation Allowance		2,000
	Sold Molson Coors Brewing Company shares at a gain.		

Elm Corporation would report the Gain on Sale of Long-Term Investment as an "Other gain or loss" in the non-operating section of the income statement.

✓ JUST CHECKING

4. Focus Ltd. completed the following investment transactions during 2013 and 2014. Journalize the transactions, providing explanations.

2013

Oct. 16   Purchased 10,000 of the 60,000 outstanding common shares of Levell Inc. at a price of $45.00 per share; Levell Inc. is known for its generous dividends, so Focus Ltd. plans to hold the investment for more than one year. Commissions were $425.

Dec. 1   Received a cash dividend of $2.00 per share on the Levell Inc. shares.

     31   At Focus Ltd.'s year end, adjusted the investment to its fair value of $46.00 per share.

2014

Feb. 15   Suddenly needing cash, Focus Ltd. sold half the Levell Inc. shares for $49.00 per share. Commissions were $260.

Just Checking Solutions appear at the end of this chapter and on MyAccountingLab.

Long-Term Share Investments Accounted for by the Equity Method

An investor may make an investment in the investee by purchasing from 20 to 50 percent of the investee's voting shares. In this case, the investor will likely be able to exert a *significant influence* over the investee and how the investee operates the business. Such an investor can likely affect the investee's decisions on dividend policy, product lines, sources of supply, and other important matters. We use the **equity method for investments** to account for investments in which the investor can significantly influence the decisions of the investee.

The ability to influence matters more than the actual percentage of ownership. In certain circumstances, an investor with less than a 20-percent holding may still exert significant influence if there are many other shareholders who all own a small number of shares. In another case, a shareholder with a larger holding, such as a 30-percent holding, may exert no significant influence if another shareholder owns 51 percent of the shares and thus has control of the corporation. In this situation, the cost or fair-value method would be used to account for this investment rather than the equity method since there is no significant influence.

Investment   Investments accounted for by the equity method are recorded initially at cost. Suppose Saturna Corp. pays $4,000,000 for 30 percent of the common shares of Galiano Corporation. Brokerage commissions are $5,000. Saturna Corp.'s entry to record the purchase of this investment is

---

LO ③
What is the equity method, and how do we use it?

 KEY POINTS

An investor who holds 20% of a company's shares can *usually* **influence** some decisions of the board of directors and gain influence in company decisions. With more than 50% ownership (majority ownership), the investor can *usually* **control** the affairs of the company.

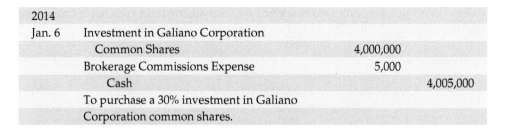

2014			
Jan. 6	Investment in Galiano Corporation		
	Common Shares	4,000,000	
	Brokerage Commissions Expense	5,000	
	Cash		4,005,000
	To purchase a 30% investment in Galiano		
	Corporation common shares.		

Recording a Share of Income/Loss Under the equity method, Saturna Corp., as the investor, applies its percentage of ownership, 30 percent in our example, in recording its share of the investee's net income and dividends. If Galiano Corporation reports net income of $1,000,000 for the year, Saturna Corp. records 30 percent of this amount as an increase in the investment account and as equity-method investment revenue, as follows:

KEY POINTS

A simple T-account illustrates transaction balances for equity-method investments:

**Equity Method
Investment in Galiano Corp.**

Original cost	Share of losses
Share of income	Share of dividends

2014			
Dec. 31	Investment in Galiano Corporation		
	Common Shares	300,000	
	Equity-Method Investment Revenue		300,000
	To record 30% of Galiano Corporation net		
	income, $300,000 ($1,000,000 × 0.30).		

Equity-Method Investment Revenue is specifically identified separately as an Investment Revenue account. It is put into its own account for the same reason as we distinguish Sales Revenue from Service Revenue—to get better management information from the financial statements.

The investor increases the Investment account and records Investment Revenue when the investee reports income because of the close relationship between the two companies. As the investee's shareholders' equity increases, so does the Investment account on the books of the investor.

Recording a Share of Dividends Saturna Corp. records its proportionate part of cash dividends received from Galiano Corporation. Assuming Galiano Corporation declares and pays a cash dividend of $600,000, Saturna Corp. receives 30 percent of this dividend, recording it as follows:

2014			
Dec. 31	Cash	180,000	
	Investment in Galiano Corporation		
	Common Shares		180,000
	To record receipt of 30% of Galiano Corporation		
	cash dividend, $180,000 ($600,000 × 0.30).		

Observe that the Investment account is credited for the receipt of a dividend on an equity-method investment. Why? It is because the dividend decreases the investee's shareholders' equity and so it also reduces the investor's investment. In effect, the investor received cash for this portion of the investment.

After the above entries are posted, Saturna Corp.'s Investment account reflects its equity in the net assets of Galiano Corporation (also known as its *carrying value*):

Investment in Galiano Corporation Common Shares					
2014					
Jan. 6	Purchase	4,000,000	Dec. 31	Dividends	180,000
Dec. 31	Net income	300,000			
2014					
Dec. 31	Balance	4,120,000			

Gain or Loss on the Sale of an Equity-Method Investment   The gain or loss on sale is measured as the difference between the sale proceeds and the carrying value of the investment. For example, sale of one-tenth of the Galiano Corporation common shares owned by Saturna Corp. for $400,000 with brokerage fees of $500 would be recorded as follows:

2015			
Feb. 13	Cash	399,500	
	Brokerage Commissions Expense	500	
	Loss on Sale of Investment	12,000	
	Investment in Galiano Corporation		
	Common Shares		412,000
	Sold one-tenth of investment in Galiano		
	Corporation common shares at a loss of $12,000		
	[$400,000 − ($4,120,000 × 1/10)].		

Companies with investments accounted for by the equity method often refer to the investee as an **affiliated company**. The account titles Investments in Affiliated Companies or Investments Subject to Significant Influence also refer to investments that are accounted for by the equity method.

Write-downs   Sometimes a company must write down an investment accounted for by the equity method due to what is expected to be a permanent decline in the value of the asset. These **write-downs** are rare. The following was reported about Kinross Gold Corporation and its 100 percent investment in the Tasiast Mine in Mauritania:

> Kinross Gold Corp. (TSX:K) reported a loss of US$2.78 billion in its latest quarter as it wrote down the value of its delayed Tasiast project in Africa, but the gold miner also increased its dividend amid record production and revenue last year. … The writedown announced Wednesday reflects the company's estimate of what the project is now worth as it moves to expand the mine over the next few years.[4]

A write-down means there was a credit (decrease) to the asset account and a debit to an expense account, which reduces profit on the income statement.

Joint Ventures—Accounted for by Proportionate Consolidation

A *joint venture* is a separate entity or project owned and operated by a small group of businesses. Joint ventures are common in risky endeavours such as the petroleum, mining, and construction industries. Moreover, they are widely used in developing countries such as Brazil, Russia, India, and China (the BRIC countries), where the political and economic systems are not the same as in North America. Many Canadian and U.S. companies that do business abroad enter into joint ventures.

Section 3055 of Part II of the *CICA Handbook* requires the use of **proportionate consolidation** when accounting for a joint venture. Proportionate consolidation means the venturer combines its proportionate interest in the assets, liabilities, revenues, and expenses of a joint venture with its own assets, liabilities, revenues, and expenses.[5] For example, assume V Ltd. has inventory of $500,000 and a 40-percent interest in a joint venture. The joint venture has inventory of $200,000. V Ltd. would report inventory on its consolidated financial statements of $580,000 ($500,000 + 40% of $200,000).

Private enterprises can choose to use the equity method or the cost method to account for joint ventures if the costs of using proportionate consolidation outweighed the benefits.

Kinross Gold Corporation reported in its December 31, 2011, Annual Report that it is participating in a joint venture with a company in Brazil.

---

[4] Craig Wong, "Kinross Gold Takes Hit on Tasiast Writedown, But Increases Dividend," February 15, 2012, Canadian Press report posted on the *Canadian Business* website at http://www.canadian-business.com/article/71262--kinross-gold-takes-hit-on-tasiast-writedown-but-increases-dividend, accessed October 18, 2012.

[5] The CICA is currently reviewing this treatment. This information is current at the time of publishing. Students are advised to check on the progress of the amendments at the CICA website, www.cica.ca.

Long-Term Share Investments Accounted for by the Consolidation Method

A **controlling** (or **majority**) **interest** is normally the ownership of more than 50 percent of the investee's voting shares. Such an investment enables the investor to elect a majority of the investee's board of directors and so control the investee. In such a situation, the investor is called the **parent company**, and the investee company is called the **subsidiary**. The financial statements of subsidiaries are normally *consolidated* with those of the parent. For example, Galen Weston and other shareholders own George Weston Limited. In turn, that company owns 63 percent of Loblaw Companies Limited and 100 percent of Weston Foods, as diagrammed in Exhibit 16–4. It can be said that George Weston Limited has control over both Loblaw Companies Limited and Weston Foods.

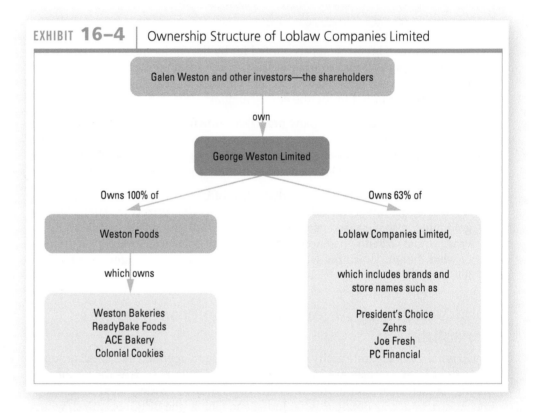

EXHIBIT 16–4 | Ownership Structure of Loblaw Companies Limited

Why have subsidiaries? Why not have the corporation take the form of a single legal entity? Subsidiaries may limit the parent's liabilities in a risky venture; may make mergers, acquisitions, and sales easier; and may ease expansion into foreign countries. For example, George Weston Limited sold off Neilson Dairy to Saputo Limited for $465 million and purchased ACE Bakery for $110 million. These deals would have been much more complex if they were all part of one big company. Exhibit 16–5 shows selected subsidiaries of three major Canadian companies.

Consolidation accounting is a method of combining the financial statements of two or more companies that are controlled by the same owners. This method implements the entity concept by reporting a single set of financial statements for the consolidated entity, which carries the name of the parent company.

ASPE allows parent companies to account for their subsidiaries using the equity method or the cost method if the cost of providing consolidated financial statements is greater than the benefits for users who are able to gain access to financial information directly from the parent company. However, the *CICA Handbook* emphasizes consolidation for companies with controlling interest, so we focus on consolidation accounting in such situations. The entire next section of this textbook will focus on how to do this.

The *CICA Handbook* provides guidance about how to record transactions and present financial information. It is not exclusively a book of rules. There are often alternatives from which companies need to choose based on what provides the best information to readers of financial statements at the most reasonable cost. In this case, there is an emphasis (or recommendation) to consolidate when there is controlling interest but it is not the only choice.

EXHIBIT 16–5 | Selected Subsidiaries of Three Canadian Companies

Parent Company	Selected Subsidiaries
TD Bank Group	TD Securities TD Life Insurance Company Meloche Monnex Inc. TD Waterhouse Canada Inc. TD Mortgage Corporation TD Asset Management Inc.
Kinross Gold Corporation	Echo Bay Minerals (USA) Aurelian Ecuador Compania Minear Maricunga (Chile) Chiranco Gold Mines (Ghana) Fairbanks Gold Mining Inc (USA) Northern Gold LLC (Russian Federation)
Bombardier Inc.	Bombardier Aerospace Corporation Bombardier Corporate Financial Services—Reykjavik Bombardier Sifang (Qingdao) Transportation Ltd. Bombardier Transport France S.A.S. Bombardier Transportation Canada Inc. Learjet Inc.

So far we have introduced several types of ownership and several methods for recording and reporting information. Exhibit 16–6 illustrates another way to remember the accounting method used generally for share investments according to the percentage of the investor's ownership in the investee company.

EXHIBIT 16–6 | Accounting Methods for Share Investment by Percentage of Ownership

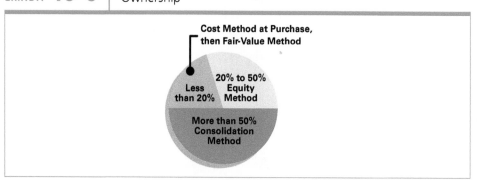

✓ JUST CHECKING

5. Identify the appropriate accounting method for each of the following situations involving investments in common shares:

   a. Purchase of 25 percent and investor plans to hold as a long-term investment
   b. Investor intends to sell three months after year end
   c. Purchase of more than 50 percent of investee's shares

6. Investor Ltd. paid $140,000 to acquire 40 percent of the common shares of Investee Ltd. The investment is subject to significant influence. At the end of the first year, Investee Ltd.'s net income was $180,000, and Investee Ltd. declared and paid cash dividends of $140,000. Journalize Investor Ltd.'s (a) purchase of the investment, (b) share of Investee Ltd.'s net income, (c) receipt of dividends from Investee Ltd., and (d) sale of all the Investee Ltd. shares for $160,000.

Just Checking Solutions appear at the end of this chapter and on MyAccountingLab.

Consolidated Financial Statements

LO ④

What is consolidation, and how do we perform a simple consolidation?

Many published financial reports include consolidated statements. To understand the statements you are likely to encounter, you need to know the basic concepts underlying consolidation accounting. **Consolidated statements** combine the balance sheets, income statements, and other financial statements of the parent company with those of the subsidiaries into an overall set as if the parent and its subsidiaries were a single entity. The goal is to provide a better perspective on operations than could be obtained by examining the separate reports of each of the individual companies. The assets, liabilities, revenues, and expenses of each subsidiary are added to the parent's accounts. The consolidated financial statements present the combined account balances. For example, the balance in the Cash account of Loblaw Companies Limited is added to the balance in the George Weston Limited Cash account, and the sum of the two amounts is presented as a single amount in the consolidated balance sheet of George Weston Limited. Each account balance of a subsidiary loses its identity in the consolidated statements. George Weston Limited financial statements are entitled "George Weston Limited and Consolidated Subsidiaries." Loblaw Companies Limited and the names of all other George Weston Limited subsidiaries do not appear in the statement titles. But the names of the subsidiary companies are listed in the parent company's annual report. A reader of corporate annual reports cannot hope to understand them without knowing how consolidated statements are prepared. Exhibit 16–7 diagrams a corporate structure where the parent corporation owns controlling interests in five subsidiary companies and an equity-method investments in two other investee companies.

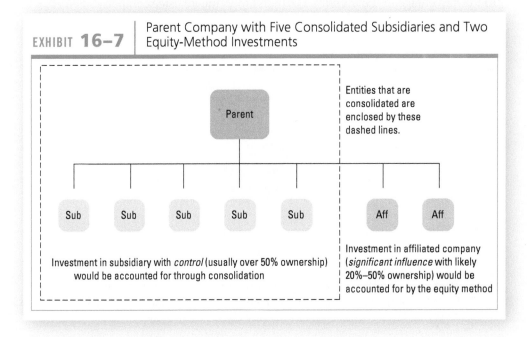

EXHIBIT 16–7 | Parent Company with Five Consolidated Subsidiaries and Two Equity-Method Investments

Entities that are consolidated are enclosed by these dashed lines.

Investment in subsidiary with *control* (usually over 50% ownership) would be accounted for through consolidation

Investment in affiliated company (*significant influence* with likely 20%–50% ownership) would be accounted for by the equity method

REAL WORLD EXAMPLE

Buying shares is not the only way to purchase a company. It is also possible to buy the assets, but this alternative is covered in Finance courses.

Consolidated Balance Sheet—Parent Owns All Subsidiary's Shares Suppose that Parent Corporation purchased all the outstanding common shares of Subsidiary Corporation at its book value of $1,200,000 on June 14. In addition, Parent Corporation lent Subsidiary Corporation $640,000 on June 30. The $1,200,000 is paid to the *former* owners (the shareholders) of Subsidiary Corporation as private investors. The $1,200,000 *is not* an addition to the existing assets and shareholders' equity of Subsidiary Corporation. *That is, the books of Subsidiary Corporation are completely unaffected by Parent Corporation's initial investment and Parent's subsequent accounting for that investment. Subsidiary Corporation is not dissolved. It lives on as a separate legal entity but with a new owner, Parent Corporation.*

Parent Corporation Books			
June 14	Investment in Subsidiary Corporation	1,200,000	
	Cash		1,200,000
June 30	Note Receivable from Subsidiary Corp.	640,000	
	Cash		640,000

Subsidiary Corporation Books			
June 14	No entry		
June 30	Cash	640,000	
	Note Payable to Parent Corp.		640,000

Each legal entity has its individual set of books. The consolidated entity does not keep a separate set of books. Instead, a work sheet is used to prepare the consolidated statements. A major concern in consolidation accounting is this: *Do not double-count—that is, do not include the same item twice.*

Companies may prepare a consolidated balance sheet immediately after acquisition. The consolidated balance sheet shows all the assets and liabilities of the parent and the subsidiary. The Investment in Subsidiary account on the parent's books represents all the assets and liabilities of Subsidiary Corporation. The consolidated statements cannot show both the investment account and the amounts for the subsidiary's assets and liabilities. Doing so would count the same net resources twice. To avoid this double-counting, we eliminate (a) the $1,200,000 Investment in Subsidiary Corporation on the parent's books, and the $1,200,000 shareholders' equity on the subsidiary's books ($800,000 Common Shares and $400,000 Retained Earnings), and (b) the intercompany $640,000 note.

Explanation of Elimination-Entry (a) Exhibit 16–8 shows the *work sheet* for consolidating the balance sheet. (Notice this is a much different sort of work sheet than what was shown in Chapter 4!) Consider the elimination entry for the parent–subsidiary ownership accounts, which are intercompany accounts. Entry (a) credits the parent's Investment account to eliminate its debit balance. It also eliminates the subsidiary's shareholders' equity accounts by debiting Common Shares for $800,000 and Retained Earnings for $400,000. The resulting consolidated balance sheet reports no Investment in Subsidiary Corporation account, and the Common Shares and Retained Earnings are those of Parent Corporation only. The consolidated amounts are in the final column of the consolidation work sheet.

KEY POINTS

Each subsidiary company keeps its own set of books and pays its own taxes, just as the parent company does; however, for reporting purposes, the parent and subsidiary companies are treated as one economic unit when they are consolidated. Intercompany transactions must be eliminated.

EXHIBIT 16–8 | Work Sheet for Consolidated Balance Sheet—Parent Corporation Owns All Subsidiary Corporation's Shares

	Parent Corporation	Subsidiary Corporation	Eliminations Debit	Eliminations Credit	Consolidated Amounts
Assets					
Cash	96,000	144,000			240,000
Notes receivable from Subsidiary Corp.	640,000	—		(b) 640,000	—
Inventory	832,000	728,000			1,560,000
Investment in Subsidiary Corp.	1,200,000	—		(a) 1,200,000	—
Other assets	1,744,000	1,104,000			2,848,000
Total	4,512,000	1,976,000			4,648,000
Liabilities and Shareholders' Equity					
Accounts payable	344,000	136,000			480,000
Notes payable	1,520,000	640,000	(b) 640,000		1,520,000
Common shares	1,408,000	800,000	(a) 800,000		1,408,000
Retained earnings	1,240,000	400,000	(a) 400,000		1,240,000
Total	4,512,000	1,976,000	1,840,000	1,840,000	4,648,000

REAL WORLD EXAMPLE

Notice that in the consolidation worksheet there are no dollar signs. That is because this is an internal working document and not a formal financial statement, and because all amounts are stated in dollars.

Explanation of Elimination-Entry (b) Parent Corporation lent $640,000 to Subsidiary Corporation, and Subsidiary Corporation signed a note payable to Parent Corporation. Therefore, Parent Corporation's balance sheet includes a $640,000 note receivable and Subsidiary Corporation's balance sheet reports a note payable for this amount. This loan was entirely within the consolidated entity and so must be eliminated. Entry (b) in Exhibit 16–8 accomplishes this. The $640,000 credit in the elimination column of the work sheet offsets Parent Corporation's debit balance in Notes Receivable from Subsidiary Corporation. After this work sheet entry, the consolidated amount for notes receivable is zero. The $640,000 debit in the elimination column offsets the credit balance of Subsidiary Corporation's notes payable, and the resulting consolidated amount for notes payable is the amount owed to those outside the consolidated entity.

Examine Exhibit 16–8. Why does the consolidated shareholders' equity ($1,408,000 + $1,240,000) exclude the equity of Subsidiary Corporation ($800,000 + $400,000)? This is because the shareholders' equity of the consolidated entity is that of the parent only, and because the subsidiary's equity and the parent company's investment balance represent the same resources. Therefore, including them both would amount to double-counting.

Parent Buys Subsidiary's Shares and Pays for Goodwill A company may acquire a controlling interest in a subsidiary by paying a price above the fair value of the subsidiary's net assets (assets minus liabilities), which we assume is equal to the book value of the subsidiary's shareholders' equity. This excess is called goodwill. Accounting for goodwill was introduced in Chapter 10 on page 603.

The subsidiary does not record goodwill; only the purchaser does. The goodwill is shown as a separate line of the work sheet in the process of consolidating the parent and subsidiary financial statements.

Let's look at a new example in Exhibit 16–9 of a work sheet for a consolidated balance sheet when goodwill is involved. Suppose Par Corporation paid $2,700,000 to acquire 100 percent of the common shares of Sub Corporation, which had Common Shares of $1,200,000 and Retained Earnings of $1,080,000. Par's payment included $420,000 for goodwill ($2,700,000 − $1,200,000 − $1,080,000 = $420,000).[6]

EXHIBIT 16–9 | Work Sheet for Consolidated Balance Sheet—Par Corporation Owns All Sub Corporation's Shares and Paid for Goodwill

	Par Corporation	Sub Corporation	Eliminations Debit	Eliminations Credit	Consolidated Amounts
Assets					
Cash	880,000	100,000			980,000
Inventory	500,000	1,500,000			2,000,000
Investment in Sub Corp	2,700,000	—		2,700,000	—
Goodwill	—	—	420,000		420,000
Other assets	816,000	785,000			1,601,000
Total	4,896,000	2,385,000			5,001,000
Liabilities and Shareholders' Equity					
Accounts payable	426,000	25,000			451,000
Notes payable	1,000,000	80,000			1,080,000
Common shares	1,280,000	1,200,000	1,200,000		1,280,000
Retained earnings	2,190,000	1,080,000	1,080,000		2,190,000
Total	4,896,000	2,385,000	2,700,000	2,700,000	5,001,000

---

[6] For simplicity, we are assuming the fair market value of the subsidiary's net assets (Assets − Liabilities) equals the book value of company's shareholders' equity. Advanced courses consider other situations.

Assume that Par Corporation recorded the purchase as follows:

Par Corporation Books

Investment in Sub Corporation	2,700,000	
Cash		2,700,000

The entry to eliminate Par Corporation's Investment account against Sub Corporation's equity accounts is

Common Shares, Sub Corporation	1,200,000	
Retained Earnings, Sub Corporation	1,080,000	
Goodwill	420,000	
Investment in Sub Corporation		2,700,000

To eliminate cost of investment in Sub Corporation against Sub Corporation's equity balances and goodwill.

In *actual* practice, this entry would be made only on the consolidation work sheet. Here we show it in general journal form for instructional purposes.

The asset goodwill is reported as a separate line item on the consolidated balance sheet. For example, Kinross Gold Corporation's December 31, 2011, consolidated balance sheet includes goodwill of $3,420.3 million as a separate line item in the non-current-assets section of the balance sheet.

Consolidated Balance Sheet—Parent Owns Less Than 100 Percent of Subsidiary's Shares When a parent company owns more than 50 percent (a majority) of the subsidiary's shares but less than 100 percent of them, a new category of balance sheet account, called *non-controlling interest*, must appear on the consolidated balance sheet. Suppose P Corporation buys 75 percent of S Corporation's common shares. The non-controlling interest is the remaining 25 percent of S Corporation's equity. Thus, **non-controlling interest** (sometimes called **minority interest)** is the subsidiary's equity that is held by shareholders other than the parent company. While the *CICA Handbook* is silent on where non-controlling interest should be disclosed on the balance sheet, accepted practice is to list it as a liability between liabilities and shareholders' equity. This is illustrated in Exhibit 16–11 on page 1008.

Assume P Ltd. buys 75 percent of S Ltd.'s common shares for $1,440,000 and there is no goodwill. Also, P Ltd. owes $600,000 on a note payable to S Ltd. P Ltd. would record this purchase as follows:

P Ltd.'s Books

Investment in S. Ltd	1,440,000	
Cash		1,440,000

Exhibit 16–10 is the consolidation work sheet. Again, focus on the Eliminations columns and the Consolidated Amounts.

- Entry (a) eliminates P Ltd.'s Investment balance of $1,440,000 against the $1,920,000 shareholders' equity of S Ltd. Observe that all S Ltd.'s equity is eliminated even though P Ltd. holds only 75 percent of S Ltd.'s shares. The remaining 25 percent interest in S Ltd.'s equity is credited to Non-controlling Interest ($1,920,000 × 0.25 = $480,000). Thus, entry (a) reclassifies 25 percent of S Ltd.'s equity as non-controlling interest.

- Entry (b) eliminates S Ltd.'s $600,000 note receivable against P Ltd.'s note payable of the same amount. The consolidated amount of notes payable ($504,000) is the amount that S Ltd. owes to outsiders.

The consolidated balance sheet of P Ltd., shown in Exhibit 16–11, is based on the work sheet of Exhibit 16–10. The consolidated balance sheet reveals that ownership of P Ltd. and its consolidated subsidiary is divided between P Ltd.'s shareholders (common shares and retained earnings totalling $4,056,000) and the non-controlling shareholders of S Ltd. ($480,000).

LEARNING TIPS

The accounts that *would* appear on consolidated financial statements:

Non-Controlling Interest—the non-controlling shareholders' share of the company

Goodwill—excess of the purchase price of the subsidiary over the fair value of its net assets

The accounts that *would not* appear on the consolidated financial statements: the investment account, inter-company transactions, and the shareholders' equity of the subsidiary.

KEY POINTS

The balance sheet elimination entry requires, at most, five steps:

(1) Eliminate intercompany receivables and payables.

(2) Eliminate the shareholders' equity accounts of the subsidiary.

(3) Eliminate the Investment in Subsidiary account.

(4) Record goodwill.

(5) Record non-controlling interest.

EXHIBIT **16–10** Work Sheet for Consolidated Balance Sheet: Parent (P Ltd.) Owns Less Than 100 Percent of Subsidiary's (S Ltd.'s) Shares

	P Ltd.	S Ltd.	Eliminations Debit	Eliminations Credit	Consolidated Amounts
Assets					
Cash	396,000	216,000			612,000
Notes receivable from P Ltd.	—	600,000		(b) 600,000	—
Accounts receivable, net	648,000	468,000			1,116,000
Inventory	1,104,000	792,000			1,896,000
Investment in S Ltd.	1,440,000	—		(a)1,440,000	—
Property, plant, and equipment, net	2,760,000	1,476,000			4,236,000
Total	6,348,000	3,552,000			7,860,000
Liabilities and Shareholders' Equity					
Accounts payable	1,692,000	1,128,000			2,820,000
Notes payable	600,000	504,000	(b) 600,000		504,000
Non-controlling interest	—	—		(a) 480,000	480,000
Common shares	2,040,000	1,200,000	(a)1,200,000		2,040,000
Retained earnings	2,016,000	720,000	(a) 720,000		2,016,000
Total	6,348,000	3,552,000	2,520,000	2,520,000	7,860,000

EXHIBIT **16–11** | Consolidated Balance Sheet of P Ltd.

P LTD.
Consolidated Balance Sheet
December 31, 2014

Assets		
Current assets		
Cash	$ 612,000	
Accounts receivable, net	1,116,000	
Inventory	1,896,000	
Total current assets		$3,624,000
Property, plant, and equipment, net		4,236,000
Total assets		$7,860,000
Liabilities and Shareholders' Equity		
Current liabilities		
Accounts payable		$2,820,000
Long-term liabilities		
Notes payable		504,000
Total liabilities		3,324,000
Non-controlling interest		480,000
Shareholders' equity		
Common shares	$2,040,000	
Retained earnings	2,016,000	
Total shareholders' equity		4,056,000
Total liabilities and shareholders' equity		$7,860,000

Income of a Consolidated Entity The income of a consolidated entity is the net income of the parent plus the parent's proportion of the subsidiaries' net income. Suppose Mega-Parent Inc. owns all the shares of Subsidiary S-1 Inc. and 60 percent of the shares of Subsidiary S-2 Inc. During the year just ended, Mega-Parent Inc. earned net income of $1,980,000, Subsidiary S-1 Inc. earned

$900,000, and Subsidiary S-2 Inc. had a net loss of $600,000. Mega-Parent Inc. would report net income of $2,520,000, computed as follows:

	Net Income (Net Loss)	Mega-Parent Inc. Shareholders' Ownership	Mega-Parent Inc. Net Income (Net Loss)
Mega-Parent Inc.	$1,980,000	100%	$1,980,000
Subsidiary S-1 Inc.	900,000	100	900,000
Subsidiary S-2 Inc.	(600,000)	60	(360,000)
Consolidated net income			$2,520,000

The parent's net income is the same amount that would be recorded under the equity method. However, the equity method stops short of reporting the investee's assets and liabilities on the parent balance sheet because, with an investment in the range of 20 to 50 percent, the investor owns less than a controlling interest in the investee company.

The procedures for preparation of a consolidated income statement parallel those outlined above for the balance sheet. The consolidated income statement is discussed in an advanced accounting course.

WHY IT'S DONE THIS WAY

Having seen how to do consolidations, we can turn to the accounting framework described in Chapter 1 (and repeated on the back inside cover of this book) to understand why consolidations are done and why they are done the way they are.

Why is it important to consolidate the financial results of companies under common control? The consolidated financial statements communicate useful information to interested users to help them assess the success of the company—this is the **Level 1** objective of the accounting framework. To properly assess the success of a parent company, users need to look at the entire picture. If the parent company provided financial information on each of its subsidiaries on a company-by-company basis only, users would find it very difficult to pull all the pieces together on their own. Intercompany transactions would be difficult to identify unless a user had direct access to the same information as internal managers.

In the accounting framework, the **Level 4** economic entity consideration directs us to eliminate intercompany transactions because these occur *within* the economic entity (which is the consolidated group of companies) and would cause double-counting errors if they were not eliminated. The economic-entity consideration guides the parent and its subsidiaries to consolidate results into one set of financial statements accurately.

Some financial-statement users might argue that it is difficult to analyze the success of a company by looking only at the parent company's consolidated financial statements. They might ask, for example, how users know that all parts of the parent's business are operating successfully if they only have access to consolidated statements. The framework's **Level 3** characteristic of understandability promotes disclosure in the notes to the financial statements, which are required under ASPE as well as IFRS. As mentioned in this chapter, the parent company's notes to the financial statements must list the subsidiary companies and the parent's percentage of ownership of each. ASPE and IFRS also require that companies provide **segmented information** in their financial-statement notes. This segmented information is either by industry or by geography, and it is reported by companies that operate in different industries or regions of the world, including parent and subsidiary companies. By presenting details about a parent company's subsidiaries and segmented information in the notes, consolidated financial statements do communicate useful information to users to help them assess the success of the company, meeting the **Level 1** objective of the reporting framework.

✓ JUST CHECKING

7. Answer these questions about consolidated financial statements:

   a. Whose name appears on the consolidated statements—the parent company's, the subsidiary company's, or both?

   b. Why does consolidated shareholders' equity (contributed capital + retained earnings) exclude the equity of a subsidiary corporation?

   c. Suppose A Ltd. owns 90 percent of B Ltd. What are the remaining 10 percent of B Ltd.'s shares called, and where do they appear, if at all, in A Ltd.'s consolidated financial statements?

   d. Suppose C Ltd. paid $2,000,000 to acquire D Ltd., whose shareholders' equity (which has the same fair value as net assets) totalled $1,400,000. What is the $600,000 excess called? Which company reports the excess? Where in the consolidated financial statements is the excess reported?

8. Parent Corp. paid $400,000 for all the common shares of Subsidiary Corp., and Parent Corp. owes Subsidiary Corp. $60,000 on a note payable. Assume the fair value of Subsidiary Corp.'s net assets is equal to book value. Complete the following consolidation work sheet:

	Parent Corp.	Subsidiary Corp.	Eliminations Debit	Eliminations Credit	Consolidated Amounts
Assets					
Cash	28,000	36,000			
Note receivable from Parent Corp	—	60,000			
Investment in Subsidiary Corp	400,000	—			
Goodwill	—	—			
Other assets	432,000	396,000			_____
Total	860,000	492,000			_____
Liabilities and Shareholders' Equity					
Accounts payable	60,000	32,000			
Notes payable	60,000	120,000			
Common shares	560,000	240,000			
Retained earnings	180,000	100,000	_____	_____	_____
Total	860,000	492,000	_____	_____	_____

Just Checking Solutions appear at the end of this chapter and on MyAccountingLab.

Investments in Bonds and Notes[7]

LO ⑤

How do we record investments in bonds?

Industrial and commercial companies invest far more in shares than they do in bonds. The major investors in bonds are financial institutions, such as pension plans, trust companies, and insurance companies. The relationship between the issuer and the investor may be diagrammed as follows:

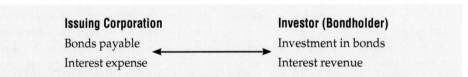

Issuing Corporation	Investor (Bondholder)
Bonds payable	Investment in bonds
Interest expense	Interest revenue

The dollar amount of a bond transaction is the same for the issuer and the investor, but the accounts debited and credited differ. For example, the issuer's interest expense is the investor's interest revenue. We saw these transactions from the perspective of the issuer in Chapter 11 (notes) and Chapter 15 (bonds).

---

[7] Section 3856 of Part II of the *CICA Handbook* addresses **financial instruments**. Much of the discussion is beyond the scope of this text and is covered in advanced accounting courses.

Short-Term Investments in Bonds Short-term investments in bonds are rare, since the purpose of investing in bonds is to provide a stream of investment income over the life of the bonds, and bonds typically have a life that is longer than one year. We covered accounting for short-term bonds using the fair-value method on page 995. Therefore, we focus here on long-term investments in bonds and notes, using bonds for the examples.

Long-Term Investments in Bonds The accounting treatment of long-term bond investments is typically referred to as the **amortized cost method,** which involves the following entries:

- Long-term bond investments are recorded at cost, which includes the purchase price and brokerage fees.
- The accountant records amortization on the cash interest dates and at year end, along with the accrual of interest receivable.
- The discount or premium is amortized to account more precisely for interest revenue over the period the bonds will be held. The journal entries would be

Discount:	Investment in Bonds
	Interest Revenue
Premium:	Interest Revenue
	Investment in Bonds

- Long-term investments in bonds are reported at their *amortized cost*, which determines the carrying amount.
- At maturity, the investor will receive the face value of the bonds.

Amortization of Discount/Premium The amortization of the discount or the premium on a bond investment affects Interest Revenue and the carrying amount of the bonds in the same way as for the company that issued the bonds. The entries bring the investment balance to the bond's face value on the maturity date and record the correct amount of interest revenue each period. Recall that in Exhibit 15–5 on page 933 we looked at bond discounts from the perspective of the seller. Exhibit 16–12 shows the same amortization of the discount except from the perspective of the purchaser in the Xpress Trucking Ltd. bonds example used below.

KEY POINTS

The company purchasing the bonds can amortize the discount or premium using the straight-line or effective-interest amortization method.

EXHIBIT **16–12** | Amortization of a Bond Discount by a Purchaser

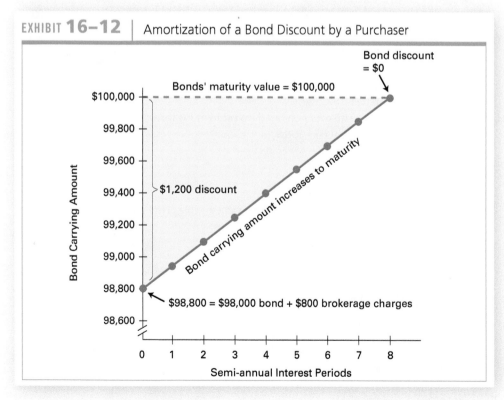

Consider the following scenario to illustrate accounting for a bond investment:

- $100,000 of 6-percent Xpress Trucking Ltd. bonds were purchased on April 1, 2014, at a price of 98 (98 percent of par value)
- Interest dates are April 1 and October 1
- Bonds mature on April 1, 2018 (outstanding for 48 months)
- Brokerage charges cost $800 and are added to the cost
- Purchaser's year end is December 31
- Use the straight-line method of amortization for the premium or discount. It is calculated the same way as it is calculated for bonds payable (see Chapter 15, pages 928–930).

The transactions for the bond investment are recorded as follows:[8]

2014			
Apr. 1	Investment in Bonds	98,800	
	Cash		98,800
	To purchase long-term bond investment		
	($100,000 × 0.98) + $800 brokerage fee.		
Oct. 1	Cash	3,000	
	Interest Revenue		3,000
	To receive semiannual interest		
	($100,000 × 0.06 × $\frac{6}{12}$).		
1	Investment in Bonds	150	
	Interest Revenue		150
	To amortize discount on bond investment for		
	six months		
	([($100,000 − $98,800) ÷ 48] × 6).		

At December 31, 2014, the year-end adjustments are as follows:

Dec. 31	Interest Receivable	1,500	
	Interest Revenue		1,500
	To accrue interest revenue for three months		
	($100,000 × 0.06 × $\frac{3}{12}$).		
31	Investment in Bonds	75	
	Interest Revenue		75
	To amortize discount on bond investment for three		
	months ([($100,000 − $98,800) ÷ 48] × 3).		

---

[8] Companies sometimes record the investment at par value and the premium or discount in a separate account. If so, the April 1 entry would be

Investment in Bonds	100,000	
Discount on Investment in Bonds		1,200
Cash		98,800

The entries on October 1 would be:

Discount on Investment in Bonds	150	
Interest Revenue		150
Cash	3,000	
Interest Revenue		3,000

Reporting Long-Term Investments in Bonds The financial statements at December 31, 2014, report the following effects of this long-term investment in bonds, where $99,025 = $98,800 + $150 + $75 (assume the bonds' market price is 102):

Balance sheet at December 31, 2014:

Current assets:	
Interest receivable	$ 1,500
Total current assets	x,xxx
Investments in bonds—Note 6	99,025

Note 6: Investments in Bonds
Investments in bonds are reported at their amortized cost. At December 31, 2014, the current market value of the investments in bonds was $102,000.

Interest revenue is $4,725 = $3,000 + $150 + $1,500 + $75.

Income statement (multiple-step) for the year ended December 31, 2014:

Other revenues:	
Interest revenue	$4,725

Write-down If the market value of a long-term bond investment declines below cost and the decline is considered to be other than temporary (thus it is an impairment), the investment should be *written down to market*. Suppose the market price for the bonds at December 31, 2014, was 97 (instead of the 102 noted above). The journal entry to write down the investment would be

2014			
Dec. 31	Impairment Loss	2,025	
	Investment in Bonds		2,025
	To record reduction in bond value not considered		
	to be temporary ($99,025 book value – $97,000).		

If there is a subsequent improvement in the value, it is possible to reverse the adjustment and increase the book value of the investment to its amortized cost.

✓ JUST CHECKING

9. On April 30, 2014, Cana Corp. paid 97.50 for 4-percent bonds of Starr Limited as an investment. The maturity value of the bonds is $100,000 at October 31, 2019; they pay interest on April 30 and October 31. At December 31, 2014, the bonds' market value is 98.25. Cana Corp. plans to hold the bonds until they mature.
    a. What accounting treatment should Cana Corp. use to account for the bonds?
    b. Using the straight-line method of amortizing the discount, journalize all transactions on the bonds for 2014.
    c. Show how the investment in Starr Limited bonds would be reported on the Cana Corp. balance sheet at December 31, 2014.
10. Cana Corp. purchased $50,000 of 4% bonds from Xylomax Inc. on June 1, 2014. It paid $46,490 and intends to hold the bonds for three years or more. There were no brokerage fees. Interest is paid semi-annually on December 1 and June 1. Using the partial amortization schedule below, prepare the journal entries for June 1, 2014, and December 1, 2014.

Annual Interest Period	Interest Revenue 4.00%	Period Interest Revenue	Discount Amort.	Discount Balance	Bond Carrying Value
Jun. 1, 2014				$3,510	$46,490
Dec. 1, 2014	$1,000	$1,395	$395	3,115	46,885
Jun. 1, 2015	1,000	1,407	407	2,708	47,292

Just Checking Solutions appear at the end of this chapter and on MyAccountingLab.

Foreign-Currency Transactions

—— LO ⑥ ——
How do we record transactions with foreign currencies?

Accounting for business activities across national boundaries makes up the field of *international accounting*. Did you know that Bombardier earned more than 94 percent of revenues outside of Canada in 2011? And Lululemon Athletica earned 48 percent of its revenues outside Canada in 2010? It is common for Canadian companies to do a large part of their business abroad. Alcan Aluminum, McCain Foods, and others are very active in other countries.

The economic environment varies from country to country. Canada may be booming while other countries may be depressed economically. International accounting must deal with such differences.

Foreign Currencies and Foreign-Currency Exchange Rates

Most countries use their own national currency. When companies engage in business transactions across national borders, there are no rules about which currency should be used. The choice of currency is just one of many business management decisions to be made. Assume BlackBerry sells 1,000 of its BlackBerry wireless devices to a U.S. retailer. Will BlackBerry receive Canadian dollars or U.S. dollars? If the transaction takes place in Canadian dollars, the U.S. retailer must buy Canadian dollars in order to pay BlackBerry in Canadian currency. If the transaction takes place in U.S. dollars, BlackBerry will receive U.S. dollars and then exchange them for Canadian dollars. In either case, a step has been added to the transaction: one company must convert domestic currency into foreign currency, or the other company must convert foreign currency into domestic currency.

The price of one nation's currency can be stated in terms of another country's monetary unit. The price of a foreign currency is called the **foreign-currency exchange rate**. In Exhibit 16–13, the Canadian dollar value of a Japanese yen is $0.010208. This means that one Japanese yen could be bought for approximately one cent. Other currencies, such as the pound and the euro, are also listed in Exhibit 16–13.

We use the exchange rate to convert the price of an item stated in one currency to its price in a second currency. We call this conversion a **translation**. Suppose an item costs 200 euros. To compute its cost in dollars, we multiply the amount in euros by the conversion rate: 200 euros × $1.30431 = $260.86.

To aid the flow of international business, a market exists for foreign currencies. Traders buy and sell Canadian dollars, U.S. dollars, euros, and other currencies in the same way that they buy and sell other commodities such as beef, corn, cotton, and automobiles. And just as supply and demand cause the prices of these other commodities to shift, so supply and demand for a particular currency cause exchange rates to fluctuate daily—even minute by minute. When the demand for a nation's currency exceeds the supply of that currency, its exchange rate rises. When supply exceeds demand, the currency's exchange rate falls.

LEARNING TIPS

Notice that the exchange rates are quoted to at least 5 decimal places in Exhibit 16–13. When using exchange rates in calculations, do not round calculations until the last step.

EXHIBIT **16–13** | Foreign-Currency Exchange Rates

Country	Monetary Unit	Cost in Canadian Dollars	Country	Monetary Unit	Cost in Canadian Dollars
United States	Dollar	$ 0.98871	Britain	Pound	$1.56515
European			Japan	Yen	0.010208
Union	Euro	1.30431	Denmark	Krone	0.17547

Source: OANDA.com, Currency Converter, accessed March 5, 2012. ©2012 OANDA Corporation. Used with permission.

Currencies are often described in the financial press as "strong" or "weak." What do these terms mean? The exchange rate of a **strong currency** is rising relative to other nations' currencies. The exchange rate of a **weak currency** is falling relative to other currencies. Looking at the long term, we can look at the relationship between the Canadian and U.S. dollar and come to the conclusion that it has taken fewer Canadian dollars to buy a U.S. dollar over time if we look at the starting and ending rates presented in the blue box below. In other words, the Canadian dollar was *stronger* than the U.S. dollar over this period.

REAL WORLD EXAMPLE

A stronger Canadian dollar at $0.9912 makes travel to the United States more attractive to Canadians than when the U.S. dollar was at $1.5480 Canadian.

> March 1, 2001 exchange rate was $1 U.S. = $1.5480 Canadian
> March 1, 2012 exchange rate was $1 U.S. = $0.9912 Canadian

Exchange rates can rise and fall dramatically within a short period. Exhibit 16–14 shows how the U.S. dollar has had periods in which it is rising and then falling. Buying goods in U.S. dollars in April 2012 and paying for them in May 2012 makes money for the Canadian company because the exchange rate has decreased, so each U.S. dollar costs less. Buying goods in May 2012 and paying for them in June 2012 costs money for the Canadian company because the exchange rate has increased, so each U.S. dollar costs more.

EXHIBIT 16–14 | Canadian Dollar–U.S. Dollar Exchange Rate (Monthly Closing) from October 2011 to September 2012

Source: Created with data from the Bank of Canada's website at http://www.bankofcanada.ca/rates/exchange/us-can-summary/, retrieved October 19, 2012.

Foreign-Currency Transactions

When a Canadian company transacts business with a foreign company, the transaction price can be stated either in Canadian dollars or in the national currency of the other company or in any other currency that is stipulated by contract. This adds risk to the transactions because, as we just saw, exchange rates fluctuate over time. Lululemon Athletica Inc. presented the following estimate of the risk to its corporation from exchange-rates changes:

> Because we recognize net revenue from sales in Canada in Canadian dollars, if the Canadian dollar weakens against the U.S. dollar it would have a negative impact on our Canadian operating results upon translation of those results into U.S. dollars for the purposes of consolidation. The exchange rate of the Canadian dollar against the U.S. dollar has increased over fiscal 2010 and our results of operations have benefited from the strength in the Canadian dollar. If the Canadian dollar were to weaken relative to the U.S. dollar, our net revenue would decline and our income from operations and net income could be adversely affected. A 10% depreciation in the relative value of the Canadian dollar compared to the U.S. dollar would have resulted in lost income from

operations of approximately $11.3 million in fiscal 2010 and approximately $11.2 million in fiscal 2009. (March 2012 10K Filing)

First we will look at how to record transactions when foreign currencies are exchanged, and then we will look briefly at ways to minimize foreign-exchange risk.

Paying Cash in a Foreign Currency

If the transaction price is stated in units of the foreign currency, the Canadian company encounters two accounting steps. First, the transaction price must be translated into Canadian dollars for recording in the accounting records. Second, these transactions usually cause the Canadian company to experience a **foreign-currency transaction gain** or **foreign-currency transaction loss**. This type of gain or loss occurs when the exchange rate changes between the date of the purchase or sale on account and the date of the subsequent payment or receipt of cash.

If a company purchases products from a supplier in another country, Accounts Payable is created. It is recorded at the exchange rate in effect at the time of the transaction. Later, when the company pays the invoice, the exchange rate has almost certainly changed. Accounts Payable is debited for the amount recorded earlier, and Cash is credited for the amount paid at the current exchange rate. A debit difference is a loss, and a credit difference is a gain.

Purchase Date Suppose on December 13, 2013, The Petit Parfum Boutique in Barrie imports Shalimar perfume from a French supplier at a price of 75,000 euros (which can also be shown as €75,000). If the exchange rate is $1.56 per euro, the Boutique records this credit purchase as follows:

2013			
Dec. 13	Inventory	117,000	
	Accounts Payable		117,000
	To record a purchase on credit (€75,000 × $1.56 per euro).		

The Boutique translates the euro price of the merchandise (€75,000) into Canadian dollars ($117,000) for recording the purchase and the related account payable.

If the Boutique were to pay this account immediately (which is unlikely in international commerce and most business scenarios), the Boutique would debit Accounts Payable and credit Cash for $117,000. Suppose, however, that the credit terms specify payment within 60 days and suppose as well that the Boutique's year end is January 31, 2014. It is almost certain that the exchange rate for the euro will be different on the year-end and payment dates.

Year End On January 31, 2014, the payable must be reported at its current dollar value. Suppose the exchange rate at January 31, 2014, has changed to $1.57 per euro. The Boutique's payable would be $117,750 (€75,000 × $1.57 per euro), which is $750 higher than the amount of the payable recorded originally. The entry to record this change in the euro exchange rate at year end is

2014			
Jan. 31	Foreign-Currency Transaction Loss	750	
	Accounts Payable		750
	To record the change in the exchange rate of the euro at year end (€75,000 × ($1.57 − $1.56)).		

Payment Date On February 2, 2014, when the Boutique pays this debt, suppose the exchange rate has changed to $1.58 per euro. The Boutique's payment entry is

KEY POINTS

For an accounts payable transaction, there is a *loss* if the exchange rate has moved *higher* in the period between the purchase and the payment. There is a *gain* if the exchange rate has moved *lower*.

Feb. 2	Accounts Payable	117,750	
	Foreign-Currency Transaction Loss	750	
	Cash		118,500
	To record payment of the account for a credit purchase (€75,000 × $1.58).		

The Boutique has a loss because the company has settled the debt with more dollars than the amount of the original account payable. If on the payment date the exchange rate of the euro was less than $1.56, the Boutique would have paid fewer dollars than the $117,750 year-end valuation of the payable. The company would have recorded a gain on the transaction as a credit to Foreign-Currency Transaction Gain.

Collecting Cash in a Foreign Currency

International sales on account also may be measured in foreign currency.

Sale Date Suppose Bombardier sells some products to an American customer on January 30, 2014. The price of the products is US$140,000, and the exchange rate is $1.04. Bombardier's sale entry is

Jan. 30	Accounts Receivable	145,600	
	Sales Revenue		145,600
	To record a sale on account (US$140,000 × $1.04).		

Collection Date Assume Bombardier collects from the American customer on March 2, 2014, when the exchange rate has fallen to $1.02. Bombardier receives fewer Canadian dollars than the recorded amount of the receivable and so experiences a foreign-currency transaction loss. The collection entry is

Mar. 2	Cash	142,800	
	Foreign-Currency Transaction Loss	2,800	
	Accounts Receivable		145,600
	To record collection of a receivable (US$140,000 × $1.02).		

Foreign-currency transaction gains and losses are combined for each accounting period. The net amount of gain or loss can be reported as Other Revenue and Expense on the income statement.

Year End Adjustment In addition, the year-end balance for accounts receivable must be updated to show any foreign currency amounts at the exchange rate in effect on the date of the financial statements. The gain or loss would be recorded to the same accounts as shown above.

Hedging—A Strategy to Avoid Foreign-Currency Transaction Losses

One way for Canadian companies to avoid foreign-currency transaction losses is to insist that international transactions be settled in Canadian dollars. This requirement puts the burden of currency translation on the foreign party. However, such a strategy may alienate customers and decrease sales, or it may cause customers to demand unreasonable credit terms to compensate for the risk they would need to take in the transaction. Another way for a company to protect itself from the effects of fluctuating foreign-currency exchange rates is by hedging.

Hedging means protecting oneself from losing money in one transaction by engaging in a **counterbalancing transaction**—a second, related transaction to offset the risk of the first one. In this case, if there is a way to guarantee the future

KEY POINTS

When a subsidiary prepares financial statements in a currency other than Canadian dollars, the subsidiary must translate the financial statements into Canadian dollars for the consolidated financial statements at the exchange rate in effect on the date of the financial statements.

REAL WORLD EXAMPLE

If a company wants to protect the value of a receivable **denominated** in a foreign currency, the company will most likely purchase a **forward contract**. A forward contract is an obligation to buy or sell a specific amount of currency at a predetermined rate at a specific future date. The advantage here is that it allows the company to project cash flows more accurately.

Chiquita ships more than a billion dollars worth of bananas annually. A small change in currency rates can mean a big change in profits. Therefore, Chiquita purchases **currency options** to hedge the foreign-currency exchange risk. The currency options give Chiquita the right to buy foreign currencies at prescribed prices and thus enable the company to minimize losses due to any changes in the exchange rate.

exchange rates, then there would be no risk. Such an arrangement can be set up using one of several tactics.

Let's go back to The Boutique example for a moment. If the company sold goods online to be paid for in Mexican pesos, it would expect to receive a fixed number of pesos in the future. If the peso is losing value, the Canadian company would expect the pesos to be worth fewer dollars than the amount of the receivable—an expected loss situation. However, since The Boutique will accumulate payables stated in a different foreign currency—the euro, in this case—losses on the receipt of pesos may be approximately offset by gains on the payment of euros to the French supplier.

If this is not an option (most companies do not have equal amounts of receivables and payables in foreign currency), there is another way to obtain a more precise hedge: some companies buy **futures contracts**, which are contracts for foreign currencies to be received in the future. This removes the risk of unanticipated changes in exchange rates in the future. These arrangements can be set up through a local financial institution. Many companies that do business internationally use hedging techniques to manage the risk related to currency translations.

Further discussion of foreign-currency and international transactions is beyond the scope of this text and will be covered in more advanced accounting and finance courses.

✓ JUST CHECKING

11. In each of the following situations, determine whether the Canadian company will experience a foreign-currency transaction gain or loss, and explain why.

    a. A Canadian company purchased car parts from a German supplier at a price of 200,000 euros. On the date of the credit purchase, the exchange rate of the euro was $1.0891. On the payment date, the exchange rate of the euro is $1.0723. The payment is in euros.

    b. A Canadian company sold merchandise to a Danish company at a price of 500,000 krones. On the date of the credit sale, the exchange rate of the krone was $0.20962. On the day the payment is received in krones, the exchange rate of the krone is $0.21325.

    c. A Canadian company purchased electronics from a Japanese supplier at a price of 1,200,000 yen. On the date of the credit purchase, the exchange rate of the yen was $0.01172. On the payment date, the exchange rate of the yen is $0.01221. The payment is in yen.

    d. A Canadian company sold merchandise to a U.S. company at a price of US$15,000. On the date of the credit sale, the exchange rate of the U.S. dollar was $1.0891. On the day the payment is received in U.S. dollars, the exchange rate of the U.S. dollar is $1.0624.

12. In each of the situations in the previous question, did the Canadian dollar strengthen or weaken against the foreign currency?

13. Suppose Zippy Ltd. sells maple syrup to a British company on May 16. Zippy agrees to accept 80,000 British pounds sterling. On the date of sale, the pound is quoted at $1.7831. Zippy collects half the receivable on June 19, when the pound is worth $1.7614. Then, on July 16, when the price of the pound is $1.7792, Zippy collects the final amount. Journalize these three transactions for Zippy; include an explanation. Overall, did Zippy have a net foreign-currency gain or loss?

Just Checking Solutions appear at the end of this chapter and on MyAccountingLab.

The Impact on Accounting for Investments of International Financial Reporting Standards (IFRS)

There are a number of diverse topics included in this chapter for which there are differences between accounting standards for private enterprises (ASPE) and IFRS. Given that this is an extremely complex topic, it can be summarized at a high level as follows:

Chapter Topic	IFRS and ASPE Differences
Equity Investments	
Where there is no significant influence (non-strategic investments)	IFRS requires that most *financial instruments* must be measured at fair value (market value). In many cases, determining the fair value can be difficult and costly. There is no option to measure at cost as there is under ASPE. Gains and losses are recorded under Other Comprehensive Income rather than under Net Income, as is done when following ASPE.
Where there is significant influence (strategic investments)	IFRS allows only the equity method. ASPE permits the cost method when it is more appropriate. Significant influence is a **rebuttable presumption**. Under IFRS, it is *presumed* that if an investor holds, directly or indirectly, 20% or more of the voting power of the investee, it has significant influence, unless it can be clearly demonstrated that this is not the case. There is not the same presumption under ASPE. IFRS also requires the reversal of impairment losses. This is not done under ASPE.
Joint ventures	IFRS differentiates between *joint operations* and *joint ventures*. *Joint ventures* are accounted for using the equity method instead of the proportionate consolidation method used when following ASPE. *Joint operations* are accounted for by recording the owners' share of each of the accounts of the business according to the IFRS treatment for each account.
Where there is control (majority interest)	Under IFRS and ASPE, the parent company must consolidate its subsidiaries' financial results. There are some limited circumstances under which this might not happen. While APSE does not say where to report minority interest, IFRS requires that it be presented within the equity section, but separate from the parent's shareholders' equity.

(*Continued*)

Chapter Topic	IFRS and ASPE Differences

Investments in Debt Instruments

Short-term investments in bonds

The standards are converged. Both suggest that these investments are measured and reported at fair value. (Use the cost method if no market price is available.)

Long-term investments in bonds

Both standards use the amortized cost method. IFRS requires the use of the effective-interest-rate method while ASPE allows either straight-line amortization or the effective-interest-rate method.

Foreign-currency transactions

IFRS introduces some different terminology. There is a gain or loss when the **functional currency** rate (the currency in which the transaction takes place or the currency of the country in which the firm operates) is different from the **presentation currency** rate (the currency used for the financial statements). Translation gains or losses are recorded in Other Comprehensive Income.

The two sets of standards differ somewhat in their requirements for accounting for hedges.

✓ JUST CHECKING

14. What is the main difference between IFRS and ASPE for short-term investments?
15. What is the main difference between IFRS and ASPE for equity investments where there is significant influence?
16. What is the main difference between IFRS and ASPE for investments in subsidiaries?

Just Checking Solutions appear at the end of this chapter and on MyAccountingLab.

Summary Problems for Your Review

1. Journalize the following transactions of Canada Corp.:

2013

Nov. 16   Purchased equipment on account for US$40,000 when the exchange rate was $1.07 per U.S. dollar.

27   Sold merchandise on account to a Swiss company for 700,000 Swiss francs. Each Swiss franc is worth $0.81.

Dec. 22   Paid the U.S. company when the U.S. dollar's exchange rate was $1.05.

31   Adjusted for the change in the exchange rate of the Swiss franc. Its current exchange rate is $0.80.

2014

Jan. 4   Collected from the Swiss company. The exchange rate is $0.82.

2. In the 2013 transactions, did the following currencies become stronger or weaker by the end of the year? Did they strengthen or weaken during 2014?

   a. U.S. dollar

   b. Swiss franc

   c. Canadian dollar

SOLUTIONS

1. Entries for transactions stated in foreign currencies:

2013			
Nov. 16	Equipment	42,800	
	Accounts Payable		42,800
	To record a purchase on credit (40,000 × $1.07).		
27	Accounts Receivable	567,000	
	Sales Revenue		567,000
	To record a sale on account (700,000 × $0.81).		
Dec. 22	Accounts Payable	42,800	
	Cash		42,000
	Foreign-Currency Transaction Gain		800
	To record payment of a credit purchase (40,000 × $1.05).		
31	Foreign-Currency Transaction Loss	7,000	
	Accounts Receivable		7,000
	Year-end exchange rate adjustment [700,000 × ($0.81 − $0.80)].		
2014			
Jan. 4	Cash	574,000	
	Accounts Receivable		560,000
	Foreign-Currency Transaction Gain		14,000
	Collection of account receivable [Cash = (700,000 × $0.82) = $574,000]		
	Accounts Receivable = ($567,000 − $7,000) = $560,000		
	Gain = [700,000 × ($0.92 − $0.90)] = $14,000]		

Always use the exchange rates in effect on the date of a transaction. When journalizing the payment or receipt for a foreign-currency transaction, calculate the cash payment or receipt amount first.
Then,
Cash payment > Payable
→ F-C transaction loss

Cash payment < Payable
→ F-C transaction gain

Cash receipt > Receivable
→ F-C transaction gain

Cash receipt < Receivable
→ F-C transaction loss

If an exchange rate expressed in Canadian $ declines over time
→ foreign currency is getting weaker
If an exchange rate expressed in Canadian $ increases over time
→ foreign currency is getting stronger

2. Based on the transactions shown, during 2013:

   a. U.S. dollar—weaker   b. Swiss franc—weaker   c. Canadian dollar—stronger

During 2014, the Swiss franc strengthened and the Canadian dollar weakened.

Summary

(1) **Learning Objective 1: Account for short-term investments**

How do we account for short-term investments?

- Use the fair-value (or market-value) method
- Change in value at year end is an unrealized gain or loss in the non-operating section of the income statement under "Other gains and losses"
- Dividends and interest are recorded as income

Pg. 993

(2) Learning Objective 2: Account for long-term share investments

How do we account for long-term share investments?	Percentage investment in shares	Accounting method	Pg. 996
	< 20%	Fair value, or market value	
	20% to 50%	Equity	
	> 50%	Consolidation	
	Joint venture	Proportionate consolidation	

(3) Learning Objective 3: Use the equity method to account for investments

What is the equity method, and how do we use it?

- Use when there is "significant influence" or ownership of 20 to 50 percent of the shares.
- Investee income is recorded by the investor by debiting the Investment account and crediting the Equity-Method Investment Revenue account.
- The investor records the receipt of dividends from the investee by crediting the Investment account.

Pg. 999

(4) Learning Objective 4: Describe and create consolidated financial statements

What is consolidation, and how do we perform a simple consolidation?

- Ownership of more than 50 percent of the voting shares—*consolidation* method must be used.
- Parent has "control" over the subsidiary
- The subsidiary's financial statements are included in the consolidated statements of the parent company.
- Two features of consolidation accounting are
  (1) Addition of the parent and subsidiary accounts to prepare the parent's consolidated statements, and
  (2) Elimination of intercompany items.
- When a parent owns less than 100 percent of the subsidiary's shares, the portion owned by outside investors is called a *non-controlling interest.*

Pg. 1004

(5) Learning Objective 5: Account for investments in bonds

How do we record investments in bonds?

- Long-term investments in bonds are *recorded at cost.* Fees are capitalized.
- They are reported at their *amortized cost,* which means the discount or premium is amortized to account more precisely for interest revenue over the period the bonds will be held.
- The amortization of the discount or premium on a bond investment affects Interest Revenue and the carrying amount of the bonds in the same way as for the company that issued the bonds.
- At maturity the investor will receive the face value of the bonds.

Pg. 1010

(6) Learning Objective 6: Account for foreign-currency transactions

How do we record transactions with foreign currencies?

Foreign-currency transaction gains:
- When a company receives foreign currency worth *more* in Canadian dollars than the amount of the receivable recorded earlier.
- When a company pays foreign currency that costs *less* in Canadian dollars than the amount of the payable recorded earlier.

Foreign-Currency transaction losses:
- When a company receives foreign currency worth *less* in Canadian dollars than the amount of the receivable recorded earlier.
- When a company pays foreign currency that costs *more* in Canadian dollars than the amount of the payable recorded earlier.

Pg. 1014

(7) Learning Objective 7: Identify the impact on accounting for investments of international financial reporting standards (IFRS)

How does IFRS apply to investments and international transactions?

- In general, IFRS and ASPE require the same or similar treatment of investments and foreign-currency transactions.
- In many cases, ASPE allows companies more options for accounting for their investments.

Pg. 1019

Check Accounting Vocabulary on page 1024 for all key terms used in Chapter 16 and the Glossary on page 1246 for all key terms used in the textbook.

CHAPTER REVIEW:

MyAccountingLab   Student PowerPoint Slides

MyAccountingLab   Audio Chapter Summary

Note: All MyAccountingLab resources can be found in the Chapter Resources section and the Multimedia Library.

SELF-STUDY QUESTIONS

Test your understanding of the chapter by marking the best answer for each of the following questions:

1. Short-term investments are reported on the balance sheet (p. 995)
   a. Immediately after inventory
   b. Immediately after accounts receivable
   c. Immediately after cash
   d. Immediately after current assets

2. Byforth Inc. distributes a stock dividend. An investor who owns Byforth Inc. shares as a short-term investment should (p. 993)
   a. Debit Short-Term Investments and credit Dividend Revenue for the book value of the shares received in the dividend distribution
   b. Debit Short-Term Investments and credit Dividend Revenue for the market value of the shares received in the dividend distribution
   c. Debit Cash and credit Short-Term Investments for the market value of the shares received in the dividend distribution
   d. Make a memorandum entry to record the new cost per share of Byforth Inc. shares held

3. Short-term investments are reported at the (pp. 994–995)
   a. Total cost of the portfolio
   b. Total fair value of the portfolio
   c. Lower of total cost or total fair value of the portfolio, or lower of cost or fair value on an investment-by-investment basis
   d. Total equity value of the portfolio

4. Mulgarvey Corporation owns 30 percent of the voting shares of Turner Inc. Turner Inc. reports net income of $200,000 and declares and pays cash dividends of $80,000. Which method should Mulgarvey Corporation use to account for this investment? (p. 999)
   a. Cost   c. Fair Value
   b. Equity   d. Consolidation

5. Refer to the facts of the preceding question. What effect do Turner Inc.'s income and dividends have on Mulgarvey Corporation's net income? (pp. 999–1000)
   a. Increase of $24,000
   b. Increase of $36,000
   c. Increase of $60,000
   d. Increase of $84,000

6. In applying the consolidation method, elimination entries are (pp. 1002–1003)
   a. Necessary
   b. Required only when the parent has a receivable from or a payable to the subsidiary
   c. Required only when there is a minority interest
   d. Required only for the preparation of the consolidated balance sheet

7. Parent Corp. reports net income of $200,000. Sub A Ltd., of which Parent Corp. owns 90 percent, reports net income of $80,000, and Sub B Ltd., of which Parent Corp. owns 60 percent, reports net income of $100,000. What is Parent Corp.'s consolidated net income? (pp. 1008–1009)
   a. $200,000   c. $335,000
   b. $332,000   d. $380,000

8. On May 16, the exchange rate of the euro was $1.50. On May 20, the exchange rate is $1.52. Which of the following statements is true? (p. 1014)
   a. The Canadian dollar has risen against the euro.
   b. The Canadian dollar has fallen against the euro.
   c. The Canadian dollar is stronger than the euro.
   d. The Canadian dollar and the euro are equally strong.

9. A strong Canadian dollar encourages (p. 1014)
   a. Travel to Canada by foreigners
   b. Purchase of Canadian goods by foreigners
   c. Canadians to save dollars
   d. Canadians to travel abroad

10. Canadian Furniture Inc. purchased dining room suites from an English supplier at a price of 400,000 British pounds sterling. On the date of the credit purchase, the exchange rate of the British pound was $1.75. On the payment date, the exchange rate of the pound is $1.77. If payment is in pounds, Canadian Furniture experiences (pp. 1016–1017)
    a. A foreign-currency transaction gain of $8,000
    b. A foreign-currency transaction loss of $8,000
    c. Neither a transaction gain nor loss because the debt is paid in Canadian dollars
    d. None of the above

Answers to Self-Study Questions

1. c 2. d 3. b 4. b 5. c ($200,000 × 0.30 = $60,000; dividends have no effect on investor net income under the equity method) 6. a 7. b [$200,000 + ($80,000 × 0.90) + ($100,000 × 0.60) = $332,000] 8. b 9. d 10. b [400,000 × ($1.77 − $1.75) = $8,000; a loss since cash payment > payable]

ACCOUNTING VOCABULARY

Actively traded   Financial instruments that are easily bought or sold because there are a lot of them in the market and it is easy to find someone who is willing to engage in a transaction   (*p. 992*).

Affiliated company   An investment in a company in which there is significant influence and 20-to-50-percent ownership. These investments are accounted for using the equity method   (*p. 1001*).

Amortized cost method   To account for long-term bond investments, the discount or premium is amortized to more accurately reflect the interest revenue. These bonds are reported at their amortized cost   (*p. 1011*).

Certificate of deposit (CD)   A secure form of investment with a fixed interest rate and term. Unlike a bank account, they must be held to maturity   (*p. 992*).

Companion account   An account that is typically paired up with another account   (*p. 994*).

Consolidated statements   Financial statements of the parent company plus those of majority-owned subsidiaries as if the combination were a single legal entity   (*pp. 989, 1004*).

Controlling interest   Ownership of more than 50 percent of an investee company's voting shares. Also called *majority interest*   (*p. 1002*).

Counterbalancing transaction   Engaging in a second transaction to offset the risk of the first transaction   (*p. 1017*).

Currency options   A contract that can be purchased to guarantee the right to a future exchange rate   (*p. 1018*).

Denominated   To be expressed in terms of a monetary unit   (*p. 1017*).

Equity method for investments   The method used to account for investments in which the investor generally has 20 to 50 percent of the investor's voting shares and can significantly influence the decisions of the investee. The investment account is debited for ownership in the investee's net income and credited for ownership in the investee's dividends   (*p. 992*).

Fair-value method   The method of accounting for shares held as short-term investments that values them at their fair, or market, value on the year-end balance sheet date. Any gain or loss resulting from the change in fair value is recognized in net income for the period in which it arises, and fair value becomes the new carrying value of the shares. Also called the *market-value method*   (*p. 993*).

Financial instrument   A contract that creates an asset for one party and a liability or equity for another   (*p. 1010*).

Foreign-currency exchange rate   The measure of one currency against another currency   (*p. 1014*).

Foreign-currency transaction gain   The gain that occurs when a cash payment is less than the related account payable or a cash receipt is greater than the related account receivable due to a change in exchange rate between the transaction date and the payment date   (*p. 1016*).

Foreign-currency transaction loss   The loss that occurs when a cash payment is greater than the related account payable or a cash receipt is less than the related account receivable due to a change in exchange rate between the transaction date and the payment date   (*p. 1016*).

Forward contract   An agreement to purchase at a specified future date and price   (*p. 1017*).

Functional currency   The main currency used by a business for most transactions and reporting   (*p. 1020*).

Futures contract   A contract that can be purchased to guarantee the right to a product at a specified price in the future   (*p. 1018*).

Hedging   A way to protect oneself from losing money in a foreign-currency transaction by engaging in a counterbalancing foreign-currency transaction   (*p. 1017*).

Long-term investments   Investments that a company intends to hold for more than one year   (*p. 992*).

Majority interest   Another name for controlling interest   (*p. 1002*).

Market-value method   Another name for the fair-value method of accounting for short-term investments in shares   (*p. 993*).

Minority interest   Another name for non-controlling interest   (*p. 1007*).

Money market fund   An investment product generally considered safe because it invests in short-term debt securities, such as certificates of deposit   (*p. 992*).

Non-controlling interest   A subsidiary company's equity that is held by shareholders other than the parent company. Also called *minority interest*   (*p. 1007*).

Parent company   An investor company that generally owns more than 50 percent of the voting shares of a subsidiary company   (*p. 1002*).

Presentation currency   The currency in which the financial statements are presented   (p. 1020).

Proportionate consolidation   The venturer combines its share of the interest in the assets, liabilities, revenues, and expenses of a joint venture with its own assets, liabilities, revenues, and expenses in its consolidated financial statements   (p. 1001).

Rebuttable assumption   A conclusion that something is true unless proven that it isn't   (p. 1019).

Segmented information   Financial information presented in the notes to the financial statements either by industry or by geography   (p. 1009).

Short-term investments   Investments that management intends to hold for less than one year   (p. 992).

Significant influence   When a company participates in the decision making of another company without having full control over it   (p. 992).

Strong currency   A currency that is rising relative to other nations' currencies   (p. 1015).

Subsidiary   An investee company in which a parent company owns more than 50 percent of the voting shares   (p. 1002).

Translation   Another term for a currency conversion or foreign-currency exchange   (p. 1014).

Treasury bills   A short-term debt obligation issued by a government   (p. 992).

Weak currency   A currency that is falling relative to other nations' currencies   (p. 1015).

Write-down   An accounting entry to recognize the decrease in the value of an asset by debiting an expense account and crediting the asset account (p. 1001).

SIMILAR ACCOUNTING TERMS

Controlling interest	Majority interest
Fair-value method	Market-value method
Minority interest	Non-controlling interest
Short-term investments	Marketable securities; Temporary investments
Translation	Foreign-currency conversion

Assignment Material

QUESTIONS

1. If a company buys the shares of another company as an investment, what is the investor's cost of 1,000 Royal Bank of Canada non-cumulative preferred shares at $20.50 with a brokerage commission of $300?

2. What distinguishes a short-term investment in shares from a long-term investment in shares?

3. Show the positions of short-term investments and long-term investments on the balance sheet.

4. At the end of a fiscal period, all equity investments that are traded on public stock exchanges must be revalued on the balance sheet to their market value. Does this policy provide better information for the investor? Explain.

5. How does an investor record the receipt of a cash dividend on an investment accounted for by the fair-value method? How does this investor record receipt of a stock dividend?

6. An investor paid $30,000 for 1,000 common shares and later that same year received a 10-percent stock dividend. Compute the gain or loss on sale of 500 common shares for $15,000 before the year end.

7. Are the short-term and long-term equity investment portfolios mixed on the balance sheet, or are they kept separate?

8. When is an investment accounted for by the equity method? Outline how to apply the equity method. Include in your answer how to record the purchase of the investment, the investor's proportion of the investee's net income, and receipt of a cash dividend from the investee. Indicate how a gain or loss on the sale of the investment would be measured.

9. Identify three transactions that cause debits or credits to an equity-method investment account.

10. What are two special features of the consolidation method for investments?

11. Why are intercompany items eliminated from consolidated financial statements? Name two intercompany items that are eliminated.

12. Name the account that expresses the excess of cost of an investment over the fair market value of the subsidiary's net assets. What type of account is this, and where in the financial statements is it reported?

13. When a parent company buys more than 50 percent but less than 100 percent of a subsidiary's shares, a certain type of equity is created. What is it called and how do most companies report it?

14. How would you measure the net income of a parent company with three subsidiaries? Assume that two subsidiaries are wholly (100 percent) owned and that the parent owns 60 percent of the third subsidiary.

15. Weel Soo purchases Canadian Utilities Inc. bonds as a long-term investment. Suppose the face amount of the bonds is $300,000 and the purchase price is 101.30. The bonds pay interest at the stated annual rate of 8 percent. How much did Soo pay for the bonds? How much principal will Soo collect at maturity?

16. The purchase date of the bond investment in the preceding question was August 1, 2014. The bonds pay semiannual interest on January 31 and July 31. How much interest will Soo earn during the year ended December 31, 2014?

17. Mentacos Inc. purchased inventory from a French company, agreeing to pay 150,000 euros. On the purchase date, the euro was quoted at $1.55. When Mentacos Inc. paid the debt, the price of a euro was $1.57. What account does Mentacos Inc. debit for the $3,000 difference between the cost of the inventory and the amount of cash paid?

18. Which of the following situations results in a foreign-currency transaction gain for a Canadian business? Which situation results in a loss?

    a. Credit purchase denominated in pesos, followed by weakness in the peso

    b. Credit purchase denominated in pesos, followed by weakness in the dollar

    c. Credit sale denominated in pesos, followed by weakness in the peso

    d. Credit sale denominated in pesos, followed by weakness in the dollar

MyAccountingLab   Make the grade with MyAccountingLab: The Starters, Exercises, and Problems marked in red can be found on MyAccountingLab. You can practise them as often as you want, and most feature step-by-step guided instructions to help you find the right answer.

STARTERS

Computing the cost of an investment in shares
① ②
a. $9,075
b. $52,800

Starter 16–1 Compute the cost of each of the following short-term investments. Round to the nearest dollar.

a. 550 shares of Grey Ltd. at $16.50 per share. Brokerage fees were $175.

b. 600 shares of Red Corp. at $88.00 per share. Red Corp. pays a cash dividend of $0.66 per year. Brokerage fees were $550.

c. 1,000 shares of White Inc. at $55.10 per share. Brokerage fees were $560.

d. 70 shares of Tangerine Ltd. at $35.50 per share. Brokerage fees were $250.

Classifying investments as short term or long term
① ②

Starter 16–2 Baines Corp. purchased 1,000 common shares in each of three companies:

a. Investment in Cullen Corp. to be sold within the next 9 to 12 months.

b. Investment in Gerson Canada Ltd. to be sold within the next 90 days.

c. Investment in Arnold Ltd. to be sold within the next two years.

Classify each investment as a current asset or a long-term asset. None of these investments is subject to significant influence.

Accounting for a short-term investment

Jan 27, 2014, gain on sale $1,000

Starter 16–3 Heat Publishing Ltd. completed the following transactions during 2013 and 2014.

2013

Dec. 6   Purchased 1,000 shares of Georgian Graphics Inc. at a price of
          $41.00 per share, intending to sell the investment within
          three months. Brokerage fees were $350.

     23   Received a cash dividend of $1.10 per share on the
          Georgian Graphics Inc. shares.

     31   Adjusted the investment to its fair value of $45.00 per
          share.

2014

Jan. 27   Sold the Georgian Graphics Inc. shares for $46.00 per
          share, less brokerage fees of $370.

Journalize Heat Publishing Ltd.'s investment transactions. Explanations
are not required.

Starter 16–4   McBain Electronics completed the following investment transactions
during 2013 and 2014.

Accounting for a short-term
investment
①

2. Jan. 16, 2014, loss on sale
$3,750

2013

Dec. 12   Purchased 1,500 shares of Blackmore Ltd. at a price of $62.00
          per share, intending to sell the investment within the next
          year. Commissions were $510.

     21   Received a cash dividend of $0.48 per share on the Blackmore
          Ltd. shares.

     31   Adjusted the investment to its fair value of $61.50 per share.

2014

Jan. 16   Sold the Blackmore Ltd. shares for $59.00 per share, less com-
          missions of $490.

1. Classify McBain's investment as short term or long term.
2. Journalize McBain's investment transactions. Explanations are not
   required.

Starter 16–5   Gerber Ltd. buys 2,000 of the 100,000 shares of Efron Inc., paying $35.00
per share. Suppose Efron distributes a 10-percent stock dividend. Later
the same year, Gerber Ltd. sells the Efron shares for $30.00 per share.
Disregard commissions on the purchase and sale.

Measuring gain or loss on the
sale of a share investment after
receiving a stock dividend
①

2. Loss on sale $4,000

1. Compute Gerber Ltd.'s new cost per share after receiving the stock
   dividend.
2. Compute Gerber Ltd.'s gain or loss on the sale of this long-term
   investment.

Starter 16–6   Match the following situations with the appropriate measurement
method (letters may be used more than once):

Matching reporting methods
① ② ③ ④ ⑤

1. Bonds held to maturity   A. Equity method
2. More than 50 percent ownership   B. Consolidation
3. Bonds held for less than one year   C. Fair-value method
4. Between 20 and 50 percent ownership
5. Less than 20 percent ownership   D. Proportionate consolidation
6. Joint venture   E. Amortized cost

Starter 16–7   Marsland Inc. completed these long-term investment transactions during
2014. Disregard commissions.

Accounting for a long-term
investment's unrealized gain
or loss
②

1. Dec. 31, 2014, unrealized
gain $9,750

2014

Jan. 14   Purchased 1,000 shares of Crew Ltd., paying $41.00 per
          share. Marsland intends to hold the investment for the
          indefinite future.

Aug. 22   Received a cash dividend of $3.28 per share on the Crew
          Ltd. shares.

Dec. 31   Adjusted the Crew Ltd. investment to its current fair value
          of $50,750.

1. Journalize Marsland's investment transactions. Explanations are not required. Marsland Inc. exerts no significant influence on Crew Ltd.
2. Show how to report the investment and any unrealized gain or loss on Marsland's balance sheet at December 31, 2014.

Accounting for the sale of a long-term investment
②
1. Gain on sale $2,250

Starter 16–8 Use the data given in Starter 16–7. On August 4, 2015, Marsland Inc. sold its investment in Crew Ltd. for $53.00 per share. Disregard commissions.
1. Journalize the sale. No explanation is required.
2. How does the gain or loss that you recorded differ from the gain or loss that was recorded at December 31, 2014 (in Starter 16–7)?

Accounting for a 40-percent investment in another company
③
3. Bal. $5,400,000

Starter 16–9 Suppose on January 6, 2014, Ling Corp. paid $5,000,000 for its 40-percent investment in True World Inc. Assume True World earned net income of $1,800,000 and paid cash dividends of $800,000 during 2014. Disregard commissions.
1. What method should Ling Corp. use to account for the investment in True World Inc.? Give your reason.
2. Journalize these three transactions on the books of Ling Corp. Include an explanation for each entry.
3. Post to the Investment in True World Inc. Common Shares T-account. What is its balance after all the transactions are posted?

Understanding consolidated financial statements
④

Starter 16–10 Answer these questions about consolidation accounting:
1. Define "parent company." Define "subsidiary."
2. Which company's name appears on the consolidated financial statements? How much of the subsidiary's shares must the parent own before reporting consolidated statements?
3. How do consolidated financial statements differ from the financial statements of a single company?

Working with a bond investment
⑤
3. Annual interest revenue $66,000

Starter 16–11 Heinz Ltd. owns vast amounts of corporate bonds. Suppose the company buys $1,000,000 of Kuzawa Corporation bonds on January 2, 2014, at a price of 97. The Kuzawa bonds pay cash interest at the annual rate of 6 percent and mature on December 31, 2018.
1. How much did Heinz Ltd. pay to purchase the bond investment? How much will Heinz Ltd. collect when the bond investment matures?
2. How much cash interest will Heinz Ltd. receive each year from Kuzawa Corporation?
3. Compute Heinz Ltd.'s annual interest revenue on this bond investment. Use the straight-line method to amortize the discount on the investment.

Recording bond investment transactions
⑤
b. Cash Interest received $60,000

Starter 16–12 Return to Starter 16–11, the Heinz Ltd. investment in Kuzawa Corporation bonds. Journalize the following transactions on Heinz Ltd.'s books, along with an explanation:

a. Purchase of the bond investment on January 2, 2014. As Heinz Ltd. expects to hold the investment to maturity, it is classified as a long-term investment.
b. Receipt of the annual cash interest on December 31, 2014.
c. Amortization of the discount on December 31, 2014.
d. Collection of the investment's face value at its maturity date on December 31, 2018. (Assume that the interest and amortization of discount for 2018 have already been recorded, so you may ignore these entries.)

Accounting for transactions stated in a foreign currency
⑥
Net foreign-currency gain $10,000

Starter 16–13 Suppose Fleetstar Ltd. sells athletic shoes to a German company on March 14. Fleetstar agrees to accept 2,000,000 euros. On the date of sale, the euro is quoted at $1.56. Fleetstar collects half the receivable on April 19, when the euro is worth $1.55. Then, on May 10, when the price of the euro is $1.58, Fleetstar collects the final amount.

Journalize these three transactions for Fleetstar; include an explanation. Overall, did Fleetstar have a net foreign-currency gain or loss?

Starter 16–14 Fill in the blanks to indicate how investments are reported under IFRS.

IFRS reporting of investments

⑦

a. Financial instruments are measured at _____.

b. Gains or losses on equity investments with no significant influence are recorded under _____.

c. Significant influence is a rebuttable assumption. It is presumed if an investor holds (directly or indirectly) _____ or more of the votes.

d. Joint ventures are accounted for using the _____ method.

e. Minority interest is shown on the balance sheet _____ but separate from the parent's _____.

f. Short-term investments in bonds are measured and reported at _____.

g. Long-term investments in bonds are amortized using the _____.

EXERCISES

MyAccountingLab

Exercise 16–1

Cummins Corp. reports its annual financial results on June 30 each year. Cummins Corp. purchased 1,000 shares in each of three companies. Classify each investment as a short-term or long-term investment.

Classifying equity investments

① ②

a. Investment to be sold within the next 9 to 12 months.

b. Investment to be sold within the next 90 days.

c. Investment to be sold within the next two years.

Exercise 16–2

Journalize the following investment transactions of Russell Corp.:

Accounting for a short-term investment

①

June 14, 2015 gain on sale
$3,900

2014

Nov. 6 Purchased 1,200 common shares of Aveda Corporation at $78.00 per share, with brokerage commission of $500. The shares will be sold early in 2015.

30 Received a cash dividend of $3.85 per share on the Aveda Corporation investment.

Dec. 31 The share price for Aveda Corporation's common shares was $76.25 on December 31, 2014, which is Russell Corp.'s year end.

2015

Jun. 14 Sold the Aveda Corporation shares for $79.50 per share. Brokerage fees were $400.

Exercise 16–3

Research in Motion (RIM) Limited (now called BlackBerry) reported the following (adapted) information in the notes accompanying its 2011 financial statements:

Reporting investments at fair value

①

Current Assets	(in millions of U.S. dollars)
Cash	$ 288
Short-term investments (fair value)	$2,410

Assume that the carrying value of RIM's short-term investments is $2,405 million prior to the year-end adjustment to fair value.

Required Write a note to identify the method used to report short-term investments, and to disclose cost and fair value. Show the journal entry that would have been made by RIM if you determine that a journal entry was needed at year end.

Exercise 16–4

Accounting for a short-term
investment
①

Jan. 20, 2015 gain on sale
$1,000

Suppose Carlton Ltd. completed the following investment transactions in 2014 and 2015:

2014

Nov.	6	Purchased 2,000 McGill Corporation common shares for $60,000. Carlton plans to sell the shares in the near future to meet its operating-cash-flow requirements. Commissions on the purchase were $800.
	30	Received a quarterly cash dividend of $1.50 per share on the McGill Corporation shares.
Dec.	31	Current fair value of the McGill common shares is $62,000.

2015

Jan.	20	Sold the McGill Corporation shares for $63,000, less commissions on the sale of $900.

Required

1. Make the entries to record Carlton Ltd.'s investment transactions. Explanations are not required. Carlton Ltd.'s year end is December 31.
2. Show how Carlton Ltd. would report its investment in the McGill Corporation shares on the balance sheet at December 31, 2014.

Exercise 16–5

Journalizing transactions for a
long-term investment
②

Dec. 4, 2014 gain on sale
$6,120

Journalize the following investment transactions of Vantage Inc.:

2014

Aug.	6	Purchased 900 Rhodes Corporation common shares as a long-term investment, paying $90.00 per share. Vantage Inc. exerts no significant influence on Rhodes Corporation. Commissions on the purchase were $900.
Sept.	12	Received cash dividends of $1.60 per share on the Rhodes Corporation investment.
Nov.	23	Received 90 Rhodes Corporation common shares in a 10-percent stock dividend.
Dec.	4	Unexpectedly sold all the Rhodes Corporation shares for $88.00 per share, less commissions on the sale of $750.

Exercise 16–6

Journalizing transactions under
the equity method
③

Kinross Gold Corp., introduced in the chapter-opening story, owns equity-method investments in several companies. Suppose Kinross paid $12,000,000 to acquire a 40-percent investment in Minecraft Ltd. Further, assume Minecraft Ltd. reported net income of $1,780,000 for the first year and declared and paid cash dividends of $650,000. Record the following entries in Kinross's general journal: (a) purchase of the investment, (b) Kinross's proportion of Minecraft Ltd.'s net income, and (c) receipt of the cash dividends. Disregard commissions on the purchase.

Exercise 16–7

Recording equity-method
transactions in the accounts
③

Gain on sale $648,000

Using the information from Exercise 16–6, calculate the balance in the Investment in Minecraft Ltd. Common Shares account. Assume that after all the above transactions took place, Kinross sold its entire investment in Minecraft Ltd. common shares for $13,100,000 cash. Journalize the sale of the investment. Disregard commissions on sale.

Exercise 16–8

Applying the appropriate
accounting method for
investments
② ③

Windsor Corporation paid $760,000 for a 35-percent investment in the common shares of Semmi Systems Inc. For the first year, Semmi Systems Inc. reported net income of $360,000 and at year end declared and paid cash dividends of $105,000. On the balance sheet date, the fair value of Windsor Corporation's investment in Semmi Systems Inc. shares was $780,000.

Required

1. Which method is appropriate for Windsor Corporation to use in accounting for its investment in Semmi Systems Inc.? Why?
2. Show everything that Windsor Corporation would report for the investment and any investment revenue in its year-end financial statements.
3. What role does the fair value of the investment play in this situation?

Exercise 16–9

Penfold Ltd. owns all the common shares of Simmons Ltd. Prepare a consolidation work sheet, using the following information. Assume that the fair value of the assets and liabilities of Simmons Ltd. are equal to their book values.

Excel Spreadsheet Template

Completing a consolidation work sheet with 100 percent ownership

④

Total consolidated assets $7,932,000

	Penfold Ltd.	Simmons Ltd.
Assets		
Cash	$ 225,000	$ 55,000
Accounts receivable, net	360,000	264,000
Note receivable from Simmons Ltd	76,000	—
Inventory	258,000	159,000
Investment in Simmons Ltd	2,350,000	—
Property, plant, and equipment, net	3,590,000	2,900,000
Total	$6,859,000	$3,378,000
Liabilities and Shareholders' Equity		
Accounts payable	$ 357,000	$ 180,000
Notes payable	462,000	759,000
Other liabilities	78,000	210,000
Common shares	1,980,000	670,000
Retained earnings	3,982,000	1,559,000
Total	$6,859,000	$3,378,000

Exercise 16–10

Pettigrew Holdings Ltd. owns an 80-percent interest in Shortland Inc. Prepare a consolidation work sheet using the information below. Assume that the fair values of Shortland Inc.'s assets and liabilities are equal to their book values.

Completing a consolidation work sheet with non-controlling interest

④

Total consolidated assets $2,086,800

	Pettigrew Holdings Ltd.	Shortland Inc.
Assets		
Cash	$ 96,000	$ 36,000
Accounts receivable, net	210,000	144,000
Note receivable from Shortland Inc.	60,000	—
Inventory	246,000	216,000
Investment in Shortland Inc.	228,000	—
Property, plant, and equipment, net	720,000	312,000
Other assets	48,000	42,000
Total	$1,608,000	$750,000
Liabilities and Shareholders' Equity		
Accounts payable	$ 108,000	$ 66,000
Notes payable	120,000	96,000
Other liabilities	204,000	324,000
Non-controlling interest	—	—
Common shares	780,000	204,000
Retained earnings	396,000	60,000
Total	$1,608,000	$750,000

Exercise 16–11

Credit Crunchers Ltd. has a large investment in corporate bonds. Suppose Credit Crunchers Ltd. buys $6,000,000 of Government of Alberta bonds at a price of 98. The Government of

Working with a bond investment

⑤

4. Annual interest revenue $192,000

Alberta bonds pay cash interest at the annual rate of 3.0 percent and mature in 10 years. Credit Crunchers Ltd. plans to hold the bonds until maturity.

1. How much did Credit Crunchers Ltd. pay to purchase the bond investment? How much will Credit Crunchers Ltd. collect when the bond investment matures?
2. How much cash interest will Credit Crunchers Ltd. receive each year from the Government of Alberta?
3. Will Credit Crunchers Ltd.'s annual interest revenue on the bond investment be more or less than the amount of cash interest received each year? Give your reason.
4. Compute Credit Crunchers Ltd.'s annual interest on this bond investment. Use the straight-line method to amortize the discount on the investment.

Exercise 16–12

Recording bond investment transactions using straight-line method
⑤

2. Dec. 31, 2014 bond discount amort. amount $97

On March 31, 2014, Kingpin Corp. paid 98.25 for 4-percent bonds of Quest Limited as an investment. The maturity value of the bonds is $100,000 at September 30, 2018; they pay interest on March 31 and September 30. At December 31, 2014, the bonds' market value is 99.25. The company plans to hold the bonds until they mature.

Required

1. How should Kingpin Corp. account for the bonds?
2. Using the straight-line method of amortizing the discount, journalize all transactions on the bonds for 2014.
3. Show how the investment would be reported by Kingpin Corp. on the balance sheet at December 31, 2014.

Exercise 16–13

Recording bond investment transactions using the effective-interest method
⑤

Ace Properties Ltd, purchased a 5-year, 4.5% Scotia bond on May 1, 2014, and intends to hold it until it matures. The market rate at the time was 5.2 percent. Interest is paid annually each April 30. Information about the bond appears in the table below. Journalize the purchase and the April 30, 2015 entries. Assume there were no brokerage fees.

Annual Interest Period	Interest Revenue 4.50%	Period Interest Revenue	Discount Amort.	Discount Balance	Bond Carrying Value
May 1, 2014				$30,100	$ 969,900
April 30, 2015	$ 45,000	$ 50,435	$ 5,435	24,665	975,335
April 30, 2016	45,000	50,717	5,717	18,948	981,052
April 30, 2017	45,000	51,015	6,015	12,933	987,067
April 30, 2018	45,000	51,327	6,327	6,606	993,394
April 30, 2019	45,000	51,606	6,606	0	1,000,000
Total	$225,000	$255,100	$30,100		

Exercise 16–14

Journalizing foreign-currency transactions
⑥

Dec. 31, 2014, foreign-currency transaction loss $2,400

Journalize the following foreign-currency transactions for Kingsway Import Inc.:

2014

Nov. 17   Purchased goods on account from a Japanese company. The price was 500,000 yen, and the exchange rate of the yen was $0.0117.

Dec. 16   Paid the Japanese supplier when the exchange rate was $0.0120.

19   Sold merchandise on account to a French company at a price of 80,000 euros. The exchange rate was $1.57.

31   Adjusted for the decrease in the value of the euro, which had an exchange rate of $1.54. Kingsway Import Inc.'s year end is December 31.

2015

Jan. 14   Collected from the French company. The exchange rate was $1.58.

Exercise 16–15

Indicate the appropriate financial reporting standard by completing each sentence with either "ASPE" or "IFRS" in the blank.

Differences between ASPE and IFRS
① ② ③ ⑤ ⑦

a. Gains and losses are recorded under "other comprehensive income" under _____.

b. Equity investments with no significant influence can only be recorded at cost under _____.

c. Equity investments with over 20 percent ownership must be treated as having significant influence unless proven otherwise under _____.

d. When there is significant influence, impairment losses must be reversed under _____.

e. Joint ventures are accounted for using the proportionate consolidation method under _____.

f. For long-term investments in bonds, the straight-line amortization method is not allowed under _____.

SERIAL EXERCISE

This exercise continues the Kerr Consulting Corporation situation from Exercise 15–20 of Chapter 15. If you did not complete Exercise 15–20, you can still complete Exercise 16–16 as it is presented.

Exercise 16–16

After issuing bonds in Chapter 15, Kerr Consulting Corporation has some excess cash on hand. Alex Kerr, the Corporation's major shareholder, intends to invest some of the cash for different time periods to get better returns than from the bank and to have cash available when needed to expand the business into a new market. Assume Kerr Consulting Corporation completed the following investment transactions:

Investment transactions
① ② ③ ⑤
2. Dec. 10, 2015 balance, $59,000

2015

Apr. 15 The business purchased 300 common shares of Canadian Tire Corporation, Limited for $74.00 per share. Alex Kerr intends to hold this investment for less than a year. He thinks the share value will increase and knows Kerr Consulting will need the cash for operations in less than a year.

Jun. 2 Purchased 2,000 of the 6,000 common shares of Landers Consulting Ltd. at a cost of $40,000. Landers Consulting is a company formed by a colleague of Kerr, so Kerr hopes the investment will lead to future business opportunities for Kerr Consulting.

15 Purchased $10,000 of 6-percent, four-year bonds of Consulting Suppliers Inc. at 115. Kerr intends to hold these to maturity since the effective interest rate is still better than other investments he assessed.

Jul. 1 Received the quarterly cash dividend of $0.05 per share on the Canadian Tire investment.

Dec. 10 Received an annual dividend of $0.50 per share from Landers Consulting Ltd. Also received word that at November 30, Landers' year end, net income was $60,000.

15 Received semiannual interest of $300 on the Consulting Suppliers Inc. bonds. Amortized the premium using the straight-line method.

Required

1. Record the transactions in the general journal of Kerr Consulting Corporation. Disregard any commissions on purchases and sales of investments.
2. Post entries to the Investment in Landers Consulting Ltd. Common Shares T-account. Determine its balance at December 10, 2015, after the transaction shown on that date.

CHALLENGE EXERCISE

Exercise 16–17

Analyzing long-term investments
(3)

2014 dividends $840

Canfor Corporation is a major integrated forest products company based in Vancouver. Suppose Canfor's financial statements reported the following items for affiliated companies whose shares Canfor owns in various percentages between 20 and 50 percent:

	(In thousands of dollars)	
	2014	**2013**
Balance Sheet (adapted)		
Equity-method investments	$6,950	$6,800
Cash Flow Statement		
Increase in equity-method investments	350	325
Income Statement		
Equity earnings in affiliates	640	400

Assume no sales of equity-method investments during 2013 or 2014.

Required

Prepare a T-Account for Equity-Method Investments to determine the amount of dividends Canfor Corporation received from investee companies during 2014. The company's year end is December 31. Show your calculations.

BEYOND THE NUMBERS

Beyond the Numbers 16–1

Analyzing long-term investments
(4)

Sophie Bu inherited some investments, and she has received the annual reports of the companies in which the funds are invested. The financial statements of the companies are puzzling to Sophie, and she asks you the following questions:

a. The companies label their financial statements as *consolidated* balance sheet, *consolidated* income statement, and so on. What are consolidated financial statements?
b. Notes to the statements indicate that "certain intercompany transactions, loans, and other accounts have been eliminated in preparing the consolidated financial statements." Why does a company eliminate transactions, loans, and accounts? Sophie states that she thought a transaction was a transaction and that a loan obligated a company to pay real money. She wonders if the company is juggling the books to defraud Canada Revenue Agency.
c. The balance sheet lists the asset Goodwill. What is goodwill? Does this mean that the company's shares have increased in value?

Required

Respond to each of Sophie Bu's questions.

ETHICAL ISSUE

Sherman Inc. owns 18 percent of the voting shares of Arbor Corporation. The remainder of the Arbor Corporation shares are held by numerous investors with small holdings. Ken Tung, president of Sherman Inc. and a member of Arbor Corporation's Board of Directors, heavily influences Arbor Corporation's policies.

Under the fair-value method of accounting for investments, Sherman Inc.'s net income increases if or when it receives dividends from Arbor Corporation. Sherman Inc. pays Mr. Tung, as president, a bonus computed as a percentage of Sherman Inc.'s net income. Therefore, Tung can control his personal bonus to a certain extent by influencing Arbor Corporation's dividends.

Sherman Inc. has a bad year in 2014, and corporate income is low. Tung uses his power to have Arbor Corporation pay a large cash dividend. This action requires Arbor Corporation to borrow a substantial sum one month later to pay operating costs.

Required

1. In getting Arbor Corporation to pay the large cash dividend, is Tung acting within his authority as a member of the Arbor Corporation Board of Directors? Are Tung's actions ethical? Whom can his actions harm?

2. Discuss how using the equity method of accounting for investments would decrease Tung's potential for manipulating his bonus.

PROBLEMS (GROUP A)   MyAccountingLab

Problem 16–1A

Oliver Corp., the conglomerate, owns numerous investments in the shares of other companies. Assume Oliver Corp. completed the following investment transactions:

Journalizing transactions under the fair-value and equity methods ① ② ③

Feb. 6, 2015 loss on sale $18,457

2014

May	1	Purchased 12,000 common shares (total issued and outstanding common shares, 50,000) of Larson Corp. at a cost of $950,000. Commissions on the purchase were $20,000.
Jul.	2	Purchased 2,000 Larson Corp. common shares at a cost of $162,000. Commissions on the purchase were $1,500.
Sept.	15	Received semiannual cash dividend of $3.20 per share on the Larson Corp. investment.
Oct.	12	Purchased 1,000 Hurley Ltd. common shares as a short-term investment, paying $33.00 per share plus brokerage commission of $1,000.
Dec.	14	Received semiannual cash dividend of $1.50 per share on the Hurley Ltd. investment.
	31	Received annual report from Larson Corp. Net income for the year was $800,000. Of this amount, Oliver Corp.'s proportion is 28 percent. The current market value for 1,000 Hurley Ltd. shares is $31,000.

2015

Feb.	6	Sold 2,000 Larson Corp. shares for cash of $166,000, less commissions of $1,550.

Required

Record the transactions in the general journal of Oliver Corp.; the company's year end is December 31.

Problem 16–2A

The balance sheet of Spottified Corp. recently included:

Applying the fair-value method and the equity method ① ② ③

3. Dec. 31, 2014 balance $525,000

Investments in significantly influenced and other companies	$2,500,000

Spottified Corp. included its short-term investments among the current assets; the investments described above were long-term. Assume the company completed the following investment transactions during 2014:

Mar.	3	Purchased 8,000 common shares as a short-term investment, paying $25.00 per share plus brokerage commission of $500.
	4	Purchased additional shares in a company that is significantly influenced by Spottified Corp. at a cost of $600,000 plus brokerage commission of $4,500.
May	14	Received semiannual cash dividend of $1.70 per share on the short-term investment purchased March 3.

Jun.	15	Received cash dividend of $55,000 from a significantly influenced company.
Aug.	28	Sold the short-term investment (purchased on March 3) for $24.00 per share, less brokerage commission of $500.
Oct.	24	Purchased other short-term investments for $275,000, plus brokerage commission of $400.
Dec.	15	Received cash dividend of $30,000 from a significantly influenced company.
	31	Received annual reports from significantly influenced companies. Their total net income for the year was $1,300,000. Of this amount, Spottified Corp.'s proportion is 30 percent.

Required

1. Record the transactions in the general journal of Spottified Corp.
2. Post entries to the Investments in Significantly Influenced and Other Companies T-account, and determine its balance at December 31, 2014.
3. Assume the beginning balance of Short-Term Investments was at a cost of $250,000. Post entries to the Short-Term Investments T-account and determine its balance at December 31, 2014.
4. Assuming the market value of the short-term investment portfolio is $510,000 at December 31, 2014, show how Spottified Corp. would report short-term investments and investments in significantly influenced and other companies on the December 31, 2014, balance sheet. Use the following format:

Cash	$XXX
Short-term investments, at fair value	☐
Accounts receivable (net)	XXX
⌇	⌇
Total current assets	XXX
Investments in significantly influenced and other companies	☐

Problem 16–3A

Compare accounting methods as share ownership percentage varies

① ② ③

Case B year-end balance in the investments account $292,250

The accounting for equity investments changes with the amount of shares held. BF Ltd has a total of 30,000 shares outstanding. Complete the chart below to show the accounting differences between two different scenarios and how MW2 Ltd should record the transaction and balances if it owns different amounts of BF Ltd shares as a long-term investment.

	Case A: 3,600 Shares	Case B: 10,500 Shares
Which accounting method should be used for this long-term investment?		
Journal entry to record purchase of shares at $27 each. No commissions.		
Journal entry to recognize share of $25,000 in dividends declared and paid.		
Journal entry to recognize $50,000 in net income declared by BF Ltd.		
Journal entry to recognize the year-end market value of $30 per share.		
What is the balance in the investments account at year end?		

Problem 16–4A

Pluto Corp. paid $750,000 to acquire all the common shares of Saturn Inc., and Saturn Inc. owes Pluto Corp. $170,000 on a note payable. The fair market value of Saturn Inc.'s net assets equalled the book value. Immediately after the purchase on May 31, 2014, the two companies' balance sheets were as follows:

Excel Spreadsheet Template

Preparing a consolidated balance sheet; goodwill; no non-controlling interest

④

Total consolidated assets $2,420,000

	Pluto Corp.	Saturn Inc.
Assets		
Cash	$ 60,000	$ 100,000
Accounts receivable, net	210,000	150,000
Note receivable from Saturn Inc.	170,000	—
Inventory	300,000	440,000
Investment in Saturn Inc.	750,000	—
Property, plant, and equipment, net	600,000	500,000
Total	$2,090,000	$1,190,000
Liabilities and Shareholders' Equity		
Accounts payable	$ 250,000	$ 40,000
Notes payable	400,000	210,000
Note payable to Pluto Corp.	—	170,000
Other liabilities	156,000	80,000
Common shares	800,000	500,000
Retained earnings	484,000	190,000
Total	$2,090,000	$1,190,000

Required

Prepare a consolidation work sheet.

Problem 16–5A

On July 18, 2014, Patrone Holdings Ltd. paid $1,920,000 to purchase 90 percent of the common shares of Smirnoff Inc., and Smirnoff Inc. owes Patrone Holdings Ltd. $240,000 on a note payable. All historical cost amounts are equal to their fair market value on July 18, 2014. Immediately after the purchase, the two companies' balance sheets were as follows:

Excel Spreadsheet Template

Preparing a consolidated balance sheet with goodwill and non-controlling interest

④

Total consolidated assets $8,299,600

	Patrone Holdings Ltd.	Smirnoff Inc.
Assets		
Cash	$ 200,000	$ 340,000
Accounts receivable, net	720,000	480,000
Note receivable from Smirnoff Inc.	240,000	—
Inventory	1,480,000	920,000
Investment in Smirnoff Inc.	1,920,000	—
Property, plant, and equipment, net	2,190,000	1,540,000
Goodwill	—	—
Total	$6,750,000	$3,280,000
Liabilities and Shareholders' Equity		
Accounts payable	$1,060,000	$ 680,000
Notes payable	1,680,000	320,000
Note payable to Patrone Holdings Ltd.	—	240,000
Other liabilities	260,000	384,000
Common shares	1,540,000	1,060,000
Retained earnings	2,210,000	596,000
Total	$6,750,000	$3,280,000

Required

Prepare a consolidation work sheet.

Problem 16–6A

Accounting for a long-term
bond investment purchased
at a discount

2. Carrying value $1,019,500

Financial institutions such as insurance companies and pension plans hold large quantities of bond investments. Suppose Sun Life Insurance Company purchases $1,000,000 of 3.00 percent bonds of Hydro-Québec at 102.00 on July 1, 2014. These bonds pay interest on January 1 and July 1 each year. They mature on July 1, 2034. At December 31, 2014, the market price of the bonds is 101.00. Sun Life plans to hold these bonds to maturity. Disregard commissions.

Required

1. Journalize Sun Life's purchase of the bonds as a long-term investment in bonds on July 1, 2014 and accrual of interest revenue and amortization of the discount for six months at December 31, 2014. Assume the straight-line method is appropriate for amortizing the discount.
2. Calculate the carrying value of the Hydro-Québec bonds at December 31, 2014.

Problem 16–7A

Computing the cost of a bond
investment and journalizing its
transactions using the effective-
interest method of amortizing
a discount

Carrying amount at Dec. 31,
2015, $651,863

On December 31, 2014, when the market interest rate is 6 percent, an investor purchases $700,000 of Tennis Bubbles Ltd. 10-year, 5-percent bonds at issuance for $647,929. Interest is paid semi-annually. Assume that the investor plans to hold the investment to maturity. Disregard commissions.

Required

Prepare a schedule for amortizing the discount on the bond investment through December 31, 2015. The investor uses the effective-interest amortization method. Use Exhibit 15-4 on page 931 as a guide. Journalize the purchase on December 31, 2014, the first semiannual interest receipt on June 30, 2015, and the year-end interest receipt on December 31, 2015.

Problem 16–8A

Journalizing foreign-currency
transactions and reporting the
transaction gain or loss

1. Foreign-currency transaction
loss at Dec. 31, 2014, $9,400

Global Networking Corporation completed the following transactions:

2014

Dec. 1 Sold equipment on account to a Japanese company for $45,000. The exchange rate of the Japanese yen is $0.0113, and the Japanese company agrees to pay in Canadian dollars.

10 Purchased supplies on account from a U.S. company at a price of US$125,000. The exchange rate of the U.S. dollar is $1.06, and payment will be in U.S. dollars.

17 Sold equipment on account to an English firm for 220,000 British pounds. Payment will be in pounds, and the exchange rate of the pound is $1.61.

22 Collected from the Japanese company. The exchange rate of the yen has not changed since December 1.

31 Adjusted the accounts for changes in foreign-currency exchange rates. Current rates: U.S. dollar, $1.10; British pound, $1.59.

2015

Jan. 18 Paid the U.S. company. The exchange rate of the U.S. dollar is $1.08.

24 Collected from the English firm. The exchange rate of the British pound is $1.63.

Required

1. Record these transactions in Global Networking Corporation's general journal, and show how to report the transaction gain or loss on the income statement for the fiscal year ended December 31, 2014. For simplicity, use Sales Revenue as the credit.
2. How will what you have learned in this problem help you structure international transactions?

Problem 16–9A

Sparta Investments Ltd. had the following short-term investments in marketable securities at fair value at December 31, 2013:

Accounting for short-term
investments using the fair-value
method and long-term
investments in bonds
① ⑤

Dec. 31, 2014 fair-value
valuation allowance $107,727

Alberta Energy Co.	$310,000
Finning Ltd.	180,000
Canadian National Railway	285,000
Total short-term investments	$775,000

Sparta Investments Ltd. had the following investment transactions during 2014:

2014

Jan.	5	Purchased 5,000 shares (2 percent) of HHN Ltd. as a short-term investment. The shares were purchased at $51.00 and the commission was $500.
	31	HHN Ltd. reported net income of $7,000,000 and declared a cash dividend of $2,100,000.
Feb.	15	Received $42,000 from HHN Ltd. as a cash dividend.
Apr.	1	Purchased $400,000 (face value) of bonds at 99 as a long-term investment. The bonds pay 5 percent interest (2.5 percent semiannually) on October 1 and April 1. Sparta Investments Ltd. plans to hold the bonds until maturity in two years. The company chooses to use the straight-line method to amortize the discount.
Aug.	31	Received a 10-percent stock dividend from HHN Ltd.
Oct.	1	Received the interest on the bonds.
Nov.	1	HHN Ltd. declared and distributed a 2-for-1 stock split.
Dec.	15	Sold 4,000 shares of HHN Ltd. for $28.00 per share and the commission was $1,500.
	31	Recorded the adjustment for accrued interest on the bonds.
	31	The fair values of the investments were

Alberta Energy Co.	$ 280,000
Finning Ltd.	187,000
Canadian National Railway	290,000
HHN Ltd	288,000
Total short-term investments	$1,045,000

Required

Prepare the general journal entries required to record the transactions of 2014.

PROBLEMS (GROUP B)   MyAccountingLab

Problem 16–1B

Big Seven Insurance Ltd. owns numerous investments in the shares of other companies. Assume Big Seven Insurance Ltd. completed the following investment transactions:

Journalizing transactions
under the fair-value and
equity methods
① ② ③

2014

Feb.	12	Purchased 30,000 (total issued and outstanding common shares, 120,000) common shares of Earl Mfg. Ltd. at a cost of $2,550,000. Commissions on the purchase were $15,000.
Jul.	2	Purchased 6,000 additional Earl Mfg. Ltd. common shares at a cost of $88.00 per share. Commissions on the purchase were $400.
Aug.	9	Received the annual cash dividend of $2.00 per share on the Earl Mfg. Ltd. investment.
Oct.	16	Purchased 2,000 Excellence Ltd. common shares as a short-term investment, paying $63.00 per share plus brokerage commission of $500.

Nov.	30	Received the semiannual cash dividend of $2.50 per share on the Excellence Ltd. investment.
Dec.	31	Received the annual report from Earl Mfg. Ltd. Net income for the year was $1,160,000. Of this amount, Big Seven Insurance Ltd.'s proportion is 30 percent.
	31	The current market value of the Excellence shares is $140,000.
2015		
Jan.	14	Sold 5,000 Earl Mfg. Ltd. shares for $460,000, less commissions of $800.

Required

Record the transactions in the general journal of Big Seven Insurance Ltd. The company's year end is December 31.

Problem 16–2B

Applying the fair-value method and the equity method
① ② ③

The December 31, 2013, balance sheet of Fire Towing Corporation included

Investments—Associated Companies at Equity	$15,000,000

Suppose the company completed the following investment transactions during the year:

2014		
Mar.	2	Purchased 2,000 common shares as a short-term investment, paying $38.00 per share plus brokerage commission of $900.
	5	Purchased additional shares in an associated company at a cost of $1,600,000. Commissions on the purchase were $30,000.
Jul.	21	Received the semiannual cash dividend of $1.50 per share on the short-term investment purchased March 2.
Aug.	17	Received a cash dividend of $160,000 from an associated company.
Oct.	16	Sold 1,100 shares of the short-term investment (purchased on March 2) for $36.00 per share, less brokerage commission of $600.
Nov.	8	Purchased short-term investments for $310,000, plus brokerage commission of $5,000.
	17	Received a cash dividend of $280,000 from an associated company.
Dec.	31	Received annual reports from associated companies. Their total net income for the year was $6,900,000. Of this amount, Fire Towing's proportion is 24 percent.

Required

1. Record the transactions in the general journal of Fire Towing Corporation.
2. Post entries to the Equity Investments T-account and determine its balance at December 31, 2014.
3. Assume the beginning balance of Short-Term Investments was cost of $104,000. Post entries to the Short-Term Investments T-account and determine its balance at December 31, 2014.
4. Assuming the market value of the short-term investment portfolio is $425,000 at December 31, 2014, show how Fire Towing Corporation would report short-term investments and investments in associated companies on the ending balance sheet. (No journal entry is required.) Use the following format:

Cash	$XXX
Short-term investments, at fair value	
Accounts receivable (net)	XXX
Total current assets	XXX
Investments—Associated companies at equity	

Problem 16–3B

The accounting for equity investments changes with the amount of shares held. Hughes Ltd has a total of 35,000 shares outstanding. Complete the chart below to show the accounting differences between two different scenarios and how Soochow Corp should record the transaction and balances if it owns different amounts of Hughes Ltd shares as a long-term investment:

Compare accounting methods as share ownership percentage varies ① ② ③

	Case A: 3,800 Shares	Case B: 11,900 Shares
Which accounting method should be used for this long-term investment?		
Journal entry to record purchase of shares at $35 each. No commissions.		
Journal entry to recognize share of $40,000 in dividends declared and paid.		
Journal entry to recognize $75,000 in net income declared by Hughes Ltd.		
Journal entry to recognize the year-end market value of $34 per share.		
What is the balance in the investments account at year end?		

Problem 16–4B

Pisa Inc. paid $1,040,000 to acquire all the common shares of Sienna Ltd., and Sienna Ltd. owes Pisa Inc. $120,000 on a note payable. The fair market value of Sienna's net assets equalled the book value. Immediately after the purchase on June 30, 2014, the two companies' balance sheets were as shown below.

Excel Spreadsheet Template

Preparing a consolidated balance sheet; goodwill, no non-controlling interest ④

	Pisa Inc.	Sienna Ltd.
Assets		
Cash	$ 80,000	$ 72,000
Accounts receivable, net	288,000	144,000
Note receivable from Sienna Ltd.	120,000	—
Inventory	480,000	388,000
Investment in Sienna Ltd.	1,040,000	—
Property, plant, and equipment, net	608,000	720,000
Total	$2,616,000	$1,324,000
Liabilities and Shareholders' Equity		
Accounts payable	$ 192,000	$ 128,000
Notes payable	588,000	224,000
Note payable to Pisa Inc.	—	120,000
Other liabilities	204,000	12,000
Common shares	880,000	440,000
Retained earnings	752,000	400,000
Total	$2,616,000	$1,324,000

Required

Prepare a consolidation work sheet.

Excel Spreadsheet Template

Preparing a consolidated balance sheet; goodwill with non-controlling interest ④

Problem 16–5B

On March 22, 2014, Primary Investments Corp. paid $1,575,000 to purchase 70 percent of the common shares of Secondary Products Inc., and Primary Investments Corp. owes Secondary Products Inc. $400,000 on a note payable. The fair market value of Secondary

Products Inc.'s net assets equalled the book value. Immediately after the purchase, the two companies' balance sheets were as follows:

	Primary Investments Corp.	Secondary Products Inc.
Assets		
Cash	$ 570,000	$ 150,000
Accounts receivable, net	540,000	440,000
Note receivable from Primary Investments Corp.	—	400,000
Inventory	750,000	540,000
Investment in Secondary Products Inc.	1,575,000	—
Property, plant, and equipment, net	1,797,000	1,520,000
Total	$5,232,000	$3,050,000
Liabilities and Shareholders' Equity		
Accounts payable	$ 480,000	$ 420,000
Notes payable	1,077,000	270,000
Note payable to Secondary Products Inc.	400,000	—
Other liabilities	155,000	230,000
Non-controlling interest	—	—
Common shares	1,170,000	540,000
Retained earnings	1,950,000	1,590,000
Total	$5,232,000	$3,050,000

Required

Prepare a consolidation work sheet.

Problem 16–6B

Accounting for a bond investment purchased at a premium
⑤

Financial institutions such as insurance companies and pension plans hold large quantities of bond investments. Suppose Meridian Credit Union purchases $2,000,000 of 3.0-percent bonds of the Province of Manitoba at 105 on January 1, 2014. These bonds pay interest on January 1 and July 1 each year. They mature on January 1, 2024. Meridian plans to hold the bonds to maturity. Disregard commissions.

Required

1. Journalize Meridian's purchase of the bonds as a long-term investment on January 1, 2014, receipt of cash interest and amortization of premium on July 1, 2014, and accrual of interest revenue and amortization of premium at October 31, 2014, the fiscal year end. Assume the straight-line method is appropriate for amortizing the premium as there is no material difference from the effective-interest method.
2. Calculate the book value of the investment in the Province of Manitoba bonds at October 31, 2014.

Problem 16–7B

Computing the cost of a long-term bond investment and journalizing its transactions using the effective-interest method of amortizing a discount
⑤

Suppose, on December 31, 2014, when the market interest rate is 6 percent, an investor purchases $5,000,000 of Belmont Products Inc.'s six-year, 5.5-percent bonds at issuance for $4,873,675. Interest is payable semiannually. The investor plans to hold these bonds to maturity. Disregard commissions.

Required

Prepare a schedule for amortizing the discount on the bond investment through December 31, 2015. The investor uses the effective-interest amortization method. Use Exhibit 15-4 on page 931 as a guide. Journalize the purchase on December 31, 2014; the first semiannual interest receipt on June 30, 2015; and the year-end interest receipt on December 31, 2015.

Problem 16–8B

Suppose Pickel Corp. completed the following transactions:

Journalizing foreign-currency transactions and reporting the transaction gain or loss

2014

Dec. 4 Sold product on account to a Mexican company for $110,000. The exchange rate of the Mexican peso was $0.078, and the customer agreed to pay in Canadian dollars.

13 Purchased inventory on account from a U.S. company at a price of US$240,000. The exchange rate of the U.S. dollar was $1.05, and payment will be in U.S. dollars.

20 Sold goods on account to an English firm for 180,000 British pounds. Payment will be in pounds, and the exchange rate of the pound was $1.66.

27 Collected from the Mexican company. The exchange rate of the Mexican peso was $0.075.

31 Adjusted the accounts for changes in foreign-currency exchange rates. Current rates: U.S. dollar, $1.07; British pound, $1.65.

2015

Jan. 21 Paid the American company. The exchange rate of the U.S. dollar was $1.06.

Feb. 17 Collected from the English firm. The exchange rate of the British pound was $1.69.

Required

1. Record these transactions in Pickel Corp.'s general journal, and show how to report the transaction gain or loss on the income statement for the year ended December 31, 2014.
2. How will what you have learned in this problem help you structure international transactions?

Problem 16–9B

Portal Holdings Ltd. had the following short-term investments in marketable securities on December 31, 2013, at fair value and book value:

Accounting for short-term investments using the fair-value method; investments in bonds

Canadian Utilities Limited	$310,000
TELUS Communications Inc.	425,000
Talisman Energy Ltd.	160,000
Total short-term investments	$895,000

Portal Holdings Ltd. had the following investment transactions during 2014:

Jan. 5 Purchased 5,000 shares (2 percent) of Salmon Ltd. as a short-term investment. The shares were purchased at $50.00 and the commission was $300.

31 Salmon Ltd. reported net income of $1,500,000 and declared a cash dividend of $900,000.

Feb. 15 Received $18,000 from Salmon Ltd. as a cash dividend.

Apr. 1 Purchased $300,000 (face value) of bonds at 100 as a long-term investment. The bonds pay 6 percent interest (3 percent semiannually) on October 1 and April 1 and mature in two years.

Aug. 31 Received a 10-percent stock dividend from Salmon Ltd.

Oct. 1 Received the interest on the bonds.

Nov. 1 Salmon Ltd. declared and distributed a 2-for-1 stock split.

Dec. 15 Sold 3,300 shares of Salmon Ltd. at $48.00 and the commission was $200.

31 Recorded the adjustment for accrued interest on the bonds.

Dec.	31	The fair values of the investments were

Canadian Utilities Limited	$ 290,000
TELUS Communications Inc.	420,000
Salmon Ltd.	270,000
Talisman Energy Ltd.	175,000
Total short-term investments	$1,155,000

Required

Prepare the general journal entries required to record the transactions of 2014.

CHALLENGE PROBLEMS

Problem 16–1C

Accounting for ownership of
shares in another company
① ② ③ ④

The text lists general rules for accounting for long-term investments in the voting shares of another corporation. However, the management of the investing company may decide that, in their judgment, the rules do not apply in a particular situation.

Required

1. Identify a situation where an investing company that owns less than 20 percent might believe that the equity method was appropriate.
2. Identify a situation where an investing company that owns between 20 percent and 50 percent might believe that the fair-value method was appropriate.
3. Identify a situation where an investing company that owns more than 50 percent might believe that the fair-value method was appropriate.

Problem 16–2C

Accounting for foreign
operations
⑥

Canadian exporters are pleased when the Canadian dollar weakens against the U.S. dollar, while the federal and provincial ministers of finance are likely not happy when this happens.

Required

Explain why a weakening Canadian dollar makes Canadian exporters happy. Why would a weaker Canadian dollar make the finance ministers unhappy?

Extending Your Knowledge

DECISION PROBLEMS

Understanding the fair-value and
equity methods of accounting
for investments
① ② ③

Margaret Joyce is the owner of Trickle Music Holdings Ltd., a newly formed company whose year end is December 31. The company made two investments during the first week of January 2014. Both investments are to be held for at least the next five years as investments. Information about each of the investments follows:

a. Trickle Music Holdings Ltd. purchased 30 percent of the common shares of Old Times Ltd. for its book value of $600,000. During the year ended December 31, 2014, Old Times Ltd. earned $240,000 and paid a total dividend of $150,000.

b. Trickle Music Holdings Ltd. purchased 10 percent of the common shares of Mountain Music Inc. for its book value of $150,000. During the year ended December 31, 2014, Mountain Music Inc. paid Trickle Music Holdings Ltd. a dividend of $10,000. Mountain Music Inc. earned a profit of $225,000 for that period. The market value of Trickle Music Holdings Ltd.'s investment in Mountain Music Inc. was $204,000 at December 31, 2014.

1044 Part 3 Accounting for Partnerships and Corporate Transactions

Joyce has come to you as her auditor to ask you how to account for the investments. Trickle Music Holdings Ltd. has never had such investments before. You attempt to explain the proper accounting to her by indicating that different accounting methods apply to different situations.

Required

Help Joyce understand by

1. Describing the methods of accounting applicable to investments such as these.
2. Identifying which method should be used to account for the investments in Old Times Ltd. and Mountain Music Inc.

FINANCIAL STATEMENT CASES

Financial Statement Case 1

Gildan Activewear Inc.'s financial statements appear in Appendix A at the end of this book and on MyAccountingLab.

Investments and foreign-currency transactions

Required

1. The financial statements are labelled "consolidated." What evidence can you find in the financial statements that reveals how Gildan Activewear Inc. accounts for its subsidiaries?
2. How does Gildan Activewear Inc. account for goodwill?
3. Does Gildan Activewear Inc. have any foreign-currency transactions? How do you know?

Financial Statement Case 2

The Rainmaker Entertainment Inc. December 31, 2011, financial statements appear on MyAccountingLab.

Investments and foreign-currency transactions

Required

1. What information can you find about Rainmaker Entertainment Inc.'s policy on foreign-currency transactions?
2. Does Rainmaker Entertainment Inc. have any subsidiaries as of December 31, 2011? How can you tell?
3. Does the company have any firms over which it exerts *significant influence*? If so, how is it accounted for? How do you know?

Comprehensive Problem for Part 3

1. ACCOUNTING FOR CORPORATE TRANSACTIONS

Greyhawk Investments Inc.'s articles of incorporation authorize the company to issue 1,000,000 common shares and 400,000 $9.00 preferred shares. During the first quarter of operations, Greyhawk Investments Inc. completed the following selected transactions:

2014
Oct. 1   Issued 50,000 common shares for cash of $30.00 per share.
      4   Signed a capital lease for equipment. The lease requires a down payment of $600,000, plus 20 quarterly lease payments of $60,000. The present value of the future lease payments is $981,086 at an annual interest rate of 8 percent.

Oct.	6	Issued 2,000 preferred shares, receiving cash of $300,000.
	22	Purchased land from the Province of Manitoba for $300,000 cash.
	30	Purchased 5,000 (25 percent) of the outstanding common shares of Big Sky Ltd. as a long-term investment, $270,000.
Nov.	1	Issued $1,000,000 of 6-percent, 10-year bonds payable at 98.
	16	Purchased short-term investments in the common shares of TELUS Communications Inc., $85,000, and ATCO Ltd., $87,000.
	19	Purchased $1,000,000 of inventory on account. Greyhawk Investments Inc. uses a perpetual inventory system.
	20	Repurchased 2,000 of the company's common shares at $15.00 per share for cancellation.
Dec.	1	Received cash dividends of $1,800 on the TELUS investment.
	16	Sold 1,000 of the company's common shares for cash of $24.00 per share.
	29	Received a report from Big Sky Ltd. indicating the combined net income for November and December was $25,000.
	30	Sold merchandise on account, $2,148,000. Cost of the goods was $945,000. Operating expenses totalled $557,000, with $498,000 of this amount paid in cash. Greyhawk Investments Inc. uses a perpetual inventory system.
	31	Accrued interest and amortized discount (straight-line method) on the bonds payable.
	31	Accrued interest on the capital lease liability.
	31	Amortized the equipment acquired by the capital lease. The company uses the double-declining-balance method.
	31	Market values of short-term investments: TELUS Communications Inc. shares, $84,000 and ATCO Ltd. shares, $93,000.
	31	Accrued income tax expense of $240,000. Credit the Income Tax Payable account.
	31	Closed all revenues, expenses, and losses to Retained Earnings in a single closing entry.
	31	Declared a quarterly cash dividend of $2.25 per share on the preferred shares. Record date is January 11, 2015, with payment scheduled for January 19.

Required

1. Record these transactions in the general journal. Explanations are not required. Disregard commissions.
2. Prepare a single-step income statement for the quarter ended December 31, 2014, including earnings per share. (Hint: Use T-accounts to calculate account balances.)
3. Report the liabilities and the shareholders' equity as they would appear on the balance sheet at December 31, 2014.

JUST CHECKING Solutions for Chapter 16

1. a. $18.70 per share ($18,700 ÷ 1,000 shares; the commission is expensed, not included in the price per share)
   b. $9.35 per share ($18,700 ÷ 2,000 shares)
   c. $8.00 per share ($16,000 ÷ 2,000 shares)
   d. $10.00 per share ($20,000 ÷ 2,000 shares; the commission is expensed, not included in the price per share)

2.

2013			
Sept. 30	Short-Term Investments	43,200	
	Commission Expense	125	
	Cash		43,325
	Purchased 1,200 common shares of Betam Ltd. at $36.00 per share (1,200 × $36.00 = $43,200) plus commission of $125.		

Dec. 21	Cash		108	
	Dividend Revenue			108
	Received $0.09 per share cash dividend			
	(1,200 × $0.09) on Betam Ltd. common shares.			
Dec. 31	Unrealized Loss on			
	Fair-Value Adjustment		3,000	
	Fair-Value Valuation			
	Allowance			3,000
	Adjusted Betam Ltd. investment to fair value			
	[1,200 × ($36.00 − $33.50)].			

2014

Apr. 13	Cash		37,080	
	Loss on Sale of Investment		3,000	
	Fair-Value Valuation			
	Allowance		3,000	
	Commission Expense		120	
	Short-Term Investments			43,200
	Sold all the Betam Ltd. common shares held for $31.00 per share. Carrying value of the common shares sold was $40,200 ($43,200 − $3,000). Loss on sale was $3,000 (1,200 × $31.00 − $40,200). Commission expense was $120.			

3. Determine the unrealized gain or loss in the carrying value for each investment in the portfolio. Then create the journal entry for any change from carrying value to fair value, or market value.

Shares	Carrying Value	Current Fair Value
All Seasons Hotels	$ 88,000	$ 97,000
Tangerine Manufacturing Corp.	140,000	124,000
Prairie Grocers Inc.	74,000	76,000
Totals	$302,000	$297,000

Report the investments at fair value, $297,000, and report an unrealized loss of $5,000 ($297,000 − $302,000) in the non-operating section of the income statement. The adjusting journal entry would be:

Unrealized Loss on Fair-Value Adjustment		5,000	
Fair-Value Valuation Allowance			5,000*
Adjusted short-term investments to fair value.			

*Since most companies account for each investment separately, the $5,000 total gain is calculated as:

All Seasons Hotels: unrealized gain	$ 9,000
Tangerine Manufacturing Corp.: unrealized loss	(16,000)
Prairie Grocers Inc.: unrealized gain	2,000
Total (unrealized loss)	$ (5,000)

4. **2013**

Oct. 16	Long-Term Investments		450,000	
	Commission Expense		425	
	Cash			450,425
	Purchased 10,000 common shares of Levell Inc. at $45.00 per share (10,000 × $45.00 = $450,000) plus commission of $425.			
Dec. 1	Cash		20,000	
	Dividend Revenue			20,000
	Received $2.00 per share cash dividend (10,000 × $2.00) on Levell Inc. common shares.			
Dec. 31	Fair-Value Valuation			
	Allowance		10,000	
	Unrealized Gain on			
	Fair-Value Adjustment			10,000
	Adjusted Levell Inc. investment to fair value [10,000 × ($46.00 − $45.00)].			

2014

Feb. 15	Cash		244,740	
	Commission Expense		260	
	Short-Term Investments			225,000
	Fair-Value Valuation			
	Allowance			5,000
	Gain on Sale of Investment			15,000
	Sold 5,000 of the Levell Inc. common shares held for $49.00 per share. Carrying value of the common shares sold was $230,000 [50% × ($450,000 + $10,000)]. Gain on sale was $15,000 (5,000 × $49.00 − $230,000). Commission expense was $260.			

5. Recall that for equity investments, the general rules are:
Less than 20% —> Fair-value
20% to 50% —> Equity
Greater than 50% —> Consolidation

a. An investment subject to significant influence is usually accounted for by the equity method.
b. Fair-value method
c. Consolidation

6. For a 40% equity-method investment, the Investment in Investee Ltd. Common Shares account includes:
The cost of the investment + 40% of the investee's net income − 40% of the investee's cash dividends

Remember that cash dividends received from an equity-method investment are credited to Investment in Investee Ltd. Common Shares, *not to Dividend Revenue.*

a.
Investment in Investee Ltd.			
Common Shares		140,000	
Cash			140,000
To purchase 40 percent investment in Investee Ltd. common shares.			

6. b. Investment in Investee Ltd.
        Common Shares   72,000
            Equity-Method Investment
                Revenue   72,000
        To record 40 percent of Investee Ltd. net income
        ($180,000 × 0.40).

    c. Cash   56,000
            Investment in Investee Ltd.
                Common Shares   56,000
        To record receipt of 40 percent of Investee Ltd.
        cash dividend ($140,000 × 0.40).

    d. Cash   160,000
            Investment in Investee Ltd.
                Common Shares   156,000
                Gain on Sale of Investment   4,000
        Sold investment in Investee Ltd. common shares
        ($140,000 + $72,000 − $56,000).

7. a. Parent company only.
    b. The shareholders' equity of the consolidated entity excludes the shareholders' equity of a subsidiary because the shareholders' equity of the consolidated entity is that of the parent only, and because the subsidiary's equity and the parent company's investment balance represent the same resources. Therefore, including them both would amount to double-counting.
    c. Non-controlling or minority interest—reported on A Ltd.'s (parent) consolidated balance sheet between the liabilities and shareholders' equity sections.
    d. Goodwill—reported on C Ltd.'s (parent) consolidated balance sheet as an asset.

8. For a consolidation work sheet: Eliminate all parent-and-subsidiary intercompany transactions to avoid double-counting items when consolidating. Check for goodwill by comparing the net assets purchased (represented by the subsidiary's shareholders' equity balance) with the amount paid. Check for non-controlling interest by verifying whether less than 100% of the subsidiary's common shares were purchased.

	Parent Corp.	Subsidiary Corp.	Eliminations Debit	Eliminations Credit	Consol. Amounts
Assets					
Cash	28,000	36,000			64,000
Note receivable from Parent Corp.	—	60,000		(a) 60,000	—
Investment in Subsidiary Corp.	400,000	—		(b)400,000	—
Goodwill	—	—	(b) 60,000*		60,000
Other assets	432,000	396,000			828,000
Total	860,000	492,000			952,000
Liabilities and Shareholders' Equity					
Accounts payable	60,000	32,000			92,000
Notes payable	60,000	120,000	(a) 60,000		120,000
Common shares	560,000	240,000	(b)240,000		560,000
Retained earnings	180,000	100,000	(b)100,000		180,000
Total	860,000	492,000	460,000	460,000	952,000

*$60,000 = $400,000 − ($240,000 + $100,000)

9. a. Cana Corp. should account for the bonds at amortized cost.
    b. 2014
        Apr. 30 Investment in Bonds   97,500
                     Cash   97,500
                 Purchased long-term Starr Limited bond
                 investment ($100,000 × 0.975).

        Oct. 31 Cash   2,000
                     Interest Revenue   2,000
                 Received semi-annual interest
                 ($100,000 × 0.04 × 6/12).

        Oct. 31 Investment in Bonds   227
                     Interest Revenue   227
                 To amortize discount on bond investment for
                 six months [($100,000 − $97,500) ÷ 66 × 6].

        Dec. 31 Interest Receivable   667
                     Interest Revenue   667
                 To accrue interest revenue for two months
                 ($100,000 × 0.04 × 2/12).

        Dec. 31 Investment in Bonds   76
                     Interest Revenue   76
                 To amortize discount on bond investment for
                 two months [($100,000 − $97,500) ÷ 66 × 2].

    c. **Balance Sheet at December 31, 2014:**

Current assets:	
Interest receivable	$667
Total current assets	x,xxx
Investment in bonds—Note 3	97,803

        Note 3: Investment in Bonds
        Long-term bond investments are reported at amortized cost. At December 31, 2014, the current market value of long-term investments in bonds was $98,250.

10.

June 1	Investment in Bonds		46,490	
	Cash			46,490
	To record purchase of bond held as a long-term investment.			
Dec. 1	Investment in Bonds		1,000	
	Interest Revenue			1,000
	To accrue interest revenue for six months ($50,000 × 0.04 × 6/12).			
Dec. 1	Investment in Bonds		395	
	Interest Revenue			395
	To amortize bond discount using effective-interest method according to the table provided.			

11. a. Foreign-currency translation gain—the payment is made in fewer Canadian dollars than when the purchase was recorded.
   b. Foreign-currency translation gain—the payment is received in more Canadian dollars than when the sale was recorded.
   c. Foreign-currency translation loss—the payment is made in more Canadian dollars than when the purchase was recorded.
   d. Foreign-currency translation loss—the payment is received in fewer Canadian dollars than when the sale was recorded.

12. a. The Canadian dollar strengthened against the euro in this situation—the Canadian company was able to buy more euros on the payment date with one Canadian dollar.
   b. The Canadian dollar weakened against the krone in this situation—the Canadian company was able to buy fewer krone on the receipt date with one Canadian dollar.
   c. The Canadian dollar weakened against the yen in this situation—the Canadian company was able to buy fewer yen on the payment date with one Canadian dollar.
   d. The Canadian dollar strengthened against the U.S. dollar in this situation—the Canadian company was able to buy more U.S. dollars on the receipt date with one Canadian dollar.

13.

May 16	Accounts Receivable		142,648	
	Sales Revenue			142,648
	To record a sale on account (80,000 × $1.7831).			
June 19	Cash		70,456	
	Foreign-Currency Transaction Loss		868	
	Accounts Receivable			71,324
	To record receipt of half the amount receivable (40,000 × $1.7614).			
July 16	Cash		71,168	
	Foreign-Currency Transaction Loss		156	
	Accounts Receivable			71,324
	To record receipt of the remaining amount receivable (40,000 × $1.7792).			

Overall, Zippy had a net foreign-currency loss of $1,024 ($868 + $156).

14. Under IFRS, most short-term financial instruments must be measured at fair value. Under ASPE, actively traded equity securities (shares) are valued at fair value. For any other short-term investments where there is no active market, the cost method can be used under ASPE.

15. IFRS and ASPE both require that investments where there is significant influence be accounted for by the equity method. ASPE additionally permits the use of the cost method to account for significantly influenced investments.

16. For investments in subsidiaries, IFRS requires that the parent prepare consolidated financial statements that include the financial results of its subsidiaries. Under ASPE, the *Handbook* emphasizes consolidation, but the parent is allowed to report its investment in subsidiaries using either the cost or equity method as well.

17 The Cash Flow Statement

KEY QUESTIONS	LEARNING OBJECTIVES
What is a cash flow statement?	**1** Identify the purposes of the cash flow statement
What are the main cash flows in a business?	**2** Identify cash flows from operating, investing, and financing activities
What is the direct method, and how is it used to prepare a cash flow statement?	**3** Prepare a cash flow statement by the direct method
What are the cash effects of different business transactions?	**4** Compute the cash effects of a wide variety of business transactions
What is the indirect method, and how is it used to prepare a cash flow statement?	**5** Prepare a cash flow statement by the indirect method
How does IFRS affect the cash flow statement?	**6** Describe the impact on the cash flow statement of international financial reporting standards (IFRS)

Manulife Centre

M anulife Financial Corporation is a large Canada-based financial services group with principal operations in Asia, Canada, and the United States. The company operates as Manulife Financial in Canada and Asia, and primarily as John Hancock in the United States. The company offers insurance to individuals and businesses, employee benefits plans to employers, as well as wealth-management products and services, including mutual funds, guaranteed investment certificates, savings accounts, and other banking products. Funds under management by Manulife Financial and its subsidiaries were $500 billion at December 31, 2011.

The income statement indicates to users whether an enterprise is profitable; the cash flow statement indicates whether or not the enterprise is generating enough cash to pay the bills. During 2010, Manulife Financial suffered a net loss of $1.526 billion and a decline in its cash flows of $6.619 billion. Since the company had cash of more than $18 billion at the beginning of 2010, it was able to start 2011 with cash of $11.322 billion. Results in 2011 were better: net income was $245 million and cash flows improved to $766 million. The improvement in 2011 was due in part to increasing the prices on new products, and expanding the company's equity-market and interest-rate hedging programs to reduce the effects of interest-rate changes in the financial markets.

Companies like Manulife Financial Corporation raise cash in different ways. As we discussed in earlier chapters, a company can raise cash by issuing shares if it is a corporation or by issuing debt in the form of bonds. Manulife raised cash of $391 million by issuing preferred shares during 2011. However, a company's most important ongoing source of cash to run its business must come from successfully operating its business. Manulife Financial's $766 million increase in cash flows during 2011 includes $9.333 billion of cash flows from operations, a good sign that shows the company is generating enough cash to pay its bills.[1]

---

[1] Manulife Financial Corporation *2011 Annual Report*, p. 2 and p. 4.

①	②	③	④	⑤	⑥
Identify the purposes of the cash flow statement	Identify cash flows from operating, investing, and financing activities	Prepare a cash flow statement by the direct method	Compute the cash effects of a wide variety of business transactions	Prepare a cash flow statement by the indirect method	Describe the impact on the cash flow statements of international financial reporting standards (IFRS)
What is a cash flow statement? page 1054	*What are the main cash flows in a business?* page 1056	*What is the direct method, and how is it used to prepare a cash flow statement?* page 1062	*What are the cash effects of different business transactions?* page 1067	*What is the indirect method, and how is it used to prepare a cash flow statement?* page 1076	*How does IFRS affect the cash flow statement?* page 1082
The Cash Flow Statement: Basic Concepts, page 1054	Operating, Investing, and Financing Activities, page 1056	The Cash Flow Statement: The Direct Method, page 1062	Computing Individual Amounts for the Cash Flow Statement, page 1067	The Cash Flow Statement: The Indirect Method, page 1076	The Impact on the Cash Flow Statement of International Financial Reporting Standards, page 1082
Purpose of the Cash Flow Statement, page 1055	Noncash Investing and Financing Activities, page 1059				
	Measuring Cash Adequacy: Free Cash Flow, page 1060				
	Format of the Cash Flow Statement, page 1060				
		MyAccountingLab **Animation:** Creating Cash Flow Statements by the Direct Method		MyAccountingLab **Animation:** Creating Cash Flow Statements by the Indirect Method	

MyAccountingLab

- Chapter 17: DemoDoc covering Operating, Investing, and Financing Activities
- Chapter 17: Student PowerPoint Slides
- Chapter 17: Audio Chapter Summary

All MyAccountingLab resources can be found in the Chapter Resources section and the Multimedia Library.

The **Summary** for Chapter 17 appears on page 1085.
Accounting Vocabulary with definitions appears on page 1087.

The cash flow statement, a required financial statement,

reports where cash came from and how the company spent it. Like the income statement and the balance sheet, the cash flow statement provides important information about an organization. For Manulife Financial Corporation, the results seem positive overall because operations are generating positive cash flow, especially when compared to the previous year when the company suffered huge losses in both net income and cash flow (see Exhibit 17–1). Positive cash flow from operations is a positive signal about any company because operations should be the main source of cash. Manulife ended 2011 with a positive cash flow of $776 million; however, the net income for 2011 was only $245 million and it could have been a loss if the company had not improved operations by raising its product prices and improving its hedging in 2011.

MANULIFE FINANCIAL CORPORATION
Consolidated Statements of Cash Flows (Adapted)
For the Years Ended December 31, 2011 and 2010

	(in millions)	
Cash flows from operating activities:	**2011**	**2010**
Net income	$ 245	$ (1,526)
Add transactions not involving cash outlays (e.g., amortization)	10,235	11,991
Change in noncash working capital	(1,147)	1,094
Net cash inflow from operating activities	9,333	11,559
Cash flows from investing activities:		
Purchases and mortgage advances	(82,830)	(76,090)
Disposals and repayments	71,851	54,533
Changes in investment broker net receivables and payables	1,757	83
Net cash decrease from purchase of subsidiaries	—	(28)
Net cash outflow from investing activities	(9,222)	(21,502)
Cash flows from financing activities:		
Issue of long-term debt, net	—	2,024
Repayment of long-term debt	(396)	(1)
Issue of capital instruments, net	547	—
Repayment of capital instruments	(550)	—
Changes in bank deposits, net	1,603	1,574
Shareholder dividends paid in cash	(717)	(691)
Common shares issued, net	2	3
Preferred shares issued, net	391	—
Other financing activities	(225)	415
Net cash inflow from financing activities	655	3,324
Cash and cash equivalents:		
Cash flow from operating, investing, and financing activities	766	(6,619)
Effect of exchange rate on cash and cash equivalents	198	(337)
Net change in cash and cash equivalents	964	(6,956)
Cash and cash equivalents, beginning of year	11,849	18,805
Cash and cash equivalents, end of year	$12,813	$11,849

We begin this chapter by explaining the cash flow statement format preferred by the accounting standards for private enterprises (ASPE) described in the *CICA Handbook*. It is very clear and is called the *direct method*. We end the chapter with the more common format of the cash flow statement, the *indirect method*. The method used by Manulife Financial Corporation in the chapter-opening vignette is the indirect method. By the time you have worked through this chapter, you will be better able to analyze the cash flows of any company you might encounter.

The cash flow statement reports where cash came from and how it was spent. We learned in Chapter 1 (pp. 23–24) that the cash flow statement is a required financial statement. Like the other two major financial reports—the income statement and the balance sheet—the cash flow statement enables investors and creditors to make informed decisions about a company. The income statement might present one picture of the company: relatively high income; while the cash flow statement might present a different picture: not enough cash. This example underscores the challenge of financial analysis: that a company's signals may point in different directions. Astute investors and creditors know what to look for; increasingly they are focusing on cash flows.

The Cash Flow Statement: Basic Concepts

LO ①
What is a cash flow statement?

The balance sheet reports a company's cash balance at the end of the period. By comparing the beginning and ending balance sheets, you can tell whether cash increased or decreased during the period. However, the balance sheet does not indicate *why* the cash balance changed. The income statement reports revenues, expenses, and net income (or net loss)—clues about the sources and uses of cash—but does not tell *why* cash increased or decreased.

The **cash flow statement** reports the entity's **cash flows**—cash receipts and cash payments—during the period.

- It shows where cash came from (receipts) and how cash was spent (payments).
- It reports why cash increased or decreased during the period.
- It covers a period of time and is dated "For the Month Ended xxx" or "For the Year Ended xxx," the same as the income statement.

The cash flow statement is a summary of all the transactions that affected the Cash account for a period of time. Exhibit 17–2 shows the Cash T-account and some of the types of transactions that affect its balance during a period.

Exhibit 17–3 illustrates the relationships among the balance sheet, the income statement, and the cash flow statement, and the time periods covered by each.

EXHIBIT 17–2 | Some Transactions that Affect the Cash Account

Cash (and cash equivalents)	
Beginning cash balance	Payments to suppliers
Collections from customers	Payments to employees
Interest received on notes	Payments for income tax
Issuance of shares	Payments for assets
Issuance of bonds	Loan to another company
Receipt of dividends	Payment of dividends
	Repayment of a bank loan
	Repayment of long-term loans
Ending cash balance	

KEY POINTS

The end of the day on December 31 of this year is considered to be the same as the beginning of the day on January 1 of next year.

EXHIBIT 17–3 | Timing of the Financial Statements

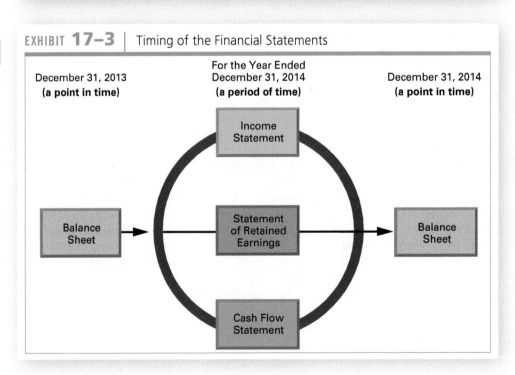

Purpose of the Cash Flow Statement

How do people use cash flow information? The cash flow statement helps to

1. *Predict future cash flows.* It takes cash to pay the bills or take advantage of opportunities. In many cases, past cash receipts and cash payments help predict future cash flows.

2. *Evaluate management decisions.* Wise decisions lead to profits and strong cash flows. Unwise decisions often bring bankruptcy. One of the areas that the cash flow statement reports on is the investments a company is making in itself and in outside companies so shareholders and other interested financial-statement users can assess management's investment decisions.

3. *Determine the company's ability to pay dividends and debts.* Shareholders are interested in receiving dividends on their investments in the company's shares. Creditors want to receive their principal and interest amounts on time. The cash flow statement helps investors and creditors predict whether the business can make dividend and debt payments.

4. *Show the relationship between net income and cash flow.* Usually, cash and net income move together. High profits tend to lead to increases in cash, and vice versa. However, a company's cash balance can decrease when net income is high, and cash can increase when net income is low. The failures of companies that were earning net income but had insufficient cash have pointed to the need for cash flow information.

It is clear that cash flows are important to a company's survival. A cash shortage is usually the most pressing problem of a struggling organization. Abundant cash allows a company to expand, invest in research and development, and hire the best employees. How, then, do investors (and their representatives, financial analysts) and creditors use cash flow information for decision making?

Neither cash flow data, net income information, balance sheet figures, nor the financial statement notes tell investors all they need to know about a company. Decision making is much more complex than inserting a few numbers into a simple formula. To decide whether to invest in a company's shares, investors analyze:

- A company's financial statements
- Articles in the financial press
- Data about the company's industry
- Predictions about the world and local economy

To evaluate a loan request, a bank loan officer may interview a company's top managers to decide whether they are trustworthy and whether their projections for the future of the company are reasonable. Both investors and creditors are interested mainly in a company's future. They want to make predictions about a company's future net income and future cash flows.

It has been said that cash-flow data help to spot losers better than winners. This is often true. When a company's business is booming, profits are high and cash flows are usually improving. In almost all cases, a negative cash flow from operations warrants investigation. A cash downturn in a *single* year is not necessarily a danger signal. But negative cash flows for two or more *consecutive* years may lead to bankruptcy. Without cash flow from operations, a business simply cannot survive.

You may ask, "Can't the business raise money by issuing shares or by borrowing?" The answer is often no, because if operations cannot generate enough cash, then investors will not buy the company's shares. Bankers will not lend it money. *Over the long run, if a company cannot generate cash from operations, it is doomed.*

KEY POINTS

A business operates for profit, and it must operate profitably to be a going concern. Information about net income (using the accrual basis) is found on the income statement. However, a business must have cash to pay suppliers, employees, and so on. Information about cash flows is found on the cash flow statement. A company can manipulate numbers on the income statement to some degree with estimates and accruals, but cash amounts are difficult to manipulate. The cash flow statement is very reliable when it is created correctly.

Cash and Cash Equivalents

On the financial statements, *Cash* has a broader meaning than just cash on hand and cash in the bank. It includes **cash equivalents** (discussed in Chapter 8), which are highly liquid short-term investments convertible into cash with little delay. Because their liquidity is one reason for holding these investments, they are treated as cash. Examples of cash equivalents are investments in money-market funds and investments in Government of Canada Treasury Bills. Businesses invest their extra cash in these types of liquid assets to earn interest income rather than let cash remain idle. Throughout this chapter, the term *cash* refers to cash and cash equivalents.

✓ JUST CHECKING

1. Refer to the Manulife Financial Corporation cash flow statements illustrated in Exhibit 17–1 and answer the following questions:

   a. What is the period of time covered by Manulife Financial Corporation's cash flow statements?

   b. What was Manulife Financial Corporation's net income during the periods covered by the cash flow statement?

   c. In the "investing activities" section, on what did Manulife Financial Corporation spend most of its cash? How much cash did the company spend on this category of investment? (Note that cash outflows, or cash payments, are indicated by dollar amounts in parentheses.)

   d. In the "financing activities" section, on what did Manulife Financial Corporation spend most of its cash? How much cash did the company spend on this category?

   e. What amount of cash and cash equivalents did Manulife Financial Corporation report on its balance sheet at December 31, 2011, and on December 31, 2010?

2. Indicate whether each of the following items would increase (I) or decrease (D) the balance of cash and cash equivalents.

   ___ Payment of dividends   ___ Payments for assets

   ___ Issuance of shares   ___ Repayment of a bank loan

   ___ Payment to employees   ___ Issuance of bonds

   ___ Collections from customers

Just Checking Solutions appear at the end of this chapter and on MyAccountingLab.

Operating, Investing, and Financing Activities

LO ②
What are the main cash flows in a business?

KEY POINTS

Once the business is up and running, *operations* are the most important activity, followed by *investing activities* and *financing activities*. Investing activities are generally more important than financing activities because *what* a company invests in is usually more important than how the company finances the investment.

A business engages in three basic categories of business activities:

- Operating activities
- Investing activities
- Financing activities

The cash flow statement has a section for each category of cash flows. Here is what each section reports:

Operating Activities

- Create revenues, expenses, gains, and losses
- Affect net income on the income statement
- Affect current assets and current liabilities on the balance sheet
- Are the most important category of cash flows because they reflect the day-to-day operations that determine the future of an organization

Investing Activities

- Increase and decrease long-term assets, such as computers, software, land, buildings, and equipment, and purchases and sales of these long-term assets
- Include purchases and sales of long-term share investments
- Include long-term notes receivable in the form of loans to others as well as the collection of long-term loans
- Next most important after operating activities

Financing Activities

- Increase and decrease long-term liabilities and owners' equity
- Include issuing shares, paying dividends, and repurchasing a company's own shares
- Include borrowing money and paying off loans
- Are least important of all the activities because what a company invests in is usually more important than how the company finances the investment

Exhibit 17–4 shows the relationships among operating, investing, and financing cash flows and the various parts of the balance sheet.

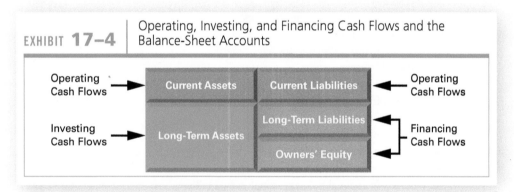

| EXHIBIT **17–4** | Operating, Investing, and Financing Cash Flows and the Balance-Sheet Accounts |

As you can see, operating cash flows affect the current accounts. Investing cash flows affect the long-term assets. Financing cash flows affect long-term liabilities and owners' equity.

The cash flow statement in Exhibit 17–5 shows how cash receipts and payments are divided into operating activities, investing activities, and financing activities for Capilano Ltd., a small manufacturer of glass products and the company we will refer to throughout this chapter. Exhibit 17–5 shows that each set of activities includes both cash inflows (receipts) and cash outflows (payments). Outflows have parentheses to indicate that payments are subtracted. Each section of the statement reports a net cash inflow (net cash receipt) or a net cash outflow (net cash payment).

Exhibit 17–5 shows that Capilano Ltd.'s net cash inflow from operating activities is $168,000. A large positive cash inflow from operations is a good sign about a company. *In the long run, operations must be the main source of a business's cash.* The acquisition of long-term assets dominates Capilano Ltd.'s investing activities, which produce a net cash outflow of $612,000. Financing activities of Capilano Ltd. brought in net cash receipts of $400,000. One thing to watch among financing activities is whether the business is borrowing heavily. Excessive borrowing has been the downfall of many companies. Overall, Capilano Ltd.'s cash decreased by $44,000 during 2014. The company began the year with cash of $101,000 and ended with $57,000.

Each of these categories of activities—operating, investing, and financing— includes both cash receipts and cash payments, as shown in Exhibit 17–6. The exhibit lists the more common cash receipts and cash payments that appear on the cash flow statement. (All amounts in the exhibit are in thousands of dollars.)

EXHIBIT **17–5** | Cash Flow Statement (Direct Method for Operating Activities)

CAPILANO LTD.
Cash Flow Statement
For the Year Ended December 31, 2014

Cash flows from operating activities		(In thousands)
Receipts:		
Collections from customers	$650	
Interest received on notes receivable	24	
Dividends received on investments in shares	22	
Total cash receipts		$696
Payments:		
To suppliers for merchandise for resale	(270)	
To suppliers for operating expenses	(44)	
To employees	(140)	
For interest	(38)	
For income tax	(36)	
Total cash payments		(528)
Net cash inflow from operating activities		168
Cash flows from investing activities		
Acquisition of property, plant, and equipment, and intangible assets	(735)	
Loan to another company	(26)	
Cash received from selling property, plant, and equipment, and intangible assets	149	
Net cash outflow from investing activities		(612)
Cash flows from financing activities		
Cash received from issuing common shares	242	
Cash received from issuing long-term notes payable	226	
Payment of long-term debt*	(27)	
Payment of dividends	(41)	
Net cash inflow from financing activities		400
Net increase (decrease) in cash and cash equivalents		(44)
Cash and cash equivalents at beginning of 2014		101
Cash and cash equivalents at end of 2014		$ 57

* This would also include the current portion of long-term debt payable, which is NIL in this case.

LEARNING TIPS

When preparing the cash flow statement, compare beginning and ending cash. Has it increased or decreased? An increase during the period means the statement will show a "net increase in cash."

Discontinued Operations

Just as discontinued operations are to be shown separately on the income statement, they are to be shown separately on the cash flow statement. The cash inflow or outflow resulting from discontinued operations should be shown as part of operating, investing, or financing activities, as is appropriate.

Interest and Dividends as Operating Activities

You may be puzzled by the inclusion of cash receipts of interest and dividends as operating activities. After all, these cash receipts result from investing activities. Interest comes from investments in loans, and dividends come from investments in shares. Equally puzzling is listing the payment of interest as part of operations. Interest expense results from borrowing money—a financing activity. *However, interest and dividends are included as operating activities because they affect the computation of net income.* Interest revenue and dividend revenue increase net income, and interest expense decreases income. Therefore, cash receipts of interest

EXHIBIT **17–6** | Cash Receipts and Payments on the Cash Flow Statement

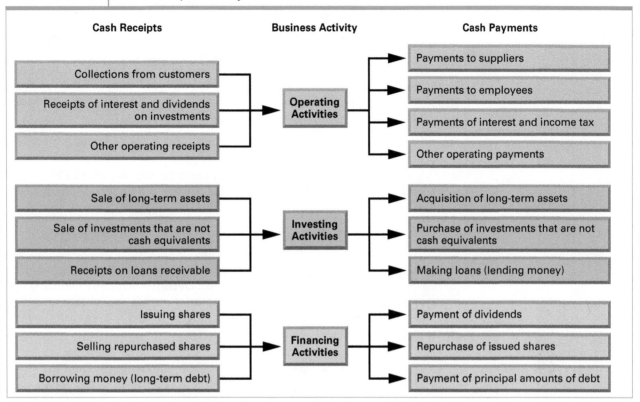

and dividends and cash payments of interest are reported as operating activities on the cash flow statement.

In contrast, note that dividend payments are reported as a financing activity. This is because they do not enter into the computation of net income but rather are payments to the entity's shareholders, who finance the business by purchasing its shares.

Noncash Investing and Financing Activities

Companies make investments that do not require cash. For example, they may issue a note payable to buy land, or they may pay off a loan by issuing shares. Our examples thus far included none of these transactions.

Suppose Capilano Ltd. issued common shares with a stated value of $730,000 to acquire a warehouse. Capilano Ltd. would make this journal entry:

Warehouse	730,000	
Common Shares		730,000

Since this transaction has no net effect on the cash flow statement, Paragraph 1540.48 in Part II of the *CICA Handbook* requires that noncash investing and financing activities be disclosed elsewhere in the financial statements in a way that provides all the relevant information about these investing and financing activities. This can be done in a note to the financial statements in a summary as illustrated in Exhibit 17–7.

When there is a cash component to a transaction, it is appropriate to show only the net effect of the transaction on the cash flow statement. For example, if the purchase of the building had been for common shares of $700,000 and for cash of

KEY POINTS

Noncash investing and financing activities, such as issuing debt for an asset, are reported in the notes to the financial statements.

| EXHIBIT **17–7** | Noncash Investing and Financing Activities (All Amounts Assumed for Illustration Only) |

Noncash investing and financing activities	Thousands
Acquisition of building by issuing common shares	$ 730
Acquisition of land by issuing note payable	172
Payment of long-term debt by transferring investments to the creditor	250
Acquisition of equipment by issuing short-term note payable	89
Total noncash investing and financing activities	$1,241

$30,000, it would be appropriate to show only the net effect on cash of $30,000 and the other components of the transaction in the notes to the financial statements.

Measuring Cash Adequacy: Free Cash Flow

So far, we have focused on cash flows from operating, investing, and financing activities. Some investors want to know how much cash a company can "free up" for new opportunities. **Free cash flow** is the amount of cash available from operations after paying for planned investments in long-term assets. Free cash flow can be computed as follows:

	Net cash provided		**Cash payments planned for**
Free cash flow =	**by operating**	**−**	**investments in property, plant,**
	activities		**equipment, and other long-term assets**

PepsiCo, Inc. uses free cash flow as part of a financial management strategy to manage its operations. Suppose PepsiCo expects net cash provided by operations of $2.9 billion. Assume PepsiCo plans to spend $2.3 billion to modernize its bottling factories. In this case, PepsiCo's free cash flow would be $0.6 billion ($2.9 billion – $2.3 billion). If a good investment opportunity comes along, PepsiCo should have $0.6 billion to invest in the opportunity. A large amount of free cash flow is preferable because it means a lot of cash is available for new investments.

Format of the Cash Flow Statement

There are two ways to format operating activities on the cash flow statement:

- The **direct method**, which reports all the cash receipts and all the cash payments from operating activities
- The **indirect method** (sometimes called the **reconciliation method**), which reconciles net income to net cash provided by operating activities

The direct method, illustrated in Exhibit 17–5 on page 1058, is the method preferred by the *CICA Handbook* because it reports where cash came from and how it was spent on operating activities, for example, cash collected directly from customers.

In keeping with ASPE, companies' accounting systems are designed for accrual, rather than cash-basis, accounting. To use the direct method, a company must be able to access information on cash inflows and cash outflows. However, accrual-based accounting systems make it easy for companies to compute cash flows from operating activities using the indirect method, which starts with net income and reconciles to cash flows from operating activities. Exhibit 17–8 gives an overview of the process of converting from accrual-basis income to the cash basis for the cash flow statement.

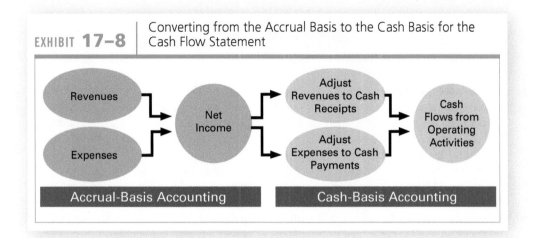

The direct method is easier to understand, and it provides better information for decision making, and the Accounting Standards Board and most financial analysts prefer it. However, accounting systems often don't produce the cash flow data easily. By learning how to compute the cash flow amounts for the direct method, you will be learning something far more important: how to determine the cash effects of business transactions. This is a critical skill for analyzing financial statements because accrual-basis accounting often hides cash effects. Then, after you have a firm foundation in cash flow analysis, it is easier to learn the indirect method. If your instructor chooses to focus solely on the indirect method, you can study that method, which begins on page 1076, with a minimum of references to earlier sections of this chapter.

The indirect and direct methods:

- Use different computations but produce the same amount of cash flow from operations, and
- Have no effect on investing activities or financing activities—they show the same net change in cash for the period.

✓JUST CHECKING

3. Identify each of the following transactions as either an operating activity (O), an investing activity (I), a financing activity (F), or an activity that is not reported on a cash flow statement (N). Assume the direct method is used to report cash flows from operating activitties.

_____ Payment of income taxes

_____ Issuance of preferred shares

_____ Payment of employee salaries

_____ Collections of accounts receivable

_____ Payment for a delivery truck

_____ Repayment of a long-term bank loan (principal only)

_____ Receipt of loan interest

_____ Payment of accounts payable

4. For the items listed in the previous question, indicate whether the transaction would increase (+), decrease (−), or have no effect (N) on cash.

Just Checking Solutions appear at the end of this chapter and on MyAccountingLab.

WHY IT'S DONE THIS WAY

Having seen the contents of the cash flow statement, we can turn to the accounting framework described in Chapter 1 (and repeated on the back inside cover of this book) to understand why the cash flow statement is one of the required financial statements for all companies.

Level 1 of the accounting framework states the objective of financial reporting is to communicate financial information that is useful in evaluating investment decisions and in assessing the success of a company. Supporting this objective, **Level 2** of the framework describes the characteristics that financial statements must have to be useful. Two of those characteristics are *relevance* and *reliability*.

In previous chapters, we discussed the role of the income statement in providing relevant and reliable information. Does the cash flow statement provide relevant and reliable information? Many investors feel that the cash flow statement provides the most relevant information of all of the financial statements. Why? While the income statement provides information about how much income was earned during the period, it does not state clearly how much cash was generated by the company. The income statement uses accruals to match revenues and expenses, and report them in the proper time period in which they were earned or incurred. However, the cash generated by a company and the use of that cash in the business is a significant predictor of future financial performance. As a result, companies need to provide the cash flow statement to show this information. We make the cash flow statement even more relevant and informative by classifying the cash flows as coming from operating, investing, or financing activities.

The cash flow statement is reliable since it deals only with cash transactions, and, typically, cash transactions are easy to verify. There are no accrual assumptions to assess when dealing with cash transactions.

Thus, by being both relevant and reliable, the cash flow statement is critical to achieving the accounting framework's **Level 1** objective of providing information to help users make investment decisions and assess company success.

The Cash Flow Statement: The Direct Method

LO ③

What is the direct method, and how is it used to prepare a cash flow statement?

There are two ways used in this text to illustrate the preparation of the cash flow statement: one way is to start with two years of financial statements and finding the cash transactions by explaining the changes in the balances from the first year to the next. The other way is to start with the results of such a comparison. Let's see how to prepare the cash flow statement by the direct method illustrated in Exhibit 17–5 on page 1058 using the second method. Suppose Capilano Ltd. has assembled the summary of 2014 transactions in Exhibit 17–9. These transactions give data for both the income statement and the cash flow statement. Some transactions affect one statement, some the other. Sales, for example, are reported on the income statement, but cash collections appear on the cash flow statement. Other transactions, such as the cash receipt of dividend revenue, affect both. *The cash flow statement reports only those transactions with cash effects* (those with an asterisk in Exhibit 17–9).

To prepare the cash flow statement, follow these three steps:

1. Identify the activities that increased cash or decreased cash—those items with asterisks in Exhibit 17–9.

2. Classify each cash increase and each cash decrease as an operating activity, an investing activity, or a financing activity.

3. Identify the cash effect of each transaction.

Cash Flows from Operating Activities

KEY POINTS

Note that cash collections from customers are not the same as sales. Cash collections from customers could include collections from sales that were made last year (beginning accounts receivable) but not credit sales from the current year that have not yet been collected (ending accounts receivable).

Operating cash flows are listed first because they are the most important source of cash for most businesses. The failure of operations to generate the bulk of cash inflows for an extended period may signal trouble for a company. Exhibit 17–5

EXHIBIT **17-9** | Summary of Capilano Ltd.'s 2014 Transactions

Operating Activities:

1. Sales on account, $682,000.
*2. Collections of accounts receivable and cash sales, $650,000.
3. Interest revenue on notes receivable, $29,000.
*4. Collection of interest receivable, $24,000.
*5. Cash receipt of dividend revenue on investments in shares, $22,000.
6. Cost of goods sold, $360,000.
7. Purchases of inventory on credit, $353,000.
*8. Payments to suppliers for merchandise, $270,000, and operating expenses, $44,000.
9. Salaries expense, $134,000.
*10. Payments of salaries, $140,000.
11. Amortization expense, $43,000.
12. Other operating expense, $41,000.
*13. Interest expense and payments, $38,000.
*14. Income tax expense and payments, $36,000.

Investing Activities:

*15. Cash payments to acquire property, plant, and equipment, and intangible assets, $735,000.
*16. Loan to another company, $26,000.
*17. Cash receipts from sale of property, plant, and equipment, and intangible assets, $149,000, including a $19,000 gain.

Financing Activities:

*18. Cash receipts from issuing common shares, $242,000.
*19. Cash receipts from issuing a long-term note payable, $226,000.
*20. Payment of long-term debt, $27,000.
*21. Declaration and payment of cash dividends, $41,000.

*Indicates a cash flow transaction is to be reported on the cash flow statement

shows that Capilano Ltd. is sound; its operating activities generated the greatest amount of cash, $696,000 in operating receipts. Capilano's cash flows from operating activities section from Exhibit 17–5 is repeated here for reference. Refer to it as we apply the three steps listed above to the transactions shown in Exhibit 17–9. We will go through it line by line.

Cash flows from operating activities	(In thousands)	
Receipts:		
Collections from customers	$650	
Interest received on notes receivable	24	
Dividends received on investments in shares	22	
Total cash receipts		$696
Payments:		
To suppliers for merchandise for resale	(270)	
To suppliers for operating expenses	(44)	
To employees	(140)	
For interest	(38)	
For income tax	(36)	
Total cash payments		(528)
Net cash inflow from operating activities		$168

Cash Collections from Customers Cash sales bring in cash immediately. Credit sales bring in cash later, when cash is collected. "Collections from customers" include both cash sales and collections of accounts receivable from credit sales—$650,000.

Cash Receipts of Interest Interest revenue is earned on notes receivable. The income statement reports interest revenue. As time passes, interest revenue accrues, but *cash* interest is received only on specific dates. Only the cash receipts of interest appear on the cash flow statement—$24,000.

Cash Receipts of Dividends Dividends are earned on share investments. Dividend revenue is ordinarily recorded on the income statement when cash is received. This cash receipt is reported on the cash flow statement—$22,000. (Dividends *received* are part of operating activities, but dividends *paid* are a financing activity.)

These cash receipts add to the total cash receipts of $696,000.

Cash Payments to Suppliers Payments to suppliers include all cash payments for inventory and most operating expenses, but not for interest, income taxes, and employee compensation expenses. *Suppliers* are entities that provide the business with its inventory and essential services. For example, a clothing store's payments to Levi Strauss & Co., Nygard International, and Stanfield are payments to suppliers. Other suppliers provide advertising, utilities, and other services. Payments to suppliers *exclude* payments to employees, payments for interest, and payments for income taxes because these are separate categories of operating cash payments. Capilano Ltd.'s payments to suppliers are $270,000 for merchandise for resale and $44,000 for operating expenses.

Cash Payments to Employees Salaries, wages, commissions, and other forms of employee compensation require payments to employees. Accrued amounts are excluded because they have not yet been paid. The income statement reports the expense, including accrued amounts. The cash flow statement reports only the cash payments $(140,000).

Cash Payments for Interest Expense and Income Tax Expense These cash payments are reported separately from the other expenses. In the Capilano Ltd. example, interest and income tax expenses equal the cash payments. Therefore, the same amount appears on the income statement and the cash flow statement. In practice, this is rarely the case. Year-end accruals and other transactions usually cause the expense and cash payment amounts to differ. The cash flow statement reports the cash payments for interest $(38,000) and income tax $(36,000).

Amortization Expense This expense is not listed on the cash flow statement because it does not affect cash. Amortization is recorded by debiting the expense and crediting Accumulated Amortization (there is no debit or credit to the Cash account).

Cash Flows from Investing Activities

Investing activities are important because a company's investments determine its future. Purchases of tangible assets such as property, plant, and equipment, as well as intangible assets such as patents, indicate the company is expanding, which is usually a good sign about the company. Low levels of investing activities over a lengthy period mean the business is not replenishing its property, plant, and equipment, or intangible assets. Knowing the cash flows from investing activities helps investors and creditors evaluate the direction that managers are charting for the business.

Capilano's cash flows from investing activities section from Exhibit 17–5 is repeated here for reference. Refer to it as we go through this section line by line.

Cash flows from investing activities		
Acquisition of property, plant, and equipment, and intangible assets	$(735)	
Loan to another company	(26)	
Cash received from selling property, plant, and equipment, and intangible assets	149	
Net cash outflow from investing activities		$(612)

KEY POINTS

Using the direct method, cash receipts from issuing shares are a *financing activity*. Payment of dividends is also considered a *financing activity*. Cash receipts from and payments of short- or long-term borrowing are *financing activities*. But interest expense on these borrowings is considered an *operating* activity.

Cash Payments for Property, Plant, and Equipment, and Intangible Assets, Investments, and Loans to Other Companies   All these cash payments acquire a long-term asset. The first investing activity reported by Capilano Ltd. on its cash flow statement is the purchase of property, plant, and equipment, and intangible assets, such as land, buildings, equipment, and patents $(735,000). The second transaction is a $26,000 loan; Capilano Ltd. obtains a note receivable. These are investing activities because the company is investing in assets for business use rather than for resale. These transactions have no immediate direct effect on revenues or expenses and thus are not reported on the income statement. The other typical transaction in this category—not shown—is a purchase of long-term investments.

Cash Received from the Sale of Property, Plant, and Equipment, and Intangible Assets, Investments, and the Collection of Loans   These transactions are the opposite of making acquisitions of property, plant, and equipment, acquisitions of intangible assets, investments, and loans. They are cash receipts from investment transactions.

The sale of the property, plant, and equipment, and intangible assets needs explanation. The cash flow statement reports that Capilano Ltd. received $149,000 cash on the sale of these assets. The income statement shows a $19,000 gain on this transaction. What is the appropriate amount to show on the cash flow statement? It is $149,000, the cash received from the sale. If we assume Capilano Ltd. sold equipment that cost $155,000 and had accumulated amortization of $25,000, the following journal entry would record the sale:

Cash	149,000	
Accumulated Amortization	25,000	
Equipment		155,000
Gain on Sale of Equipment (from income statement)		19,000

The analysis indicates the equipment cost $155,000 and its accumulated amortization was $25,000. Thus, the book value of the equipment was $130,000 ($155,000 − $25,000). However, the book value of the asset sold is not reported on the cash flow statement. Only the cash proceeds of $149,000 are reported on the cash flow statement. For the income statement, only the gain is reported.

Because a gain occurred, you may wonder why this cash receipt is not reported as part of operations. Operations consist of buying and selling merchandise or rendering services to earn revenue. Investing activities are the acquisition and disposition of assets used in operations. Therefore, the cash received from the sale of property, plant, and equipment, and intangible assets, and the sale of investments should be viewed as cash inflows from investing activities. Any gain or loss on the sale is not cash, but rather an accounting amount based on the asset's book value in the accounting records.

Investors and creditors are often critical of a company that sells large amounts of its property, plant, and equipment, and intangible assets. Such sales may signal an emergency need for cash and negative news. But selling property, plant, and equipment or tangible assets may be positive news if the company is selling an unprofitable division or a useless property, plant, and equipment asset. Whether sales of property, plant, and equipment or intangible assets are positive news or negative news should be evaluated in light of a company's net income (or net loss), financial position, and other cash flows.

Cash Flows from Financing Activities

Readers of the financial statements want to know how the entity obtains its financing. Cash flows from financing activities include several specific items. The majority are related to obtaining money from investors and lenders and paying them back.

Capilano's cash flows from financing activities section from Exhibit 17–5 is repeated here for reference. Refer to it as we go through this section line by line.

LEARNING TIPS

Notice the entry to record the sale of equipment. Any time Cash is debited in a journal entry, it must appear on the cash flow statement as a cash inflow. Likewise, a credit signals an outflow. To think it through, make journal entries, but note that the entries are not to be posted and are merely a way to help you understand the cash effect of the transaction.

Cash flows from financing activities		
Cash received from issuing common shares	$242	
Cash received from issuing long-term notes payable	226	
Payment of long-term debt	(27)	
Payment of dividends	(41)	
Net cash inflow from financing activities		$400

Cash Received from Issuing Shares and Debt Issuing shares (preferred and common) and debt are two common ways to finance operations. Capilano Ltd. issued common shares for cash of $242,000 and long-term notes payable for cash of $226,000.

Payment of Debt and Repurchases of the Company's Own Shares The payment of debt decreases Cash, which is the opposite of borrowing money. Capilano Ltd. reports debt payments of $27,000. Other transactions in this category are repurchases of the company's shares.

KEY POINTS

The *payment* of cash dividends, not the *declaration*, appears as a cash outflow on the cash flow statement.

Payment of Cash Dividends The payment of cash dividends decreases Cash and is therefore reported as a cash payment. Capilano Ltd.'s $41,000 payment is an example. A dividend in another form—such as a stock dividend—has no effect on Cash and is either *not* reported on the cash flow statement or is reported in the noncash financing and investing section described earlier in this chapter.

✓ JUST CHECKING

5. Suppose Markham Corp. sold land at a $3 million gain. The land cost Markham Corp. $2 million when it was purchased in 1995. What amount will Markham Corp. report as an investing activity on the cash flow statement?

6. Matheson Corporation's accounting records include the information shown below for the year ended December 31, 2014. Prepare Matheson Corporation's income statement and cash flow statement for the year ended December 31, 2014. Follow the cash flow statement format of Exhibit 17–5, using the direct method for operating cash flows and follow the single-step format for the income statement (grouping all revenues together and all expenses together, as shown in Exhibit 17–10 on page 1067). Net income is $61,000.

   a. Salary expense, $290,000.

   b. Amortization expense on property, plant, and equipment, $104,000.

   c. Cash received from issuing common shares, $87,000.

   d. Declaration and payment of cash dividends, $62,000.

   e. Collection of interest on notes receivable, $20,000.

   f. Payments of salaries, $308,000.

   g. Collections from credit customers, $1,030,000.

   h. Loan to another company, $118,000.

   i. Cash received from selling property, plant, and equipment, $50,000, including a $3,000 loss.

   j. Payments to suppliers, $893,000.

   k. Income tax expense and payments, $45,000.

   l. Credit sales, $1,005,000.

   m. Cash sales, $258,000.

   n. Interest revenue, $22,000.

   o. Cash received from issuing short-term debt, $106,000.

   p. Payments of long-term debt, $160,000.

   q. Interest expense and payments, $31,000.

   r. Loan collections, $143,000.

   s. Cash received from selling investments, $61,000, including a $36,000 gain.

   t. Purchase of inventory on credit, $832,000.

(Continued)

(Continued)

    u. Dividends received in cash, on investments in shares, $8,000.

    v. Cash payments to acquire property, plant, and equipment, $232,000.

    w. Cost of goods sold, $795,000.

    x. Cash balance: December 31, 2013—$230,000

                      December 31, 2014—$144,000

Note that, for simplicity, uncollectible accounts have been ignored.

Just Checking Solutions appear at the end of this chapter and on MyAccountingLab.

Computing Individual Amounts for the Cash Flow Statement

How do we compute the amounts for the cash flow statement? We use the income statement and *changes* in the related balance sheet accounts. For the *operating* cash flow amounts, the adjustment process follows this basic approach:

Revenue or expense from the income statement	±	Adjustment for the change in the related balance sheet account(s)	=	Amount for the cash flow statement

This is called the T-account approach and it will be illustrated in the next section beginning with the Sales and Accounts Receivable connection. Learning to analyze T-accounts is one of the most useful accounting skills you will acquire. It will enable you to measure the cash effects of a wide variety of transactions.

The following discussions use Capilano Ltd.'s income statement in Exhibit 17–10, comparative balance sheet in Exhibit 17–11, and cash flow statement in Exhibit 17–12

LO ④

What are the cash effects of different business transactions?

LEARNING TIPS

The cash flow statement reports the changes in all noncash accounts. To make sure that all changes have been accounted for, place a check mark by each account on the balance sheet after you have used it in preparing the statement. If a check mark is missing, further investigation may be required.

EXHIBIT 17–10 | Income Statement

CAPILANO LTD. Income Statement For the Year Ended December 31, 2014 (amounts in thousands)		
Revenues and gains:		
Sales revenue	$682	
Interest revenue	29	
Dividend revenue	22	
Gain on sale of property, plant, and equipment,		
and intangible assets	19	
Total revenues and gains		$752
Expenses:		
Cost of goods sold	360	
Salaries expense	134	
Amortization expense	43	
Other operating expenses	41	
Interest expense	38	
Total expenses		616
Net income before income taxes		136
Income tax expense		36
Net income		$100

CAPILANO LTD.
Balance Sheet
December 31, 2014 and 2013
(amounts in thousands)

Assets	2014	2013	Increase (Decrease)	Changes in the following:
Current				
Cash	$ 57	$ 101	$ (44)	
Accounts receivable	224	192	32	Current assets—**Operating**
Interest receivable	8	3	5	
Inventory	323	330	(7)	
Prepaid expenses	18	17	1	
Long-term receivable from another company	26	—	26	Noncurrent assets—**Investing**
Property, plant, and equipment, net of amortization	1,087	525	562	
Total	$1,743	$1,168	$ 575	
Liabilities				
Current				Current liabilities— **Operating** and change in current portion of long-term debt—**Financing**
Accounts payable	$ 220	$ 137	$ 83	
Salaries payable	6	12	(6)	
Accrued liabilities	5	7	(2)	
Long-term debt	384	185	199	Most long-term liabilities and contributed capital—**Financing**
Shareholders' Equity				
Common shares	861	619	242	Change due to net income—**Operating** and change due to dividends— **Financing**
Retained earnings	267	208	59	
Total	$1,743	$1,168	$ 575	

KEY POINTS

Exhibit 17–4 highlights the same information shown in the "Changes in" section of Exhibit 17–11.

LEARNING TIPS

A *decrease* in Accounts Receivable indicates that cash collections were greater than sales. The decrease is *added* to Sales. An *increase* in Accounts Receivable indicates that cash collections were less than sales. The increase is *deducted* from Sales.

(which is a repeat of Exhibit 17–5 for your convenience). First, trace the $101,000 and $57,000 cash amounts on the balance sheet in Exhibit 17–11 to the bottom part of the cash flow statement in Exhibit 17–12. You see that the beginning and ending cash amounts come from the balance sheets. Now let's compute the cash flows from operating activities.

Computing the Cash Amounts of Operating Activities

Cash Collections from Customers Collections can be computed by converting sales revenue (an accrual-basis amount) to the cash basis. Capilano Ltd.'s income statement (Exhibit 17–10) reports sales of $682,000. Exhibit 17–11 shows that Accounts Receivable increased from $192,000 at the beginning of the year to $224,000 at year end, a $32,000 increase. Based on those amounts, Cash Collections equals $650,000, as shown in the Accounts Receivable T-account:

Accounts Receivable

Beginning balance	192,000		
Sales	682,000	Collections	650,000
Ending balance	224,000		

CAPILANO LTD.
Cash Flow Statement
For the Year Ended December 31, 2014

Cash flows from operating activities	(In thousands)	
Receipts:		
Collections from customers	$650	
Interest received on notes receivable	24	
Dividends received on investments in shares	22	
Total cash receipts		$696
Payments:		
To suppliers for merchandise for resale	(270)	
To suppliers for operating expenses	(44)	
To employees	(140)	
For interest	(38)	
For income tax	(36)	
Total cash payments		(528)
Net cash inflow from operating activities		168
Cash flows from investing activities		
Acquisition of property, plant, and equipment, and intangible assets	(735)	
Loan to another company	(26)	
Cash received from selling property, plant, and equipment, and intangible assets	149	
Net cash outflow from investing activities		(612)
Cash flows from financing activities		
Cash received from issuing common shares	242	
Cash received from issuing long-term debt	226	
Payment of long-term debt*	(27)	
Payment of dividends	(41)	
Net cash inflow from financing activities		400
Net increase (decrease) in cash and cash equivalents		(44)
Cash and cash equivalents at beginning of 2014		101
Cash and cash equivalents at end of 2014		$ 57

*This would also include the current portion of long-term debt payable, which is NIL in this case.

Another explanation: Accounts Receivable increased by $32,000, so Capilano Ltd. must have received $32,000 less cash than sales revenue for the period.

The following equation shows another way to compute cash collections from customers:

Accounts Receivable

Beginning balance	+	Sales	−	Collections	=	Ending balance
$192,000	+	$682,000	−	X	=	$224,000
				−X	=	$224,000 − $192,000 − $682,000
				X	=	$650,000

A decrease in Accounts Receivable would mean that the company received more cash than the amount of sales revenue. This computation is summarized as the first item in Exhibit 17–13 on page 1072.

LEARNING TIPS

Remember that each account contains four basic elements:

    Beginning Balance
    + Increases
    − Decreases
    = Ending Balance

Apply this relationship to Accounts Receivable for Capilano Ltd.

Compute collections.

Beg. A/R	$ 192,000
+ Sales	682,000
− Collections*	?
= Ending Balance	$ 224,000

*Collections = $650,000

All collections of receivables are computed in the same way. In our example, Capilano Ltd.'s income statement, Exhibit 17–10, reports interest revenue of $29,000. Interest Receivable's balance in Exhibit 17–11 increased $5,000. Cash receipts of interest must be $24,000 (Interest Revenue of $29,000 minus the $5,000 increase in Interest Receivable). Exhibit 17–13 on page 1072 summarizes this computation.

Payments to Suppliers   This computation includes two parts, payments for inventory related to Cost of Goods Sold and payments for operating expenses.

Payments for inventory are computed by converting cost of goods sold to the cash basis. We must analyze the Inventory and Accounts Payable accounts. To "analyze" an account means to explain each amount in the account. For companies that purchase inventory on short-term notes payable, we must also analyze Short-Term Notes Payable in the same manner as Accounts Payable. The computation of Capilano Ltd.'s cash payments for inventory is given by this analysis of the T-accounts (again, we are using Exhibit 17–10 and Exhibit 17–11 for our numbers):

Inventory				Accounts Payable			
Beg. Inventory	330,000	Cost of goods	Payments for		Beg. bal.	137,000
Purchases	353,000	sold 360,000	inventory 270,000		Purchases	353,000 ◄
End. Inventory	323,000				End. bal.	220,000

The first equation details the activity in the Inventory account to compute Purchases, as follows:

Inventory

Beginning inventory	+	Purchases	−	Cost of goods sold	=	Ending inventory
$330,000	+	X	−	$360,000	=	$323,000
		X			=	$323,000 − $330,000 + $360,000
		X			=	$353,000

Now we can insert the purchases figure into Accounts Payable to compute the amount of cash paid for inventory, as follows:

Accounts Payable

Beginning balance	+	Purchases	−	Payments for inventory	=	Ending balance
$137,000	+	$353,000	−	X	=	$220,000
				$-X$	=	$220,000 − $137,000 − $353,000
				X	=	$270,000

Beginning and ending inventory amounts come from the balance sheet, and Cost of Goods Sold comes from the income statement. Exhibit 17–13 on page 1072 shows the general approach to compute the payments to suppliers of inventory (fourth item).

Payments for inventory appear in the Accounts Payable account, but we must first work through the Inventory account to calculate payments to suppliers of inventory.

Payments for Operating Expenses   Payments for operating expenses other than interest and income tax can be computed as "plug figures," or differences, by analyzing Prepaid Expenses and Accrued Liabilities, as follows for Capilano Ltd. (again, all numbers are taken from Exhibit 17–10 and Exhibit 17–11). The assumption here is that all prepaid items, such as rent, insurance, and advertising or all accrued liabilities, such as entertainment, telephone, and utilities, flow through the one Other Operating Expenses account.

LEARNING TIPS

For the situation opposite to the example given, an ↑ in Inventory indicates more inventory has been purchased than sold. A ↓ in Inventory indicates that purchases are less than COGS.

LEARNING TIPS

The COGS calculation requires two adjustments. The adjustment for inventory gives the amount of purchases; the adjustment for accounts payable gives the payments for inventory.

The question is how much cash did Capilano pay for operating expenses? An assumption is made regarding operating expenses in the following example. It assumes that all the prepaid expenses at the beginning of the year ($17,000) expired during the year and were adjusted in the current year. We know that accrued expenses during the year were $5,000 so we have enough data to determine how much cash was paid out for these operating expenses combined ($44,000).

Prepaid Expenses				Accrued Liabilities				Operating Expenses (other than Salaries, Wages, and Amortization)	
Beg. bal.	17,000	Expiration of		Payments	7,000	Beg. bal.	7,000	Accrual of	
		prepaid				Accrual of		expense at	
Payments	18,000	expense	17,000			expense at		year end	5,000
End. bal.	18,000					year end	5,000	Expiration of	
						End. bal.	5,000	prepaid	
								expense	17,000
								Payments	19,000
								End. bal.	41,000

Total payments for operating expenses = $44,000
$18,000 + $7,000 + $19,000 = $44,000

The following equations show another way to calculate payments for operating expenses.

Prepaid Expenses

$$\text{Beginning balance} + \text{Payments} - \text{Expiration of prepaid expense} = \text{Ending balance}$$

$17,000	+	X	−	$17,000	= $18,000
		X			= $18,000 − $17,000 + $17,000
		X			= $18,000

Accrued Liabilities

$$\text{Beginning balance} + \text{Accrual of expense at year end} - \text{Payments} = \text{Ending balance}$$

$7,000	+	$5,000	−	X	= $5,000
				−X	= $5,000 − $7,000 − $5,000
				X	= $7,000

Operating Expenses

$$\text{Accrual of expense at year end} + \text{Expiration of prepaid expense} + \text{Payments} = \text{Ending balance}$$

$5,000	+	$17,000	+	X	= $41,000
				X	= $41,000 − $5,000 − $17,000
				X	= $19,000

The expense total for operating expenses is $41,000. Once we remove the prepaid expirations and the expense accruals, the remaining balance must be the cash payments for expenses.

Payments to Employees Companies keep separate accounts for salaries, wages, and other forms of employee compensation. It is convenient to combine all compensation amounts into one account for presentation purposes. Capilano Ltd.'s calculation adjusts Salaries Expense for the change in Salaries Payable, as shown in the following T-account:

Salaries and Wages Payable

		Beginning balance	12,000
Payments to employees	140,000	Salaries expense	134,000
		Ending balance	6,000

Salaries and Wages Payable

Beginning balance	+	Salaries expense	−	Payments	=	Ending balance
$12,000	+	$134,000	−	X	=	$6,000
				$-X$	=	$6,000 - $12,000 - $134,000
				X	=	$140,000

Exhibit 17–13 summarizes this computation under Payments to Employees.

Payments of Interest and Income Tax   In our example, the expense and payment amount is the same for interest and income tax. Therefore, no analysis is required to determine the payment amount—we can use the expense amounts on the income statement for the cash flow statement. However, if the expense and the payment differ, the payment can be computed by analyzing the related liability or prepayment account. The payment computation follows the pattern illustrated for payments to employees; Exhibit 17–13 summarizes the procedure for interest and income tax.

Exhibit 17–13 shows how to compute operating cash flows under the direct method.

Computing the Cash Amounts of Investing Activities

Investing activities affect long-term asset accounts, such as Property, Plant, and Equipment, intangible assets, Investments, and Notes Receivable. Cash flows from

---

LEARNING TIPS

Increases and decreases in other payables (Salary Payable, Interest Payable, and Income Tax Payable) are treated in the same way as increases and decreases in Accounts Payable and Accrued Liabilities. A *decrease* in the payable indicates that payments for salaries/interest/income taxes were greater than the expense. The decrease is *added* to the expense. An *increase* in the payable indicates that payments for salaries/interest/income taxes were less than the expense. The increase is *deducted* from the expense.

EXHIBIT 17-13 | Direct Method of Determining Cash Flows from Operating Activities

Cash Receipts and Payments	From the Income Statement (Exhibit 17–10)	From the Balance Sheet (Exhibit 17–11)	
CASH RECEIPTS			
From customers	Sales Revenue	+ Decrease in Accounts Receivable − Increase in Accounts Receivable	
Of interest	Interest Revenue	+ Decrease in Interest Receivable − Increase in Interest Receivable	
Of dividends	Dividend Revenue	+ Decrease in Dividends Receivable − Increase in Dividends Receivable	
CASH PAYMENTS			
To suppliers of inventory	Cost of Goods Sold	+ Increase in Inventory − Decrease in Inventory	+ Decrease in Accounts Payable − Increase in Accounts Payable
To suppliers of other items	Operating Expense	+ Increase in Prepaids − Decrease in Prepaids	+ Decrease in Accrued Liabilities − Increase in Accrued Liabilities
To employees	Salaries (Wages) Expense	+ Decrease in Salaries (Wages) Payable − Increase in Salaries (Wages) Payable	
For interest	Interest Expense	+ Decrease in Interest Payable − Increase in Interest Payable	
For income tax	Income Tax Expense	+ Decrease in Income Tax Payable − Increase in Income Tax Payable	

Source: Suggestion of Barbara Gerrity

investing activities can be computed by analyzing these accounts. The income statement and beginning and ending balance sheets provide the data.

Acquisitions and Sales of Tangible and Intangible Assets Companies keep separate accounts for Land, Buildings, Equipment, and other tangible and intangible assets. It is helpful to combine these accounts into a single summary for computing the cash flows from acquisitions and sales of these assets. Also, we often subtract accumulated amortization from the assets' cost and work with a net figure for property, plant, and equipment, and amortizable intangible assets. This approach allows us to work with a single total for tangible and intangible assets.

To illustrate, observe that Capilano Ltd.'s balance sheet (Exhibit 17–11) reports beginning property, plant, and equipment, net of amortization, of $525,000 and an ending net amount of $1,087,000. The income statement in Exhibit 17–10 shows amortization of $43,000 and a $19,000 gain on sale of property, plant, and equipment. Further, the acquisitions are $735,000, an amount provided by the accounting records. How much are the proceeds from the sale of property, plant, and equipment? First, we must compute the book value of property, plant, and equipment sold as follows:

KEY POINTS

Changes in asset accounts, other than those used to compute cash flow from operating activities, are investing activities. An increase in an asset represents a cash outflow; a decrease in an asset represents a cash inflow.

LEARNING TIPS

Recall that to calculate the book value, subtract "Accumulated Amortization," which is shown as a contra-asset on the balance sheet.

Property, Plant, and Equipment (net)

Beginning balance (net)	525,000	Accumulated Amortization	43,000
Acquisitions	735,000	Book value of assets sold	130,000
Ending balance (net)	1,087,000		

Property, Plant, and Equipment, Net

Beginning balance	+ Acquisitions	−	Accumulated Amortization	−	Book value of assets sold	=	Ending balance
$525,000	+ $735,000	−	$43,000	−	X	=	$1,087,000
					−X	=	$1,087,000 − $525,000 − $735,000 + $43,000
					X	=	$130,000

Now we can compute the proceeds from the sale of property, plant, and equipment as follows:

$$\text{Sale proceeds} = \text{Book value of assets sold} + \text{Gain} - \text{Loss}$$
$$= \$130,000 \qquad + \$19,000 - \$0$$
$$= \$149,000$$

Trace the sale proceeds of $149,000 to the cash flow statement in Exhibit 17–12. If the sale had resulted in a loss of $6,000, the sale proceeds would be $124,000 ($130,000 – $6,000), and the cash flow statement would report $124,000 as a cash receipt from this investing activity.

KEY POINTS

When an asset is sold, the asset account is decreased by the asset's original cost, not the selling price. Proceeds from the sale of an asset need not equal the asset's book value. Remember:

Book value + Gain = Proceeds

Book value − Loss = Proceeds

The book value information comes from the balance sheet, the gain or loss from the income statement.

Acquisitions and Sales of Long-Term Investments, and Long-Term Loans and Loan Collections The cash amounts of long-term investment and loan transactions can be computed in the manner illustrated for property, plant, and equipment, and intangible assets. Investments are easier to analyze, because there is no amortization to account for, as shown by the following T-account:

Investments

Beginning balance*	xxx		
Purchases**	xxx	Cost of investments sold	xxx
Ending balance*	xxx		

*From the balance sheet
**From the accounting records, used to create the cash flow statement

Long-Term Investments (amounts assumed for illustration only)

Beginning balance	+	Purchases	−	Cost of investments sold	=	Ending balance
$200,000	+	$100,000	−	X	=	$280,000
				$-X$	=	$280,000 − $200,000 − $100,000
				X	=	$20,000

$$\text{Sale proceeds} = \text{Cost of investments sold} + \text{Gain} - \text{Loss}$$
$$= \$20,000 \qquad\qquad + \$6,000 \quad - \$0$$
$$= \$26,000$$

Loan transactions follow the pattern described on pages 1068–1069 for collections from customers. New loans made increase the receivable and decrease the amount of cash. Collections decrease the receivable and increase the amount of cash, as follows:

Loans and Notes Receivable (Long-Term)

Beginning balance*	xxx		
New loans made**	xxx	Collections	xxx
Ending balance*	xxx		

*From the balance sheet
**From the accounting records, used to create the cash flow statement

Loans and Notes Receivable (amounts assumed for illustration only)

Beginning balance	+	New loans made	−	Collections	=	Ending balance
$180,000	+	$20,000	−	X	=	$60,000
				$-X$	=	$60,000 − $180,000 − $20,000
				X	=	$140,000

Computing the Cash Amounts of Financing Activities

Financing activities affect the long-term liability and shareholders' equity accounts, such as Notes Payable, Bonds Payable, Long-Term Debt, Common Shares, and Retained Earnings. To compute the cash flow amounts, analyze these accounts.

Issuances and Payments of Long-Term Debt Notes Payable, Bonds Payable, and Long-Term Debt accounts are related to borrowing, a financing activity. Their balances come from the balance sheet. If either the amount of new issuances or the amount of the payments is known, the other amount can be computed. New debt issuances totalled $226,000 for Capilano Ltd. as provided by the accounting records. Debt payments are computed from the Long-Term Debt T-account, using amounts from Capilano Ltd.'s balance sheet, Exhibit 17–11:

KEY POINTS

Changes in liability and shareholders' equity accounts, other than those used to compute cash flow from operating activities, are financing activities.

Long-Term Debt

		Beginning balance	185,000
Payments	27,000	Issuance of new debt	226,000
		Ending balance	384,000

Long-Term Debt

$$\underset{\text{balance}}{\text{Beginning}} + \underset{\text{new debt}}{\text{Issuance of}} - \underset{\text{of debt}}{\text{Payments}} = \text{Ending balance}$$

$185,000	+	$226,000	− X	= $384,000
			−X	= $384,000 − $185,000 − $226,000
			X	= $27,000

Issuances and Repurchases of Shares These financing activities are computed from the various share accounts. It is convenient to work with a single summary account for shares. Using data from Exhibit 17–11 and Exhibit 17–12, we have

Common Shares

		Beginning balance	619,000
Retirements of shares	0	Issuance of new shares	242,000
		Ending balance	861,000

Common Shares

$$\underset{\text{balance}}{\text{Beginning}} + \underset{\text{new share}}{\text{Issuance of}} - \underset{\text{of shares}}{\text{Retirements}} = \text{Ending balance}$$

$619,000	+	$242,000	− X	= $861,000
			−X	= $861,000 − $619,000 − $242,000
			X	= $0

Dividend Payments If the amount of the dividends is not given elsewhere (for example, in a statement of retained earnings), it can be computed as follows:

LEARNING TIPS

Retained Earnings

		Beginning balance	208,000
Dividend declaration	41,000	Net income	100,000
		Ending balance	267,000

Dividends Payable

		Beginning balance	0
Dividend payments	41,000	Dividend declaration	41,000
		Ending balance	0

How are you able to tell, by referring to the balance sheet, if the amount of dividends paid is different from the dividends declared? If there is not a Dividend Payable account (or no change in the Dividend Payable account), then the dividends declared are equal to the dividends paid. Remember, only dividends *paid* appear on the cash flow statement, not dividends *declared*.

First, we must compute dividend declarations by analyzing Retained Earnings. Then we can solve for dividend payments with the Dividends Payable account. Capilano Ltd. has no Dividends Payable account, so dividend payments are the same as declarations. The following computations show how to compute Capilano Ltd.'s dividend payments.

Retained Earnings

$$\underset{\text{balance}}{\text{Beginning}} + \text{Net income} - \underset{\text{declarations}}{\text{Dividend}} = \text{Ending balance}$$

$208,000	+	$100,000	− X	= $267,000
			−X	= $267,000 − $208,000 − $100,000
			X	= $41,000

✓JUST CHECKING

7. Pardies Limited reported the following current-asset and current-liability amounts at year end:

	December 31, 2014	December 31, 2013
Current assets		
Cash and cash equivalents	$38,000	$ 6,000
Accounts receivable	44,000	46,000
Inventories	68,000	62,000
Prepaid expenses	2,000	6,000
Current liabilities		
Notes payable (for inventory purchases)	$22,000	$14,000
Accounts payable	48,000	38,000
Accrued liabilities	14,000	18,000
Income and other taxes payable	22,000	20,000

Use this information to answer the following questions about the company:

i. Compute collections from customers during 2014. Sales totalled $240,000 and all sales were on credit.

ii. Compute payments for inventory during 2014, assuming the change in Accounts Payable is due to inventory. Cost of goods sold was $140,000.

iii. Compute payments for income taxes during 2014. Income tax expense for 2014 was $20,000.

iv. Compute payments for prepaid expenses during 2014. Prepaid expenses of $8,000 expired during 2014.

8. Bolin Corp. reported the following (amounts in thousands):

Retirement of Bolin Corp. preferred shares	$ 90
Sale of bonds issued by Blue Ltd	224
Payment of interest on mortgage note to bank	22
Purchase of land	316
Payment of income taxes	76
Sale of Bolin Corp. common shares	210
Collection of long-term note receivable	126
Payment of dividends	300

a. What is Bolin Corp.'s net change in cash from investing activities?

b. Categorize the other items.

9. Refer to the Bolin Corp. data in the previous question. What is Bolin Corp.'s net change in cash from financing activities?

Just Checking Solutions appear at the end of this chapter and on MyAccountingLab.

The Cash Flow Statement: The Indirect Method

LO ⑤
What is the indirect method, and how is it used to prepare a cash flow statement?

The indirect method of reporting cash flows from operating activities is a conversion or a reconciliation from net income to net cash inflow (or outflow) from operating activities. It is a conversion of accrual-based net income to the cash-based net income, which shows how the company's net income is related to net cash flow from operating activities. Exhibit 17–14 shows the reconciliation for Capilano Ltd.

CAPILANO LTD.
Reconciliation of Net Income to Net Cash Inflow from Operating Activities
For the Year Ended December 31, 2014
(In thousands)

Net income		$100
Add (subtract) items that affect net income and cash flow differently:		
Amortization	$43	
Gain on sale of property, plant, and equipment, and intangible assets	(19)	
Increase in accounts receivable	(32)	
Increase in interest receivable	(5)	
Decrease in inventory	7	
Increase in prepaid expenses	(1)	
Increase in accounts payable	83	
Decrease in salaries payable	(6)	
Decrease in accrued liabilities	(2)	68
Net cash inflow from operating activities		$168

The end result—net cash inflow from operating activities of $168,000—is the same as the result we derived earlier under the *direct* method (see Exhibit 17–12). The reconciliation is also the same as the *indirect* method of computing operating cash flows. We now turn to the indirect method.

The indirect method starts with net income from the income statement and reconciles to operating cash flows.

This method shows the link between net income and cash flow from operations better than the direct method. Many companies use the indirect method for that reason. The main drawback of the indirect method is that it does not report the detailed operating cash flows—collections from customers and other cash receipts, payments to suppliers, payments to employees, and payments for interest and taxes. Although the Accounting Standards Board prefers the direct method, the vast majority of Canadian companies (and U.S. companies) use the indirect method.

These two methods (direct and indirect) of preparing the cash flow statement affect only the operating activities section of the statement. No difference exists for investing activities or financing activities.

Exhibit 17–15 is Capilano Ltd.'s cash flow statement prepared by the indirect method. Only the operating section of the statement differs from the direct-method format in Exhibit 17–12. The new items Ⓐ, Ⓑ, and Ⓒ are keyed to their explanations, which are discussed below. For ease of reference, we repeat Capilano Ltd.'s income statement and balance sheet here as Exhibits 17–16 and 17–17.

Theory behind the Indirect Method

The indirect-method cash flow statement begins with accrual-basis net income, from the income statement. Additions and subtractions follow. These are labelled "Add (subtract) items that affect net income and cash flow differently." We discuss these items in the following sections. Refer to Exhibit 17–15.

Amortization Expenses Ⓐ These expenses are added back to net income to compute cash flow from operations. Let's see why.

KEY POINTS

These two methods (direct and indirect) of preparing the cash flow statement affect only the operating activities section of the statement. No difference exists for investing activities or financing activities.

CAPILANO LTD.
Cash Flow Statement
For the Year Ended December 31, 2014

		(in thousands)	
Cash flows from operating activities			
Net income		$100	
Add (subtract) items that affect net income and cash flow differently:			
(A) Amortization		$ 43	
(B) Gain on sale of property, plant, and equipment, and intangible assets		(19)	
Increase in accounts receivable		(32)	
Increase in interest receivable		(5)	
Decrease in inventory		7	
(C) Increase in prepaid expenses		(1)	
Increase in accounts payable		83	
Decrease in salaries payable		(6)	
Decrease in accrued liabilities		(2)	68
Net cash inflow from operating activities			168
Cash flows from investing activities			
Acquisition of property, plant, and equipment and intangible assets		(735)	
Loan to another company		(26)	
Cash received from selling property, plant, and equipment, and intangible assets		149	
Net cash outflow from investing activities			(612)
Cash flow from financing activities			
Cash received from issuing common shares		242	
Cash received from issuing long-term debt		226	
Payment of long-term debt		(27)	
Payment of dividends		(41)	
Net cash inflow from financing activities			400
Net increase (decrease) in cash and cash equivalents			(44)
Cash and cash equivalents at beginning of 2014			101
Cash and cash equivalents at end of 2014			$ 57

From Exhibit 17–12

Amortization was originally recorded as follows:

Amortization Expense	43,000	
Accumulated Amortization		43,000

REAL WORLD EXAMPLE

Other adjustments commonly made to net income are for amortization of bond premium/discount and equity-method revenue.

This entry neither debits nor credits Cash because amortization has no cash effect. However, amortization expense is deducted from revenues to compute income. Therefore, in going from net income to cash flows from operations, we add amortization back to net income. The addback cancels the earlier deduction.

The following example should help clarify this practice: Suppose a company had only two transactions during the period, a $5,000 cash sale and amortization expense of $1,000. Net income is $4,000 ($5,000 – $1,000). But cash flow from operations is $5,000. To go from net income ($4,000) to cash flow ($5,000), we must add back the amortization amount of $1,000.

Gains and Losses on the Sale of Assets (B)   Sales of property, plant, and equipment and of intangible assets are investing activities on the cash flow statement. Refer to the calculations on pages 1073 and 1074 regarding the sale of the Capilano Ltd.

EXHIBIT **17–16** | Income Statement

CAPILANO LTD. Income Statement For the Year Ended December 31, 2014 (amounts in thousands)		
Revenues and gains:		
Sales revenue	$682	
Interest revenue	29	
Dividend revenue	22	
ⒷGain on sale of property, plant, and equipment, and intangible assets	19	
Total revenues and gains		$752
Expenses:		
Cost of goods sold	360	
Salaries expense	134	
ⒶAmortization expense	43	
Other operating expenses	41	
Interest expense	38	
Total expenses		616
Net income before income taxes		136
Income tax expense		36
Net income		$100

equipment with a book value of $130,000 for $149,000, producing a gain of $19,000. The $19,000 gain is reported on the income statement and is therefore included in net income. The cash receipt, or proceeds from the sale, is $149,000, and that is what we report on the cash flow statement. The $149,000 of cash received also includes the $19,000 gain on the sale. Gains and losses are bookkeeping amounts that we track on the income statement. They do not represent the cash received of $149,000 from the sale, which is what we want to show in the investing section. Starting with net income, we subtract the gain, which removes the gain's earlier effect on income. The sale of property, plant, and equipment and of intangible assets is reported as a $149,000 cash receipt from an investing activity, as shown in Exhibit 17–15.

A loss on the sale of property, plant, and equipment and of intangible assets is also an adjustment to net income on the cash flow statement. A loss is *added back* to income to compute cash flow from operations. The cash received from selling the property, plant, and equipment and intangible assets is reported under investing activities on the cash flow statement.

To convert net income from accrual basis to cash basis:

- **Expenses with no cash effects, such as accruals, are added back to net income on the cash flow statement.**

- **Revenues that do not provide cash, such as accrued income, are subtracted from net income.**

- **Items are either added or subtracted by calculating differences in current assets and current liabilities between the opening and closing amounts.**

Changes in the Current Asset and Current Liability Accounts Ⓒ Most current assets and current liabilities result from operating activities. Changes in the current accounts are reported as adjustments to net income on the cash flow statement. The following rules apply:

CAPILANO LTD.
Balance Sheet
December 31, 2014 and 2013
(amounts in thousands)

Assets	2014	2013	Increase (Decrease)	Changes in the following:
Current				
Cash	$ 57	$ 101	$ (44)	
©Accounts receivable	224	192	32	
©Interest receivable	8	3	5	Current assets—**Operating**
©Inventory	323	330	(7)	
©Prepaid expenses	18	17	1	
Long-term receivable from another company	26	—	26	
Property, plant, and equipment, net of amortization	1,087	525	562	Noncurrent assets—**Investing**
Total	$1,743	$1,168	$ 575	
Liabilities				
Current				
©Accounts payable	$ 220	$ 137	$ 83	Current liabilities—**Operating**
©Salaries payable	6	12	(6)	and current portion of
©Accrued liabilities	5	7	(2)	long-term debt—**Financing**
Long-term debt	384	185	199	Most long-term liabilities and contributed
Shareholders' Equity				capital—**Financing**
Common shares	861	619	242	
Retained earnings	267	208	59	Due to net income— **Operating** and change due to dividends—**Financing**
Total	$1,743	$1,168	$ 575	

1. **An increase in a current asset other than cash is subtracted from net income to compute cash flow from operations.** Suppose a company makes a sale. Income is increased by the sale amount. However, collection of less than the full amount increases Accounts Receivable. For example, Exhibit 17–17 reports that Capilano Ltd.'s Accounts Receivable increased by $32,000 during 2014. To compute the impact of revenue on Capilano Ltd.'s cash flows, we must subtract the $32,000 increase in Accounts Receivable from net income in Exhibit 17–15. The reason is this: We have *not* collected this $32,000 in cash. The same logic applies to the other current assets. If they increase during the period, subtract the increase from net income.

Remember this:[2]

KEY POINTS

The additions and subtractions of current assets and current liabilities in the operating section are not inflows and outflows of cash. They are adjustments to net income to convert it to the cash basis.

Current asset other than Cash	↑	Cash ↓
(Accounts Receivable, Inventory, Supplies, etc.)		

---

[2] The authors thank Mari S. duToit for suggesting these displays.

2. **A decrease in a current asset other than cash is added to net income.** Suppose Capilano Ltd.'s Accounts Receivable balance decreased by $8,000 during the period. Cash receipts cause Accounts Receivable to decrease and Cash to increase, so decreases in Accounts Receivable and the other current assets are *added* to net income.

Symbolically,

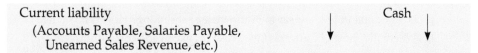

Current asset other than Cash   Cash ↑
   (Accounts Receivable, Inventory, Supplies, etc.) ↓

3. **A decrease in a current liability is subtracted from net income.** The payment of a current liability decreases both Cash and the current liability, so decreases in current liabilities are subtracted from net income. For example, in Exhibit 17–15, the $2,000 decrease in Accrued Liabilities is *subtracted* from net income to compute net cash inflow from operating activities.

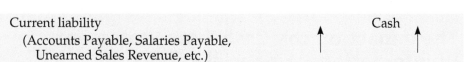

Current liability   Cash ↓
   (Accounts Payable, Salaries Payable,
      Unearned Sales Revenue, etc.) ↓

4. **An increase in a current liability is added to net income.** Capilano Ltd.'s Accounts Payable increased during the year. This increase can occur only if cash is not spent to pay this liability, which means that cash payments are less than the related expense. As a result, we have more cash on hand. Thus, increases in current liabilities are *added* to net income.

Current liability   Cash ↑
   (Accounts Payable, Salaries Payable,
      Unearned Sales Revenue, etc.) ↑

KEY POINTS

In the direct method, an increase in short-term debt is a financing activity. However, in the indirect method, it is classified in operations for simplicity as it is classified as a current liability.

Computing net cash inflow or net cash outflow from *operating* activities by the indirect method takes a path that is very different from the direct-method computation. However, both methods arrive at the same amount of net cash flow from operating activities, as shown in Exhibits 17–12 and 17–15: both report a net cash inflow of $168,000.

Exhibit 17–18 summarizes the adjustments needed to convert net income to net cash inflow (or net cash outflow) from operating activities by the indirect method.

If you are studying *only* the indirect method for operating cash flows, please turn to pages 1064–1065 and pages 1065–1066 for coverage of investing and financing activities.

MyAccountingLab

DemoDoc: Operating, Investing, and Financing Activities

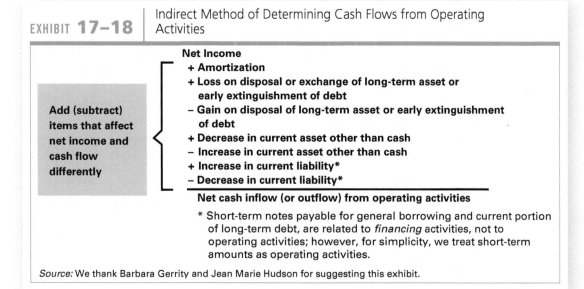

EXHIBIT 17–18 | Indirect Method of Determining Cash Flows from Operating Activities

Net Income

Add (subtract) items that affect net income and cash flow differently
- + Amortization
- + Loss on disposal or exchange of long-term asset or early extinguishment of debt
- – Gain on disposal of long-term asset or early extinguishment of debt
- + Decrease in current asset other than cash
- – Increase in current asset other than cash
- + Increase in current liability*
- – Decrease in current liability*

Net cash inflow (or outflow) from operating activities

* Short-term notes payable for general borrowing and current portion of long-term debt, are related to *financing* activities, not to operating activities; however, for simplicity, we treat short-term amounts as operating activities.

Source: We thank Barbara Gerrity and Jean Marie Hudson for suggesting this exhibit.

✓ JUST CHECKING

10. The information listed below is taken from the financial statements of Vista Corp. for the year ended December 31, 2014, when net income is $150. All amounts are in thousands of dollars:

	Dec. 31, 2014	Jan. 1, 2014
Cash	$45	$15
Accounts Receivable	12	18
Inventory	66	48
Accounts Payable	20	9
Wages Payable	24	39

Compute cash flow from operating activities using the indirect method.

11. Examine Capilano Ltd.'s cash flow statement, Exhibit 17–15, and answer these questions:

  a. Does Capilano Ltd. appear to be growing or shrinking? How can you tell?

  b. Where did most of Capilano Ltd.'s cash for expansion come from?

  c. Suppose Accounts Receivable decreased by $80,000 (instead of increasing by $32,000) during the current year. What would Capilano Ltd.'s cash flow from operating activities be?

Just Checking Solutions appear at the end of this chapter and on MyAccountingLab.

The Impact on the Cash Flow Statement of International Financial Reporting Standards (IFRS)

LO ⑥

How does IFRS affect the cash flow statement?

As we saw earlier in this chapter under accounting standards for private enterprises (ASPE), receipts of interest and dividends, and payments of interest are operating activities. Payment of dividends is a financing activity. Under IFRS, a company may choose to classify receipts of interest and dividends as either operating or investing activities. Similarly, a company may choose to report payments of interest and dividends as either operating or financing activities. Once a company chooses its accounting policy, it must apply the policy consistently to all similar transactions. Under IFRS, there is no preference for the direct or indirect method of reporting cash flows from operating activities; either method is acceptable.

Under ASPE, the statement showing cash inflows and outflows is called the *Cash Flow Statement*; under IFRS, it is called the *Statement of Cash Flows*. However, this is a very minor difference as both sets of standards allow some flexibility in naming the statements. In practice, *Cash Flow Statement* and *Statement of Cash Flows* are used interchangeably.

✓ JUST CHECKING

12. Under IFRS, what options does an entity have for classifying cash inflows from interest and dividends on the statement of cash flows? How does this differ from ASPE?

13. Under IFRS, what options does an entity have for classifying cash payments of interest and dividends on the statement of cash flows? How does this differ from ASPE?

Just Checking Solutions appear at the end of this chapter and on MyAccountingLab.

Summary Problem for Your Review

Prepare the 2014 cash flow statement for Valemont Corporation, using the indirect method to report cash flows from operating activities.

Transaction data for 2014

Amortization expense	$ 40,000	Payment of cash	
Issuance of long-term note		dividends	$ 72,000
payable to borrow cash	28,000	Net income	104,000
Issuance of common shares		Purchase of long-term	
for cash	76,000	investment	32,000
Cash received from sale		Issuance of long-term note	
of building	296,000	payable to purchase	
Repurchase of own shares	20,000	patent	148,000
Loss on sale of building	8,000	Issuance of common shares	
Purchase of equipment	392,000	to retire $52,000 of bonds	52,000

	December 31,		For the indirect method, calculate
	2014	**2013**	the dollar change in all *noncash* current asset and current liability accounts.
Current assets			
Cash and cash equivalents	$ 76,000	$ 12,000	
Accounts receivable	88,000	92,000	$(4,000)
Inventories	136,000	124,000	12,000
Prepaid expenses	4,000	12,000	(8,000)
Current liabilities			
Notes payable (for inventory purchases)	$ 44,000	$ 28,000	$16,000
Accounts payable	96,000	76,000	20,000
Accrued liabilities	28,000	36,000	(8,000)
Income and other taxes payable	40,000	40,000	0

SOLUTION

Recall:

The title must include the name of the company, "Cash Flow Statement," and the specific period of time covered. There are three sections: Cash flows from operating, investing, and financing activities.

For the indirect method, always begin with accrual-basis net income from the income statement (or from data given, in this case).

Add back noncash items: amortization and losses; deduct gains

Reflect changes in current assets and liabilities as follows:
Current asset increases—deduct
Current asset decreases—add
Current liability increases—add
Current liability decreases—deduct

For cash flows from investing activities, look for activities that have a cash impact on long-term asset accounts. Brackets indicate cash outflows (purchases).

For cash flows from financing activities, look for activities that have a cash impact on short-term debt (or note) accounts, long-term liability accounts, and equity accounts. Brackets indicate cash outflows. The end result should equal the December 31, 2014, balance sheet amount of cash and cash equivalents, given as part of Current assets. If it does not, there is an error in the cash flow statement.

VALEMONT CORPORATION
Cash Flow Statement
For the Year Ended December 31, 2014

Cash flows from operating activities

Net income		$104,000
Add (subtract) items that affect net income and		
cash flow differently:		
Amortization	$ 40,000	
Loss on sale of building	8,000	
Decrease in accounts receivable	4,000	
Increase in inventories	(12,000)	
Decrease in prepaid expenses	8,000	
Increase in notes payable, short-term	16,000	
Increase in accounts payable	20,000	
Decrease in accrued liabilities	(8,000)	76,000
Net cash inflow from operating activities		180,000
Cash flows from investing activities		
Purchase of equipment	(392,000)	
Sale of building	296,000	
Purchase of long-term investment	(32,000)	
Net cash outflow from investing activities		(128,000)
Cash flows from financing activities		
Issuance of long-term note payable	28,000	
Issuance of common shares	76,000	
Payment of cash dividends	(72,000)	
Repurchase of Valemont Corporation common shares	(20,000)	
Net cash inflow from financing activities		12,000
Net increase in cash and cash equivalents		$ 64,000
Cash and cash equivalents at beginning of 2014		12,000
Cash and cash equivalents at end of 2014		$ 76,000

In the notes to the financial statements:
1. During the year, the company issued a long-term note payable in the amount of $148,000 in payment for a patent.
2. During the year, the company issued common shares in the amount of $52,000 to retire bonds payable in the same amount.

Summary

Check Accounting Vocabulary on page 1087 for all key terms used in Chapter 17 and the Glossary on page 1246 for all key terms used in the textbook.

CHAPTER REVIEW:

MyAccountingLab   DemoDoc covering Operating, Investing, and Financing Activities

MyAccountingLab   Student PowerPoint Slides

MyAccountingLab   Audio Chapter Summary

Note: All MyAccountingLab resources can be found in the Chapter Resources section and the Multimedia Library.

SELF-STUDY QUESTIONS

Test your understanding of the chapter by marking the correct answer for each of the following questions:

1. The income statement and the balance sheet (p. 1054)
   a. Report the cash effects of transactions
   b. Fail to report why cash changed during the period
   c. Report the sources and uses of cash during the period
   d. Are divided into operating, investing, and financing activities

2. The purpose of the cash flow statement is to (p. 1055)
   a. Predict future cash flows
   b. Evaluate management decisions
   c. Determine the ability to pay liabilities and dividends
   d. Do all the above

3. A successful company's major source of cash should be (p. 1056)
   a. Operating activities   b. Investing activities
   c. Financing activities   d. A combination of the above

4. Dividends paid to shareholders are usually reported on the cash flow statement as a(n) (pp. 1058–1059)
   a. Operating activity
   b. Investing activity
   c. Financing activity
   d. Combination of the above

5. Which of the following appears as a line on a cash flow statement prepared by the direct method? (p. 1063)
   a. Amortization expense
   b. Decrease in accounts receivable
   c. Loss on sale of property, plant, and equipment, and intangible assets
   d. Cash payments to suppliers

6. Falcon Lake Copy Centre had accounts receivable of $40,000 at the beginning of the year and $50,000 at year end. Revenue for the year totalled $150,000. How much cash did Falcon Lake Copy Centre collect from customers? (pp. 1063–1064)
   a. $160,000   b. $190,000
   c. $200,000   d. $140,000

7. Tancredi Ltd. sold a long-term investment for $50,000; the selling price included a loss of $2,500. The cash flow from investing activities will show (p. 1074)
   a. An increase of $50,000
   b. An increase of $47,500
   c. A decrease of $52,500
   d. None of the above

8. Herdsman Corp. borrowed $100,000, issued common shares for $40,000, and paid dividends of $30,000. What was Herdsman Corp.'s net cash provided (used) by financing activities? (pp. 1074–1075)
   a. $0   b. $110,000
   c. $(30,000)   d. $140,000

9. In preparing a cash flow statement by the indirect method, the accountant will treat an increase in inventory as a(n) (pp. 1080–1081)
   a. Increase in investment cash flows
   b. Decrease in investment cash flows
   c. Decrease in operating cash flows
   d. Increase in operating cash flows

10. Net income is $40,000, and amortization is $12,000. In addition, the sale of property, plant, and equipment generated a $8,000 gain. Current assets other than cash increased by $12,000, and current liabilities increased by $16,000. What was the amount of cash flow from operations using the indirect method? (pp. 1078–1081)
    a. $64,000   b. $48,000
    c. $40,000   d. $72,000

Answers to Self-Study Questions

1. b
2. d
3. a
4. c
5. d
6. d
7. a
8. b
9. c
10. b ($40,000+$12,000−$8,000−$12,000+$16,000= $48,000)

ACCOUNTING VOCABULARY

Cash equivalents Highly liquid short-term investments that can be converted into cash with little delay *(p. 1056)*.

Cash flow statement Reports cash receipts and cash payments classified according to the entity's major activities: operating, investing, and financing *(p. 1054)*.

Cash flows Cash receipts and cash payments (disbursements) *(p. 1054)*.

Direct method Format of the operating activities section of the cash flow statement that shows cash receipts from and cash payments for operating activities *(p. 1060)*.

Financing activity Activity that obtains the funds from investors and creditors needed to launch and sustain the business; a section of the cash flow statement *(p. 1057)*.

Free cash flow The amount of cash available from operations after paying for planned investments in plant, equipment, and other long-term assets *(p. 1060)*.

Indirect method Format of the operating activities section of the cash flow statement that starts with net income and shows the reconciliation from net income to operating cash flows. Also called the *reconciliation method (p. 1060)*.

Investing activity Activity that increases and decreases the long-term assets available to the business; a section of the cash flow statement *(p. 1057)*.

Operating activity Activity that creates revenue or expense in the entity's major line of business. A section of the cash flow statement. Operating activities affect the income statement *(p. 1056)*.

Reconciliation method Another name for the indirect method of formatting the operating activities section of the cash flow statement *(p. 1076)*.

SIMILAR ACCOUNTING TERMS

Cash flows	Cash receipts and cash payments
Cash flow statement	Statement of cash flows; Statement of changes in financial position
Cash payments	Disbursements
Cash receipts	Proceeds
Indirect method	Reconciliation method

Assignment Material

QUESTIONS

1. What information does the cash flow statement report that is not shown on the balance sheet, the income statement, or the statement of retained earnings?

2. Identify four purposes of the cash flow statement.

3. Identify and briefly describe the three types of activities that are reported on the cash flow statement.

4. How is the cash flow statement dated and why?

5. What is the check figure for the cash flow statement? In other words, which figure do you check to make sure you've done your work correctly? Where is it obtained, and how is it used?

6. What is the most important source of cash for most successful companies?

7. How can cash decrease during a year when income is high? How can cash increase when income is low? How can investors and creditors learn these facts about the company?

8. How should issuance of a note payable to purchase land be reported in the financial statements? Identify three other transactions that fall into this same category.

9. What is free cash flow, and how is it calculated?

10. Fort Inc. prepares its cash flow statement using the *direct* method for operating activities. Identify the section of Fort Inc.'s cash flow statement where the results of each of the following transactions will appear. If the transaction does not appear on the cash flow statement, give the reason.

a. Cash	14,000	
Note Payable, Long-Term		14,000
b. Salary Payable	7,300	
Cash		7,300
c. Cash	28,400	
Sales Revenue		28,400
d. Amortization Expense	6,500	
Patent		6,500
e. Accounts Payable	1,400	
Cash		1,400

11. Why is amortization expense *not* reported on a cash flow statement that reports operating activities by the direct method? Why and how are these expenses reported on a statement prepared by the indirect method?

12. Winford Distributing Corp. collected cash of $102,000 from customers and $8,000 interest on notes receivable. Cash payments included $28,000 to employees, $18,000 to suppliers, $11,000 as dividends to shareholders, and $10,000 as a long-term loan to another company. How much was Winford Distributing Corp.'s net cash inflow from operating activities?

13. Summarize the major cash receipts and cash payments in the three categories of activities that appear on the cash flow statement prepared by the direct method.

14. Nelson Inc. recorded salary expense of $54,000 during a year when the balance of Salary Payable decreased from $8,000 to $2,000. How much cash did Nelson Inc. pay to employees during the year? Where on the cash flow statement should Nelson Inc. report this item?

15. Trail Corporation's beginning Property, Plant, and Equipment balance, net of accumulated amortization, was $200,000, and the ending amount was $180,000. Trail Corporation recorded amortization of $35,000 and sold property, plant, and equipment with a book value of $10,000. How much cash did Trail Corporation pay to purchase property, plant, and equipment during the period? Where on the cash flow statement should Trail Corporation report this item?

16. Which format of the cash flow statement gives a clearer description of the individual cash flows from operating activities? Which format better shows the relationship between net income and operating cash flow?

17. An investment that cost $150,000 was sold for $160,000, resulting in a $10,000 gain. Show how to report this transaction on a cash flow statement prepared by the indirect method.

18. Using the indirect method, identify the cash effects of net increases and net decreases in current assets other than cash. What are the cash effects of net increases and net decreases in current liabilities?

19. Aggasiz Corporation earned net income of $90,000 and had amortization expense of $24,000. Also, noncash current assets decreased by $18,000, and current liabilities decreased by $12,000. Using the indirect method, what was Aggasiz Corporation's net cash flow from operating activities?

20. What is the difference between the direct method and the indirect method of reporting investing activities and financing activities?

21. Degrout Corp. reports operating activities by the direct method. Does this method show the relationship between net income and cash flow from operations? If so, state how. If not, how can Greenwood Corp. satisfy this purpose of the cash flow statement?

MyAccountingLab   Make the grade with MyAccountingLab: The Starters, Exercises, and Problems marked in red can be found on MyAccountingLab. You can practise them as often as you want, and most feature step-by-step guided instructions to help you find the right answer.

STARTERS

Purposes of the cash flow statement

Starter 17–1 Describe how the cash flow statement helps investors and creditors perform each of the following functions:

1. Predict future cash flows.
2. Evaluate management decisions.
3. Predict the ability to make debt payments to lenders and pay dividends to shareholders.
4. Show the relationship of net income to cash flow.

Starter 17–2   Answer these questions about the cash flow statement.

    a. List the categories of cash flows in order of importance.

    b. What is the "check figure" for the statement of cash flows? Where do you get this check figure?

    c. What is the first dollar amount to report for the direct method?

    d. What is the first dollar amount to report for the indirect method?

Classifying cash flow items

Starter 17–3   Latham Company expects the following for 2014:

- Net cash provided by operating activities of $120,000
- Net cash provided by financing activities of $48,000
- Net cash used for investing activities of $64,000 (no sales of long-term assets)

How much free cash flow does Latham Company expect for 2014?

Free cash flow

Free cash flow $56,000

Starter 17–4   Memmot Health Labs Inc. began 2014 with cash of $65,000. During the year, Memmot earned service revenue of $650,000 and collected $660,000 from customers. Expenses for the year totalled $470,000, of which Memmot paid $460,000 in cash to suppliers and employees. Memmot also paid $150,000 to purchase equipment and paid a cash dividend of $40,000 to its shareholders during 2014.

    Prepare the company's cash flow statement for the year ended December 31, 2014. Format operating activities by the direct method.

Preparing a cash flow statement—direct method

Net increase in cash $10,000

Starter 17–5   (Starter 17–6 is an alternate.) Napanee Resources Inc. has assembled the following data for the year ended June 30, 2014.

Payment of dividends	$ 12,000
Cash received from issuing shares	40,000
Collections from customers	400,000
Cash received from sale of land..	120,000
Payments to suppliers	220,000
Purchase of equipment..	80,000
Payments to employees..	140,000
Payment of note payable..	60,000

    Prepare only the *operating* activities section of Napanee's cash flow statement for the year ended June 30, 2014. Napanee uses the direct method for operating cash flows.

Computing operating cash flows—direct method

Net cash provided $40,000

Starter 17–6   Use the data in Starter 17–5 to prepare Napanee Resources Inc.'s complete cash flow statement for the year ended June 30, 2014. Napanee uses the *direct* method for operating activities. Use Exhibit 17–12 on page 1069 as a guide, but you may stop after determining the net increase (or decrease) in cash.

Preparing a cash flow statement—direct method

Net increase in cash $48,000

Starter 17–7   Refer to the Equipment T-account below. For the items to be reported on the cash flow statement, indicate the section where they are reported.

Preparing a cash flow statement—investing

Equipment

Beginning Balance	$100,000		
July 1	200,000		
		July 15	$50,000
Aug. 1	57,000		
Ending balance	$307,000		

July 1 and July 15 were cash transactions.
August 1 was a purchase with a long-term note.

Computing operating cash
flows—direct method

a. Collections from customers
$402,000

Starter 17–8 Hasbra Toys Ltd. had the following comparative balance sheet:

HASBRA TOYS LTD.						
Balance Sheet						
December 31, 2014 and 2013						
Assets	**2014**	**2013**	**Liabilities**		**2014**	**2013**
Current			Current			
Cash	$ 57,000	$ 48,000	Accounts payable	$	141,000	$ 126,000
Accounts receivable	162,000	144,000	Salary payable		69,000	63,000
Inventory	240,000	232,000	Accrued liabilities		24,000	33,000
Prepaid expenses	9,000	6,000	Long-term notes			
			payable		198,000	204,000
Long-term investments	225,000	270,000	**Shareholders' Equity**			
Property and			Common shares		120,000	111,000
equipment, net	675,000	575,000	Retained earnings		816,000	738,000
Total	$1,368,000	$1,275,000	Total		$1,368,000	$1,275,000

Compute for Hasbra Toys Ltd:

a. Collections from customers during 2014. Sales totalled $420,000.

b. Payments for inventory during 2014, assuming the change in Accounts Payable is due to inventory. Cost of goods sold was $240,000.

Computing financing cash flows

c. Dividends $42,000

Starter 17–9 Use the Hasbra Toys Ltd. data in Starter 17–8 to compute the following:

a. New borrowing or payment of long-term note payable, with Hasbra having only one long-term note payable transaction during the year.

b. Issuance of common shares, with Hasbra having only one common share transaction during the year.

c. Payment of cash dividends. Net income for the year ended December 31, 2014 was $120,000.

d. Calculate the net cash provided by operating activities using the direct method. Ignore Prepaid Expenses, Salary Payable, and Accrued Liabilities.

Computing investing and
financing cash flows
④
a. Acquisitions $16,500

Starter 17–10 Hubert Media Corporation had the following income statement and balance sheet for 2014:

HUBERT MEDIA CORPORATION	
Income Statement	
For the Year Ended December 31, 2014	
Service revenue	$120,000
Amortization expense	9,000
Other expenses	81,000
Net income	$ 30,000

HUBERT MEDIA CORPORATION					
Balance Sheet					
December 31, 2014 and 2013					
Assets	**2014**	**2013**	**Liabilities**	**2014**	**2013**
Current:			Current:		
Cash	$ 7,500	$ 6,000	Accounts payable	$ 12,000	$ 9,000
Accounts receivable	15,000	9,000	Long-term notes		
Equipment, net	112,500	105,000	payable	15,000	18,000
			Shareholders' equity		
			Common shares	33,000	30,000
			Retained earnings	75,000	63,000
	$135,000	$120,000		$135,000	$120,000

Compute for Hubert during 2014:

a. Acquisition of equipment. Hubert sold no equipment during the year.
b. Payment of a long-term note payable. During the year, Hubert issued a $7,500 note payable.

Starter 17–11 Werstiner Corporation is preparing its cash flow statement by the *indirect* method. The company has the following items for you to consider in preparing the statement. Identify each item as

- Operating activity—addition to net income (O+), or subtraction from net income (O–)
- Investing activity (I)
- Financing activity (F)
- Activity that is not used to prepare the cash flow statement (N)

Answer by placing the appropriate symbol in the blank space.

Identifying items for reporting cash flows from operations—indirect method

a. O+
j. O–

_____ a. Loss on sale of land   _____ f. Increase in accounts payable

_____ b. Amortization expense   _____ g. Payment of dividends

_____ c. Increase in inventory   _____ h. Decrease in accrued liabilities

_____ d. Decrease in accounts receivable   _____ i. Issuance of common shares

_____ e. Purchase of equipment   _____ j. Gain on sale of building

Starter 17–12 Urgent Printers reported the following data for 2014:

Computing cash flows from operating activities—indirect method

Net cash provided $61,000

Income Statement	
Net income	$63,000
Amortization expense	10,000
Balance sheet	
Increase in Accounts Receivable	7,000
Decrease in Accounts Payable	5,000

Compute Urgent Printers' net cash provided by operating activities, using the indirect method.

Starter 17–13 Donna's Gourmet Shops earned net income of $88,000, which included amortization of $16,500. Donna's paid $132,000 for a building and borrowed $66,000 on a long-term note payable. How much did Donna's cash balance increase or decrease during the year?

Computing a cash increase or decrease—indirect method

Increased $38,500

Starter 17–14 (Starter 17–15 is an alternate.) Hwyn Resources Inc. accountants have assembled the following data for the year ended June 30, 2014.

Computing operating cash flows—indirect method

Net cash provided $70,000

Payment of dividends .... $12,000   Net income $100,000

Cash receipt from issuance   Purchase of equipment....................... 80,000

   of common shares 40,000   Decrease in current liabilities 10,000

Increase in current   Payment of note payable.................... 60,000

   assets other than cash 60,000   Cash receipt from sale of land......... 120,000

Repurchase of Hwyn shares.............. 10,000   Amortization expense 40,000

Prepare the *operating* activities section of Hwyn Resources Inc.'s cash flow statement for the year ended June 30, 2014. Hwyn uses the *indirect* method for operating cash flows.

Preparing a cash flow
statement—indirect method
⑤
Net increase in cash $68,000

Starter 17–15 Use the data in Starter 17–14 to prepare Hwyn Resources Inc.'s cash flow statement for the year ended June 30, 2014. Hwyn uses the *indirect* method for operating activities. Use Exhibit 17–15 as a guide, but you may stop after determining the net increase (or decrease) in cash.

Using a cash flow statement
①

Starter 17–16 Which company shown below is likely a start-up company rather than an established company? Give reasons for your answer.

	Company X	Company Y
Cash inflow (outflow)—operating activities	$ (10,000)	$50,000
Cash inflow (outflow)—investing activities	(100,000)	30,000
Cash inflow (outflow)—financing activities	80,000	(20,000)
Income (loss) for the year	20,000	20,000

EXERCISES MyAccountingLab

Exercise 17–1

Identifying the purposes of the
cash flow statement
①

Hazelton Properties Ltd., a real estate developer, has experienced ten years of growth in net income. Nevertheless, the business is facing bankruptcy. Creditors are calling all Hazelton Properties Ltd.'s outstanding loans for immediate payment, and the cash is simply not available. Where did Hazelton Properties Ltd. go wrong? Managers placed too much emphasis on net income and gave too little attention to cash flows.

Required

Write a brief memo, in your own words, to explain for Hazelton Properties Ltd. managers the purposes of the cash flow statement.

Exercise 17–2

Using a cash flow statement
①

Suppose Whiteshell Inc.'s cash flow statement showed a net cash outflow from operations of $6,000,000.

Required

1. Suggest possible reasons for the cash outflow from operations.
2. What is the main danger signal this situation reveals?
3. Suppose Whiteshell Inc. has two more years with the cash flows mentioned above. What is likely to happen to the company?

Exercise 17–3

Distinguishing among operating, investing, and financing
activities
②

Describe operating activities, investing activities, and financing activities. For each category, give an example of (a) a cash receipt and (b) a cash payment.

Exercise 17–4

Identifying activities for the cash
flow statement
② ③
a. NIF
e. I–
g. O+

Identify each of the following transactions as an operating activity (O), an investing activity (I), a financing activity (F), a noncash investing and financing activity (NIF), or a transaction that is not reported on the cash flow statement (N). For each cash flow, indicate whether the item increases (+) or decreases (–) cash. Assume the direct method is used to report cash flows from operating activities.

Activity	(+)/(−)	Transactions
a.	_____	Acquisition of a building by issuance of common shares
b.	_____	Issuance of common shares for cash
c.	_____	Payment of accounts payable
d.	_____	Acquisition of equipment by issuance of note payable
e.	_____	Purchase of long-term investment
f.	_____	Payment of wages to employees
g.	_____	Collection of cash interest
h.	_____	Distribution of stock dividend
i.	_____	Repurchase of common shares
j.	_____	Amortization of bond discount
k.	_____	Collection of accounts receivable

Exercise 17–5

Use the information provided to prepare a cash flow statement for Starr Karaoke using the direct method for December 31, 2014. Assume that the beginning balance of cash is $55,000. Identify by letter which entry matched the line item on the cash flow statement.

Preparing a cash flow statement—direct method

③

a. Cash balance end of the year $73,000.

a.	Land	185,000	
	Cash		185,000
b.	Dividends Payable	40,000	
	Cash		40,000
c.	Furniture and Fixtures	43,000	
	Note Payable, Short-Term		43,000
d.	Salaries Expense	19,000	
	Cash		19,000
e.	Equipment	137,000	
	Cash		137,000
f.	Cash	125,000	
	Long-Term Investment in Bonds		125,000
g.	Bonds Payable	80,000	
	Cash		80,000
h.	Building	210,000	
	Note Payable, Long-Term		210,000
i.	Cash	85,000	
	Accounts Receivable		85,000
j.	Accounts Payable	39,000	
	Cash		39,000
k.	Cash	140,000	
	Common Shares		140,000
l.	Cash	8,000	
	Interest Revenue		8,000

Exercise 17–6

The accounting records of Koltire Auto Parts Ltd. reveal the following:

Computing cash flows from operating activities—direct method

③

Net cash inflow from operating activities $60,000

Acquisition of land........................	$ 89,000	Loss on sale of land.....................	$ 6,000	
Amortization...............................	50,000	Net income	78,000	
Cash sales	78,000	Payment of accounts payable....	110,000	
Collection of accounts		Payment of dividends	25,000	
receivable...................................	186,000	Payment of income tax	8,000	
Collection of dividend revenue..	4,000	Payment of interest.....................	14,000	
Decrease in current liabilities	52,000	Payment of salaries		
Increase in current assets		and wages.................................	76,000	
other than cash	48,000			

Required

Compute cash flows from operating activities by the direct method. Use the format of the operating activities section of Exhibit 17–12.

Exercise 17–7

Identifying items for the cash flow statement—direct method

Selected accounts of Acorn Storage Centres show the following:

Accounts Receivable

Beginning balance	27,000	Cash receipts from customers	354,000
Service revenue	360,000		
Ending balance	33,000		

Land

Beginning balance	640,000	
Acquisitions paid with cash	81,000	
Ending balance	721,000	

Long-Term Debt

Payments	207,000	Beginning balance	819,000
		Issuance of debt for cash	249,000
		Ending balance	861,000

Required

For each account, identify the item or items that should appear on a cash flow statement prepared by the direct method. Also, state each item's amount and where to report the item.

Exercise 17–8

Preparing a cash flow statement—direct method

3. Net increase in cash $100,000

Tech Arts Ltd. began 2014 with cash of $112,000. During the year, the company earned service revenue of $2,400,000 and collected $2,360,000 from clients. Expenses for the year totalled $1,760,000, of which the company paid $1,640,000 in cash to employees and $60,000 in cash for supplies. Tech Arts Ltd. also paid $480,000 to purchase computer equipment and paid a cash dividend of $80,000 to its shareholders during 2014.

Required

1. Compute net income for the year.
2. Determine the cash balance at the end of the year.
3. Prepare the company's cash flow statement for the year. Format operating activities by the direct method.

Exercise 17–9

Preparing a cash flow statement—direct method

Net cash from operating $288,000; investing $(182,000); financing $(86,000)

The income statement and additional data of Flashpoint Consulting Ltd. follow:

FLASHPOINT CONSULTING LTD. Income Statement For the Year Ended September 30, 2014		
Revenues		
Consulting revenue		$548,000
Expenses		
Salaries expense	$296,000	
Amortization expense	58,000	
Rent expense	14,000	
Office supplies expense	16,000	
Insurance expense	4,000	
Interest expense	4,000	
Income tax expense	36,000	428,000
Net income		$120,000

Additional data:

a. Collections from clients were $114,000 more than revenues.

b. Increase in cash balance, $20,000.

c. Payments to employees are $8,000 less than salaries expense.

d. Interest expense and income tax expense equal their cash amounts.

e. Acquisition of computer equipment is $232,000. Of this amount, $202,000 was paid in cash, $30,000 by signing a long-term note payable.

f. Cash received from sale of land, $20,000.

g. Cash received from issuance of common shares, $84,000.

h. Payment of long-term note payable, $40,000.

i. Payment of cash dividends, $130,000.

j. Payments for rent and insurance were equal to expense.

k. Payment for office supplies was $12,000 more than expense.

Prepare Flashpoint Consulting Ltd.'s cash flow statement by the direct method and the note to the financial statements giving the summary of noncash investing and financing activities. Evaluate Flashpoint's cash flow for the year. Mention all three categories of cash flows and the reason for your evaluation.

Exercise 17–10

Compute the following items for the cash flow statement:

Computing amounts for the cash flow statement—direct method

③ ④

a. $104,000

a.	Beginning Accounts Receivable	$25,000
	Ending Accounts Receivable	21,000
	Credit sales for the period	100,000
	Cash collections	?
b.	Cost of goods sold	$80,000
	Beginning Inventory balance	20,000
	Ending Inventory balance	16,000
	Beginning Accounts Payable	12,000
	Ending Accounts Payable	8,000
	Cash payments for inventory	?

Exercise 17–11

Compute the following items for the cash flow statement:

Computing investing and financing amounts for the cash flow statement

④

a. $45,000

a.	Beginning Retained Earnings	$120,000
	Ending Retained Earnings	160,000
	Net income for the period	150,000
	Stock dividends	65,000
	Cash dividend payments	?
b.	Beginning Property, Plant, and Equipment	$320,000 net
	Ending Property, Plant, and Equipment	365,000 net
	Amortization for the period	36,000
	Acquisitions of new property, plant, and equipment	104,000
	Property, plant, and equipment was sold at an $8,000 loss.	
	What was the amount of the cash receipt from the sale?	

Exercise 17–12

Identify each of the following transactions as an operating activity (O), an investing activity (I), a financing activity (F), a noncash investing and financing activity (NIF), or a transaction that is not reported on the cash flow statement (N). For each cash flow, indicate whether the item increases (+) or decreases (–) cash. Assume the *indirect* method is used to report cash flows from operating activities.

Identifying activities for the cash flow statement

② ⑤

a. O+
e. F+
g. O+

Activity	(+)/(−)	Transactions
a.	——	Amortization of equipment
b.	——	Sale of long-term investment at a loss
c.	——	Payment of cash dividend
d.	——	Increase in inventory
e.	——	Issuance of preferred shares for cash
f.	——	Prepaid expenses decreased during the year
g.	——	Accrual of salaries expense
h.	——	Issuance of long-term note payable to borrow cash
i.	——	Cash sale of land
j.	——	Payment of long-term debt

Exercise 17–13

Computing net income using cash flows from operating activities—indirect method

Repage Inc. reported a net cash flow from operating activities of $40,625 on its cash flow statement for the year ended December 31, 2014. The following information was reported in the Cash Flows from Operating Activities section of the cash flow statement, using the *indirect* method:

Decrease in legal fees payable...........................	$1,000
Increase in prepaid expenses............................	400
Amortization.......................................	3,350
Loss on sale of equipment.............................	1,500
Increase in accounts payable	600
Decrease in inventories	2,175
Increase in trade accounts receivable.............	2,000

Determine the net income reported by Repage Inc. for the year ended December 31, 2014.

Exercise 17–14

Classifying transactions for the cash flow statement

② ③ ⑤

Indicate whether or not each of the items below would be shown on a cash flow statement, with operating activities reported using the *indirect* method. Indicate whether the adjustment is added to, deducted from, or has no effect on the cash flow statement. If the transaction affects the cash flow statement, state whether it relates to operating activities, investing activities, or financing activities. Provide the reason for your answer.

a. The payment of interest on long-term debt.

b. The declaration and distribution of a common stock dividend.

c. A decrease in accounts payable.

d. The sale of office equipment for its book value.

e. The borrowing of funds for future expansion through the sale of bonds.

f. A gain on the sale of property, plant, and equipment.

g. The purchase of equipment in exchange for common shares.

h. Amortization expense—buildings.

i. A decrease in merchandise inventory.

j. An increase in prepaid expenses.

k. Amortization of the premium on bonds payable.

l. An investment in a money-market fund.

m. The receipt of interest on long-term investments.

n. The purchase of office equipment.

o. Receiving funds for future expansion through the sale of common shares.

p. Amortization of intangible assets.

Exercise 17–15

The accounting records of Iberia Corporation reveal the following:

Acquisition of land.................	$ 444,000	Increase in current assets	
Amortization...........................	156,000	other than cash	$252,000
Cash sales	108,000	Loss on sale of land......................	60,000
Collection of accounts		Net income	288,000
receivable.............................	1,116,000	Payment of accounts payable......	576,000
Collection of dividend		Payment of dividends	84,000
revenue	108,000	Payment of income tax.................	96,000
Decrease in current		Payment of interest.......................	192,000
liabilities	276,000	Payment of salaries and wages...	432,000

Compute cash flows from operating activities by the indirect method. Use the format of the operating activities section of Exhibit 17–15. Then evaluate Iberia Corporation's operating cash flows as strong or weak.

Computing cash flows from operating activities—indirect method

Cash outflows from operating activities $(24,000)

Exercise 17–16

Two transactions of LRT Logistics Inc. are recorded as follows:

a. Cash..	80,000	
Accumulated Amortization—Computer Equipment.........	830,000	
Computer Equipment...		870,000
Gain on Sale of Computer Equipment..........................		40,000
b. Land	2,900,000	
Cash...		1,300,000
Note Payable..		1,600,000

Classifying transactions for the cash flow statement

Required

1. Indicate where, how, and in what amount to report these transactions on the cash flow statement and accompanying schedule of noncash investing and financing activities. Are they cash receipts or payments? LRT Logistics Inc. reports cash flows from operating activities by the *direct* method.

2. Repeat Requirement 1, assuming that LRT Logistics Inc. reports cash flows from operating activities by the *indirect* method.

Exercise 17–17

Use the income statement of Flashpoint Consulting Ltd. in Exercise 17–9, plus these additional data during fiscal year 2014:

a. Acquisition of computer equipment was $232,000. Of this amount, $202,000 was paid in cash, $30,000 by signing a long-term note payable. Flashpoint Consulting Ltd. sold no computer equipment during fiscal year 2014.

b. Cash received from sale of land, $20,000.

c. Cash received from issuance of common shares, $84,000.

d. Payment of long-term note payable, $40,000.

e. Payment of dividends, $130,000.

f. Change in cash balance, $?.

g. From the comparative balance sheet:

Preparing the cash flow statement by the indirect method

Net cash flow from operating $288,000; investing $(182,000); financing $(86,000)

FLASHPOINT CONSULTING LTD.		
Balance Sheet (partial)		
September 30, 2014 and 2013		
	2014	**2013**
Current assets:		
Cash	$56,000	$ 36,000
Accounts receivable	30,000	144,000
Office supplies	18,000	6,000
Prepaid expenses	10,000	10,000
Current liabilities:		
Accounts payable	$68,000	$ 56,000
Accrued liabilities	38,000	42,000

Required

1. Prepare Flashpoint Consulting Ltd.'s cash flow statement for the year ended September 30, 2014, using the indirect method.

2. Evaluate Flashpoint Consulting Ltd.'s cash flows for the year. In your evaluation, mention all three categories of cash flows, and give the reason for your evaluation.

Exercise 17–18

Computing cash flows from operating activities—indirect method

⑤

Net cash outflow from operating activities $21,000

Witbey Printing Ltd.'s year end is February 28. The accounting records of Witbey Printing Ltd. at March 31, 2014, include the selected accounts shown below.

Cash			
Mar. 1	75,000	Dividend	24,000
Collections	126,000	Payments	138,000
Mar. 31	39,000		

Accounts Receivable			
Mar. 1	54,000		
Sales	228,000	Collections	126,000
Mar. 31	156,000		

Inventory			
Mar. 1	57,000		
Purchases	111,000	Cost of sales	108,000
Mar. 31	60,000		

Equipment		
Mar. 1	279,000	
Mar. 31	279,000	

Accumulated Amortization—Equipment		
	Mar. 1	78,000
	Amortization	9,000
	Mar. 31	87,000

Accounts Payable			
		Mar. 1	42,000
Payments	96,000	Purchases	111,000
		Mar. 31	57,000

Accrued Liabilities			
		Mar. 1	27,000
Payments	42,000	Expenses	33,000
		Mar. 31	18,000

Retained Earnings			
Quarterly		Mar. 1	192,000
dividend	24,000	Net income	69,000
		Mar. 31	237,000

Required

Compute Witbey Printing Ltd.'s net cash inflow or outflow from operating activities during March 2014. Use the *indirect* method. Does Witbey Printing Ltd. have trouble collecting receivables or selling inventory? How can you tell?

Exercise 17–19

Interpreting a cash flow statement—indirect method

⑤

Consider three independent cases for the cash flow data of Rennie Recreation Products Inc.:

	Case A	Case B	Case C
Cash flows from operating activities:			
Net income	$ 120,000	$ 12,000	$ 120,000
Amortization	44,000	44,000	44,000
Increase in current assets	(4,000)	(28,000)	(76,000)
Decrease in current liabilities	0	(32,000)	(24,000)
	160,000	(4,000)	64,000

(Continued)

(Continued)

	Case A	Case B	Case C
Cash flows from investing activities:			
Acquisition of property, plant, and equipment	(364,000)	(364,000)	(364,000)
Sales of property, plant, and equipment	16,000	16,000	388,000
	(348,000)	(348,000)	24,000
Cash flows from financing activities:			
New borrowing	200,000	516,000	64,000
Payment of debt	(36,000)	(116,000)	(84,000)
	164,000	400,000	(20,000)
Net increase (decrease) in cash	$ (24,000)	$ 48,000	$ 68,000

Required For each case, identify from the cash flow statement how Rennie Recreation Products Inc. generated the cash to acquire new property, plant, and equipment.

Exercise 17–20

Refer to the data in Exercise 17–19 for Rennie Recreation Products Inc. Which case indicates the best financial position? Give the reasons for your answer by analyzing each case.

Interpreting cash flow statements—indirect method

Exercise 17–21

The income statement and additional data of Klayquot Consulting Ltd. follow:

Preparing the cash flow statement under IFRS— direct method

Net cash from operating $39,500; investing $(45,500); financing $11,000

KLAYQUOT CONSULTING LTD.		
Income Statement		
For the Year Ended December 31, 2014		
Revenues:		
Consulting revenue		$137,000
Expenses:		
Salaries expense	$74,000	
Depreciation expense	14,500	
Rent expense	6,000	
Office supplies expense	1,500	
Insurance expense	1,000	
Interest expense	1,000	
Income tax expense	9,000	107,000
Net income		$ 30,000

Additional data:

a. Collections from clients are $3,500 more than revenues.

b. Increase in cash balance, $5,000.

c. Payments to employees are $2,000 less than salaries expense.

d. Interest expense and income tax expense equal their cash amounts.

e. Acquisition of property, plant, and equipment is $58,000. Of this amount, $50,500 is paid in cash, $7,500 by signing a long-term note payable.

f. Cash received from sale of land, $5,000.

g. Cash received from issuance of common shares, $21,000.

h. Payment of long-term note payable, $10,000.

i. Payment of cash dividends, $7,500.

j. Payments for rent and insurance are equal to expense.

k. Payment for office supplies is $3,000 more than expense.

l. Opening cash balance, $8,000.

Required

Assume Klayquot Consulting Ltd. has adopted IFRS and elects to classify as operating activities all cash inflows and outflows for interest and dividends. Prepare Klayquot Consulting Ltd.'s cash flow statement by the direct method for operating activities, and a note to the financial statements providing a summary of noncash investing and financing activities.

SERIAL EXERCISE

This exercise continues the Kerr Consulting Corporation situation from Exercise 16–16 of Chapter 16. If you did not complete Exercise 16–16, you can still complete Exercise 17–22 as it is presented.

Exercise 17–22

Preparing the cash flow statement—indirect method
⑤

Net cash from operating $39,900; investing $(83,000); financing $40,000

Suppose, at December 31, 2014, Kerr Consulting Corporation has the following comparative balance sheet.

KERR CONSULTING CORPORATION
Balance Sheet
December 31, 2014 and 2013

	2014	2013
Current assets		
Cash	$ 5,000	$ 8,100
Accounts receivable	2,200	1,700
Supplies	420	300
Equipment	10,000	2,000
Furniture	3,600	3,600
Building	55,000	—
Less: accumulated amortization	(2,753)	(93)
Land	20,000	—
Total assets	$93,467	$15,607
Current liabilities		
Accounts payable	$ 350	$ 3,900
Salary payable	2,500	—
Long-term liabilities		
Notes payable	40,000	—
Shareholders' equity		
Common shares	20,000	10,000
Retained earnings	30,617	1,707
Total liabilities and shareholders' equity	$93,467	$15,607

Additional information: Kerr Consulting Corporation declared and paid $10,000 in dividends during 2014. Net income for the year ended December 31, 2014, was $38,910.

Required

Using this information, prepare the cash flow statement for Kerr Consulting Corporation using the indirect method for operating activities.

CHALLENGE EXERCISE

Exercise 17–23

Canadian Tire Corporation, Limited's cash flow statement for the years ended December 31, 2011, and January 1, 2011, is reproduced below:

Analyzing an actual company's cash flow statement

① ② ③ ⑤

CANADIAN TIRE CORPORATION, LIMITED
Consolidated Cash Flow Statement (adapted)

For the Years Ended (Dollars in millions)	December 31, 2011	January 1, 2011
Cash generated from (used for):		
Operating activities		
Net earnings	$ 467.0	$ 444.2
Items not affecting cash		
Impairment on loans receivable	352.0	347.0
Depreciation of property and equipment	229.8	223.8
Income tax expense	162.9	142.6
Net finance costs	132.2	135.7
Amortization of intangible assets	66.3	50.3
Changes in fair value of derivative instruments	(3.1)	(16.0)
Other	(7.0)	10.3
Cash generated from operations	1,400.1	1,337.9
Changes in working capital and other	219.6	(293.1)
Interest paid	(176.6)	(190.5)
Interest received	26.1	6.7
Income taxes paid	(63.7)	(131.5)
Cash generated from operating activities	1,405.5	729.5
Investing activities		
Acquisition of FGL Sports	(739.9)	—
Acquisition of short-term investments	(334.8)	(215.5)
Acquisition of long-term investments	(123.1)	(70.5)
Additions to property and equipment	(230.5)	(237.9)
Additions to intangible assets	(128.9)	(70.4)
Long-term receivables and other assets	(3.2)	16.5
Proceeds from the disposition of long-term investments	18.1	—
Proceeds from the disposition of short-term investments	364.0	124.0
Other	16.9	10.6
Cash used for investing activities	(1,161.4)	(443.2)
Financing activities		
Issuance of long-term debt	—	262.8
Issuance of short-term borrowings	2,676.8	1,160.3
Repayment of short-term borrowings	(2,666.7)	(1,222.7)
Issuance of loans payable	129.3	248.4
Repayment of loans payable	(187.6)	(318.8)
Issuance of share capital	11.6	16.7
Repurchase of share capital	(11.9)	(25.4)
Dividends paid	(89.6)	(68.5)
Repayment of long-term debt	(355.6)	(690.8)
Cash used for financing activities	(493.7)	(638.0)
Cash used in the year	(249.6)	(351.7)
Cash and cash equivalents, beginning of year	450.6	802.6
Cash and cash equivalents, end of year	$ 201.0	$ 450.9

Required

1. Which format did Canadian Tire Corporation, Limited use for reporting cash flows from operating activities?
2. What was Canadian Tire's largest source of cash during the year ended December 31, 2011? During the previous year January 1, 2011?
3. What was Canadian Tire's largest use of cash during the year ended December 31, 2011? During the year ended January 1, 2011?
4. The operating activities section of the statement lists (in millions of dollars) "Changes in working capital and other, $219.6." This amount includes in part:

Trade and other receivables	$(31.4)
Trade and other payables	242.1

Did these accounts' balances increase or decrease during the year ended December 31, 2011? How can you tell?

5. During the year ended December 31, 2011, Canadian Tire has a large negative cash flow from investing activities. Does this mean Canadian Tire is expanding, down-sizing, or remaining stable?
6. Why are Canadian Tire's year ends shown as December 31, 2011, and January 1, 2011?

BEYOND THE NUMBERS

Beyond the Numbers 17–1

Using cash flow data to evaluate an investment

Gillam Ltd. and Genoway Inc. are asking you to recommend their shares to your clients. Gillam Ltd. and Genoway Inc. earn about the same net income and have similar financial positions, so your decision depends on their cash flow statements, summarized as follows:

	Gillam Ltd.		Genoway Inc.	
Net cash inflows from operating activities		$ 90,000		$50,000
Net cash inflows (outflows) from investing activities:				
Purchase of property, plant, and equipment	$(100,000)		$(20,000)	
Sale of property, plant, and equipment	10,000	(90,000)	40,000	20,000
Net cash inflows (outflows) from financing activities:				
Issuance of common shares	30,000		—	
Issuance of long-term debt	—		80,000	
Repayment of long-term debt	—	30,000	(120,000)	(40,000)
Net increase in cash		$ 30,000		$30,000

Based on their cash flows, which company looks better? Give your reasons.

ETHICAL ISSUE

Eurocheapo Travel Ltd. is experiencing a bad year. Net income is only $60,000. Also, two important clients are falling behind in their payments to Eurocheapo Travel Ltd., and the agency's accounts receivable are increasing dramatically. The company desperately needs a loan. The company's board of directors is considering ways to put the best face on the company's financial statements. The company's bank closely examines cash flow from operations. Trent Belland, a director, suggests reclassifying as long term the receivables from the slow-paying clients. He explains to the other members of the board that removing the $40,000 rise in accounts receivable will increase net cash inflow from operations. This approach will increase the company's cash balance and may help Eurocheapo Travel Ltd. get the loan.

Required

1. Using only the amounts given, compute net cash inflow from operations both with-out and with the reclassification of the receivables. Which reporting makes Eurocheapo Travel Ltd. look better?

2. Where else in Eurocheapo's cash flow statement will the reclassification of the receivable be reported? What cash flow effect will this item report? What effect would the reclas-sification have on overall cash flow from all activities?

3. Under what condition would the reclassification of the receivables be ethical? Unethical?

PROBLEMS (GROUP A)   MyAccountingLab

Problem 17–1A

Top managers of Upland Communications Corp. are reviewing company performance for 2014. The income statement reports an 18 percent increase in net income, which is excellent. The balance sheet shows modest increases in assets, liabilities, and shareholders' equity. The assets with the largest increases are plant and equipment because the company is halfway through an expansion program. No other assets and no liabilities are increasing dramatically. A summarized version of the cash flow statement reports the following:

Using cash flow information to evaluate performance

Net cash inflow from operating activities	$1,240,000
Net cash outflow from investing activities	(1,140,000)
Net cash inflow from financing activities	280,000
Increase in cash during 2014	$ 380,000

Required   Write a memo to give top managers of Upland Communications Corp. your assessment of 2014 and your outlook for the future. Focus on the information content of the cash flow data.

Preparing the cash flow statement—direct method

1. Net cash from operating $(240,000), investing $307,800, financing $401,200

Problem 17–2A

Coyle Products Ltd. accountants have developed the following data from the company's accounting records for the year ended July 31, 2014:

a. Salaries expense, $631,800.

b. Cash payments to purchase property, plant, and equip-ment, $1,035,000.

c. Proceeds from issuance of long-term debt, $264,600.

d. Payments of long-term debt, $112,800.

e. Proceeds from sale of property, plant, and equipment, $358,200.

f. Interest revenue, $72,600.

g. Cash receipt of dividend revenue on investments in shares, $66,200.

h. Payments to suppliers, $4,129,800.

i. Interest expense and payments, $226,800.

j. Cost of goods sold, $2,886,600.

k. Collection of interest revenue, $20,200.

l. Acquisition of equipment by issuing short-term note payable, $213,000.

m. Payment of salaries, $804,000.

n. Credit sales, $3,648,600.

o. Income tax expense and payments, $338,400.

p. Amortization expense, $309,600.

q. Collections on accounts receivable, $4,038,600.

r. Collection of long-term notes receivable, $446,400.

s. Proceeds from sale of investments, $538,200.

t. Payment of long-term debt by issuing preferred shares, $900,000.

u. Cash sales, $1,134,000.

v. Proceeds from issuance of common shares, $589,400.

w. Payment of cash dividends, $340,000.

x. Cash balance: July 31, 2013—$654,800 July 31, 2014—$?

Required

1. Prepare Coyle Products Ltd.'s cash flow statement for the year ended July 31, 2014. Follow the format of Exhibit 17–12, but do *not* show amounts in thousands. Include a note to the financial statements giving a summary of noncash investing and financing activities.

2. Evaluate 2014 in terms of cash flow. Give your reasons.

Problem 17–3A

The 2014 comparative balance sheet and income statement of Orangeville Group Inc. follow:

Preparing the cash flow
statement—direct method
② ③ ④

1. Net cash from operating
$666,000, investing $(526,000),
financing $(249,000)

ORANGEVILLE GROUP INC.
Balance Sheet
December 31, 2014 and 2013

	2014	2013
Current assets		
Cash and cash equivalents	$ 47,000	$ 156,000
Accounts receivable	415,000	431,000
Interest receivable	6,000	9,000
Inventories	993,000	899,000
Prepaid expenses	17,000	22,000
Plant and equipment, net	1,009,000	937,000
Land	401,000	200,000
Total assets	$2,888,000	$2,654,000
Current liabilities		
Accounts payable	$ 114,000	$ 179,000
Interest payable	63,000	67,000
Salaries payable	71,000	14,000
Other accrued liabilities	181,000	187,000
Income tax payable	73,000	38,000
Long-term liabilities		
Notes payable	450,000	650,000
Shareholders' equity		
Common shares	1,411,000	1,223,000
Retained earnings	525,000	296,000
Total liabilities and shareholders' equity	$2,888,000	$2,654,000

ORANGEVILLE GROUP INC.
Income Statement
For the Year Ended December 31, 2014

Revenues:		
Sales revenue		$4,380,000
Interest revenue		17,000
Total revenues		4,397,000
Expenses:		
Cost of goods sold	$1,952,000	
Salaries expense	814,000	
Amortization expense	253,000	
Other operating expenses	497,000	
Interest expense	246,000	
Income tax expense	169,000	
Total expenses		3,931,000
Net income		$ 466,000

Orangeville Group had no noncash investing and financing transactions during 2014. During the year, there were no sales of land or plant and equipment, no issuances of notes payable, and no repurchase of common shares.

Required

1. Prepare the 2014 cash flow statement, formatting operating activities by the direct method.
2. Evaluate the 2014 cash flow for this company.

Problem 17–4A

Use the Orangeville Group Inc. data from Problem 17–3A.

Required

1. Prepare the 2014 cash flow statement by the indirect method. If your instructor also assigned Problem 17–3A, prepare only the operating activities section.
2. Evaluate the 2014 cash flow for this company.

Problem 17–5A

Accountants for Blondies Confectionary Ltd. have assembled the following data for the year ended December 31, 2014:

Excel Spreadsheet
Template

Preparing the cash flow
statement—indirect method
② ③ ⑤

1. Net cash from
operating $666,000,
investing $(526,000),
financing $(249,000)

Preparing the cash flow
statement—indirect method
② ⑤

Net cash from operating
$17,775, investing $(21,575),
financing $4,150

	December 31,	
	2014	2013
Current accounts (all result from operations)		
Current assets		
Cash and cash equivalents	$ 9,050	$ 8,700
Accounts receivable	17,025	18,425
Inventories	29,625	24,125
Prepaid expenses	800	525
Current liabilities		
Notes payable (for inventory purchases)	7,575	9,200
Accounts payable	18,025	16,875
Income tax payable	1,475	1,950
Accrued liabilities	12,075	5,800

Transaction data for 2014:

Acquisition of building by issuing long-term note payable	$33,000	Issuance of preferred shares for cash	$14,050
Acquisition of equipment	18,500	Net income	12,625
Acquisition of long-term investment	11,200	Payment of cash dividends	10,700
Amortization expense	5,075	Payment of long-term debt	16,950
Collection of loan	2,575	Retirement of bonds payable by issuing common shares	22,350
Gain on sale of investment	875	Sale of long-term investment for cash	5,550
Issuance of long-term debt to borrow cash	17,750	Stock dividends	3,150

Required

1. Prepare Blondies Confectionary Ltd.'s cash flow statement, using the *indirect* method to report operating activities. Include a note regarding noncash investing and financing activities.
2. Evaluate Blondies Confectionary Ltd.'s cash flows for the year. Mention all three categories of cash flows, and give the reason for your evaluation.

Problem 17–6A

Preparing the cash flow statement—direct and indirect methods

③ ⑤

1. Net cash from operating $84,100, investing $(51,500), financing $(44,500)

To prepare the cash flow statement, accountants for Nottingham Sales Ltd. have summarized 2014 activity in two T-accounts as follows:

Cash

Beginning balance	87,100	Payments of operating	
Sale of common shares	80,800	expenses	46,100
Receipts of dividends	17,900	Payment of long-term debt	78,900
Sale of investments	28,400	Repurchase of common shares	30,400
Receipts of interest	22,200	Payment of income tax	6,000
Collections from customers	307,000	Payments on accounts payable	101,600
		Payments of dividends	16,000
		Payments of salaries and wages	67,500
		Payments of interest	41,800
		Purchase of equipment	79,900
Ending balance	75,200		

Common Shares

Repurchase of common shares	30,400	Beginning balance	103,500
		Issuance for cash	80,800
		Issuance to acquire land	64,500
		Issuance to retire long-term debt	31,600
		Ending balance	250,000

Nottingham Sales Ltd.'s 2014 income statement and selected balance sheet data follow:

NOTTINGHAM SALES LTD.
Income Statement
For the Year Ended December 31, 2014

Revenues and gains:		
Sales revenue		$317,000
Interest revenue		22,200
Dividend revenue		17,900
Gain on sale of investments		700
Total revenues and gains		357,800
Expenses:		
Cost of goods sold	$103,600	
Salaries and wages expense	66,800	
Amortization expense	10,900	
Other operating expenses	44,700	
Interest expense	44,100	
Income tax expense	9,200	
Total expenses		279,300
Net income		$ 78,500

NOTTINGHAM SALES LTD.
Balance Sheet Data
For the Year Ended December 31, 2014

	Increase (Decrease)
Current assets	
Cash and cash equivalents	$?
Accounts receivable	10,000
Inventories	5,700
Prepaid expenses	(1,900)

(Continued)

(Continued)

NOTTINGHAM SALES LTD. Balance Sheet Data For the Year Ended December 31, 2014	Increase (Decrease)
Investments	$ (27,700)
Plant and equipment, net	69,000
Land	75,000
Current liabilities	
Accounts payable	$ 7,700
Interest payable	2,300
Salaries payable	(700)
Other accrued liabilities	(3,300)
Income tax payable	3,200
Long-term debt	(100,000)
Common shares	146,500
Retained earnings	62,500

Required

1. Prepare Nottingham Sales Ltd.'s cash flow statement for the year ended December 31, 2014, using the *direct* method to report operating activities. Also prepare a note to the financial statements summarizing the noncash investing and financing activities.

2. Prepare a schedule showing cash flows from operating activities using the *indirect* method. All activity in the current accounts results from operations.

Problem 17–7A

Mill Bay Inc.'s comparative balance sheet at September 30, 2014, and its 2014 income statement are shown below.

Preparing the cash flow statement—direct and indirect methods

1. Net cash from operating $243,600, investing $(12,800), financing $(132,400)

MILL BAY INC. Balance Sheet September 30, 2014 and 2013	2014	2013
Current assets		
Cash	$ 194,800	$ 96,400
Accounts receivable	167,600	164,000
Interest receivable	16,400	11,200
Inventories	486,800	467,600
Prepaid expenses	34,400	37,200
Long-term investments	204,400	55,200
Plant and equipment, net	527,600	416,400
Land	188,400	297,200
	$1,820,400	$1,545,200
Current liabilities		
Notes payable, short-term	$ 40,000	$ 0
Accounts payable	247,200	281,200
Income tax payable	47,200	46,400
Accrued liabilities	71,600	116,400

(Continued)

(Continued)

MILL BAY INC.
Balance Sheet
September 30, 2014 and 2013

	2014	2013
Interest payable	$ 18,000	$ 12,800
Salaries payable	6,000	4,400
Long-term note payable	492,000	525,600
Common shares	543,600	336,000
Retained earnings	354,800	222,400
	$1,820,400	$1,545,200

MILL BAY INC.
Income Statement
For the Year Ended September 30, 2014

Sales revenue		$1,468,400
Cost of goods sold		646,000
Gross margin		822,400
Operating expenses:		
Amortization	$ 34,000	
Salaries	253,600	
Other	118,400	406,000
Operating income		416,400
Other revenues and expenses:		
Revenues and gains:		
Interest	29,200	
Gain on sale of land	43,600	72,800
		489,200
Interest expense		54,000
Income before income taxes		435,200
Income tax expense		85,600
Net income		$ 349,600

Other information for the year ended September 30, 2014:

a. Acquired equipment by issuing long-term note payable, $89,200, and paying $16,000 cash.

b. Paid long-term note payable, $122,800.

c. Received $207,600 cash for issuance of common shares.

d. Paid cash dividends, $217,200.

e. Acquired equipment by issuing short-term note payable, $40,000.

Required

1. Prepare Mill Bay Inc.'s cash flow statement for the year ended September 30, 2014, using the *direct* method to report operating activities. Also prepare a note to the financial statements giving a summary of noncash investing and financing activities. All current accounts, except short-term notes payable, result from operating transactions.

2. Prepare a supplementary schedule showing the cash flows from operating activities using the *indirect* method.

Problem 17–8A

The financial statements for Facetime Corp. for the year ended December 31, 2014, are as follows:

Distinguishing among operating, investing, and financing activities; using the financial statements to compute the cash effects of a wide variety of business transactions; preparing a cash flow statement by the indirect method

② ④ ⑤

1. Net cash from operating $586,000, investing $(204,000), financing $(430,000)

FACETIME CORP.
Balance Sheet
December 31, 2014 and 2013

	2014	2013
Assets		
Cash	$ 10,000	$ 18,000
Investment in money market fund	0	40,000
Accounts receivable	189,000	175,000
Merchandise inventory	280,000	610,000
Prepaid expenses	30,000	23,000
Plant and equipment	1,798,000	1,654,000
Less accumulated amortization	(160,000)	(120,000)
Land	200,000	0
Goodwill	90,000	100,000
Total assets	$2,617,000	$2,500,000
Liabilities		
Accounts payable	$ 176,000	$ 120,000
Salaries payable	110,000	100,000
Loan payable	350,000	400,000
Total liabilities	636,000	620,000
Shareholders' equity		
Preferred shares	500,000	500,000
Common shares	800,000	500,000
Retained earnings	501,000	880,000
Total shareholders' equity	1,981,000	1,880,000
Total liabilities and shareholders' equity	$2,617,000	$2,500,000

FACETIME CORP.
Income Statement
For the Year Ended December 31, 2014

Net sales	$1,600,000
Cost of goods sold	840,000
Gross margin	760,000
Operating expenses:	
Selling expenses	350,000
Administrative expenses	230,000
Interest expense	40,000
Total operating expenses	620,000
Operating income	140,000
Income taxes	39,000
Net income	$ 101,000

Additional information:

a. The administrative expenses included:
   Amortization expense on plant and equipment, $100,000.
   Writedown of goodwill, $10,000.

b. Sold equipment for its book value. The equipment cost $430,000 and had been amortized for $60,000.

c. Purchased additional equipment in December for $574,000.

d. Issued common shares for land valued at $200,000.

e. Declared and paid cash dividends: Preferred, $230,000; Common, $250,000.

f. Sold 20,000 common shares for $5.00 per share.

g. Paid $90,000 (of which $40,000 was interest) on the loans.

Required

1. Prepare a cash flow statement for Facetime Corp. for the year ended December 31, 2014, using the *indirect* method. The investment in the money market fund is a cash equivalent.

2. Did the company improve its cash position in 2014? Give your reasons.

Problem 17–9A

Preparing the cash flow statement under IFRS— direct method
⑥

1. Net cash from operating $(33,200), investing $131,400, financing $84,800

Manji Products Ltd.'s accountants have developed the following data from the company's accounting records for the year ended December 31, 2014:

a. Salaries expense, $210,600.

b. Cash payments to purchase property, plant, and equipment, $345,000.

c. Proceeds from issuance of long-term debt, $88,200.

d. Payments of long-term debt, $37,600.

e. Proceeds from sale of property, plant, and equipment, $119,400.

f. Interest revenue, $24,200.

g. Cash receipt of dividend revenue on investments in shares, $5,400.

h. Payments to suppliers, $1,376,600.

i. Interest expense and payments, $75,600.

j. Cost of goods sold, $962,200.

k. Collection of interest revenue, $33,400.

l. Acquisition of equipment by issuing short-term note payable, $91,000.

m. Payment of salaries, $468,000.

n. Credit sales, $1,216,200.

o. Income tax expense and payments, $112,800.

p. Depreciation expense, $103,200.

q. Collections on accounts receivable, $1,346,200.

r. Collection of long-term notes receivable, $138,800.

s. Proceeds from sale of investments, $179,400.

t. Payment of long-term debt by issuing preferred shares, $400,000.

u. Cash sales, $578,000.

v. Proceeds from issuance of common shares, $209,800.

w. Payment of cash dividends, $100,000.

x. Cash balance:
   December 31, 2013—$151,600
   December 31, 2014—$?

Required Assume that Manji Products Ltd. has adopted IFRS and elected to classify cash inflows from interest and dividends as investing activities, and cash outflows for the payment of interest and dividends as financing activities. Prepare Manji's cash flow statement for the year ended December 31, 2014, reporting operating activities by the direct method. Include a note to the financial statements providing a summary of noncash investing and financing activities.

PROBLEMS (GROUP B)   MyAccountingLab

Problem 17–1B

Using cash flow information to evaluate performance
①

Top managers of Domino Delivery Ltd. are reviewing company performance for 2014. The income statement reports a 20-percent increase in net income over 2013. However, most of the net income increase resulted from an unusual gain of $60,000 on the sale of equipment.

The cash proceeds were $180,000. The balance sheet shows a large increase in receivables. The cash flow statement, in summarized form, reports the following:

Net cash outflow from operating activities..........................	$(330,000)
Net cash inflow from investing activities............................	300,000
Net cash inflow from financing activities...........................	150,000
Increase in cash during 2014...	$ 120,000

Required

Write a memo to give the managers of Domino Delivery Ltd. your assessment of 2014 operations and give your outlook for the future. Focus on the information content of the cash flow data.

Problem 17–2B

Accountants for Kitchen Guys Builders' Supply Ltd. have developed the following data from the company's accounting records for the year ended April 30, 2014:

Preparing the cash flow statement—direct method

a. Credit sales, $728,125.

b. Income tax expense and payments, $47,375.

c. Cash payments to acquire property, plant, and equipment, $49,250.

d. Cost of goods sold, $478,250.

e. Cash received from issuance of long-term debt, $85,000.

f. Payment of cash dividends, $80,500.

g. Collection of interest, $34,250.

h. Acquisition of equipment by issuing short-term note payable, $40,500.

i. Payment of salaries, $129,500.

j. Cash received from sale of property, plant, and equipment, $28,000, including an $8,500 loss.

k. Collections on accounts receivable, $578,250.

l. Interest revenue, $4,750.

m. Cash receipt of dividend revenue on investment in shares, $25,125.

n. Payments to suppliers, $460,625.

o. Cash sales, $214,875.

p. Amortization expense, $78,500.

q. Cash received from issuance of short-term debt, $69,500.

r. Payments of long-term debt, $62,500.

s. Interest expense and payments, $16,625.

t. Salaries expense, $119,125.

u. Collections of notes receivable, $35,000.

v. Cash received from sale of investments, $11,375, including $2,500 gain.

w. Payment of short-term note payable by issuing long-term note payable, $78,750.

x. Cash balance: May 1, 2013—$99,125
               April 30, 2014—$?

Required

1. Prepare Kitchen Guys Builders' Supply Ltd.'s cash flow statement for the year ended April 30, 2014. Follow the format of Exhibit 17–12, but do not show amounts in thousands. Include a note regarding the noncash investing and financing activities.

2. Evaluate 2014 from a cash flow standpoint. Give your reasons.

Problem 17–3B

The 2014 comparative income statement and balance sheet of New Design Ltd. follow:

Preparing the cash flow
statement—direct method
② ③ ④

NEW DESIGN LTD.		
Income Statement		
For the Year Ended December 31, 2014		
Revenues:		
Sales revenue		$257,000
Interest revenue		13,600
Total revenues		270,600
Expenses:		
Cost of goods sold	$76,600	
Salaries expense	27,800	
Amortization expense	4,000	
Other operating expenses	10,500	
Interest expense	16,600	
Income tax expense	27,800	
Total expenses		163,300
Net income		$107,300

NEW DESIGN LTD.		
Balance Sheet		
December 31, 2014 and 2013		
	2014	**2013**
Current assets		
Cash and cash equivalents	$ 7,200	$ 6,300
Accounts receivable	31,600	26,900
Interest receivable	1,900	700
Inventories	33,600	57,200
Prepaid expenses	2,500	1,900
Plant and equipment, net	66,500	49,400
Land	103,000	54,000
Total assets	$246,300	$196,400
Current liabilities		
Accounts payable	$ 31,400	$ 28,800
Interest payable	4,400	4,900
Salaries payable	3,100	6,600
Other accrued liabilities	13,700	16,000
Income tax payable	8,900	7,700
Long-term liabilities		
Notes payable	75,000	95,000
Shareholders' equity		
Common shares	68,300	34,700
Retained earnings	41,500	2,700
Total liabilities and shareholders' equity	$246,300	$196,400

New Design Ltd. had no noncash financing and investing transactions during 2014. During the year, there were no sales of land or plant and equipment, and no issuances of notes payable.

Required

1. Prepare the 2014 cash flow statement, formatting operating activities by the direct method.
2. Evaluate the 2014 cash flow for this company.

Problem 17–4B

Use the New Design Ltd. data from Problem 17–3B.

Excel Spreadsheet Template

Preparing the cash flow statement—indirect method
② ③ ⑤

Required

1. Prepare the 2014 cash flow statement by the indirect method. If your instructor also assigned Problem 17–3B, prepare only the operating activities section of the statement.
2. Evaluate the 2014 cash flow for this company.

Problem 17–5B

Roanoke Ltd.'s accountants have assembled the following data for the year ended December 31, 2014:

Preparing the cash flow statement—indirect method
② ⑤

	December 31, 2014	December 31, 2013
Current accounts (all result from operations)		
Current assets		
Cash and cash equivalents	$ 75,500	$ 56,750
Accounts receivable	174,250	155,500
Inventories	271,500	212,500
Prepaid expenses	13,250	10,250
Current liabilities		
Notes payable (for inventory purchases)	56,500	45,750
Accounts payable	132,250	139,500
Income tax payable	96,500	41,750
Accrued liabilities	38,750	68,000

Transaction data for 2014:

Acquisition of building	$325,750	Issuance of long-term note payable to borrow cash	$ 36,000
Acquisition of land by issuing long-term note payable	237,500	Loss on sale of equipment	16,750
Acquisition of long-term investment	79,000	Net income	199,000
Amortization expense	60,250	Payment of cash dividends	90,750
Collection of loan	71,750	Repurchase and retirement of common shares	85,750
Issuance of common shares for cash	123,000	Retirement of bonds payable by issuing common shares...	157,500
Stock dividends	79,500	Sale of equipment for cash	145,000

Required

1. Prepare Roanoke Ltd.'s cash flow statement, using the *indirect* method to report operating activities. Note any additional disclosures that are required.
2. Evaluate Roanoke Ltd.'s cash flows for the year. Mention all three categories of cash flows, and give the reason for your evaluation.

Problem 17-6B

To prepare the cash flow statement, accountants for Tofino Inc. have summarized activity for the year 2014 in two accounts as follows:

Cash

Beginning balance	64,320	Payments on accounts payable	447,720
Collection of loan	39,600	Payments of dividends	52,640
Sale of investment	31,440	Payments of salaries and wages	172,560
Receipts of interest	39,120	Payments of interest	56,280
Collections from customers	814,440	Purchase of equipment	37,680
Issuance of common shares	33,360	Payments of operating expenses	41,160
Receipts of dividends	25,400	Payment of long-term debt	73,560
		Repurchase of common shares	20,280
		Payment of income tax	22,680
Ending balance	123,120		

Common Shares

Repurchase of shares	20,280	Beginning balance	101,280
		Issuance for cash	33,360
		Issuance to acquire land	77,320
		Issuance to retire long-term debt	42,800
		Ending balance	234,480

Tofino Inc.'s income statement and selected balance sheet data follow:

TOFINO INC.		
Income Statement		
For the Year Ended December 31, 2014		
Revenues:		
Sales revenue		$847,560
Interest revenue		39,120
Dividend revenue		25,400
Total revenues		912,080
Expenses and losses:		
Cost of goods sold	$420,720	
Salaries and wages expense	180,960	
Amortization expense	29,160	
Other operating expenses	52,920	
Interest expense	58,560	
Income tax expense	19,440	
Loss on sale of investments	3,720	
Total expenses		765,480
Net income		$146,600

TOFINO INC.	
Balance Sheet Data	
For the Year Ended December 31, 2014	
	Increase (Decrease)
Current assets	
Cash and cash equivalents	$?
Accounts receivable	33,120
Inventories	(14,160)

(Continued)

(Continued)

TOFINO INC.
Balance Sheet Data
For the Year Ended December 31, 2014

	Increase (Decrease)
Prepaid expenses	$ 720
Loan receivable	(39,600)
Long-term investments	(35,160)
Plant and equipment, net	8,520
Land	97,320
Current liabilities	
Accounts payable	$(41,160)
Interest payable	2,280
Salaries payable	8,400
Other accrued liabilities	12,480
Income tax payable	(3,240)
Long-term debt	(96,360)
Common shares	133,200
Retained earnings	93,960

Required

1. Prepare the cash flow statement of Tofino Inc. for the year ended December 31, 2014, using the *direct* method to report operating activities. Also prepare a summary of noncash investing and financing activities that will be part of a note to the financial statements.

2. Use the data from Tofino Inc.'s 2014, income statement and the selected balance sheet data to prepare a supplementary schedule showing cash flows from operating activities by the *indirect* method. All activity in the current accounts results from operations.

Problem 17–7B

Sugar Barrel Antiques Ltd.'s comparative balance sheet at June 30, 2014, and its 2014 income statement are as follows:

Preparing the cash flow statement—direct and indirect methods
③ ④ ⑤

SUGAR BARREL ANTIQUES LTD.
Balance Sheet
June 30, 2014 and 2013

	2014	2013
Current assets		
Cash	$ 188,000	$ 43,000
Accounts receivable	370,000	241,500
Interest receivable	14,500	18,000
Inventories	343,000	301,000
Prepaid expenses	18,500	14,000
Long-term investment	50,500	26,000
Plant and equipment, net	422,500	368,000
Land	212,000	480,000
	$1,619,000	$1,491,500

(Continued)

(Continued)

SUGAR BARREL ANTIQUES LTD.
Balance Sheet
June 30, 2014 and 2013

	2014	2013
Current liabilities		
Notes payable, short-term		
(for general borrowing)	$ 67,000	$ 90,500
Accounts payable	234,500	201,500
Income tax payable	69,000	72,500
Accrued liabilities	41,000	48,500
Interest payable	18,500	14,500
Salaries payable	4,500	13,000
Long-term note payable	237,000	470,500
Common shares	319,500	256,000
Retained earnings	628,000	324,500
	$1,619,000	$1,491,500

SUGAR BARREL ANTIQUES LTD.
Income Statement
For the Year Ended June 30, 2014

Net sales		$1,327,000
Cost of goods sold		402,000
Gross margin		925,000
Operating expenses:		
Salaries expense	$194,000	
Amortization expense	27,000	
Other expenses	210,000	431,000
Operating income		494,000
Other revenues and expenses:		
Revenues and gains:		
Interest revenue		53,000
Expenses and losses:		
Interest expense	(30,500)	
Loss on sale of land	(33,500)	(64,000)
Income before income taxes		483,000
Income tax expense		49,500
Net income		$ 433,500

Other information for the year ended June 30, 2014:

a. Acquired equipment by issuing a long-term note payable, $76,500, and paying $5,000 cash.

b. Purchased a long-term investment for cash.

c. Received cash for issuance of common shares, $40,000.

d. Only cash dividends were issued during the year.

e. Paid short-term note payable by issuing common shares.

Required

1. Prepare the cash flow statement of Sugar Barrel Antiques Ltd. for the year ended June 30, 2014, using the *direct* method to report operating activities. Also prepare a note to the financial statements providing a summary of noncash investing and financing activities. All current accounts, except short-term notes payable, result from operating transactions.

2. Prepare a supplementary schedule showing cash flows from operations by the *indirect* method.

Problem 17–8B

Cloverdale Sales Corp. had the financial statements for the year ended December 31 shown below.

Distinguishing among operating, investing, and financing activities; using the financial statements to compute the cash effects of a wide variety of business transactions; preparing a cash flow statement by the indirect method
② ④ ⑤

CLOVERDALE SALES CORP.
Income Statement
For the Year Ended December 31, 2014

Net sales	$267,000
Cost of goods sold	120,000
Gross margin	147,000
Operating expenses	
Selling expenses	73,800
Administrative expenses	43,500
Interest expense	8,700
Total operating expenses	126,000
Operating income	21,000
Income taxes	8,400
Net income	$ 12,600

CLOVERDALE SALES CORP.
Balance Sheet
December 31, 2014 and 2013

	2014	2013
Assets		
Cash	$ 6,000	$ 27,600
Investments in money-market funds	1,500	4,500
Accounts receivable	12,700	34,200
Merchandise inventory	45,900	107,815
Prepaid expenses	3,600	2,850
Plant and equipment	285,600	235,535
Less accumulated amortization	(24,000)	(15,000)
Land	90,000	0
Goodwill	18,000	22,500
Total assets	$439,300	$420,000
Liabilities		
Accounts payable	$ 21,300	$ 22,500
Salaries payable	34,000	21,000
Loans payable	84,000	99,000
Total liabilities	139,300	142,500
Shareholders' equity		
Common shares	165,000	150,000
Retained earnings	135,000	127,500
Total shareholders' equity	300,000	277,500
Total liabilities and shareholders' equity	$439,300	$420,000

Additional information:

a. The administrative expenses included:
   Amortization expense on plant and equipment = $24,000
   Writedown of goodwill   = $4,500

b. Sold equipment for its net book value. The equipment cost $44,685 and had been amortized for $15,000.

c. Purchased additional equipment for $94,750.

d. Exchanged common shares for land valued at $90,000.

e. Declared and paid cash dividends on common shares, $5,100.

f. Repurchased common shares for $75,000.

g. Paid $23,700 (of which $8,700 was interest) on the loans.

Required

1. Prepare a cash flow statement for Cloverdale Sales Corp. for the year ended December 31, 2014, using the *indirect* method. Consider the investments in money market funds to be a cash equivalent.

2. Comment on the results indicated by the cash flow statement.

Problem 17–9B

Preparing the cash flow statement under IFRS—direct method
⑥

Accountants for Giovanni's Builders' Supply Ltd. have developed the following data from the company's accounting records for the year ended December 31, 2014.

a. Credit sales, $291,950.

b. Income tax expense and payments, $18,950.

c. Cash payments to acquire property, plant, and equipment, $29,700.

d. Cost of goods sold, $191,300.

e. Cash received from issuance of long-term debt, $34,000.

f. Payment of cash dividends, $24,200.

g. Collection of interest, $13,700.

h. Acquisition of equipment by issuing short-term note payable, $18,200.

i. Payment of salaries, $43,800.

j. Cash received from sale of property, plant, and equipment, $11,200, including a $3,400 loss.

k. Collections on accounts receivable, $231,300.

l. Interest revenue, $1,900.

m. Cash receipt of dividend revenue on investment in shares, $2,050.

n. Payments to suppliers, $184,250.

o. Cash sales, $85,950.

p. Depreciation expense, $31,400.

q. Cash received from issuance of short-term debt, $29,800.

r. Payments of long-term debt, $25,000.

s. Interest expense and payments, $16,650.

t. Salaries expense, $47,650.

u. Collections of notes receivable, $24,000.

v. Cash received from sale of investments, $4,550, including $1,000 gain.

w. Payment of short-term note payable by issuing long-term note payable, $31,500.

x. Cash balance: December 31, 2013—$39,650 December 31, 2014—$?

Required

Assume that Giovanni's Builders' Supply Ltd. has adopted IFRS and elected to classify cash inflows from interest and dividends as investing activities, and cash outflows for the payment of interest and dividends as financing activities. Prepare Giovanni's cash flow statement for the year ended December 31, 2014, reporting operating activities by the direct method. Include a note to the financial statements giving a summary of noncash investing and financing activities.

CHALLENGE PROBLEMS

Distinguishing between the direct method and indirect method
③ ⑤

Problem 17–1C

Both the Accounting Standards Board (AcSB) in Canada and the Financial Accounting Standards Board (FASB) in the United States prefer the direct method of preparing the operating activities portion of the cash flow statement. Yet most companies use the indirect method when preparing their cash flow statement.

Required

Discuss why you think companies use the indirect method when the direct method is the method preferred by the standard-setting bodies.

Problem 17–2C

Initially, the *CICA Handbook* did not require financial statements to include information about noncash investing and financing activities. The financial statements reported only changes in working capital (defined as current assets less current liabilities) and so transactions such as the use of long-term debt to purchase property, plant, and equipment, or conversion of debt into equity were excluded.

Accounting for noncash financing and investing activities
④

Required

Discuss the present *CICA Handbook's* requirements with respect to disclosure of noncash financing and investing decisions, and explain why you think the required disclosure does or does not benefit users.

Extending Your Knowledge

DECISION PROBLEMS

Decision Problem 1

The 2014 comparative income statement and the 2014 comparative balance sheet of Eclipse Golf Inc. have just been distributed at a meeting of the company's board of directors.

In discussing the company's results of operations and year-end financial position, the members of the board of directors raise a fundamental question: Why is the cash balance so low? This question is especially puzzling to the board members because 2014 showed record profits. As the controller of the company, you must answer the question.

Preparing and using the cash flow statement to evaluate operations
④ ⑤

1. Net cash from operating $60,000, investing $(66,500), financing $(18,500)

ECLIPSE GOLF INC. Income Statement For the Years Ended December 31, 2014 and 2013 (amounts in thousands)		
	2014	**2013**
Revenues and gains:		
Sales revenue	$222.0	$155.0
Gain on sale of equipment (sale price, $17.5)	—	9.0
Total revenues and gains	222.0	164.0
Expenses and losses:		
Cost of goods sold	110.5	81.0
Salaries expense	24.0	14.0
Amortization expense	28.5	16.5
Interest expense	6.5	10.0
Loss on sale of land (sale price, $30.5)	—	17.5
Total expenses and losses	169.5	139.0
Net income	$ 52.5	$ 25.0

ECLIPSE GOLF INC.
Balance Sheet
December 31, 2014 and 2013
(amounts in thousands)

Assets	2014	2013
Cash	$ 6.5	$ 31.5
Accounts receivable, net	46.0	30.5
Inventories	97.0	90.5
Property, plant, and equipment, net	74.0	30.5
Patents, net	88.5	94.0
Total assets	$312.0	$277.0
Liabilities and Shareholders' Equity		
Notes payable, short-term (for general borrowing)	$ 16.0	$ 50.5
Accounts payable	31.5	28.0
Accrued liabilities	6.0	8.5
Notes payable, long-term	73.5	81.5
Common shares	74.5	30.5
Retained earnings	110.5	78.0
Total liabilities and shareholders' equity	$312.0	$277.0

Required

1. Prepare a cash flow statement for 2014 in the format that best shows the relationship between net income and operating cash flow. The company sold no capital assets or long-term investments and issued no notes payable during 2014. The changes in all current accounts except short-term notes payable arose from operations. There were no noncash financing and investing transactions during the year. Show all amounts in thousands. Amortization expense on the patent was $5,500.

2. Answer the board members' question: Why is the cash balance so low? In explaining the business's cash flows, identify two significant cash receipts that occurred during 2013 but not in 2014. Also point out the two largest cash payments during 2014.

3. Considering net income and the company's cash flows during 2014, was it a good year or a bad year for Eclipse Golf Inc.? Give your reasons.

Decision Problem 2

Using the cash flow statement to evaluate a company's operations
①

The cash flow statement, in the not-too-distant past, included information in only two categories: sources of funds and uses of funds. Funds were usually defined as working capital (current assets minus current liabilities). The present-day statement provides information about cash flows from operating activities, investing activities, and financing activities. The earlier statement permitted the information to be about changes in working capital or in cash, while today's cash flow statement deals specifically with information about flows in cash and cash equivalents.

Required

1. Explain why you think the present-day cash flow statement, with its disclosure of the three different kinds of activities, is or is not an improvement over the earlier model that showed only sources and uses of funds.

2. Is information about cash flows more informative to users than information about working capital flows?

3. Briefly explain why comparative balance sheets and a cash flow statement are more informative than just comparative balance sheets.

FINANCIAL STATEMENT CASES

Financial Statement Case 1

Using the cash flow statement
② ④

Gildan Activewear Inc.'s Consolidated Statements of Cash Flow appear in Appendix A at the end of this book and on MyAccountingLab. Use these statements along with the other material in the Annual Report to answer the following questions.

1. By which method of reporting does Gildan report net cash flows from operations? How can you tell?

2. Did Gildan improve its cash position in the year ended October 2, 2011? If so, by how much? If not, by how much did it decline?

3. By how much did Gildan's cash from operations increase or decrease in the year ended October 2, 2011? Why is it important for cash from operating activities to be a positive number?

4. What were the major investing activities during fiscal 2011? Financing activities?

5. Was Gildan expanding or contracting in fiscal 2011? Support your answer with specific references to the financial statements.

Financial Statement Case 2

Using the cash flow statement
② ④

Rainmaker Entertainment Inc.'s Statements of Cash Flows appear on MyAccountingLab. Use these statements along with the other material in the Annual Report to answer the following questions.

1. By which method of reporting does Rainmaker report net cash flows from operations? How can you tell?

2. Did Rainmaker improve its cash position in 2011? If so, by how much?

3. Rainmaker, and many other companies, reports items differently in the operating section than the method illustrated or described in the chapter. Explain.

4. Explain the cause for the large inflow in the investing section, and discuss.

5. Was Rainmaker expanding, contracting, or holding steady in 2011? Support your answer with specific references to the financial statements.

IFRS MINI-CASE

The income statement and additional data of ENVIRO Consulting Ltd. follow:

ENVIRO CONSULTING LTD.		
Income Statement		
For the Year Ended December 31, 2014		
Revenues:		
Consulting revenue		$274,000
Expenses:		
Salaries expense	$148,000	
Depreciation expense	29,000	
Rent expense	12,000	
Office supplies expense	3,000	
Insurance expense	2,000	
Interest expense	2,000	
Income tax expense	18,000	214,000
Net income		$ 60,000

Additional data:

a. Collections from clients are $7,000 more than revenues.

b. Increase in cash balance, $10,000.

c. Payments to employees are $4,000 less than salaries expense.

d. Interest expense and income tax expense equal their cash amounts.

e. Acquisition of property, plant, and equipment is $116,000. Of this amount, $101,000 is paid in cash, $15,000 by signing a long-term note payable.

f. Cash received from sale of land, $10,000.

g. Cash received from issuance of common shares, $42,000.

h. Payment of long-term note payable, $20,000.

i. Payment of cash dividends, $15,000.

j. Payments for rent and insurance are equal to expense.

k. Payment for office supplies is $6,000 more than expense.

l. Opening cash balance, $16,000.

Required

1. Assume ENVIRO Consulting Ltd. has adopted IFRS and elects to classify as operating activities all cash inflows and outflows for interest and dividends. Prepare ENVIRO Consulting Ltd.'s cash flow statement by the direct method for operating activities, and a note to the financial statements providing a summary of noncash investing and financing activities.

2. Assume ENVIRO Consulting Ltd. has adopted IFRS and elects to classify as investing or financing activities all cash inflows and outflows for interest and dividends. Prepare ENVIRO Consulting Ltd.'s cash flow statement by the direct method for operating activities, and a note to the financial statements providing a summary of noncash investing and financing activities.

3. Compare and summarize the effects of the accounting choice in Requirement 1 with that of Requirement 2. Can ENVIRO change the method used and classifications from one year to the next?

JUST CHECKING Solutions for Chapter 17

1. a. Two years: 2011 and 2010.
   b. Net income of $245 million in 2011 and net loss of $1,526 million in 2010
   c. Purchases and mortgage advances: $82.83 million in 2011 and $76,090 million in 2010
   d. Shareholder dividends: $717 million in 2011 and $691 million in 2010
   e. $12,813 million in 2011 and $11,849 million in 2010

2.
D	Payment of dividends
I	Issuance of shares
D	Payment to employees
I	Collections from customers
D	Payments for assets
D	Repayment of a bank loan
I	Issuance of bonds

3.
O	Payment of income taxes
F	Issuance of preferred shares
O	Payment of employee salaries
O	Collections of accounts receivable
I	Payment for a delivery truck
F	Repayment of a long-term bank loan (principal only)
O	Receipt of loan interest
O	Payment of accounts payable

4.
−	Payment of income taxes
+	Issuance of preferred shares
−	Payment of employee salaries
+	Collections of accounts receivable
−	Payment for a delivery truck
−	Repayment of a long-term bank loan (principal only)
+	Receipt of loan interest
−	Payment of accounts payable

5. Markham Corp. will report a cash receipt of $5 million (cost of $2 million plus the gain of $3 million).
6. To create the income statement, select revenues, expenses, gains, and losses from the list of items a to x. Items can be listed in order of declining balances or in alphabetical order. Income tax expense is almost always shown separately, as the last item before net income.

Matheson Corporation
Income Statement
For the Year Ended December 31, 2014

Item (Reference Letter)		(amounts in thousands)	
	Revenue and gains:		
l., m.	Sales revenue ($1,005 + $258)	$1,263	
s.	Gain on sale of investments	36	
n.	Interest revenue	22	
u.	Dividend revenue	8	
	Total revenues and gains		$1,329
	Expenses and losses:		
w.	Cost of goods sold	795	
a.	Salary expense	290	
b.	Amortization expense	104	
q.	Interest expense	31	
i.	Loss on sale of property, plant, and equipment	3	
	Total expenses		1,223
	Net income before income tax		106
k.	Income tax expense		45
	Net income		$ 61

In a cash flow statement:

- Brackets indicate a cash outflow (a cash payment).
- When using the direct method of calculating cash flows from operating activities, look for activities that have a cash impact on revenues (cash receipts) and expenses (cash payments).
- For cash flows from financing activities, look for activities that have a cash impact on short-term debt accounts, long-term liability accounts, and equity accounts.
- For cash flows from investing activities, look for activities that have a cash impact on long-term asset accounts.
- The cash balance at December 31, 2014, calculated at the end of the cash flow statement should equal the December 31, 2014, balance sheet amount, given as part of item x. If it does not, there is an error in the cash flow statement.

Matheson Corporation
Cash Flow Statement
For the Year Ended December 31, 2014

Item (Reference Letter)		(amounts in thousands)	
	Cash flows from operating activities		
	Receipts:		
g., m.	Collections from customers ($1,030 + $258)	$1,288	
e.	Interest received on notes receivable	20	
u.	Dividends received on investments in shares	8	
	Total cash receipts		$ 1,316
	Payments:		
j.	To suppliers	(893)	
f.	To employees	(308)	
q.	For interest	(31)	
k.	For income tax	(45)	
	Total cash payments		(1,277)
	Net cash inflow from operating activities.		39

(Continued)

(Continued)

<table>
<tr><th colspan="3">Matheson Corporation</th></tr>
<tr><th colspan="3">Cash Flow Statement</th></tr>
<tr><th colspan="3">For the Year Ended December 31, 2014</th></tr>
<tr><td></td><td colspan="2">Cash flows from investing activities</td></tr>
<tr><td>v.</td><td>Acquisition of property, plant, and equipment</td><td>$(232)</td><td></td></tr>
<tr><td>h.</td><td>Loan to another company</td><td>(118)</td><td></td></tr>
<tr><td>s.</td><td>Cash received from sale of investments</td><td>61</td><td></td></tr>
<tr><td>i.</td><td>Cash received from sale of property, plant,</td><td></td><td></td></tr>
<tr><td></td><td>and equipment</td><td>50</td><td></td></tr>
<tr><td>r.</td><td>Collection of loans</td><td>143</td><td></td></tr>
<tr><td></td><td>Net cash outflow from investing activities</td><td></td><td>(96)</td></tr>
<tr><td></td><td colspan="2">Cash flows from financing activities</td></tr>
<tr><td>o.</td><td>Cash received from issuing short-term debt</td><td>106</td><td></td></tr>
<tr><td>c.</td><td>Cash received from issuing common shares</td><td>87</td><td></td></tr>
<tr><td>p.</td><td>Payments of long-term debt</td><td>(160)</td><td></td></tr>
<tr><td>d.</td><td>Dividends declared and paid</td><td>(62)</td><td></td></tr>
<tr><td></td><td>Net cash outflow from financing activities</td><td></td><td>(29)</td></tr>
<tr><td></td><td>Net decrease in cash</td><td></td><td>(86)</td></tr>
<tr><td>x.</td><td>Cash balance at beginning of 2014</td><td></td><td>230</td></tr>
<tr><td>x.</td><td>Cash balance at end of 2014</td><td></td><td>$ 144</td></tr>
</table>

7. i. Cash collections from customers:

Accounts Receivable Beginning Balance	+	Sales	−	Collections	=	Accounts Receivable Ending Balance
$46,000	+	$240,000	−	X	=	$44,000
				−X	=	$44,000 − $46,000 − $240,000
				X	=	$242,000

ii. Payments for inventory:

Inventory Beginning Balance	+	Purchases	−	Cost of Goods Sold	=	Inventory Ending Balance
$62,000	+	X	−	$140,000	=	$68,000
				X	=	$68,000 − $62,000 + $140,000
				X	=	$146,000

Accounts and Notes Payable Beginning Balance	+	Purchases	−	Payments for Inventory	=	Accounts and Notes Payable Ending Balance
$52,000	+	$146,000	−	X	=	$70,000
				−X	=	$70,000 − $52,000 − $146,000
				X	=	$128,000

iii. Payments for income taxes:

Income and Other Taxes Payable Beginning Balance	+	Income Tax Expense	−	Payments	=	Income and Other Taxes Payable Ending Balance
$20,000	+	$20,000	−	X	=	$22,000
				−X	=	$22,000 − $20,000 − $20,000
				X	=	$18,000

iv. Payments for prepaid expenses:

Prepaid Expenses Beginning Balance	+	Payments	−	Expiration of Prepaid Expenses	=	Prepaid Expenses Ending Balance
$6,000	+	X	−	$8,000	=	$2,000
				X	=	$2,000 − $6,000 + $8,000
				X	=	$4,000

8. a. Net change in cash from investing activities (amounts in thousands):

Sale of bonds issued by Blue Ltd.	$ 224
Purchase of land	(316)
Collection of long-term note receivable	126
	$ 34 a net increase

b. *Operating activities:* Payment of interest, payment of income taxes.

Financing activities: Retirement of preferred shares, sale of common shares, payment of dividends.

9. Net change in cash from financing activities (amounts in thousands):

Retirement of Bolin Corp. preferred shares	$ (90)
Sale of Bolin Corp. common shares	210
Payment of dividends	(300)
	$(180) a net decrease

10. Computation of cash flow from operating activities using the indirect method:

Net income	$150
Add (subtract):	
Decrease in Accounts Receivable	6
Increase in Inventory	(18)
Increase in Accounts Payable	11
Decrease in Wages Payable	(15)
Cash flow from operating activities	$134

11. a. Capilano Ltd. appears to be growing. The company acquired more property, plant, and equipment, and intangible assets ($735,000) than it sold during the year ($149,000), and current assets changed very little.

b. Most of the cash for expansion came from issuing common shares ($242,000) and from borrowing ($226,000). However, cash from the balance on January 1, 2014, and cash from operating activities could have been used for expansion too.

c. Accounts Receivable ↓, Cash ↑

Therefore, net cash inflow from operating activities would be $280,000 ($168,000 + $80,000 + $32,000).

12. Under IFRS, an entity may choose to report cash inflows from interest and dividends as either operating activities or investing activities. Once an accounting policy is chosen, it must be applied consistently to all transactions of a similar nature.

IFRS differs from ASPE in that ASPE requires that the receipt of interest and dividends be reported as operating activities on the cash flow statement.

13. Under IFRS, an entity may choose to report cash payments for interest and dividends as either operating activities or financing activities. Once an accounting policy is chosen, it must be applied consistently to all transactions of a similar nature.

IFRS differs from ASPE in that ASPE requires that payments of interest be reported as an operating activity on the cash flow statement and that payments of dividends be reported in the financing-activities section.

18 Financial Statement Analysis

KEY QUESTIONS	LEARNING OBJECTIVES
How do we compare several years of financial information?	**1** Perform a horizontal analysis of financial statements
What is a vertical analysis, and how do we perform one?	**2** Perform a vertical analysis of financial statements
What are common-size financial statements, and how do we use them?	**3** Prepare and use common-size financial statements
How do we compute standard financial ratios, and what do they mean?	**4** Compute the standard financial ratios
What is the impact of IFRS on financial statement analysis?	**5** Describe the impact on financial statement analysis of international financial reporting standards (IFRS)

Winpak Ltd., based in Winnipeg, is a Canadian success story. We will examine Winpak's financial statements throughout this chapter.

Winpak manufactures and sells high-quality packaging materials and innovative packaging machines. Customers use Winpak packaging for perishable foods, beverages, pharmaceuticals, and medical applications. Most Winpak products are sold in the United States and Canada. Customers include Proctor & Gamble, McCain Foods Limited, High Liner Foods Inc., and Maple Leaf Foods.

Investors and management of Winpak compare the performance of the most recent period against prior periods. This is a common form of financial analysis and is the reason that at least two years of financial results are presented in annual reports. Winpak's 2011 Annual Report states that "In each of the past four years, Winpak's net income has aggressively surpassed the prior year's standings. For 2011, net income attributable to common shareholders of $63.8 million or 98 cents per share, outpaced 2010's performance by 15.3 percent or 13 cents per share. Of further distinction, quarterly earnings per share for each of the past 15 consecutive quarters have exceeded the preceding year's achievements. . ."[1] This analysis also compared Winpak's earnings to its number of shareholders to measure success. By comparing different amounts of earnings against different numbers of shareholders, *relative* performance is considered rather than just the total dollar amounts, which is another form of analysis.

---

[1] Winpak Ltd.'s 2011 Annual Report, Report to Shareholders section, p. 1.

①	②	③	④	⑤
Perform a horizontal analysis of financial statements	Perform a vertical analysis of financial statements	Prepare and use common-size financial statements	Compute the standard financial ratios	Describe the impact on financial statement analysis of international financial reporting standards (IFRS)
How do we compare several years of financial information? page 1130	*What is a vertical analysis, and how do we perform one? page 1134*	*What are common-size financial statements, and how do we use them? page 1136*	*How do we compute standard financial ratios, and what do they mean? page 1139*	*What is the impact of IFRS on financial statement analysis? page 1155*
The Objectives of Financial Statement Analysis, page 1129	Vertical Analysis, page 1134	Common-Size Statements, page 1136	Using Ratios to Make Decisions, page 1139	The Impact on Financial Statement Analysis of International Financial Reporting Standards (IFRS), page 1155
Methods of Analysis, page 1130		Benchmarking, page 1137	Limitations of Financial Analysis, page 1150	
Horizontal Analysis, page 1130			Efficient Markets, Nonfinancial Reports, and Investor Decisions, page 1151	

MyAccountingLab

- Chapter 18: DemoDoc covering Financial Statement Analysis
- Chapter 18: Student PowerPoint Slides
- Chapter 18: Audio Chapter Summary

All MyAccountingLab resources can be found in the Chapter Resources section and the Multimedia Library.

The **Summary** for Chapter 18 appears on page 1157.
Accounting Vocabulary with definitions appears on page 1161.

Investors and creditors also compare Winpak against its competitors in the same field of business and the industry in general. Managers also use the financial information prepared by accountants to make business decisions. For example, inventory levels are analyzed to see if they are too high so that operations managers can adjust production, marketing managers can see whether changes to advertising results in increased sales, and human resources managers can see if labour costs are in line with other companies in the industry. Financial analysis is performed in many different situations and by many different people! In this chapter, we will explore ratios and other forms of financial statement analysis.

As the opening vignette illustrates, managers rely on accounting information to make business decisions. Investors and creditors also rely on accounting information. Often they want to compare two or more similar companies. The way to compare companies of different sizes is to use *standard* measures. In earlier chapters, we have discussed financial ratios, such as the current ratio, inventory turnover, and return on shareholders' equity. These ratios are standard measures that enable investors to compare companies of similar sizes or different sizes, or companies that operate in the same or different industries. In this chapter, we discuss most of the basic ratios and related measures that managers use to run a company. Investors and lenders use the same tools to search for good investments and loan prospects. It is important to know how ratios are calculated to better understand and interpret the results of financial statement analysis.

The Objectives of Financial Statement Analysis

Financial statement analysis focuses on techniques used by internal managers and by analysts external to the organization. A major source of their information is the annual report. Annual reports usually contain:

1. The basic financial statements: balance sheet, income statement, statement of retained earnings, and cash flow statement, and the notes to the financial statements, including a statement of significant accounting policies;
2. Comparative financial information for at least the prior year;
3. The auditor's report;
4. Management's discussion and analysis (MD&A) of the past financial results and expectations for the future;
5. A management report; and
6. Other financial and nonfinancial information about the company, such as information relating to environmental affairs.

Websites for public corporations often include financial information such as annual reports and news releases. This information is usually found in a section called "shareholder information" or "investor relations."

Investors who purchase a company's shares expect to receive dividends and hope the shares' value will increase. Creditors make loans with the expectation of receiving cash for the interest and principal. Both groups bear the risk they will not receive their expected returns. They use financial statement analysis to (1) predict the amount of expected returns and (2) assess the risks associated with those returns.

Creditors generally expect to receive specific fixed amounts and have the first claim on a company's assets if the company goes bankrupt, so creditors are most concerned with assessing *short-term liquidity* and *long-term solvency*. **Short-term liquidity** is an organization's ability to meet current payments as they become due. **Long-term solvency** is the ability to generate enough cash to pay long-term debts as they mature.

In contrast, *investors* are more concerned with profitability, dividends, and future share prices. Why? Because dividends and future share prices depend on profitable operations. Creditors also assess profitability because profitable operations are the company's prime source of cash to repay loans.

However, investors and creditors cannot evaluate a company by looking at only one year's data. This is one reason why most financial statements present results for at least two periods. This chapter illustrates some of the analytical tools for charting a company's progress over time.

Exhibit 18–1 on the next page shows graphical data taken from the 2011 annual report of Winpak Ltd. Management presents information this way to show how the company performed over the 10 years ended December 25, 2011.

REAL WORLD EXAMPLE

The SEDAR website makes available annual reports and other financial information for Canadian corporations at www.sedar.com.

KEY POINTS

When performing financial analysis, it is important to not look at only one period or one ratio. Think of analysis as solving a mystery, where one clue leads to another until a conclusion can be reached based on all the clues fitting together.

EXHIBIT **18–1** | Financial Data from Winpak Ltd.'s 2011 Annual Report

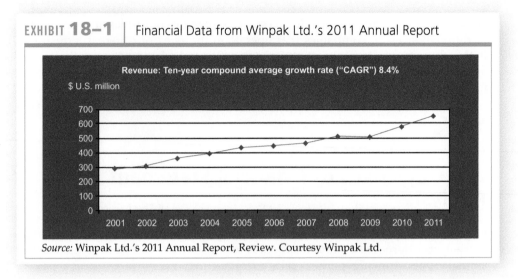

Source: Winpak Ltd.'s 2011 Annual Report, Review. Courtesy Winpak Ltd.

How can we decide what we really think about Winpak's performance? We need some way to analyze a company's performance

- From year to year
- Compared with a competing company
- Compared with the company's industry

Then, we can better judge the company's situation now and predict what might happen in the near future.

Methods of Analysis

There are three main ways to analyze financial statements:

- Perform horizontal analysis to provide a year-to-year comparison of performance in different periods.
- Perform vertical analysis to compare different companies.
- Calculate and interpret financial ratios.

Horizontal Analysis

── LO ① ──
How do we compare several
years of financial information?

KEY POINTS

Horizontal analysis often involves a
percentage change, calculated as:

$$\frac{\$ \text{ change}}{\text{Base year } \$} \times 100 = \% \text{ change}$$

It is important to consider both
dollar changes and percentage
changes in horizontal analysis. The
dollar increase may be growing,
but the percentage change may be
growing less because the base is
greater each year.

Many managerial decisions hinge on whether the numbers—revenues, expenses, and net income—are increasing or decreasing. Have revenues risen from last year? By how much? The fact revenues may have risen by $20,000 may be interesting, but considered alone it is not very useful for decision making. Did $2,000,000 or $200,000 in revenues increase by $20,000? The *percentage change* in the net revenues over time is more useful because it shows the changes over time in *relative* terms. It is more useful to know that revenues increased by 20 percent than to know that revenues increased by $20,000.

The study of percentage changes in comparative statements is called **horizontal analysis**. Computing a percentage change in comparative statements requires three steps:

1. Lay out at least two periods of financial statement information side by side.
2. Compute the dollar amount of the change from the earlier period to the later period.
3. Divide the dollar amount of the change by the earlier-period amount and multiply by 100. We call the earlier period the *base period*.

Let's look at how horizontal analysis, which is illustrated for Winpak Ltd. in Exhibit 18–2 and Exhibit 18–3, is done.

Step 1: Organize financial information into a chart format, as shown here:

	(U.S. dollar amounts in millions)		Increase (Decrease)	
	2011	2010	Amount	Percent
Sales	$652	$579		
Net earnings	65	57		

Step 2: Compute the dollar amount of change in each account during the most recent year.

	(U.S. dollar amounts in millions)		Increase (Decrease)	
	2011	2010	Amount	Percent
Sales	$652	$579	$73	
Net earnings	65	57	8	

Step 3: Divide the dollar amount of change by the base-period amount and multiply by 100 to compute the percentage change during the later period. For sales, the calculation is as follows:

$$\text{Percentage change} = \frac{\text{Dollar amount of change}}{\text{Base-year amount}} = \frac{\$73}{\$579} \times 100 = 12.6 \text{ percent}$$

	(U.S. dollar amounts in millions)		Increase (Decrease)	
	2011	2010	Amount	Percent
Sales	$652	$579	$73	12.6
Net earnings	65	57	8	14.0

The comparative income statement for Winpak Ltd. shown in Exhibit 18–2 shows that sales increased by $73 million or 12.6 percent. Since the cost of goods sold (cost of sales) increased by a lesser amount ($57 million or 14.0 percent), earnings from operations increased by $16 million, or 20.3 percent.

REAL WORLD EXAMPLE
Spreadsheet programs such as Excel are ideal for performing horizontal analysis.

EXHIBIT 18–2 | Comparative Income Statement—Horizontal Analysis

WINPAK LTD.
Consolidated Statements of Income (adapted)
For the Years Ended December 25, 2011, and December 26, 2010
(U.S. dollar amounts in millions except per-share amounts)

	2011	2010	Increase (Decrease) Amount	Increase (Decrease) Percent
Sales	$ 652	$ 579	$ 73	12.6%
Cost of sales	464	407	57	14.0
Gross margin	188	172	16	9.3
Expenses				
Selling, general, & administrative	79	79	0	0
Research and technical	13	13	0	0
Pre-production	1	1	0	0
Earnings from operations	95	79	16	20.3
Interest	1	1	0	0
Earnings before income taxes	96	79*	17	21.5
Income tax expense	31	22	9	40.9
Net earnings	$ 65	$ 57	$ 8	14.0
Earnings per share (basic and fully diluted)	$0.98	$0.85	$0.13	15.3

* Numbers may not add up due to rounding to the nearest million.

The comparative balance sheet in Exhibit 18–3 shows that there was a change between 2010 and 2011. Total assets increased by $60 million, or 11.8 percent, and total liabilities increased by $13 million, or 11.1 percent. The increase in retained earnings was $48 million, or 13.3 percent.

EXHIBIT 18–3 | Comparative Balance Sheet—Horizontal Analysis

WINPAK LTD.
Consolidated Balance Sheet (adapted)*
December 25, 2011, and December 26, 2010
(U.S. dollar amounts in millions)

	2011	2010	Increase (Decrease) Amount	Increase (Decrease) Percent
Assets				
Current assets:				
Cash and equivalents	$127	$ 90	$37	41.1%
Accounts receivable	84	77	7	9.1
Income taxes receivable	—	2	(2)	(100.0)
Inventory	78	76	2	2.6
Prepaid expenses	3	2	1	50.0
	292	249	43	17.3
Property, plant, and equipment	257	235	22	9.4
Other assets, intangible assets, and goodwill	10	24	(14)	(58.3)
Total assets	**$568**	**$508**	**$60**	**11.8**
Liabilities and Shareholders' Equity				
Current liabilities:				
Accounts payable and accrued liabilities	61	53	8	15.1
Income taxes payable	5	2	3	150.0
	66	55	11	20.0
Noncurrent liabilities:				
Employee benefit plan liabilities	13	7	6	85.7
Deferrals	27	31	(4)	(12.9)
Provisions	8	8	0	0
Noncontrolling interest	16	17	(1)	(5.9)
	63	63	0	0
Total liabilities	130	117	13	11.1
Shareholders' equity:				
Common shares	29	29	0	0
Retained earnings	409	361	48	13.3
Total shareholders' equity	438	391	47	12.0
Total liabilities and shareholders' equity	$568	$508	$60	11.8

Percentage changes are typically not computed for shifts from a negative amount to a positive amount, and vice versa.

* Slight differences are due to rounding throughout the statement.

Note: A decrease from any number to zero is a decrease of 100 percent. We will treat an increase from zero to any positive number as an increase of 100 percent.

KEY POINTS

There are no equal sign lines for the total in the Percent column. This column will never add up because a separate percentage has been calculated for each item, as is always done in horizontal analysis.

Trend Percentages

Trend percentages are a form of horizontal analysis. Trends are important indicators of the direction a business is taking. How have sales changed over a five-year period? What trend does gross margin show? These questions can be answered by analyzing trend percentages over a recent period, such as the most recent five years or 10 years. To gain a realistic view of the company, it is often necessary to examine more than just a two- or three-year period.

Trend percentages are computed by selecting a base year. The base-year amounts are set to 100 percent. The amounts for each following year are expressed as a percent of the base amount. To compute trend percentages, divide each item for following years by the base-year amount and multiply by 100 percent.

$$\text{Trend \%} = \frac{\text{Any year \$}}{\text{Base-year \$}} \times 100\text{ \%}$$

Using financial statements from more than one year, we can create a summary chart to show Winpak sales and earnings from operations for the past five years:

	(Amounts in millions)				
	2011	**2010**	**2009**	**2008**	**2007**
Sales	$652	$579	$506	$512	$466
Earnings from operations	95	79	66	46	34
Net earnings	65	57	42	29	24

We want trend percentages for a four-year period, 2008 through 2011, so we use 2007 as the base year. Trend percentages for sales are computed by dividing each sales amount by the 2007 amount of $466 million. Likewise, dividing each year's earnings from operations amount by the base-year amount, $34 million, yields the trend percentages for earnings from operations. The same steps are done for net earnings. The resulting trend percentages follow:

	2011	**2010**	**2009**	**2008**	**2007**
Sales	140%	124%	109%	110%	100%
Earnings from operations	279	232	194	135	100
Net earnings	271	238	175	121	100

Winpak's sales have trended upward from 2007; 2011 sales are 140 percent of 2007 sales. Earnings from operations have trended upward from 2007. Net earnings also followed the same upwards trend, from $24 million in 2007 to $65 million in 2011; 2011's net earnings were 271 percent of 2007's net earnings. Sales, earnings from operations, and net earnings have all trended upwards. Further analysis would need to be completed to confirm whether the trend is expected to continue upward.

You can perform a trend analysis on any item you consider important. Trend analysis may be used to predict the future by seeing the direction things are going. Because it is unwise to assume that the future can be predicted, this sort of forward-looking assumption must be used with caution.

KEY POINTS

Trend percentages indicate the change between a base year and any later year:

$$\text{Trend \%} = \frac{\text{Any year \$}}{\text{Base-year \$}} \times 100\%$$

To calculate the % change from the base year, subtract 100% from the trend %.

In this example, sales increased 40% from 2007 to 2011 (140% − 100%).

✓ JUST CHECKING

1. Perform a horizontal analysis of the comparative income statement of Umoja Inc. State whether 2014 was a good year or a bad year and give your reasons.

UMOJA INC.
Income Statement
For the Years Ended December 31, 2014 and 2013

	2014	2013
Net sales	$275,000	$225,000
Expenses:		
Cost of goods sold	194,000	165,000
Engineering, selling, and administrative expenses	54,000	48,000
Interest expense	5,000	5,000
Income tax expense	9,000	3,000
Other expense (income)	1,000	(1,000)
Total expenses	263,000	220,000
Net income	$ 12,000	$ 5,000

2. Suppose Umoja Inc. reported the following revenues and net income amounts:

	(in thousands)			
	2014	2013	2012	2011
Revenues (net sales)	$275,000	$225,000	$210,000	$200,000
Net income	12,000	5,000	6,000	3,000

   a. Show Umoja Inc.'s trend percentages for revenues and net income. Use 2011 as the base year.

   b. Which measure increased faster between 2011 and 2014?

Just Checking Solutions appear at the end of this chapter and on MyAccountingLab.

Vertical Analysis

— LO ② —
What is a vertical analysis, and how do we perform one?

As we have seen, horizontal analysis and trend percentages highlight changes in an item over time. However, no single technique provides a complete picture of a business. Another way to analyze a company is called vertical analysis.

Vertical analysis of a financial statement reveals the relationship of each statement item to a base, which is the 100 percent figure.

$$\text{Vertical analysis \%} = \frac{\text{Each account}}{\text{Base amount*}} \times 100\%$$

* Base amount for an income statement is Sales. Base amount for a balance sheet is Total Assets.

For example, when an income statement for a merchandising company is subjected to vertical analysis, net sales is usually the base. Every other item on the income statement is then reported as a percentage of that base.

Suppose under normal conditions a company's gross margin is 40 percent of net sales. A drop in gross margin to 30 percent of net sales may cause the company to report a net loss on the income statement. Management, investors, and creditors view a large decline in gross margin with alarm. If analysis were performed using just dollar amounts, it is possible that this decline would be missed because an increase in sales and gross margin might not show the relative decline in the gross margin. Exhibit 18–4 shows the vertical analysis of Winpak's income statement as a percentage of sales. Notice that there was a decline in the gross margin percentage even though there was an increase in the dollar amount of gross margin.

KEY POINTS

While horizontal analysis shows the relationship among several years, vertical analysis shows the relationship among numbers on the financial statements for the same year.

EXHIBIT **18–4** | Comparative Income Statement—Vertical Analysis

WINPAK LTD.
Consolidated Statement of Income (adapted)
For the Years Ended December 25, 2011, and December 26, 2010
(U.S. dollar amounts in millions)

	2011		2010	
	Amount	Percent*	Amount	Percent*
Sales	$ 652	100.0%	$ 579	100.0%
Cost of sales	464	71.2	407	70.3
Gross margin	188	28.8	172	29.7
Expenses:				
Selling, general, & administrative	79	12.1	79	13.6
Research and technical	13	2.0	13	2.2
Pre-production	1	0.2	1	0.2
Earnings from operations	95	14.6	79	13.6
Interest	1	0.2	1	0.2
Earnings before income taxes	96	14.7	79	13.6
Income tax expense	31	4.8	22	3.8
Net earnings	$ 65	10.0	$ 57	9.8
Earnings per share (basic and fully				
diluted)	$0.98		$0.85	

* Percentages may not add up due to rounding.

The 2011 comparative income statement (Exhibit 18–4) reports that cost of sales increased from 70.3 percent of sales in 2010 to 71.2 percent of sales in 2011. Note that earnings from operations increased from 13.6 percent of sales in 2010 to 14.6 percent of sales in 2011. With sales and profits, increases are good!

The vertical analysis of Winpak's balance sheet in Exhibit 18–5 shows that current assets increased from 49.0 percent of total assets in 2010 to 51.4 percent of total assets in 2011. This is good because it means more money is available to pay short-term bills. We can also see that the company is profitable (retained earnings went from 71.1 percent in 2010 to 72.0 percent of total assets in 2011, as shown on page 1136).

EXHIBIT **18–5** | Comparative Balance Sheet—Vertical Analysis

WINPAK LTD.
Consolidated Balance Sheet (adapted)
December 25, 2011, and December 26, 2010
(U.S. dollar amounts in millions)

	2011		2010	
	Amount	Percent*	Amount	Percent*
Assets				
Current assets:				
Cash and equivalents	$127	22.4%	$ 90	17.7%
Accounts receivable	84	14.8	77	15.2
Income taxes receivable	—	—	2	0.4
Inventory	78	13.7	76	15.0
Prepaid expenses	3	0.5	2	0.4
	292	51.4	249	49.0
Property, plant, and equipment	257	45.3	235	46.3
Other assets, intangible assets, and goodwill	10	1.9	24	4.7
Total assets	$568	100.0%	$508	100.0%

KEY POINTS

To show the *relative* importance of each item on a financial statement, vertical analysis presents everything on that statement as a percentage of one total amount. On an income statement, all amounts are presented as a percentage of net sales. On a balance sheet, all amounts are presented as a percentage of total assets.

(*Continued*)

EXHIBIT **18–5** | Comparative Balance Sheet—Vertical Analysis (Continued)

	2011		2010	
	Amount	Percent*	Amount	Percent*
Liabilities and Shareholders' Equity				
Current liabilities:				
Accounts payable and accrued liabilities	$ 61	10.7	$ 53	10.4
Income taxes payable	5	0.9	2	0.4
	66	11.6	55	10.8
Noncurrent liabilities				
Employee benefit plan liabilities	13	2.3	7	1.4
Deferrals	27	4.8	31	6.1
Provisions	8	1.4	8	1.6
Noncontrolling interest	16	2.8	17	3.4
	63	11.1	63	12.4
Total liabilities	130	22.9	117	23.0
Shareholders' equity:				
Common shares	29	5.1	29	5.7
Retained earnings	409	72.0	361	71.1
Total shareholders' equity	438	77.1	391	77.0
Total liabilities and shareholders' equity	$568	100.0%	$508	100.0%

* Percentages may not add up due to rounding.

✓ JUST CHECKING

3. Refer to the Umoja Inc. information in Just Checking Question 1. Perform a vertical analysis of the comparative income statement. Was 2014 a good year or a bad year? Give your reasons.

Just Checking Solutions appear at the end of this chapter and on MyAccountingLab.

Common-Size Statements

LO ③

What are common-size financial statements, and how do we use them?

KEY POINTS

A common-size statement is a form of vertical analysis used to facilitate comparison between different companies by making all amounts relative to some base amount.

Horizontal analysis and vertical analysis provide useful data about a company. As we have seen, Winpak's percentages depict a successful company. But the Winpak data apply only to one business.

To compare one company to another we can use a common-size statement. A **common-size statement** reports only percentages—the same percentages that appear in a vertical analysis. For example, Winpak's common-size income statement could be created by removing the dollar amounts from Exhibit 18–4 and presenting just the percentages.

On a common-size income statement, each item is expressed as a percentage of the net sales (or revenues) amount. Net sales (or revenues) is the *common size* to which we relate the statement's other amounts. On the balance sheet, the *common size* is total assets *or* the sum of total liabilities and shareholders' equity.

To create a partial common-size balance sheet, some amounts from Exhibit 18–5 were summarized as shown in Exhibit 18–6. Common-size statements provide information useful for analyzing the changes in account balances over time irrespective of the dollar amounts in each account. For example, the inventory balance increased from $76 to $78 million but Exhibit 18–6 shows that the inventory has decreased from 15.0 percent of total assets in 2010 to 13.7 percent of total assets in 2011. If the decrease in inventory was not planned, this would be important information for management to see to get the right amount of inventory on hand. A common-size statement also eases the comparison of different companies because their amounts are stated as percentages. If Winpak's competitors held inventory that was 20% of their total assets, then Winpak might be holding too little.

EXHIBIT 18–6 | Common-Size Analysis of Current Assets

WINPAK LTD. Partial Common-Size Balance Sheet December 25, 2011, and December 26, 2010		
	Percent of Total Assets	
	2011	2010
Current assets:		
Cash and equivalents	22.4%	17.7%
Accounts receivable	14.8	15.2
Inventory	13.7	15.0
Other (includes income tax receivable and prepaid expenses)	0.5	1.1
Total current assets	51.4%	49.0%

REAL WORLD EXAMPLE

Spreadsheet programs such as Excel are ideal for performing vertical analysis and for creating common-size financial statements. Most spreadsheet programs also have a graphing function, making it easy to create pie graphs and other types of graphs.

Benchmarking

Benchmarking is the practice of comparing any part of a company's performance with that of other leading companies. There are two main types of benchmarks in financial statement analysis: against another company and against an industry average.

Benchmarking Against Another Company   A company's financial statements show past results and help investors predict future performance. Still, that knowledge may be limited to that one company. We may learn that gross margin and net income have increased. This information is helpful, but it does not consider how other companies in the same industry have fared over the same period. Have competitors profited even more? Is there an industry-wide increase in net income? Managers, investors, creditors, and other interested parties need to know how one company compares with other companies in the same line of business.

We can look at the Internet service industry for an example. Google Inc. and YAHOO! Inc. are competitors who could be compared to see which one is more profitable, but the different sizes of the companies would make a direct comparison very complex. Google's revenues in 2011 were almost $38 billion, YAHOO!'s revenues were under $5 billion. So how does Google's net income of $9.7 billion compare to Yahoo's $1 billion net income? Exhibit 18–7 on the next page presents their common-size income statements. YAHOO!'s net income is 21.0 percent of revenue while Google's net income is 25.7 percent of revenue. From this analysis, we can see that YAHOO! is less profitable than Google when compared with the amount of revenues each earns.

	Google Inc.	YAHOO! Inc.
Revenues	100.0%	100.0%
Cost of revenues	29.9	30.1
Gross margin	**70.1**	**69.9**
Sales and marketing expense	12.1	22.7
General and administrative expense	7.2	9.8
Research and development expense	13.6	20.2
Other expense	6.2	1.0
Income before income taxes	31.0	16.2
Income tax expense (revenue)	5.3	(4.9)
Net income	25.7%	21.0%

Google Inc.

Net income 25.7%
Cost of revenues 29.9%
Income tax 5.3%
Other expense 6.2%
R & D expense 13.6%
G & A expense 7.2%
Sales and marketing expense 12.1%

YAHOO! Inc.

Net income 21.0%
Income tax 4.9%
Other expense 1.0%
Cost of revenues 30.1%
R & D expense 20.2%
G & A expense 9.8%
Sales and marketing expense 22.7%

When the same information—the common-size income statement data—is presented in a graph, we can also notice other differences in the companies, such as the fact that YAHOO! invests a greater percentage of its revenues into research and development than does Google.

Benchmarking Against the Industry Average   The industry average can also serve as a useful benchmark for evaluating a company. An industry comparison would show how Google is performing compared with the industry. The *RMA Annual Statement Studies*, published by The Risk Management Association, provides common-size statements for most industries.

Information Sources

Financial analysts draw their information from various sources.

- Annual and quarterly reports offer readers a good look at an individual business's operations. The SEDAR website (www.sedar.com) makes available annual reports and other financial information for Canadian corporations.

- Publicly held companies must submit annual and quarterly reports to the provincial securities commission in each province where they are listed on a stock exchange (for example, the Ontario Securities Commission for the Toronto Stock Exchange).

- Business publications such as *The National Post* and *The Globe and Mail* Report on Business carry information about individual companies and Canadian industries.

- Credit agencies, like Dun & Bradstreet Canada, for example, offer industry averages as part of their financial service.

- Online financial databases, such as LexisNexis, Financial Post DataGroup, and globeinvestor.com, offer quarterly financial figures for hundreds of public corporations going back as far as 10 years.

REAL WORLD EXAMPLE

Benchmarks can also be found in industry-specific publications. For example, on its website, the National Automobile Dealers Association provides some industry averages for car dealerships.

✓ JUST CHECKING

4. Refer to the vertical analysis of Umoja Inc. performed in Just Checking Question 3. Suppose Compet Ltd. is a competitor of Umoja Inc. in the same industry. Use the Compet Ltd. information given below to create its common-size income statement. How do the results of Umoja Inc. compare with those of Compet Ltd.?

COMPET LTD. Income Statement For the Year Ended December 31, 2014	
Net sales	$580,000
Expenses:	
Cost of goods sold	395,000
Engineering, selling, and administrative expenses	100,000
Interest expense	30,000
Income tax expense	23,000
Other expense (income)	1,800
Total expenses	549,800
Net income	$ 30,200

Just Checking Solutions appear at the end of this chapter and on MyAccountingLab.

Using Ratios to Make Decisions

— LO ④ —
How do we compute standard financial ratios, and what do they mean?

An important part of financial analysis is the calculation and interpretation of ratios. A ratio is a useful way to show the relationship of one number to another. For example, if the balance sheet shows current assets of $100,000 and current liabilities of $25,000, the ratio of current assets to current liabilities is $100,000 to $25,000. We could simplify this numerical expression to the ratio of 4 to 1, which may also be written 4:1 and 4/1. Other acceptable ways of expressing this ratio include "current assets are 400 percent of current liabilities," "the business has four dollars in current assets for every one dollar in current liabilities," or simply, "the current ratio is 4.0."

A manager, a lender, or a financial analyst may use any ratio that is relevant to a particular decision. Many companies include ratios in a special section of their annual report. The ratios we discuss in this chapter may be classified as follows:

LEARNING TIPS

Notice that there are many different ways to say the same thing! Practise using each of the different ways.

- Measuring ability to pay current liabilities (short-term **liquidity**)

- Measuring ability to sell inventory and collect receivables (efficiency)

- Measuring ability to pay long-term debt (long-term solvency)

- Measuring profitability

- Analyzing shares as an investment (value)

All the ratios discussed in this chapter are summarized on page 1159, after the Summary for this chapter. You may want to tab or mark the ratios table for easy reference.

Measuring Ability to Pay Current Liabilities

Working capital is calculated as:

MyAccountingLab

DemoDoc: Financial Statement Analysis

$$\text{Working capital} = \text{Current assets} - \text{Current liabilities}$$

Working capital measures the company's ability to meet short-term obligations with current assets. The working capital amount considered alone, however, does not give a complete picture of the entity's working capital position. Consider two companies with equal working capital.

	Company A	Company B
Current assets	$100,000	$200,000
Less current liabilities	50,000	150,000
Working capital	$ 50,000	$ 50,000
Working capital as a percent of current liabilities	100%	33%

Both companies have working capital of $50,000, but Company A's working capital is as large as its current liabilities. Company B's working capital, on the other hand, is only one-third as large as its current liabilities. Which business has a better level of working capital? Company A, because its working capital is a higher percentage of current assets and current liabilities. Two decision tools based on working capital data are the *current ratio* and the *acid-test ratio*.

Current Ratio   The most common ratio using current asset and current liability data is the **current ratio**, which is total current assets divided by total current liabilities. We introduced the current ratio in Chapter 4 (p. 206). Recall the makeup of current assets and current liabilities. Current assets consist of cash, short-term investments, net receivables, inventory, and prepaid expenses. Current liabilities include accounts payable, short-term notes payable, unearned revenues, and all types of accrued liabilities. The current ratio measures the company's ability to pay bills that are due to be paid in the coming year with items that can be turned into cash easily in the coming year.

Exhibits 18–8 and 18–9 give the comparative income statement and balance sheet, respectively, of Sofawerks Furniture Inc. We will use this information to calculate several key ratios for the company. Let's start with the current ratio.

EXHIBIT 18–8 | Comparative Income Statement

SOFAWERKS FURNITURE INC.
Income Statement
For the Years Ended December 31, 2014 and 2013

	2014	2013
Net sales	$858,000	$803,000
Cost of goods sold	513,000	509,000
Gross margin	345,000	294,000
Operating expenses:		
Selling expenses	116,000	104,000
General expenses	118,000	123,000
Total operating expenses	234,000	227,000
Income from operations	111,000	67,000
Interest revenue	4,000	—
Less interest expense	34,000	24,000
Income before income taxes	81,000	43,000
Income tax expense	33,000	17,000
Net income	$ 48,000	$ 26,000

EXHIBIT **18–9** | Comparative Balance Sheet

SOFAWERKS FURNITURE INC.
Balance Sheet
December 31, 2014 and 2013

Assets	2014	2013
Current assets:		
Cash	$ 39,000	$ 42,000
Accounts receivable, net	114,000	85,000
Inventories	113,000	111,000
Prepaid expenses	6,000	8,000
Total current assets	272,000	246,000
Long-term investments	18,000	9,000
Property, plant, and equipment, net	507,000	399,000
Total assets	$797,000	$654,000
Liabilities		
Current liabilities:		
Notes payable	$ 42,000	$ 27,000
Accounts payable	83,000	78,000
Accrued liabilities	27,000	31,000
Total current liabilities	152,000	136,000
Long-term debt	289,000	198,000
Total liabilities	441,000	334,000
Shareholders' Equity		
Common shares	186,000	186,000
Retained earnings	170,000	134,000
Total shareholders' equity	356,000	320,000
Total liabilities and shareholders' equity	$797,000	$654,000

The current ratios for 2014 and 2013 are calculated below. The result decreased slightly during 2014. A high current ratio indicates a strong financial position and that the business has sufficient **liquid assets** to maintain normal business operations.

Formula	Current Ratio of Sofawerks Furniture Inc.		Retail Furniture Industry Average
	2014	2013	
Current ratio $= \dfrac{\text{Current assets}}{\text{Current liabilities}}$	$\dfrac{\$272,000}{\$152,000} = 1.79$	$\dfrac{\$246,000}{\$136,000} = 1.81$	1.68

What is an acceptable current ratio? The answer to this question depends on the nature of the business. The current ratio should generally exceed 1.0, while the norm for most companies is around 1.50. In most industries, a current ratio of 2.0 is considered very good. Sofawerks Furniture Inc.'s current ratio in excess of 1.75 is within the range of those values. We can look at the ratios for some real companies from a variety of industries:

Company	Current Ratio
Canadian Tire Corporation, Limited (December 2011)	1.68
Research in Motion Limited (March 2012)	2.08
Lululemon Athletica Inc. (January 2012)	5.10
Tim Hortons (January 2012)	1.30

LEARNING TIPS

The current ratio measures the company's ability to pay current liabilities with current assets. So it should make sense that the result of the calculation of the current ratio should always be greater than 1. In other words, we need at least as much current assets as current liabilities or short-term payments cannot be made.

Acid-Test Ratio The **acid-test ratio** (or **quick ratio**) tells us whether the entity could pay all its current liabilities if they came due immediately. We saw in Chapter 9 (p. 543) that the higher the acid-test ratio, the better able the business is to pay its current liabilities. That is, *could the company pass this acid test*? To do so, the company would have to convert its most liquid assets to cash.

To compute the acid-test ratio, we add cash, short-term investments, and net current receivables (accounts and notes receivable, net of allowances) and divide by total current liabilities. Inventory and prepaid expenses are *not* included in the acid-test computations because a business may not be able to convert them to cash immediately to pay current liabilities. The acid-test ratio measures liquidity using fewer assets than the current ratio does.

Sofawerks Furniture Inc.'s acid-test ratios for 2014 and 2013 are as follows:

Formula	Acid-Test Ratio of Sofawerks Furniture Inc.		Retail Furniture Industry Average
	2014	**2013**	
Acid-test ratio = $\dfrac{\text{Cash + Short-term investments + Net current receivables}}{\text{Current liabilities}}$	$\dfrac{\$39{,}000 + \$0 + \$114{,}000}{\$152{,}000} = 1.01$	$\dfrac{\$42{,}000 + \$0 + \$85{,}000}{\$136{,}000} = 0.93$	0.60

KEY POINTS

How do we assess a ratio? We must consider prior years, industry averages, budgeted ratios, and so on—only then does a ratio have meaning.

The company's acid-test ratio improved considerably during 2014 and is significantly better than the industry average. Compare Sofawerks Furniture Inc.'s 1.01 acid-test ratio with the acid-test ratios of some well-known companies:

Company	Acid-Test Ratio
Canadian Tire Corporation, Limited	1.3
Research in Motion Limited	1.6
Lululemon Athletica Inc	4.0
Tim Hortons	0.6

An acid-test ratio of 0.90 to 1.00 is considered good in most industries. Note the range for the companies listed here is from a low of 0.6 to a high of 4.0.

Measuring the Ability to Sell Inventory and Collect Receivables

The ability to sell inventory and collect receivables is fundamental to the business success of a merchandiser. (Recall the operating cycle: cash to inventory to receivables and back to cash in Chapter 5, p. 261). This section discusses three ratios that measure the ability to sell inventory and collect receivables.

Inventory Turnover Companies generally seek to achieve the quickest possible return on their investments. A return on an investment in inventory—usually a substantial amount—is no exception. The faster inventory sells, the sooner the business creates accounts receivable, and the sooner it collects cash. In addition, companies make a profit each time they sell inventory. The more often they sell inventory, the greater the total amount of profit.

Inventory turnover measures the number of times a company sells its average level of inventory during a year. It is also used as a measure of the efficiency of a company in managing its inventory. We introduced inventory turnover in Chapter 5, pages 281–282. A high rate of turnover indicates ease in selling inventory; a low turnover indicates slower sales and may indicate difficulty in selling. Of course, there is a relationship between turnover and the product; Dollarama will have a higher rate of turnover than a company such as Finning International Inc. of Vancouver, which sells heavy equipment. A value of 6 means that the company sold its average level of inventory six times during the year. A business

REAL WORLD EXAMPLE

High turnover has been the recipe for success for companies like Walmart and Dollarama. Students who have taken a marketing course may recognize this pricing strategy—these are low-cost, high-volume retailers.

also strives for the *most profitable* rate of inventory turnover, not necessarily the *highest* rate.

To compute inventory turnover, we divide cost of goods sold by the average inventory for the period. We use the cost of goods sold—not sales—because both cost of goods sold and inventory are stated *at cost*. Sales at *retail* are not comparable to inventory at *cost*.

Sofawerks Furniture Inc.'s inventory turnover for 2014 is

Formula	Inventory Turnover of Sofawerks Furniture Inc.		Retail Furniture Industry Average
Inventory turnover = $\dfrac{\text{Cost of goods sold}}{\text{Average inventory}}$	$\dfrac{\$513,000}{(\$111,000 + \$113,000)/2}$	= 4.58 times	2.70 times

Cost of goods sold appears in the income statement (Exhibit 18–8). Average inventory is calculated by averaging the beginning inventory of 2014 (which is the balance at the end of 2013), $111,000, and ending inventory in 2014 of $113,000, from Exhibit 18–9. If inventory levels vary greatly from month to month, compute the average by adding the 12 monthly balances and dividing this sum by 12.

Inventory turnover varies widely with the nature of the business. Companies that remove natural gas from the ground hold their inventory for a very short period of time and have an average turnover of 30. Sofawerks Furniture Inc.'s turnover of 4.58 times a year is high for its industry, which has an average turnover of 2.70. Sofawerks Furniture Inc.'s high inventory turnover results from its policy of keeping little inventory on hand. The company takes customer orders and has its suppliers ship directly to customers.

LEARNING TIPS

Another helpful way to analyze inventory is to compare the inventory turnover days:

$$\frac{365 \text{ days}}{\text{Inventory turnover}}$$

The calculation for Sofawerks Furniture Inc. for 2014 would be

$$\frac{365 \text{ days}}{4.58} = 80 \text{ days}$$

It took the company approximately 80 days to sell all the items in inventory.

Accounts-Receivable Turnover Accounts-receivable turnover measures the company's ability to collect cash from credit customers. It is also used as a measure of the efficiency of a company to manage its cash collections. The higher the ratio is, the faster are the cash collections. However, a receivable turnover that is too high may indicate that credit is too tight, causing the loss of sales to good customers.

To compute the accounts-receivable turnover, we divide net credit sales by average net accounts receivable. The resulting ratio indicates how many times during the year the average level of receivables was turned into cash.

Sofawerks Furniture Inc.'s accounts-receivable turnover ratio for 2014 is computed as follows:

Formula	Accounts-Receivable Turnover of Sofawerks Furniture Inc.		Retail Furniture Industry Average
Accounts-receivable turnover = $\dfrac{\text{Net credit sales}}{\text{Average net accounts receivable}}$	$\dfrac{\$858,000}{(\$85,000 + \$114,000)/2}$	= 8.62 times	22.2 times

The net credit sales figure comes from the income statement. Sofawerks Furniture Inc. makes all sales on credit. (If a company makes both cash and credit sales, this ratio is best computed using only net *credit* sales. *Credit* means "on account"—it does not mean "using a credit card.") Average net accounts receivable is calculated by adding the beginning net accounts receivable balance ($85,000) and the ending balance ($114,000), then dividing by 2. If accounts receivable balances exhibit a seasonal pattern, compute the average using the 12 monthly balances added together and divided by 12.

Sofawerks Furniture Inc.'s accounts-receivable turnover of 8.62 times is much lower than the industry average. Why the difference? Sofawerks is a home-town store that sells to local people who tend to pay their bills over a period of time.

LEARNING TIPS

Recall that net accounts receivable is computed by subtracting the allowance for doubtful accounts from the accounts receivable total.

REAL WORLD EXAMPLE

When a business's accounts receivable turnover is different from the industry average, one must look past the ratio before deciding if a result is "good" or "bad." In the case of Sofawerks, the industry average might be high due to the use of *factors* rather than faster collection. If this industry is dominated by large stores, then the industry average is not a reasonable benchmark for Sofawerks.

Many larger furniture stores sell their receivables to other companies called **factors**. This practice keeps receivables low and receivable turnover high. In return for receiving the cash sooner, companies that factor (sell) their receivables receive less than face value for the receivables.

Days' Sales in Receivables   The **days'-sales-in-receivables** ratio measures the ability to collect receivables. This ratio tells us how many days' credit sales remain in Accounts Receivable. Recall from Chapter 9 (p. 543) that days' sales in receivables indicates how many days it takes to collect the average level of receivables. To compute the ratio, we can follow a two-step process.

① Divide net credit sales by 365 days to calculate average sales for one day.

② Divide this average day's sales amount into the average net accounts receivable.

The data to compute this ratio for Sofawerks Furniture Inc. for 2014 are taken from the income statement and the balance sheet (Exhibits 18–8 and 18–9).

Formulas	Days' Sales in Accounts Receivable of Sofawerks Furniture Inc. for 2014	Retail Furniture Industry Average
① One day's sales $= \dfrac{\text{Net sales}}{\text{365 days}}$	$\dfrac{\$858,000}{\text{365 days}} = \$2,351$	
② Day's sales in average accounts receivable $= \dfrac{\text{Average net accounts receivable}}{\text{One day's sales}}$	$\dfrac{(\$85,000\ +\ \$114,000)/2}{\$2,351} = 42 \text{ days}$	16 days

Days' sales in average receivables can also be computed in a single step:

$$((\$85,000 + \$114,000)/2) \div (\$858,000 \div 365 \text{ days}) = 42 \text{ days}.$$

Sofawerks Furniture Inc.'s ratio tells us that 42 days' sales remained in average accounts receivable during the year, or that it takes 42 days to collect receivables. The company will increase its cash inflow if it can decrease this ratio. Ways to do this include offering discounts for early payments, tightening credit policies to disallow slow-paying customers, using more aggressive collection procedures, and selling receivables to factors. The days' sales in receivables is higher (worse) than the industry average because the company collects its own receivables. Other furniture stores may sell their receivables or carry fewer days' sales in receivables. Sofawerks Furniture Inc. remains competitive because of the personal relationship with customers. Without their good paying habits, the company's cash flow would suffer.

LEARNING TIPS

Days' sales in receivables and accounts receivables turnover are both "saying the same thing in a different way." Notice that when turnover is 8.62 times, that is $365 \div 8.62 = 42$ days!

Measuring the Ability to Pay Long-Term Debt (Solvency)

Most businesses also have long-term debt. Two key indicators of a business's ability to pay long-term liabilities are the *debt ratio* and *times-interest-earned ratio*.

Debt Ratio   Suppose you are a loan officer at a bank and you are evaluating loan applications from two companies with equal sales and equal total assets of $1,000,000. Both A Co. and B Co. have asked to borrow $500,000 and have agreed to repay the loan over a five-year period. A Co. already owes $900,000 to another bank. B Co. owes only $250,000. Other things being equal, you would be more likely to lend money to B Co. because B Co. owes less money than A Co. owes. This relationship between total liabilities and total assets—called the **debt ratio**—shows the proportion of the company's assets that it has financed with debt. We introduced the debt ratio in Chapter 4, page 206. If the debt ratio is 0.90, as shown in the margin for A Co., then debt has been used to finance most of the assets. A debt ratio of 0.25 means that the company has borrowed to finance one quarter its assets; the owners have financed three-quarters of the assets. The higher the debt ratio is, the higher the strain of paying interest each year and the principal amount at maturity.

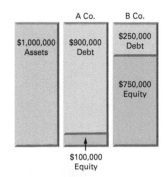

Creditors view a high debt ratio with caution. To help protect themselves, creditors generally charge higher interest rates on borrowings to companies with an already-high debt ratio.

Sofawerks Furniture Inc.'s debt ratios at the end of 2014 and 2013 are as follows:

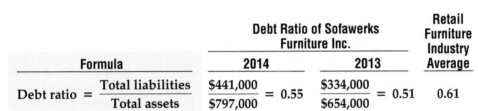

| Formula | Debt Ratio of Sofawerks Furniture Inc. | | Retail Furniture Industry Average |
	2014	2013	
Debt ratio = $\dfrac{\text{Total liabilities}}{\text{Total assets}}$	$\dfrac{\$441,000}{\$797,000} = 0.55$	$\dfrac{\$334,000}{\$654,000} = 0.51$	0.61

Sofawerks Furniture Inc. expanded operations by financing the purchase of buildings and fixtures through borrowing, which is common. This expansion explains the company's increased debt ratio. Even after the increase in 2014, the company's debt is not very high. The average debt ratio for most industries ranges around 0.57 to 0.67, with relatively little variation from company to company. Sofawerks Furniture Inc.'s 0.55 debt ratio indicates a fairly low-risk debt position in comparison with the retail furniture industry average of 0.61.

The **equity ratio** provides complementary information to the debt ratio. By dividing total shareholders' equity by total assets, the equity ratio provides investors with the amount of assets financed by the owners of the company. Sofawerks Furniture Inc. has a debt ratio of 55% in 2014, which means that the company has a 45% equity ratio. The debt and equity ratios must total 100%. All assets are financed either by debt or by equity. The debt ratio and the equity ratio give lenders and investors an indication of how the company is financed.

Equity ratio = $\dfrac{\text{Total shareholders' equity}}{\text{Total assets}}$

Times-Interest-Earned Ratio The debt ratio indicates nothing about the ability to pay interest expense. Analysts use a second ratio—the **times-interest-earned ratio**—to relate income to interest expense. This ratio is sometimes called the *interest-coverage ratio*. It measures the number of times that operating income can cover interest expense. A high times-interest-earned ratio indicates ease in paying interest expense; a low value suggests difficulty.

Calculation of Sofawerks Furniture Inc.'s times-interest-earned ratios follow:

| Formula | Times-Interest-Earned Ratio of Sofawerks Furniture Inc. | | Retail Furniture Industry Average |
	2014	2013	
Times-interest-earned ratio = $\dfrac{\text{Income from operations}}{\text{Interest expense}}$	$\dfrac{\$111,000}{\$34,000} = 3.26$ times	$\dfrac{\$67,000}{\$24,000} = 2.79$ times	2.00 times

The company's times-interest-earned ratio increased in 2014. This is a favourable sign about the company, especially since the company's liabilities rose substantially during the year. Sofawerks Furniture Inc.'s new buildings and fixtures, we conclude, have earned more in operating income than they have cost the business in interest expense. The company's times-interest-earned ratio of 3.26 is much better than the 2.00 average for furniture retailers. The norm for businesses, as reported by Robert Morris Associates, falls in the range of 2.00 to 3.00 for most companies. Based on its debt ratio and times-interest-earned ratio,

KEY POINTS

Note the numerator in the times-interest-earned ratio: *income from operations* (not net income), often calculated by the formula:

Income from operations = Net income + Interest expense + Income tax expense

Sofawerks Furniture Inc. appears to have little difficulty **servicing its debt**, that is, paying its liabilities.

What makes a corporation with a lot of debt a more risky loan prospect than one with a lot of equity? For a corporation with a lot of debt, interest on debt is contractual and must be paid; it is not discretionary. If interest on debt is not paid, creditors can force the company into bankruptcy. With equity, dividends are discretionary and do not have to be declared.

Measuring Profitability

REAL WORLD EXAMPLE

The Co-operators Group Limited, an insurance company, was ranked as the number one corporate citizen in Canada in 2011. At the same time it managed to make over $120 million in net income.

We often hear that the fundamental goal of business is to earn a profit. This is not the only objective of a business. Managers attempt to meet the needs of shareholders who require a sufficient return on their investment and to support other goals related to corporate social responsibility—to earn money to spend for the greater good (to support charities or environmental causes, for example). Ratios that measure profitability are reported in the business press, by investment services, and in annual reports. We examine four profitability measures.

Rate of Return on Net Sales   In business, the term *return* is used broadly as a measure of profitability. Consider a ratio called the **rate of return on net sales,** or simply **return on sales (ROS)**. (The word *net* is usually omitted for convenience, even though net sales is used to compute the ratio.) It is also called the *profit margin*. This ratio shows the percentage of each sales dollar earned as net income, or the amount of profit per dollar of sales. The rate-of-return-on-sales ratios for Sofawerks Furniture Inc. follow:

Formula	Rate of Return on Sales of Sofawerks Furniture Inc.		Retail Furniture Industry Average
	2014	**2013**	
Rate of return on net sales $= \dfrac{\text{Net income}}{\text{Net sales}}$	$\dfrac{\$48,000}{\$858,000} = $ 0.056, or 5.6%	$\dfrac{\$26,000}{\$803,000} = $ 0.032, or 3.2%	0.008, or 0.8%

Companies strive for a high rate of return on sales. The higher the rate of return, the more sales dollars are providing profit. The increase in Sofawerks Furniture Inc.'s return on sales is significant and identifies the company as more successful than the average furniture store. Compare Sofawerks Furniture Inc.'s rate of return on sales to the rates of some leading companies in other industries:

Company	Rate of Return on Sales
Canadian Tire Corporation, Limited	0.0450, or 4.50%
Research in Motion Ltd.	0.0631, or 6.31%
Lululemon Athletica Inc.	0.1848, or 18.48%
Tim Hortons Inc.	0.3686, or 36.86%

KEY POINTS

The denominator for rate of return on total assets is *average* total assets. Income is earned throughout the year. For the denominator to be stated for the same time period as the numerator, an average of assets for the year is used.

As these numbers indicate, the rate of return on sales varies widely from industry to industry, from 4.5 percent to 36.86 percent.

Rate of Return on Total Assets   The **rate of return on total assets** or, simply **return on assets (ROA)**, measures success in using assets to earn a profit. We first discussed rate of return on total assets in Chapter 13, page 831. Two groups finance a company's assets. Creditors have lent money to the company, and they earn interest on this money. Shareholders have invested in shares, and their rate of return is the company's net income.

The sum of interest expense and net income is thus the return to the two groups that have financed the company's assets. Computation of the rate of return on total assets for Sofawerks Furniture Inc. for 2014 follows:

	Formula	Rate of Return on Total Assets of Sofawerks Furniture Inc.		Retail Furniture Industry Average
Rate of return on total assets	= $\dfrac{\text{Net Income} + \text{Interest expense}}{\text{Average total assets}}$	$\dfrac{\$48,000 + \$34,000}{(\$797,000 + \$654,000)/2}$ =	0.113, or 11.3%	0.078, or 7.8%

Net income and interest expense are taken from the income statement (Exhibit 18–8). Average total assets is the average of beginning and ending total assets from the comparative balance sheet (Exhibit 18–9). Compare Sofawerks Furniture Inc.'s 11.3 percent rate of return on assets to the rates of some other companies, which range from 4.08 percent to 29.07 percent:

Company	Rate of Return on Assets
Canadian Tire Corporation, Limited	0.0408, or 4.08%
Research in Motion Ltd.	0.0926, or 9.26%
Lululemon Athletica Inc.	0.2907, or 29.07%
Tim Hortons Inc.	0.1663, or 16.63%

Rate of Return on Common Shareholders' Equity   A popular measure of profitability is the **rate of return on common shareholders' equity**, often shortened to **return on shareholders' equity**, or simply **return on equity (ROE)**. We examined this ratio in detail in Chapter 13, page 831.

This ratio shows the relationship between net income and common shareholders' investment in the company—how much income is earned for every dollar invested by the common shareholders. To compute this ratio, we first subtract preferred dividends from net income. The remainder is net income available to the common shareholders. Then divide net income available to common shareholders by the average common shareholders' equity during the year. The 2014 rate of return on common shareholders' equity for Sofawerks Furniture Inc. follows:

KEY POINTS

Return on shareholders' equity measures how much income is earned for every $1 invested by the *common* shareholders (both contributed capital and retained earnings).

	Formula	Rate of Return on Common Shareholders' Equity of Sofawerks Furniture Inc.		Retail Furniture Industry Average
Rate of return on common shareholders' equity	= $\dfrac{\text{Net income} - \text{Preferred dividends}}{\text{Average common shareholders' equity}}$	$\dfrac{\$48,000 - \$0}{(\$356,000 + \$320,000)/2}$ =	0.142, or 14.2%	0.121, or 12.1%

Average equity is the average of the beginning and ending balances [($356,000 + $320,000)/2 = $338,000]. Common shareholders' equity is equal to total equity minus preferred equity.

Observe that Sofawerks Furniture Inc.'s return on equity, 14.2 percent, is higher than its return on assets, 11.3 percent. This difference results from borrowing from the bank and paying interest at a rate of 8 percent, and investing the funds to earn a higher rate, such as the firm's 14.2 percent return on shareholders' equity. This practice is called **trading on the equity**, or using **leverage**. It is directly related to the debt ratio. The higher the debt ratio, the higher the financial leverage. Companies that finance operations with debt are said to *leverage* their positions.

Leverage usually increases profitability because a company can earn more with the borrowed money than the interest it pays for the borrowed money. Leverage could have a negative impact on profitability. If revenues drop, debt and interest expense must still be paid. Therefore, leverage can have positive and negative effects on profits, increasing profits during good times but increasing risk during bad times due to higher fixed interest payments. Compare Sofawerks Furniture Inc.'s rate of return on common shareholders' equity with rates of other companies:

Company	Rate of Return on Common Shareholders' Equity
Canadian Tire Corporation, Limited	0.1110, or 11.10%
Research in Motion Ltd.	0.1223, or 12.23%
Lululemon Athletica Inc.	0.3698, or 36.98%
Tim Hortons Inc.	0.3285, or 32.85%

Sofawerks Furniture Inc. is more profitable than some of these leading companies. A return on equity of 15 to 20 percent year after year is considered excellent in most industries.

Earnings per Common Share *Earnings per common share* or, simply, **earnings per share (EPS)** is perhaps the most widely quoted of all financial statistics. It was introduced in Chapter 14, page 876. While accounting standards for private enterprises (ASPE) do not require that corporations disclose EPS figures on the income statement or in a note to the financial statements, many corporations do provide this information because investors and financial analysts use it to assess a corporation's profitability. EPS is the amount of net income per *common* share. Earnings per share is computed by dividing net income available to common shareholders by the weighted average number of common shares outstanding during the year. Preferred dividends are subtracted from net income because the preferred shareholders have a prior claim to their dividends.

If the company has bonds or preferred shares that are convertible into common shares, the company must also disclose *fully diluted* earnings per share.

Sofawerks Furniture Inc. has no preferred shares outstanding and so has no preferred dividends. Computations of the firm's EPS for 2014 and 2013 follow (the company had 10,000 common shares outstanding throughout both years):

KEY POINTS

Preferred dividends *must* be deducted to give the net income earned by the common shareholders if they have been declared, or, if they have not been declared, if they are cumulative.

	Formula	Earnings per Share of Sofawerks Furniture Inc.	
		2014	**2013**
Earnings per common share (EPS)	=	Net income − Preferred dividends / Weighted average number of common shares outstanding	$\dfrac{\$48,000 - \$0}{10,000} = \$4.80$	$\dfrac{\$26,000 - \$0}{10,000} = \$2.60$

Sofawerks Furniture Inc.'s EPS increased 85 percent from 2013 to 2014. (This is calculated as the change from 2013 to 2014: ($4.80 − $2.60) ÷ $2.60 = 85%). Its shareholders should not expect such a large increase in EPS every year. Most companies strive to increase EPS by 10 to 15 percent annually, and strong companies do so. However, even the most successful companies have an occasional bad year.

Analyzing Shares as an Investment

Investors purchase shares to earn a return on their investment. This return consists of two parts: (1) gains (or losses) from selling the shares at a price that is different from the investors' purchase price, and (2) dividends, the periodic distributions to shareholders. The ratios we examine in this section help analysts evaluate investments in shares.

Price/Earnings Ratio   The **price/earnings (P/E) ratio** is the ratio of the market price of a common share to the company's earnings per share. The P/E ratio appears on websites giving stock information, such as that of the Toronto Stock Exchange. The P/E ratio plays an important part in evaluating decisions to buy, hold, and sell shares. It indicates the market price of $1.00 of earnings. If earnings are negative, the P/E ratio is not applicable.

The calculations for the P/E ratios of Sofawerks Furniture Inc. follow. The market price of its common shares was $50.00 at the end of 2014 and $35.00 at the end of 2013. These prices can be obtained from financial publications, a stockbroker, or elsewhere on the Internet.

	Formula	Price/Earnings Ratio of Sofawerks Furniture Inc.	
		2014	**2013**
Price/ earnings = ratio	Market price per common share / Earnings per share	$\dfrac{\$50.00}{\$4.80} = 10.4$	$\dfrac{\$35.00}{\$2.60} = 13.5$

Recall that earnings per share (EPS) is calculated as (Net income − Preferred dividends) ÷ Weighted average number of common shares outstanding.

Given Sofawerks Furniture Inc.'s 2014 P/E ratio of 10.4, we would say that the company's shares are "selling at 10.4 times earnings." The decline from the 2013 P/E ratio of 13.5 is a concern but not a cause for alarm because the market price of the shares is not under Sofawerks Furniture Inc.'s control. Net income is more controllable, and it increased during 2014. Like most other ratios, P/E ratios vary from industry to industry. They range from 14.43 for WestJet Airlines, to 57.72 for Lululemon Athletica Inc., to negative earnings for Kinross Gold Corp., with a result of −1.85.

The higher a share's P/E ratio, the higher its **downside risk**—the risk that the share's market price will fall. Some investors interpret a sharp increase in a share's P/E ratio as a signal to sell the shares.

REAL WORLD EXAMPLE

These ratios were retrieved May 19, 2011, from *The Globe and Mail* website at www.theglobeandmail. com/globe-investor. Check to see how these companies are doing now!

Dividend Yield   The **dividend yield** is the ratio of dividends per share to the share's market price. This ratio measures the percentage of a share's market value that is returned annually as dividends, an important concern of shareholders. *Preferred shareholders,* who invest primarily to receive dividends, pay special attention to this ratio.[2]

Sofawerks Furniture Inc. paid annual cash dividends of $1.20 per share in 2014 and $1.00 in 2013 and market prices of the company's common shares were $50.00 in 2014 and $35.00 in 2013. Calculation of the company's dividend yields on common shares is as follows:

	Formula	Dividend Yield on Common Shares of Sofawerks Furniture Inc.	
		2014	**2013**
Dividend yield on = common shares	Dividend per common share / Market price per common share	$\dfrac{\$1.20}{\$50.00} = \begin{array}{l}0.024 \\ \text{or } 2.4\%\end{array}$	$\dfrac{\$1.00}{\$35.00} = \begin{array}{l}0.029 \\ \text{or } 2.9\%\end{array}$

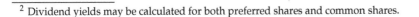

[2] Dividend yields may be calculated for both preferred shares and common shares.

Investors who buy Sofawerks Furniture Inc.'s common shares for $50.00 can expect to receive almost 2.5 percent of their investment annually in the form of cash dividends. Dividend yields vary widely, from more than 5.0 percent for older established firms (for example, BCE Inc. at 5.35 percent) down to 1.23 percent for a growth company like Gildan Activewear Inc. Sofawerks Furniture Inc.'s dividend yield places the company somewhere in the middle.

Book Value per Common Share   **Book value per common share** is simply common shareholders' equity divided by the number of common shares outstanding. Common shareholders' equity equals total shareholders' equity less preferred equity including cumulative preferred dividends. Sofawerks Furniture Inc. has no preferred shares outstanding. Recall that 10,000 common shares were outstanding throughout 2013 and 2014. Calculations of its book value per common share ratios are as follows:

	Formula	Book Value per Common Share of Sofawerks Furniture Inc.	
		2014	**2013**
Book value per common share	= $\dfrac{\text{Total shareholders' equity} - \text{Preferred equity}}{\text{Number of common shares outstanding}}$	$\dfrac{\$356,000 - \$0}{10,000} = \$35.60$	$\dfrac{\$320,000 - \$0}{10,000} = \$32.00$

Book value indicates the recorded accounting amount for each common share outstanding. Some experts argue that book value is not useful for investment analysis. Recall from Chapter 13, page 828, that book value depends on historical costs, while market value depends on investors' outlook for dividends and an increase in the share's market price. Book value bears no relationship to market value and provides little information beyond shareholders' equity reported on the balance sheet. However, some investors base their investment decisions on book value. For example, some investors rank shares on the basis of the ratio of market price to book value. To these investors, the lower the ratio, the lower the risk, and the more attractive the shares. These investors who focus on the balance sheet are called "value" investors, as contrasted with "growth" investors, who focus more on trends in a company's net income.

Limitations of Financial Analysis

Business decisions are made in a world of uncertainty. As useful as ratios may be, they do have limitations. When a physician reads a thermometer, 39°C indicates that something is wrong with the patient, but the temperature alone does not indicate what the problem is or how to cure it. The same is true of ratios.

In financial analysis, a sudden drop in a company's current ratio usually signals that *something* is wrong, but this change does not identify the problem or show how to correct it. The business manager and users of the financial statements must analyze he figures that go into the ratio to determine whether current assets have decreased, current liabilities have increased, or both. If current assets have dropped, is the problem a cash shortage? Are accounts receivable down? Are inventories too low? Is the condition temporary? This process can be shown in a figure:

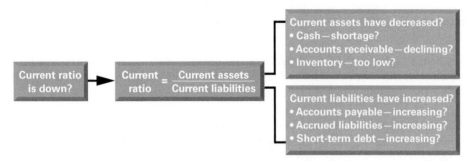

By analyzing the individual items that make up the ratio, managers can determine how to solve the problem and users of the financial statements can determine whether the company is a good investment or a credit risk. The managers and users of the financial statements must evaluate data on all ratios in the light of other information about the company and about its particular line of business, such as increased competition or seasonality or a slowdown in the economy.

Legislation, international affairs, competition, scandals, and many other factors can turn profits into losses, and vice versa. To be most useful, ratios should also be analyzed over a period of years to take into account a representative group of these factors. Any one year, or even any two years, may not be representative of the company's performance over the long term.

Efficient Markets, Nonfinancial Reports, and Investor Decisions

An **efficient capital market** is one in which the market prices reflect the impact of all information available to the public. Market efficiency means that managers cannot fool the market with accounting gimmicks. If the information is available, the market as a whole can translate accounting data into a "fair" price for the company's shares.

Suppose you are the president of CompSys Ltd. Reported earnings per share are $4.00 and the share price is $40.00—so the P/E ratio is 10. You believe the corporation's shares are underpriced in comparison with other companies in your industry. What if you are considering changing from accelerated to straight-line amortization to give the market a more accurate reflection of the company's value? The accounting change will increase earnings per share to $5.00. Will the shares then rise to $50.00? Probably not. The share price will likely remain at $40.00 because the market can understand that the change in amortization method, not improved operations, caused earnings to increase.

In an efficient market, the search for "underpriced" shares is fruitless unless the investor has relevant private information. Moreover, it is unlawful to invest based on *insider* information—information that is available only to corporate management.

Users of financial statements should be aware of potential problems in companies they might want to invest in or lend money to. Users of a company's financial statements should also consider the following additional information when evaluating the company.

Nonfinancial Reports

There is more to analyzing financial statements than performing horizontal and vertical analyses and computing the standard ratios. The nonquantitative parts of the annual report may hold more important information than the financial statements. For example, the president's letter may describe a turn-over of top managers. The management's discussion and analysis will reveal management's opinion of the year's results. And the auditor's report may indicate a major problem with the company. Let's consider each of these parts of a corporate annual report.

President's Letter to the Shareholders   The president of the company gives his or her view of the year's results and outlines the direction top management is charting for the company. In 2011, Winpak's President wrote:

> Records are meant to be broken! Each year, for the past four years, Winpak's net income has aggressively surpassed the prior year's standings. . . .
> There is a new buzz at the Company originating from the resolve to see Winpak's revenue escalate to one billion dollars by the year 2015. The Corporation's new battle cry is the "Billion Dollar Commitment" and its acronym "BDC" is entrenched in the spirit and work ethic of the entire Winpak team. This enthusiasm and dedication to the cause is backed by Winpak's Board of Directors having endorsed a capital program, which will provide plant expansions and state-of-the-art manufacturing equipment, allowing Winpak to remain at the forefront of technical breakthroughs.[3]

A shift in top management or a major change in the company's direction is important to investors.

Management's Discussion and Analysis (MD&A)   The people who know the most about a company are its executives. For this reason, the shareholders want to know what management thinks about the company's net income (or net loss), cash flows, and financial position. The MD&A section of the annual report discusses *why* net income was up or down, how the company invested the shareholders' money, and plans for future spending. Through the MD&A, investors may learn of the company's plan to discontinue a product line or to expand into new markets. These forward-looking data are not permitted in the historical financial statements, which are based on past transactions.

Auditor's Report   Both the president's letter and the MD&A express the views of corporate insiders. The financial statements are also produced by the management of the company. These people naturally want to describe the company in a favourable light. Therefore, all the information coming from the company could be slanted to make the company look good.

Investors are aware of the possibility for management bias in the financial statements. For this reason, the various provincial securities acts require that all financial statements of public corporations be audited by independent accountants. The auditors are not employees of the companies they audit, so they can be objective. After auditing the Winpak Ltd. financial statements, PricewaterhouseCoopers (PwC), an international accounting firm, issued its professional opinion on the Winpak statements. PwC stated that the Winpak statements present fairly the financial position, financial performance, and cash flows in accordance with International Financial Reporting Standards. This is how investors in Canada and other developed countries gain *assurance* that they can rely on a company's financial statements. If the survival of Winpak were in doubt, PwC would ensure that the notes to the financial statements would alert investors to the difficulty.

---

[3] Winpak Ltd.'s 2011 Annual Report, Report to Shareholders section, p. 1.

Management's Report to the Shareholders Appearing just before the Auditor's Report is the Management's Report to the Shareholders, in which management acknowledges its responsibility for the financial information presented in the financial statements. Management also highlights that an independent audit has been completed and directs shareholders to the Auditor's Report.

Look for Red Flags When Analyzing Financial Statements

Recent accounting scandals highlight the importance of *red flags* that may signal financial trouble. Watch out for the following conditions:

- **Changes in Sales, Inventory, and Receivables.** Sales, receivables, and inventory generally move together. Increased sales lead to higher receivables and require more inventory to meet demand. Unusual increases in receivables without an increase in sales may indicate trouble.
- **Earnings Problems.** Has net income decreased significantly for several years in a row? Has income turned into a loss? Most companies cannot survive consecutive annual losses.
- **Decreased Cash Flow.** Is cash flow from operations consistently lower than net income? Are the sales of property, plant, and equipment assets a major source of cash? If so, the company may face a cash shortage.
- **Too Much Debt.** How does the company's debt ratio compare with that of major competitors and with the industry average? If the debt ratio is too high, the company may be unable to pay its debts.
- **Inability to Collect Receivables.** Are days' sales in receivables growing faster than for other companies in the industry? A cash shortage may be looming.
- **Buildup of Inventories.** Is inventory turnover too slow? If so, the company may be unable to sell goods, or it may be overstating inventory. Recall from the cost-of-goods-sold lesson that one of the easiest ways to overstate net income is to overstate ending inventory.

WHY IT'S DONE THIS WAY

This final chapter of the book discusses the many ways that a user of the financial statements can analyze results. As we have shown in the chapters prior to this one, the accounting framework has allowed us to develop financial statements that are useful to interested users—this is the **Level 1** objective of the accounting framework.

For assessing the success of a company, however, the financial statements are a starting point. To evaluate appropriately the success of a company, we must perform a thorough analysis of the various aspects of the business. We also need to compare the performance of the company in the current year against the performance in previous years and against the performance of its competitors.

As we have seen throughout this book, the reporting framework has provided guidance to preparers of financial statements. From establishing guidelines for recording transactions in **Level 4**, to the characteristics we desire to see in our financial statements described in **Level 2**, the framework is a resource for preparers and standard setters. ASPE and IFRS provide the detailed guidance in financial statement preparation, but supporting the standards is the accounting framework. A solid understanding of the framework, combined with professional judgment acquired through experience in the accounting profession, allows accountants to provide financial information that is highly useful to investors and other users, achieving **Level 1** of the accounting framework.

✓ JUST CHECKING

5. For each of the following ratios, indicate whether it is a liquidity, efficiency, solvency, or profitability ratio by checking off the appropriate column:

Ratio	Liquidity	Efficiency	Solvency	Profitability
Return on common shareholders' equity				
Inventory turnover				
Current ratio				
Debt ratio				
Acid-test ratio				
Accounts-receivable turnover				
Return on net sales				

6. For each of the following unrelated situations, indicate if the change is positive for the company or negative.

Situation	Positive change	Negative change
A decrease in return on equity		
A decrease in days' sales in inventory		
An increase in the debt ratio		
An increase in the acid-test ratio		
A decrease in receivables turnover		

7. a) Suppose JMT Ltd. has a current ratio of 2.00 and an acid-test ratio of only 0.70. Which account explains the big difference between these two measures of ability to pay current liabilities? Explain.

   b) If JMT Ltd. has 42 days' sales in receivables, is this good or bad? Explain. Does your answer change if the terms are 60 days? Or 30 days?

8. Big Bend Picture Frames Inc. has asked you to determine whether the company's ability to pay its current liabilities and total liabilities has improved or deteriorated during 2014. To answer this question, you gather the following data:

	2014	2013
Cash	$ 50,000	$ 47,000
Short-term investments	27,000	—
Net receivables	128,000	124,000
Inventory	237,000	272,000
Total assets	480,000	490,000
Total current liabilities	295,000	202,000
Long-term note payable	44,000	56,000
Income from operations	170,000	168,000
Interest expense	46,000	33,000

Compute the following ratios for 2014 and 2013:
   a) Current ratio
   b) Acid-test ratio
   c) Debt ratio
   d) Times-interest-earned ratio

Just Checking Solutions appear at the end of this chapter and on MyAccountingLab.

The Impact on Financial Statement Analysis of International Financial Reporting Standards (IFRS)

Procedures

The tools and procedures for analyzing financial statements remain the same whether financial information is reported and presented under accounting standards for private enterprises (ASPE) or under IFRS. This is the case because financial analysis involves determining relationships between various components of the financial statements to determine the company's current financial position and to predict future performance. While the numbers in the financial statements under ASPE and IFRS may differ, the procedures for analyzing the relationships among the reported numbers remain unchanged. That being said, calculating the dividend yield may require an additional step if the business follows ASPE. As we saw earlier, earnings per share is not required to be shown on financial statements prepared under ASPE, so it would have to be calculated first before calculating dividend yield.

LO ⑤
What is the impact of IFRS on financial statement analysis?

Limitations

However, when conducting their investigation, financial analysts and investors must be aware of the limitations of financial statements and adjust for these as appropriate. For example, under ASPE, land and buildings *must* be carried at their historical cost. In their evaluation, analysts may substitute an approximate market value for land and buildings to make predictions. The values for these items in an IFRS balance sheet *may* already reflect the market values. Because valuation is a choice under IFRS, analysts must read the notes to the financial statements carefully because these assets could be recorded at their historic cost or at market value.

American Companies

Another issue facing investors who consider owning shares in American companies and managers who use American firms for benchmarks is that American companies use their own U.S. GAAP, which is only partially converged with IFRS at this time. It is important to know this so that comparisons are made cautiously. Knowing which rules are followed and which accounting choices were made (as indicated in the notes to the financial statements) will lead to better decisions.

Changing Standards

A bigger issue stems from companies changing their financial reporting from ASPE to IFRS. Ratios can change and impact financial covenants [promises or conditions]. For example, most loan agreements include a number of covenants, or conditions, in which the borrower agrees to do certain things and not to do other things, such as agreeing to maintain a minimum current ratio of 1.5:1. If these covenants were agreed upon based on the financial results of statements prepared under ASPE, the covenants might not be maintained if the financial statements are prepared under IFRS and some financial-statement amounts change. The reported income and the value of certain assets and liabilities will depend to some extent on the set of standards used—ASPE or IFRS. In this situation, lenders and borrowers should renegotiate covenants ahead of time to avoid unintentional defaults arising simply from the adoption of a different set of accounting standards.

✓ JUST CHECKING

9. Are there procedural differences when analyzing financial statements prepared under ASPE and financial statements prepared under IFRS? Why or why not?

Just Checking Solutions appear at the end of this chapter and on MyAccountingLab.

Summary Problem for Your Review

Bazinga Inc., which operates a chain of clothing stores, reported these figures:

BAZINGA INC. Five-Year Selected Financial Data For the Years Ended January 31, (Dollar amounts in thousands)					
	2014	2013	2012	2011	2010
Operating Results					
Net sales	$2,960	$2,519	$1,934	$1,587	$1,252
Cost of goods sold	1,856	1,496	1,188	1,007	814
Interest expense (net)	4	4	1	3	3
Income from operations	340	371	237	163	126
Income taxes	129	141	92	65	52
Net income	211	230	145	98	74
Cash dividends	44	41	30	23	18
Financial Position					
Merchandise inventory	366	314	247	243	193
Total assets	1,379	1,147	777	579	481
Working capital	355	236	579	129	434
Shareholders' equity	888	678	466	338	276
Current ratio	2.06:1	1.71:1	1.39:1	1.69:1	1.70:1
Average number of common shares outstanding (in thousands)	144	142	142	141	145

Required

Refer to page 1159 for the ratios mentioned in this chapter and their formulas.

Compute the following ratios for 2011 through 2014, and evaluate Bazinga Inc.'s operating results. Are operating results strong or weak? Did they improve or deteriorate during the four-year period?

1. Gross margin percentage
2. Rate of return on net sales
3. Earnings per share
4. Inventory turnover
5. Times-interest-earned ratio
6. Rate of return on shareholders' equity

SOLUTION

For 1. Remember to add the previous year's ending inventory balance and the current year's ending balance and divide by two when calculating average inventory in the inventory turnover ratio.

For 2. Add the previous year's shareholders' equity and current year's shareholder's equity and divide by two when calculating average shareholders' equity in the rate of return on shareholders' equity.

	2014	2013	2012	2011
1. Gross margin percentage	$\dfrac{\$2,960 - \$1,856}{\$2,960}$ $= 37.3\%$	$\dfrac{\$2,519 - \$1,496}{\$2,519}$ $= 40.6\%$	$\dfrac{\$1,934 - \$1,188}{\$1,934}$ $= 38.6\%$	$\dfrac{\$1,587 - \$1,007}{\$1,587}$ $= 36.5\%$
2. Rate of return on net sales	$\dfrac{\$211}{\$2,960} = 7.1\%$	$\dfrac{\$230}{\$2,519} = 9.1\%$	$\dfrac{\$145}{\$1,934} = 7.5\%$	$\dfrac{\$98}{\$1,587} = 6.2\%$
3. Earnings per share	$\dfrac{\$211}{144} = \$1.47$	$\dfrac{\$230}{142} = \$1.62$	$\dfrac{\$145}{142} = \$1.02$	$\dfrac{\$98}{141} = \$0.70$
4. Inventory turnover	$\dfrac{\$1,856}{(\$366 + \$314)/2}$ $= 5.5$ times	$\dfrac{\$1,496}{(\$314 + \$247)/2}$ $= 5.3$ times	$\dfrac{\$1,188}{(\$247 + \$243)/2}$ $= 4.8$ times	$\dfrac{\$1,007}{(\$243 + \$193)/2}$ $= 4.6$ times
5. Times-interest-earned ratio	$\dfrac{\$340}{\$4} = 85$ times	$\dfrac{\$371}{\$4} = 93$ times	$\dfrac{\$237}{\$1} = 237$ times	$\dfrac{\$163}{\$3} = 54$ times
6. Rate of return on shareholders' equity	$\dfrac{\$211}{(\$888 + \$678)/2}$ $= 26.9\%$	$\dfrac{\$230}{(\$678 + \$466)/2}$ $= 40.2\%$	$\dfrac{\$145}{(\$466 + \$338)/2}$ $= 36.1\%$	$\dfrac{\$98}{(\$338 + \$276)/2}$ $= 31.9\%$

Evaluation: During this four-year period, Bazinga Inc.'s operating results were outstanding. Operating results improved, with all ratio values higher in 2014 than in 2011 except return on shareholders' equity. Moreover, all the performance measures indicate high levels of income and return to investors.

For the six ratios calculated, think of the results as "the higher the ratio, the better." When these ratios increase each year, it is a positive trend and indicates good news.

Remember to evaluate all ratios along with other information about the company. One ratio will not tell the complete story.

Summary

(1) Learning Objective 1: Perform a horizontal analysis of financial statements

How do we compare several years of financial information?

- *Horizontal analysis* is the study of percentage changes in financial statement items from one period to the next.   Pg. 1130
  - (1) Calculate the dollar amount of the change from the base (earlier) period to the later period, and
  - (2) Divide the dollar amount of change by the base-period amount and multiply by 100.
- *Trend percentages* are a form of horizontal analysis.

(2) Learning Objective 2: Perform a vertical analysis of financial statements

What is a vertical analysis, and how do we perform one?	*Vertical analysis* shows the relationship of each statement item to a specified base, which is the 100 percent figure.	**Pg. 1134**

- On an income statement, net sales (or revenues) is usually the base.
- On a balance sheet, total assets is usually the base.

(3) Learning Objective 3: Prepare and use common-size financial statements

What are common-size financial statements, and how do we use them?	Common-size financial statements:	**Pg. 1136**

- Report only percentages, not dollar amounts
- Ease the comparison of different companies
- May signal the need for corrective action

Benchmarking is the practice of comparing a company's performance with that of other companies, usually in the same industry.

(4) Learning Objective 4: Compute the standard financial ratios.

How do we compute standard financial ratios, and what do they mean?	A ratio expresses the relationship of one item to another.	**Pg. 1139**

The most important financial ratios measure:

- **Liquidity:** a company's ability to pay current liabilities
  (current ratio, acid-test ratio)
- **Efficiency:** its ability to sell inventory and collect receivables
  (inventory turnover, accounts-receivable turnover, days' sales in receivables)
- **Solvency:** its ability to pay long-term debt
  (debt ratio, times-interest-earned ratio)
- **Profitability**
  (rate of return on net sales, rate of return on total assets, rate of return on common shareholders' equity, earnings per common share)
- **Value as an investment**
  (price/earnings ratio, dividend yield, book value per common share).

The formulas for these ratios are listed on the next page.

(5) Learning Objective 5: Describe the impact on financial statement analysis of international financial reporting standards (IFRS)

What is the impact of IFRS on financial statement analysis?	The procedures for analyzing the relationships among the reported numbers are the same.	**Pg. 1155**

Debt covenants and other contractual arrangements may be affected by the numbers reported under the different sets of standards. Therefore, covenants should be checked and renegotiated if necessary to avoid unintentional defaults.

Check Accounting Vocabulary on page 1161 for all key terms used in Chapter 18 and the Glossary on page 1246 for all key terms used in the textbook.

CHAPTER REVIEW:

MyAccountingLab   DemoDoc covering Financial Statement Analysis

MyAccountingLab   Student PowerPoint Slides

MyAccountingLab   Audio Chapter Summary

Note: All MyAccountingLab resources can be found in the Chapter Resources section and the Multimedia Library.

Ratios Used in Financial Statement Analysis

Name	Formula	Interpretation
Measuring the company's ability to pay current liabilities (liquidity):		
1. Current ratio	$\dfrac{\text{Current assets}}{\text{Current liabilities}}$	Measures ability to pay current liabilities with current assets.
2. Acid-test (quick) ratio	$\dfrac{\text{Cash} + \text{Short-term investments} + \text{Net current receivables}}{\text{Current liabilities}}$	Shows ability to pay all current liabilities if they come due immediately.
Measuring the company's ability to sell inventory and collect receivables (efficiency):		
3. Inventory turnover	$\dfrac{\text{Cost of goods sold}}{\text{Average inventory}}$	Indicates saleability of inventory— the number of times a company sells its average amount of inventory during a year.
4. Accounts-receivable turnover	$\dfrac{\text{Net credit sales}}{\text{Average net accounts receivable}}$	Measures ability to collect cash from credit customers.
5. Days' sales in receivables	① One day's sales = Net sales/365 days ② $\dfrac{\text{Average net accounts receivable}}{\text{One day's sales}}$	Shows how many days' sales remain in Accounts Receivable—how many days it takes to collect the average level of receivables.
Measuring the company's ability to pay long-term debt (solvency):		
6. Debt ratio	$\dfrac{\text{Total liabilities}}{\text{Total assets}}$	Indicates percentage of assets financed with debt.
7. Times-interest-earned ratio	$\dfrac{\text{Income from operations}}{\text{Interest expense}}$	Measures the number of times operating income can cover interest expense.
Measuring the company's profitability:		
8. Rate of return on net sales (profit margin)	$\dfrac{\text{Net income}}{\text{Net sales}}$	Shows the percentage of each sales dollar earned as net income.
9. Rate of return on total assets	$\dfrac{\text{Net income} + \text{Interest expense}}{\text{Average total assets}}$	Measures how profitably a company uses its assets.
10. Rate of return on common shareholders' equity	$\dfrac{\text{Net income} - \text{Preferred dividends}}{\text{Average common shareholders' equity}}$	Gauges how much income is earned for each dollar invested by common shareholders.
11. Earnings per common share	$\dfrac{\text{Net income} - \text{Preferred dividends}}{\text{Weighted average number of common shares outstanding}}$	Gives the amount of earnings earned for each of the company's common shares.
Analyzing the company's shares as an investment (value):		
12. Price/earnings ratio	$\dfrac{\text{Market price per common share}}{\text{Earnings per share}}$	Indicates the market price of $1 of earnings.
13. Dividend yield	$\dfrac{\text{Annual dividends per common (or preferred) share}}{\text{Market price per common (or preferred) share}}$	Shows the percentage of the market price of each share returned as dividends to shareholders each period.
14. Book value per common share	$\dfrac{\text{Total shareholders' equity} - \text{Preferred equity}}{\text{Number of common shares outstanding}}$	Indicates the recorded accounting amount for each common share outstanding.

SELF-STUDY QUESTIONS

Test your understanding of the chapter by marking the correct answer for each of the following questions:

1. Net income for PJ Ltd. was $240,000 in 2012, $210,000 in 2013, and $252,000 in 2014. The change from 2013 to 2014 is a(n) (*p. 1130*)
   a. Increase of 5 percent
   b. Increase of 20 percent
   c. Decrease of 10 percent
   d. Decrease of 12.5 percent

2. Vertical analysis of a financial statement shows (*p. 1134*)
   a. Trend percentages
   b. The percentage change in an item from period to period
   c. The relationship of an item to a base amount on the statement
   d. Net income expressed as a percentage of shareholders' equity

3. Common-size statements are useful for comparing (*p. 1136*)
   a. Changes in the makeup of assets from period to period
   b. Different companies
   c. A company to its industry
   d. All of the above

4. Benchmarking allows a user of the financial statements of a company to (*pp. 1137–1138*)
   a. Compare the performance of the company against that of its key competitors
   b. Compare the performance of the company against best practices
   c. Compare the performance of the company against average performance
   d. Do all of the above

5. The following figures were taken from the 2014 balance sheet of Plateau Golf Academy Ltd. Cash is $10,000, net accounts receivable amount to $22,000, inventory is $55,000, prepaid expenses total $3,000, and current liabilities are $40,000. What is the acid-test ratio? (*pp. 1141–1142*)
   a. 0.25   c. 2.18
   b. 0.80   d. 2.25

6. Inventory turnover is computed by dividing (*p. 1143*)
   a. Sales revenue by average inventory
   b. Cost of goods sold by average inventory
   c. Credit sales by average inventory
   d. Average inventory by cost of goods sold

7. Garnet Motors Ltd. is experiencing a severe cash shortage because of its inability to collect accounts receivable. The decision tool most likely to help identify the appropriate corrective action is the (*p. 1144*)
   a. Acid-test ratio
   b. Inventory turnover
   c. Times-interest-earned ratio
   d. Day's sales in receivables

8. Analysis of Sanjay Corp.'s financial statements over five years reveals that sales are growing steadily, the debt ratio is higher than the industry average and is increasing, interest coverage is decreasing, return on total assets is declining, and earnings per common share is decreasing. Considered together, these ratios suggest that (*pp. 1153–1154*)
   a. Sanjay Corp. should pursue collections of receivables more vigourously
   b. Competition is taking sales away from Sanjay Corp.
   c. Sanjay Corp. is in a declining industry
   d. The company's debt burden is hurting profitability

9. Which of the following is most likely to be true? (*pp. 1146–1147*)
   a. Return on common equity > return on total assets.
   b. Return on total assets > return on common equity.
   c. Return on total assets = return on common equity.
   d. None of the above is true.

10. How are financial ratios used in decision making? (*pp. 1139–1140*)
    a. They remove the uncertainty of the business environment.
    b. They give clear signals about the appropriate action to take.
    c. They can help identify the reasons for success and failure in business, but decision making requires information beyond the ratios.
    d. They are not useful because decision making is too complex.

Answers to Self-Study Questions

1. b $252,000 − $210,000 = $42,000;
   $42,000 ÷ $210,000 = 0.20, or 20%
2. c
3. d
4. d
5. b ($10,000 + $22,000) ÷ $40,000 = 0.80
6. b
7. d
8. d
9. a
10. c

1160 Part 4 Analysis of Accounting Information

ACCOUNTING VOCABULARY

Accounts-receivable turnover Ratio of net credit sales to average net accounts receivable. Measures ability to collect cash from credit customers *(p. 1143)*.

Acid-test ratio Ratio of the sum of cash plus short-term investments plus net current receivables to current liabilities. Tells whether the entity could pay all its current liabilities if they came due immediately. Also called the *quick ratio* *(p. 1142)*.

Benchmarking Comparison of current performance with some standard. The standard often is the performance level of a leading outside organization or industry average *(p. 1137)*.

Book value per common share Common shareholders' equity divided by the number of common shares outstanding *(p. 1150)*.

Common-size statement A financial statement that reports only percentages (no dollar amounts); a type of vertical analysis *(p. 1136)*.

Current ratio Current assets divided by current liabilities. Measures the ability to pay current liabilities from current assets *(p. 1140)*.

Days' sales in receivables Ratio of average net accounts receivable to one day's sales. Tells how many days' sales remain in Accounts Receivable awaiting collection *(p. 1144)*.

Debt ratio Ratio of total liabilities to total assets. Tells the proportion of a company's assets that it has financed with debt *(p. 1144)*.

Dividend yield Ratio of dividends per share to the share's market price per share. Tells the percentage of a share's market value that the company pays to shareholders as dividends *(p. 1149)*.

Downside risk An estimate of the potential loss from a change in market conditions *(p. 1149)*.

Earnings per share (EPS) Amount of a company's net income per outstanding common share *(p. 1148)*.

Efficient capital market One in which the market prices fully reflect the impact of all information available to the public *(p. 1151)*.

Equity ratio Ratio of total shareholders' equity to total assets. Tells the proportion of assets financed by the owners of the company *(p. 1145)*.

Factors Companies that purchase other firms' accounts receivable at a discount. Receivables are sold so that the cash can be received more quickly *(p. 1144)*.

Horizontal analysis The calculation and use of percentage changes in comparative financial statements *(p. 1130)*.

Inventory turnover Ratio of cost of goods sold to average inventory. Measures the number of times a company sells its average level of inventory during a year *(p. 1142)*.

Leverage Earning more income on borrowed money than the related expense, thereby increasing the earnings for the owners of the business. Another name for *trading on the equity* *(p. 1147)*.

Liquid assets Assets that can be converted to cash quickly. Often they are financial instruments that can be sold without a discount *(p. 1141)*.

Liquidity Ability to meet current payments as they come due *(p. 1139)*.

Long-term solvency The ability to generate enough cash to pay long-term debts as they mature *(p. 1129)*.

Price/earnings (P/E) ratio Ratio of the market price of a common share to the company's earnings per share. Measures the value that the stock market places on $1 of a company's earnings *(p. 1149)*.

Quick ratio Ratio of the sum of cash plus short-term investments plus net current receivables to current liabilities. Tells whether the entity could pay all its current liabilities if they came due immediately. Another name for the *acid-test ratio* *(p. 1142)*.

Rate of return on common shareholders' equity Net income minus preferred dividends, divided by average common shareholders' equity. A measure of profitability. Also called *return on common shareholders' equity* or *return on equity (ROE)* *(p. 1147)*.

Rate of return on net sales Ratio of net income to net sales. A measure of profitability. Also called *return on sales* *(p. 1146)*.

Rate of return on total assets The sum of net income plus interest expense divided by average total assets. This ratio measures the success a company has in using its assets to earn income for the persons who finance the business. Also called *return on assets* *(p. 1146)*.

Return on assets (ROA) Another name for *rate of return on total assets* *(p. 1146)*.

Return on equity (ROE) Another name for *rate of return on common shareholders' equity* *(p. 1147)*.

Return on sales (ROS) Another name for *rate of return on net sales* *(p. 1146)*.

Return on shareholders' equity Another name for *rate of return on common shareholders' equity* *(p. 1147)*.

Servicing its debt Phrase that means the repayment of principal and interest on loans or bonds *(p. 1146)*.

Short-term liquidity Ability to meet current payments as they come due *(p. 1129)*.

Times-interest-earned ratio Ratio of income from operations to interest expenses. Measures the number of times that operating income can cover interest expense. Also called the interest-coverage ratio   (p. 1145).

Trading on the equity   Earning more income on borrowed money than the related expense, thereby increasing the earnings for the owners of the business. Also called *leverage*   (p. 1147).

Vertical analysis   Analysis of a financial statement that reveals the relationship of each statement item to a total, which is 100 percent   (p. 1134).

Working capital   Current assets minus current liabilities; measures a business's ability to meet its short-term obligations with its current assets   (p. 1139).

SIMILAR ACCOUNTING TERMS

Acid-test ratio	Quick ratio
Current ratio	Working-capital ratio
Leverage	Trading on the equity
Earnings per share	Earnings per common share; EPS
Rate of return on common shareholders' equity	Return on common shareholders' equity; Return on equity; ROE
Rate of return on net sales	Return on sales; ROS; Profit margin
Rate of return on total assets	Return on assets; ROA
Solvency	Long-term solvency
Times-interest-earned ratio	Interest-coverage ratio

Assignment Material

QUESTIONS

1. Identify three groups of users of accounting information and the decisions they base on accounting data.

2. Name the three broad categories of analytical tools that are based on accounting information.

3. Briefly describe horizontal analysis. How do decision makers use this analytical tool?

4. What is vertical analysis and what is its purpose?

5. What is the purpose of common-size statements?

6. What is benchmarking? Give an example of its use.

7. Why are ratios an important tool of financial analysis? Give an example of an important financial ratio.

8. Identify two ratios used to measure a company's ability to pay current liabilities. Show how they are computed.

9. Why is the acid-test ratio given that name?

10. What does the inventory-turnover ratio measure?

11. Suppose the days'-sales-in-receivables ratio of Peanuts Inc. increased from 33 days at January 1 to 45 days at December 31. Is this a good sign or a bad sign about the company? What might Peanut Inc.'s management do in response to this change?

12. Janner Inc.'s debt ratio has increased from 0.40 to 0.75. Identify a decision maker to whom this increase is important, and state how the increase affects this party's decisions about the company.

13. Which ratio measures the effect of debt on (a) financial position (the balance sheet) and (b) the company's ability to pay interest expense (the income statement)?

14. Freshie Ltd. is a chain of grocery stores and Benjamin's Inc. is a furniture store. Which company is likely to have the higher (a) current ratio, (b) inventory turnover, (c) rate of return on sales? Give your reasons.

15. Identify four ratios used to measure a company's profitability. Show how to compute these ratios and state what information each ratio provides.

16. Recently, the price/earnings ratio of WestJet Airlines was 10.1, and the price/earnings ratio of the Bank of Nova Scotia was 11.4. Which company did the stock market favour? Explain.

17. Recently, TransCanada Corporation paid cash dividends of $0.42 per share when the market price of the company's shares was $41.00 per share. What was the dividend yield on TransCanada's shares? What does dividend yield measure?

18. Hold all other factors constant and indicate whether each of the following situations generally signals good or bad news about a company. Explain your answer.

    a. Increase in return on sales
    b. Decrease in earnings per share
    c. Increase in price/earnings ratio
    d. Increase in book value per share
    e. Increase in current ratio
    f. Decrease in inventory turnover
    g. Increase in debt ratio
    h. Decrease in interest-coverage ratio

19. Explain how an investor might use book value per share in making an investment decision.

20. Describe how decision makers use ratio data. What are the limitations of ratios?

MyAccountingLab Make the grade with MyAccountingLab: The Starters, Exercises, and Problems marked in red can be found on MyAccountingLab. You can practise them as often as you want, and most feature step-by-step guided instructions to help you find the right answer.

STARTERS

Starter 18–1   Match each of the following terms with its description. Place the letter for the description in the blank beside the term.

Match terms with definitions
①②④

Terms	Description
_____ 1. Horizontal analysis	a. Ability to meet current payments as they come due.
_____ 2. Quick ratio	b. Ratio of cost of goods sold to average inventory.
_____ 3. Vertical analysis	c. Ratio of total liabilities to total assets.
_____ 4. Debt ratio	d. Ratio of the sum of cash plus short-term investments plus net current receivables to current liabilities.
_____ 5. Inventory turnover	e. Analysis of a financial statement that reveals the relationship of each statement item to a total, which is 100 percent.
_____ 6. Liquidity	f. Earning more income on borrowed money than the related expense, thereby increasing the earnings for the owners of the business.
_____ 7. Leverage	g. The use of percentage changes in comparative financial statements.

Starter 18–2   Sun-Rype Products Ltd. reported the following on its 2011 comparative income statement:

Horizontal analysis of revenues and gross margin
①
2011 net sales increased 6.7%

	(in millions)		
	2011	**2010**	**2009**
Net sales	$147.5	$138.2	$147.7
Cost of sales	126.3	104.8	110.8

Perform a horizontal analysis of net sales, cost of sales, and gross margin, both in dollar amounts and in percentages, for 2011 and 2010.

Starter 18–3   Sun-Rype Products Ltd. reported the following net sales and net income amounts:

Trend analysis of revenues and net income
①
1. 2011 net sales 100%

	(in millions)		
	2011	**2010**	**2009**
Net sales	$147.5	$138.2	$147.7
Net income	(5.7)	4.8	6.8

1. Show Sun-Rype's trend percentages for net sales and net income. Use 2009 as the base year.
2. Did sales and income grow or decline in unison?

Starter 18–4 Sporting Apparel Inc. reported the following amounts on its balance sheet at December 31, 2014.

	2014
Cash and receivables	$24,000
Inventory	19,000
Property, plant, and equipment, net	48,000
Total assets	$91,000

Perform a vertical analysis of the company's assets at the end of 2014.

Common-size income
statements of two
companies
(2)

Net income as % of sales:
HomePro 6.2%

Starter 18–5 Compare HomePro Corp. and Away Inc. by converting their income statements to common size.

	(in thousands)	
	HomePro Corp.	**Away Inc.**
Net sales	$18,978	$39,072
Cost of goods sold	11,570	28,202
Other expenses	6,228	8,994
Net income	$ 1,180	$ 1,876

Which company earns more net income? Which company's net income is a higher percentage of its net sales?

Starter 18–6 For each of the following ratios, indicate with a check mark if a higher result is considered "good."

_____ Current ratio   _____ Debt ratio

_____ Inventory turnover   _____ Earnings per common share

_____ Return on total assets   _____ Return on net sales

_____ Book value per common share _____ Days' sales in receivables

Use the following data for Starters 18–7 through 18–11. **CoCo Roofers Inc., a roofing-supplies chain, reported these summarized figures (in millions):**

COCO ROOFERS INC.
Income Statement
For the Year Ended December 31, 2014

Net sales	$61.6
Cost of goods sold	42.4
Interest expense	0.6
All other expenses	15.0
Net income	$ 3.6

COCO ROOFERS INC.
Balance Sheet
December 31

	2014	2013		2014	2013
Cash	$ 2.8	$ 1.6	Total current liabilities	$ 8.8	$ 7.2
Short-term investments	0.4	0.5	Long-term liabilities	8.6	8.3
Accounts receivable	0.5	0.4	Total liabilities	17.4	15.5
Inventory	9.2	8.0	Common shares	5.2	4.8
Other current assets	0.8	0.6	Retained earnings	15.7	11.8
Total current assets	13.7	11.1	Total equity	20.9	16.6
All other assets	24.6	21.0	Total liabilities		
Total assets	$38.3	$32.1	and equity	$38.3	$32.1

Starter 18–7 Use the CoCo Roofers Inc. balance sheet data given on the previous page.

1. Compute the company's current ratio at December 31, 2014 and 2013.
2. Did CoCo Roofers Inc.'s current ratio value improve, deteriorate, or hold steady during 2014?

Evaluating a company's
current ratio

1. 2014 current ratio 1.56

Starter 18–8 Use the CoCo Roofers Inc. data to compute the following (amounts in millions):

a. The rate of inventory turnover for 2014.
b. Days' sales in average receivables during 2014. All sales are made on account. Round dollar amounts to three decimal places.

Computing inventory turnover
and days' sales in receivables

(4)

a. 4.9 times

Starter 18–9 Use the financial statements of CoCo Roofers Inc.

1. Compute the debt ratio at December 31, 2014.
2. Is CoCo Roofers Inc.'s ability to pay its liabilities strong or weak? Explain your reasoning.

Measuring ability to
pay liabilities

(4)

Debt ratio. 0.45

Starter 18–10 Use the financial statements of CoCo Roofers Inc.

1. Compute these profitability measures for 2014:
   a. Rate of return on net sales.
   b. Rate of return on total assets. Interest expense for 2014 was $0.6 million.
   c. Rate of return on common shareholders' equity.
2. Are these rates of return strong or weak? Explain.

Measuring profitability

(4)

a. ROS = 5.8%

Starter 18–11 Use the financial statements of CoCo Roofers Inc., plus the following item (in millions):

Number of common shares outstanding 0.8

1. Compute earnings per share (EPS) for CoCo Roofers Inc. Round to the nearest cent.
2. Compute CoCo Roofers Inc.'s price/earnings ratio. The price of a CoCo Roofers Inc. common share is $131.00.

Computing EPS and the price/
earnings ratio

(4)

1. $4.50

Starter 18–12 A summary of Pasmore Ltd.'s income statement appears as follows:

Using ratio data to reconstruct
an income statement

(4)

(D) Net income $342

Income Statement	
Net sales	$3,600
Cost of goods sold	(A)
Selling and administrative expenses	855
Interest expenses	(B)
Other expenses	75
Income before taxes	500
Income tax expenses	(C)
Net income	$ (D)

Use the following ratio data to complete Pasmore Ltd.'s income statement:

a. Inventory turnover was 5.50 (beginning inventory was $395, ending inventory was $375).
b. Rate of return on sales is 0.095, or 9.5 percent.

Using ratio data to reconstruct
a balance sheet
④

(C) Total current assets $735

Starter 18–13 A summary of Pasmore Ltd.'s balance sheet appears as follows:

Balance Sheet			
Cash	$ 25	Total current liabilities	$1,050
Receivables	(A)	Long-term note payable	(E)
Inventories	375	Other long-term liabilities	410
Prepaid expenses	(B)		
Total current assets	(C)		
Property, plant, and equipment, net	(D)		
Other assets	1,075	Shareholders' equity	1,200
Total assets	$3,400	Total liabilities and equity	$ (F)

Use the following ratio data to complete Pasmore Ltd.'s balance sheet:

a. Current ratio is 0.70.

b. Acid-test ratio is 0.30.

EXERCISES

MyAccountingLab

Exercise 18–1

Computing year-to-year changes
in working capital
①

2014 increase in working
capital 1.9%

Compute the dollar change and the percentage change in Navin Ltd.'s working capital each year during 2013 and 2014. Is this trend favourable or unfavourable?

	2014	2013	2012
Total current assets	$92,250	$87,000	$78,750
Total current liabilities	39,000	34,750	42,500

Exercise 18–2

Excel Spreadsheet
Template

Horizontal analysis of an
income statement
①

2014 net income increased
19.8%

Prepare a horizontal analysis of the comparative income statement of Keesha Shoes Inc. Round percentage changes to the nearest one-tenth percent (three decimal places).

Why was the percentage increase in net income higher than that in total revenue during 2014?

KEESHA SHOES INC.		
Income Statement		
For the Years Ended December 31, 2014 and 2013		
	2014	2013
Net sales	$533,000	$465,000
Expenses		
Cost of goods sold	235,000	202,000
Selling and general expenses	140,000	135,000
Interest expense	10,000	6,000
Wages expense	51,000	41,000
Total expenses	436,000	384,000
Net income	$ 97,000	$ 81,000

Exercise 18–3

Computing trend percentages
①

2014 net sales grew 24.6%

Compute trend percentages for Ceder Inc.'s net sales and net income for the following five-year period, using 2010 as the base year:

	2014	2013	2012	2011	2010
	(Amounts in thousands)				
Net sales	$1,625	$1,469	$1,375	$1,200	$1,304
Net income	149	131	100	82	105

Which measure grew more during the period, net sales or net income? By what percentage did net sales and net income grow from 2010 to 2014?

Exercise 18-4

Sumanishi Corp. has requested that you perform a vertical analysis of its balance sheet. Determine the component percentages of its assets, liabilities, and shareholders' equity.

Vertical analysis of a
balance sheet
②
Total current assets are 26.2%
of total assets

SUMANISHI CORP.
Balance Sheet
December 31, 2014

Assets	
Total current assets	$109,000
Property, plant, and equipment, net	267,000
Other assets	40,000
Total assets	$416,000
Liabilities	
Total current liabilities	$ 85,000
Long-term debt	156,000
Total liabilities	241,000
Shareholders' Equity	
Total shareholders' equity	175,000
Total liabilities and shareholders' equity	$416,000

Exercise 18-5

Prepare a comparative common-size income statement for Keesha Shoes Inc. using the 2014 and 2013 data of Exercise 18-2 and rounding percentages to one-tenth of a percent (three decimal places).

Excel Spreadsheet
Template

Preparing a common-size
income statement
③

2014 net income is 18.2% of
net sales.

Exercise 18-6

Prepare a common-size analysis to compare the asset composition of Bhagwan Inc. and Bigwig Ltd. (amounts in millions).

Common-size analysis of assets
③

Cash and equiv. as % of total
assets:
Bhagwan Inc. 4.1%
Bigwig Ltd. 2.4%

Assets	Bhagwan Inc.	Bigwig Ltd.
Current assets:		
Cash and equivalents	$ 462	$ 472
Short-term investments	—	804
Accounts receivable, net	2,898	882
Inventories	2,082	5,380
Other current assets	408	134
Total current assets	5,850	7,672
Property, plant, and equipment, net	4,960	11,280
Goodwill and other intangibles	206	226
Other assets	302	540
Total assets	$11,318	$19,718

To which company are *current assets* more important? Which company places more emphasis on its *property, plant, and equipment?*

Exercise 18-7

Compare the results of two years of ratios for Limited Inc.:

Interpreting ratio results
④

Ratio	2014	2013	Change + or −	Benchmark	Performance + or −
Current ratio	1.5	1.7		2:1	
Acid-test ratio	0.83	0.85		0.95	
Inventory turnover	8	7		10	
Accounts-receivable turnover	12	14		13	
Debt ratio	0.3	0.2		0.7	
Times-interest-earned ratio	7	6		4	
Rate of return on total assets	0.06	0.04		0.05	
Rate of return on common shareholders' equity	0.24	0.23		0.14	

Required

1. Identify whether the change from 2013 to 2014 was good (+) or bad (−).
2. Assess whether the performance in 2014 is good (+) or bad (−) compared to the industry average presented in the benchmark column.

Excel Spreadsheet
Template

Computing five ratios
④

a. 1.54

Exercise 18–8

The financial statements of Baca Bay Ltd. include the following items:

	2014	2013
Balance sheet		
Cash	$ 11,500	$ 14,500
Short-term investments	6,500	10,500
Net receivables	39,000	35,000
Inventory	45,500	38,500
Prepaid expenses	3,500	3,500
Total current assets	$106,000	$102,000
Total current liabilities	$ 69,000	$ 46,000
Income statement		
Net credit sales	$248,500	
Cost of goods sold	138,500	

Required

Compute the following ratios for 2014: (a) current ratio, (b) acid-test ratio, (c) inventory turnover, (d) accounts receivable turnover, and (e) days' sales in average receivables.

Exercise 18–9

Compute ratios and analyze
a company
④

a. 2014: 2.04
2013: 1.78

Grewers Automotive Products Ltd. has requested that you determine whether the company's ability to pay its current liabilities and long-term debt has improved or deteriorated during 2014. To answer this question, compute the following ratios for 2014 and 2013: (a) current ratio, (b) acid-test ratio, (c) debt ratio, and (d) times-interest-earned ratio. Summarize the results of your analysis in a paragraph explaining what the results of the calculations mean.

	2014	2013
Cash	$ 13,000	$ 25,500
Short-term investments	15,000	—
Net receivables	59,500	65,500
Inventory	125,000	135,000
Prepaid expenses	9,000	5,500
Total assets	275,000	260,000
Total current liabilities	108,500	130,000
Total liabilities	137,000	143,000
Income from operations	99,000	82,500
Interest expense	22,500	21,000

Exercise 18–10

Analyzing profitability
④

EPS: 2014 $0.34
2013 $0.71

Compute four ratios that measure the ability to earn profits for Gardener Farm Supplies Ltd., whose comparative income statement appears on the next page. Additional data follow.

GARDENER FARM SUPPLIES LTD.
Income Statement
For the Years Ended December 31, 2014 and 2013

	2014	2013
Net sales	$195,000	$174,000
Cost of goods sold	101,500	91,750
Gross margin	93,500	82,250
Selling and general expenses	50,200	40,000
Income from operations	43,300	42,250
Interest expense	25,400	12,050
Income before income tax	17,900	30,200
Income tax expense	4,475	7,550
Net income	$ 13,425	$ 22,650

Additional data	2014	2013
a. Average total assets	$230,000	$222,000
b. Average common shareholders' equity	102,000	98,000
c. Preferred dividends	5,000	5,000
d. Number of common shares outstanding	25,000	25,000

Did the company's operating performance improve or deteriorate during 2014?

Exercise 18–11

Evaluate the common shares of Payment Software Inc. as an investment. Specifically, use the three share ratios to determine whether the shares have increased or decreased in attractiveness during the past year.

Evaluating shares as an investment
④

	2014	2013
Net income	$ 33,000	$ 27,000
Dividends (25% to preferred shareholders)	19,000	13,000
Common shareholders' equity at year end (75,000 shares)	275,000	250,000
Preferred shareholders' equity at year end	50,000	50,000
Market price per common share at year end	$ 4.83	$ 3.89

Dividend yield:
2014 3.9%
2013 3.3%

Exercise 18–12

Homburg Invest Inc. is an international real estate investment and development company headquartered in Halifax, Nova Scotia. For the year ended December 31, 2008, Homburg prepared two sets of financial statements—one in accordance with Canadian GAAP in place at that time (similar to ASPE), the other in accordance with IFRS.

Excerpts from Homburg Invest Inc.'s Canadian ASPE-based financial statements and IFRS-based financial statements appear below and on the following pages.

Computing ratios under ASPE and IFRS
⑤

Current ratio:
1. (a) Under ASPE, 0.39
2. (a) Under IFRS, 0.62

ASPE-Based Financial Statements:

HOMBURG INVEST INC.
Consolidated Balance Sheet
($ amounts in thousands)

	December 31 2008	December 31 2007
Assets		
Investment properties	$3,310,317	$2,939,960
Development properties	360,562	293,955
Long term investments	40,086	39,562
Intangible assets	110,067	100,619
Goodwill		33,036
Restricted cash	25,969	27,704
Cash	16,359	17,927
Receivables and other	138,397	78,845
Currency guarantee receivable	28,165	
	$4,029,922	$3,531,608

(Continued)

(Continued)

HOMBURG INVEST INC.
Consolidated Balance Sheet
($ amounts in thousands)

	December 31, 2008	December 31, 2007
Liabilities		
Long term debt	$2,952,124	$2,094,122
Accounts payable and other liabilities	268,796	579,373
Construction financing	102,433	66,393
Future income taxes	129,097	110,578
Intangible liabilities	15,429	12,234
Liabilities of discontinued operations	28,903	28,903
Derivative instrument liability	19,427	
	3,516,209	2,891,603
Shareholders' equity	513,713	640,005
	$4,029,922	$3,531,608

HOMBURG INVEST INC.
Consolidated Statement of Earnings (Loss)
For the Year Ended December 31
($ amounts in thousands)

	2008	2007
Property revenue	$309,579	$207,331
Sale of properties developed for resale	191,260	229,139
Dividend income and distributions	2,992	2,011
Gain on fair value increase in investments		938
Other income	1,849	3,857
Foreign exchange gain		18,305
Gain on derivative instrument		2,303
Gain on sale of assests	443	2,051
	506,123	465,935
Property operating expenses	84,421	45,173
Cost of sale of properties developed for resale	142,841	147,677
Interest on long-term debt	154,899	106,818
Interest and financing costs	11,916	13,053
Depreciation and amortization	62,860	39,278
General and administrative	23,956	11,051
Stock-based compensation	307	5,288
Foreign exchange loss	19,656	
Loss on derivative instruments	18,542	
Goodwill impairment loss	63,456	
Loss on fair value decrease in investments	23,133	
	605,987	368,338
Earnings (loss) before income taxes	(99,864)	97,597
Total income taxes (recovery)	(3,781)	16,270
Net earnings (loss) from continuing operations	(96,083)	81,327
Net loss from discontinued operations		(2,159)
Net earnings (loss)	$ (96,083)	$ 79,168

IFRS-Based Financial Statements:

HOMBURG INVEST INC.
Consolidated Balance Sheet
($ amounts in thousands)

	December 31 2008	December 31 2007
Assets		
Non-current assets		
Investment properties	$3,549,744	$3,304,880
Development properties	224,285	126,522
Currency guarantee receivable	28,165	
Goodwill		48,594
Investments	40,086	39,562
Restricted cash	25,969	27,704
	3,868,249	3,547,262
Current assets		
Cash	16,359	17,927
Construction properties being developed for resale	194,638	225,596
Receivables and other	65,390	26,694
	276,387	270,217
Total assets	$4,144,636	$3,817,479
Equity and Liabilities		
Total equity	$ 606,768	$ 886,271
Non-current liabilities		
Long-term debt	2,901,348	1,910,668
Derivatives	19,427	
Deferred tax liabilities	143,930	145,559
Other liabilities	29,727	28,602
	3,094,432	2,084,829
Current liabilities		
Accounts payable and other	255,585	561,122
Income taxes payable	5,739	6,507
Liabilities of discontinued operations	28,903	28,903
Construction financing	102,433	66,393
Current portion of long-term debt	50,776	183,454
	443,436	846,379
Total liabilities	3,537,868	2,931,208
Total equity and liabilities	$ 4,144,636	$3,817,479

HOMBURG INVEST INC.
Consolidated Income Statement
For the Year Ended December 31
($ amounts in thousands)

	2008	2007
Property revenue	$ 310,466	$211,025
Sales of properties developed for resale	186,350	191,139
Total revenues	496,816	402,164
Property operating expenses	88,414	51,854
Cost of sale of properties developed for resale	143,131	131,677
	231,545	183,531
Gross income from operations	265,271	218,633
General and administrative	(23,956)	(11,051)
Stock-based compensation	(307)	(5,288)
Other income, net	1,849	3,857
Dividend income and distributions	2,992	2,011
Net adjustment to fair value of investment properties	(286,060)	55,757
Gain on sale of investment properties	443	924
Goodwill impairment loss	(48,594)	
Net adjustment to fair value of held-for-trading financial assets	(23,133)	938
Net adjustment to fair value of derivative financial instruments	(18,542)	2,303
Interest expense	(166,815)	(119,871)
Exchange differences, net	(19,656)	18,305
Income (loss) before income taxes	(316,508)	166,518
Total income taxes (recovery)	(39,855)	23,864
Net income (loss) from continuing operations	(276,653)	142,654
Net loss from discontinued operations		(2,159)
Net income (loss)	$ (276,653)	$140,495

Notice that the presentation of the financial statements differs somewhat, as well as some of the recorded balances. These differences arise because ASPE and IFRS rules measure certain transactions differently. However, the focus of this question is the impact on ratios of using a different set of accounting rules. Investors need to understand that if two companies in the same industry are being compared, their results could be very different depending upon whether IFRS or ASPE is used in the preparation of the financial information.

Required

1. Compute the following ratios for 2008 based on Homburg's financial statements prepared in accordance with ASPE. For the purpose of this exercise, assume that "cash" and "receivables and other assets" are current assets, and that "accounts payable and other liabilities," "construction financing," and "liabilities of discontinued operations" are current liabilities. Include both "interest on long-term debt" and "interest and financing costs" in your computations for part d.

   a. Current ratio

   b. Acid-test ratio

   c. Debt ratio

   d. Rate of return on total assets

2. Compute the same ratios as in question 1 for 2008 based on Homburg's IFRS financial statements.

Exercise 18–13

Suppose, at December 31, 2014, Kerr Consulting Corporation has the following balance sheet.

Computing six ratios

④

(a) 2.67

KERR CONSULTING CORPORATION
Balance Sheet
December 31, 2014

Assets

Current assets:	
Cash	$ 5,000
Accounts receivable	2,200
Supplies	420
Total current assets	7,620
Equipment	10,000
Furniture	3,600
Building	55,000
Less accumulated amortization	(2,753)
Land	20,000
Total assets	$93,467

Liabilities and Shareholders' Equity

Current liabilities:	
Accounts payable	$ 350
Salary payable	2,500
Total current liabilities	2,850
Long-term liabilities:	
Notes payable	40,000
Shareholders' equity:	
Common shares	20,000
Retained earnings	30,617
Total liabilities and shareholders' equity	$93,467

Additional information: Kerr Consulting Corporation incurred interest expense of $2,400 during 2014. Net income for the year ended December 31, 2014, was $38,910. The market price of Kerr Consulting Corporation's 1,500 common shares is $50.00 per share on December 31, 2014.

Required

Using this information, calculate the following ratios for Kerr Consulting Corporation:

a. Current ratio

b. Debt ratio

c. Earnings per share

d. Price/earnings ratio

e. Rate of return on total assets

f. Rate of return on common shareholders' equity

CHALLENGE EXERCISE

Exercise 18–14

Using ratio data to reconstruct
a company's balance sheet
② ③ ④
Current Liabilities $13,999

The following data (dollar amounts in thousands) are from the financial statements of Joachim's Equipment Manufacturing Ltd.

Total liabilities	$29,204
Preferred shares	0
Total current assets	$24,498
Accumulated amortization	$ 7,854
Debt ratio	55.312%
Current ratio	1.75:1

Required

Complete the following condensed balance sheet. Report amounts to the nearest thousand dollars:

Current assets		$?
Property, plant, and equipment	$?	
Less accumulated amortization	?	?
Total assets		$?
Current liabilities		$?
Long-term liabilities		?
Shareholders' equity		?
Total liabilities and shareholders' equity		$?

BEYOND THE NUMBERS

Beyond the Numbers 18–1

Understanding the components
of accounting ratios
④

Consider the following unrelated business situations.

1. Teresa Chan has asked you about the shares of a particular company. She finds them attractive because they have a high dividend yield relative to another company's shares that she is also considering. Explain to her the meaning of the ratio and the danger of making a decision based on it alone. Suggest other information (ratios) Teresa should consider as she makes the investment decision.

2. Saskatoon Plumbing Supplies Ltd.'s owners are concerned because the number of days' sales in receivables has increased over the previous two years. Explain why the ratio might have increased.

Beyond the Numbers 18–2

Taking unethical action to
improve accounting ratios
④

Moe Sahota is the controller of Forochar Ltd., whose year end is December 31. Sahota prepares cheques for suppliers in December and posts them to the appropriate accounts in that month. However, he holds on to the cheques and mails them to the suppliers in January. What financial ratio(s) are most affected by the action? What is Sahota's purpose in undertaking the activity?

ETHICAL ISSUE

Harrison Outfitters Inc.'s (HOI) long-term debt agreements make certain demands on the business. For example, HOI may not repurchase company shares in excess of the balance of Retained Earnings. Long-term debt may not exceed shareholders' equity, and the current ratio may not fall below 1.60. If HOI fails to meet these requirements, the company's lenders have the authority to take over management of the corporation.

Changes in consumer demand have made it hard for HOI to sell its products. Current liabilities have increased faster than current assets, causing the current ratio to fall to 1.45. Prior to releasing financial statements, HOI management is scrambling to improve the current ratio. The controller points out that an equity investment can be classified as either long term or short term, depending on management's intention. By deciding to convert an investment to cash within one year, HOI can classify the investment as short term (a current asset). On the controller's recommendation, HOI's board of directors votes to reclassify the long-term equity investments as short-term equity investments.

Required

1. What effect will reclassifying the investment have on the current ratio? Is Harrison Outfitters Inc.'s financial position stronger as a result of reclassifying the investment?

2. Shortly after releasing the financial statements, sales improve and so, then, does the current ratio. As a result, HOI management decides not to sell the investments it had reclassified as short term. Accordingly, the company reclassifies the investments as long term. Has management behaved unethically? Give your reason.

PROBLEMS (GROUP A)   MyAccountingLab

Problem 18–1A

Net sales, net income, and common shareholders' equity for Naturah Products Ltd. for a six-year period follow:

Trend percentages, return on common equity, and comparison with the industry

2. Return on common shareholders' equity 2014, 16.0%

	2014	2013	2012	2011	2010	2009
			(Amounts in thousands)			
Net sales	$1,806	$1,757	$1,606	$1,704	$1,638	$1,588
Net income	144	120	89	126	100	96
Ending common shareholders' equity	940	860	772	684	628	600

Required

1. Compute trend percentages for 2010 through 2014, using 2009 as the base year.

2. Compute the rate of return on average common shareholders' equity for 2010 through 2014, rounding to three decimal places. In this industry, rates of 12 percent are average, rates above 15 percent are considered good, and rates above 20 percent are viewed as outstanding.

3. How does Naturah Products Ltd.'s return on common shareholders' equity compare with the industry's?

Common-size statements,
analysis of profitability, and
comparison with the industry
② ③ ④

2014 current assets are 64.1%
of total assets

Problem 18–2A

Fixxit Ltd. has asked for your help in comparing the company's profit performance and financial position with the computer services industry average. The manager has given you the company's income statement and balance sheet, and also the following industry average data for computer services companies:

FIXXIT LTD. Income Statement For the Year Ended December 31, 2014		
	Fixxit Ltd.	Industry Average
Net sales	$425,625	100.0%
Cost of goods sold	250,375	53.2
Gross margin	175,250	46.8
Operating expenses	87,300	21.3
Operating income	87,950	25.5
Other expenses	20,500	5.2
Net income	$ 67,450	20.3%

FIXXIT LTD. Balance Sheet December 31, 2014		
	Fixxit Ltd.	Industry Average
Current assets	$162,750	62.5%
Property and equip., net	85,250	35.2
Other assets	6,000	2.3
Total assets	$254,000	100.0%
Current liabilities	$112,500	42.5%
Long-term liabilities	62,500	32.5
Shareholders' equity	79,000	25.0
Total liabilities and shareholders' equity	$254,000	100.0%

Required

1. Prepare a two-column common-size income statement and a two-column common-size balance sheet for Fixxit Ltd. The first column of each statement should present Fixxit Ltd.'s common-size statement, and the second column should show the industry averages.

2. For the profitability analysis, compute Fixxit Ltd.'s (a) ratio of gross margin to net sales, (b) ratio of operating income to net sales, and (c) ratio of net income to net sales. Compare these figures to the industry averages. Is Fixxit Ltd.'s profit performance better or worse than the industry average?

3. For the analysis of financial position, compute Fixxit Ltd.'s (a) ratio of current assets to total assets, and (b) ratio of shareholders' equity to total assets. Compare these ratios to the industry averages. Is Fixxit Ltd.'s financial position better or worse than the industry averages?

Problem 18–3A

Financial statement data of MKR Bakery Supplies Ltd. include the following items:

Cash	$ 68,000
Accounts receivable, net	97,500
Inventories	129,000
Prepaid expenses	6,000
Total assets	625,000
Short-term notes payable	39,000
Accounts payable	109,500
Accrued liabilities	27,000
Long-term liabilities	204,000
Net income	103,000
Number of common shares outstanding	40,000 shares

Required

1. Compute MKR Bakery Supplies Ltd.'s current ratio, debt ratio, and earnings per share.

2. Compute each of the three ratios after evaluating the effect of each transaction that follows. Consider each transaction *separately*.

   a. Purchased merchandise of $43,000 on account, debiting Inventory.
   b. Paid long-term liabilities, $40,000.
   c. Declared, but did not pay, a $60,000 cash dividend on common shares.
   d. Borrowed $50,000 on a long-term note payable.
   e. Issued 10,000 common shares at the beginning of the year, receiving cash of $140,000.
   f. Received cash on account, $29,000.
   g. Paid short-term notes payable, $25,000.

Set up a table in the following format for your answers:

Transaction	Current Ratio	Debt Ratio	Earnings per Share

Problem 18–4A

Comparative financial statement data of Main Street Antiques Ltd. appear below:

Using ratios to evaluate a share investment

(4)

1. a. 2014, 2.45
      2013, 2.07

MAIN STREET ANTIQUES LTD.
Income Statement
For the Years Ended December 31, 2014 and 2013

	2014	2013
Net sales	$311,850	$297,000
Cost of goods sold	148,850	147,000
Gross margin	163,000	150,000
Operating expenses	79,250	77,000
Income from operations	83,750	73,000
Interest expense	12,500	14,000
Income before income tax	71,250	59,000
Income tax expense	17,850	14,600
Net income	$ 53,400	$ 44,400

MAIN STREET ANTIQUES LTD.
Balance Sheet
December 31, 2014 and 2013
(selected 2012 amounts given for computation of ratios)

	2014	2013	2012
Current assets:			
Cash	$ 27,500	$ 25,000	
Current receivables, net	67,500	62,500	$ 52,500
Inventories	127,500	117,500	95,000
Prepaid expenses	5,000	4,000	
Total current assets	227,500	209,000	
Property, plant, and equipment, net	100,500	98,000	
Total assets	$328,000	$307,000	295,500
Total current liabilities	$ 93,000	$100,725	
Long-term liabilities	117,500	127,500	
Total liabilities	210,500	228,225	
Preferred shares, $1.25	5,000	5,000	
Common shares	50,000	37,500	17,500
Retained earnings	62,500	36,275	25,000
Total liabilities and shareholders' equity	$328,000	$307,000	

Other information:

- Market price of Main Street Antiques Ltd. common shares: $24.00 at December 31, 2014, and $12.00 at December 31, 2012.

- Common shares outstanding: 10,000 during 2014 and 7,500 during 2013. There are 1,000 preferred shares outstanding at December 31, 2014 and 2013.

- All sales are on credit.

Required

1. Compute the following ratios for 2014 and 2013:

   a. Current ratio
   b. Inventory turnover
   c. Accounts-receivable turnover
   d. Times-interest-earned ratio
   e. Return on assets

   f. Return on common shareholders' equity
   g. Earnings per common share
   h. Price/earnings ratio
   i. Book value per common share at year end

2. Decide (a) whether Main Street Antiques Ltd.'s financial position improved or deteriorated during 2014, and (b) whether the investment attractiveness of its common shares appears to have increased or decreased.

3. How will what you have learned in this problem help you evaluate an investment?

Problem 18–5A

Using ratio data to complete a set of financial statements ④

Net income $4,954,000

Incomplete and adapted versions of the comparative financial statements of Canadarch Ltd. follow (amounts in thousands).

CANADARCH LTD. Income Statement For the Year Ended May 31, 2014	
Net sales	$30,718
Cost of goods sold	(a)
Gross margin	(b)
Selling and general expenses	9,654
Other expense (income)	1,130
Income before income tax	(c)
Income tax expense (25%)	(d)
Net income	$ (e)

CANADARCH LTD. Balance Sheet May 31, 2014 and 2013		
Assets	2014	2013
Current:		
Cash	$ (f)	$ 300
Short-term investments	1,852	1,630
Receivables, net	4,224	3,726
Inventories	1,300	1,046
Prepaid expenses	(g)	168
Total current assets	(h)	6,870
Property, plant, and equipment, net	22,354	19,248
Total assets	$ (i)	$26,118

(Continued)

1178 Part 4 Analysis of Accounting Information

(Continued)

CANADARCH LTD.
Balance Sheet
May 31, 2014 and 2013

	2014	2013
Liabilities		
Current liabilities	$ 9,270	$ 7,434
Long-term liabilities	(j)	15,964
Total liabilities	(k)	23,398
Shareholders' Equity		
Common shareholders' equity	(l)	2,720
Total liabilities and shareholders' equity	$ (m)	$26,118

CANADARCH LTD.
Cash Flow Statement
For the Year Ended May 31, 2014

Net cash inflow from operating activities	$4,324
Net cash outflow from investing activities	(2,464)
Net cash outflow from financing activities	(1,130)
Net increase (decrease) in cash during 2014	$ (n)

Ratio data:

- Current ratio at May 31, 2014, is 0.9276, or 92.76 percent.
- Inventory turnover for the year ended May 31, 2014, is 11.362.
- Debt ratio at May 31, 2014, is 0.7521, or 75.21 percent.

Required

Complete the financial statements. Start with the income statement, then go to the cash flow statement. Complete the balance sheet last.

Problem 18–6A

Assume you are purchasing an investment and have decided to invest in a company in the home renovation business. Suppose you have narrowed the choice to BildRite Ltd. and Highbuild Homes Ltd. You have assembled the following selected data:

Selected income statement data for current year

	BildRite Ltd.	Highbuild Homes Ltd.
Net sales (all on credit)	$323,050	$231,875
Cost of goods sold	187,700	154,250
Income from operations	89,500	48,750
Interest expense	15,000	2,500
Net income	70,000	36,550

Excel Spreadsheet Template

Using ratios to decide between two share investments
④

a. BildRite 1.86, Highbuild 2.56

Selected balance sheet and market price data at end of current year

	BildRite Ltd.	Highbuild Homes Ltd.
Current assets:		
Cash	$ 17,250	$ 18,500
Short-term investments	11,500	9,750
Current receivables, net	32,300	26,100
Inventories	60,950	55,775
Prepaid expenses	2,000	1,250
Total current assets	$124,000	$111,375
Total assets	$225,000	$169,000
Total current liabilities	66,750	43,500
Total liabilities	97,500	68,500
Preferred shares: $3.00 (250 shares)	12,500	
Common shares (4,000 shares)		15,000
Common shares (7,000 shares)	17,500	
Total shareholders' equity	127,500	100,500
Market price per common share	$ 10.00	$ 10.00

Selected balance sheet data at beginning of current year

	BildRite Ltd.	Highbuild Homes Ltd.
Current receivables, net	$ 30,250	$ 16,000
Inventories	52,500	52,500
Total assets	240,000	192,500
Preferred shareholders' equity, $3.00 (250 shares)	12,500	—
Common shares (4,000 shares)		15,000
Common shares (7,000 shares)	17,500	
Total shareholders' equity	90,000	87,500

Your investment strategy is to purchase the shares of companies that have low price/earnings ratios but appear to be in good shape financially. Assume you have analyzed all other factors, and your decision depends on the results of the ratio analysis to be performed.

Required

Compute the following ratios for both companies for the current year and decide which company's shares better fits your investment strategy:

a. Current ratio

b. Acid-test ratio

c. Inventory turnover

d. Day's sales in average receivables

e. Debt ratio

f. Times-interest-earned ratio

g. Return on net sales

h. Return on total assets

i. Return on common shareholders' equity

j. Earnings per common share

k. Book value per common share

l. Price/earnings ratio

Problem 18–7A

Natural Microwave Products Ltd.'s financial statements for the year ended December 31, 2014, are shown below.

Preparing a horizontal and vertical analysis of a financial statement, computing the standard financial ratios used for decision making, using ratios in decision making
① ② ④
3. a. 8.64

NATURAL MICROWAVE PRODUCTS LTD.
Income Statement
For the Year Ended December 31, 2014

Net sales	$945,000
Cost of goods sold	610,000
Gross margin	335,000
Operating expenses:	
Selling expenses	128,200
Administrative expenses	78,000
Interest expense	22,000
Total operating expenses	228,200
Operating income	106,800
Income taxes (25%)	26,700
Net income	$ 80,100

NATURAL MICROWAVE PRODUCTS LTD.
Statement of Retained Earnings
For the Year Ended December 31, 2014

Retained earnings, January 1, 2014		$162,000
Add net income for 2014		80,100
		242,100
Less dividends: Preferred	$25,000	
Common	9,000	34,000
Retained earnings, December 31, 2014		$208,100

NATURAL MICROWAVE PRODUCTS LTD.
Balance Sheet
December 31, 2014 and 2013

	2014	2013
Assets		
Cash	$ 92,000	$ 45,000
Accounts receivable	84,000	92,000
Merchandise inventory	102,000	118,000
Prepaid expenses	8,000	6,000
Property, plant, and equipment	498,000	474,000
Less accumulated amortization	(106,000)	(70,000)
Goodwill	40,000	40,000
Total assets	$718,000	$705,000
Liabilities		
Accounts payable	$ 30,100	$ 43,000
Notes payable (due in 30 days)	3,000	10,000
Mortgage payable	68,800	130,000
Total liabilities	101,900	183,000

(Continued)

(Continued)

NATURAL MICROWAVE PRODUCTS LTD.
Balance Sheet
December 31, 2014 and 2013

	2014	2013
Shareholders' equity		
Preferred shares (1,200 shares, $10.00		
callable at $210.00 per share)	$240,000	$240,000
Common shares		
(2014—12,000 shares; 2013—6,000 shares)	168,000	120,000
Retained earnings	208,100	162,000
Total shareholders' equity	616,100	522,000
Total liabilities and shareholders' equity	$718,000	$705,000

Required

1. Perform a horizontal analysis of the comparative balance sheets. Comment on the analysis.

2. Perform a vertical analysis of the income statement. The industry standards are gross margin of 35 percent and net income of 12 percent. Comment on the results

3. Calculate each of the following ratios for the year ended December 31, 2014. The industry standards are provided in parentheses for some of the ratios.

   a. Current ratio (3:1)
   b. Acid-test ratio
   c. Inventory turnover
   d. Days' sales in receivables
   e. Debt ratio (0.50)
   f. Times-interest-earned ratio
   g. Rate of return on net sales

   h. Rate of return on total assets
   i. Rate of return on common shareholders' equity
   j. Price/earnings ratio—the market price per share is $30.00 at year end, when dividends were paid (5.0)
   k. Dividend yield (5%)

4. Comment on your calculations for Natural Microwave Products Ltd. in Requirement 3. Include comments for those ratios for which industry standards were provided.

PROBLEMS (GROUP B)   MyAccountingLab

Problem 18–1B

Trend percentages, return on sales, and comparison with the industry
① ④

Net sales, net income, and total assets for River Holdings Ltd. for a six-year period follow.

	2014	2013	2012	2011	2010	2009
			(Amounts in thousands)			
Net sales	$804	$912	$662	$714	$616	$604
Net income	112	92	65	82	68	58
Total assets	654	610	522	470	462	410

Required

1. Compute trend percentages for 2010 through 2014. Use 2009 as the base year.

2. Compute the return on net sales for 2010 through 2014, rounding to three decimal places. In this industry, rates above 8 percent are considered good, and rates above 10 percent are viewed as outstanding.

3. How does River Holdings Ltd.'s return on net sales compare to the industry's?

Problem 18–2B

Top managers of Russian Steel Fabricators Inc., a specialty steel fabricating company, have asked for your help in comparing the company's profit performance and financial position with the average for the steel fabricating industry. The accountant has given you the company's income statement and balance sheet, and also the average data for the steel fabricating industry (amounts in millions).

Common-size statements, analysis of profitability, and comparison with the industry
② ③ ④

RUSSIAN STEEL FABRICATORS INC. Income Statement For the Year Ended December 31, 2014		
	Russian Steel Fabricators Inc.	Industry Average
Net sales	$29.2	100.0%
Cost of goods sold	17.6	65.9
Gross margin	11.6	34.1
Operating expenses	8.4	28.1
Operating income	3.2	6.0
Other expenses	0.2	0.4
Net income	$ 3.0	5.6%

RUSSIAN STEEL FABRICATORS INC. Balance Sheet December 31, 2014		
	Russian Steel Fabricators Inc.	Industry Average
Current assets	$10.4	66.6%
Property, plant, equip., net	8.0	32.3
Other assets	0.2	1.1
Total assets	$18.6	100.0%
Current liabilities	$ 6.2	35.6%
Long-term liabilities	5.2	19.0
Shareholders' equity	7.2	45.4
Total liabilities and shareholders' equity	$18.6	100.0%

Required

1. Prepare a two-column common-size income statement and a two-column common-size balance sheet for Russian Steel Fabricators Inc. The first column of each statement should present Russian Steel Fabricators Inc.'s common-size statement, and the second column should show the industry averages.

2. For the profitability analysis, compare Russian Steel Fabricators Inc.'s (a) ratio of gross margin to net sales, (b) ratio of operating income (loss) to net sales, and (c) ratio of net income (loss) to net sales. Compare these figures with the industry averages. Is Russian Steel Fabricators Inc.'s profit performance better or worse than the average for the industry?

3. For the analysis of financial position, compare Russian Steel Fabricators Inc.'s (a) ratio of current assets to total assets and (b) ratio of shareholders' equity to total assets. Compare these ratios with the industry averages. Is Russian Steel Fabricators Inc.'s financial position better or worse than the average for the industry?

Problem 18–3B

Financial statement data of Xi Supplies Inc. as at December 31, 2014, include the following items:

Effects of business transactions on selected ratios

Cash	$ 53,000
Accounts receivable, net	127,000
Inventories	251,000
Prepaid expenses	10,000
Total assets	922,000
Short-term notes payable	80,000
Accounts payable	91,000
Accrued liabilities	64,000
Long-term liabilities	248,000
Net income	147,000
Number of common shares outstanding	44,000 shares

Required

1. Compute Xi Supplies Inc.'s current ratio, debt ratio, and earnings per share. Round all ratios to two decimal places.

2. Compute each of the three ratios after evaluating the effect of each transaction that follows. Consider each transaction *separately*.

a. Borrowed $100,000 on a long-term note payable.

b. Issued 12,000 common shares on January 2, 2015, receiving cash of $180,000.

c. Received cash on account, $29,000.

d. Paid short-term notes payable, $50,000.

e. Purchased merchandise costing $62,000 on account, debiting Inventory.

f. Paid long-term liabilities, $15,000.

g. Declared, but did not pay, a $40,000 cash dividend on the common shares.

Set up a table in the following format for your answers:

Transaction	Current Ratio	Debt Ratio	Earnings per Share

Problem 18–4B

Using ratios to evaluate a share investment
④

Comparative financial statement data of Avenger Hardware Ltd. are as follows:

AVENGER HARDWARE LTD.
Income Statement
For the Years Ended December 31, 2014 and 2013

	2014	2013
Net sales	$351,500	$310,000
Cost of goods sold	201,000	155,000
Gross margin	150,500	155,000
Operating expenses	65,000	71,000
Income from operations	85,500	84,000
Interest expense	26,000	20,000
Income before income tax	59,500	64,000
Income tax expense	19,000	22,500
Net income	$ 40,500	$ 41,500

AVENGER HARDWARE LTD.
Balance Sheet
December 31, 2014 and 2013
(Selected 2012 amounts given for computation of ratios)

	2014	2013	2012
Current assets:			
Cash	$ 21,000	$ 25,000	
Current receivables, net	116,000	80,500	$ 62,500
Inventories	149,000	137,000	86,000
Prepaid expenses	6,000	9,000	
Total current assets	292,000	251,500	
Property, plant, and equipment, net	154,500	143,500	
Total assets	$446,500	$395,000	351,500
Total current liabilities	$141,000	$138,500	
Long-term liabilities	114,500	121,000	
Total liabilities	255,500	259,500	
Preferred shares, $1.50	30,000	30,000	
Common shares	75,000	60,000	60,000
Retained earnings	86,000	45,500	19,000
Total liabilities and shareholders' equity	$446,500	$395,000	

Other information:

- Market price of Avenger Hardware Ltd. common shares: $19.00 at December 31, 2014, and $31.00 at December 31, 2013.
- Weighted-average number of common shares outstanding: 15,000 during 2014 and 12,000 during 2013.
- There are 2,000 preferred shares outstanding.
- All sales are on credit.

Required

1. Compute the following ratios for 2014 and 2013:

   a. Current ratio
   b. Inventory turnover
   c. Accounts-receivable turnover
   d. Times-interest-earned ratio
   e. Return on assets

   f. Return on common shareholders' equity
   g. Earnings per common share
   h. Price/earnings ratio
   i. Book value per common share at year end

2. Decide (a) whether Avenger Hardware Ltd.'s ability to pay its debts and to sell inventory improved or deteriorated during 2014 and (b) whether the investment attractiveness of its common shares appears to have increased or decreased.

3. How will what you have learned in this problem help you evaluate an investment?

Problem 18–5B

Incomplete and adapted versions of the financial statements of Horseshoe Landscaping Ltd. follow (amounts in thousands).

Using ratio data to complete a set of financial statements

④

Ratio data:

- Current ratio at December 31, 2014, is 0.7547.
- Inventory turnover for 2014 was 5.284.
- Debt ratio at December 31, 2014, is 0.5906.

HORSESHOE LANDSCAPING LTD.
Balance Sheet
December 31, 2014 and 2013

	2014	2013
Assets		
Current:		
Cash	$ (f)	$ 2,528
Short-term investments	1,702	1,702
Receivables, net	3,600	2,984
Inventories	2,428	2,196
Prepaid expenses	(g)	204
Total current assets	(h)	9,614
Property, plant, and equipment, net	19,632	17,336
Total assets	$ (i)	$26,950
Liabilities		
Current liabilities	$14,204	$11,684
Long-term liabilities	(j)	4,416
Total liabilities	(k)	16,100
Shareholders' Equity		
Common shareholders' equity	(l)	10,850
Total liabilities and shareholders' equity	$ (m)	$26,950

HORSESHOE LANDSCAPING LTD.
Income Statement
For the Year Ended December 31, 2014

Net sales	$32,548
Cost of goods sold	(a)
Gross margin	(b)
Selling and general expenses	13,624
Other expense (income)	480
Income before income tax	(c)
Income tax expense (35%)	(d)
Net income	$ (e)

HORSESHOE LANDSCAPING LTD.
Cash Flow Statement
For the Year Ended December 31, 2014

Net cash inflow from operating activities	$ 6,640
Net cash outflow from investing activities	(2,420)
Net cash outflow from financing activities	(4,094)
Net increase (decrease) in cash during 2014	$ (n)

Required

Complete the financial statements. Start with the income statement. Then go to the cash flow statement. Complete the balance sheet last.

Excel Spreadsheet
Template

Using ratios to decide between
two share investments
(4)

Problem 18–6B

Assume that you are purchasing shares in a company in the variety store and gas bar supply business. Suppose you have narrowed the choice to BFI Trading Ltd. and Lin Corp. and have assembled the following data:

Selected income statement data for the year ended December 31, 2014

	BFI Trading Ltd.	Lin Corp.
Net sales (all on credit)	$1,060,000	$1,246,000
Cost of goods sold	602,000	722,000
Income from operations	186,000	202,000
Interest expense	40,000	10,000
Net income	82,000	124,000

Selected balance sheet and market price data for the year ended December 31, 2014

	BFI Trading Ltd.	Lin Corp.
Current assets:		
Cash	$ 134,000	$ 110,000
Short-term investments	0	24,000
Current receivables, net	312,000	392,000
Inventories	424,000	448,000
Prepaid expenses	24,000	28,000
Total current assets	$ 894,000	$1,002,000
Total assets	$ 2,070,000	$2,344,000
Total current liabilities	748,000	800,000
Total liabilities	1,444,000	1,508,000
Preferred shares, $10.00 (300 shares)	60,000	
Common shares (75,000 shares)		450,000
Common shares (10,000 shares)	100,000	
Total shareholders' equity	626,000	836,000
Market price per common share	$ 84.00	$ 55.00

Selected balance sheet data at January 1, 2014

	BFI Trading Ltd.	Lin Corp.
Current receivables, net	$ 330,000	$ 280,000
Inventories	448,000	470,000
Total assets	1,970,000	1,720,000
Preferred shareholders' equity, $10.00 (300 shares)	60,000	
Common shares (75,000 shares)		450,000
Common shares (10,000 shares)	100,000	
Total shareholders' equity	560,000	720,000

Your investment strategy is to purchase the shares of companies that have low price/earnings ratios but appear to be in good shape financially. Assume you have analyzed all other factors, and your decision depends on the results of the ratio analysis to be performed.

Required

Compute the following ratios for both companies for the current year and decide which company's shares better fit your investment strategy:

a. Current ratio

b. Acid-test ratio

c. Inventory turnover

d. Days' sales in average receivables

e. Debt ratio

f. Times-interest-earned ratio

g. Return on net sales

h. Return on total assets

i. Return on common shareholders' equity

j. Earnings per common share

k. Book value per common share

l. Price/earnings ratio

Problem 18–7B

Jens Hardware Inc.'s financial statements for the year ended December 31, 2014, are shown below.

Preparing a horizontal and vertical analysis of a financial statement, computing the standard financial ratios used for decision making, using ratios in decision making

① ② ④

JENS HARDWARE INC.	
Income Statement	
For the Year Ended December 31, 2014	
Net sales	$330,000
Cost of goods sold	190,000
Gross margin	140,000
Operating expenses:	
Selling expenses	40,000
Administrative expenses	23,000
Interest expense	6,000
Total operating expenses	69,000
Operating income	71,000
Income taxes (30%)	21,300
Net income	$ 49,700

JENS HARDWARE INC.
Statement of Retained Earnings
For the Year Ended December 31, 2014

Retained earnings, January 1, 2014		$48,100
Add net income for 2014		49,700
		97,800
Less dividends: Preferred	$16,000	
Common	23,150	39,150
Retained earnings, December 31, 2014		$58,650

JENS HARDWARE INC.
Balance Sheet
December 31, 2014 and 2013

	2014	2013
Assets		
Cash	$ 21,600	$ 15,600
Accounts receivable	33,050	21,000
Merchandise inventory	38,000	42,000
Prepaid expenses	1,000	1,500
Property, plant, and equipment	170,000	157,000
Less accumulated amortization	(34,000)	(24,000)
Goodwill	15,000	15,000
Total assets	$244,650	$228,100
Liabilities		
Accounts payable	$ 15,000	$ 18,500
Notes payable (due in 30 days)	2,000	3,500
Mortgage payable	40,000	45,000
Total liabilities	57,000	67,000
Shareholders' equity		
Preferred shares (8,000 shares; $2.00, callable at $15.00 per share)	48,000	48,000
Common shares (2014—12,000 shares; 2013—8,000 shares)	81,000	65,000
Retained earnings	58,650	48,100
Total shareholders' equity	187,650	161,100
Total liabilities and shareholders' equity	$244,650	$228,100

Required

1. Perform a horizontal analysis of the comparative balance sheets. Comment on the analysis.
2. Perform a vertical analysis of the comparative balance sheets. The industry standards are a gross margin of 45 percent and net income of 15 percent. Comment on the analysis.

3. Calculate each of the following ratios for the year ended December 31, 2014. The industry standards are provided in parentheses for some of the ratios.

   a. Current ratio (2:1)

   b. Acid-test ratio

   c. Inventory turnover

   d. Days' sales in receivables

   e. Debt ratio (0.47)

   f. Times-interest-earned ratio

   g. Rate of return on net sales

   h. Rate of return on total assets

   i. Rate of return on common shareholders' equity

   j. Price/earnings ratio—the market price per share is $9.00 at year end, when dividends were paid (14.0)

   k. Dividend yield (4%)

4. Comment on your calculations for Jens Hardware Inc. Include comments for those ratios for which industry standards were provided.

CHALLENGE PROBLEMS

Problem 18–1C

Recently newspapers carried stories about a company that fired three top executives for management fraud. The three had been using improper accounting practices to overstate profits. The improper practices included improperly recording assets on the company's balance sheet, overstating sales, and understating cost of goods sold by inflating inventory numbers. When inventory got out of line, the executives would debit property, plant, and equipment and credit inventory to further hide their fraud.

Using horizontal analysis to assess whether a company is using improper accounting practices

The company had been growing at a very rapid pace, outdistancing its competitors. However, there were warning signals or "red flags" that revealed that all was not well with the company and that suggested that the books might have been "cooked" in order to report the rapid growth. For example, sales, which were almost all on credit, grew much faster than did accounts receivable when these balances on the company's financial statements were compared with industry data. Inventory turnover was lower than that of competitors while sales were unusually low relative to property, plant, and equipment. A final "red flag" was that management bonuses were tied to sales increases.

Required

1. Which items would be misstated in a horizontal analysis of the company's income statement? Which items would be misstated in a horizontal analysis of the company's balance sheet? Indicate the direction of the misstatement.

2. Why do you think the issue of management bonuses is considered a "red flag"?

Problem 18–2C

You are a senior staff member of a public accounting firm, and you have been asked by one of the firm's partners to discuss the impact of improper accounting practices on the financial statements of a company to new junior staff accountants. Using the information given in Problem 18–1C, use the following questions to frame your comments to the new juniors.

Understanding the impact of improper accounting practices on the financial statements of a company

Required

1. Sales grew faster than receivables. Would this situation create an unusually high or unusually low accounts receivable turnover?

2. Why was the fact that sales grew faster than receivables relative to other companies in the industry a "red flag"?

3. Explain why inventory turnover was too low.

4. Why was the fact that inventory turnover was low relative to other companies a "red flag"?

5. Compare the company's receivables turnover with inventory turnover. Does the comparison suggest a "red flag"? If so, what is it?

Extending Your Knowledge

DECISION PROBLEM

Identifying action to cut losses
and establish profitability
② ④

Suppose you manage WinterWorld Inc., a ski and snowboard store, which lost money during the past year. Before you can set the business on a successful course, you must first analyze the company and industry data for the current year in an effort to learn what is wrong. The data appear below.

Required

On the basis of your analysis of these figures, suggest three courses of action WinterWorld Inc. should take to reduce its losses and establish profitable operations. Give your reasons for each suggestion.

WinterWorld Inc. Income Statement Data

	WinterWorld Inc.	Industry Average
Net sales	100.0%	100.0%
Cost of sales	(61.2)	(55.4)
Gross margin	38.8	44.6
Operating expense	(40.2)	(38.6)
Operating income (loss)	(1.4)	6.0
Interest expense	(3.1)	(1.2)
Other revenue	0.8	0.4
Income (loss) before income tax	(3.7)	5.2
Income tax (expense) saving	1.3	(1.8)
Net income (loss)	(2.4)%	3.4%

WinterWorld Inc. Balance Sheet Data

	WinterWorld Inc.	Industry Average
Cash and short-term investments	0.2%	8.0%
Accounts receivable	20.0	15.5
Inventory	67.1	57.5
Prepaid expenses	0.5	0.6
Total current assets	87.8	81.6
Property, plant, and equipment, net	10.2	14.4
Other assets	2.0	4.0
Total assets	100.0%	100.0%
Bank loan, 6%	18.0%	14.0%
Notes payable, short-term, 8%	6.0	0.0
Accounts payable	18.2	22.3
Accrued liabilities	6.9	8.4
Total current liabilities	49.1	44.7
Long-term debt, 8%	16.0	14.0
Total liabilities	65.1	58.7
Common shareholders' equity	34.9	41.3
Total liabilities and shareholders' equity	100.0%	100.0%

FINANCIAL STATEMENT CASE

Sun-Rype Products Ltd's website gives a Five-Year Historical Review, with data for the fiscal years ended December 31, 2007, to December 31, 2011. Portions of the Five-Year Historical Review are reproduced below.

Measuring profitability and analyzing shares as an investment
(4)

SUN-RYPE PRODUCTS LTD.

Five-Year Historical Review

For the Years Ended December 31

(dollar amounts in thousands except per-share amounts)

Operating Results	2011	2010	2009[1]	2008[1]	2007[1]
Net Sales	$147,529	$138,185	$147,696	$125,368	$135,134
Earnings (loss) before interest, income taxes and depreciation ("EBITDA")	(2,683)	10,326	14,874	(12,780)	11,108
Net earnings (loss)	(5,687)	4,503	6,767	(11,673)	4,636
Financial Position at December 31					
Net Working Capital	28,084	23,522	20,803	20,709	15,548
Total Assets	96,139	82,318	60,986	73,622	56,884
Interest-bearing debt	25,562	7,701	5,145	27,696	500
Shareholders' equity	46,379	52,119	35,745	28,978	41,023
Per Share Information					
Average number of common shares outstanding (000's)	10,808	10,818	10,828	10,828	10,828
EBITDA	$ (0.25)	$ 0.95	$ 1.37	$ (1.18)	$ 1.03
Net earnings (loss)	(0.53)	0.42	0.62	(1.08)	0.43
Cash flow from operating activities	(0.53)	0.94	2.09	(2.48)	1.32
Book value	4.29	4.82	3.30	2.68	3.79
Share price—high	8.75	10.25	9.79	11.70	14.00
Share price—low	5.51	8.05	5.79	4.94	11.03
Share price—close	6.23	8.45	8.71	5.79	11.50

[1] The Company adopted International Financial Reporting Standards ("IFRS") with a transition date of January 1, 2010. Amounts for prior years have not been restated to reflect IFRS and as such certain amounts may not be comparable. An explanation of how the transition to IFRS has affected the financial position, financial performance and cash flows of the Company is included in the notes to the consolidated financial statements for the year ended December 31, 2011.

Prospective investors should note that this information has been extracted from Sun-Rype's audited consolidated financial statements and may not give a complete profile of Sun-Rype. This information includes non-IFRS financial measures that do not have a standardized meaning prescribed by IFRS and therefore may not be comparable to similar measures presented by other companies. It should be read in conjunction with Management's Discussion and Analysis, as well as the audited consolidated financial statements and the accompanying notes for the years, which are available for viewing on the Canadian Securities Administrators' website (www.sedar.com) and on Sun-Rype's website (www.sunrype.com).

Required

1. Using the Five-Year Historical Review, perform a four-year trend analysis of
   a. Net sales
   b. Net earnings (loss)
   c. EBITDA per common share

   Start with 2008 and end with 2011; use 2007 as the base year.

2. Evaluate Sun-Rype Products Ltd.'s profitability trend during this four-year period.

IFRS MINI-CASE

Blue Jay Metals Inc. is a small Canadian manufacturer of parts used in the construction of machinery. For the year ended December 31, 2014, Blue Jay Metals prepared two sets of financial statements—one in accordance with ASPE for its Canadian business associates, the other in accordance with IFRS, which it requires for doing business overseas. It is considering adopting IFRS as a one-time change so that it no longer has to prepare two sets of statements. Excerpts from Blue Jay Metals Inc.'s financial statements appear below.

ASPE-Based Financial Statements:

Blue Jay Metals Inc.
Consolidated Balance Sheet
December 31, 2014 and 2013

($ amounts in thousands)	December 31, 2014	December 31, 2013
Assets		
Cash	$ 40,000	$ 30,000
Securities	85,000	85,000
Accounts receivable, net	100,000	95,000
Inventory	375,000	370,000
Total current assets	600,000	580,000
Plant and equipment, net	600,000	520,000
Total assets	$1,200,000	$1,100,000
Liabilities		
Accounts payable	$ 100,000	$ 110,000
Bank loans	125,000	135,000
Accrued expenses	25,000	25,000
Total current liabilities	250,000	250,000
Bonds payable	500,000	450,000
Total liabilities	750,000	700,000
Shareholders' equity		
Shareholders' equity	450,000	400,000
Total liabilities and shareholders' equity	$1,200,000	$1,100,000

Key information from the 2014 Consolidated Statement of Earnings:
Net income = $91,000
Interest expense = $94,000

IFRS-Based Financial Statements:

Blue Jay Metals Inc.		
Consolidated Statement of Financial Position		
December 31, 2014 and 2013		
($ amounts in thousands)	December 31, 2014	December 31, 2013
Assets		
Non-current assets		
Investments	$ 70,000	$ 85,000
Plant and equipment, net	850,000	750,000
Total non-current assets	920,000	835,000
Current assets		
Cash	40,000	30,000
Marketable securities	5,000	3,000
Receivables, net	100,000	95,000
Inventory	375,000	370,000
Total current liabilities	520,000	498,000
Total assets	$1,440,000	$1,333,000
Equity and Liabilities		
Total equity	$ 680,000	$ 505,000
Non-current liabilities		
Bonds payable	500,000	550,000
Current liabilities		
Accounts payable and other	100,000	110,000
Bank loans	125,000	135,000
Accrued expenses	35,000	33,000
Total current liabilities	260,000	278,000
Total liabilities	760,000	828,000
Total equity and liabilities	$1,440,000	$1,333,000

Key information from the 2014 Consolidated Statement of Comprehensive Income:
Net Income = $31,000
Interest expense = $94,000

Notice that the presentation of the financial statements differs somewhat, as well as some of the recorded balances. These differences arise because ASPE and IFRS rules measure certain transactions differently. However, the focus of this question is the impact on ratios of using a different set of accounting rules. Investors need to understand that if two companies in the same industry are being compared, their results could be very different depending upon whether IFRS or ASPE is used in the preparation of the financial information.

Required

1. Compute the following ratios for 2014 based on Blue Jay Metals' financial statements prepared in accordance with ASPE.

    a. Current ratio   b. Acid-test ratio   c. Debt ratio   d. Rate of return on total assets

2. Compute the same ratios as in Requirement 1 for 2014 based on Blue Jay Metals' IFRS financial statements.

3. What effect did the different standards have on the results? Should Blue Jay Metals switch to IFRS?

Comprehensive Problem for Part Four

ANALYZING A COMPANY FOR ITS INVESTMENT POTENTIAL

In its 2011 annual report, Gildan Activewear Inc. included a five-year summary of its operating and financial record highlights.

Analyze the company's Financial Highlights for the fiscal years 2007 to 2011 to decide whether to invest in the common shares of Gildan Activewear Inc. Include the following sections in your analysis and fully explain your final decision:

- Trend analysis (use 2007 as the base year). Analyses for net sales, net earnings (loss), total assets, and shareholders' equity are suggested.
- Profitability analysis. Returns on sales, return on assets, return on equity, and diluted earnings per share would be key.

(in US$ millions, except per share data and ratios)	2011	2010	2009	2008	2007
INCOME STATEMENT					
Net sales	**1,726.0**	1,311.5	1,038.3	1,249.7	964.4
EBITDA[1]	**312.5**	278.4	160.6	249.8	194.0
Net earnings	**239.9**	198.2	95.3	146.4	129.1
Diluted earnings per share[2]	**1.96**	1.63	0.79	1.20	1.06
Adjusted net earnings[1]	**245.5**	203.6	99.7	151.3	156.4
Adjusted diluted earnings per share[1][2]	**2.01**	1.67	0.82	1.24	1.29
CASH FLOW					
Operating cash flow[3]	**310.8**	270.6	159.5	191.2	167.7
Change in non-cash working capital balances	**(129.2)**	30.9	9.7	47.7	(79.1)
Capital expenditures	**(164.7)**	(127.9)	(44.9)	(97.0)	(134.3)
Free cash flow[1]	**7.3**	175.9	132.2	148.4	(43.5)
FINANCIAL POSITION					
Total assets	**1,889.7**	1,327.5	1,074.5	1,085.7	867.7
Long-term debt (including current portion)	**209.0**	—	4.4	53.0	59.7
Net indebtedness (Cash in excess of total indebtedness)[1]	**120.2**	(258.4)	(95.3)	40.6	50.4
Shareholders' equity	**1,327.3**	1,114.4	910.8	811.5	661.1
FINANCIAL RATIOS					
EBITDA margin	**18.1%**	21.2%	15.5%	20.0%	20.1%
Net debt to EBITDA	**0.4x**	n.a.	n.a.	0.2x	0.3x
Net earnings margin[4]	**14.2%**	15.5%	9.6%	12.1%	16.2%
Return on shareholders' equity[5]	**20.0%**	20.2%	11.3%	19.8%	22.0%

(1) EBITDA, Adjusted net earnings, Adjusted diluted earnings per share, Free cash flow and Net indebtedness/(Cash in excess of total indebtedness) are non-GAAP measures. See "Definition and Reconciliation of Non-GAAP Measures" on page 45 of the 2011 Management's Discussion and Analysis.
(2) All per share data reflect the effect of the stock split in May 2007.
(3) Cash flows from operating activities before net changes in non-cash working capital balances.
(4) Adjusted net earnings divided by net sales.
(5) Adjusted net earnings divided by average shareholders' equity for the period.
   n.a. Not applicable.
   Certain minor rounding variances exist between the financial statements and this summary.

1. Horizontal analysis compares 2014 with 2013 to determine the changes in each income statement item in dollar amounts and percent ($ and %).

   $ change = 2014 $ amount − 2013 $ amount
   % change = $ change ÷ 2013 $ amount
   Large or unusual changes in $ or % should be investigated.

UMOJA INC.
Horizontal Analysis of Comparative Income Statement
For the Years Ended December 31, 2014 and 2013

			Increase (Decrease)	
	2014	2013	Amount	Percent
Net sales	$275,000	$225,000	$50,000	22.2%
Expenses: Cost of goods sold	$194,000	$165,000	$29,000	17.6
Engineering, selling, and administrative expenses	54,000	48,000	6,000	12.5
Interest expense	5,000	5,000	—	—
Income tax expense	9,000	3,000	6,000	200.0
Other expense (income)	1,000	(1,000)	2,000	—*
Total expenses	263,000	220,000	43,000	19.5
Net income	$ 12,000	$ 5,000	$ 7,000	140.0%

*Percentage changes are typically not computed for shifts from a negative amount to a positive amount, and vice versa.

The net earnings increase of 140% occurred because the dollar amounts are quite small. Income tax expense increased 200%, which should be investigated.

The horizontal analysis shows that net sales increased 22.2 percent. This percentage increase was greater than the 19.5 percent increase in total expenses, resulting in a 140 percent increase in net income. This indicates 2014 was a good year.

2. a)

	(in thousands)			
	2014	2013	2012	2011
Revenues (net sales)	138%	113%	105%	100%
Net income	400%	167%	200%	100%

b) Net income increased faster than revenues (net sales).

3. Vertical analysis expresses net income and expenses as a percentage of net sales.

   % of net sales = Each expense $ (and net income $) ÷ Net sales $

   The percentages for 2014 are compared with those of 2013. Any large or unexpected differences should be reviewed.

UMOJA INC.
Vertical Analysis of Comparative Income Statement
For the Years Ended December 31, 2014 and 2013

	2014		2013	
	Amount	Percent	Amount	Percent
Net sales	$275,000	100.0%	$225,000	100.0%
Expenses: Cost of goods sold	$194,000	70.5	$165,000	73.3
Engineering, selling, and administrative expenses	54,000	19.6	48,000	21.3
Interest expense	5,000	1.8	5,000	2.2
Income tax expense	9,000	3.3	3,000	1.4*
Other expense (income)	1,000	0.4	(1,000)	(0.4)
Total expenses	263,000	95.6	220,000	97.8
Net income	$ 12,000	4.4%	$ 5,000	2.2%

*Number rounded up.

The vertical analysis shows decreases in the percentages of net sales consumed by

- cost of goods sold (from 73.3 percent in 2013 to 70.5 percent in 2014)
- engineering, selling, and administrative expenses (from 21.3 percent in 2013 to 19.6 percent in 2014).

These two items are Umoja Inc.'s largest dollar expenses, so their percentage decreases are important positive changes.

The 2014 net income rose to 4.4 percent of sales, compared with 2.2 percent the preceding year. The analysis shows that 2014 was significantly better than 2013.

4.

Common-Size Income Statement of Umoja Inc. and Compet Ltd.
For the Year Ended December 31, 2014

	UMOJA INC.	COMPET LTD.
Net sales	100.0%	100.0%
Expenses: Cost of goods sold	70.5	68.1
Engineering, selling, and administrative expenses	19.6	17.2
Interest expense	1.8	5.2
Income tax expense	3.3	4.0
Other expense (income)	0.4	0.3
Total expenses	95.6	94.8
Net income	4.4%	5.2%

Umoja Inc.'s results are similar to those of Compet Ltd., although they are, in general, not quite as good. Umoja's cost of goods sold and engineering, selling, and administrative expenses are slightly higher than Compet's, perhaps reflecting efficiencies that Compet might have from being a larger company (its sales are more than twice those of Umoja's). Except for interest expense, Compet's expenses as a proportion of net sales are not as great as Umoja's. Compet's net income percentage would have been almost double that of Umoja if Compet did not have such a high proportion of interest expenses. As a result of this benchmarking against a competitor, Umoja should explore ways to further reduce its cost of goods sold and engineering, selling, and administrative expenses to improve its future performance.

5.

Ratio	Liquidity	Efficiency	Solvency	Profitability
Return on common shareholders' equity				✓
Inventory turnover		✓		
Current ratio	✓			
Debt ratio			✓	
Acid-test ratio	✓			
Accounts-receivable turnover		✓		
Return on net sales				✓

6.

Situation	Positive change	Negative change
A decrease in return on equity		✓
A decrease in days' sales in inventory	✓	
An increase in the debt ratio*		✓
An increase in acid-test ratio	✓	
A decrease in receivables turnover		✓
*This could also be a positive change depending on a company's situation.		

7. a) If JMT Ltd. has a current ratio of 2.00 and an acid-test ratio of only 0.70, Inventory is the account that explains the big difference between these two measures of ability to pay current liabilities. Inventory is included in the current ratio, but not in the acid-test ratio. Prepaid expenses may also explain part of the difference, but inventory is likely the more important explanation.

   b) Whether it is good or bad if JMT Ltd. has 42 days' sales in receivables depends on the credit period. If the credit period is 60 days, then this ratio is good. If the credit period is 30 days, then JMT Ltd. must alter its credit/collection policies. To a creditor of JMT Ltd., the important point is that it takes 42 days for the cash from JMT Ltd.'s receivables to become available to pay off a debt.

8.

a) Current ratio:

2014: $$\frac{\$50,000 + \$27,000 + \$128,000 + \$237,000}{\$295,000} = 1.50$$

2013: $$\frac{\$47,000 + \$124,000 + \$272,000}{\$202,000} = 2.19$$

b) Acid-test ratio:

2014: $$\frac{\$50,000 + \$27,000 + \$128,000}{\$295,000} = 0.69$$

2013: $$\frac{\$47,000 + \$124,000}{\$202,000} = 0.85$$

c) Debt ratio:

2014: $$\frac{\$295,000 + \$44,000}{\$480,000} = 0.71$$

2013: $$\frac{\$202,000 + \$56,000}{\$490,000} = 0.53$$

d) Times-interest-earned ratio:

2014: $$\frac{\$170,000}{\$46,000} = 3.70 \text{ times}$$

2013: $$\frac{168,000}{33,000} = 5.09 \text{ times}$$

Summary: The company's ability to pay its current liabilities has deteriorated based on the comparison of current and acid-test ratios 2014 over 2013. The ability to cover long-term debt has also deteriorated as evidenced by the higher debt ratio and the lower times-interest-earned ratio in 2014 compared to 2013.

9. The procedures for analyzing financial statements under ASPE and IFRS are the same. While the absolute numbers may differ, the method for determining the relationships between them and among them is the same. For example, computing a current ratio involves dividing current assets by current liabilities, regardless of the value of current assets and current liabilities.

GILDAN

Part of

2011
annual
report

*your
life*

MANAGEMENT'S RESPONSIBILITY FOR FINANCIAL REPORTING

The accompanying Consolidated Financial Statements have been prepared by management and approved by the Board of Directors of the Company. The Consolidated Financial Statements were prepared in accordance with Canadian generally accepted accounting principles and, where appropriate, reflect management's best estimates and judgments. Where alternative accounting methods exist, management has chosen those methods deemed most appropriate in the circumstances. Management is responsible for the accuracy, integrity and objectivity of the Consolidated Financial Statements within reasonable limits of materiality, and for maintaining a system of internal controls over financial reporting as described in "Management's Annual Report on Internal Control Over Financial Reporting" on page 37 of the 2011 Annual Management's Discussion and Analysis. Management is also responsible for the preparation and presentation of other financial information included in the 2011 Annual Report and its consistency with the Consolidated Financial Statements.

The Audit and Finance Committee, which is appointed annually by the Board of Directors and comprised exclusively of independent directors, meets with management as well as with the independent auditors and internal auditors to satisfy itself that management is properly discharging its financial reporting responsibilities and to review the Consolidated Financial Statements and the independent auditors' report. The Audit and Finance Committee reports its findings to the Board of Directors for consideration in approving the Consolidated Financial Statements for presentation to the shareholders. The Audit and Finance Committee considers, for review by the Board of Directors and approval by the shareholders, the engagement or reappointment of the independent auditors.

The Consolidated Financial Statements have been independently audited by KPMG LLP, Chartered Accountants, on behalf of the shareholders, in accordance with Canadian generally accepted auditing standards and the standards of the Public Company Accounting Oversight Board (United States). Their report outlines the nature of their audit and expresses their opinion on the Consolidated Financial Statements of the Company. In addition, our auditors have issued an attestation report on the Company's internal controls over financial reporting as at October 2, 2011. KPMG LLP has direct access to the Audit and Finance Committee of the Board of Directors.

(signed)
Glenn J. Chamandy
President and Chief Executive Officer

(signed)
Laurence G. Sellyn
Executive Vice-President,
Chief Financial and Administrative Officer

December 9, 2011

REPORT OF INDEPENDENT REGISTERED PUBLIC ACCOUNTING FIRM

To the Shareholders and Board of Directors of Gildan Activewear Inc.

We have audited the accompanying consolidated balance sheets of Gildan Activewear Inc. (the "Company") and subsidiaries as at October 2, 2011 and October 3, 2010 and the related consolidated statements of earnings and comprehensive income, shareholders' equity and cash flows for the years ended October 2, 2011, October 3, 2010 and October 4, 2009. These consolidated financial statements are the responsibility of the Company's management. Our responsibility is to express an opinion on these consolidated financial statements based on our audits.

We conducted our audits in accordance with Canadian generally accepted auditing standards and the standards of the Public Company Accounting Oversight Board (United States). Those standards require that we plan and perform the audit to obtain reasonable assurance about whether the financial statements are free of material misstatement. An audit includes examining, on a test basis, evidence supporting the amounts and disclosures in the financial statements. An audit also includes assessing the accounting principles used and significant estimates made by management, as well as evaluating the overall financial statement presentation. We believe that our audits provide a reasonable basis for our opinion.

In our opinion, the consolidated financial statements referred to above present fairly, in all material respects, the financial position of the Company and subsidiaries as at October 2, 2011 and October 3, 2010, and the results of their operations and their cash flows for the years ended October 2, 2011, October 3, 2010 and October 4, 2009, in conformity with Canadian generally accepted accounting principles.

We have also audited, in accordance with the standards of the Public Company Accounting Oversight Board (United States), the Company's internal control over financial reporting as at October 2, 2011, based on criteria established in *Internal Control - Integrated Framework issued by the Committee of Sponsoring Organizations of the Treadway Commission* (*COSO*), and our report dated November 30, 2011 expressed an unqualified opinion on the effectiveness of the Company's internal control over financial reporting.

KPMG LLP

Chartered Accountants
Montréal, Canada
November 30, 2011

KPMG LLP is a Canadian limited liability partnership and a member firm of the KPMG network of independent member firms affiliated with KPMG International Cooperative ("KPMG International"), a Swiss entity. KPMG Canada provides services to KPMG LLP.

REPORT OF INDEPENDENT REGISTERED PUBLIC ACCOUNTING FIRM

To the Shareholders and Board of Directors of Gildan Activewear Inc.

We have audited Gildan Activewear Inc.'s internal control over financial reporting as at October 2, 2011, based on the criteria established in *Internal Control - Integrated Framework issued by the Committee of Sponsoring Organizations of the Treadway Commission (COSO)*. Gildan Activewear Inc.'s management is responsible for maintaining effective internal control over financial reporting and for its assessment of the effectiveness of internal control over financial reporting as presented in the section entitled "Management's Annual Report on Internal Control over Financial Reporting" included in Management's Discussion and Analysis. Our responsibility is to express an opinion on the Company's internal control over financial reporting based on our audit.

We conducted our audit in accordance with the standards of the Public Company Accounting Oversight Board (United States). Those standards require that we plan and perform the audit to obtain reasonable assurance about whether effective internal control over the financial reporting was maintained in all material respects. Our audit included obtaining an understanding of internal control over financial reporting, assessing the risk that a material weakness exists, and testing and evaluating the design and operating effectiveness of internal control based on the assessed risk. Our audit also included performing such other procedures as we considered necessary in the circumstances. We believe that our audit provides a reasonable basis for our opinion.

A company's internal control over financial reporting is a process designed to provide reasonable assurance regarding the reliability of financial reporting and the preparation of financial statements for external purposes in accordance with generally accepted accounting principles. A company's internal control over financial reporting includes those policies and procedures that (1) pertain to the maintenance of records that, in reasonable detail, accurately and fairly reflect the transactions and dispositions of the assets of the company; (2) provide reasonable assurance that transactions are recorded as necessary to permit preparation of financial statements in accordance with generally accepted accounting principles, and that receipts and expenditures of the Company are being made only in accordance with authorizations of management and directors of the Company; and (3) provide reasonable assurance regarding prevention or timely detection of unauthorized acquisition, use, or disposition of the Company's assets that could have a material effect on the financial statements.

Because of its inherent limitations, internal control over financial reporting may not prevent or detect misstatements. Also, projections of any evaluation of effectiveness to future periods are subject to the risk that controls may become inadequate because of changes in conditions, or that the degree of compliance with the policies or procedures may deteriorate.

In our opinion, Gildan Activewear Inc. maintained, in all material respects, effective internal control over financial reporting as at October 2, 2011, based on criteria established in *Internal Control - Integrated* Framework issued by the Committee of Sponsoring Organizations of the Treadway Commission (COSO).

Management has excluded from its assessment of the effectiveness of internal control over financial reporting as of October 2, 2011 the internal control over financial reporting of Gold Toe Moretz Holdings Corp. ("Gold Toe Moretz") which Gildan Activewear Inc. acquired on April 15, 2011. The total assets and total net sales of Gold Toe Moretz represent approximately 24% of the consolidated total assets and approximately 7% of the consolidated net sales included in the consolidated financial statements of Gildan Activewear Inc. as of and for the year ended October 2, 2011. Our audit of internal control over financial reporting of Gildan Activewear Inc. also excluded an evaluation of the internal control over financial reporting of Gold Toe Moretz.

We also have conducted our audits on the consolidated financial statements in accordance with Canadian generally accepted auditing standards and the standards of the Public Company Accounting Oversight Board (United States). Our report dated November 30, 2011 expressed an unqualified opinion on those consolidated financial statements.

KPMG LLP

Chartered Accountants
Montréal, Canada
November 30, 2011

*CA Auditor permit no 20408

KPMG LLP is a Canadian limited liability partnership and a member firm of the KPMG network of independent member firms affiliated with KPMG International Cooperative ("KPMG International"), a Swiss entity. KPMG Canada provides services to KPMG LLP.

GILDAN ACTIVEWEAR INC.
CONSOLIDATED BALANCE SHEETS
As at October 2, 2011 and October 3, 2010
(in thousands of U.S. dollars)

	2011	2010
Current assets:		
Cash and cash equivalents	$ 88,802	$ 258,442
Trade accounts receivable	191,594	145,684
Income taxes receivable	515	-
Inventories (note 3)	575,594	332,542
Prepaid expenses and deposits	10,966	9,584
Future income taxes (note 15)	11,666	6,340
Other current assets	9,307	9,079
	888,444	761,671
Property, plant and equipment (note 4)	565,398	479,292
Assets held for sale (note 16)	13,142	3,246
Intangible assets (note 5(b))	256,467	61,321
Goodwill (note 5(a))	153,219	10,197
Other assets (note 6)	13,051	11,805
Total assets	$ 1,889,721	$ 1,327,532
Current liabilities:		
Accounts payable and accrued liabilities	$ 315,269	$ 186,205
Income taxes payable	-	5,024
	315,269	191,229
Long-term debt (note 8)	209,000	-
Future income taxes (note 15)	26,575	10,816
Non-controlling interest in consolidated joint venture	11,562	11,058
Commitments and contingencies (note 13)		
Shareholders' equity (note 10):		
Share capital	100,436	97,036
Contributed surplus	16,526	10,091
Retained earnings	1,184,781	982,764
Accumulated other comprehensive income	25,572	24,538
	1,210,353	1,007,302
	1,327,315	1,114,429
Total liabilities and shareholders' equity	$ 1,889,721	$ 1,327,532

See accompanying notes to consolidated financial statements.

On behalf of the Board of Directors:

(signed)
Director
Glenn J. Chamandy

(signed)
Director
William D. Anderson

GILDAN ACTIVEWEAR INC.
CONSOLIDATED STATEMENTS OF EARNINGS AND COMPREHENSIVE INCOME
Years ended October 2, 2011, October 3, 2010 and October 4, 2009
(in thousands of U.S. dollars, except per share data)

	2011	2010	2009
Net sales	$ 1,726,041	$ 1,311,463	$ 1,038,319
Cost of sales (note 20(c))	1,288,293	947,206	807,986
Gross profit	437,748	364,257	230,333
Selling, general and administrative expenses	199,132	154,674	134,785
Restructuring and acquisition-related costs (note 16)	8,465	8,705	6,199
Operating income	230,151	200,878	89,349
Financial expense (income), net (note 22(b))	5,485	751	(304)
Non-controlling interest in consolidated joint venture	504	3,786	110
Earnings before income taxes	224,162	196,341	89,543
Income taxes (note 15)	(15,742)	(1,904)	(5,786)
Net earnings	239,904	198,245	95,329
Other comprehensive income (loss), net of related income taxes (note 17)	1,034	(1,710)	-
Comprehensive income	$ 240,938	$ 196,535	$ 95,329
Earnings per share:			
Basic EPS (note 18)	$ 1.97	$ 1.64	$ 0.79
Diluted EPS (note 18)	$ 1.96	$ 1.63	$ 0.79

See accompanying notes to consolidated financial statements.

GILDAN ACTIVEWEAR INC.
CONSOLIDATED STATEMENTS OF SHAREHOLDERS' EQUITY
Years ended October 2, 2011, October 3, 2010 and October 4, 2009
(in thousands or thousands of U.S. dollars)

	Share capital		Contributed surplus	Accumulated other comprehensive income	Retained earnings	Total shareholders' equity
	Number	Amount				
Balance, October 5, 2008	120,536	$ 89,377	$ 6,728	$ 26,248	$ 689,190	$ 811,543
Stock-based compensation related to stock options and Treasury restricted share units	-	-	3,007	-	-	3,007
Shares issued under employee share purchase plan	58	781	-	-	-	781
Shares issued pursuant to exercise of stock options	54	125	-	-	-	125
Shares issued pursuant to vesting of Treasury restricted share units	315	2,759	(2,759)	-	-	-
Net earnings	-	-	-	-	95,329	95,329
Balance, October 4, 2009	120,963	$ 93,042	$ 6,976	$ 26,248	$ 784,519	$ 910,785
Stock-based compensation related to stock options and Treasury restricted share units	-	-	4,081	-	-	4,081
Recovery related to repricing of stock options previously exercised (note 11(b))	-	-	1,159	-	-	1,159
Shares issued under employee share purchase plan	24	628	-	-	-	628
Shares issued pursuant to exercise of stock options	183	1,251	(10)	-	-	1,241
Shares issued pursuant to vesting of Treasury restricted share units	182	2,115	(2,115)	-	-	-
Other comprehensive loss (note 17)	-	-	-	(1,710)	-	(1,710)
Net earnings	-	-	-	-	198,245	198,245
Balance, October 3, 2010	121,352	$ 97,036	$ 10,091	$ 24,538	$ 982,764	$ 1,114,429
Stock-based compensation related to stock options and Treasury restricted share units	-	-	4,899	-	-	4,899
Shares issued under employee share purchase plan	23	642	-	-	-	642
Shares issued pursuant to exercise of stock options	379	3,594	(219)	-	-	3,375
Shares issued pursuant to vesting of Treasury restricted share units	26	588	(588)	-	-	-
Shares issued as consideration for costs incurred in a business acquisition (note 19(c))	30	1,065	-	-	-	1,065
Shares repurchased and cancelled (note 10(d))	(400)	(337)	-	-	(10,200)	(10,537)
Share repurchases (note 10(e))	(79)	(2,152)	2,152	-	-	-
Other comprehensive income (note 17)	-	-	-	1,034	-	1,034
Dividends declared	-	-	191	-	(27,687)	(27,496)
Net earnings	-	-	-	-	239,904	239,904
Balance, October 2, 2011	121,331	$ 100,436	$ 16,526	$ 25,572	$ 1,184,781	$ 1,327,315

See accompanying notes to consolidated financial statements.

GILDAN ACTIVEWEAR INC.
CONSOLIDATED STATEMENTS OF CASH FLOWS
Years ended October 2, 2011, October 3, 2010 and October 4, 2009
(in thousands of U.S. dollars)

	2011	2010	2009
Cash flows from (used in) operating activities:			
Net earnings	$ 239,904	$ 198,245	$ 95,329
Adjustments for non-cash items (note 19(a))	70,851	72,360	64,178
	310,755	270,605	159,507
Changes in non-cash working capital balances:			
Trade accounts receivable	(18,861)	16,018	45,608
Inventories	(182,080)	(32,280)	16,742
Prepaid expenses and deposits	698	2,020	(1,191)
Other current assets	1,883	(168)	2,743
Accounts payable and accrued liabilities	74,496	52,127	(22,731)
Income taxes payable	(5,341)	(6,771)	(31,499)
	181,550	301,551	169,179
Cash flows from (used in) financing activities:			
Increase (decrease) in amounts drawn under revolving long-term credit facility	209,000	-	(45,000)
Dividends paid	(27,496)	-	-
Increase in other long-term debt	-	43	44
Repayment of other long-term debt	-	(4,430)	(3,661)
Proceeds from the issuance of shares	4,017	1,869	906
Repurchase and cancellation of shares (note 10(d))	(10,537)	-	-
Repurchase of shares (note 10(e))	(2,152)	-	-
Recovery related to repricing of stock options previously exercised	-	1,159	-
	172,832	(1,359)	(47,711)
Cash flows from (used in) investing activities:			
Purchase of property, plant and equipment	(159,946)	(126,855)	(43,877)
Purchase of intangible assets	(4,776)	(1,026)	(1,061)
Business acquisitions (note 2)	(349,639)	(15,850)	(1,196)
Payment of contingent consideration (note 19(d))	(5,815)	-	-
Restricted cash related to a business acquisition	-	254	3,958
Purchase of corporate asset, net of proceeds (note 19(a))	(3,693)	-	-
Proceeds on disposal of assets held for sale	1,125	4,708	6,349
Net (increase) decrease in other assets	(1,193)	(2,477)	1,629
	(523,937)	(141,246)	(34,198)
Effect of exchange rate changes on cash and cash equivalents denominated in foreign currencies	(85)	(236)	105
Net (decrease) increase in cash and cash equivalents during the year	(169,640)	158,710	87,375
Cash and cash equivalents, beginning of year	258,442	99,732	12,357
Cash and cash equivalents, end of year	$ 88,802	$ 258,442	$ 99,732

Supplemental disclosure of cash flow information (note 19)

See accompanying notes to consolidated financial statements.

NOTES TO CONSOLIDATED FINANCIAL STATEMENTS

Years ended October 2, 2011, October 3, 2010 and October 4, 2009
(Tabular amounts in thousands or thousands of U.S. dollars except per share data, unless otherwise indicated)

Gildan Activewear Inc. (the "Company") is incorporated under the *Canada Business Corporations Act*. Its principal business activity is the manufacture and sale of activewear, socks and underwear. The Company's fiscal year ends on the first Sunday following September 28. All references to 2011, 2010 and 2009 represent the fiscal years ended October 2, 2011, October 3, 2010 and October 4, 2009, respectively.

1. SIGNIFICANT ACCOUNTING POLICIES:

The consolidated financial statements are expressed in U.S. dollars and have been prepared in accordance with Canadian generally accepted accounting principles. The Company's functional currency is the U.S. dollar. The principal accounting policies of the Company are summarized as follows:

(a) Basis of presentation:
The accompanying consolidated financial statements include the accounts of the Company and its subsidiaries. The consolidated financial statements also include the accounts of a yarn spinning joint venture with Frontier Spinning Mills, Inc., CanAm Yarns LLC ("CanAm"), as the Company is considered the primary beneficiary of this entity. All significant intercompany balances and transactions have been eliminated on consolidation.

(b) Future accounting standards:
In February 2008, the Canadian Accounting Standards Board (AcSB) confirmed that International Financial Reporting Standards as issued by the International Accounting Standards Board (IFRS), will replace Canadian generally accepted accounting principles for publicly accountable enterprises effective for fiscal years beginning on or after January 1, 2011. As a result, the Company will be required to change over to IFRS for its fiscal 2012 interim and annual consolidated financial statements beginning October 3, 2011 with comparative information for fiscal 2011.

(c) Cash and cash equivalents:
The Company considers all liquid investments with maturities of three months or less when acquired to be cash equivalents.

(d) Trade accounts receivable:
Trade accounts receivable consist of amounts due from our normal business activities. We maintain an allowance for doubtful accounts to reflect expected credit losses. We provide for bad debts based on collection history and specific risks identified on a customer-by-customer basis. Uncollected accounts are written off through the allowance for doubtful accounts.

(e) Inventories:
Inventories are stated at the lower of First-In First-Out cost and net realizable value. Inventory costs include the purchase price and other costs directly related to the acquisition of raw materials used in the manufacturing process, and the cost of purchased finished goods. Inventory costs also include the costs directly related to the conversion of materials to finished goods, such as direct labour, and a systematic allocation of fixed and variable production overhead, including manufacturing depreciation expense. The allocation of fixed production overheads to the cost of inventories is based on the normal capacity of the production facilities. Normal capacity is the average production expected to be achieved over a number of periods under normal circumstances.

(f) Property, plant and equipment:
Property, plant and equipment are initially recorded at cost. Depreciation and amortization are recorded on a straight-line basis over the following estimated useful lives:

Asset	Useful life
Buildings and improvements	5 to 40 years
Manufacturing equipment	3 to 10 years
Other equipment	2 to 10 years

1. SIGNIFICANT ACCOUNTING POLICIES (continued):

(f) Property, plant and equipment (continued):

Assets not yet utilized in operations include expenditures incurred to date for plant expansions which are still in process and equipment not yet placed into service as at the balance sheet date. Depreciation on these assets commences when the assets are put into service.

(g) Assets held for sale:

Long-lived assets are classified as held for sale when certain criteria are met, which include: the Company's commitment to a plan to sell the assets; the assets are available for immediate sale in their present condition; an active program to locate buyers and other actions to sell the assets have been initiated; the sale of the assets is probable and their transfer is expected to qualify for recognition as a completed sale within one year; the assets are being actively marketed at reasonable prices in relation to their fair value; and it is unlikely that significant changes will be made to the plan to sell the assets or that the plan will be withdrawn.

The Company measures assets held for sale at the lower of carrying amount or fair value less cost to sell. These assets are not depreciated.

(h) Intangible assets:

Intangible assets include identifiable intangible assets acquired in a business combination, which are initially recorded at fair value at the date of acquisition, and include trademarks, license agreements, customer contracts and customer relationships, and non-compete agreements. Intangible assets also include the cost of computer software that is not an integral part of the related hardware. Intangible assets with finite lives are depreciated on a straight-line basis over the following estimated useful lives:

Asset	Useful life
Customer contracts and customer relationships	20 years
License agreements	7 years
Computer software	4 years
Non-compete agreements	2 years

Trademarks are not amortized as they are considered to be indefinite life intangible assets, and are tested for impairment annually, or more frequently if events or changes in circumstances indicate that the asset might be impaired.

The costs of information technology projects including internally developed computer software are capitalized and included in intangible assets commencing at the point at which the following criteria are met: the technical feasibility of completing the projects have been achieved; the Company intends to complete the information technology projects and is capable of using the software internally; the software will generate probable future economic benefits; the Company has adequate technical, financial and other resources to complete development of the projects; and the Company has the ability to reliably measure the expenditures attributable to the information technology projects during development. The Company does not capitalize pilot projects where it believes that future economic benefits are less than probable or projects that do not meet the above criteria. The costs of information technology projects that are capitalized include the cost of software tools and licenses used in the development of the projects as well as direct payroll and consulting costs. The capitalization of costs ceases and depreciation commences when the assets are put into service.

(i) Impairment of long-lived assets:

Property, plant and equipment and intangible assets with finite lives are reviewed for potential impairment if events or changes in circumstances indicate that the carrying amounts of such assets may not be recoverable. An impairment loss would be recognized when the estimated undiscounted future cash flows expected to result from the use of an asset (or asset group for which identifiable cash flows are largely independent of the cash flows of other assets and liabilities) and its eventual disposition are less than its carrying amount. The amount of the impairment loss recognized is measured as the amount by which the carrying value for an asset exceeds the fair value of the asset or asset group, with fair value being determined based on the present value of expected future cash flows or appraised values, depending on the nature of the asset or asset group. The annual impairment test for trademarks, which are considered to be intangible assets with indefinite lives, consists of a comparison of the fair value of the trademarks, using the present value of expected future cash flows, with the carrying amount of the trademarks. If the carrying amount of the trademarks exceeds their fair value, an impairment loss is recognized in an amount equal to the excess.

1. SIGNIFICANT ACCOUNTING POLICIES (continued):

(i) Impairment of long-lived assets (continued):

Assessing the impairment of long-lived assets requires the Company to make significant estimates and assumptions, including, but not limited to, the expected future cash flows that the asset or asset group will generate based on internal plans, which incorporate management's judgments as to the remaining service potential of the long-lived assets, and their fair value on an open market. Changes in circumstances, such as technological advances, adverse changes in third party licensing arrangements, changes to the Company's business strategy, and changes in economic conditions can result in actual useful lives and future cash flows differing significantly from estimates and could result in increased charges for amortization or impairment.

(j) Goodwill:

Goodwill recorded in connection with business combinations represents the excess of the purchase price over the fair value of net assets acquired, and is assigned to a reporting unit at the time of acquisition. Goodwill is not amortized and is tested for impairment on an annual basis, or more frequently if an event or circumstance occurs that more likely than not reduces the fair value of a reporting unit below its carrying amount. The annual goodwill impairment test involves a two-step process. First, the fair value of a reporting unit is compared with its carrying amount, including goodwill, in order to identify a potential impairment. The fair value of the reporting unit under the first step is determined based on the present value of expected future cash flows. The second step is required if the carrying amount of a reporting unit exceeds its fair value as determined in the first step, in which case the estimated fair value of the reporting unit is allocated to all of the assets and liabilities of the reporting unit, including the implied fair value of any intangible assets that would be recorded had the reporting unit been acquired in a business acquisition. Any fair value in excess of amounts allocated to the reporting unit's net assets represents the implied fair value of goodwill for that reporting unit. If the carrying value of the goodwill exceeds the implied fair value, the carrying value is written down by an amount equal to such excess.

The goodwill impairment testing process involves the use of significant assumptions, estimates and judgments with respect to a variety of factors, including expected sales, gross margins, selling, general and administrative expenses, capital expenditures, cash flows and the selection of an appropriate discount rate, all of which are subject to inherent uncertainties and subjectivity. The assumptions are based on annual business plans and other forecasted results as well as discount rates which are used to reflect market-based estimates of the risks associated with the projected cash flows, based on the best information available as of the date of the impairment test. If the future was to adversely differ from management's best estimate of key economic assumptions, and if associated cash flows were to materially decrease, the Company may be required to record impairment charges related to its goodwill.

(k) Foreign currency translation:

Monetary assets and liabilities of the Canadian and foreign operations denominated in currencies other than U.S. dollars are translated at the rates of exchange at the balance sheet date. Other balance sheet items denominated in currencies other than U.S. dollars are translated at the rates prevailing at the respective transaction dates. Income and expenses denominated in currencies other than U.S. dollars are translated at average rates prevailing during the year. Gains or losses on foreign exchange are recorded in net earnings.

The Company's foreign subsidiaries are considered to be integrated foreign operations, and their accounts have been translated using the temporal method with translation gains and losses included in net earnings. The Company does not currently have any self-sustaining foreign subsidiaries.

(l) Revenue recognition:

Revenue is recognized upon shipment of products to customers, since title passes upon shipment, and to the extent that the selling price is fixed or determinable. At the time of sale, estimates are made for customer price discounts and volume rebates based on the terms of existing programs. Accruals required for new programs, which relate to prior sales, are recorded at the time the new program is introduced. Sales are recorded net of these program costs and a provision for estimated sales returns, which is based on historical experience, current trends and other known factors, and exclude sales taxes.

1. SIGNIFICANT ACCOUNTING POLICIES (continued):

(m) Cost of sales and gross profit:

Cost of sales includes all raw material costs, manufacturing conversion costs, including manufacturing depreciation expense, sourcing costs, inbound freight and inter-facility transportation costs, and outbound freight to customers. Cost of sales also includes the cost of purchased finished goods, costs relating to purchasing, receiving and inspection activities, manufacturing administration, third-party manufacturing services, sales-based royalty costs, insurance, inventory write-downs, and customs and duties.

Gross profit is the result of sales less cost of sales. The Company's gross profit may not be comparable to this metric as reported by other companies, since some entities exclude depreciation expense, outbound freight to customers and royalty costs from cost of sales.

(n) Selling, general and administrative expenses:

Selling, general and administrative (SG&A) expenses include warehousing and handling costs, selling and administrative personnel costs, advertising and marketing expenses, costs of leased facilities and equipment, professional fees, non-manufacturing depreciation and amortization expense, and other general and administrative expenses. SG&A expenses also include bad debt expense, and amortization of customer-related intangible assets, license agreements and non-compete agreements.

(o) Advertising and product introduction expenditures:

Advertising and co-op advertising expenses are expensed as incurred in selling, general and administrative expenses. Product introduction expenditures are one-time fees paid to retailers to allow the Company's products to be placed on store shelves. These fees are recognized as a reduction in revenue when incurred unless the Company receives a benefit over a period of time and certain other criteria are met, such as identifiable contractual rights which are enforceable and recoverable. In this case, these fees are recorded as an asset and are amortized as a reduction of revenue over the term of the arrangement. The Company evaluates the recoverability of these assets on a quarterly basis.

(p) Cotton and yarn procurements:

The Company contracts to buy cotton and yarn with future delivery dates at fixed prices in order to reduce the effects of fluctuations in the prices of cotton used in the manufacture of its products. These contracts are not used for trading purposes and are not considered to be financial instruments. The Company commits to fixed prices on a percentage of its cotton and yarn requirements up to eighteen months in the future. If the cost of committed prices for cotton and yarn plus estimated costs to complete production exceed current selling prices, a loss is recognized for the excess as a charge to cost of sales.

(q) Financial instruments and hedging relationships:

All financial instruments are classified into one of the following five categories: held-for-trading, held-to-maturity investments, loans and receivables, available-for-sale financial assets or other financial liabilities. All financial instruments, including derivatives, are included on the consolidated balance sheet and are measured at fair value with the exception of loans and receivables, held-to-maturity investments and other financial liabilities, which are measured at amortized cost. Subsequent measurement and recognition of changes in fair value of financial instruments depend on their initial classification. Held-for-trading financial investments are measured at fair value and all gains and losses are included in net earnings in the period in which they arise. Available-for-sale financial instruments are measured at fair value with revaluation gains and losses included in other comprehensive income until the asset is removed from the balance sheet or is determined to be impaired. Financial assets and liabilities measured at fair value use a fair value hierarchy to prioritize the inputs used in measuring fair value. Level 1, defined as observable inputs such as quoted prices in active markets; Level 2, defined as inputs other than quoted prices in active markets that are either directly or indirectly observable; and Level 3, defined as unobservable inputs in which little or no market data exists, therefore requiring an entity to develop its own assumptions.

1. SIGNIFICANT ACCOUNTING POLICIES (continued):

(q) Financial instruments and hedging relationships (continued):

Derivative instruments are recorded as either assets or liabilities measured at their fair value unless exempted from derivative treatment as a normal purchase and sale. Certain derivatives embedded in other contracts must also be measured at fair value. All changes in the fair value of derivatives are recognized in net earnings unless specific hedge criteria are met, which requires that a company must formally document, designate and assess the effectiveness of transactions that receive hedge accounting. Derivatives that qualify as hedging instruments must be designated as either a "cash flow hedge," when the hedged item is a future cash flow, or a "fair value hedge," when the hedged item is a recognized asset or liability. The effective portion of unrealized gains and losses related to a cash flow hedge are included in other comprehensive income. For a cash flow hedge, when hedging instruments become ineffective before their maturity or the hedging relationship is terminated, any gains, losses, revenues or expenses associated with the hedging item that had previously been recognized in other comprehensive income as a result of applying hedge accounting are carried forward to be recognized in net earnings in the same period as the hedged item affects net earnings, to the extent that it is probable that the forecasted cash flows will occur. For a fair value hedge, both the derivative and the hedged item are recorded at fair value in the consolidated balance sheet and the unrealized gains and losses from both items are included in net earnings. Any derivative instrument that does not qualify for hedge accounting is recorded at fair value at each reporting date with the change in fair value for the period being included in net earnings.

When the Company utilizes derivatives in hedge accounting relationships, the Company formally documents all relationships between hedging instruments and hedged items, as well as its risk management objective and strategy for undertaking various hedge transactions. This process includes linking all derivatives to specific assets and liabilities on the balance sheet or to specific firm commitments or anticipated transactions. The Company also formally assesses, both at the hedge's inception and on an ongoing basis, whether the derivatives that are used in hedging transactions are effective in offsetting cash flows of hedged items.

(r) Comprehensive income:

Comprehensive income, which consists of net earnings and other comprehensive income, is defined as the change in shareholders' equity from transactions and other events from non-owner sources. Other comprehensive income refers to items recognized in comprehensive income but that are excluded from net earnings calculated in accordance with generally accepted accounting principles and includes unrealized gains and losses on financial assets classified as available for sale, unrealized foreign currency translation gains and losses arising from self-sustaining foreign subsidiaries and changes in the fair value of the effective portion of qualifying cash flow hedging instruments.

(s) Income taxes:

The Company utilizes the asset and liability method for accounting for income taxes which requires the establishment of future tax assets and liabilities, measured at substantively enacted tax rates, for all temporary differences caused when the tax bases of assets and liabilities differ from those reported in the financial statements. The Company recognizes future income tax assets only to the extent that, in management's opinion, it is more likely than not that the future income tax assets will be realized, based on estimates of future taxable income in applicable jurisdictions and other assumptions. A valuation allowance is provided to the extent that it is determined that it is no longer more likely than not that the asset will be realized. Future income tax assets and future income tax liabilities are offset if they relate to the same taxable entity and the same taxation authority.

The Company's income tax provision is based on interpretations of applicable tax laws, including income tax treaties between various countries in which the Company operates as well as underlying rules and regulations with respect to transfer pricing. These interpretations involve judgments and estimates and may be challenged through government taxation audits that the Company is regularly subject to. The Company recognizes the benefits of uncertain tax filing positions in its financial statements when it is considered likely that the tax position will be sustained upon examination by tax authorities, including the resolution of any related appeals or litigation processes, based on the technical merits of the position. The tax benefits recognized from such positions are measured at the best estimate of the amounts expected to be realized upon ultimate resolution. The Company periodically reviews and adjusts its estimates and assumptions of income tax assets and liabilities as circumstances warrant, such as changes to tax laws, administrative guidance, change in management's assessment of the technical merits of its positions due to new information, and the resolution of uncertainties through either the conclusion of tax audits or expiration of prescribed time limits within relevant statutes. Previously recognized tax benefits relating to uncertain tax filing positions are derecognized if it becomes likely that the Company's tax position will no longer be upheld.

1. SIGNIFICANT ACCOUNTING POLICIES (continued):

(t) Stock-based compensation and other stock-based payments:

The Company follows the fair value-based method to account for all transactions where services are received in exchange for stock-based compensation and other stock-based payments. For stock options and Treasury restricted share units, compensation cost is measured at the fair value at the date of grant, net of estimated forfeitures, and is expensed over the award's vesting period. The fair value of stock options granted is estimated on the date of grant using the Black-Scholes pricing model, and the fair value of Treasury restricted share units granted is equal to the market price of the common shares of the Company on the date of grant. For non-Treasury restricted share units, the compensation cost is ultimately measured based on the market price of the Company's shares at the vesting date, net of estimated forfeitures, and is expensed over the award's vesting period. The offsetting liability is marked to the underlying market price until the vesting date with any changes in the market value of the Company's shares resulting in a change in the measure of compensation cost for these awards until vested, which is recorded in the periods in which these changes occur. The measurement of the compensation cost for certain Treasury and non-Treasury restricted share units, for which the vesting is partially contingent on the achievement of performance conditions, includes the probability of achieving the performance conditions, net of estimated forfeitures.

For employee share purchase plans, the Company's contribution, on the employee's behalf, is recognized as compensation expense with an offset to share capital, and consideration paid by employees on purchase of stock is also recorded as an increase to share capital.

(u) Employee future benefits:

The Company offers group defined contribution plans to eligible employees whereby the Company matches employees' contributions up to a fixed percentage of the employee's salary. Contributions by the Company to trustee-managed investment portfolios or employee associations are expensed as incurred.

In connection with the acquisition of Gold Toe Moretz in April 2011 as described in note 2, the Company acquired a funded qualified defined benefit plan ("Retirement Plan") covering certain employees of Gold Toe Moretz. The Retirement Plan has been frozen since January 1, 2007, and as such no additional employees became participants in the Retirement Plan and existing participants in the Retirement Plan ceased accruing any additional benefits after that date. The pension obligation is actuarially determined using the projected benefit method to determine plan obligations and related periodic costs. Assets of the Retirement Plan are invested in high quality money market funds and are recorded at fair value. Plan valuations require economic assumptions, including expected rates of return on plan assets, discount rates to value plan obligations, and participant demographic assumptions including mortality rates. Because the Retirement Plan is frozen, salary escalation is not considered in the actuarial valuation, and there are no current service costs incurred. The actuarial assumptions used may differ materially from actual results due to changing market and economic conditions. Actual results that differ from the actuarial assumptions are reflected as unrecognized gains and losses. Unrecognized gains and losses that exceed 10% of the greater of the plan's projected benefit obligations or market value of assets at the beginning of the period are amortized to earnings over the estimated service life of the remaining plan participants.

The Company also maintains a liability for statutory severance and pre-notice benefit obligations for active employees located in the Caribbean Basin and Central America which is payable to the employees in a lump sum payment upon termination of employment. The liability is based on management's best estimates of the ultimate costs to be incurred to settle the liability and is based on a number of assumptions and factors, including historical trends, actuarial assumptions and economic conditions.

(v) Earnings per share:

Basic earnings per share are computed by dividing net earnings by the weighted average number of common shares outstanding for the year. Diluted earnings per share are computed using the treasury stock method. Under the treasury stock method, the weighted average number of common shares outstanding for the period is increased to include additional shares from the assumed exercise of options and the issuance of Treasury restricted share units, if dilutive. The number of additional shares is calculated by assuming that all outstanding options are exercised and all outstanding Treasury restricted share units have vested, and that the proceeds from such exercises, as well as the amount of unrecognized stock-based compensation which is considered to be assumed proceeds under the treasury stock method, are used to repurchase common shares at the average share price for the period. For Treasury restricted share units, only the unrecognized stock-based compensation is considered assumed proceeds since there is no exercise price paid by the holder.

1. SIGNIFICANT ACCOUNTING POLICIES (continued):

(w) Environmental expenditures:

Environmental expenditures that relate to current operations are expensed or capitalized as appropriate. Expenditures that extend the life of the related property or mitigate or prevent future environmental contamination are capitalized in property, plant and equipment and are generally amortized over the remaining useful life of the underlying asset. Expenditures that relate to an existing condition caused by past operations and which are not expected to contribute to current or future operations are expensed. Liabilities are recorded when environmental assessments and/or remedial efforts are likely, and when the costs, based on a specific plan of action in terms of the technology to be used and the extent of the corrective action required, can be reasonably estimated.

The Company may be obliged to incur certain future removal and site restoration costs should it decide to discontinue some of its activities. Where there is a legal obligation associated with the retirement of property, plant and equipment, and the fair value of the obligation can be reasonably estimated, a liability is initially recognized at its estimated fair value and a corresponding asset retirement cost is added to the carrying value of the related asset and amortized over the remaining life of the underlying asset. The Company had no recognized asset retirement obligations as at October 2, 2011 and October 3, 2010, as the Company plans to continue its activities for an indeterminate period and the range of possible methods of restoration are not conclusive at this time. As such, the information available to the Company is insufficient to reasonably estimate the fair value of a conditional asset retirement obligation.

(x) Business acquisitions:

The Company accounts for business acquisitions using the purchase method. Accordingly, the purchase price of a business acquisition, including direct and incremental costs incurred to effect the business combination, is allocated to its identifiable net assets, including certain restructuring and integration costs of the acquired business, on the basis of estimated fair values as at the date of purchase, with any excess being assigned to goodwill. When the amounts assigned to identifiable net assets exceed the cost of the purchase, resulting in negative goodwill, the excess is applied, to the extent possible, to certain non-current assets, with the balance recorded as an extraordinary gain.

(y) Use of estimates:

The preparation of financial statements in conformity with generally accepted accounting principles requires management to make estimates and assumptions that affect the reported amounts of assets and liabilities and disclosure of contingent liabilities and fair values of financial instruments at the date of the financial statements, and the reported amounts of revenues and expenses during the reporting period. These estimates involve varying degrees of judgment and uncertainty, and are based on a number of factors, including historical experience, current events and industry trends, information available from outside sources, management's business plans, and other assumptions that management believes are reasonable based on information available at the time they are made. Given the inherent uncertainty involved in making estimates, actual results reported in future periods could differ materially from these estimates.

Significant areas requiring the use of management estimates and assumptions include: the allowance for doubtful accounts and accruals for sales promotional programs; the valuation of inventory at the lower of cost and net realizable value; the useful life and valuation of property, plant and equipment and intangible assets with finite lives; actuarial and economic assumptions used in determining pension costs and accrued pension liabilities; the composition and valuation of future income tax assets and liabilities; and the assumptions used in impairment tests on long-lived assets and indefinite life intangible assets and goodwill.

2. BUSINESS ACQUISITIONS:

Gold Toe Moretz Holdings Corp.

On April 15, 2011, the Company acquired 100% of the capital stock of Gold Toe Moretz Holdings Corp. ("Gold Toe Moretz"), a leading supplier of high-quality branded athletic, casual and dress socks for national chains, mass-market retailers, price clubs, department stores and specialty sporting goods stores in the United States.

2. BUSINESS ACQUISITIONS (continued):

Gold Toe Moretz Holdings Corp. (continued)

The aggregate purchase price of $349.6 million, net of cash acquired, included direct acquisition related costs of $7.3 million. The purchase agreement provides for an additional purchase price consideration of up to 150,000 common shares which have been issued in the form of treasury restricted share units ("Treasury RSUs") at closing, with a fair value of approximately $4 million as at October 2, 2011. The vesting of the Treasury RSUs is contingent on specified future events. This contingent consideration has not been reflected in the purchase price of the acquisition on the basis that the outcome of the contingency cannot be determined beyond a reasonable doubt at this time. Any additional purchase price consideration paid by the Company will be accounted for as an increase to goodwill. The Company financed the acquisition by using approximately $100 million of cash on hand and approximately $250 million drawn on the Company's revolving long-term credit facility.

The Company accounted for this acquisition using the purchase method and the results of Gold Toe Moretz have been consolidated with those of the Company from the date of acquisition. The Company has allocated the purchase price to the assets acquired and liabilities assumed based on management's best estimate of their fair values and taking into account all relevant information available at that time.

The following table summarizes the estimated fair value of assets acquired and liabilities assumed at the date of acquisition:

Assets acquired:		
Trade accounts receivable	$	28,150
Income taxes receivable		208
Inventories		57,549
Prepaid expenses and deposits		2,080
Future income taxes, current		10,810
Other current assets		122
Property, plant and equipment		3,523
Intangible assets (i)		204,700
Other assets		495
		307,637
Liabilities assumed:		
Accounts payable and accrued liabilities		(54,828)
Future income taxes, net, non-current		(40,377)
		(95,205)
Net identifiable assets acquired		212,432
Goodwill		137,207
Purchase price	$	349,639
Consideration:		
Cash paid at closing, net of cash acquired of $3,576	$	342,368
Direct acquisition costs		7,271
	$	349,639

Goodwill recorded in connection with this acquisition is not deductible for tax purposes.

2. BUSINESS ACQUISITIONS (continued):

Gold Toe Moretz Holdings Corp. (continued)

(i) The estimated fair value of intangible assets of $204.7 million included in the purchase price allocation above consists of the following:

Trademarks (not subject to amortization)	$	94,000
License agreements		51,000
Customer relationships		58,000
Non-compete agreements		1,700
	$	204,700

Shahriyar Fabric Industries Limited

Effective March 31, 2010, the Company acquired 100% of the common shares of Shahriyar Fabric Industries Limited ("Shahriyar"), a vertically-integrated knitting, dyeing, finishing, cutting and sewing facility for the manufacture of high-quality ring-spun T-shirts near Dhaka, Bangladesh, for a total consideration of $15.9 million.

The Company accounted for this acquisition using the purchase method and the results of Shahriyar have been consolidated with those of the Company from the date of acquisition. The Company has allocated the purchase price to the assets acquired based on their fair value and taking into account all relevant information available at that time.

The following table summarizes the estimated fair value of assets acquired and liabilities assumed at the date of acquisition:

Assets acquired:		
Trade accounts receivable	$	1,392
Inventories		1,120
Other current assets		1,383
Property, plant and equipment		12,181
		16,076
Liabilities assumed:		
Accounts payable and accrued liabilities		(3,714)
Net identifiable assets acquired		12,362
Goodwill		3,488
Purchase price	$	15,850
Consideration:		
Payment to shareholders	$	3,250
Repayment of debt on behalf of the selling shareholders at closing		12,000
Direct acquisition costs		600
	$	15,850

The Company's repayment of the debt on behalf of the selling shareholders at closing was funded through a short-term banking facility of $12 million. This facility bore interest at 9.5% per annum, and was secured by a restricted cash deposit. As at October 3, 2010 the amount drawn under the short-term banking facility amounted to $9.9 million with a corresponding restricted cash deposit of the same amount, and the Company offset these amounts owing under the short-term banking facility against the collateral deposit in the consolidated balance sheet since the Company had the legal right of offset and used the collateral deposit to repay the bank facility in fiscal 2011. As at October 2, 2011, there were no amounts drawn under the short-term banking facility.

Goodwill recorded in connection with this acquisition is not deductible for tax purposes.

3. INVENTORIES:

Inventories were comprised of the following:

	2011	2010
Finished goods	$ 469,600	$ 240,884
Raw materials and spare parts inventories	74,284	54,353
Work in process	31,710	37,305
	$ 575,594	$ 332,542

The amount of inventory recognized as an expense and included in cost of sales was $1,262.9 million (2010 - $928.9 million; 2009 - $795.0 million), which included an expense of $6.2 million (2010 - $7.1 million; 2009 - $8.1 million) related to the write-down of inventory to net realizable value.

4. PROPERTY, PLANT AND EQUIPMENT:

2011	Cost	Accumulated depreciation	Net book value
Land	$ 35,549	$ -	$ 35,549
Buildings and improvements	196,531	47,124	149,407
Manufacturing equipment	511,543	227,935	283,608
Other equipment	99,256	49,970	49,286
Assets not yet utilized in operations	47,548	-	47,548
	$ 890,427	$ 325,029	$ 565,398

2010	Cost	Accumulated depreciation	Net book value
Land	$ 34,923	$ -	$ 34,923
Buildings and improvements	169,865	42,010	127,855
Manufacturing equipment	413,287	176,686	236,601
Other equipment	73,599	38,005	35,594
Assets not yet utilized in operations	44,319	-	44,319
	$ 735,993	$ 256,701	$ 479,292

Assets not yet utilized in operations include expenditures incurred to date for plant expansions which are still in process and equipment not yet placed into service as at the balance sheet date.

5. GOODWILL AND INTANGIBLE ASSETS:

(a) Goodwill:

The change in the carrying amount of goodwill is as follows:

	2011	2010
Balance, beginning of year	$ 10,197	$ 6,709
Goodwill acquired (note 2)	137,207	3,488
Payment of contingent consideration (note 19(d))	5,815	-
Balance, end of year	$ 153,219	$ 10,197

5. GOODWILL AND INTANGIBLE ASSETS (continued):

(b) Intangible assets:

2011	Cost	Accumulated amortization	Net book value
Customer contracts and customer relationships	$ 121,526	$ 14,446	$ 107,080
Trademarks (not subject to amortization)	94,000	-	94,000
License agreements	51,000	3,484	47,516
Computer software	26,038	19,477	6,561
Non-compete agreements	1,700	390	1,310
	$ 294,264	$ 37,797	$ 256,467

2010	Cost	Accumulated amortization	Net book value
Customer contracts and customer relationships	$ 63,526	$ 9,966	$ 53,560
Computer software	26,453	18,692	7,761
	$ 89,979	$ 28,658	$ 61,321

Computer software includes $3.9 million (2010 – nil) of expenditures incurred to date for information technology projects which are still in process and not yet placed into service as at the balance sheet date.

6. OTHER ASSETS:

	2011	2010
Prepaid lease deposit	$ 6,073	$ 1,500
Long-term prepaid expenses and other	3,069	3,564
Deferred financing charges	2,789	-
Long-term non-trade receivable	1,120	953
Restricted cash related to the acquisition of Prewett (note 19(d))	-	5,788
	$ 13,051	$ 11,805

7. REVOLVING LINE OF CREDIT:

The Company's joint venture, CanAm, has a revolving line of credit in the amount of $4.0 million. Borrowings are due on demand and bear interest at LIBOR plus 2.0%, with a minimum interest rate of 4.0%, resulting in an initial rate of 4.0% per annum. The line of credit is secured by a first ranking security interest on the assets of CanAm. There were no amounts drawn under the line of credit at October 2, 2011 and October 3, 2010.

8. LONG-TERM DEBT:

In June 2011, the Company increased its existing unsecured revolving long-term credit facility from $400 million to $800 million. The amended facility has a maturity date of June 2016. Amounts drawn under the revised facility bear interest at a variable banker's acceptance or U.S. LIBOR-based interest rate plus a spread ranging from 125 to 200 basis points. The Company incurred certain costs related to the revolving long-term credit facility. These charges are recorded at cost and are being amortized as a financial expense on a straight-line basis over the term of the related facility. The deferred financing charges are included in other assets on the consolidated balance sheet. At October 2, 2011, $209.0 million (October 3, 2010 - nil) was drawn under this facility bearing a combined effective interest rate for the period of 2.3%, including the impact of interest rate swaps. In addition, an amount of $5.8 million (October 3, 2010 - $12.7 million) has been committed against this facility to cover various letters of credit as described in note 14.

Under various financing arrangements with its bankers and other long-term lenders, including the revolving long-term credit facility, the Company is required to meet certain financial covenants. The revolving long-term credit facility requires the Company to maintain a net debt to trailing twelve months EBITDA ratio below 3.0:1, although the facility provides that this limit may be exceeded in the short term under certain circumstances, and to maintain an interest coverage ratio. The Company was in compliance with all financial covenants as at October 2, 2011 and October 3, 2010.

9. EMPLOYEE BENEFIT PLANS:

Defined Benefit Plan

The Company has a funded qualified defined benefit pension plan ("Retirement Plan") covering certain employees of Gold Toe Moretz. At the time of the acquisition of Gold Toe Moretz in April 2011, the Retirement Plan was in a net deficit position of $21.8 million, which was included in accounts payable and accrued liabilities. Management's intention is to fully fund the deficit, and subsequently liquidate and wind-up the Retirement Plan within the next twelve months. An actuarial valuation was performed at the date of acquisition and at October 2, 2011 with liabilities determined on a plan termination basis. The last valuation for funding purposes was performed on January 1, 2011, and the next valuation for funding purposes is expected to be performed on January 1, 2012. The Company has made funding contributions of $19 million, and has begun de-risking the Retirement Plan through settlement payments totaling $39 million for the period from April 15, 2011 to October 2, 2011. The Company expects to contribute approximately $5.5 million to the Retirement Plan in fiscal 2012 followed by the termination and wind-up of the Retirement Plan shortly thereafter.

At October 2, 2011, the funded status of the Company's Retirement Plan was as follows:

		October 2, 2011
Benefit obligation at April 15, 2011	$	55,975
Interest cost		900
Actuarial loss		1,574
Settlement charge		545
Benefits paid		(1,879)
Plan settlements		(39,004)
Benefit obligation at end of year	$	18,111
Fair value of plan assets at April 15, 2011	$	34,181
Employer contributions		19,000
Plan settlements		(39,004)
Actual return on plan assets		267
Benefits paid		(1,879)
Fair value of plan assets at end of year	$	12,565
Funded status - plan deficit	$	(5,546)
Unamortized actuarial loss		1,574
Accrued benefit liability - included in accounts payable and accrued liabilities	$	(3,972)

9. EMPLOYEE BENEFIT PLANS (continued):

The plan assets are invested entirely in high quality money market funds.

Net periodic pension expense of the Company's Retirement Plan for the year ended October 2, 2011 includes the following components:

		2011
Interest cost	$	900
Expected return on plan assets		(267)
Settlement charge		545
Net periodic pension expense - included in restructuring and acquisition-related costs	$	1,178

Weighted-average assumptions to determine benefit obligations and net periodic benefit cost:

	2011
Benefit obligation:	
Discount rate	4.84%
Net periodic benefit cost:	
Discount rate	3.74%
Rate of return on plan assets	3.50%

Defined Contribution Plan
For the year ended October 2, 2011, defined contribution expenses were $2.0 million (October 3, 2010 - $1.4 million; October 4, 2009 - $1.4 million).

Statutory Severance
During fiscal 2011, the Company expensed $12.2 million (2010 - $9.1 million; 2009 - $7.1 million) in cost of sales, representing management's best estimate of the cost of statutory severance and pre-notice benefit obligations accrued for active employees located in the Caribbean Basin and Central America. As at October 2, 2011, an amount of $12.6 million (October 3, 2010 - $10.2 million) has been included in accounts payable and accrued liabilities.

10. SHAREHOLDERS' EQUITY:

(a) The Company has a shareholder rights plan which provides the Board of Directors and the shareholders with additional time to assess any unsolicited take-over bid for the Company and, where appropriate, pursue other alternatives for maximizing shareholder value.

(b) Accumulated other comprehensive income:

At the commencement of fiscal 2004, the Company adopted the U.S. dollar as its functional and reporting currency. The change in the functional currency for the prior periods resulted in a currency translation adjustment of $26.2 million, which is reflected in the accumulated other comprehensive income. In addition, accumulated other comprehensive income includes the changes in the fair value of the effective portion of qualifying cash flow hedging instruments outstanding at the end of the period.

10. SHAREHOLDER'S EQUITY (continued):

(c) Share capital:

Authorized:
First preferred shares, without limit as to number and without par value, issuable in series and non-voting. Second preferred shares, without limit as to number and without par value, issuable in series and non-voting. As at October 2, 2011 and October 3, 2010 none of the first and second preferred shares were issued. Common shares, authorized without limit as to number and without par value.

Issued:
As at October 2, 2011, there were 121,330,544 common shares (October 3, 2010 - 121,351,998) issued and outstanding.

(d) Normal Course Issuer Bid:

In December 2010, the Company announced the reinstatement of a normal course issuer bid to repurchase up to one million outstanding common shares of the Company on the TSX and the NYSE (the "NCIB"). During fiscal 2011, the Company repurchased and cancelled a total of 0.4 million common shares for a total cost of $10.5 million. Of the total cost, $0.3 million was charged to share capital and $10.2 million was charged to retained earnings as there was no amount of contributed surplus attributable to these common shares. On December 2, 2011 the TSX approved the renewal of the Company's NCIB to purchase up to one million common shares, representing approximately 0.8% of its issued and outstanding common shares, in accordance with the requirements of the TSX. Common shares purchased under the NCIB will be cancelled.

(e) Common shares purchased as settlement for Non-Treasury RSUs:

In September 2011, the Company established a trust for the purpose of purchasing 79,108 common shares on the open market for a total cost of $2.2 million which were used to settle the vesting of non-Treasury RSUs in lieu of cash. As such, the common shares were held in trust for and on behalf of the holders of the vesting non-Treasury RSUs, and the Company reflected the common shares as held in treasury at October 2, 2011. The common shares held in treasury were subsequently re-issued in October 2011, when the Non-Treasury RSUs vested. At the time the shares were purchased, the corresponding liability recorded in the amount of $2.2 million for the Non-Treasury RSUs initially expected to be settled in cash was reclassified to contributed surplus.

11. STOCK-BASED COMPENSATION:

(a) Employee share purchase plans:

The Company has employee share purchase plans which allow eligible employees to authorize payroll deductions of up to 10% of their salary to purchase from Treasury, common shares of the Company at a price of 90% of the then current stock price as defined in the plans. Shares purchased under the plans prior to January 1, 2008 must be held for a minimum of one year. Employees purchasing shares under the plans subsequent to January 1, 2008 must hold the shares for a minimum of two years. The Company has reserved 2,800,000 common shares for issuance under the plans. As at October 2, 2011, a total of 266,925 shares (2010 - 243,702) were issued under these plans. Included as compensation costs in selling, general and administrative expenses is $0.1 million (2010 - $0.1 million; 2009 - $0.1 million) relating to the employee share purchase plans.

11. STOCK-BASED COMPENSATION (continued):

(b) Stock options and restricted share units:

The Company's Long-Term Incentive Plan (the "LTIP") includes stock options and restricted share units. The LTIP allows the Board of Directors to grant stock options, dilutive restricted share units ("Treasury RSUs") and non-dilutive restricted share units ("non-Treasury RSUs") to officers and other key employees of the Company and its subsidiaries. On February 2, 2006, the shareholders of the Company approved an amendment to the LTIP to fix at 6,000,316 the number of common shares that are issuable pursuant to the exercise of stock options and the vesting of Treasury RSUs. As at October 2, 2011, 2,530,322 common shares remained authorized for future issuance under this plan.

The exercise price payable for each common share covered by a stock option is determined by the Board of Directors at the date of the grant, but may not be less than the closing price of the common shares of the Company on the trading day immediately preceding the effective date of the grant. Stock options granted since fiscal 2007 vest equally beginning on the second, third, fourth and fifth anniversary of the grant date, with the exception of a special one-time award of 409,711 options which cliff vest on the fifth anniversary of the grant date, and expire no more than seven or ten years after the date of the grant. All stock options granted prior to fiscal 2007 have fully vested.

As previously disclosed in fiscal 2010, an internal review of all stock option grants made by the Company since its initial public offering in 1998 was conducted by a special committee of independent directors of the Board. As a result of this review, the Company determined that certain stock options granted to employees, officers and directors during fiscal years 1999 to 2003 had been awarded at prices which were inconsistent with the terms of the Company's LTIP in effect at the time, as well as with certain requirements of the Toronto Stock Exchange. The special committee of the Board concluded that there had been no intention of wrongdoing on the part of any current or former director or senior officer in the granting of stock options during the aforesaid period. However, current directors and senior executive officers who inadvertently benefitted from more favourable pricing of stock options have voluntarily reimbursed the Company for any excess gains and have agreed to the repricing of unexercised options. In addition, the Company pursued all reasonable avenues for recoveries from other parties. The steps taken by the Company resulted in: (i) the Company increasing the exercise price of 261,440 unexercised vested stock options during the second quarter of fiscal 2010, resulting in a $0.2 million increase in the aggregate exercise value of the unexercised stock options, or representing an increase to the weighted average exercise price for these stock options of $0.77 (from $6.18 to $6.95), and also resulting in an increase of $0.10 to the weighted average exercise price of all options outstanding as at April 4, 2010 (from $18.76 to $18.86), and; (ii) the Company recovering $2.2 million in cash, including $1.1 million from current senior officers during the second quarter of fiscal 2010 relating to stock options that were previously exercised, and $1.1 million from other parties during the first quarter of fiscal 2010. Amounts recovered in cash from current senior officers have been recorded as a credit to contributed surplus. No adjustment was required to prior year financial statements under either Canadian or U.S. GAAP.

Holders of Treasury RSUs, non-Treasury RSUs and deferred share units are entitled to dividends declared by the Company which are recognized in the form of additional equity awards equivalent in value to the dividends paid on common shares. The vesting conditions of the additional equity awards are subject to the same performance objectives and other terms and conditions as the underlying equity awards. The additional awards related to outstanding Treasury RSUs are credited to contributed surplus when the dividends are declared, whereas the additional awards related to outstanding non-Treasury RSUs and deferred share units are credited to accounts payable and accrued liabilities.

11. STOCK-BASED COMPENSATION (continued):

(b) Stock options and restricted share units (continued):

Outstanding stock options were as follows:

	Number		Weighted average exercise price
			(in Canadian dollars)
Stock options outstanding, October 4, 2009	1,010	$	16.21
Changes in outstanding stock options:			
Granted	498		21.77
Exercised	(183)		7.06
Forfeited	(26)		26.87
Stock options outstanding, October 3, 2010	1,299		19.57
Changes in outstanding stock options:			
Granted	69		28.64
Exercised	(379)		8.72
Forfeited	(28)		26.88
Stock options outstanding, October 2, 2011	961	$	24.28

The weighted average fair value of each stock option granted was estimated on the date of grant using the Black-Scholes pricing model with the following weighted average assumptions:

	2011	2010	2009
Risk-free interest rate	2.01%	2.69%	3.06%
Expected volatility	52.37%	42.48%	34.98%
Expected life	5.25 years	7.1 years	5.25 years
Expected dividend yield	-	-	-

The grant date weighted average fair value of stock options granted in fiscal 2011 was $13.36 (2010 – $8.51; 2009 – $9.24).

The following table summarizes information about stock options outstanding and exercisable at October 2, 2011:

Range of exercise prices (in Canadian dollars)	Options outstanding				Options exercisable		
	Number		Weighted average exercise price (in Canadian dollars)	Weighted average remaining contractual life (yrs)	Number		Weighted average exercise price (in Canadian dollars)
$ 5.40 - $ 5.72	31	$	5.53	0.25	31	$	5.53
$20.12 - $23.49	667		22.21	6.60	38		23.49
$27.17 - $39.39	263		31.75	3.33	175		31.93
	961	$	24.28		244	$	27.25

A Treasury RSU represents the right of an individual to receive one common share on the vesting date without any monetary consideration being paid to the Company. With the exception of a special, one-time award, which vests at the end of an eight-year period, all other Treasury RSUs awarded to date vest within a five-year vesting period. The vesting of at least 50% of each Treasury RSU grant is contingent on the achievement of performance conditions that are primarily based on the Company's average return on assets performance for the period as compared to the S&P/TSX Capped Consumer Discretionary Index, excluding income trusts, or as determined by the Board of Directors.

11. STOCK-BASED COMPENSATION (continued):

(b) Stock options and restricted share units (continued):

Outstanding Treasury RSUs were as follows:

	Number		Weighted average fair value per unit
Treasury RSUs outstanding, October 4, 2009	758	$	18.48
Changes in outstanding Treasury RSUs:			
Granted	202		18.57
Settled through the issuance of common shares	(182)		11.64
Forfeited	(30)		24.17
Treasury RSUs outstanding, October 3, 2010	748		19.93
Changes in outstanding Treasury RSUs:			
Granted	62		35.40
Granted for dividends declared	6		29.93
Settled through the issuance of common shares	(26)		22.68
Forfeited	(29)		25.78
Treasury RSUs granted as contingent consideration (note 2)	150		35.40
Treasury RSUs outstanding, October 2, 2011	911	$	23.34

As at October 2, 2011 and October 3, 2010, none of the outstanding Treasury RSUs were vested for which shares were issued subsequent to year-end. The compensation expense included in selling, general and administrative expenses and cost of sales, in respect of the options and Treasury RSUs, was $4.9 million (2010 - $4.1 million; 2009 - $3.0 million). The counterpart has been recorded as contributed surplus. When the shares are issued to the employees, the amounts previously credited to contributed surplus are transferred to share capital. As described in note 2, the compensation expense excludes the value of 150,000 Treasury RSUs granted in connection with the acquisition of Gold Toe Moretz as they are considered contingent consideration.

Outstanding non-Treasury RSUs were as follows:

	Number
Non-Treasury RSUs outstanding, October 4, 2009	185
Changes in outstanding non-Treasury RSUs:	
Granted	214
Settled	(70)
Forfeited	(16)
Non-Treasury RSUs outstanding, October 3, 2010	313
Changes in outstanding non-Treasury RSUs:	
Granted	151
Granted for dividends declared	3
Settled	(29)
Forfeited	(42)
Non-Treasury RSUs outstanding, October 2, 2011	396

11. STOCK-BASED COMPENSATION (continued):

(b) Stock options and restricted share units (continued):

Non-Treasury RSUs have the same features as Treasury RSUs, except that their vesting period is a maximum of three years and they are expected to be settled in cash at the end of the vesting period. The settlement amount is based on the Company's stock price at the vesting date. Beginning in fiscal 2010, 100% of Non-Treasury RSUs awarded to executive officers are dependent upon the financial performance of the Company relative to a benchmark group of Canadian publicly listed companies. In addition, up to two times the actual number of Non-Treasury RSUs awarded to executive officers can vest if exceptional financial performance is achieved. As of October 2, 2011, the weighted average fair value per non-Treasury RSU was $25.84. Non-Treasury RSUs that are expected to be settled in cash are non-dilutive as no common shares are issued from treasury. As at October 2, 2011, none (2010 – 18,911) of the outstanding non-Treasury RSUs were vested.

The compensation expense included in selling, general and administrative expenses and cost of sales, in respect of the non-Treasury RSUs, was $3.7 million (2010 - $2.9 million; 2009 - $0.8 million). The liability under this plan as at October 2, 2011, is $3.9 million (October 3, 2010 - $3.1 million) and is recorded in accounts payable and accrued liabilities.

12. DEFERRED SHARE UNIT PLAN:

The Company has a deferred share unit plan for independent members of the Company's Board of Directors who must receive at least 50% of their annual board retainers in the form of deferred share units ("DSUs"). The value of these DSUs is the market price of the Company's common shares at the time of payment of the retainers or fees. DSUs granted under the plan will be redeemable and the value thereof payable in cash only after the director ceases to act as a director of the Company. As at October 2, 2011, there were 78,416 (2010 - 53,602) DSUs outstanding at a value of $2.0 million (2010 - $1.5 million). This amount is included in accounts payable and accrued liabilities. The DSU obligation is adjusted each quarter based on the market value of the Company's common shares. The Company includes the cost of the DSU plan in selling, general and administrative expenses.

Changes in outstanding DSUs were as follows:

	Number
DSUs outstanding, October 4, 2009	36
Granted	18
DSUs outstanding, October 3, 2010	54
Granted	24
DSUs outstanding, October 2, 2011	78

13. COMMITMENTS AND CONTINGENCIES:

(a) The minimum annual lease payments under operating leases for premises, equipment and aircraft are approximately as follows:

Fiscal year	
2012	$ 12,210
2013	9,112
2014	6,555
2015	5,032
2016	4,316
Thereafter	10,750
	$ 47,975

13. COMMITMENTS AND CONTINGENCIES (continued):

(b) As at October 2, 2011, there were contractual obligations outstanding of approximately $54.9 million for the acquisition of property, plant and equipment (2010 - $76.1 million).

(c) During fiscal 2011, the United States Department of Agriculture advanced $3.3 million (2010 - $3.1 million; 2009 - $4.3 million) to CanAm, in connection with a subsidy program with the intent of assisting domestic spinning and textile manufacturers. Amounts received under this program are based on U.S. cotton consumption. The assistance provided is not repayable, provided that eligible capital investments are incurred over a certain period of time for amounts equivalent to the assistance received. All amounts received are recorded as deferred income and are included in accounts payable and accrued liabilities until there is reasonable assurance that eligible capital investments will be incurred. Once reasonable assurance is obtained, the amounts recorded in deferred income are recognized and proportionately allocated as a reduction of cost of goods sold and property, plant and equipment, using the intent of the subsidy program as a basis for the allocation. During fiscal 2011, the Company recognized $3.2 million of the subsidies received as a reduction of cost of goods sold (2010 - $6.0 million; 2009 - nil), partially offset by a charge of $1.6 million (2010 - $3.0 million; 2009 - nil) to non-controlling interest in the Company's consolidated statement of earnings to reflect the 50% non-controlling interest of the amount recognized. In addition, the Company recorded $0.5 million (October 3, 2010 - $0.7 million; October 4, 2009 - nil) as a reduction of capital expenditures as at October 2, 2011. As at October 2, 2011, financial assistance received in the amount of $0.8 million, $3.3 million, and $0.6 million is to be disbursed by CanAm no later than February 2012, February 2013 and February 2014, respectively, to finance eligible capital expenditures.

(d) Securities Class Actions:

The Company and certain of its senior officers were named as defendants in a number of class action lawsuits filed in the United States District Court for the Southern District of New York, which were subsequently consolidated, alleging claims under the U.S. securities laws, as well as in class action lawsuits filed in the Ontario Superior Court of Justice and in the Quebec Superior Court. Each of these U.S. and Canadian lawsuits alleged, among other things, that the defendants misrepresented the Company's financial condition and its financial prospects in its earnings guidance concerning the 2008 fiscal year, which guidance was subsequently revised on April 29, 2008.

On August 3, 2010, the Company announced that it had entered into an agreement to settle all claims raised in these class action lawsuits, subject to final approval from the courts, on behalf of all persons who acquired the Company's common shares between August 2, 2007 and April 29, 2008 (the "Class Members"). Final court approval of the settlement was obtained from each of the courts in February and March 2011 and all of the actions have been dismissed on terms including releases from Class Members of the claims against the Company and the named senior officers. The settlement agreement provided for a total settlement amount of $22.5 million, which has been entirely funded by the Company's insurers. Therefore no provision has been recorded in the consolidated financial statements and no amounts have been disbursed by the Company in respect of the settlement.

(e) The Company is a party to other claims and litigation arising in the normal course of operations. The Company does not expect the resolution of these matters to have a material adverse effect on the financial position or results of operations of the Company.

14. GUARANTEES:

The Company, and some of its subsidiaries, have granted corporate guarantees, irrevocable standby letters of credit and surety bonds, to third parties to indemnify them in the event the Company and some of its subsidiaries do not perform their contractual obligations. As at October 2, 2011, the maximum potential liability under these guarantees was $15.1 million (2010 - $21.8 million), of which $5.0 million (2010 - $5.1 million) was for surety bonds and $10.1 million (2010 - $16.7 million) was for corporate guarantees and standby letters of credit. The surety bonds are automatically renewed on an annual basis, the corporate guarantees and standby letters of credit mature at various dates in fiscal 2012.

As at October 2, 2011, the Company has recorded no liability with respect to these guarantees, as the Company does not expect to make any payments for the aforementioned items. Management has determined that the fair value of the non-contingent obligations requiring performance under the guarantees in the event that specified triggering events or conditions occur approximates the cost of obtaining the standby letters of credit and surety bonds.

15. INCOME TAXES:

The income tax provision differs from the amount computed by applying the combined Canadian federal and provincial tax rates to earnings before income taxes. The reasons for the difference and the related tax effects are as follows:

	2011	2010	2009
Combined basic Canadian federal and provincial income taxes	$ 64,514	$ 59,533	$ 27,884
(Decrease) increase in income taxes resulting from:			
Effect of different tax rates on earnings of foreign subsidiaries	(82,407)	(70,105)	(32,181)
Income tax (recovery) charge for prior taxation years	(413)	2,322	(6,085)
Effect of non-deductible expenses and other	2,564	6,346	4,596
	$ (15,742)	$ (1,904)	$ (5,786)

The income tax recovery of $6.1 million in fiscal 2009, relates to previously unrecognized tax positions of prior taxation years.

The components of income taxes are as follows:

	2011	2010	2009
Current income taxes	$ 3,376	$ 9,523	$ (3,352)
Future income taxes	(19,118)	(11,427)	(2,434)
	$ (15,742)	$ (1,904)	$ (5,786)

Significant components of the Company's future income tax assets and liabilities are as follows:

	2011	2010
Future income tax assets (liabilities)		
Non-capital losses	$ 67,853	$ 12,778
Taxable temporary differences related to:		
Reserves and accruals	11,666	6,340
Property, plant and equipment	(6,428)	(5,863)
Intangible assets	(91,428)	(19,751)
Other	3,428	2,020
Net future income tax liability	$ (14,909)	$ (4,476)
Presented as:		
Current assets	$ 11,666	$ 6,340
Long-term liabilities	(26,575)	(10,816)

As at October 2, 2011, the Company has non-capital loss carryforwards and taxable temporary differences available to reduce future taxable income for Canadian, and U.S. tax purposes of approximately CAD$4.9 million and $1.4 million, respectively, for which no future tax asset has been recognized. The non-capital loss carryforwards expire between 2022 and 2031.

The Company has not recognized a future income tax liability for the undistributed profits of its subsidiaries in the current or prior years because the Company currently does not expect to sell those investments, and for those undistributed profits that would become taxable, there is no intention to repatriate the profits.

16. RESTRUCTURING AND ACQUISITION-RELATED COSTS, AND ASSETS HELD FOR SALE:

	2011	2010	2009
Loss (gain) on disposal of assets held for sale	$ 634	$ 37	$ (619)
Accelerated depreciation	-	2,488	-
Asset impairment loss and write-down of assets held for sale	1,722	1,826	1,595
Employee termination costs and other benefits	2,887	744	2,180
Other exit costs	3,222	3,705	3,120
Adjustment for employment contract	-	(95)	(77)
	$ 8,465	$ 8,705	$ 6,199

During the first quarter of fiscal 2010, the Company announced plans to consolidate its distribution centres servicing retail customers at its new retail distribution centre in Charleston, South Carolina, and to close its leased retail distribution facility in Martinsville, Virginia and its retail distribution facilities in Fort Payne, Alabama. In February 2009, the Company closed its U.S. sock finishing operations in Fort Payne, Alabama, and in February 2011 the Company announced the closure of the remaining U.S. sock knitting operations in Fort Payne, Alabama.

For fiscal 2011, restructuring and acquisition-related costs totalled $8.5 million, mainly relating to the closure of the U.S. sock knitting operations mentioned above, including $2.9 million of employee termination costs, other exit costs of $2.0 million related to carrying and dismantling costs and $1.7 million of asset write-downs mainly for assets held for sale. Other exit costs also included net pension expense of $1.2 million related to Gold Toe Moretz's defined benefit pension plan which was incurred primarily as a result of the Company's plan to fully fund and de-risk the plan, and reduce future pension costs.

For fiscal 2010, restructuring and acquisition-related costs totalled $8.7 million, mainly relating to the consolidation of retail distribution facilities mentioned above, including $2.5 million of accelerated depreciation, an asset impairment loss of $1.8 million, and $0.7 million of employee termination costs. The Company also incurred other exit costs of $3.7 million for fiscal 2010 including inventory transfer costs, carrying and dismantling costs, and lease termination costs.

For fiscal 2009, restructuring and acquisition-related costs totalled $6.2 million which included $3.7 million for the closure of the Company's U.S. sock finishing operations, and $3.1 million primarily related to facility closures that occurred in previous fiscal years, including carrying costs and asset write-downs, net of a gain of $0.6 million relating to assets held for sale.

Assets held for sale of $13.1 million as at October 2, 2011 (October 3, 2010 - $3.2 million) include property, plant and equipment primarily relating to closed facilities. The Company expects to incur additional carrying costs relating to the closed facilities, which will be accounted for as restructuring charges as incurred until all property, plant and equipment related to the closures are disposed. Any gains or losses on the disposal of the assets held for sale relating to closed facilities will also be accounted for as restructuring charges as incurred.

Accounts payable and accrued liabilities include amounts relating to restructuring activities and charges to comply with an employment contract with a former officer of the Company, as follows:

Balance, October 4, 2009	$ 1,686
Employee termination and other benefits	744
Adjustment for employment contract	(95)
Foreign exchange adjustment	34
Payments	(915)
Balance, October 3, 2010	1,454
Employee termination and other benefits	2,887
Payments	(3,351)
Balance, October 2, 2011	$ 990

17. OTHER COMPREHENSIVE INCOME (LOSS):

Other comprehensive income (loss) was comprised of the following:

	2011	2010	2009
Net (loss) gain on derivatives designated as cash flow hedges	$ (4,448)	$ 2,151	$ -
Income taxes	45	(22)	-
Amounts reclassified from other comprehensive income to net earnings, and included in:			
Net sales	5,177	(2,688)	-
Selling, general and administrative expenses	(1,045)	(701)	-
Financial expense (income), net	1,360	(489)	-
Income taxes	(55)	39	-
Other comprehensive income (loss)	$ 1,034	$ (1,710)	$ -

As at October 2, 2011, approximately $2.3 million of net gains presented in accumulated other comprehensive income are expected to be reclassified to net earnings within the next twelve months.

18. EARNINGS PER SHARE:

A reconciliation between basic and diluted earnings per share is as follows:

	2011	2010	2009
Basic earnings per share:			
Basic weighted average number of common shares outstanding	121,526	121,159	120,811
Basic earnings per share	$ 1.97	$ 1.64	$ 0.79
Diluted earnings per share:			
Basic weighted average number of common shares outstanding	121,526	121,159	120,811
Plus dilutive impact of stock options and Treasury RSUs	757	821	624
Diluted weighted average number of common shares outstanding	122,283	121,980	121,435
Diluted earnings per share	$ 1.96	$ 1.63	$ 0.79

Excluded from the above calculation for the year ended October 2, 2011 are 155,848 stock options (2010 - 612,144; 2009 - 452,093) and nil Treasury RSUs (2010 - 16,375; 2009 - 236,934) which were deemed to be anti-dilutive.

19. SUPPLEMENTAL CASH FLOW DISCLOSURE:

(a) Adjustments for non-cash items:

	2011	2010	2009
Depreciation and amortization (note 20(a))	$ 79,808	$ 66,472	$ 65,407
Variation of depreciation included in inventories (note 20(a))	(3,423)	2,725	(2,437)
Restructuring charges related to assets held for sale and property, plant and equipment (note 16)	2,356	4,351	976
Loss on disposal of long-lived assets	1,877	842	561
Loss on disposal of corporate asset (i)	3,693	-	-
Stock-based compensation costs	4,899	4,081	3,007
Future income taxes	(19,118)	(11,427)	(2,434)
Non-controlling interest in consolidated joint venture	504	3,786	110
Unrealized net loss (gain) on foreign exchange and financial derivatives not designated as cash flow hedges	255	846	(1,012)
Adjustments to financial derivatives included in other comprehensive income, net of amounts reclassified to net earnings	-	684	-
	$ 70,851	$ 72,360	$ 64,178

(i) During fiscal 2011 the Company purchased a corporate aircraft pursuant to an early purchase option under its operating lease for approximately $16.9 million. Immediately following the purchase, the Company sold the corporate aircraft to an unrelated third party for proceeds of $13.2 million, resulting in a loss of $3.7 million which is included in selling, general and administrative expenses. The Company has leased a new corporate aircraft which is being accounted for as an operating lease.

(b) Cash paid during the period for:

	2011	2010	2009
Interest	$ 3,033	$ 638	$ 2,028
Income taxes	8,620	16,443	30,419

19. SUPPLEMENTAL CASH FLOW DISCLOSURE (continued):

(c) Non-cash transactions:

	2011	2010	2009
Balance of non-cash transactions:			
Additions to property, plant and equipment			
included in accounts payable and accrued liabilities	$ 5,026	$ 2,099	$ 627
Proceeds on disposal of long-lived assets included			
in other assets	-	427	808
Proceeds on disposal of long-lived assets included			
in other current assets	-	-	456
Treasury RSUs issued in lieu of cash dividends	$ 191	$ -	$ -
Non-cash ascribed value credited to share capital from			
shares issued pursuant to vesting of Treasury RSUs			
and exercise of stock options	807	2,125	2,759
Shares issued as consideration for lease termination costs			
incurred as part of the acquisition of Gold Toe Moretz	1,065	-	-

(d) In connection with the acquisition of V.I. Prewett & Son Inc. in fiscal 2008, the purchase agreement provided for an additional purchase consideration of up to $10.0 million contingent on specified future events. This amount was initially paid into escrow by the Company, but events occurring subsequent to the acquisition resulted in a reduction of the contingent purchase price and escrow deposit balance to $5.8 million. During fiscal 2011, the contingent purchase consideration was settled and paid to the selling shareholders in the amount of $5.8 million from the escrow deposit. The additional purchase price consideration paid by the Company has been accounted for as an increase in goodwill and a corresponding decrease in other assets.

(e) Cash and cash equivalents consist of:

	2011	2010	2009
Cash balances with banks	$ 87,251	$ 196,279	$ 92,608
Short-term investments, bearing interest at rates			
between 0.12% and 1.05%	1,551	62,163	7,124
	$ 88,802	$ 258,442	$ 99,732

20. OTHER INFORMATION:

(a) Depreciation and amortization (excluding accelerated depreciation, which is included in restructuring and acquisition-related costs):

	2011	2010	2009
Depreciation and amortization of property, plant and equipment and intangible assets	$ 79,808	$ 66,472	$ 65,407
Adjustment for the variation of depreciation of property, plant and equipment and intangible assets included in inventories at the beginning and end of the period	(3,423)	2,725	(2,437)
Depreciation and amortization included in the consolidated statements of earnings and comprehensive income	$ 76,385	$ 69,197	$ 62,970
Comprised of:			
Depreciation of property, plant and equipment	$ 63,283	$ 60,378	$ 53,925
Amortization of intangible assets	13,087	8,797	8,843
Amortization of financing costs and other	15	22	202
Depreciation and amortization included in the consolidated statements of earnings and comprehensive income	$ 76,385	$ 69,197	$ 62,970

(b) The Company recorded bad debt expense, net of recoveries, of $0.6 million (2010 – $2.4 million; 2009 – $6.0 million) which is included in selling, general and administrative expenses.

(c) During the fourth quarter of fiscal 2010, the Company received business interruption insurance proceeds of $8.0 million, reflecting the maximum insurance recovery available under its insurance policy related to the earthquake which struck Haiti on January 12, 2010. The earthquake impacted the Company's third-party contractor operations used to sew the majority of the fabric produced at its Dominican Republic textile facility, which resulted in lost sales opportunities due to a temporary loss of production, as well as incremental costs related to supply chain inefficiencies. Business interruption proceeds have been recorded as a reduction of cost of sales in the statement of earnings and comprehensive income.

21. RELATED PARTY TRANSACTIONS:

The Company has transactions with Frontier Spinning Mills, Inc., which manages the operations of CanAm. These transactions are in the normal course of operations and are measured at the exchange amount, which is the amount of consideration established and agreed to by the related parties. The following is a summary of the related party transactions and balances owed:

	2011	2010	2009
Transactions:			
Yarn purchases	$ 297,495	$ 156,761	$ 149,754
Management fee expense	750	750	750
Balances outstanding:			
Accounts payable and accrued liabilities	63,132	30,050	22,129

The Company leases warehouse and office space from an officer of a subsidiary of the Company under operating leases. The payments made on these leases were in accordance with the terms of the lease agreements established and agreed to by the related parties, which amounted to $0.6 million for fiscal 2011 (2010 - nil). There were no amounts owing as at October 2, 2011.

22. FINANCIAL INSTRUMENTS:

Disclosures relating to exposure to risks, in particular credit risk, liquidity risk, foreign currency risk and interest rate risk, are included in the section entitled "Financial Risk Management" of the Management's Discussion and Analysis of the Company's operations, performance and financial condition as at October 2, 2011, which is included in the Report to Shareholders along with these consolidated financial statements. Accordingly, these disclosures are incorporated into these consolidated financial statements by cross-reference.

(a) Financial instruments – carrying values and fair values:

The fair values of financial assets and liabilities, together with the carrying amounts included in the consolidated balance sheets, are as follows:

	2011		2010	
	Carrying amount	Fair value	Carrying amount	Fair value
Financial assets				
Held-for-trading financial assets:				
Cash and cash equivalents	$ 88,802	$ 88,802	$ 258,442	$ 258,442
Loans and receivables:				
Trade accounts receivable	191,594	191,594	145,684	145,684
Other current assets	6,008	6,008	7,980	7,980
Long-term non-trade receivable included in other assets	1,120	1,120	953	953
Restricted cash related to the acquisition of Prewett included in other assets	-	-	5,788	5,788
Derivative assets	3,299	3,299	1,099	1,099
Financial liabilities				
Other financial liabilities:				
Accounts payable and accrued liabilities	311,262	311,262	183,117	183,117
Long-term debt - bearing interest at variable rates	209,000	209,000	-	-
Derivative liabilities	4,007	4,007	3,088	3,088

Derivative assets and derivative liabilities consist of the fair values of forward foreign exchange contracts, interest rate swap contracts and zero-cost collar options outstanding at October 2, 2011. The Company has determined that the fair value of its short-term financial assets and liabilities approximates their respective carrying amounts as at the balance sheet dates because of the short-term maturity of those instruments. The fair values of the long-term receivable and the restricted cash included in other assets, and the Company's interest-bearing financial liabilities also approximate their respective carrying amounts. The fair values of cash and cash equivalents and derivative instruments were measured using Level 2 inputs in the fair value hierarchy. In determining the fair value of financial assets and financial liabilities, including derivative financial instruments, the Company takes into account its own credit risk and the credit risk of the counterparty.

22. FINANCIAL INSTRUMENTS (continued):

(b) Financial expense (income), net:

		2011		2010		2009
Interest expense (i)	$	2,856	$	436	$	1,824
Bank and other financial charges		2,216		1,504		1,039
Foreign exchange gain (ii)		(1,098)		(1,084)		(3,085)
Derivative loss (gain) on financial instruments not designated for hedge accounting		1,511		(105)		(82)
	$	5,485	$	751	$	(304)

(i) Interest expense (income):

		2011		2010		2009
Interest expense on long-term debt	$	3,246	$	88	$	1,800
Interest expense on short-term indebtedness		27		463		142
Interest income on held-for-trading financial assets		(434)		(132)		(103)
Interest income on loans and receivables		(80)		(80)		(80)
Other interest expense		97		97		65
	$	2,856	$	436	$	1,824

Interest income on held-for-trading financial assets consists of interest earned from cash and cash equivalents invested in short-term deposits. Interest income on loans and receivables relates to interest earned on the Company's long-term receivable included in other assets.

(ii) Foreign exchange gain:

		2011		2010		2009
Gain relating to financial assets and liabilities	$	(219)	$	(1,154)	$	(220)
Other foreign exchange (gain) loss		(879)		70		(2,865)
	$	(1,098)	$	(1,084)	$	(3,085)

(c) Derivative instruments:

The Company has entered into forward foreign exchange contracts and zero-cost collar options in order to reduce the exposure of forecasted cash flows in currencies other than the U.S. dollar. The forward foreign exchange contracts and the intrinsic value of zero-cost collar options were designated as cash flow hedges and qualified for hedge accounting. As such, the effective portion of unrealized gains and losses related to the fair value of the cash flow hedges are included in other comprehensive income, and are recognized in net earnings in the same period in which the foreign exchange impact of the forecasted cash flow affects net earnings. The gains and losses related to the time value of zero-cost collar options are immediately recognized in earnings in the same caption as the items being hedged. The forward foreign exchange contracts and zero-cost collar options outstanding as at October 2, 2011 consisted primarily of contracts to reduce the exposure to fluctuations in Mexican pesos, Euros, Australian dollars, Canadian dollars, and Pounds sterling against the U.S. dollar. As at October 2, 2011, the derivatives designated as cash flow hedges were considered to be fully effective with no resulting portions being ineffective.

22. FINANCIAL INSTRUMENTS (continued):

(c) Derivative instruments (continued):

October 2, 2011	Notional foreign currency amount equivalent	Average exchange rate	Notional U.S. $ equivalent	Other current assets	Accounts payable and accrued liabilities	0 to 6 months	7 to 12 months
					Carrying and fair value		Maturity
Forward foreign exchange contracts designated as cash flow hedges:							
Sell MXN/Buy USD	112,800	0.0832	$ 9,389	$ 1,308	$ -	$ 515	$ 793
Sell CAD/Buy USD	17,100	1.0438	17,849	1,378	-	647	731
Buy CAD/Sell USD	10,006	0.9594	9,600	31	(16)	13	2
Zero-cost collar options designated as cash flows hedges:							
Put Options							
Sell AUD/Buy USD	1,500	0.9200	1,380	84	-	84	-
Sell GBP/Buy USD	3,900	1.5636	6,098	291	-	291	-
Sell EUR/Buy USD	3,000	1.3300	3,990	207	-	207	-
Call Options							
Sell AUD/Buy USD	1,500	1.0193	1,529	-	(56)	(56)	-
Sell GBP/Buy USD	3,900	1.6259	6,341	-	(118)	(118)	-
Sell EUR/Buy USD	3,000	1.3880	4,164	-	(178)	(178)	-
			$ 60,340	$ 3,299	$ (368)	$ 1,405	$ 1,526

October 3, 2010	Notional foreign currency amount equivalent	Average exchange rate	Notional U.S. $ equivalent	Other current assets	Accounts payable and accrued liabilities	0 to 6 months	7 to 12 months
					Carrying and fair value		Maturity
Forward foreign exchange contracts designated as cash flow hedges:							
Sell AUD/Buy USD	7,908	0.8704	$ 6,883	$ -	$ (570)	$ (334)	$ (236)
Sell GBP/Buy USD	24,900	1.5443	38,454	-	(511)	(210)	(301)
Sell EUR/Buy USD	33,150	1.2964	42,977	-	(2,007)	(813)	(1,194)
Sell CAD/Buy USD	16,000	0.9938	15,900	393	-	393	-
Buy CAD/Sell USD	21,222	0.9330	19,800	706	-	368	338
			$ 124,014	$ 1,099	$ (3,088)	$ (596)	$ (1,393)

22. FINANCIAL INSTRUMENTS (continued):

(c) Derivative instruments (continued):

During fiscal 2011, the Company entered into a series of interest rate swap contracts to fix the variable interest rates on a designated portion of the borrowings under the revolving long-term credit facility. As at October 2, 2011, the interest rate swap contracts were designated as cash flow hedges and qualified for hedge accounting. As such, the effective portion of unrealized gains and losses related to the fair value of the interest rate swap contracts are included in other comprehensive income, and are recognized in earnings as a charge or credit to financial expense, in the same period as the interest payments on the amounts drawn under the revolving long-term credit facility are recognized. The following table summarizes the outstanding interest rate swap contracts as at October 2, 2011:

| | | | | | Carrying and fair value | |
Notional amount	Maturity date	Pay / Receive	Fixed rate	Floating rate	Other current assets	Accounts payable and accrued liabilities
$ 100,000	June 3, 2016	Pay fixed rate / Receive floating rate	1.88%	1-month U.S. LIBOR	$ -	$ (3,623)
15,000	June 3, 2016	Pay fixed rate / Receive floating rate	1.10%	1-month U.S. LIBOR	-	(13)
10,000	June 3, 2016	Pay fixed rate / Receive floating rate	1.08%	1-month U.S. LIBOR	-	(3)
$ 125,000					$ -	$ (3,639)

23. CAPITAL DISCLOSURES:

The Company's objective in managing capital is to ensure sufficient liquidity to pursue its organic growth strategy and undertake selective acquisitions, while at the same time taking a conservative approach towards financial leverage and management of financial risk.

The Company's capital is composed of net debt and shareholders' equity. Net debt consists of interest-bearing debt less cash and cash equivalents. The Company's primary uses of capital are to finance capital expenditures for manufacturing and distribution facilities, working capital requirements, payment of dividends, and business acquisitions. The Company currently funds these requirements out of its internally-generated cash flows and the periodic use of its revolving long-term bank credit facility.

The primary measure used by the Company to monitor its financial leverage is its ratio of net debt to earnings before interest, taxes, depreciation and amortization, non-controlling interest, and restructuring and acquisition-related costs ("EBITDA"), which it aims to maintain at less than a maximum of 3.0:1. Net debt is computed as at the most recent quarterly balance sheet date. EBITDA is based on the last four quarters ending on the same date as the balance sheet date used to compute net debt. The computations of net debt/cash in excess of total indebtedness and EBITDA as at October 2, 2011, October 3, 2010 and October 4, 2009 were as follows:

23. CAPITAL DISCLOSURES (continued):

	2011	2010	2009
Current portion of long-term debt	$ -	$ -	$ 2,803
Long-term debt	209,000	-	1,584
Less: cash and cash equivalents	(88,802)	(258,442)	(99,732)
Net debt (Cash in excess of total indebtedness)	$ 120,198	$ (258,442)	$ (95,345)

	For the last four quarters ended on		
	October 2, 2011	October 3, 2010	October 4, 2009
Net earnings	$ 239,904	$ 198,245	$ 95,329
Restructuring and acquisition-related costs	8,465	8,705	6,199
Depreciation and amortization	79,808	66,472	65,407
Variation of depreciation included in inventories	(3,423)	2,725	(2,437)
Interest, net	2,856	436	1,824
Income tax recovery	(15,742)	(1,904)	(5,786)
Non-controlling interest in consolidated joint venture	504	3,786	110
EBITDA	$ 312,372	$ 278,465	$ 160,646
Net debt to EBITDA ratio	0.4:1	n/a	n/a

The Company does not currently plan to refinance its revolving credit facility, or a portion thereof, with debt of longer maturities or to raise additional equity capital, unless uses of cash arise which are currently not anticipated. In the third quarter of fiscal 2011, the Company used its revolving credit facility to partially finance the acquisition of Gold Toe Moretz.

In order to maintain or adjust its capital structure, the Company, upon approval from its Board of Directors, may issue or repay long-term debt, issue shares, repurchase shares, pay dividends or undertake other activities as deemed appropriate under the specific circumstances.

In December 2010, the Board of Directors approved the introduction of a quarterly cash dividend. During fiscal 2011, the Company has paid an aggregate of $27.5 million of dividends. On November 29, 2011, the Board of Directors declared a quarterly dividend of $0.075 per share for an expected aggregate payment of $9.1 million which will be paid on January 6, 2012 on all of the issued and outstanding common shares of the Company, rateably and proportionately to the holders of record on December 15, 2011. The Board of Directors will consider several factors when deciding to declare quarterly cash dividends, including the Company's present and future earnings, cash flows, capital requirements and present and/or future regulatory and legal restrictions. There can be no assurance as to the declaration of future quarterly cash dividends. Although the Company's revolving long-term credit facility requires compliance with lending covenants in order to pay dividends, these covenants are not currently, and are not expected to be, a constraint to the payment of dividends under the Company's dividend policy.

The Company is not subject to any capital requirements imposed by a regulator.

24. SEGMENTED INFORMATION:

The Company manufactures and sells activewear, socks and underwear. The Company operates in one business segment, being high-volume, basic, frequently replenished, non-fashion apparel.

(a) Net sales by major product group:

	2011	2010	2009
Activewear and underwear	$ 1,406,036	$ 1,084,953	$ 795,535
Socks	320,005	226,510	242,784
	$ 1,726,041	$ 1,311,463	$ 1,038,319

(b) Major customers and revenues by geographic area:

(i) The Company has two customers accounting for at least 10% of total net sales:

	2011	2010	2009
Customer A	19.4%	21.0%	18.6%
Customer B	12.1%	14.3%	15.5%

(ii) Net sales were derived from customers located in the following geographic areas:

	2011	2010	2009
United States	$ 1,536,670	$ 1,154,776	$ 939,717
Canada	63,422	54,160	35,134
Europe and other	125,949	102,527	63,468
	$ 1,726,041	$ 1,311,463	$ 1,038,319

(c) Property, plant and equipment by geographic area are as follows:

	2011	2010
Honduras	$ 333,143	$ 243,033
Caribbean Basin	115,582	118,876
United States	84,873	81,555
Bangladesh	12,391	12,124
Canada	8,537	10,051
Other	10,872	13,653
	$ 565,398	$ 479,292

(d) Intangible assets by geographic area are as follows:

	2011	2010
United States	$ 250,060	$ 54,650
Canada	5,294	5,456
Honduras	951	907
Other	162	308
	$ 256,467	$ 61,321

24. SEGMENTED INFORMATION (continued):

(e) Goodwill by geographic area is as follows:

		2011		2010
United States	$	149,731	$	6,709
Bangladesh		3,488		3,488
	$	153,219	$	10,197

25. COMPARATIVE FIGURES:

The Company reclassified $6.3 million of future income taxes between current and non-current as at October 3, 2010.

26. SUBSEQUENT EVENT:

On November 30, 2011, the Company announced a reduction in its selling prices in the U.S. wholesale distributor channel. The Company also concurrently announced that the reduction in selling prices will be applied to existing distributor inventories, which is projected to result in a distributor inventory devaluation discount of approximately $17 million, and which will be recorded as a reduction to trade accounts receivable and net sales in the first quarter of fiscal 2012.

Appendix B

Present-Value Tables and Future-Value Tables

This appendix provides present-value tables (more complete than those appearing in Chapter 15) and future-value tables.

Table B-1   *Present Value of $1*

Periods	1%	2%	3%	4%	5%	6%	7%	8%	9%	10%	12%
1	0.990	0.980	0.971	0.962	0.952	0.943	0.935	0.926	0.917	0.909	0.893
2	0.980	0.961	0.943	0.925	0.907	0.890	0.873	0.857	0.842	0.826	0.797
3	0.971	0.942	0.915	0.889	0.864	0.840	0.816	0.794	0.772	0.751	0.712
4	0.961	0.924	0.888	0.855	0.823	0.792	0.763	0.735	0.708	0.683	0.636
5	0.951	0.906	0.883	0.822	0.784	0.747	0.713	0.681	0.650	0.621	0.567
6	0.942	0.888	0.837	0.790	0.746	0.705	0.666	0.630	0.596	0.564	0.507
7	0.933	0.871	0.813	0.760	0.711	0.665	0.623	0.583	0.547	0.513	0.452
8	0.923	0.853	0.789	0.731	0.677	0.627	0.582	0.540	0.502	0.467	0.404
9	0.914	0.837	0.766	0.703	0.645	0.592	0.544	0.500	0.460	0.424	0.361
10	0.905	0.820	0.744	0.676	0.614	0.558	0.508	0.463	0.422	0.386	0.322
11	0.896	0.804	0.722	0.650	0.585	0.527	0.475	0.429	0.388	0.350	0.287
12	0.887	0.788	0.701	0.625	0.557	0.497	0.444	0.397	0.356	0.319	0.257
13	0.879	0.773	0.681	0.601	0.530	0.469	0.415	0.368	0.326	0.290	0.229
14	0.870	0.758	0.661	0.577	0.505	0.442	0.388	0.340	0.299	0.263	0.205
15	0.861	0.743	0.642	0.555	0.481	0.417	0.362	0.315	0.275	0.239	0.183
16	0.853	0.728	0.623	0.534	0.458	0.394	0.339	0.292	0.252	0.218	0.163
17	0.844	0.714	0.605	0.513	0.436	0.371	0.317	0.270	0.231	0.198	0.146
18	0.836	0.700	0.587	0.494	0.416	0.350	0.296	0.250	0.212	0.180	0.130
19	0.828	0.686	0.570	0.475	0.396	0.331	0.277	0.232	0.194	0.164	0.116
20	0.820	0.673	0.554	0.456	0.377	0.312	0.258	0.215	0.178	0.149	0.104
21	0.811	0.660	0.538	0.439	0.359	0.294	0.242	0.199	0.164	0.135	0.093
22	0.803	0.647	0.522	0.422	0.342	0.278	0.226	0.184	0.150	0.123	0.083
23	0.795	0.634	0.507	0.406	0.326	0.262	0.211	0.170	0.138	0.112	0.074
24	0.788	0.622	0.492	0.390	0.310	0.247	0.197	0.158	0.126	0.102	0.066
25	0.780	0.610	0.478	0.375	0.295	0.233	0.184	0.146	0.116	0.092	0.059
26	0.772	0.598	0.464	0.361	0.281	0.220	0.172	0.135	0.106	0.084	0.053
27	0.764	0.586	0.450	0.347	0.268	0.207	0.161	0.125	0.098	0.076	0.047
28	0.757	0.574	0.437	0.333	0.255	0.196	0.150	0.116	0.090	0.069	0.042
29	0.749	0.563	0.424	0.321	0.243	0.185	0.141	0.107	0.082	0.063	0.037
30	0.742	0.552	0.412	0.308	0.231	0.174	0.131	0.099	0.075	0.057	0.033
40	0.672	0.453	0.307	0.208	0.142	0.097	0.067	0.046	0.032	0.022	0.011
50	0.608	0.372	0.228	0.141	0.087	0.054	0.034	0.021	0.013	0.009	0.003

Table B-1 (cont'd)

| Periods | \multicolumn{11}{c}{Present Value} |
	14%	15%	16%	18%	20%	25%	30%	35%	40%	45%	50%
1	0.877	0.870	0.862	0.847	0.833	0.800	0.769	0.741	0.714	0.690	0.667
2	0.769	0.756	0.743	0.718	0.694	0.640	0.592	0.549	0.510	0.476	0.444
3	0.675	0.658	0.641	0.609	0.579	0.512	0.455	0.406	0.364	0.328	0.296
4	0.592	0.572	0.552	0.516	0.482	0.410	0.350	0.301	0.260	0.226	0.198
5	0.519	0.497	0.476	0.437	0.402	0.328	0.269	0.223	0.186	0.156	0.132
6	0.456	0.432	0.410	0.370	0.335	0.262	0.207	0.165	0.133	0.108	0.088
7	0.400	0.376	0.354	0.314	0.279	0.210	0.159	0.122	0.095	0.074	0.059
8	0.351	0.327	0.305	0.266	0.233	0.168	0.123	0.091	0.068	0.051	0.039
9	0.308	0.284	0.263	0.225	0.194	0.134	0.094	0.067	0.048	0.035	0.026
10	0.270	0.247	0.227	0.191	0.162	0.107	0.073	0.050	0.035	0.024	0.017
11	0.237	0.215	0.195	0.162	0.135	0.086	0.056	0.037	0.025	0.017	0.012
12	0.208	0.187	0.168	0.137	0.112	0.069	0.043	0.027	0.018	0.012	0.008
13	0.182	0.163	0.145	0.116	0.093	0.055	0.033	0.020	0.013	0.008	0.005
14	0.160	0.141	0.125	0.099	0.078	0.044	0.025	0.015	0.009	0.006	0.003
15	0.140	0.123	0.108	0.084	0.065	0.035	0.020	0.011	0.006	0.004	0.002
16	0.123	0.107	0.093	0.071	0.054	0.028	0.015	0.008	0.005	0.003	0.002
17	0.108	0.093	0.080	0.060	0.045	0.023	0.012	0.006	0.003	0.002	0.001
18	0.095	0.081	0.069	0.051	0.038	0.018	0.009	0.005	0.002	0.001	0.001
19	0.083	0.070	0.060	0.043	0.031	0.014	0.007	0.003	0.002	0.001	
20	0.073	0.061	0.051	0.037	0.026	0.012	0.005	0.002	0.001	0.001	
21	0.064	0.053	0.044	0.031	0.022	0.009	0.004	0.002	0.001		
22	0.056	0.046	0.038	0.026	0.018	0.007	0.003	0.001	0.001		
23	0.049	0.040	0.033	0.022	0.015	0.006	0.002	0.001			
24	0.043	0.035	0.028	0.019	0.013	0.005	0.002	0.001			
25	0.038	0.030	0.024	0.016	0.010	0.004	0.001	0.001			
26	0.033	0.026	0.021	0.014	0.009	0.003	0.001				
27	0.029	0.023	0.018	0.011	0.007	0.002	0.001				
28	0.026	0.020	0.016	0.010	0.006	0.002	0.001				
29	0.022	0.017	0.014	0.008	0.005	0.002					
30	0.020	0.015	0.012	0.007	0.004	0.001					
40	0.005	0.004	0.003	0.001	0.001						
50	0.001	0.001	0.001								

Table B-2 *Present Value of Annuity of $1*

					Present Value						
Periods	**1%**	**2%**	**3%**	**4%**	**5%**	**6%**	**7%**	**8%**	**9%**	**10%**	**12%**
1	0.990	0.980	0.971	0.962	0.952	0.943	0.935	0.926	0.917	0.909	0.893
2	1.970	1.942	1.913	1.886	1.859	1.833	1.808	1.783	1.759	1.736	1.690
3	2.941	2.884	2.829	2.775	2.723	2.673	2.624	2.577	2.531	2.487	2.402
4	3.902	3.808	3.717	3.630	3.546	3.465	3.387	3.312	3.240	3.170	3.037
5	4.853	4.713	4.580	4.452	4.329	4.212	4.100	3.993	3.890	3.791	3.605
6	5.795	5.601	5.417	5.242	5.076	4.917	4.767	4.623	4.486	4.355	4.111
7	6.728	6.472	6.230	6.002	5.786	5.582	5.389	5.206	5.033	4.868	4.564
8	7.652	7.325	7.020	6.733	6.463	6.210	5.971	5.747	5.535	5.335	4.968
9	8.566	8.162	7.786	7.435	7.108	6.802	6.515	6.247	5.995	5.759	5.328
10	9.471	8.983	8.530	8.111	7.722	7.360	7.024	6.710	6.418	6.145	5.650
11	10.368	9.787	9.253	8.760	8.306	7.887	7.499	7.139	6.805	6.495	5.938
12	11.255	10.575	9.954	9.385	8.863	8.384	7.943	7.536	7.161	6.814	6.194
13	12.134	11.348	10.635	9.986	9.394	8.853	8.358	7.904	7.487	7.103	6.424
14	13.004	12.106	11.296	10.563	9.899	9.295	8.745	8.244	7.786	7.367	6.628
15	13.865	12.849	11.938	11.118	10.380	9.712	9.108	8.559	8.061	7.606	6.811
16	14.718	13.578	12.561	11.652	10.838	10.106	9.447	8.851	8.313	7.824	6.974
17	15.562	14.292	13.166	12.166	11.274	10.477	9.763	9.122	8.544	8.022	7.120
18	16.398	14.992	13.754	12.659	11.690	10.828	10.059	9.372	8.756	8.201	7.250
19	17.226	15.678	14.324	13.134	12.085	11.158	10.336	9.604	8.950	8.365	7.366
20	18.046	16.351	14.878	13.590	12.462	11.470	10.594	9.818	9.129	8.514	7.469
21	18.857	17.011	15.415	14.029	12.821	11.764	10.836	10.017	9.292	8.649	7.562
22	19.660	17.658	15.937	14.451	13.163	12.042	11.061	10.201	9.442	8.772	7.645
23	20.456	18.292	16.444	14.857	13.489	12.303	11.272	10.371	9.580	8.883	7.718
24	21.243	18.914	16.936	15.247	13.799	12.550	11.469	10.529	9.707	8.985	7.784
25	22.023	19.523	17.413	15.622	14.094	12.783	11.654	10.675	9.823	9.077	7.843
26	22.795	20.121	17.877	15.983	14.375	13.003	11.826	10.810	9.929	9.161	7.896
27	23.560	20.707	18.327	16.330	14.643	13.211	11.987	10.935	10.027	9.237	7.943
28	24.316	21.281	18.764	16.663	14.898	13.406	12.137	11.051	10.116	9.307	7.984
29	25.066	21.844	19.189	16.984	15.141	13.591	12.278	11.158	10.198	9.370	8.022
30	25.808	22.396	19.600	17.292	15.373	13.765	12.409	11.258	10.274	9.427	8.055
40	32.835	27.355	23.115	19.793	17.159	15.046	13.332	11.925	10.757	9.779	8.244
50	39.196	31.424	25.730	21.482	18.256	15.762	13.801	12.234	10.962	9.915	8.305

Table B-2 *(cont'd)*

					Present Value						
Periods	14%	15%	16%	18%	20%	25%	30%	35%	40%	45%	50%
1	0.877	0.870	0.862	0.847	0.833	0.800	0.769	0.741	0.714	0.690	0.667
2	1.647	1.626	1.605	1.566	1.528	1.440	1.361	1.289	1.224	1.165	1.111
3	2.322	2.283	2.246	2.174	2.106	1.952	1.816	1.696	1.589	1.493	1.407
4	2.914	2.855	2.798	2.690	2.589	2.362	2.166	1.997	1.849	1.720	1.605
5	3.433	3.352	3.274	3.127	2.991	2.689	2.436	2.220	2.035	1.876	1.737
6	3.889	3.784	3.685	3.498	3.326	2.951	2.643	2.385	2.168	1.983	1.824
7	4.288	4.160	4.039	3.812	3.605	3.161	2.802	2.508	2.263	2.057	1.883
8	4.639	4.487	4.344	4.078	3.837	3.329	2.925	2.598	2.331	2.109	1.922
9	4.946	4.772	4.607	4.303	4.031	3.463	3.019	2.665	2.379	2.144	1.948
10	5.216	5.019	4.833	4.494	4.192	3.571	3.092	2.715	2.414	2.168	1.965
11	5.453	5.234	5.029	4.656	4.327	3.656	3.147	2.752	2.438	2.185	1.977
12	5.660	5.421	5.197	4.793	4.439	3.725	3.190	2.779	2.456	2.197	1.985
13	5.842	5.583	5.342	4.910	4.533	3.780	3.223	2.799	2.469	2.204	1.990
14	6.002	5.724	5.468	5.008	4.611	3.824	3.249	2.814	2.478	2.210	1.993
15	6.142	5.847	5.575	5.092	4.675	3.859	3.268	2.825	2.484	2.214	1.995
16	6.265	5.954	5.669	5.162	4.730	3.887	3.283	2.834	2.489	2.216	1.997
17	6.373	6.047	5.749	5.222	4.775	3.910	3.295	2.840	2.492	2.218	1.998
18	6.467	6.128	5.818	5.273	4.812	3.928	3.304	2.844	2.494	2.219	1.999
19	6.550	6.198	5.877	5.316	4.844	3.942	3.311	2.848	2.496	2.220	1.999
20	6.623	6.259	5.929	5.353	4.870	3.954	3.316	2.850	2.497	2.221	1.999
21	6.687	6.312	5.973	5.384	4.891	3.963	3.320	2.852	2.498	2.221	2.000
22	6.743	6.359	6.011	5.410	4.909	3.970	3.323	2.853	2.498	2.222	2.000
23	6.792	6.399	6.044	5.432	4.925	3.976	3.325	2.854	2.499	2.222	2.000
24	6.835	6.434	6.073	5.451	4.937	3.981	3.327	2.855	2.499	2.222	2.000
25	6.873	6.464	6.097	5.467	4.948	3.985	3.329	2.856	2.499	2.222	2.000
26	6.906	6.491	6.118	5.480	4.956	3.988	3.330	2.856	2.500	2.222	2.000
27	6.935	6.514	6.136	5.492	4.964	3.990	3.331	2.856	2.500	2.222	2.000
28	6.961	6.534	6.152	5.502	4.970	3.992	3.331	2.857	2.500	2.222	2.000
29	6.983	6.551	6.166	5.510	4.975	3.994	3.332	2.857	2.500	2.222	2.000
30	7.003	6.566	6.177	5.517	4.979	3.995	3.332	2.857	2.500	2.222	2.000
40	7.105	6.642	6.234	5.548	4.997	3.999	3.333	2.857	2.500	2.222	2.000
50	7.133	6.661	6.246	5.554	4.999	4.000	3.333	2.857	2.500	2.222	2.000

Table B-3 *Future Value of $1*

					Future Value								
Periods	1%	2%	3%	4%	5%	6%	7%	8%	9%	10%	12%	14%	15%
1	1.010	1.020	1.030	1.040	1.050	1.060	1.070	1.080	1.090	1.100	1.120	1.140	1.150
2	1.020	1.040	1.061	1.082	1.103	1.124	1.145	1.166	1.188	1.210	1.254	1.300	1.323
3	1.030	1.061	1.093	1.125	1.158	1.191	1.225	1.260	1.295	1.331	1.405	1.482	1.521
4	1.041	1.082	1.126	1.170	1.216	1.262	1.311	1.360	1.412	1.464	1.574	1.689	1.749
5	1.051	1.104	1.159	1.217	1.276	1.338	1.403	1.469	1.539	1.611	1.762	1.925	2.011
6	1.062	1.126	1.194	1.265	1.340	1.419	1.501	1.587	1.677	1.772	1.974	2.195	2.313
7	1.072	1.149	1.230	1.316	1.407	1.501	1.606	1.714	1.828	1.949	2.211	2.502	2.660
8	1.083	1.172	1.267	1.369	1.477	1.594	1.718	1.851	1.993	2.144	2.476	2.853	3.059
9	1.094	1.195	1.305	1.423	1.551	1.689	1.838	1.999	2.172	2.358	2.773	3.252	3.518
10	1.105	1.219	1.344	1.480	1.629	1.791	1.967	2.159	2.367	2.594	3.106	3.707	4.046
11	1.116	1.243	1.384	1.539	1.710	1.898	2.105	2.332	2.580	2.853	3.479	4.226	4.652
12	1.127	1.268	1.426	1.601	1.796	2.012	2.252	2.518	2.813	3.138	3.896	4.818	5.350
13	1.138	1.294	1.469	1.665	1.886	2.133	2.410	2.720	3.066	3.452	4.363	5.492	6.153
14	1.149	1.319	1.513	1.732	1.980	2.261	2.579	2.937	3.342	3.798	4.887	6.261	7.076
15	1.161	1.346	1.558	1.801	2.079	2.397	2.759	3.172	3.642	4.177	5.474	7.138	8.137
16	1.173	1.373	1.605	1.873	2.183	2.540	2.952	3.426	3.970	4.595	6.130	8.137	9.358
17	1.184	1.400	1.653	1.948	2.292	2.693	3.159	3.700	4.328	5.054	6.866	9.276	10.76
18	1.196	1.428	1.702	2.026	2.407	2.854	3.380	3.996	4.717	5.560	7.690	10.58	12.38
19	1.208	1.457	1.754	2.107	2.527	3.026	3.617	4.316	5.142	6.116	8.613	12.06	14.23
20	1.220	1.486	1.806	2.191	2.653	3.207	3.870	4.661	5.604	6.728	9.646	13.74	16.37
21	1.232	1.516	1.860	2.279	2.786	3.400	4.141	5.034	6.109	7.400	10.80	15.67	18.82
22	1.245	1.546	1.916	2.370	2.925	3.604	4.430	5.437	6.659	8.140	12.10	17.86	21.64
23	1.257	1.577	1.974	2.465	3.072	3.820	4.741	5.871	7.258	8.954	13.55	20.36	24.89
24	1.270	1.608	2.033	2.563	3.225	4.049	5.072	6.341	7.911	9.850	15.18	23.21	28.63
25	1.282	1.641	2.094	2.666	3.386	4.292	5.427	6.848	8.623	10.83	17.00	26.46	32.92
26	1.295	1.673	2.157	2.772	3.556	4.549	5.807	7.396	9.399	11.92	19.04	30.17	37.86
27	1.308	1.707	2.221	2.883	3.733	4.822	6.214	7.988	10.25	13.11	21.32	34.39	43.54
28	1.321	1.741	2.288	2.999	3.920	5.112	6.649	8.627	11.17	14.42	23.88	39.20	50.07
29	1.335	1.776	2.357	3.119	4.116	5.418	7.114	9.317	12.17	15.86	26.75	44.69	57.58
30	1.348	1.811	2.427	3.243	4.322	5.743	7.612	10.06	13.27	17.45	29.96	50.95	66.21
40	1.489	2.208	3.262	4.801	7.040	10.29	14.97	21.72	31.41	45.26	93.05	188.9	267.9
50	1.645	2.692	4.384	7.107	11.47	18.42	29.46	46.90	74.36	117.4	289.0	700.2	1,084.0

Table B-4 Future Value of Annuity of $1

						Future Value							
Periods	1%	2%	3%	4%	5%	6%	7%	8%	9%	10%	12%	14%	15%
1	1.000	1.000	1.000	1.000	1.000	1.000	1.000	1.000	1.000	1.000	1.000	1.000	1.000
2	2.010	2.020	2.030	2.040	2.050	2.060	2.070	2.080	2.090	2.100	2.120	2.140	2.150
3	3.030	3.060	3.091	3.122	3.153	3.184	3.215	3.246	3.278	3.310	3.374	3.440	3.473
4	4.060	4.122	4.184	4.246	4.310	4.375	4.440	4.506	4.573	4.641	4.779	4.921	4.993
5	5.101	5.204	5.309	5.416	5.526	5.637	5.751	5.867	5.985	6.105	6.353	6.610	6.742
6	6.152	6.308	6.468	6.633	6.802	6.975	7.153	7.336	7.523	7.716	8.115	8.536	8.754
7	7.214	7.434	7.662	7.898	8.142	8.394	8.654	8.923	9.200	9.487	10.09	10.73	11.07
8	8.286	8.583	8.892	9.214	9.549	9.897	10.26	10.64	11.03	11.44	12.30	13.23	13.73
9	9.369	9.755	10.16	10.58	11.03	11.49	11.98	12.49	13.02	13.58	14.78	16.09	16.79
10	10.46	10.95	11.46	12.01	12.58	13.18	13.82	14.49	15.19	15.94	17.55	19.34	20.30
11	11.57	12.17	12.81	13.49	14.21	14.97	15.78	16.65	17.56	18.53	20.65	23.04	24.35
12	12.68	13.41	14.19	15.03	15.92	16.87	17.89	18.98	20.14	21.38	24.13	27.27	29.00
13	13.81	14.68	15.62	16.63	17.71	18.88	20.14	21.50	22.95	24.52	28.03	32.09	34.35
14	14.95	15.97	17.09	18.29	19.60	21.02	22.55	24.21	26.02	27.98	32.39	37.58	40.50
15	16.10	17.29	18.60	20.02	21.58	23.28	25.13	27.15	29.36	31.77	37.28	43.84	47.58
16	17.26	18.64	20.16	21.82	23.66	25.67	27.89	30.32	33.00	35.95	42.75	50.98	55.72
17	18.43	20.01	21.76	23.70	25.84	28.21	30.84	33.75	36.97	40.54	48.88	59.12	65.08
18	19.61	21.41	23.41	25.65	28.13	30.91	34.00	37.45	41.30	45.60	55.75	68.39	75.84
19	20.81	22.84	25.12	27.67	30.54	33.76	37.38	41.45	46.02	51.16	63.44	78.97	88.21
20	22.02	24.30	26.87	29.78	33.07	36.79	41.00	45.76	51.16	57.28	72.05	91.02	102.4
21	23.24	25.78	28.68	31.97	35.72	39.99	44.87	50.42	56.76	64.00	81.70	104.8	118.8
22	24.47	27.30	30.54	34.25	38.51	43.39	49.01	55.46	62.87	71.40	92.50	120.4	137.6
23	25.72	28.85	32.45	36.62	41.43	47.00	53.44	60.89	69.53	79.54	104.6	138.3	159.3
24	26.97	30.42	34.43	39.08	44.50	50.82	58.18	66.76	76.79	88.50	118.2	158.7	184.2
25	28.24	32.03	36.46	41.65	47.73	54.86	63.25	73.11	84.70	98.35	133.3	181.9	212.8
26	29.53	33.67	38.55	44.31	51.11	59.16	68.68	79.95	93.32	109.2	150.3	208.3	245.7
27	30.82	35.34	40.71	47.08	54.67	63.71	74.48	87.35	102.7	121.1	169.4	238.5	283.6
28	32.13	37.05	42.93	49.97	58.40	68.53	80.70	95.34	113.0	134.2	190.7	272.9	327.1
29	33.45	38.79	45.22	52.97	62.32	73.64	87.35	104.0	124.1	148.6	214.6	312.1	377.2
30	34.78	40.57	47.58	56.08	66.44	79.06	94.46	113.3	136.3	164.5	241.3	356.8	434.7
40	48.89	60.40	75.40	95.03	120.8	154.8	199.6	259.1	337.9	442.6	767.1	1,342.0	1,779.0
50	64.46	84.58	112.8	152.7	209.3	290.3	406.5	573.8	815.1	1,164.0	2,400.0	4,995.0	7,218.0

Appendix C

TYPICAL CHARTS OF ACCOUNTS FOR SERVICE PROPRIETORSHIPS AND SERVICE PARTNERSHIPS (ASPE)

ASSETS

Cash
Accounts Receivable
Allowance for
   Doubtful Accounts
Notes Receivable,
   Short-Term
Goods and Services Tax
   Recoverable
Harmonized Sales Tax
   Recoverable
Interest Receivable
Supplies
Prepaid Rent
Prepaid Insurance
Notes Receivable,
   Long-Term
Land
Furniture
Accumulated
   Amortization—
   Furniture
Equipment
Accumulated
   Amortization—
   Equipment
Building
Accumulated
   Amortization—
   Building

LIABILITIES

Accounts Payable
Notes Payable,
   Short-Term
Salaries Payable
Wages Payable
Goods and Services Tax
   Payable
Harmonized Sales Tax
   Payable
Employee Income Tax
   Payable
Employment Insurance
   Payable
Canada Pension Plan
   Payable
Quebec Pension Plan
   Payable
Employee Benefits
   Payable
Interest Payable
Unearned Service
   Revenue
Notes Payable,
   Long-Term

OWNER'S EQUITY

Owner, Capital
Owner, Withdrawals

Revenues and Gains

Service Revenue
Interest Revenue
Gain on Sale of Land (or
   Furniture, Equipment,
   or Building)

Expenses and Losses

Salaries Expense
Wages Expense
Employee Benefits
   Expense
Insurance Expense for
   Employees
Rent Expense
Insurance Expense
Supplies Expense
Bad-Debt Expense
Amortization
   Expense—Furniture
Amortization
   Expense—Equipment
Amortization
   Expense—Building
Property Tax Expense
Interest Expense
Miscellaneous Expense
Loss on Sale
   (or Exchange) of Land
   (Furniture, Equipment,
   or Buildings)

SERVICE PARTNERSHIP

Same as Service Proprietorship, except for Owners' Equity:

OWNERS' EQUITY

Partner 1, Capital
Partner 2, Capital
Partner N, Capital
Partner 1, Withdrawals
Partner 2, Withdrawals
Partner N, Withdrawals

MERCHANDISING CORPORATION

ASSETS	LIABILITIES	SHAREHOLDERS' EQUITY	

ASSETS	LIABILITIES	SHAREHOLDERS' EQUITY	Expenses and Losses
Cash	Accounts Payable	Common Shares	Cost of Goods Sold
Short-Term	Notes Payable,	Retained Earnings	Salaries Expense
Investments	Short-Term	Dividends	Wages Expense
Fair-Value Valuation	Current Portion of Bonds		Commission Expense
Allowance	Payable	**Revenues and Gains**	Payroll Benefits Expense
Allowance for Doubtful	Salaries Payable		Insurance Expense for
Accounts	Wages Payable	Sales Revenue	Employees
Notes Receivable,	Goods and Services Tax	Interest Revenue	Rent Expense
Short-Term	Payable	Dividend Revenue	Insurance Expense
Goods and Services Tax	Harmonized Sales Tax	Equity-Method	Supplies Expense
Recoverable	Payable	Investment Revenue	Bad-Debt Expense
Harmonized Sales Tax	Employee Income Tax	Gain on Sale of Investments	Depreciation
Recoverable	Payable	Unrealized Gain on	Expense—Land
Interest Receivable	Employment Insurance	Short-Term Investments	Improvements
Inventory	Payable	Gain on Sale of Land	Depreciation
Supplies	Canada Pension Plan	(Furniture and Fixtures,	Expense—Furniture
Prepaid Rent	Payable	Equipment, or Building)	and Fixtures
Prepaid Insurance	Quebec Pension Plan	Discontinued	Depreciation
Notes Receivable,	Payable	Operations—Gain	Expense—Equipment
Long-Term	Employee Benefits		Depreciation
Investment Subject to	Payable		Expense—Buildings
Significant Influence	Interest Payable		Depreciation
Long-Term	Income Tax Payable		Expense—Franchises
Investments	Unearned Service Revenue		Depreciation
Other Receivables,	Notes Payable,		Expense—Leaseholds
Long-Term	Long-Term		Incorporation Expense
Land	Bonds Payable		Income Tax Expense
Land Improvements	Lease Liability		Loss on Writedown of
Accumulated	Non-Controlling		Goodwill
Depreciation—	Interest		Loss on Sale of Investments
Land Improvements			Unrealized Loss on
Furniture and Fixtures			Short-Term Investments
Accumulated			Loss on Sale (or Exchange)
Depreciation—Furniture			of Land (or Furniture and
and Fixtures			Fixtures, Equipment, or
Equipment			Buildings)
Accumulated			Discontinued
Depreciation—			Operations—Loss
Equipment			
Buildings			
Accumulated			
Depreciation—Buildings			
Organization Cost			
Franchises			
Patents			
Leaseholds			
Goodwill			

Glossary

Accounts receivable turnover Ratio of net credit sales to average net accounts receivable. Measures ability to collect cash from credit customers (p. 1143).

Acid-test ratio Ratio of the sum of cash plus short-term investments plus net current receivables to current liabilities. Tells whether the entity could pay all its current liabilities if they came due immediately. Also called the *quick ratio* (p. 1142).

Actively traded Financial instruments that are easily bought or sold because there are a lot of them in the market and it is easy to find someone who is willing to engage in a transaction (p. 992).

Affiliated company An investment in a company in which there is significant influence and 20-to-50-percent ownership. These investments are accounted for using the equity method (p. 1001).

Amortized cost method To account for long-term bond investments, the discount or premium is amortized to more accurately reflect the interest revenue. These bonds are reported at their amortized cost (p. 1011).

Appropriations Restriction of retained earnings that is recorded by a formal journal entry (p. 884).

Arrears To be behind or overdue in a debt payment (p. 826).

Articles of incorporation The document issued by the federal or provincial government giving the incorporators permission to form a corporation (p. 811).

Asset revaluation Adjust asset values to reflect current market values usually based on an independent appraisal of the assets (p. 773).

Authorization of shares Provision in a corporation's articles of incorporation that permits a corporation to sell a certain number of shares of stock (p. 812).

Authorized shares The number of shares a corporation is allowed to sell according to the articles of incorporation (p. 812).

Bearer bonds Bonds payable to the person that has possession of them. Also called *unregistered bonds* (p. 921).

Benchmarking Comparison of current performance with some standard. The standard often is the performance level of a leading outside organization (p. 1137).

Bid price The highest price that a buyer is willing to pay for a bond (p. 922).

Blended payments Payments are a constant amount, and the amount of interest and principal that are applied to the loan change with each payment (p. 942).

Board of directors Group elected by the shareholders to set policy for a corporation and to appoint its officers (p. 812).

Bond A formal agreement in which a lender loans money to a borrower, who agrees to repay the money loaned at a future date and agrees to pay interest regularly over the life of the bond (p. 919).

Bond indenture The contract that specifies the maturity value of the bonds, the stated (contract) interest rate, and the dates for paying interest and principal (p. 919).

Bonds payable Groups of notes payable (bonds) issued to multiple lenders called bondholders (p. 919).

Book value Amount of shareholders' equity on the company's books for each share of its stock (p. 828).

Book value per common share Common shareholders' equity divided by the number of common shares outstanding (p. 1150).

Bylaws Constitution for governing a corporation (p. 812).

Callable bonds Bonds that the issuer may call or pay off at a specified price whenever the issuer wants (p. 938).

Capital lease Lease agreement that substantially transfers all the benefits and risks of ownership from the lessor to the lessee (p. 944).

Cash equivalents Highly liquid short-term investments that can be converted into cash with little delay (p. 1056).

Cash flow statement Reports cash receipts and cash payments classified according to the entity's major activities: operating, investing, and financing (p. 1054).

Cash flows Cash receipts and cash payments (disbursements) (p. 1054).

Certificate of deposit (CD) A secure form of investment with a fixed interest rate and term. Unlike a bank account, they must be held to maturity (p. 992).

Chairperson (of board) Elected person on a corporation's board of directors; usually the most powerful person in the corporation (p. 812).

Closely held Describes a corporation with only a few shareholders (p. 830).

Common-size statement A financial statement that reports only percentages (no dollar amounts); a type of vertical analysis (p. 1136).

Common shares The most basic form of share capital. In describing a corporation, the common shareholders are the owners of the business (p. 814).

Companion account An account that is typically paired with another account (p. 994).

Consolidated statements Financial statements of the parent company plus those of majority-owned subsidiaries as if the combination were a single legal entity (pp. 989, 1004).

Consolidation A decrease in the number of shares outstanding by a fixed ratio. Also called a *reverse split* (p. 867).

Contract interest rate Interest rate that determines the amount of cash interest the borrower pays and the investor receives each year. Also called the *stated interest rate* (p. 923).

Contributed capital A corporation's capital from investments by the shareholders. Also called *share capital* or *capital stock* (p. 814).

Controlling interest Ownership of more than 50 percent of an investee company's voting shares. Also called *minority interest* (p. 1002).

Convertible bonds (or notes) Bonds (or notes) that may be converted into the common shares of the issuing company at the option of the investor (p. 939).

Convertible preferred shares Preferred shares that may be exchanged by the preferred shareholders, if they choose, for another class of shares in the corporation (p. 822).

Counterbalancing transaction Engaging in a second transaction to offset the risk of the first transaction (p. 1017).

Coupon rate Represents the contractual rate of interest that the issuer must pay the bondholders (p. 920).

Cumulative preferred shares Preferred shares whose owners must receive all dividends in arrears before the corporation pays dividends to the common shareholders (p. 827).

Currency option A contract that can be purchased to guarantee the right to a future exchange rate (p. 1018).

Current ratio Current assets divided by current liabilities. Measures the ability to pay current liabilities from current assets (p. 1140).

Date of record On this date, which is a few weeks after the declaration of the dividend, the list of shareholders who will receive the dividend is compiled (p. 824).

Days' sales in receivables Ratio of average net accounts receivable to one day's sales. Tells how many days' sales remain in Accounts Receivable awaiting collection (p. 1144).

Debenture Unsecured bond, backed only by the good faith of the issuer (p. 921).

Debt ratio Ratio of total liabilities to total assets. Tells the proportion of a company's assets that it has financed with debt (p. 1144).

Declaration date The date on which the board of directors announces the dividend. There is a liability created on this date (p. 824).

Deficit Debit balance in the retained earnings account (p. 815).

Denominated To be expressed in terms of a monetary unit (p. 1017).

Direct method Format of the operating activities section of the cash flow statement that shows cash receipts from and cash payments for operating activities (p. 1060).

Discount Amount of bond's issue price under its maturity (par) value (p. 921).

Dissolution Ending of a partnership (p. 756).

Dividend yield Ratio of dividends per share to the share's market price per share. Tells the percentage of a share's market value that the company pays to shareholders as dividends (p. 1149).

Dividends Distributions by a corporation to its shareholders (p. 815).

Double taxation Corporations pay their own income taxes on corporate income. Then, the shareholders pay personal income tax on the cash dividends that they receive from corporations (p. 811).

Downside risk An estimate of the potential loss from a change in market conditions (p. 1149).

Earnings per share (EPS) Amount of a company's net income per outstanding common share (pp. 867, 1148).

Effective-interest amortization (of a bond) Amortization method in which a different amount of amortization expense is assigned to each year (or period) of the bond's life. The amount of amortization expense is the same percentage of a bond's carrying value for every period over a bond's life (p. 930).

Effective interest rate Interest rate that investors demand in order to loan their money. Also called the *market interest rate* (p. 923).

Efficient capital market One in which the market prices fully reflect the impact of all information available to the public (p. 1151).

Equity method for investments The method used to account for investments in which the investor generally has 20 to 50 percent of the investor's voting shares and can significantly influence the decisions of the investee. The investment account is debited for ownership in the investee's net income and credited for ownership in the investee's dividends (p. 992).

Equity ratio Ratio of total shareholders' equity to total assets. Tells the proportion of assets financed by the owners of the company (p. 1145).

Face value Another name for maturity value of a bond (p. 915).

Factors Companies that purchase other firms' accounts receivable at a discount. Receivables are sold so that the cash can be received more quickly (p. 1144).

Fair-value method The method of accounting for short-term investments that values them at their fair, or market, value on the year-end balance sheet date. Any gain or loss resulting from the change in fair value is recognized in net income for the period in which it arises, and fair value becomes the new carrying value of the shares. Also called the *market-value method* (p. 993).

Financial instrument A contract that creates an asset for one party and a liability or equity for another (p. 1010).

Financing activity Activity that obtains the funds from investors and creditors needed to launch and sustain the business; a section of the cash flow statement (p. 1057).

Foreign-currency exchange rate The measure of one currency against another currency (p. 1014).

Foreign-currency transaction gain The gain that occurs when a cash payment is less than the related account payable or a cash receipt is greater than the related account receivable due to a change in exchange rate between the transaction date and the payment date (p. 1016).

Foreign-currency transaction loss The loss that occurs when a cash payment is greater than the related account payable or a cash receipt is less than the related account receivable due to a change in exchange rate between the transaction date and the payment date (p. 1016).

Forward contract An agreement to purchase a product at a specified future date and price (p. 1017).

Free cash flow The amount of cash available from operations after paying for planned investments in plant, equipment, and other long-term assets (p. 1060).

Fully diluted EPS Earnings per share calculated using the number of outstanding common shares plus the number of additional common shares that would arise from conversion of convertible bonds and convertible preferred shares into common shares (p. 879).

Functional currency The main currency used by a business for most transactions and reporting (p. 1020).

Futures contract A contract that can be purchased to guarantee the right to a product at a specified price in the future (p. 1018).

General partnership A form of partnership in which each partner is an owner of the business, with all the privileges and risks of ownership (p. 759).

Hedging A way to protect oneself from losing money in a foreign-currency transaction by engaging in a counterbalancing foreign-currency transaction (p. 1017).

Horizontal analysis Study of percentage changes in comparative financial statements (p. 1130).

Indirect method Format of the operating activities section of the cash flow statement that starts with net income and shows the reconciliation from net income to operating cash flows. Also called the *reconciliation method* (p. 1060).

Initial public offering (IPO) The first time a particular class of a corporation's shares are sold to investors (p. 818).

Inventory turnover Ratio of cost of goods sold to average inventory. Measures the number of times a company sells its average level of inventory during a year (p. 1142).

Investing activity Activity that increases and decreases the long-term assets available to the business; a section of the cash flow statement (p. 1057).

Issue price The price at which shareholders first purchase shares from the corporation (p. 817).

Issued shares Shares that are offered for sale to investors (p. 817).

Lease Agreement in which the tenant (lessee) agrees to make rent payments to the property owner (lessor) in exchange for the exclusive use of the asset (p. 943).

Lessee Tenant, or user of the asset, in a lease agreement (p. 943).

Lessor Property owner in a lease agreement (p. 943).

Leverage The use of financial instruments to increase the potential return on investment; in other words, borrowing money at a particular interest rate and using it to make investments that earn a higher rate of return than that interest rate. Another name for trading on the equity (pp. 832, 1147).

Limited liability No personal obligation of a shareholder for corporation debts. The most that a shareholder can lose on an investment in a corporation's shares is the cost of the investment (p. 811).

Limited liability partnership (LLP) A partnership in which each partner's personal liability for the business's debts is limited to a certain dollar amount (p. 759).

Limited partnership A partnership with at least two classes of partners: a general partner and limited partners (p. 759).

Liquid assets Assets that can be converted to cash quickly. Often they are financial instruments that can be sold without a discount (p. 1140).

Liquidation The process of going out of business by selling the entity's assets and paying its liabilities. The final step in liquidation of a business is the distribution of any remaining cash to the owners (p. 776).

Liquidation value (redemption value or call value) The amount of capital that a preferred shareholder would receive per preferred share upon liquidation of the corporation (p. 829).

Liquidity Ability to meet current payments as they come due (p. 1139).

Long-term investments Investments that a company intends to hold for more than one year (p. 992).

Long-term liabilities Debts due to be paid in more than a year or more than one of the entity's operating cycles if an operating cycle is greater than one year (p. 919).

Long-term solvency The ability to generate enough cash to pay long-term debts as they mature (p. 1129).

Majority Interest Another name for controlling interest (p. 1002).

Market interest rate Interest rate that investors demand in order to loan their money. Also called the *effective interest rate* (p. 923).

Market value Price for which a person could buy or sell a share (p. 828).

Market-value method Another name for the fair-value method of accounting for short-term investments in shares (p. 993).

Maturity date The date on which the borrower must pay the principal amount to the lender (p. 919).

Maturity value A bond issued at par that has no discount or premium. Also another name for a bond's principal value (p. 919).

Memorandum entry A journal entry without debits and credits (p. 867).

Minority interest Another name for non-controlling interest (p. 1007).

Money market fund An investment product generally considered safe because it invests in short-term debt securities, such as certificates of deposit (p. 992).

Mortgage Borrower's promise to transfer the legal title to certain assets to the lender if the debt is not paid on schedule. A mortgage is a special type of *secured bond* (p. 921).

Mutual agency Every partner can bind the business to a contract within the scope of the partnership's regular business operations (p. 757, 811).

Non-controlling interest A subsidiary company's equity that is held by shareholders other than the parent company. Also called *minority interest* (p. 1007).

No-par-value shares Shares that do not have a value assigned to them by the articles of incorporation (p. 818).

Off-balance-sheet financing Acquisition of assets or services whose resulting debt is not reported on the balance sheet (p. 946).

Operating activity Activity that creates revenue or expense in the entity's major line of business. A section of the cash flow statement. Operating activities affect the income statement (p. 1056).

Operating lease Usually a short-term or cancelable rental agreement (p. 943).

Organization costs The costs of organizing a corporation, including legal fees, and charges by promoters for selling the shares. Organization cost is an intangible asset under ASPE but is written off as an expense under IFRS (p. 823).

Outstanding shares Shares in the hands of a shareholder (p. 817).

Par value An arbitrary value assigned when certain shares are initially offered to the public; these types of shares are not common in Canada. Also another name for maturity value of a bond (pp. 818, 919, 921).

Parent company An investor company that generally owns more than 50 percent of the voting shares of a subsidiary company (p. 1002).

Partnership An unincorporated business with two or more owners (p. 754).

Partnership agreement Agreement that is the contract between partners specifying such items as the name, location, and nature of the business; the name, capital investment, and duties of each partner; and the method of sharing profits and losses by the partners (p. 756).

Preemptive right Existing shareholders are given the right to purchase additional shares of the company before the shares are offered to others. This would give existing shareholders the opportunity to maintain the same percentage of ownership as they would have had before the new shares were issued (p. 816).

Preferred shares Shares of stock that give its owners certain advantages over common shareholders, such as the priority to receive dividends before the common shareholders and the priority to receive assets before the common shareholders if the corporation liquidates (p. 820).

Premium Excess of bond's issue price over its maturity (par) value (p. 921).

Present value Amount a person would invest now to receive a greater amount at a future date (p. 922).

Presentation currency The currency in which the financial statements are presented (p. 1020).

President Chief operating officer in charge of managing the day-to-day operations of a corporation (p. 812).

Price/earnings (P/E) ratio Ratio of the market price of a common share to the company's earnings per share. Measures the value that the stock market places on $1 of a company's earnings (p. 1149).

Price-to-earnings ratio (or price-earnings ratio, or P/E) The market price of a share divided by its earnings per share (EPS) (p. 879).

Principal value The amount a company borrows from a bondholder. Also called the bond's *maturity value*, *par value*, or *face value* (pp. 919, 921).

Private corporation A corporation that does not issue shares that are traded on a stock exchange (p. 811).

Proportionate consolidation The venturer combines its share of the interest in the assets, liabilities, revenues, and expenses of a joint venture with its own assets, liabilities, revenues, and expenses in its consolidated financial statements (p. 1001).

Proportionate share The same amount of shares in relation to others before and after an event such as a new issue of shares (p. 816).

Prospective In the future. For example, changes in accounting estimates are reflected in future financial statements, *not* in past financial statements (p. 884).

Prospectus A mandatory legal document that describes an investment to potential purchasers (p. 818).

Proxy A formal appointment of one person to cast a vote for another person (p. 813).

Public corporation A corporation that issues shares that are traded on a stock exchange (p. 810).

Quick ratio Ratio of the sum of cash plus short-term investments plus net current receivables to current liabilities. Tells whether the entity could pay all its current liabilities if they came due immediately. Another name for the acid-test ratio (p. 1142).

Rate of return on common shareholders' equity Net income minus preferred dividends, divided by average common shareholders' equity. A measure of profitability. Also called *return on equity (ROE)* or *return on common shareholders' equity* (pp. 831, 1147).

Rate of return on net sales Ratio of net income to net sales. A measure of profitability. Also called *return on sales* (p. 1146).

Rate of return on total assets The sum of net income plus interest expense divided by average total assets. This ratio measures the success a company has in using its assets to earn income for the persons who finance the business. Also called *return on assets (ROA)* (pp. 831, 1146).

Rebuttable assumption A conclusion that something is true unless proven that it isn't (p. 1019).

Reconciliation method Another name for the indirect method of formatting the operating activities section of the cash flow statement (p. 1076).

Redeemable bonds Bonds that give the purchaser the option of retiring them at a stated dollar amount prior to maturity (p. 938).

Repurchase of own shares A corporation repurchases its own shares that it issued previously (p. 869).

Retained earnings A corporation's capital that is earned through profitable operation of the business (p. 814).

Retrospective In the past. For example, changes in accounting policies are reflected in past financial-statement figures as if those policies had always been in place (p. 883).

Return on assets (ROA) Another name for *rate of return on total assets* (pp. 831, 1146).

Return on equity (ROE) Another name for *rate of return on common shareholders' equity* (pp. 831, 1147).

Return on sales (ROS) Another name for *rate of return on net sales* (p. 1146).

Return on shareholders' equity Another name for *rate of return on common shareholders' equity* (p. 1147).

Reverse split Another name for a consolidation (p. 867).

Secured bond A bond that gives the bondholder the right to take specified assets of the issuer if the issuer fails to pay principal or interest. A mortgage is a special type of secured bond (p. 921).

Segment of the business A significant part of a company (p. 875).

Segmented information Financial information presented in the notes to the financial statements either by industry or by geography (p. 1009).

Serial bond Bond that matures in installments over a period of time (p. 921).

Servicing its debt Phrase that means the repayment of principal and interest on loans or bonds (p. 1129).

Share dividend Another name for a stock dividend (p. 864).

Shareholder A person or a company who owns shares in a corporation (p. 811).

Shareholders' equity Owners' equity of a corporation (p. 814).

Shares Units into which the owners' equity of a corporation is divided (p. 811).

Short-term investments Investments that management intends to hold for less than one year (p. 992).

Short-term liquidity Ability to meet current payments as they come due (p. 1129).

Significant influence When a company participates in the decision making of another company without having full control over it (p. 992).

Stated interest rate Interest rate that determines the amount of cash interest the borrower pays and the investor receives each year Also called the *contract interest rate* (p. 923).

Stated value An arbitrary amount assigned to a share of stock when it is issued (p. 818).

Statement of equity (statement of shareholders' equity) Presents changes in all components of equity (p. 880).

Stock Shares into which the owners' equity of a corporation is divided (p. 811).

Stock dividend (or share dividend) A proportional distribution by a corporation of its own shares to its shareholders (p. 864).

Stock split An increase in the number of authorized and outstanding shares coupled with a proportionate reduction in the book value of each share (p. 867).

Straight-line (SL) amortization Allocate a bond discount or a bond premium to expense by dividing the discount or premium into equal amounts for each interest period (p. 928).

Strong currency A currency that is rising relative to other nations' currencies (p. 1015).

Subsidiary An investee company in which a parent company owns more than 50 percent of the voting shares (p. 1002).

Term bonds Bonds that all mature at the same time for a particular issue (p. 921).

Times-interest-earned ratio Ratio of income from operations to interest expenses. Measures the number of times that operating income can cover interest expense. Also called the *interest-coverage ratio* (p. 1145).

Trading on the equity Earning more income on borrowed money than the related expense, thereby increasing the earnings for the owners of the business (pp. 941, 1147).

Translation Another term for a currency conversion or foreign-currency exchange (p. 1014).

Treasury Bill A short-term debt obligation issued by a government (p. 992).

Treasury shares When a corporation repurchases its own shares and holds the shares in its treasury for resale (p. 869).

Underwriter An independent firm that is hired to sell shares on a corporation's behalf (p. 816).

Unlimited personal liability When a partnership (or a proprietorship) cannot pay its debts with business assets, the partners (or the proprietor) must use personal assets to meet the debt (p. 757).

Unregistered bonds Another name for *bearer bonds* (p. 921).

Vertical analysis Analysis of a financial statement that reveals the relationship of each statement item to the total, which is 100 percent (p. 1134).

Weak currency A currency that is falling relative to other nations' currencies (p. 1015).

Working capital Current assets minus current liabilities; measures a business's ability to meet its short-term obligations with its current assets (p. 1139).

Write-down An accounting entry to recognize the decrease in the value of an asset by debiting an expense account and crediting the asset account (p. 1001).

Yield The interest rate that an investor will receive based on a compounding period of one year (p. 922).

Index